The Protestant Reformation in Sixteenth-Century Italy

Habent sua fata libelli

Volume XLIII
of
Sixteenth Century Essays & Studies

Raymond A. Mentzer, General Editor

Composed by Thomas Jefferson University Press
at Truman State University
Cover Art and Title Page by Matt Trego of Truman State University
Manufactured in the United States of America
Text is set in Adobe Garamond 10/12.. Display type is Carter & Cone's
Mantinia

THE PROTESTANT REFORMATION IN SIXTEENTH-CENTURY ITALY

SALVATORE CAPONETTO

Translated by
Anne C. Tedeschi and John Tedeschi

VOLUME XLIII
SIXTEENTH CENTURY ESSAYS & STUDIES

Copyright © 1999 Thomas Jefferson University Press
Truman State University
100 East Normal Street, Kirksville, MO 63501-4221 USA
http://www2.truman.edu/tjup

The translation of this book was underwritten by the
American Waldensian Society
in cooperation with the
Waldensian National Board in Italy

Library of Congress Cataloging-in-Publication Data
Caponetto, Salvatore.
   [La Riforma protestante nell'Italia del Cinquecento. English]
   The Protestant Reformation in sixteenth-century Italy / Salvatore
Caponetto : Translated by Anne C. Tedeschi and John Tedeschi.
         p.   cm. – (Sixteenth century essays & studies : v. 43)
   Includes bibliographical references and index.
   ISBN 0-943549-67-1 (HB : alk. paper)
   1. Reformation–Italy. 2. Italy–Church history–16th century.
   I. Title. II. Series.
   BR390.C4613   1998   98-3776
   274.5'06–dc21   CIP

Text is set in Minion 10/12. Display type is Mantinia by Carter & Cone.
Cover and title page by Matt Trego, Truman State University designer.
Printed by Edwards Brothers, Ann Arbor, Michigan, USA

To Melina, with gratitude

They confess a single God, a single Savior, a single Holy Spirit, one Faith, one Law, one Baptism, one hope in the kingdom of the heavens ... their faith and their religion are founded wholly on the pure Word of God.... And, if it is permitted to the Turks, to the Saracens, and to the Jews (who are bitter enemies of our Lord Jesus Christ) to live and dwell among Christians in the most beautiful cities in the world, why would those who possess the holy Gospel and who worship Jesus Christ not be permitted to live in these poor mountains?

—The Waldensians to the President
of the Parliament of Turin, 1561

Heretics must not be tortured or burned, no one should be compelled to accept any faith.

—Ottaviano and Barbara Giglioli of Rovigo
to judges of the Inquisition, 1564

CONTENTS

TRANSLATORS' PREFACE

It is a pleasure to present in English translation this welcome survey of a subject, the Italian Protestant Reformation of the sixteenth century, that justifiably has received increasing critical attention in both Europe and America. The work is the culmination of a lifetime of research and writing by Salvatore Caponetto, but by no means the final contribution from this distinguished scholar's prolific pen. It is hard to imagine anyone better prepared to offer a synthesis of the Italian Reformation than Caponetto, an emeritus professor of history at the University of Florence. Caponetto's career began auspiciously, when, as a neophyte in the field, his first modestly presented investigations on the influential booklet, the *Beneficio di Cristo*, compelled that giant of Italian culture, Benedetto Croce, to retract in print a mistaken attribution Croce had previously made. Since that time, more than a half century ago, Caponetto's contributions have ranged over multiple aspects of the Italian Reformation. He has produced full-length studies of such a key reformer as Aonio Paleario and edited one of his writings never published before; clarified the circumstances of the clandestine translations into the Italian vernacular of influential works by northern reformers; investigated the progress of Reformation currents in his native Sicily and followed the fortunes of the leading proselytizers and converts to Geneva and other transalpine cities of refuge; identified the appropriation of Lutheran and Erasmian concepts in the thought of such literary figures as Francesco Berni and Ludovico Castelvetro; and produced a massive critical edition of the *Beneficio* in a splendid volume containing all its sixteenth-century versions and translations.

A lifetime of research is woven into the fabric of Caponetto's *The Protestant Reformation*. The account begins with the Italian situation on the eve of the great religious upheaval and the fertile ground on which Luther's message fell. Attention is paid to the spread of the new religious ideas through the book trade, the influence of Juan de Valdés, and the preaching activity of early Italian champions of the new ideas. The *Beneficio*, the most celebrated booklet of the Italian Reformation, comes in for its share of obligatory attention. Various modern interpretations of this little work, first published in 1543, have dubbed it, in turn, the quintessential expression of Valdesian spirituality, a weaving together of passages from the writings of northern reformers, and finally, an expression of Benedictine–Pelagian spirituality.

Much emphasis is placed on the inroads made by Protestant currents in various Italian centers from the Veneto and the Friuli in the north to Sicily in the south. The successes of Calvinism, among the Waldensians in Piedmont, at the court of the French Duchess Renée at Ferrara, and in the Republic of Lucca, which witnessed a mass exodus of its leading families to Geneva, receive separate chapters. So extensive is the diffusion that Caponetto, appropriating an old term coined by Giorgio Spini, dubs the phenomenon "The Calvinism of the Mediterranean," stretching from Geneva and Lyons through Genoa to Naples and the martyred Waldensian colonies in Calabria and Puglia, to Sardinia and Sicily. The great port city of Messina produced an entire "colony" of refugees to Geneva.

The present English translation, based on the first Italian edition (1992), has also incorporated the corrections and addenda to the second edition (1997), which appeared while our work was in progress. The major innovations consisted of bibliographical and textual appendices and a short essay by Carlo Papini on the religiosity of Lorenzo Lotto. Thus, the attentive reader should consult these brief additions updating the text and its apparatus before delving into the apposite chapters. We have corrected obvious errors and typographical slips, but with few exceptions, made no attempt to verify the accuracy of the notes, to complete the citations, or to provide a fuller bibliography,[1] although we have referred to English-language editions, where possible, of works cited in Italian translations. With a few exceptions, we did not succeed in tracking down the original French names for the many figures presented in Italian forms.

Readers without previous exposure to the subject might wish for a more linear and direct, perhaps less elusive exposition. In his desire to produce an uncluttered narrative, the author has not burdened it with the documentation that might have helped to elucidate and more firmly anchor some of the intriguing events that fill these pages. One is left to wonder, for example, how walking out of the mass after the reading of the Gospels helped to shield the true views of evangelicals still residing in papal Italy? Wouldn't such an abrupt, disruptive exodus achieve just the opposite effect (p. 258)? What possibly could have been the motive of the antitrinitarians who are said to have betrayed to Catholic authorities a fellow Piedmontese evangelical, and under what circumstances did this occur (p. 129)? The Prince of Sanseverino is said to have entered into a second marriage with a Huguenot woman in France, but we are not told that he extricated himself from his wife of many years, the virtuous, exemplary Isabella Villamarino (p. 291). These are a few of the instances that would have profited from further explanation and supporting annotation.

Admirably, Caponetto's study is based heavily on original sources, including Holy Office records. For the uninitiated, it might have been useful if the author could have brought his vast experience to bear briefly on the procedures of this tribunal, which decided or influenced the fate of so many of the book's protagonists. One is occasionally left with the mistaken impression that it was but a step between arrest and the stake, whereas in actual fact proceedings were generally drawn out and carefully supervised by the Supreme Congregation of the Inquisition in Rome. Capital punishment was reserved only for the "obdurate" and "pertinacious" who would not abandon their beliefs, or for the relapsed, persons who had experienced a previous,

[1] This can be found in the forthcoming *The Italian Reformation of the Sixteenth Century and the Diffusion of Renaissance Culture: A Bibliography of the Secondary Literature (Ca. 1750–1997)*, compiled by John Tedeschi in association with James M. Lattis, with a historiographical introduction by Massimo Firpo that will be published under the auspices of the Istituto di Studi Rinascimentali, Ferrara.

formal conviction for heresy. And only persons in this first category might be liable to the agony of being burned alive. A much more frequently dispensed sentence, one to a *carcere perpetuo*, "life" imprisonment, usually meant, as it often does today, a reclusion of only a few years.

As the title of the volume itself implies, the Reformation *in* Italy is the subject. But to the author's credit, he includes a short chapter touching on the émigrés *religionis causa*. The fact is, that long after any traces of the Reformation had been extinguished in the peninsula proper (with the Waldensian exception), the cultural achievements of the Italian religious refugees in bringing to northern Europe the thought and literature, the theological, philological, scientific, technological, juridical, and economic advances of the Italian Renaissance continued to have an impact. One needs only to think, in the realm of theology alone, of the contributions to Anglican liturgy and polity made by Peter Martyr Vermigli or to the Polish Minor Church by Fausto Sozzini, who helped to found a movement bearing his name, Socinianism, which would spread across the continent and traverse the ocean. It is the European-wide dimensions of the Italian Reformation, not only its heroic but ultimately failed penetration in the peninsula alone, which gives significance to and explains the continuing strong appeal of this field of study. *The Protestant Reformation in Sixteenth-Century Italy* is a rare, comprehensive introduction to a fascinating, still developing subject rewarding serious scholarly attention.

Anne C. Tedeschi and John Tedeschi

ACKNOWLEDGMENTS

We should like to acknowledge with gratitude the generosity of the American Waldensian Society in New York which provided the support for this translation, the unfailing cooperation of Dr. Carlo Papini, director of Claudiana Editrice, publisher of the original version of this work, and the indefatigable labors exerted on behalf of this project by Professor Robert V. Schnucker, whose intelligence and drive helped to make this publication, as well as so many others concerned with the sixteenth century, possible.

INTRODUCTION

AFTER THE PUBLICATION in 1956 of my study on the Sicilian nobleman Bartolomeo Spadafora,[2] Luigi Firpo wrote to me in Pesaro, where I was then living, urging me to attempt a history of the Reformation in Italy. Although I was flattered by his suggestion, I had to reply that the lack of specific preliminary works on the various aspects of the problem, as well as our ignorance of the documents that still might be buried in public and ecclesiastical archives, made an attempt at a synthesis premature, despite valuable preparatory writings by Thomas M'Crie, Cesare Cantù, Bartolomeo Fontana, Emilio Comba, Emmanuel-Pierre Rodocanachi, Giuseppe Morpurgo, Giovanni Jalla, Francesco Lanzoni, Arturo Pascal, Francesco Ruffini, Luigi Firpo, and Giorgio Spini. Moreover, research by Benedetto Croce, Federico Chabod, and Delio Cantimori had opened up immense vistas that needed to be explored more fully if we were to obtain a clear idea of the spread of Luther's message of protest in the Italy of Machiavelli, Ariosto, Guicciardini, Castiglione, and Michelangelo.

At the time, I was fully persuaded by Paolo Negri's view, expressed in his two early essays dating from 1910 and 1912, that a long and patient campaign of archival digging encompassing the entire peninsula would bring to light the existence of a widespread popular movement of religious protest, "as vast and grand as any that had ever inspired the Italian spirit, but an indeterminate movement, without definitive objectives and lacking in leadership."[3] Negri attributed the widespread diffusion of the reforming ideas to the efforts of "zealous missionary figures," who did not preach abstract notions, but the Gospel message, and promoted "a true conversion of souls." My own studies of the trials conducted by the Spanish Inquisition in Sicily confirmed in my mind the correctness of Negri's vision.

By 1989, thirty years after my correspondence with Firpo, our knowledge of events had become greatly enriched through a long series of monographs on individual personages of the Italian Reformation: Juan de Valdés, Bernardino Ochino, Peter Martyr Vermigli, Aonio Paleario, Pietro Carnesecchi, and Pier Paolo Vergerio. A younger generation of scholars, in the footsteps of its illustrious teachers, had dedicated themselves passionately to the study of sixteenth-century Italian religious life. The ensuing results constitute some of the major themes in twentieth-century historiography. In-depth archival investigations had been devoted to Italian geographical regions, and to such intellectual and doctrinal currents as Carlo Ginzburg's on

---

[2]"Bartolomeo Spadafora e la Riforma protestante in Sicilia nel secolo XVI," *Rinascimento* 7 (1956): 219–341.

[3]P. Negri, "Note e documenti per la storia della Riforma in Italia," *Atti della R. Accademia delle Scienze di Torino* 45 (1909–1910): 586–608; 47 (1911–1912), 57–81, at p. 66.

Nicodemism, Paolo Simoncelli's on evangelism, and Silvana Seidel Menchi's on Eras-mianism. Meanwhile, the *Corpus reformatorum italicorum* directed by Firpo and Spini, was making available critical editions of the *Beneficio di Cristo*, and writings by such key figures as Camillo Renato, Mino Celsi, and Antonio Brucioli.

It now seemed as if we had reached the *plenitudo temporum* for a reconstruction of the history of the Italian Protestant Reformation, a scholarly desideratum augured from the end of the last century apart from confessional interests. Additionally, the idea of attempting such a synthesis appealed to me because of the differences, some of them striking, between some of my own conclusions and those of eminent schol-ars in the field. While from my readings and research, I had detected manifestations of religious dissent cropping up contemporaneously in the peninsula, from the *Tren-tino* in the north to Sicily and Sardinia in the south, others denied the existence of a true Protestant movement in sixteenth-century Italy.

In 1984 Andrea Del Col expressed an opinion based on his important studies focusing on Friulan religious life during the period:

> It is highly misleading to embark on an analysis of Italian heretical history from a *schema* of an institutional and confessional type, as if it was a matter of studying the attempts made by the Protestant churches to conquer Italy, or the spread of the heretical contagion, or the diffusion of errors through the work of the devil, ideas held by prelates and inquisitors from the *Cinquecento* until today. To investigate the Reformation in Italy by these means, or from the Protestant vantage point, which sees in those con-demned or tried by the Inquisition, witnesses to truth, is tantamount to confusing the profession of historian with that of the apologist and contro-versialist theologian, who judges on the basis of a meta-historical truth. In our peninsula, in fact, there were no evangelical churches, with the excep-tion of the Waldensians who accepted the Reformation in 1532; nor was there an organized will to adhere to one or the other of the evangelical churches. What we had, rather, was a current of opinion, aspirations to reform, attempts to solve problems posed by the religious crisis which was sweeping across Europe.[4]

A serious scholar such as Del Col would probably not repeat today this rather reductionist view after examining the numerous documents cited in the first edition of this book (1992); or the studies by Achille Olivieri on Vicenza, who already in 1979 had advanced a wholly opposed opinion; or Simonetta Adorni-Braccesi's on Lucca, or Pierroberto Scaramella's on the Mezzogiorno, all of whom have expanded the horizons of our subject with new archival discoveries. More complex and nuanced are the interpretations offered by Silvana Seidel-Menchi and Massimo Firpo, who have tried to identify the special features of the Italian religious dissent against the Church of Rome.

---

[4]A. Del Col, "Fermenti di novità religiose in alcuni cicli pittorici del Pordenone e dell' Amalteo," in *Società e cultura del Cinquecento nel Friuli*, a cura di A. Del Col (Pordenone, 1984), 236–237.

The effort to interpret the significance of a spontaneous, loosely organized, complex movement that contemporaneously traversed the entire peninsula, which at the end of the nineteenth century astounded J. B. G. Galiffe for its pervasiveness beyond the borders of the Italian states, led me to conclude that the Protestant movement in Italy had nothing peculiarly national about it. Most of the confessions and abjurations extracted from prosecuted persons, and the sentences emitted by their judges, frequently take us back, in spite of ambiguities and contradictions in the statements of the defendants, to the teachings of Luther, Valdés, Calvin, and the Anabaptists, as I have attempted to show with references to the writings of the reformers. To be sure, it should not be forgotten that much of the evidence available to us was extorted under the stress of judicial torture, physical, and psychological.

In all my work, I have tried to keep uppermost in my mind the conclusions offered by Lucien Febvre in his famous book on the origins of the French Reformation. It is not possible, he wrote in 1929, to confine to "one's own small homeland a story that is as intrinsically international as that of the religious, philosophical and moral ideas of Europe, which by then had possessed a common spirituality for centuries...." And, he continued, "specificity, precedence, nationality are words that should be dropped from a historian's lexicon. They are problems without a proper subject matter, old remnants of the controversy, which we continue to drag into our scholarly writings."[5]

The first problem that I had to confront concerned the nature and dimensions of the introduction and spread of Luther's ideas of protest, and the theories of church reform advocated by Zwingli, Bucer, Calvin, and later by Italian evangelicals from Vergerio to Ochino, and from Vermigli to Curione. This is a story of ideas, books, and proselytizers, the majority of whom were ecclesiastics and schoolteachers. But we also find among them merchants, students, travelers, and artisans who would pause on their journeys returning from Germany, Switzerland, and France to describe the events they had witnessed resulting from the great religious upheaval Luther had set in motion. The message was received in the most varied cultural and social settings: the schools of the orders, universities, academies, confraternities, artisans' shops and workplaces.

In the course of the book, I discuss a significant case where a Protestant propagandist, the nobleman Filippo Campolo, succeeded in circumventing the controls imposed against the penetration of prohibited literature by concealing several of these books in a case containing jars of preserves shipped to his mother and sisters. Campolo's family may have served as intermediaries receiving clandestine works intended for the many preachers who served Messina's clandestine evangelical communities. The question of the aspects and forms assumed by the heterodox movement in the course of the century, sometimes linked and confused with the aspirations of the "*spirituali*" for the reformation of the church, is intimately connected to the penetration of books, portraits of the reformers, antipapal medals, and emblems.

---

[5]L. Febvre, "Une question mal posée: Les origines de la Réforme française et le problème des causes de la Réforme" *Revue historique,* 161 (1929): 1–73 at 63, 73.

It is essential to keep in mind the different geographical, political, and economic situations of the various states in the peninsula. The notion of Italy as one country was then only an abstraction in the poetic tradition from Dante to Machiavelli. No nationalist sentiment linked the Italian states, frequently at war among themselves, aligned on opposite sides in the chronic conflict between France and Empire. All that bound them together was the Church of Rome, with its myriad monastic orders, with their *studi* and itinerant preachers who crossed borders and roamed far and wide, especially during the Lenten seasons. Reflect on the imperial principate of Trent, closely linked to the Germanic world, the Istria of the brothers Vergerio, the Modena of Cardinal Morone, the Lucca of Vermigli, the Naples of Valdés and Sicily, dominated by the Spanish Inquisition. There are deep differences among them that should be explored more carefully than I have been able to do in the economy of a work of synthesis.

Only by studying the overall movement for reform in every region of the peninsula, in the context of their social and religious situations, have I managed to distinguish Protestant currents from the drive for Catholic reform, whether institutional, or as it was espoused by the "*spirituali,*" influenced by the thought of Valdés. I have noted the attempts at linkage made by such distant allies as the Calvinists of Vicenza and Messina, and resistance to the repressive measures of the Counter-Reformation, in spite of the losses suffered, the abjurations, the betrayals, and flights abroad of many leaders.

Scholars who have attempted to discover what is peculiar to the Italian heterodox movement have generally neglected the Waldensians, viewing the sect's adherence to Swiss Protestantism in 1532 merely as an episode in Piedmontese history. But this is wrong. When the Waldensians espoused the Reformation, they launched an energetic missionary activity throughout Piedmont, appropriated Huguenot resistance theory, and courageously fought for their own survival from impregnable mountain redoubts, and collaborated with the two pastors, Gian Luigi Pascale and Giacomo Bonello, sent by Geneva's Venerable Company of Pastors on the daring errand to reclaim for scriptural faith their brethren in Calabria and Puglia. The enterprise ended with the slaughter of the peasants in the hamlets of Montalto, San Sisto, and La Guardia, the enforced Catholicization of their co-religionaries in Puglia, and the condemnation to the stake of the two heroic missionaries.

The Protestant Reformation did not sink lasting roots in Italy due to the fragmented nature of the movement, its inability to forge a viable organization, the all-pervasive inquisitorial vigilance, and the Roman church's startling recovery, supported by and in collaboration with the Italian states, ever haunted by the specter of the civil wars and wars of religion wracking France. However, we should be hesitant to state, in a historical context, that there was no Reformation in Italy. This would be to forget the sacrifices, dreams, and actions of all those who fought for freedom of conscience and for the right to read and interpret Sacred Scripture.

In one of his last essays, Delio Cantimori, reflecting on the dramatic consequences of the break with the traditional religion on the part of the champions of justification by faith alone, with all the accompanying consequences for theology, the liturgy and ecclesiastical discipline, as well as the bloody conflicts that ensued from it, observed that all this "has almost caused to disappear and make us forget the division and break between old and new, even though it was felt acutely by the actors of the time, small and great alike...." And he concluded with this bitter thought, which I repeat here as a seal of my own long labors:

> The most recent historiography has covered up with many fine veils—cultural, sociological, ideological, philosophical, rhetorical—the story of those fierce conflicts. But the history of European civilization cannot forget them or leave them obscured, because without remembering them we cannot comprehend the significance and the value of certain humanistic and confessional-theological positions.[6]

Florence,
February 1997

---

[6]The homonymous piece is published in D. Cantimori, *Umanesimo e religione nel Rinascimento* (Turin: Einaudi, 1975), 269. [A reduced English version of the essay, entitled "Reason, Unreason and Faith: Challenges to Traditional Christianity," appeared in *The Age of the Renaissance*, ed. Denys Hay (London: Thames and Hudson, 1967), 145–62. Trans. note.]

ABBREVIATIONS

AAL	Lucca, Archivio Arcivescovile
AHSJ	*Archivum Historicum Societatis Jesu*
ASF	Florence, Archivio di Stato
ASL	*Archivio Storico Lombardo*
ASM	Modena, Archivio di Stato
ASS	*Archivio Storico Siciliano*
ASV	Venice, Archivio di Stato
BHR	*Bibliothèque d'Humanisme et Renaissance*
BSSV	*Bollettino della Società di Studi Valdesi*
Beneficio	Benedetto da Mantova, *Il beneficio di Cristo con le versioni del secolo XVI: Documenti e testimonianze*, a cura di S. Caponetto (Florence: Sansoni; & Chicago: The Newberry Library, 1972)
Considerazioni	Juan de Valdés, *Le cento e dieci divine considerazioni*, a cura di E. Cione (Milan: Bocca, 1944)
CR	*Corpus Reformatorum* (Halle, Brunswick, Berlin, Leipzig, 1834 ff)
DBI	*Dizionario Biografico degli Italiani*
FBN	Florence, Biblioteca Nazionale
Garufi I	C. A. Garufi, "Contributo alla storia dell'Inquisizione in Sicilia nei secoli XVI e XVII: Note e appunti dagli Archivi di Spagna," *ASS*, n.s. 38 (1913–14): 264–329
Garufi II	Idem, "Contributo alla storia dell'Inquisizione in Sicilia nei secoli XVI e XVII. Nota III: La Riforma religiosa," *ASS* 40 (1915–16): 304–89
Garufi III	Idem, "Contributo alla storia dell'Inquisizione in Sicilia nei secoli XVI–XVII. Nota IV: Lotte di giurisdizione fra Inquisitori e Vicerè," *ASS* 41 (1917): 389–465
GSLI	*Giornale storico della letteratura italiana*
MPG	J. P. Migne, *Patrologiae cursus completus, series Graeca* (Paris, 1857–1912)
NRS	*Nuova Rivista Storica*
"Processo Carnesecchi"	G. Manzoni, ed., "Estratto del processo di Pietro Carnesecchi," *Miscellanea di Storia Italiana* (Turin) 10 (1870): 187– 573
RSCI	*Rivista di Storia della Chiesa in Italia*
RSI	*Rivista Storica Italiana*
RSLR	*Rivista di Storia e Letteratura Religiosa*
Serie	V. La Mantia, *Serie dei rilasciati al Braccio secolare (1487–1732)* (Palermo, 1904)
WA	*Martin Luthers sämtliche Werke*, Kritische Gesamtausgabe (Weimar, 1883–1983)
WA DB	*Martin Luthers sämtliche Werke: Kritische Gesamtausgabe: Deutsche Bibel* (Weimar, 1906–61)

Rome: Castel Sant'Angelo and the Vatican at the end of the fifteenth century. Note, below, the square before the bridge of Sant'Angelo. The low tower with battlements is the Tor di Nona (detail from an engraving in H. Schedel, *Liber chronicarum* (Nuremberg, 1493).

The symbols of papal power: Castel Sant'Angelo and the prison in the Tor di Nona from an engraving by the Bohemian Hussite Wenzel von Olmütz (end of the fifteenth century, perhaps from a lost Italian original). The recovery of a monstrous animal on the banks of the Tiber on 14 January 1496 was interpreted as a portent of divine judgment on the papacy of Alexander VI Borgia. In 1545, the theme would be taken up again by Lucas Cranach the Younger for new satirical engravings of the *"papàsino"* (papal ass), with texts from Luther and Melanchthon.

A. Dürer, The triumph of Death (1510)

I

LUTHER'S MESSAGE IN THE CRISIS OF THE EARLY SIXTEENTH CENTURY

HOMO FABER FORTUNAE SUAE?

THE QUARTER CENTURY BETWEEN the discovery of America and the publication of Luther's Ninety-Five Theses (1492–1517) witnessed a rapid sequence of events of universal significance, events that overturned the framework and vision of life inherited from the Middle Ages and affected the course of human history irrevocably. The discovery of a "Nuevo Mundo," the invention of powerful firearms that could pulverize feudal castles and fortresses, advances in printing that made possible the diffusion of learning even to the lower strata of society, and humanism, which attained its fullness through a vast reappropriation of the writings of the ancients, had opened up new horizons to thought and to the sciences. Humanist civilization, with a magnificent flowering of all the branches of culture and the arts, stimulated hopes and expectations of an imminent "rebirth" of society and of the church, which had been in profound turmoil for more than a century, and dreamed as did Nicolas Cusanus, Pico della Mirandola and Erasmus of Rotterdam, of a *pax fidei* and a universal peace. Erasmus, the greatest of the sixteenth-century humanists, used sarcasm to combat tyranny, war, and violence. He proclaimed himself a citizen of the world and coined the motto: "Man is born for love and not for war."[1]

Such dreams, aspirations, and illusions were confronted by hard reality: Most pressing was the Turkish menace, encroaching upon the west after the conquest of the Balkan peninsula, reaching Vienna's very walls in 1529. Tensions in society had deepened with the growing domination of the ruling classes, rich merchants, great landowners, and bankers. They had become puppet masters, who manipulated

---

[1] Erasmo da Rotterdam, *Adagia: Sei saggi politici in forma di proverbi*, a cura di S. Seidel Menchi (Turin: Einaudi, 1980), 202–3.

princes and kings "by golden threads."[2] Charles I of Spain would never have become emperor of the Holy Roman Empire in 1519 without the financial support of the Fuggers. With the growth of commercial capitalism, the burden on peasants, laborers, and artisans became harsher. The discrepancy between classes culminated in the terrible German Peasants' War of 1525. The great calamities of war, famine, and pestilence evoked such images as the three horsemen of the Apocalypse representing divine judgment on a corrupt humanity.

The humanists' optimistic world vision dissipated before these rude realities of daily life. The Renaissance dream of a humanity made more human and more tolerant, conscious of the value of reason and intelligence, remain immortalized in the splendor of painting, culture, and literature. As Walter Binni observed discussing the poetry of Michelangelo in the sixteenth century, "a sentiment of loss and of melancholy, of delusion and frustration" took a deeper hold. Society was increasingly beset by an awareness "of an instability of values, of a failing of human effort, of the causality and hostility of fate, at the bottom of which was a reluctant consciousness of the drama of recent Italian historical events: the demise of city, state and regional independence, wars and massacres, and constant setbacks to spiritual and religious reform."[3]

Albrecht Dürer's great engraving representing Melancholy, to which Jules Michelet drew our attention, is one of the best depictions of this transformation of sentiments concerning the possibilities for intelligence and culture in the face of the mysteries of human destiny.[4] Beside a winged woman of massive proportions stand all the symbols of human resourcefulness and science, from the compass to the chisel, from the chemist's scales to the writer's inkwell. She is a meditative and sorrowful figure. The keys of power and a full purse hang uselessly from her belt. Above her, the forces of destiny clash in the celestial sphere. There is a rainbow, but below it a comet, symbol of imminent disasters. Melancholy evokes a feeling of defeat provoked by the inability to dominate events.[5] The year is 1514, the eve of the unfolding of a new religious horizon, marked by a prodigious and almost incredible flowering of scriptural studies, as well as of senseless fanaticism, and wars and crusades bent on extermination in the name of Christ. Dürer, one of the greatest among artists and humanists produced by northern Europe, was one among many who would convert to the Lutheran cause.

Turning to the art and especially the poetry of Michelangelo, we can discern virtually in its entirety the tension inherent in the Christian drama, from the consciousness of sin to the growing search for refuge in the grace of God alone. On the verso of a letter dated 8 September 1525 the artist penned this fragment of a sonnet:

Alive to sin, to me I die alone;
Being of sin, my life I cannot claim.

[2]H. Hauser and A. Renaudet, *Les débuts de l'âge moderne*, 4th ed. (Paris: Presses Universitaires de France, 1956), 363.

[3]W. Binni, *Michelangelo scrittore* (Rome: Ateneo, 1965), 11.

[4]J. Michelet, *Histoire de la France* (Paris: Marpon and Flammarion, 1869), 10:84–88.

[5]E. Panofsky, *Albrecht Dürer*, 3rd ed., 2 vols. (London: Oxford University Press, 1945). See vol. 2, fig. 209.

All good from heaven, comes from me all blame;
Swept by my will, no will at all I own.
Freedom a slave, mortality has grown
Into a god in me. O woe! O shame!
Into what wretched life, through birth, I came![6]

Another example of the cultural and spiritual crisis spreading throughout the peninsula, and with variations, in other parts of western Europe, but with a single voice proclaiming distrust in ecclesiastical institutions, is exemplified by a little-known but dramatic episode occurring in the duchy of Urbino, one of the great centers of Renaissance civilization. In 1528, the year Baldassar Castiglione published his *Cortegiano*, a book that would bring lasting fame to the court of Guidobaldo di Montefeltro and Elisabetta Gonzaga, the gentlewoman Emilia Pio died. She was the "inseparable companion of the duchess Elisabetta," according to Castiglione, her admirer, who wrote of her "in the most sympathetic light for her vivacity, for her spirit at the same time alert and resolute as one finds in a masterful leader, in whom suave discourse was often mingled with sharp bellicose skepticism."[7] The rumor quickly spread even as far as the papal court that "madame Emilia has passed away without the benefit of any sacrament of the Church."

The report was accurate. Emilia, widow of Antonio, the count of Montefeltro who was Guidobaldo's illegitimate brother, had obstinately refused confession. Sebastiano Bonaventura sent a dramatic message to the duchess of Urbino, Eleonora Gonzaga, at Fossombrone, only a few hours before the death of her friend: "Together with her lady-in-waiting we have attempted to have her draw up a testament and put her affairs in order, but until now to no avail. She has not confessed herself."[8] One can imagine the dismay at this refusal of the sacrament and its consequences as far as a church funeral was concerned. Emilia Pio's behavior was immediately explained in terms of skepticism, but actually this unequivocal suspension of mental habits had deep roots in one who had not forgotten the cruelties and infamies of Cesare Borgia during his occupation of the duchy of Urbino, and who was well aware of the resounding prophecies and denunciations of Savonarola, whose works circulated at court. It was now the eve of the Sack of Rome.

The incident of the rejected sacrament must be seen against the background of this dire episode. The Sack, striking at the very heart of the Christian world, accompanied by the unheard-of brutality of the armies of the most Catholic Charles V, exposed the fragility of the Renaissance dream of a new golden age. Such was the horror produced by the barbarism, the plundering, the killings in the magnificent

[6] *The Complete Poems of Michelangelo*. Translated into verse with notes and introduction by Joseph Tusiani (New York: The Noonday Press, 1960), 30. Cf. E. Campi, *Michelangelo e Vittoria Colonna* (Turin: Claudiana, 1994), 55–77.
[7] *Il Cortegiano del conte B. Castiglione*, annotato e illustrato da V. Cian (Florence: Sansoni, 1929), 524–25.
[8] S. Caponetto, "Motivi di riforma religiosa e Inquisizione nel ducato di Urbino nella prima metà del Cinquecento," in the author's *Studi sulla Riforma in Italia* (Florence: Università degli Studi, Dipartimento di Storia, 1987), 265.

palaces in the Rome of Julius II, Leo X, and Clement VII, by the humiliation visited on the pontiff, a prisoner in Castel Sant'Angelo, that the emperor ordered the circulation in manuscript throughout Italy of two dialogues written by his secretary, Alfonso de Valdés: *Diálogo de las cosas occuridas en Roma* and the *Diálogo de Mercurio y Caron.*

In the first of these, written between July and August 1527, Valdés attempted to exculpate the emperor, interpreting the Sack as the just punishment for the corruption of the church and of the papacy. After the peace signed at Barcelona (25 June 1529) and the accords that would lead to the imperial coronation at Bologna (24 February 1530), the two dialogues seemed anachronistic and remained unpublished. They would not see the light of day in print until 1546.

LUTHER'S MESSAGE

Under the pressure of dire events, everywhere in Christian Europe, in culture as well as in art, themes of Christian pessimism multiplied, such as that of the invincible reality of sin (examples of which both ecclesiastics and laymen offered daily spectacle) and of the necessity of penance to obtain the forgiveness of God.

The prognostications of astrologers, the prophecies of the hermits crisscrossing the cities of north central Italy, the apocalyptic tone of many preachers, the recent memory of the burning of the prophet of San Marco, spread, first among the unlettered masses but later in all classes of society, occasioning the fear of death and of the hereafter along with a sentiment of anguish and alienation. Jean Delumeau has painted a masterful picture of western society on the eve of Luther's protest.[9] Death is the encompassing theme in the iconography of the waning Middle Ages. At least fifty-two "dances of death" dating from the fifteenth and sixteenth centuries have been identified. The populace gazed on them emotionally as presages of equality and justice. Preoccupation over personal salvation became increasingly intense. The *ars moriendi* had an ever-growing success.

Even Erasmus wrote a *Treatise on the Preparation for Death.* The prince of humanists who, at the beginning of the century, with his *Enchiridion militis christiani* had charted the way for the new theology founded on Scripture, now affirmed with his edition of the original text of the New Testament (*Novum Instrumentum*, 1516) that only the *philosophia Christi* contained the true message of salvation and of life. On 18 March 1523 he wrote to a friend: "Mundus insanit in libros sacros."[10] Between 1520 and 1530 commentaries to the Pauline epistles grew in number, selling even faster than books of chivalry.

People were searching for an instrument that would be efficacious in obtaining divine forgiveness, grasping as never before at devotions, at the cult of relics in the most superstitious forms, at indulgences, at the recital of the rosary.

---

[9]J. Delumeau, *Naissance et affirmation de la Réforme* (Paris: Presses Universitaires de France, 1965).
[10]*Opus epistolarum Des. Erasmi Roterodami*, ed. P. S. Allen, H. M. Allen, and H. W. Garrod (Oxford, 1906–58), 5:1349.

Jean Delumeau put it succinctly: "Naturally, one had recourse to God made man, who had come to expiate the sins of the world."[11] Painters, sculptors, engravers, and glass workers dwelt insistently on the Passion of Christ and his suffering on the cross. The epoch of the "Beau Dieu" of Amiens had passed. Now anxious eyes were raised to Grünewald's Crucifixion, Michelangelo's *Pietà*, and Dürer's "Lamentation of Christ." This was the configuration of the age when Martin Luther made his protest; keeping this picture before us, both his message as well as the wildfire spread of the Reformation become comprehensible. Luther gave a response to the longing to know one's destiny in the hereafter and he gave it in the fullness of time. Through his commentaries on the Psalms and then on Paul's Epistles to the Romans and Galatians, the Augustinian monk discovered a new theology: "*In Christo crucifixo est vera theologia et cognitio Dei.*" The *theologia crucis* was his starting point.

To Luther, the theology of the cross revealed the utter senselessness of the church's entire penitential system. That great scriptural exegete read verse 17 in the first chapter of the Epistle to the Romans with different eyes: "For in it the righteousness of God is revealed…; as it is written, 'He who through faith is righteous shall live.'" The justice revealed in the Gospel is the grace of God, the gift of his mercy, redeemed through the price paid by his Son on the cross for sin and malediction. Justification by faith consists of believing in the work of God and accepting the free bestowal of salvation. For Luther this was the key to understanding all of Scripture, *fides fiducialis* in God's promises.

The reformer's famous trilogy was printed at Wittenberg between August and November 1520: *An Open Letter to the Christian Nobility of the German Nation*; *A Prelude on the Babylonian Captivity of the Church*; *A Treatise on Christian Liberty.* In the heat of the bitter polemic that followed the *affaire* of the indulgences in which the chief champions of Catholic theology took the field, Luther, immersed in study, meditation, and prayer, demonstrated his immense learned and spiritual qualities. Totally at home with Scripture, an acute polemicist well versed in theology, philosophy, and literature, he unleashed a linguistic barrage of incomparable richness that was cutting, telling, and sometimes coarse. As a Catholic priest, Brunero Gherardini, recently wrote: "a cry of freedom goes up in Germany and spreads all over Europe: freedom for the Gospel from curial incrustations, for the people of God from an abusive clericalism, for the Word of God from the pope and his decretals."[12]

The fundamental themes of Luther's teachings are affirmed vigorously in the trilogy: the equality before God of all baptized people without any distinction between ecclesiastics and laity; the right of every believer, desirous of comprehending divine revelation, to read and interpret Sacred Scripture; the reform of the mass, conceived as the proclamation of the Gospel and commemoration of Christ's death; and the emancipation of the Christian from all clerical mediation and ecclesiastical tyranny. This was Luther's message to a deeply troubled generation, overwhelmed by

---

[11]J. Delumeau, *Naissance et affirmation de la Réforme*, 53.
[12]B. Gherardini, *L'eredità di Lutero nell'evoluzione teologica della Riforma* (Rome: Edizioni Paoline, 1978), 54–55.

calamity, longing to hear words of assurance and consolation. His personal drama matched the great longing of his time and his message raced through Europe. With the priority it gave to Scripture, it became harnessed to the printing press, which had become, at the beginning of the century, the preeminent instrument for communication in society.

According to Lucien Febvre, Luther's message contained only major themes:[13] the use of the Bible in the vernacular and justification by grace through faith in the work of Jesus Christ. The vernacular Bible was becoming known. The living God was coming into contact with the believer through the mysterious powers of the Holy Spirit mediated by the personal reading of Scripture. It is difficult to imagine today the emotion of the faithful, hearing for the first time in everyday parlance, the words spoken of Jesus by John the Baptist: "Here is the Lamb of God, who takes upon himself the sins of the world."

To be sure, many knew neither how to read or write, but members of the ruling classes, schoolteachers, lawyers, notaries, merchants, and clerics did. Preachers, won over to the new ideas, proclaimed the Reformation message from the pulpit. Justification by faith alone freed the individual from the anxiety of sin and from the terrifying prospect of hell and purgatory. It was a revolution of ideas, a revolution of basic feelings, not a question of cold theological formulae, but of new sentiments destined to spread quickly throughout Christian Europe, to become deeply rooted in the consciousness of multitudes of men and women ready to confront prison, torture, and death for their new beliefs. Febvre summed up the phenomenon, "at the beginning of the sixteenth century, at a particularly interesting moment in the evolution of human societies, the Reformation was the sign and the product of a profound revolution in religious sentiment."[14]

THE RECEPTION IN ITALY

How was this revolutionary and unsettling message received by Italians, accustomed to look at the Church of Rome—that city of which Christ is "a citizen" (Dante *Purgatory*, XXXII, 102)—as the sole great dispenser of grace and divine forgiveness? In attempting to fathom the reasons for the widespread penetration of the Lutheran protest at all levels of Italian society, beginning in the 1520s, we must first look at the politico-religious situation of the states of the peninsula in the first three decades of the century. Never had the absence of a unified Italian nation seemed so important as after the descent of Charles VIII, who conquered Italy without resistance, with chalk (*gesso*), in the words of that perceptive observer of Italian reality and of sins of the princes, Machiavelli. The Italian states, deeply divided, oscillated between France and the Empire in their efforts to safeguard their independence. The Lombard plain became the focal point of a disastrous war between France and Spain for the

---

[13]L. Febvre, "Une question mal posée: Les origines de la Réforme française et le problème des causes de la Réforme," *Revue historique* 161 (1929): 1–73.
[14]Ibid., 28.

conquest of the Kingdom of Naples and the State of Milan. A series of great battles were fought there by the mercenary armies recruited from many states: Agnadello (1509), Ravenna (1512), Melegnano (1515), Pavia (1525), followed by the Sack of Rome in 1527 and by the fall of the glorious Florentine Republic in 1530.

The Sack of Rome and the coronation at Bologna in 1530 of Charles V as king of Italy and emperor, signaled the end of so-called "Italian liberty" and confirmed Spanish dominion over Milan, Naples, Sicily, and Sardinia. Indirectly, this jurisdiction extended over the Florence of Alessandro de' Medici, joined in marriage to Marguerite of Austria, natural daughter of Charles V, and over the republics of Genoa, Lucca, and Siena. Only Venice and the papal states succeeded, with great difficulty, in preserving their independence.

The new factor in this political situation was the importance assumed by the papacy as an Italian principate, with Julius II a protagonist in European affairs. What this represented in the long, protracted march towards Italian unity, was seen keenly and prophetically by Machiavelli in book 1, chapter 12, of the *Discorsi*: "It is the Church that has kept, and keeps, Italy divided." It became ever more difficult to distinguish the prince, with his magnificent Roman court, from the Vicar of Christ, the head of the Catholic Church. This was so even for the devout and traditionalist segments of society, who had not read the ferocious Erasmian dialogue, *Julius exclusus e coelis*, referring to Pope Julius II and his entrance into Bologna with his head encased in a Persian helmet, supporting the triple tiara.

This distinction was still clear to the two learned Venetians, Tommaso Giustiniani and Vincenzo Quirini, who became hermits in the monastery of Camaldoli. Their *Libellus ad Lionem X*, sent to the Fifth Lateran Council (1513) during its closing sessions, because of its universality and objective analysis of the ills afflicting the church in all its parts—from the pope, who was dedicating himself more to the temporal than to the spiritual dominion; to priests, both regular and secular, who were often ignorant and corrupt; to bishops, absent from their sees and usually forgetful of their spiritual duties—is one of the most significant documents produced by the Catholic Reformation. It offers a highly perceptive analysis of the profound crisis faced by the papacy and the church in Italy, and sheds light on the chief features of the Catholic reform movement. But, in the words of a leading student of the time, "the vision which the trained and prophetic eye of the high-minded Venetians beheld was too lofty both for the pope to whom they addressed themselves and for the Council assembled before their eyes. Pope and Council disappointed the hopes that had been set on them."[15] A quarter century later, after so many dramatic events, even after the schism sundering the unity of Christendom, the situation remained much the same. The *Consilium de emendanda ecclesia* issued in 1537 denounced the same ills in the church and advanced anew a program of deep-seated reform *in capite et membris*.

The two documents, despite the fact that among the signatories of the *Consilium* one finds many of the leaders of the "*spirituali*," Cardinals Pole, Contarini, Cortese,

---

[15]H. Jedin, *A History of the Council of Trent*, trans. Dom Ernest Graf O.S.B. (St. Louis: Herder, 1957), 1:130.

Sadoleto, and Fregoso, who were more open and receptive to the ideas of the Reformation, are linked in their loyalty to the pope, who in the *Libellus* was actually exalted, based on the premise of his indisputable authority, received from Christ's promise: "And I tell you, you are Peter, and on this rock I will build my Church."[16] This ecclesiology, from which no Catholic reformer would ever budge, marks the essential difference from Lutheran doctrine.

If the picture of Italian religious life in the first half of the sixteenth century drawn by Pietro Tacchi Venturi seems overly harsh, designed to create a more dramatic contrast with the shining figures of Loyola and his followers, it documents, nevertheless, the degradation of the church during the papacies of Alexander VI, Julius II, Leo X, and Clement VII.[17]

There is no point belaboring the ills besetting the church, the clerical corruption, the decadence afflicting monasteries and convents of both sexes, the illiteracy of the secular clergy, the scandalous life of the Roman Curia, and so forth. Two elements only have to be considered interdependent: episcopal nonresidence and the abandonment of the care of souls by parish priests. The flock had been left to its own devices. The church was not up to the task of satisfying the intense spiritual longing of the people. Who suffered especially were the lower classes, whether urban or rural, deprived of the instruction that would have permitted them to find solace outside the parish for their anxieties and bewilderment.

Due to the many dioceses, the nonresidence of bishops had more serious consequences in Italy than elsewhere in Europe. From the end of the fifteenth through the sixteenth century, there were more than 250, without counting the islands and the bishops *in partibus*, compared to 131 in France, 33 in England, Wales, and Scotland, and 34 in Ireland. This enormous horde greedily searched for benefices to supplement the modest income of the episcopal sees. Perhaps less than half the number resided in their dioceses instructing the faithful, ordaining priests, and administering the sacraments.[18]

Sixteenth-century chronicles and pastoral visitations, both before and after the Council of Trent, throw light on the religious state of the Italian populace, corroborating the judgment of the Jesuits traveling as preachers in the Abruzzi, Calabria, Puglia, and Sicily: These were the "Italian Indies," which needed to be evangelized before missions were launched to lands beyond the seas. Mountainous regions were populated by uncouth people, more pagan than Christian. The Jesuit Father Silvestro Landini traveling in 1547 through the Lunigiana and Garfagnana, where for years the peasants had neither confessed themselves nor received communion because of the neglect of their priests, reported his astonishment to his superiors in the order.[19]

In the first decades of the sixteenth century, however, currents of fervent and intense religiosity appeared in the peninsula. The "observant" movement, from late in

---

[16]Matt. 16:18.

[17]See P. Tacchi Venturi, *Storia della Compagnia di Gesù in Italia: I. La vita religiosa in Italia durante la prima età della Compagnia di Gesù* (Rome: Civiltà Cattolica, 1930).

[18]See D. Hay, *The Church in Italy in the Fifteenth Century* (Cambridge: Cambridge University Press, 1977).

[19][See below, chap. 16, pp. 283 ff. Trans. note.]

the fifteenth century, touched the Benedictine, Dominican, Franciscan, and Augustinian orders, imposing respect for the ancient rules, calling for the renewal of discipline, joined to a powerful revival of Biblical and theological study. These were undoubtedly the first steps of the reformation preached by Aegidius of Viterbo: *"reformare homines per sacra et non sacra per homines."* These impulses, though not without opposition and internal conflicts between reformers and their opponents, would bear fruit and contribute to the affirmation of the Catholic Reformation.

Alongside the conventuals, and occasionally linked to them, movements tending towards personal reform, such as the Oratory of Divine Love, active in Genoa and Rome, also came into being, led by members of the noble and bourgeois classes and high prelates, who espoused ideals of charity and mercy, but did not as yet preoccupy themselves with the reform of ecclesiastical institutions. The same can be said about the many lay confraternities, which advocated prayer and solidarity and attempted to make up for the deficiencies of the parish clergy. Towards mid–sixteenth century, the new doctrines, with their challenge to the cult of saints and superfluous devotions, penetrated a few of these bodies.

BIBLIOGRAPHICAL NOTE

For this introductory chapter, in addition to the general works cited in the notes, see the synthesis by E. Garin, *La cultura del Rinascimento* (Bari: Laterza, 1967), which summarizes his fundamental studies on the Renaissance. Of the immense recent bibliography on Luther, I limit myself to citing J. Atkinson, *Martin Luther and the Birth of Protestantism* (Atlanta: Knox Press, 1981; 1st ed., 1968).

H. Holbein, the Younger, The Triumph of Death (sixteenth century)

Enlarged from the printer's mark of Jodocus Badius von Assch, used on the title pages of
various books printed by him, 1507–35.

2

THE IMAGE OF LUTHER AND THE ORIGINS OF THE ITALIAN REFORMATION

THE LUTHER "AFFAIR"

NOT LONG AFTER the nailing of the Ninety-Five Theses to the castle church door at Wittenberg, news of the monk who had rebelled against pope, church, and traditional theology crossed Germany's borders and began to spread throughout Europe. Luther's booklets and pamphlets produced at Wittenberg in 1519 were soon joined by an edition of his Latin works printed by Johannes Froben, the publisher friend of Erasmus. Their refutation by orthodox writers followed at an ever-increasing pace. By frequently reproducing substantial portions of the works they were attacking, they inadvertently helped to propagate their teachings. Luther now found himself embroiled in a bitter controversy, and the "Luther affair" quickly ceased being a concern only for papal diplomacy and theology to become the object of popular curiosity and then of discussion and debate involving persons able to read Latin: school teachers, men of letters, jurists, notaries, physicians, and members of such educated families as the Buonvisi of Lucca and the Panciatichi of Florence.

As the scandal widened, after the daring professor of Scripture burned a papal bull and books of canon law (10 December 1520) in the presence of his colleagues and applauding students, his fame also spread among the lower classes everywhere in western Europe. The diffusion of Luther's works in Italy followed rapidly. The efforts of the bookseller Francesco Minizio Calvo of Como, who struck an agreement with Froben for the distribution of the reformer's works, are well known.[1] But soon they also began to be printed in Venice. Even though only one of these, the *Appellatio ad*

---

[1] See the biographical sketch by F. Barberi, *DBI* 17:38–40.

concilium, reprinted in 1518, carried the author's name on the title page, Luther's teachings spread quickly to every part of the peninsula.[2]

The first image of the rebellious monk was the one offered by the theologians who had thrown themselves acrimoniously against "the arrogant, ignorant and reckless German." The earliest confutation, which appeared in Florence in 1520, came from the pen of the Sienese Dominican, Ambrogio Catarino (Lancillotto de' Politi), in which *mendax, vanus,* and *imperitus* are the least violent expressions used.[3] The very next year, Cristoforo Marcelli, archbishop of Corfù, produced his vindication of papal authority, also published in Florence, a place that earlier had witnessed the demise of another rebellious monk.[4] In the treatment accorded to Luther by the major controversialist writers—Tommaso Radini Tedeschi, Christophorus Langolius, and Giovanni da Fano—his image gained in specificity and was also transformed: he becomes the new Savonarola, a newly sprung Catiline, overthrower of the church and society, precursor of the Antichrist.[5] Thanks to preachers responding to a constant stream of briefs from Clement VII against the introduction of Lutheran works in Italy, this image also spread among the people. An anonymous popular poem that appeared in print about 1530 must have provided great material for strolling players:

Men, women, great and small
Seem with fervor to await
This renegade dog and wicked mastiff
Who seeks to devour our souls
One says: let that Martin finally come
So that I may take two wives.
Another says: I'll take two husbands.
O ye, blind to all and from the faith departed.[6]

But this type of acrimonious polemic proved to be a double-edged sword. It drove the supporters of the reformer, especially among the members of the Augustinian order, cognizant of the theological distortions and calumnies being uttered against their daring brother-member, to counterattack from the pulpit and to hearken back to Augustine's teaching on grace. Eventually, both laity and ecclesiastics had

[2]S. Seidel Menchi, "Le traduzioni di Lutero nella prima metà del Cinquecento," *Rinascimento*, n.s. 17 (1977): 36.
[3]A. Catharinus Politus, *Apologia pro veritate catholicae et apostolicae fidei doctrinae adversus impia ac valde pestifera Martini Lutheri dogmata*. Ed. J. Schweizer. Corpus Catholicorum, 27 (Münster, 1956), 181. The work dates from 1520.
[4]C. Marcelli, *De authoritate Summi pontificis et his quae ad illam pertinent, adversus impia Martini Lutheri dogmata*. Florentiae per Haeredes Philippi Juntae, A. Domini 1521.
[5]See T. Radini Tedeschi, *Orazione contro Filippo Melantone*, a cura di R. Ghizzoni (Brescia: Paideia, 1973) (Luther is the new Savonarola); A. Biondi, "Il Ciceroniano e l'eversore: Una lettura politica di Lutero nell'orazione di Cristoforo Longolio: 'Ad Luterianos quosdam iam damnatos (1521),'" in *Lutero in Italia: Studi storici nel V centenario della nascita*, a cura di L. Perrone (Casale Monferrato: Marietti, 1983), 27–46; S. Cavazza, "'Luthero fidelissimo inimico de messer Jesu Christo.' La polemica contro Lutero nella letteratura religiosa in volgare della prima metà del Cinquecento," ibid, 65–94.
[6]S. Seidel Menchi, "Le traduzioni," 108.

his writings printed pseudonymously and circulated them. Even those who wished to confute Luther's message, as we noted, often reproduced it in extenso. In 1532, for example, Giovanni da Fano gave a detailed exposition of the doctrines and causes underlying his protest, and some readers began to question the correctness of excommunicating such a learned interpreter of Scripture.

The original negative opinion of Luther gradually became transformed in the milieu of the Savonarolans, Erasmians, antipapal republicans, and humanists. The same year that Politi published his attack, the Florentine Bartolomeo Cerretani, an old follower of Savonarola despite his loyalty to the Medici, wrote a fictional dialogue between two *Piagnoni* of Florence, Lorenzo and Girolamo, and Giovanni Rucellai in the home of Francesco Guicciardini, governor of Modena. The two friends have been traveling about Europe since 1512 and have just returned from visiting Erasmus. They decide to go to Germany and meet Martin Luther, whose writings they had read in Bologna, "first that one against indulgences, just as miraculous as they are full of a true and stable doctrine." For these two former Savonarolans, the reformer is not the son of iniquity, but rather "a venerable man of religion," "exceedingly worthy because of his habits, learning and piety."[7]

Marin Sanudo's diaries, in contrast to the silence of the Italian chronicles of the day, recorded much of the information emanating from Rome that was controlled by the papal curia. But he also expressed an opinion worth remarking upon: Luther founded his beliefs on the Gospels alone. Reporting the Christmas sermon of 1520 by the Augustinian Andrea Bauria, delivered at Venice in the square of Santo Stefano, in which he "spoke ill of the pope and the papal court," Sanudo commented: "This person espouses the teachings of Martin Luther who is in Germany, a very learned man who follows Saint Paul and is strongly opposed to the pope; because of it he has been excommunicated by the pope."[8]

"LUTHERAN" AUGUSTINIANS

The first proselytizers for the Reformation were Luther's brother-members in his order. The network of Augustinians who preached Lutheran doctrines extended throughout Italy, from Venice to Sicily. In 1529 Fra Geremia da Tripedi was tried at Palermo and Fra Alessio da Fivizzano (Alessio Casani, 1491–1570) at Florence. The latter's unpublished memoirs are a precious source for knowledge of heretical writings on the part of members of the Augustinian order who had already become acquainted with the Inquisition thanks to their "scandalous sermons." Casani, imprisoned in Florence in 1530 but later absolved and pardoned by the Medici pope Clement VII, to whose family he would always remain devoted, obviously outgrew

---

[7]See the biographical sketch by P. Malanima in *DBI* 23: 806–9; J. Schnitzer, *Quellen und Forschungen zur Geschichte Savonarolas, III: B. Cerretani* (Münich: J. J. Lentner'schen, 1904), 83–105.

[8]O. Niccoli, "il mostro di Sassonia: Conoscenza e non conoscenza di Lutero in Italia nel Cinquecento (1520–1530 ca.)," in *Lutero in Italia*, 18–23, and the biography by F. Gaeta in *DBI* 7:296–97.

these vague, early sympathies. But the information Casani furnished in his memoirs is of crucial importance concerning his master and superior, Agostino da Fivizzano.[9] Here we read an astonishing fact. Shortly before he died, Agostino, who had studied in Paris in the 1520s, gave Casani nearly fifty "Lutheran" books which he kept concealed in a chest. The good monk hastened to Rome to show them to the general of the order, Girolamo Seripando, who retained a few and ordered the destruction of the rest. Unfortunately for us, Fra Alessio, by then wholly subservient to the discipline of the Catholic Church, left no further information about this intriguing cache of books.

A majority of the Augustinians who fell foul of the Inquisition had been won over by Luther's teachings. This explains the great success of their preaching, based on Scripture and on the theology of the cross, compared with the Lenten orators who articulated intricate philosophical views which often ended with vague quotations from Aristotle.

Although there were differences among these theologian supporters of Luther, a good example of their preaching is offered by the recent discovery of two books of *Prediche* by Giulio della Rovere (1504–81, Giulio da Milano), containing his last Lenten sermons delivered at Venice in 1541 before his trial and flight from prison at the end of February 1543. In these texts the Augustinian takes a positive stand and avoids polemics. His presentation hinges on the threefold theme of "*sola fide, sola gratia, sola Scriptura*," against which he juxtaposes pretentious reason, carnal judgment, and the theological positions of hypocrites.[10]

Ugo Rozzo, to whom we owe the in-depth research on Giulio della Rovere, hypothesizes a common strategy of proselytization on the part of an "organizational nucleus" of Augustinians, all confirmed supporters of Luther. This suggestion finds credence if we consider the large number of monks who became suspects, bringing the entire order into ill repute between 1530 and 1550: Agostino da Fivizzano, Francesco da Gambassi, Andrea da Volterra (Andrea Ghetti), Gabriele da Bergamo, Stefano da Mantova, Pietro Gratalaro, Giovanni Gigliuto, Andrea di Lanza, Giulio della Rovere, Giuliano da Colle (Giuliano Brigantino), Agostino da Treviso (Agostino Museo), Ambrogio da Milano (Ambrogio Cavalli), Ambrogio da Palermo (Ambrogio Bolognesi), Nicolò da Verona, Agostino Mainardi, to mention only the better known, masters of theology, superiors in their convents, professors in the most prestigious seats of learning of their order, and leading cultural figures, all exerted an influence in the religious debate which far surpassed that of any other monastic order.

After painful and humiliating trials, imprisonment, suspension from teaching and preaching, anguished by the rift in the body of Christ, almost all dropped their quest for doctrinal reforms outside the church, submitted to Roman obedience, and placed their hopes in the pending council desired by all, Protestant and Catholic

---

[9]S. Bondi, "Alessio Casani da Fivizzano OSA (1491–1570) e le sue Memorie inedite," *Analecta Augustiniana* 50 (1987): 5–44.

[10]See U. Rozzo, "Le 'Prediche' veneziane di Giulio da Milano," *BSSV,* n. 152 (1983): 3–30.

alike. But not all felt they could sacrifice "liberty of conscience," as Melanchthon wrote in his *Loci Communes theologici* in 1521.[11]

Agostino Mainardi (1482–1563), after a period of disputation and controversy with his adversaries in Asti and Pavia, where he had converted Celio Secondo Curione, crossed over to the territory of the Grisons in 1541. Here he became the first acknowledged preacher to the evangelical community of Chiavenna. With an open mind, he conducted an indefatigable ministry, even when confronted by dissident and subtle disputants, until the age of eighty-one.

Giulio della Rovere fled from a Venetian prison in February 1543 and also found refuge in the Grisons, easily accessible from Lombardy, where he had a long career as pastor at Poschiavo and missionary throughout the Valtellina, and was highly esteemed for his upright habits, his preaching and reforming zeal. He died at the age of seventy-six.

The situation differed for Ambrogio Cavalli ((1500?–1556). Rehabilitated after a Roman trial in 1537, he was again arrested at Venice in 1537 for sermons delivered on the island of Nicosia. Even though this trial ended with his solemn abjuration, he was not wholly able to eradicate the new faith from his mind. He settled at Ferrara in the court of Duchess Renée where he served as her almoner from 1547 to 1554. When the Calvinist conventicle there was dispersed by the duke, he moved on to the Grisons and then to Geneva. Returning to Italy, perhaps to give support to Renée, who was being coerced by her husband and the Jesuits to abandon the reformed faith, Ambrogio was arrested and brought to Rome. He was executed on 15 June 1556 as an impenitent heretic, after refusing to hear mass and receive confession, declaring that "he was dying for the glory of God."[12]

The reactions to the sermons and disputations of these tenacious proselytizers over a period of many years, interspersed with the appeals of the generals of the order, Gabriele Della Volta, and Girolamo Seripando, to desist from preaching Lutheran heresies, and their vacillations, and return to controversial themes are described for us in a colorful letter from Lorenzo Davidico to Ignatius Loyola, dated 25 April 1550, apropos Fra Giuliano Brigantino of Colle Valdelsa (1510?–52?)[13]:

> Every day something new turns up against Master Zuliano, especially by means of one of his students, a monk *eiusdem ordinis*, whom I believe the vicar will keep in prison for a few days. One of his brothers [in the order] told one of them, in whom he reposed a certain confidence: 'if we were not afraid of the flames, we would all be living Luther's way.' Another of these monks told a certain gentleman, worthy of credence, in conversation: 'To tell the truth, we all hold Martin Luther to be a great saint.' I can tell you that *in angulis et conventiculis* he has caused much harm. Thus, I beg you to reveal to the world for the glory of God the charity which is resplendent in

[11]"*Nam ut christiana libertas est conscientiae libertas, ita christianorum servitus est conscientiae servitus,*" in the *Loci communes* (1521 ed.), repr. in *Melanchthons Werke in Auswahl*, ed. R. Stupperich (Gütersloh: Mohn, 1978), 2 Band, 1 teil, 78.
[12]See the biography by U. Rozzo in *DBI* 22: 713–14.
[13]See the biography by V. I. Comparato in *DBI* 14: 262–63.

you, and act with all your strength for the sake of the honor of God and of so many of his poor sheep. It is necessary to take action at once, and not lose time in this.

I commend myself to the chaste and fervent prayers of all of you, leaving you in the most pure blood of the slaughtered lamb, and beseeching you to have this diabolical fox seized, who *scienter* has told a hundred lies in his last sermon, and many errors.[14]

This is a glimpse of the sentiments among these Lutheran sympathizers in a city such as Florence, where the echo of Savonarola was not yet extinguished. Fra Giuliano, a participant in clandestine meetings of Protestants and Valdesians in Venice, after his "Lutheran" sermons that were not unlike the Lenten preaching taking place in Verona, Parma, Milan, Ferrara, and Venice, was summoned to Rome to defend himself. In 1552, he was ordered to return to Florence to make a solemn recantation from the pulpit of the convent of Santo Spirito, which closed with the words: "*Extra ecclesiam nulla salus.*" Moreover, we also know of the tumult caused in Siena by the preaching of Agostino Museo, and the subsequent intervention and involvement of such personages as Lattanzio Tolomei, Tullio Crispoldi, Gasparo Contarini, and Marcantonio Flaminio.[15]

The trial against the provincial of the Augustinians of Palermo, Ambrogio Bolognesi (1507–56) attests to the thread of continuity among "Lutheran" preachers of the order, even after the decree on justification was approved by the Council of Trent (13 January 1547) sealing the defeat of the reform party.[16] His highly skillful and learned defense, which argued that the points of doctrine considered scandalous were actually authentic Augustinian teaching, did not save him from being confined in a small convent in the environs of Palermo.

On the morning of 20 January 1552, the day of Saint Sebastian, in the church of the Nunziata in Palermo, the provincial, the highest authority of the order in Palermo, delivered a sermon before a great crowd of spectators, among whom mingled the youthful professors from the Jesuit College, zealous custodians of orthodoxy. To refute beyond a shadow of a doubt the opinions of Pelagius, which affirmed the sovereignty of the grace of God, the speaker took as his authorities the Council of Orange, which, meeting on 3 July 1529, had condemned semi-Pelagianism, and three scriptural texts: Isa. 10:15, Ps. 44:2, and the classic Gospel reference: "*Sine me nihil potesti facere*" (John 15:5). Without going into the particulars of his exegesis, borrowed from Alfonso di Castro, we know from evidence supplied by the Spaniard Pietro de Riva del Neyda, how it was received by the public: "He declared that our *libero arbitrio* was like a small child who does not know how to write and the grace of God was like the teacher, which takes the child's hand guiding it and teaching it to

---

[14]*Monumenta Historica Societatis Jesu, Epistulae mixtae* 1:382–83. On L. Davidico, cf. the biographical sketch by C. von Flüe, in *DBI* 43:157–60.

[15]See the biography by M. Rosa in *DBI* 1:489–91; V. Marchetti, *Gruppi ereticali senesi del Cinquecento* (Florence: "La Nuova Italia," 1975), 18–24.

[16]S. Caponetto, "Dell'agostiniano Ambrogio Bolognesi e del suo processo d'eresia a Palermo," *BHR* 20 (1958): 310–43 (repr. in the author's *Studi sulla Riforma*, 143–76).

make marks...." Bystanders must have been stupefied when Master Ambrogio, in an indignant outburst, inveighed against those who entrusted their salvation to their own works rather than to Jesus Christ, pretending to be justified by their "cursed *pater nosters*," an unambiguous allusion to the recent introduction of the rosary.

The trial of Ambrogio Bolognesi, the culmination of a long process in the diffusion of Lutheran teachings on the island, brings us back to an environment of bitter polemics, opposition by the ecclesiastical authorities to ideas that had been espoused by many, sometimes even in the solitary meditation of the cloister, as seems to have been the case with Fra Ambrogio. The investigation did not turn up evidence that he had ties with persons who harbored erroneous opinions in matters of the faith.

Nevertheless, his was not an isolated case among Sicilian Augustinians. In 1543 Pietro Granata was reconciled in Messina and Giacomo Anfulio in Salemi; in 1549 it was the turn of Filippo Carboni. Giovanni Grasso, prior of the convent in Messina, was condemned in 1568 to wear the penitential garment for six years. He may have been related to the gentleman Melchiorre Grasso, who fled to Geneva in 1563 together with his son Colantuono, and to Norella Grasso, wife of the weaver Antonio, reconciled to the church the same year. Later yet, in 1574, Fra Giovanni Pietro Perrone of Messina, who had probably died in prison awaiting the conclusion of his trial, was burned in effigy.[17]

Bibliographical Note

For the crisis experienced by the Augustinian order in the sixteenth century, the fundamental work is H. Jedin, *Girolamo Seripando*, 2 vols., Würzburg, 1937, also available in a reduced English translation: *Papal Legate at the Council of Trent: Cardinal Seripando*, tr. F. C. Eckhoff (St. Louis: Herder, 1947). See also D. Gutiérrez, "Hieronymi Seripandi, 'Diarium de vita sua' (1513–62)," *Analecta Augustiniana* 25 (1963).

[17]See S. Caponetto, "Bartolomeo Spadafora e la Riforma protestante in Sicilia nel secolo XVI," *Rinascimento*, 7 (1956): 219–341 (repr. in the author's *Studi sulla Riforma*, 5–139, passim).

Luther's coat of arms: a rose with a cross at the center.

3

FROM THE SPOKEN ᵀᴼ THE WRITTEN WORD

THE IMPACT OF PRINTING

"RARELY HAS ONE INVENTION had more decisive influence than that of printing on the Reformation."[1] The reformers, beginning with Luther, considered it a divine gift. In 1563 John Foxe wrote in his *Book of Martyrs*: "the Lord began to work for his church, not with sword and target to subdue his exalted adversary, but with printing, writing, and reading....Wherefore, I suppose, that either the pope must abolish printing, or he must seek a new world to reign over; for else, as this world stands, printing doubtless will abolish him."[2]

In Italy too, in this early phase when the new ideas circulated primarily through the spoken word from the pulpit, even though the name of the excommunicated German monk was never mentioned, there was a desire to learn more about him and his teachings, to read with one's own eyes his assertion that a true reform of the church required a return to the Gospel of Christ.

A document uncommon for its clarity and simplicity provides a glimpse of daily life in the 1520s, with its longings, preoccupations, and anxieties provoked by the religious revolution in Germany. I allude to a letter written to his father in Padua, on 18 February 1524 by Girolamo, brother of Francesco Negri, future author of the *Tragedia del libero arbitrio*, who was at the time a Benedictine in the monastery of Santa Giustina in Padua under his religious name of Fra Simeone da Bassano. Girolamo had gone to visit his brother at San Giorgio Maggiore in Venice where he was attending to some business of his religious house. Girolamo had been sent by their father to inquire about rumors that Simeone was an admirer of Martin Luther, even to the

---

[1] E. Eisenstein, *The Printing Press as an Agent of Change: Communications and Cultural Transformations in Early-Modern Europe*, 2 vols. (Cambridge: Cambridge University Press, 1978), 1:309.

[2] *The Acts and Monuments of the Church: Containing the History and Sufferings of the Martyrs* (New York: Worthington, N.D.), 355.

point of contemplating a trip to Germany to meet him. In Venice, while occupied purchasing "nuts and rice" to send back to Bassano, between one topic and another, Girolamo asked his brother: "And about brother Martin, is anything much being said, because in Padua we hear such tales..." After smiling at gossip that Luther was recruiting soldiers for the king of France, to Girolamo's specific question, "All right then, what's your opinion about his teachings?" Fra Simeone replied, as he had done on other occasions, "His teachings seem a good thing to me, because in truth they are founded totally on Sacred Scripture."

Girolamo's letter to his father, written to calm down the fantasies he had imagined, concluded: "He says that the teachings of Martin Luther are based on Holy Scripture and that he is trying to get some of his books. These notions, in my opinion, are held by all those who have read some work of this Martin, because, in fact, I have spoken with many who have read something of his, and they all say the same thing: namely, that Martin's writings are founded on Scripture, and that, if they could obtain them, they would gladly buy them."[3]

Luther had become the man of the hour just a few years after the publication of his famous trilogy in 1520, circulated with missionary zeal by his supporters and followers and with extraordinary business acumen by the booksellers in northern Italy, where lively commercial relations with Germany and Switzerland were maintained. Whether what was being said about him was good or bad, it was no longer confined to the universities of Padua, Pavia, Siena, Turin, or Bologna, which were attended by foreign students in great numbers. Talk about brother Martin could be heard on church steps, in artisans' shops, in the taverns, grocers' shops, and marketplaces.

Menato's quip in Ruzante's *La Moscheta*, a play performed during the 1528 carnival season, would have been incomprehensible to spectators, among whom were many from the lower classes, were it not for the echo it contained of the reformer's *De servo arbitrio*, his reply to Erasmus in 1525 in their quarrel over free will. Menato, complaining that he has been bewitched by Betta, Ruzante's wife, exclaims: "Bah, but these women really do have great power, who drag men around where they want, to our vexation. And then she claims that there is free will!" (act 1, scene 1). And again in 1528, Ruzante, in his second oration before Cardinal Francesco Cornaro, lamenting the ruin of the church, which was depicted as overgrown with thorns and briars, blamed "that German Martinello the lutist," because many people no longer went to confession or to Vespers.[4]

In 1541 the Venetian jeweler Alessandro Caravia, poet and admirer of popular verse, had a short composition of his own published, for which he would be tried in 1556. The *Sogno* or "Dream" reflects discussions in Venice about Luther and his

[3]Cited by G. Zonta, "Francesco Negri l'eretico e la sua tragedia 'Il libero arbitrio,'" *GSLI* 67 (1916), 274–76. A second installment is cited at note 27 in this chapter.
[4]See L. Zorzi, *Ruzante, Teatro* (Turin: Einaudi, 1967), 1393–95, and note 15. Obviously, the image of the German reformer, competent lutist, and despised for this by the Anabaptists, as attested by the schoolteacher of Rothenburg, Valentin Jekelsheimer, in a violent pamphlet of 1525, from which Ruzante took his expression, had reached the German *Fondaco* in Venice. Cf. the *Flugschrift: Clag etlicher Brüder*, ed. E. L. Enders in *Aus der Kampf der Schwärmer gegen Luther*, Flugschriften aus der Reformationszeit, 10 (Halle, 1895), 48.

popularity among artisans, especially jewelers who had established among themselves a clandestine association so that they could discuss religious questions at their ease.

In the confession made at Venice in 1567 by Teofilo Panarelli, to whom we shall return later, who had been arrested as one of the Protestant leaders, we read: "There was a company among the jewelers, who held as a clear and certain fact that man was saved without works, and that to do any good works including prayer which moved the spirit, was not a useful thing for the soul, but only gave sign of a perfect and charitable faith, about which they glorified themselves."[5] Luther's *sola fides* was praised by Caravia's *Il sogno* in these verses:

> One hears nothing else except disputation
> About this Martin, and his new laws
> Which I beseech God will come to prevail here
> Who can live by them, and doing so does not want the proofs,
> By now it is time to restore
> The holy faith of the eternal Jove,
> Now it is time that the great majority
> Who lives in this world should govern itself right....
> This Martin, from what we hear,
> Excels in all branches of learning,
> He abandons not the pure Gospel.
> Luther has confused the minds of many:
> One says that only Christ can pardon us,
> Another that Paul III and Clement may.
> There are those who pull and those who yield,
> Who speak the truth, who lie through their teeth.[6]

THE FIRST ITALIAN TRANSLATIONS

In 1525 a small anonymous anthology of Lutheran writings entitled *Uno Libretto volgare, con la dechiaratione de li dieci comandamenti, del Credo, del Pater noster, con una breve annotatione del vivere christiano* was published by the Venetian press of Nicolò di Aristotile, detto Zoppino. Six editions were produced in a period of roughly thirty years: three anonymously and three under the name of Erasmus. When Luther first saw the book, he exclaimed enthusiastically, according to his follower and table companion Johann Mathesius: "Blessed are the hands which wrote it, the eyes which saw it, the hearts which will believe what is written in this book,

[5]Cited by E. Pommier, "La société venitienne et la Réforme protestante au XVI siècle," *Bollettino dell'Istituto di storia della società e dello Stato veneziano* 1 (1959): 18.
[6]*Il sogno dil Caravia*. In Vinegia: nelle case di Giovanni Antonio di Nicolini da Sabbio, 1541, verses 344 and 349. Quoted from E. Benigni Clementi, "Il processo del gioielliere veneziano Alessandro Caravia," *NRS* 65 (1981): 638. On Caravia, see the biographical sketch by L. Zorzi in *DBI* 19:672, and F. Ambrosini, "Ortodossia cattolica e tracce di eterodossia nei testamenti veneziani del Cinquecento," *Archivio Veneto*, ser. 5, 136 (1991): 35–46.

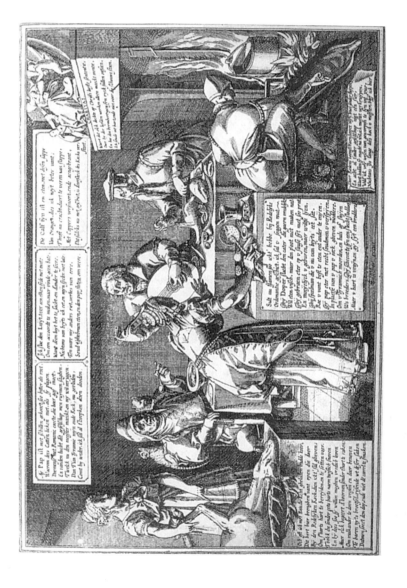

Engraving by the Dutchman C. J. Visscher (c. 1570), Anabaptist in inspiration, invoking toleration and religious peace. In the great kitchen every religious faction (the pope, Luther, Calvin, and the Anabaptist) is allowed to prepare its own repast. Note Luther playing the lute (Herzog August Bibliothek, Wolfenbüttel).

and who then praise God."[7] This modest work, imbued with an ardent Christocentric piety and eschewing any sort of virulent polemic against Rome, was a valuable propaganda instrument, suitable in its simplicity for all readers and in harmony with the message being preached by Augustinians from the pulpit, soon to be joined by Franciscans, and in southern Italy by the Minims of San Francesco di Paola.

A few years later in 1533, when the possibility of imperial approval of the Augsburg Confession had passed, Luther's major controversialist work, *An Open Letter to the Christian Nobility of the German Nation*, first published in 1520, appeared in Italian at Strasbourg as *Libro de la emendatione et correctione dil stato christiano*. This writing, revised for the better comprehension on the part of an Italian public, has been judged by Silvana Seidel Menchi to be "a successful transplanting of the Protestant message into Italian soil, a work of a very high level, even literarily."[8]

But the book that in these early days spread Lutheran teaching throughout the peninsula better than all others was the ingenious synthesis compiled by Philipp Melanchthon, his *Loci communes theologici*, originally published at Wittenberg in 1521. This little work, translated into elegant Italian by one of the great literary critics and writers of the century, Ludovico Castelvetro, appeared between 1530 and 1534, emanating from the printing shop of Paolo Manuzio. It was published with the clever and original title of *I Principii de la Theologia di Ippofilo da Terra Negra*, a play on Melanchthon's family name of Schwarzerd.[9] The 1521 *Loci* represent the first attempt to systematize the essential points of Lutheran doctrine, the first *summa* of the Reformation, written in an extremely clear Latin, and possessed with logic and structure that even today fill the reader with admiration. The *Loci* constitute an anguished reflection on the finiteness of man before God, on the impossibility of knowing God "in wisdom through wisdom," and on the need to abandon ourselves, with Saint Paul, "to the scandal of the Gospel message." Melanchthon, a professor of Greek, who had put aside Plato and Aristotle, recognized the unbridgeable chasm between the Gospel message and humanism. Nevertheless, he realized that the humanistic method of returning *ad fontes* remained valid, in fact appeared to him indispensable for the new faith, based as it was on Sacred Scripture and on the life of the apostolic church in its first centuries, not yet corrupted by pagan philosophy and Scholasticism. Castelvetro saw in this synthesis, both reasoned and polemical, vis-à-vis the Roman church, a guide in the search for a faith that was not "historical," but "living and true" in the "benefit of Christ," that is, in the gift of salvation through his death on the cross. The *Loci* led him to the heart of the Gospel message, to the realistic awareness of the tragedy of human destiny, and the abandonment of the Renaissance myth of the *homo faber fortunae suae*.

[7]S. Seidel Menchi, "Le traduzioni," 40ff.
[8] Ibid., 80. The translation has been attributed to Bartolomeo Fonzio (see chap. 4, p. 43).
[9]See S. Caponetto, *Due opere di Melantone tradotte da Ludovico Castelvetro: "I Principii de la Theologia di Ippofilo da Terra Negra," e "Dell'autorità della Chiesa e degli scritti degli antichi,"* NRS 70 (1986): 253–74, repr. in idem, *Studi sulla Riforma,* 351–74. My edition of the sixteenth-century Italian version of the *Loci communes* was published by the Istituto storico italiano per l'età moderna e contemporanea with the title *I principii della teologia* (Rome, 1992).

The *Loci* marked a decisive stage in Castelvetro's cultural journey. And not just for him but also for other humanists, men of letters such as Teofilo Folengo, Marcantonio Flaminio, and Aonio Paleario, who read Melanchthon's text in the original or in Castelvetro's beautiful translation. In the latter form it traveled widely throughout the peninsula, from Venice to Rome, from Modena to Lucca and Siena, and from Florence to Naples. The great French philologist and humanist, Joseph Scaliger, son of Julius Caesar Scaliger who had converted to Calvinism in 1562, met many learned persons during an Italian journey in 1565, among whom was Serafino Rezalio Olivario, who had been born in Lyons, but was living in Italy in the service of the papal curia. Rezalio recounted to Scaliger an amusing story of many years before. For more than a year, the *Principii* was being sold openly in Rome without anyone noticing that the book was Melanchthon's *Loci*, until a Franciscan exposed this. So many copies were subsequently burned and so thorough was the destruction that the work does not even appear in any of the Indices of Prohibited Books.

What role precisely did this fascinating work play in the early days of the Reformation in Italy? It is clear, even after a cursory reading, that the Lutheran doctrine of justification by faith alone and the spirituality of the "benefit of Christ," through Melanchthon and Castelvetro, had received the first systematic theological exposition, before the *Sommario della Sacra Scrittura* (1537), before the circulation in manuscript of the works of Juan de Valdés, and at least ten years before the publication at Venice in 1543 of the *Trattato utilissimo del beneficio di Gesù Christo crocifisso*, the title of which it certainly had anticipated in affirming that "scholastic theologians" had with their ruminations "obscured the message and benefits of Christ."[10]

Roughly in the years between 1519 and 1530, knowledge of Luther's ideas and works was limited to persons who were in a position to read the writings of the Catholic controversialists. If we reflect further, that the few books by Luther translated into Italian presented him as a theologian of fervent Christocentric piety, but did not reveal the great polemicist, the destroyer of the hierarchical and sacramental edifice of the Church of Rome, then the edifying function of Castelvetro's clear, logical, and elegant translation becomes obvious. The *Loci* are, as the author underlines, a commentary on Sacred Scripture, to which they allude continually as "a sweet and pure spring." The translator never omits references to Luther and to his works, nor does he leave out Melanchthon's own opinion that the condemnation of Luther, preacher of the message of grace, was contrary to divine law and without validity for Christians.

The translation efficaciously conveys the polemical thrust of the original against the sophistry of the Scholastics, against the theologians of the Sorbonne, against humanists who claim to know God by means of reason. "Philosophy is a chaos of carnal dreams.... As far as I can understand, the human mind cannot by itself determine anything certain about God." The attack on Roman tyranny is even sharper here than in the "second age" of the 1535 *Loci*: the translator does not neglect a single syllable. It is enough to quote, apropos the mass as sacrifice and offering for the living and for the dead, the damning statement: "The priestly celebrants are the prophets of

---

[10]*I principii della teologia*, 26; Caponetto, *Studi sulla Riforma*, 359.

Jezebel, that is, of Rome." The work contains a fervent appeal for the "freedom of conscience," the rights of the believer, the permissibility of rebelling against ecclesiastical and civil laws, inasmuch as they trample on the conscience of the Christian who has received the seal of the Holy Spirit: "And you have appropriated the not obscure statements of Scripture which teach us that consciences must not be bound by human traditions" (1 Cor. 3).[11] This is a vindication of human freedom and dignity, reacquired through the redeeming act of Christ, a reaffirmation without equivocation of the Erasmian theme of the liberation of man from the tyranny of human traditions, a message that did not remain confined to the world of the cultural elites.

About the year 1540, the Sicilian Lorenzo Romano, yet another Augustinian, who had divested himself of the habit of his order, set out for Germany "to prepare himself better." He returned imbued with Luther's teachings and enthusiastic about Melanchthon. In 1549, approximately, he opened a school in Piedimonte, near Caserta, attended by "many gentlemen." He taught from the *Logica* (i.e. *Loci*) of Melanchthon and the *Chronica* of Johann Carion, translated into Italian by Pietro Lauro (Venice: M. Tramezzino, 1548). Lorenzo would be condemned in Rome for Lutheranism in 1552.

An in-depth examination of Melanchthon's impact would not stop with the mention of his works in the lists of books confiscated and burned in the public squares of Italian cities. There is much other evidence such as that of the Modenese physician who, in 1547, considered the *praeceptor Germaniae* as "the most learned man which Germany possessed," or that dating from two decades earlier, of the priest and man of letters Lucio Paolo Rosello, who wrote to Melanchthon, at the time of the Diet of Augsburg in 1530, exhorting him to defend the cause of the reform of the church "*tamquam omnium evangelicorum caput,*" even at the cost of his life.[12]

THE MODERATE CONTROVERSY

Hermann Bodius's *Unio dissidentium*, reprinted in Venice in 1532 by Agostino de Bindonis, was a work that supported the Melanchthonian position. Originally appearing at Antwerp in 1527, and immediately condemned by the Sorbonne after the publication of the French version in 1531, it enjoyed twenty-four editions within a period of roughly forty years. The book is an immense anthology of passages taken from Scripture and from the church fathers on fundamental theological themes. The selections were made from a strictly Lutheran point of view and achieve a notable impact, furnishing the reader an imposing apparatus of *auctoritates* in defense of the new faith. It circulated widely, even in Italy.[13]

The great number of inquisitorial trials held in the peninsula and the islands, from the 1530s to the early decades of the seventeenth century, and the many inventories of books confiscated from booksellers and defendants, despite the general

---

[11] *I principii della teologia*, 85; Caponetto, *Studi sulla Riforma*, 360–61.
[12] Caponetto, *Studi sulla Riforma*, 353–54.
[13] P. F. Grendler, *The Roman Inquisition and the Venetian Press, 1540–1605* (Princeton: Princeton University Press, 1977), 75.

scarcity of documents, reveal the massive circulation in Italy of works by the great reformers and their major collaborators: Luther, Melanchthon, Bucer, Zwingli, Calvin, Brenz, Urbanus Rhegius, Erasmus Sarcerius, Ullrich Hutten, Johannes Bugenhagen, Georg Rörer, and many others. To these, after 1542, should be added the books and sermons of the Italians Ochino, Vermigli, Negri, Curione, Giulio della Rovere, Girolamo Donzellino, Antonio Brucioli, Pier Paolo Vergerio, Francesco Betti, Girolamo Cato, among others, concealed under pseudonyms or total anonymity. From Venice, the most important European center of book production, originated a network for the clandestine diffusion of heretical literature that arguably was without equal anywhere in Europe. From Augsburg, Lyons, Strasbourg, Basel, Geneva, Poschiavo, Bern, and Zurich flowed a stream of contraband literature that successfully overcame the obstacles thrown up by both civic and ecclesiastical authorities. In the Italian states, until the establishment of the Roman Inquisition in 1542, booksellers did not experience serious difficulties disposing of heretical works. The demand was so great as to constitute a lucrative business for them as well as for printers and publishers, many of whom were not supporters of the Reformation, but were eager to take advantage of the market. But some booksellers were favorable to the Protestant cause, such as Andrea di Giorgio Arrivabene, or the publisher, Pietro Perna, who emigrated to Basel and became the channel between that Swiss city and Venice, Bergamo, Padua, and Lucca.

By midcentury, especially in outlying areas, places of collection and distribution of prohibited books sprang up. This was the case at Consandolo, belonging to Ferrara, where, with the aid of the Calvinist duchess Renée, a repository of Protestant books was established. Alessandro Ressa of Imola disclosed this during his trial in 1551. When he asked the duchess's steward "if he had some Scriptural novelty," the latter replied: "As of now I don't have anything, but this coming month there might be something new, because every year couriers come down from Germany with some work or other of Scripture. And they make Consandolo their headquarters, from where they go to visit the Christian congregations and churches." Ressa had then requested that when one of them came, he should be sent to Imola, where he should ask for Nocento da Tossignano. The network provided not only for books and missions of proselytization but aid for victims of the Inquisition. A shoemaker at Consandolo "furnished a haven for all the persecuted and then sent them on to Ferrara, and then from place to place until they reached the land of the Lutherans."[14] This is at midcentury, when Italian reformers were still trying to organize, a phase to which we shall return.

Just as was the case at Consandolo, other small centers for the clandestine collection of heretical books sprang up in many Italian cities: Brescia, Venice, Padua, Verona, Florence, Lucca, Siena, Naples, and Messina. Methods, both simple and highly complex, were devised to circumvent customs agents and the surveillance of the Inquisition. Books, Bibles, pamphlets, fragments of Scripture, anticlerical engravings, and portraits of Luther were concealed in merchants' bales. Prohibited

---

[14]G. F. Cortini, "La Riforma e l'Inquisizione in Imola," *La Romagna* 16–17 (1927–28): 19.

books were shipped alongside and under cover of orthodox titles. There is the well-known joke played on Ignatius Loyola, who in 1551 received two cases of legitimate books under which were concealed some "pernicious works" of the Protestants.

In spite of the numerous bonfires lit in Turin, Venice, Milan, Florence, Naples, Palermo, and Messina, and the boast by the Venetian inquisitor, Fra Marino da Venezia that in the eight years of his term (1542–50) he had destroyed an "infinite number" of books,[15] rigorous measures such as the inspection of all the bookshops, and in Sicily the searching of ships arriving at the port of Messina had to be continued to the very end of the century.

Two Supportive Works: The "Dottrina vecchia e dottrina nuova" and the "Sommario della Santa Scrittura."

The enormous clandestine diffusion of the heretical book points to numerous readers, at least in the urban centers, exceeding by far what has been commonly believed. Two main types of publication were involved, directed at different levels of society: the more educated and the popular. The first included the original writings of the great reformers in Latin and in Italian translations. The second comprised works in the vernacular, suitable for persons of middling education, but intended also for artisans, laborers, and peasants. Among the latter, one work has been almost totally forgotten.

The *Opera utilissima intitolata dottrina vecchia et nuova* is the title given by the anonymous Italian translator to the small work by Urban König or Rhegius (1489–1541), which first appeared in Latin in 1526, the *Novae doctrinae ad veterem Collatio*.[16] The humanist and theologian Rhegius, who had been educated at Basel, preached the Reformation in Augsburg and Lünenburg. He resurrected the accusation with which the Jews had admonished Jesus, that he was preaching a "new doctrine," which, on the contrary, Rhegius felt, "was the true one," and he attacked the adversaries of the pure "message of Grace and glory of God." His book, which reduced the religious controversy to simple terms, claimed that the doctrine now called evangelical was actually the original Roman one, namely that preached by Jesus and the apostles.

---

[15]The book burnings had begun in the 1520s. About 1529 mass destruction occurred for 250 copies of works by Melanchthon, J. Jonas, Agricola, Bugenhagen, Zwingli (*De eucarestia*), Oecolampadius, 13 works by Luther, 7 by Zwingli, works of Hus and J. Lonicer. Cf. T. Elze, *Geschichte der protestantischen Bewegungen und der deutschen Evangelischen Gemeinde A.C. in Venedig* (Bielefeld: Belhagen, 1883), 9 ff. (2d rev. and expanded ed. by E. Lessing [Florence, 1941]).

[16]Published by K. Benrath, "Dottrina nuova e dottrina vecchia, compendio di controversia del sec. XVI," *Rivista Cristiana* 3 (1875): 137–58, 185–207. The book had more than ninety European editions. Three other works by this author appeared in Italian: the *Medicina dell'anima* (1545); the *Libretto consolatorio a li perseguitati per la confessione della verità evangelica* (1545); *Dottrina verissima tolta dal cap. IV. a Rom. per consolar le afflitte conscientie* (n.d.). After Luther, Rhegius is the most translated German writer, his mission to provide a pastoral program for the new believers. His *Medicina* was especially popular. It was printed on three occasions at Venice by Comin da Trino (1545) and by Valgrisi (1545, 1551).

The book stayed carefully within the boundaries of the church, appealing for its reformation, in which everything should be demonstrated "by the Word of God and by the Catholic Church," without discrediting or altering the foundations established by the fathers, at least those not contrary to "the cultivation of piety." The work goes on to affirm justification by faith alone, rejecting the efficacy of works, which are compared to "a polluted garment" (Isaiah 64:6). The Lord's Supper should be a remembrance of the benefit of redemption: to eat the body and to drink the blood of Jesus Christ means believing, in the manner of Zwingli, in the Word of Christ, "the price of our redemption, our satisfaction and justice." An irenic spirit transpires from the work, which mentions neither Luther, nor explicitly the Church of Rome. The *Novae doctrinae* enjoyed great success prior to the Diet of Augsburg in 1530. First prohibited in England in 1529 under the name of its actual author, and then anonymously in almost all subsequent *Indices of Prohibited Books*, it is found recorded by the Italian title in the Lucca *Index* of 1545. It soon went out of print and was superseded by the course of events, but it efficaciously assisted the Augustinian sympathizers of Luther in their proselytizing activities, as well as others who aspired to a reformation of the Roman church without a major rupture.

The *Sommario della santa Scrittura*, which appeared anonymously in 1534, without typographical information of any kind,[17] was another work that aided the missionary work of the Augustinians and Franciscans who had been converted to Lutheran teachings and supported the *Confessio Augustana*. The booklet made its first appearance in Modena in 1537 and subsequently everywhere else in Italy as far south as Naples, and was attacked by the Dominican Lancillotto de' Politi. Hundreds of copies were burned in the 1540s, but the work continued to circulate, at least in Modena, until 1567 to 1568. The *Sommario* is not an original composition, but the translation from the French of an anonymous writing, which had appeared in Dutch at Leiden in 1523: *De Summa der Godliker Scrifturen*. The champions of the new ideas saw the translation of this work as integral to their program of proselytization. The book asserted in simple words the doctrine of justification by faith alone, moderately criticized monasticism and its degradation, but mentioned neither the pope nor the Lutheran controversy. On that account it seemed a highly suitable vehicle for evangelizing the masses, just as the translation of Melanchthon's *Loci* was thought appropriate for theologians and educated persons. It is not improbable that the *Sommario* was translated in Modena alongside Castelvetro's Italian version of the *Loci communes*.

The *Sommario* enjoyed great popularity among the lower classes, because a somewhat theological first section is followed by a second entitled "*l'ordinario dei cristiani*," a brief manual of Christian ethics, which examines how one should act in different social situations. It discusses some of the liveliest questions of the day—marriage and conjugal life, the upbringing of children, exalting the Lutheran conception of manual labor: "In the entire world no life is more Christian and more in

---

[17]See *Il Sommario della santa Scrittura e l'ordinario dei cristiani*, a cura di C. Bianco, con una introduzione di J. Trapman (Turin: Claudiana, 1988).

harmony with the Gospel message than the life of common people, artisans and laborers, who by their own hands and the sweat of their brows (Gen. 3:19) earn their bread and sustenance."[18] The entire life of society is shown to be founded on their work and on their sacrifices. Artisans and laborers feed the clergy, nobles, and soldiers, as well as thieves and prostitutes, who do not labor themselves but exploit the work of others. This message probably explains the book's great success among the common people of the Garfagnana and Lunigiana, of Modena, the Veneto and Lombardy.

THE BRUCIOLI BIBLE

An exceptional role was played by the vernacular translations of Sacred Scripture in the propaganda wars waged through the printing press: the Italian versions of Antonio Brucioli and Massimo Teofilo and, for the Waldensians, the French translation in 1535 by Louis Olivier, known as Pierre Robert Olivétan, a cousin of John Calvin. The latter participated in this monumental publishing enterprise with two prefatory letters of exhortation, one to the princes and people, "subjects in the empire of Christ," and the other to the Jews, as well as with an introduction to the New Testament readings.

Similarly, the two Italian versions by Brucioli and Teofilo opened with prefaces by their translators or from Reformation texts, with the obvious intent of guiding the reader to discover the centrality of Jesus Christ in divine revelation. Brucioli's translation of the New Testament printed at Venice in 1530, followed two years later by the entire Bible, became one of the most successful vehicles for the dissemination of Reformation doctrines. Reprinted many times with an impressive commentary between 1540 and 1546, it penetrated all levels of Italian society, and was read in the rarefied culture of the courts at Urbino, Mantua, Ferrara, and Florence, in the stately homes of professional men and merchants, as well as in the poor dwellings of scarcely literate artisans, laborers, and peasants. The Florentine translator Brucioli addressed himself especially to the lower classes with simple language accessible to all. In the preface to the 1538 reprinting, dedicated to Princess Anna d'Este, the daughter of Renée of France, duchess of Ferrara, he stated:

> "Let the people then receive the sweet and loving visitation from Jesus Christ, in the celestial light of the Gospel, which is the true guide for Christians, a guide for life, a guide for salvation...in the knowledge that men and their learning count for nothing, except to the extent that they serve to confirm and fortify the Word of God...If we are all one in Christ, why should we not all eat of that evangelical bread, so that our minds become satiated for our edification?...
>
> "Some may indeed exclaim that it is an unworthy thing for a woman, or a shoemaker to speak of Sacred Scriptures and attempt to comprehend it through their own reading. Let us consider, also, who were Christ's listeners,

[18]Ibid., 156.

Left: Original illustration by Lucas Cranach the Elder for Luther's New Testament (printed by Melchior Lotter the Younger, Wittenberg, 1522). The engraving concerns chap. 11 of the Apocalypse and recalls Dürer's iconography: John measures God's temple and counts those worshipping within; on the first floor the two witnesses of Christ who are prophesying are attacked and killed by the beast rising up from the abyss. *Right:* The corresponding engraving in Brucioli's New Testament (Venice, 1532). Note that the timid allusion to the crown on the monster's head in Cranach, here has become emphatically a papal tiara.

oh, do we not find a varied multitude of blind men, cripples, mendicants, publicans, centurions, craftsmen, women, and children?

"Should Christ now be deprived of being read by those by whom he wanted to be heard? And why may they not approach the abundance of that great Jesus Christ of ours, the beggar, the smith, the peasant, the mason, the fisherman, publicans, and all the states of men and women, who had been worthy of hearing them from the mouth of Christ himself? I do not know how it cannot appear ridiculous that women and men, just like parrots, should whisper by rote their Psalms and their prayers in Latin or Greek, understanding nothing of what they are uttering, so that they are unable to edify their minds in any way...."[19]

Brucioli's dedication, reprinted in many subsequent editions, expressed his deepest feelings. Despite his vacillations and abjurations, he played a significant role in the diffusion of Reformation teachings through his Bible, which, even if not a literary masterpiece, dominated the book trade for more than a quarter century. But the work also helped to spread the doctrines of Luther and Calvin through revisions, adaptations, and even plagiarism, as Tommaso Bozza has once again recently demonstrated.[20]

P. P. Vergerio in his *Otto defensioni* recounts an episode that demonstrates the excitement aroused in the lowest classes by the reading of Scripture, for whom the printed word made concrete the message of salvation that they had only heard spoken of in church, in the homes of friends, or in their own shops. At the beginning of the 1540s a poor shoemaker of Pirano (Istria), somewhat literate, had purchased a book containing the Gospels in both the vernacular and Latin and read it often with his family. This fact was resented by some monks of the town, who went to his house and tore the book from his hands, proclaiming "that a man in his station should not be reading the Word of God."[21]

The Antichrist

Without wanting to overly simplify, one might say that roughly between 1540 and 1570, in the brief period during which the Italian Reformation movement made its greatest effort to expand throughout the peninsula by organizing religious

---

[19]Quoted from G. Spini, *Tra Rinascimento e Riforma: Antonio Brucioli* (Florence: "La Nuova Italia," 1940), 216–17.

[20]T. Bozza, *Calvino in Italia* (Rome: Arti grafiche italiane, 1966), 3–10.

[21]Quoted from A. J. Schutte, *Pier Paolo Vergerio: The Making of an Italian Reformer* (Geneva: Droz, 1977), 181. For the entire century Catholic preachers inveighed against illiterate "mechanics" and the "dregs of the populace" who dared to debate the "loftiest doctrines of our faith." See the sermon by A. Castiglioni, cited in D. Cantimori, "Le idee religiose del Cinquecento: La storiografia," in *Storia della letteratura italiana, V: Il Seicento* (Milan: Garzanti, 1967), 45–46 (repr. 1979, 37–38).

communities outside the jurisdiction of the Church of Rome, the effort to prose-lytize through the printed word changed course profoundly.

Undoubtedly the different strategy, with respect to the initial phase of accom-modation with the religious and social realities of the country, presupposed an orga-nized homogeneous movement, and not merely a movement of ideas. Nevertheless, it should be remembered that some of the leaders and protagonists of this second phase were the same persons who had acknowledged the defeat of their aspirations for a reformation of the church and a reunification of the body of Christ: the Augus-tinians Agostino Mainardi, Giulio della Rovere, Peter Martyr Vermigli, Ortensio Lando; Bernardino Ochino, ex-general of the Capuchins who had fled, no longer content to preach "a disguised Christ"; Pier Paolo Vergerio, the former bishop of Capodistria, who under the accusation of Lutheranism had seen the collapse of his experiment to reform his diocese; Francesco Negri, a former Benedictine, who wrote the *Tragedia del libero arbitrio*. After the collapse at Ratisbon in 1541 of the Erasmian and Melanchthonian dream of the reunification of all Christians under the authority of the Word of God, and the establishment in 1542 of the Roman Inquisition, the situation changed dramatically. Under the impetus of the Swiss-Rhenish Reforma-tion, which the Piedmontese Waldensians joined at the assembly of Chanforan in 1532, the printed word became an arm of unfettered violent controversy, without the subtleties and ambiguities of the *Beneficio di Cristo* and the silences of the *Sommario della santa Scrittura*. The pope was now singled out as the Antichrist and the Church of Rome as the Babylon of Revelation.

Alongside the books by reformers and their leading collaborators, Italy was over-run by small works in the vernacular, pamphlets, broadsides, medals, and engravings deriding the Catholic Church and its acolytes. Translations of Protestant booklets were also clandestinely produced. To be sure, for the rest of the century the circula-tion of more edifying literature continued, from the *Paraphrases* of Erasmus, to Luther's commentaries, from such works of Juan de Valdés as the *Alfabeto cristiano* and the *Cento e dieci divine considerazioni*, to the sermons of Ochino. But the pasqui-nades, Vergerio's vituperative booklets, the attacks against Nicodemism by Vergerio, F. Negri, and A. Trissino also multiplied.

Among this popular propaganda, a satirical writing by Ochino entitled *Imagine di Antechristo*, first printed at Geneva by Jean Gérard in 1542, later translated into French and German (1545), Spanish (1557), and Latin (1558), enjoyed special suc-cess. The central argument unfolds through a series of juxtapositions easily compre-hensible even by the uneducated. The sequences recall intimately Lucas Cranach's *Passional Christi und Antichristi* (1521): Christ paid his tribute so as not to cause scandal; the Antichrist will enrage the entire world with extortions exacted through tithes and crushing taxes; Christ preached peace but the Antichrist foments war among Christians; "Christ's sword is the Word of God, the Antichrist's is the inven-tion of men"; Christ triumphed on the cross and the Antichrist in his pleasures; Christ carried the cross to die on it and the Antichrist holds it over his shoes to force the faithful to kiss them and kneel before him; Christ called him "Abomination" (Matt. 24:15) and Saint Paul, "man of sin and son of perdition, violator of the laws of nature such as marriage" (Dan. 12:11; 1 Thess. 2:3–10 and 1 Tim. 4:1–5).[22] Ochino's pasquinade circulated widely since its *editio princeps* was placed as an appendix to his Genevan *Prediche* of 1542, brought to Florence by Ludovico Manna, together with the *Considerations* of Juan de Valdés.

This is not the place to attempt a description of the entire controversialist literature with which the Italian reformers, primarily those who had chosen exile, and who had the requisite theological and literary preparation, vigorously attacked the Roman church and Curia. But we cannot avoid discussing at least two of the works which enjoyed enormous popularity in Italy and abroad, namely Celio Secondo Curione's *Pasquino in estasi* and Francesco Negri's *Tragedia del libero arbitrio*.

The *Pasquino* began to circulate in Italy in 1543, the year of the first edition which appears to be no longer extant. It was followed, in 1546, with a second version revised to reflect political and religious circumstances in the peninsula, following the failure of irenic hopes for reconciliation, and the opening of the Council of Trent (1545) without Protestant participation. Recalling themes from a collection of satirical pasquinades that he had published in two volumes at Basel in 1544, Curione imagined that the statue of Pasquino in Rome becomes transformed through a magical intervention into a human being who has fallen into ecstasy. In this trance, an angel accompanies him on an extraterrestrial voyage towards heaven. But first the angel shows him the paradise of the popes, placed at the spiritual and physical extremities of God's heaven. The visit reveals all the deceit and misdeeds of popes, monks, theologians, and canonists, distributed around the circles of an immense mountain, resembling Dante's purgatory.

As Albano Biondi has cogently argued,[23] the *Pasquino in estasi* is a destructive and iconoclastic representation of the Roman ecclesiastical edifice, a book of harsh propaganda by one of the great humanist writers of the Reformation, where Erasmian humor fuses admirably with popular anticlericalism and the Protestant pamphlet literature. The booklet presents the fundamental principles of the Reformation with an uncommon elegance and persuasiveness, thus making it acceptable both to intellectuals capable of grasping such Erasmian subtleties in the Silenic opening as the contrast between appearance and reality in the church ("Outside I am one thing, inside, another"), and to less educated people, more familiar with anticlerical barbs and caricatures.

In an age when Renaissance culture had reached its fullness, no reader could miss the revolutionary significance of the following initial statement: "Who is there who does not know that in past times, when good letters and study slept, all Christians considered these [monks] as God's own nephews? And that they esteemed more highly their teachings than God's? They did not know Christ, who has revealed the Gospel to us, which they kept concealed. Thus, since they alone administered the

[22]Repr. in B. Ochino, *I "dialogi sette" e altri scritti del tempo della fuga*, a cura di U. Rozzo (Turin: Claudiana, 1985), 147–52.
[23]See A. Biondi, "Il 'Pasquillus extaticus' di C. S. Curione nella vita religiosa italiana della prima metà del '500," *BSSV* 91 (1970), n. 128, and the author's biographical sketch of Curione in *DBI* 31:442–48.

book of peace and freedom, people thought that they took all things from that book...." On the contrary, "with false and invented purgatories," they kept the innocent populace gripped by fear and constrained to bear laws even heavier than the Jewish law. Against the cult of saints and all the superstitions attached to it, the central doctrine of Revelation is reaffirmed: salvation only by means of faith in the sacrifice of Jesus Christ. Christ is everything: savior, master, pastor, pontiff, sole mediator, selected by the Father as his beloved Son. "Why should we want to seek for other advocates? Are we not committing an offense against the Father?" The salvation freely given through faith destroys the illegitimate commerce of indulgences and the priestly invention of purgatory. "Through the Word of God you will find no other purgatory than the Blood of Christ; since through it all sins are perfectly pardoned, great is the sin of those who allege that there is another purgatory, and enormous and most harmful is the stupidity of those who believe it." A timeless devotional practice that had been perpetuated by the church for the purification of the souls of the dead is thus branded as sinful. To search for another purgatory signifies "voiding his passion and saying that his works are imperfect." At this point there is no possibility that the Church of Rome can be reformed; it has been revealed as the Babylon of Revelation and the pope as Antichrist.

Pasquino's barbs are not directed only against priests and monks, cardinals and popes. His targets are also lords and princes, the powerful and their allies who rule over the humble. They too, just like the popes and their acolytes, have ended up in hell, but for "lordly sins, such as *verbi gratia* never forgiving injuries, carrying on vendettas, being...the reason for the deaths of so many peoples just to satisfy their own appetites, violating their vassals' women, punishing the good, rewarding the bad, despising virtue and favoring vice, and other such *peccadillos.*"

Under such circumstances, while the cause of the Gospel was progressing elsewhere in Europe, there was little hope for Italy where persecution raged against such courageous witnesses as Girolamo Galateo and compelled, out of fear, many who had preached the new faith to return to the fold. But there was still one hope for the seven thousand who had not knelt before Baal, namely that the Venetian Republic would resist the papal tyranny, which compelled it to condemn to death its own subjects as heretics and thus sacrifice its own freedom of action: "If they [the Venetians] had not shown so much respect to that tyrant [the pope], they would now be lords of all Italy; and this could still happen if they would only embrace the Gospel of Jesus Christ, bestower of all power and wealth."[24] We will see many of these ideas repeated in the confessions of persons accused and condemned for "Lutheranism" in the trials held everywhere in Italy.

Antonio Rotondò, comparing the *Pasquino in estasi* with declarations made by defendants in trials held in the Modena area, has cogently emphasized the book's contribution to bringing about the repudiation of the old ecclesiastical institutions,

---

[24][C. S. Curione], *Pasquino in estasi nuovo e molto più pieno ch'el primo* [n.p., but with the false indication of Rome, 1546], 52, 163, 184–85, 222, 229, 261–65.

starting with the twin premises of freely bestowed justification and the individual's right to a personal reading of Scripture.[25]

Francesco Negri (1500–63) experienced his crisis, concerning which we quoted earlier from the illuminating letter written by his brother Girolamo to their father, in the spring of 1525 when Francesco abandoned the Benedictine monastery of Santa Giustina in Padua and headed for Germany, attracted by Luther's fame. From 1529 to 1531 he lived in Strasbourg where he eagerly attended the lectures in theology given by Wolfgang Capito and Martin Bucer. To support himself and his family (he had married Cunegonda Fessi), he worked as a weaver.

In 1531 Capito wrote to Zwingli asking him to find a position in the Grisons for Negri, given his solid educational preparation and gifts as a preacher. In 1538 Negri did settle in Chiavenna, where he started a school and taught Latin and Greek. Here he remained until 1555, when he moved to the neighboring town of Tirano. In 1562 he abandoned the Grisons for Poland, but died the following year at Pinczów, where he had tried to minister to an *"ecclesiola italica,"* which vanished with him. The literary career of the restless former Benedictine took place entirely during his years in Chiavenna. Negri was a humanist, and also, like Paleario, an elegant Latin poet, whose verse composition, *Rhetia*, was esteemed highly. G. Zonta has emphasized the contrast between this rustic poem, imbued with the exile's nostalgia for his homeland and his need for peace and solitude, and the polemical *Tragedia del libero arbitrio*, "a bitter invective reeking with hate and rancor against the Church, of which he had once been a member, and against its head, the pope, whom he and his comrades called the 'Antichrist.'"[26]

The *Tragedia* was first published in 1546 and reprinted clandestinely by Antonio Brucioli in 1547. A second edition, expanded and revised by the author, was produced by the presses of Dolfin Landolfi at Poschiavo in 1550. Just like the *Pasquino in estasi* it circulated all over Europe. It was placed on the *Index* by Giovanni Della Casa in 1548, published in French versions in 1558 and 1559, translated into Latin by the author, and finally into English in 1589.

The *Tragedia* is the offspring of the Italian and German pasquinades collected by Curione. It has nothing either theatrical or poetic about it. As opposed to the *Pasquino* where gracious descriptions and literary images are plentiful, here the allegorical personages are inhuman abstractions. King Free Will, worried about rebellions in the realm, which had been conferred upon him by the pope in centuries past, convokes a council in Saint Peter's Square to determine what measures he should take. But his attempts to quell the rebellion fomented by Germany in his eight provinces (Monkdom, Cult of Saints, Construction of Religious Places, Penance, Fasting, Prayer, Charity, the Mass) are all in vain. God sends justifying Grace to slay King Free Will. After this, the existence of the Antichrist, namely the pope, the vicar not of Christ but of the devil, the beast of Revelation, will be disclosed to the world. This

---

[25]See A. Rotondò, "Anticristo e Chiesa romana: Diffusione e metamorfosi d'un libello antiromano del Cinquecento," *Forme e destinazione del messaggio religioso: Aspetti della propaganda religiosa del Cinquecento*, a cura di A. Rotondò (Florence: Olschki, 1991), 19–164, esp. 55ff.

[26]G. Zonta, "Francesco Negri," 300.

slender structure is exploited to distribute, over five acts, the satirical and damaging description of all the doctrinal inventions from which the pope and his theologians profit. It was precisely this polemical force that made this small work so fascinating for religious dissidents.[27]

It is understandable that the *Tragedia* should have been found on the bookshelves of the educated classes, which grasped its message and found amusement in the barbs aimed at curial writers and such Catholic reformers as Reginald Pole and the bishops Grimani and Soranzo, who knew justification by faith, but remained "adorers" of the pope and practitioners of the mass. But that the work should also arouse the interest of artisans and that it should be read in their shops during the hours of work, is further proof of the tremendous interest in religious questions pervading all social classes.

In early 1567, for example, a family named Locatelli, but known as "*Catinari*" from their work with wooden vessels (*catini*), which hailed from Mapello in the Bergamo region, was put on trial. On May 31, Giacomo Locatelli, together with a baker and a comb maker, was convicted of having read the *Tragedia*. Locatelli's house was razed to the ground and in its place a column of infamy was erected. His entire family was thus made to feel the consequences of his heretical readings. On October 26, Sebastiano Locatelli, his brother Giovanni, his son Francesco, and a certain Pietro Martire Providon were forced to abjure their errors in the cathedral of Forlì.[28] As we shall see later on, Negri's book was circulating in Faenza in the hands of such ecclesiastics and professional men as Don Girolamo Dal Pozzo and the doctor of laws, Giovanni Evangelista Calderoni.

The network for the diffusion of the new religious ideas through the agency of the printing press reached every corner of the peninsula. Alongside the pamphlet literature, here barely touched upon, Ugo Rozzo and Silvana Seidel Menchi have identified fifty-four so-called "hybrid books," all as yet unstudied.[29] The compilers of these publications inserted into perfectly orthodox works passages from the writings of prohibited authors, from Erasmus to Luther and Calvin, and, among the Italians, such authors as Antonio Brucioli, Ortensio Lando, or the anonymous translator of the two *Dialogues* by Alfonso de Valdés, to which we shall return. The intended recipients of this concealed controversialist literature were persons of a certain cultural level, in whom it was hoped doubts could be insinuated about traditional theology and those teachings of the Roman church which did not conform to Scripture.

An operation of this type was attempted by a certain Girolamo Cato of Pesaro, about whom we know nothing besides his condemnation to prison before December 1550 and his escape from the *rocca* Costanza in Pesaro with the aid of friends from that city and Gubbio.[30] Cato had been tried for having his translation of two works

---

[27]Idem, *GSLI* 68 (1916): 108–59.

[28]F. Lanzoni, *La Controriforma nella città e diocesi di Faenza* (Faenza: F. Lega, 1925), 175.

[29]U. Rozzo and S. Seidel Menchi, "Livre et Réforme en Italie," J.-F. Gilmont, ed., *La Réforme et le livre* (Paris: Cerf, 1990), 327–74.

[30]On G. Cato, who may have some connection with Costantino Cato, tried at Venice on the charge of Lutheranism in 1559 and 1562 (ASV, Sant'Uffizio, b. 14 and b. 18), see my "Motivi di riforma religiosa," 271–73.

by Cyprian printed at Venice in 1547: the *De habitu virginum* and the *De singularitate clericorum*, a spurious writing as demonstrated by Erasmus who had edited three editions of that church father's *Opera omnia*. Cato's translations are preceded by a dedication to the Vicentine gentleman Matteo Pigafetta, who belonged to a family, which along with the da Thiene, was implicated in the Reformation movement in Vicenza and Venice. Pigafetta, a severe critic of corrupt clergy, had allegedly beseeched the author to translate the two works as a response to those persons who sustained the validity of sacraments administered by unworthy priests.

The language in the dedication is that of the *"spirituali"* of the Catholic reform movement, but its author is a Protestant pamphleteer, skillfully hiding behind the facade of a holy martyr. This can be seen easily by reading a section placed at the end of the book, the "Hundred conclusions, some gathered from the teachings of Cyprian the martyr taken from his translated works and others from the understanding of the authority of Scripture amply cited therein...." These pages are unnumbered and could be detached from the main body of the work and circulated separately. The first of these "Conclusions" restates a Reformation teaching: that prohibition of marriage and of foods created by God is a demonic doctrine and those who uphold it are false prophets—a belief of the Antichrist, Bernardino Ochino had written a few years earlier. This may be the key to understanding the decidedly antifeminist tone of "To the women, virgins, married and widowed," which served as a preface to the *De habitu virginum*, where it is stated that "chastity and virginity" are a gift of God, and where the Lutheran and Erasmian teaching of the superiority of the matrimonial over the virginal state of monks and nuns is insinuated.

It is highly probable that Cato was familiar with the religious restlessness pervading the court of Urbino. Certainly Cardinal Federico Fregoso, bishop of Gubbio, who had dedicated to Duchess Eleonora the *Pio et cristianissimo trattato della oratione*, printed posthumously at Venice in 1542, exercised a profound influence there. This booklet, written in a simple, clear style in the vernacular of the *Beneficio di Cristo*, is the expression of a personal piety that reminds one of the spirituality imbuing Erasmus's *Enchiridion militis Christiani*. But the *Trattato* also contains outbursts against the custom of the people and of "our modern church" to implore divine assistance through the invocation of the Virgin, angels, and saints. "In no way can it nor should it be called praying," because it is a false worship, "damned in the ancient Scriptures, and even more so by Jesus Christ in his true exposition of it, whereby God the Creator is abandoned in favor of prayers to created things." Alongside strong opposition against the devotional practices connected with the rosary, the central features of the booklet are a constant appeal to the Sacred Scriptures, because they alone cannot err; to faith in the mercy of God and in redemption by Jesus Christ for our salvation, since the justice of men is like "a filthy and contaminated rag in the eyes of God" according to Isaiah; and to the imitation of Jesus Christ and his example of humility and poverty.

That the *Trattato* contains echoes of Erasmus and of the young Luther seems undeniable. But we do not discern in it the resolve to break with Rome that permeates the work of the reformers. Rather, we detect a retreat into a personal sort of renewal and the longing for a return to the teachings and customs of the "primitive church." This discourse on prayer reflects conversations held with the duchess of Urbino and her court by the bishop of Gubbio and Agostino Steuco, theologian and Hebraist, an adversary of Erasmus and Luther. The reputation of Duchess Eleonora Gonzaga, the sister of Cardinal Ercole, and participant in the pre-Tridentine move-ment of Catholic reform sympathetic to certain aspects of the Reformation, such as the doctrine of justification by faith, was well known in the circles of the *"spirituali"* and of the religious dissenters.

To be sure, Girolamo Cato, residing in Venice, was aware of the protection that the duchess had offered to Antonio Brucioli, who in 1537 had dedicated to her his Isaiah commentary (*Libro di Iesaia profeta*) and in 1538 his metaphysical dialogues (*Dialogi metafisicali)*, where she appears as an interlocutor, together with Fregoso, in dialogues XVI ("Of the Presence of God"), XVII ("Of the Providence of God"), and XIX ("Of the Divine Light"). Cato, a modest literary figure, might possibly have aspired to insert himself in the entourage of the court of Urbino, but without the tes-timony of his trial records, it is impossible to go beyond this conjecture.

There may be no link between this trial and the inquest, ordered by the Inquisi-tion in February 1551, against Pietro Panfilo, seneschal and confidant of Duchess Eleonora, who was well informed on the religious questions of the day, and fre-quently served as go-between with the court at Mantua. After the death of the duch-ess, an anonymous denunciation accused Panfilo of having spread Lutheran doctrines at Fossombrone, where he lived, and in "all those castles and places of that good lady [Eleonora], where every peasant discussed and reasoned over the Epistles of Saint Paul, about works and confession and prayers for the dead, scorning all these things…" But the denunciation proved to be unfounded as far as this faithful ser-vant, friend, and correspondent of Marcantonio Flaminio was concerned. The only person to be arrested and condemned in the duchy of Urbino, a short time before the accusations made against Panfilo, was the still unknown Girolamo Cato.

BIBLIOGRAPHICAL NOTE

For the circulation of books at a popular level, see N. Z. Davis, "Printing and the People," in her *Society and Culture in Early Modern France: Eight Essays* (Stanford: Stanford University Press, 1975), 189–226. For the diffusion of Protestant literature in Italy, see C. De Frede, "Per la storia della stampa nel Cinquecento in rapporto con la diffusione della Riforma in Italia," *Gutenberg-Jahrbuch* 29 (1964): 175–79; idem, "Tipografi, editori, librai italiani del Cinquecento coinvolti in processi di eresia," *RSCI*, 23 (1969): 21–53; E. Balmas, "Sulla fortuna editoriale di Lutero in Francia e in Italia nel XVI secolo," in *Martin Luther e il protestantesimo in Italia* (Milan: IPL, 1984), 95–100; S. Cavazza, "Libri in volgare e propaganda eterodossa: Venezia 1543–1547," in *Libri, idee e sentimenti religiosi nel Cinquecento italiano*, a cura di A.

Prosperi e A. Biondi (Ferrara: Panini, 1987), 9–28; U. Rozzo, *Linee per una storia dell'editoria religiosa in Italia (1465–1600)* (Udine: Arti Grafiche Friulane, 1993).

On Brucioli, see *Dialogi*, a cura di A. Landi (Naples: Prismi; Chicago: The Newberry Library, 1982), especially the "Nota critica," 553–88; and the sketch by R. N. Lear in *DBI* 14: 480–85.

Luther's preface to the Epistle of Paul to the Romans printed under the name of Cardinal Federico Fregoso by Comin da Trino at Venice in 1545 (Vienna, National Library).

4

THE "LUTHERAN TIDE" (1517–1546)

LUTHER'S FIRST FOLLOWERS

ACCORDING TO THE FRENCH HISTORIAN LÉONARD, that period of western European history that runs from the first promulgation of Luther's theses against indulgences (1517) to the reformer's death in 1546, can be characterized as the "Lutheran tide."[1] Despite the appearance on the scene of reformers of the stature of Ullrich Zwingli, Martin Bucer, and John Calvin during that grand phase of religious history that forever stamped the first half of the century, the greatest inspirational force behind all the reform movements outside the Roman obedience remained the great theologian and professor of Wittenberg.

Better than anyone else in the Italian milieu, this fascination for the German reformer was expressed by Pietro Carnesecchi, in one of the most tormented hours of his life. He was fully conscious of the risk he ran when he admitted to inquisitors at his Roman trial in 1567 (interrogation of 3 December): "We were of the opinion that he [Luther] was a great man because of his wisdom and eloquence, and we also held that he acted sincerely in his own way, namely that he did not deceive others if he was not first deceived by his own opinions."[2]

In Italy too, during these years, Luther's doctrines circulated widely, in part through his own writings or those of his collaborators and followers, or by word of mouth and the proselytizing efforts of numerous German students in Padua, Siena, Pavia, and Bologna, of merchants, soldiers, school teachers; or anyone else who had traveled or lived in countries where the Reformation had become rooted as the alternative Christian church to the "papist."

Only a few persons of a higher-than-average cultural level knew and appreciated the theology of Zwingli and only one of his works apparently was translated into

---

[1]E. G. Leonard, *A History of Protestantism, I: The Reformation* (London and Edinburgh: Nelson, 1965), 183.
[2]"Processo Carnesecchi," 325–26.

Italian. He does not seem to have made many Italian converts despite the affinity of his thought with that of the humanists. His military bent, crowned by death on the field of battle at Kappel in 1531, may have alienated their sympathy. In this regard, the silence of omission may be symptomatic in the oration *Pro se ipso* (1543) of such an Erasmian as Aonio Paleario, where he lists the great religious reformers from Erasmus and Luther to Bugenhagen.

In the period being examined here, all the manifestations of religious dissent, from the preaching of the Augustinian hermits to the first condemnations, were of Lutheran inspiration. Even many persons who eventually ended up in the camp of Swiss Protestantism were introduced to the Reformation by Luther. For many, the choices were dictated by practical considerations, such as the chance to find haven in the Valtellina, where Italian was spoken and it was much easier to become acclimated and find employment than in German-speaking areas. Influencing these choices were new convictions, which had matured gradually through a deeper meditation on Scripture or better acquaintance with the differences among the various Protestant sects. But almost always the impetus to conversion had come from Lutheran teachings. The fame and writings of Valdés, with the exception of the small nucleus of followers composing his Neapolitan circle, began to spread only after his death in 1541, the same year that John Calvin appeared on the European scene with his French-language edition of the *Institutio Christianae religionis*.

There is no doubt that many persons indicted as "Lutherans," either by public reputation or by the groping and still feeble local tribunals of the Roman Inquisition, previous to its reconstitution in 1542, were simple protesters, anticlericals, secret followers of Savonarola, to whom Luther appeared as a daring scourge of the papal curia and the corrupt ways of the clergy. This is certainly the case with the Florentine physician Girolamo Buonagrazia (1470–1541), Savonarolan sympathizer and fervent republican, who was already an avid reader of Luther's writings in 1523. He actually wrote to the reformer himself during the Sack of Rome, urging him to complete the destruction of the Roman ecclesiastical establishment. His trial ended in December 1531 with his reconciliation to the church. In his statement to the court, the demise of the myth of Florence as the New Jerusalem augured by the prophet of San Marco can be glimpsed, replaced by the hope of a radical reformation of the church by Luther and the emperor, envisioned as instruments of divine justice. The beginnings of Antonio Brucioli's dissent were not very different. He had been one of the participants in the subversive conversations held in the *Orti Oricellari*, the gardens of the Rucellai family in Florence, and was condemned to exile for two years for his republican views in 1529.[3]

Among the early dissidents were the opponents of ecclesiastical discipline, which they considered absurd, unscriptural, and contrary to the freedom of the Christian, as Erasmus and Luther had been asserting for years: the Latin liturgy in the mass, often beyond popular comprehension, the prohibition of Scripture in the

---

[3]See the entry by A. J. Schutte in *DBI*, 15:104–5 and S. Caponetto, *Aonio Paleario e la Riforma protestante in Toscana* (Turin: Claudiana, 1979), 43–44.

vernacular, and clerical celibacy with concubinage as its consequence. They applauded the flight of monks and nuns from convents and monasteries in Germany and Switzerland. An occasional priest began to follow the northern example by reforming the mass in the Lutheran manner. For example, Alberto Dominemi and Rolando Pisani, two clerics of Fontanella in the Cremona area, joined with laymen in 1530 to read from Scripture and discuss the heterodox declarations of an Augustinian preacher. In their celebrations of the mass, they omitted the *Confiteor*, the prayer to the Virgin, angels, and saints. They were tried and compelled to abjure their errors.[4] The label of "Lutheran" was loosely attached to laymen implicated in civic conflicts between secular and ecclesiastical powers and to churchmen themselves disputing over questions of privilege.

Alongside such cases, we find true followers of Luther advocating the reformation of the church on the basis of the doctrinal teachings clearly announced in the *Augsburg Confession*. About them gathered "new Christians" drawn from every social level, with a prevalence of ecclesiastics, schoolteachers, and merchants in the early years, who in turn became enthusiastic mobilizers of opinion and organizers of clandestine groups.

The diffusion of "Lutheran" ideas was most successful along the great mercantile routes and Alpine passes, crisscrossed for the entire half century by armies of every nation. Piedmont, Lombardy, the Veneto, Friuli, Istria, and the Trentino were Italy's gateways. For a decade approximately, beginning in 1524, all papal edicts aiming at the discovery and destruction of Lutheran books, and the arrest of their vendors and purchasers, were directed at northern Italy and the great urban centers bordering France, Switzerland, and Austria.

In addition to the land routes through which the new ideas, conveyed by men and books, traveled and spread throughout the peninsula, there were also the ports, where heretical publications in great numbers were debarked alongside more orthodox cargoes. Towards the beginning of February 1525, Charles V was informed of the arrival at a harbor in the kingdom of Granada of three Venetian galleys transporting Lutheran books. The governor of the place confiscated the ships and arrested officers and crew.[5] Venice, Genoa, Pisa, Senigallia, Naples, Messina, and Palermo were the major routes for the importation of heretical literature to the point where ships had to be inspected before their cargoes could be unloaded.

Despite the one-sidedness of the documents—almost all originated with civil and ecclesiastical authorities afflicted by fear of contagion from the "Lutheran plague," preoccupied with the dangers of social unrest and disdain for the humble "mechanics" who dared to discuss the mysteries of the faith—the denunciations and reports compiled by officials offer the possibility of measuring the reception of the new doctrines.

[4]F. Chabod, "Per la storia religiosa dello Stato di Milano durante il dominio di Carlo V," in *Lo stato e la vita religiosa a Milano nell'epoca di Carlo V* (Turin: Einaudi, 1971), 313.
[5]Cf. M. Bataillon, *Erasmo y España* (Mexico-Buenos Aires: Fondo de cultura económica, 1966), 190.

In July 1539 the governor of the State of Milan denounced to the *podestà* of Cremona a merchant, a certain Pietro Martire Sambugato, who "had ordered painted on the chimney of one of his rooms Jesus Christ Our Lord with the twelve apostles in a circle, each one of whom held keys in his hand, a truly scandalous matter and deserving exemplary punishment."[6] Clearly, the gesture was inspired by Lutheran teachings against the primacy of Peter and his "successor" the pope, which had become the principal argument of the defenders of orthodoxy.

An act of defiance on the part of Celio Secondo Curione was no less significant. Arrested in Val d'Aosta in 1523 together with two companions from the University of Turin, he was confined to the convent of San Benigno di Fruttuaria in the Canavese region to meditate upon the heretical discussions he had carried on with his friends. But instead of returning to the obedience of the church, after he had read Melanchthon's *Loci*, he removed the bones of some saints from a reliquary and replaced them with a Bible on which he wrote the caption: "This is the ark of the covenant where we find the true oracles of God; these are the true relics."[7]

THE DENUNCIATION OF GIAN PIETRO CARAFA

The fullest documentation for the preceding section is provided by a series of trials held in the Venetian dominions against the leaders of the Protestant movement operating in Venice, Padua, Cittadella, Vicenza, and the Istrian cities of Albona and Pirano. The suspects were persons who, because of their ecclesiastical, cultural, and social positions, became known to the authorities through their proselytization. But behind them "moved a vast, obscure mass of the weak, the struggling and the neglected who were relegated to mere skeletal lists of names and facts."[8]

The Republic of Venice, among all the Italian states, was the only one to have a specific political, economic, and even religious interest, if we consider the scandalous excesses of the clergy and of the monastic orders, in evaluating carefully what was transpiring beyond the Alps before joining the counteroffensive being launched by the Church of Rome. Moreover, we should not undervalue the fact that Venice, in its long history, while always remaining loyal to the teachings of the church, and having even assumed the role of champion of the Christian faith in the struggle against the Turks, had on more than one occasion, in the course of political conflict with the papacy, brought upon her head excommunication and interdict, as would occur again early in the seventeenth century. The memory of the disastrous Venetian defeat at Agnadello (1509) by the armies of the League of Cambrai, behind which was the hand of Julius II, was still fresh.

---

[6] F. Chabod, "Per la storia," 317 and 319 note 3.

[7] G. Jalla, *Storia della Riforma in Piemonte fino alla morte di Emanuele Filiberto*, 2 vols. (Florence: Claudiana, 1914–36), 1:23 (repr. Turin: Claudiana, 1982).

[8] P. Negri, "Note e documenti per la storia della Riforma in Italia: Bernardino Ochino," *Atti della R. Accademia delle Scienze di Torino* 47 (1912): 58.

When Clement VII complained to Venice over the ease with which heretical books circulated and were sold in its dominions, and about the free movements and contacts enjoyed by German and Swiss "Lutheran" students, merchants, schoolteachers, and travelers, the Council of Ten replied: "As for the Lutherans and heretics, our state and dominion is free; thus, we cannot prohibit them."[9]

In these years Venice was one of the major centers of European culture with its famous printing presses, academies, schools, and learned gatherings in the dwellings of patrician families, where every possible subject was discussed, from Holy Scripture to Machiavelli, from astrology to prophecy, from the works of Erasmus to those of the reformers. All the excitement provoked by the great religious upheaval of the century pervaded the neighboring University of Padua, as well as the religious orders, among which the Benedictines of Santa Giustina and of San Giorgio Maggiore stood out for their learning and their revitalized religiosity.

After the Sack of Rome and the demise of the Florentine republic, Venice had become a haven for Roman and Florentine political and religious exiles, Savonarolans such as Jacopo Nardi and Michelangelo, philo-Lutherans such as Brucioli, and the members of the Company of Divine Love, Gaetano da Thiene and Gian Pietro Carafa. Geographically speaking, there was no other Italian state more exposed than Venice to the reception of the Lutheran message or to learning about the political and religious developments in the north. If there were many channels for the transmission of this message, due to the intense commercial traffic with Germany and with other countries where the Reformation was taking hold, the most persistent was perceptively identified by Gian Pietro Carafa, bishop of Chieti. In a memorandum that he addressed to the pope in 1532, he called for immediate measures to deal with the corrupt body of the church, where numerous priests and apostate monks were "making a mockery of Christ's blood" and "a business of the sacraments (in which they do not even believe, however) and of miserable souls," where bishops abandoned their dioceses to a suffragan, and "a monk might shred his cloak" because profiting from these miserable conditions was that "cursed brood of monks which God, out of his goodness, selecting a few for his servants, has begun to throw into confusion."[10]

The "brood" of monks consisted of the conventual Franciscans: Girolamo Galateo; Bartolomeo Fonzio, who was supposed to have translated into Italian Luther's *To the Christian Nobility of the German Nation*; Alessandro Pagliarino di Pieve di Sacco, imprisoned at Padua; Tommaso da Casale, followed by Baldo Lupatino of Albona and Giulio Morato of Capodistria. But the group included still others who had managed to elude Carafa's Inquisition. In the Venetian dominion, to the best of our

[9]E. Comba, *I nostri protestanti, II: Durante la Riforma nel Veneto e nell'Istria* (Florence: Claudiana, 1897), 55.
[10]Johannes Petrus Carafa, "De Lutheranorum haeresi reprimenda et ecclesia reformanda ad Clementem VII (4 October 1532)," in *Concilium Tridentinum Diariorum, Actorum, Epistolarum, Tractatuum nova collectio* (Freiburg: Göress-Gesellschaft, 1906–61), 12:67–77, esp. 67–68. [The text of Carafa's memorandum is now available in English in *Reform Thought in Sixteenth Century Italy*, ed. and trans. Elisabeth G. Gleason (Chico: Scholars Press, 1981), 55–80. Trans. note.]

knowledge, Conventual Franciscans were the first proselytizers for the Lutheran faith.

FRANCISCAN CONVENTUALS AND THE EARLY MANIFESTATIONS OF LUTHERANISM

The general unrest among Franciscans, torn by the division between Conventuals and Observants, had as a consequence a sort of illuminist apocalypticism in Spain, and in Italy the founding of the Capuchins. Many members of the order became persuaded by the Lutheran protest and produced five martyrs to the movement for Italian Reform: Girolamo Galateo, Bartolomeo Fonzio, Baldo Lupatino, Giovanni Buzio, and Cornelio Giancardo.

Girolamo Galateo (1490–1541), a Venetian, educated in Padua, a master in theology, about the year 1528 embarked on a daring series of sermons. Accused by Carafa and arrested in Padua, tried by the prelate himself, he was condemned to death on 16 January 1531 at the express order of the pope. But the Council of Ten did not ratify the sentence and commuted it to imprisonment. After seven years of incarceration, the Council released him to the custody of the nobleman Antonio Paolucci, with a bond of a thousand ducats. In the latter's residence Galateo resumed writing an *Apologia* addressed to the Venetian Senate. It was probably this act that returned him to prison, where he died on 7 January 1541 and was buried at the Lio, "a place reserved for the interment of Jews and other infamous men."[11]

The *Apologia* was Galateo's defense intended for the Venetian senate against the charge of being a Lutheran. To accomplish this, he held up Sacred Scripture as the foundation for the search of truth. "Christ is our only teacher"; the "Gospel is an instrument for salvation, of true, certain and holy wisdom, of which not mortal man, but the good and great God is the author...." His exposition of key points was an extremely able and lucid popularization of Lutheran doctrine. We would only need to compare it to Melanchthon's *Loci*, or Luther's *Praefatio* to the Epistle of Paul to the Romans, which was first printed at Wittenberg in 1524, many times reissued at Strasbourg, and even appeared in an Italian version in 1545 under the name of Cardinal Federico Fregoso.[12]

A few of the chief points in dispute were faith and works: "Faith is the gift of God, and all the things of the Lord bear fruit. Thus, faith cannot be sterile and without fruit. Now good works are the fruits of faith and faith is not unfruitful. Consequently, there is no faith without good works; therefore good works are necessary." About purgatory he said, "I thank and praise the Lord who led me to know the true purgatory, Christ, who has washed and purged us of our sins in his blood"; and as for images, "I cannot adore my God and Savior, except in spirit and truth as Christ teaches.... Christ opens our eyes, so that neither heads, nor panels, nor walls, nor columns, nor stones can work miracles, but only the Lord through the hands of his holy angels and saints, and not by walls."

---

[11]E. Comba, *I nostri protestanti*, 79.
[12]S. Seidel Menchi, "Le traduzioni," 81–89.

Cautiously, subtly, but not without courage, he took up in turn confession, the Lord's Supper, indulgences, citing as his authorities Augustine, Ambrose, and John Chrysostom. The authors of the *Beneficio di Cristo* would do the same some years later. The *Apologia* concluded with an earnest plea to Venice's rulers to restore their church to the purity of apostolic times, hearkening back "to the Word and to the truth of Sacred Scripture....You, then, oh Venetian rulers, upon whom the Lord God has bestowed this beautiful and grand empire that extends over land and over the seas so that his message may travel fast and far, you, I say, defend that part of your crucified Christ and his Gospel and his Word.... The Lord who works all things in all men urges you to satisfy them."[13]

I have paused over the *Apologia*, an exceedingly rare booklet, because we shall find its teachings echoed in almost all trials held during this first phase of the movement, and especially in the Venetian Republic, where the influence of the Conventuals, disciples of Galateo, predominated. Galateo was already ranked in the *Pasquino in estasi* as one of the great reformers, together with "a Spanish knight of Caesar who became a knight for Christ, a certain Juan Valdés." The appeal to the Republic of Venice to align itself with the forces working for the reformation of Christianity would be taken up also by Pier Paolo Vergerio in his oration to Doge Francesco Donà delivered in 1546 and again in his commentary to the *Catalogo dei libri condannati* compiled by the nuncio Della Casa (1549), where Vergerio asked for "a council and a reformation of their churches," a program to be accomplished by Italians for their own country, but appropriating certain unmistakable principles of the European religious Reformation.

In Carafa's memorandum, mention is made of Bartolomeo Fonzio (1502– 1562), who had fled to Germany after he had been prohibited from preaching ("in the presence of Lutherans he had openly preached Protestant and heretical doctrines").[14] This activity had lasted from about 1528 to 1530. In his long northern journey through Augsburg, Ulm, Nuremberg, Basel, Constanz, and Strasbourg, the young, highly educated monk tried to comprehend the great changes set afoot by the German and Swiss reformers, as well as the causes for the deep divisions that had followed their revolution. The debates over the Lord's Supper especially seemed to him more the fruit of subtle speculation than of true searching for scriptural truth. He leaned towards the Lutheran position, but during his Strasbourg sojourn (1532–33) he worked with Bucer, whose friend he had become, to seek an agreement with the Zwinglians. When in 1533, tired and disillusioned, Fonzio eventually returned to Venice, he had broken with Bucer because of actions taken at Strasbourg in June of that year against the Anabaptists and Caspar Schwenckfeld. Fonzio continued to rank himself among the orthodox until 1536, always hoping, along with Galateo and many others throughout Italy, in the possibility of a council that would work for

---

[13]*Apologia, cioè Defensione di Hieronimo Galateo* (Bologna: Luca Fiorano et sui Fratelli, 1541), partially repr. by R. Freschi, "Girolamo Galateo e la sua Apologia," *Studi e materiali di storia delle religioni* 11 (1935), app., 74, 87, 89, 98, 108.
[14]E. Zille, *Gli eretici a Cittadella nel Cinquecento* (Cittadella: Rebellato, 1971), 147.

reform and reconciliation after the announcement that one would be convoked by Paul III.

During Galateo's imprisonment something occurred in Venice connected to his and Fonzio's preaching, and perhaps even to the Savonarolan Fra Zaccaria, who had been reading the Epistles of Paul in the vernacular publicly in the church of the Trinità. This episode sheds light on the social repercussions of the propagation of their ideas by the religious dissenters. The first to note it was the nuncio Girolamo Aleandro in a letter of 8 May 1533 to Jacopo Salviati: "In this city there is a Lutheran master carpenter, a man of perverse intelligence, who has on his own gathered about himself a small sect of artisans and others of the lower classes, and, what is even more dangerous, has supporters, as I have heard, even among the citizenry and some highly placed but foolish people; and among his errors, he does not believe in purgatory, the sacrament of confession, and free will."[15]

Antonio, a carpenter, "*marangone*," was so enthused with the new doctrines that he became their ardent proselytizer. Despite his modest education he owned a number of books: Luther's *Centum gravamina*, Hermann Bodius's *Unio dissidentium*, a vernacular Bible, almost certainly Antonio Brucioli's New Testament translation published in 1530. He himself declared that he had come to know the Christian truth "from Scripture and his books." A resident of the Rialto quarter, he had discussed his views openly in his home and in his place of business. He visited the neighboring shops of a smith, a barber, a tuner of instruments, to tell them of the new doctrines, urging that they adopt them. According to Aleandro, he "is a man who speaks with great confidence and intellectual force, and he seems to be saying that it is the Holy Spirit moving him to speak, and he adduces the authority of Scripture to more easily seduce the people."[16]

The carpenter, who had extended his propaganda to the churches of Santi Giovanni e Paolo, the Trinità, San Nicolò, Santa Maria, San Lio and to a bookseller's shop, won the support of several artisans, a notary, various Tuscans, and not a few Germans. This group, according to a witness at the carpenter's inquest, "go about subverting the people around the Rialto and everywhere in the squares and in the churches flaunt their opinions." It appears that they had a meeting place, where people were invited "to come to know the truth." After so much incriminating evidence was collected from witnesses and accusers, at Aleandro's insistence, on 8 May 1533, master Antonio was arrested and tried. The sentence to *carcere perpetuo* pronounced by the nuncio, the Venetian inquisitor, the patriarch's vicar, and a number of jurists, among whom was Annibale Grisonio who later would become inquisitor in Istria, was actually only promulgated a year later, on 24 June. Informing the apostolic protonotary Pietro Carnesecchi in Rome of this fact on the following day, the nuncio expressed his preoccupation about its actually being put into effect by the Venetian authorities: "Let us see what these lords will say about it; his supporters are many, not

---

[15]F. Gaeta, "Documenti da codici vaticani per la storia della Riforma in Venezia," *Annuario dell'Istituto Storico Italiano per l'età moderna e contemporanea* 7 (1956): 6–7, note 4.
[16]Ibid., 11.

so much for his own person, but for the sect which has grown so much it is almost incredible to believe."[17]

PIETRO SPECIALE

On 22 August 1543, two years after the death of Girolamo Galateo, Pietro Speciale of Cittadella (1478–1554), humanist, and respected grammarian and schoolteacher in Cittadella since 1536, was condemned in Venice. As a reader of Augustine and of Erasmus he had turned to the problems of grace and free will as early as 1512, when he began to write his *"De gratia Dei,"* completed on 17 October 1542, as he noted on the manuscript of the work now preserved in the Biblioteca Marciana in Venice. Here he gave emphatic witness to his adherence to the doctrine of justification by faith alone, to which he had come "before the name of Luther had become famous."[18] For thirty years he had read Luther, Melanchthon, and Bucer. Speciale, however, was not a solitary scholar, because, in the 1520s he had struck up a friendship with the Franciscan Bernardino Scardeone, a master of theology in Padua, and with other preachers of the day.

By the end of 1542, Venice was in tumult over the progress made by the religious dissent. The Augustinian Giulio della Rovere had ended up in prison after his Lenten sermons of 1541. Bernardino Ochino, the general of the Capuchins, the Savonarola of the sixteenth century, who had thundered his protests from Venetian pulpits when Giulio was arrested, himself had to abandon Italy and find refuge in Protestant lands. Speciale's *"De gratia Dei"* reflects this environment, even though the work was the fruit of a long personal meditation. Speciale, who was better educated than Galateo, supported fully the Erasmian position in favor of the matrimonial state, and opposed the vow of celibacy, which he held to be contrary to divine will. The *"De gratia Dei"* takes up in turn all the *loci* of the Christian faith and demonstrates its undivided agreement with Lutheran teachings.

The most serious accusation against Speciale at his inquisitorial trial did not hinge on the question of justification by faith, about which there was still much uncertainty, especially after the position assumed by the Venetian Cardinal Gasparo Contarini at Ratisbon. Rather, it concerned Speciale's refusal to believe in the dogma of transubstantiation. The *"De gratia Dei"* adopted the language and ideas expressed by Melanchthon and by the young Luther of the *coena Domini* as a *signum promissionis.*[19]

After eight years in the prison called *"Fresca Gioia"* (Fresh Joy) in Piazza San Marco, the septuagenarian scholar, his health ruined, impoverished by the confiscation of his property, at the urging of the theologian Francesco Bettoni of Cittadella, decided to make a full abjuration and retraction of his errors (14 July 1551). It is difficult to say to what point Speciale's abandonment of his heroic posture can be

---

[17]Ibid., 10, 13, 36.
[18]E. Zille, *Gli eretici*, 43, note 7, 47.
[19]Cf. the citation in E. Zille, 49, to be compared with *Melanchthons Werke*, 2:2, 522ff.

explained as a consequence of his harsh imprisonment or senile disorientation, as Emilio Comba suggested at the end of the last century with a regret tinged by a confessional lapse of objectivity.[20] What may have weighed even more on Speciale was the distress provoked by Pietro Manelfi, preaching in prison, who later claimed that he had baptized Speciale as an "Anabaptist," and who on 14 November of that same year, 1551, would betray the followers of Anabaptism to the Inquisition. If this was the case, it would not have been difficult to frighten Speciale with the prospect of the splintering of the church of Christ into many sects, and to bring him back to the Erasmian ideal of a church united and reformed. This is the gist of the letters he wrote from his cell to his old friends Francesco Negri and Baldo Lupatino. After Speciale abjured and retracted his errors, he had to serve a sentence of a few years' confinement before finally being permitted to return to his home in Cittadella, reduced to poverty and close to death. He was a shining example of someone who had engaged in a personal search for scriptural truth, a courageous witness and forerunner of the many schoolteachers who stand out among the protagonists of European Protestantism.

THE CASE OF FRANCESCO SPIERA

Pietro Speciale exerted an important influence on Cittadella, a small town neighboring Padua and its university, permeated by a climate favorable to the new ideas. At a time when they were being discussed widely, partly because of intensified Calvinist and Anabaptist proselytization and infiltration, the upsetting case of the lawyer Francesco Spiera (1502–1549) dominated events. He was a friend of Speciale, an enthusiastic convert who began to disseminate his ideas within his large family, assisted by his nephew, Girolamo Facio. Spiera wanted to promote the Scriptures among the peasants, translating "for a few poor rustics of the countryside the Pater Noster in a vernacular form that was not Latin, which was torn up."[21] The nephew was proselytizing at Asolo; he had purchased heretical books and brought them to Cittadella and Asolo. Uncle and nephew admitted to reading the *Beneficio di Cristo*, the *Dottrina vecchia e dottrina nuova*, the *Pasquino in estasi*, the *Tragedia del libero arbitrio*.

But the emotion of the situation, the solemnity of an inquisitorial trial, awesome and mysterious even for an experienced jurist, the pain and shame experienced by his family, led Spiera to abjure his faith on 26 June 1548. After what should have been a liberating act, he literally succumbed to the feeling that he had betrayed Jesus Christ and the truth of the Gospel. Neither physicians, nor Pier Paolo Vergerio who rushed to his bedside were able to reassure him. Spiera died convinced that he was a traitor, a reprobate now destined to suffer for eternity. The tale of the lawyer of

---

[20]E. Comba, *I nostri protestanti*, 251–55.
[21]Cf. E. Zille, *Gli eretici*, 75, note 15.

Cittadella circulated throughout Protestant Europe, thanks to the written account by Vergerio and the lessons drawn from it for the fainthearted by Calvin.[22]

A few years later an Anabaptist conventicle was discovered. Its head was a certain Agostino Tealdo, a student of Speciale's, possibly a notary, and a schoolteacher during the nine years that his master had been in prison. The group led a clandestine life and had a rudimentary organization, managing to celebrate the Lord's Supper for about a year. Tealdo was imprisoned and tried at Vicenza, condemned to death, and to avoid the spectacle of a public auto da fé, a disruptive spectacle shunned by Venetian authorities, was strangled in prison and his body burned on 29 August 1555. His followers, less resolute and firm in their faith, abjured their errors and were absolved.[23]

BALDO LUPATINO AND THE FRANCISCANS OF ISTRIA

At a time when the events connected with Antonio *"marangone"* were occurring in Venice, the papal nuncio was receiving sinister reports about the spread of the Lutheran heresy in the eastern corner of the Venetian dominion, Istria, adjacent to Carniola where the Reformation had taken hold thanks to the efforts of the Slovenian Primus Trubar. The two centers from which the Protestant currents emanated were the convents of the Minor Conventuals of Albona and Pola. Their members, preachers "roaming from convent to convent, from parish to parish" for the series of Advent and Lenten sermons, together with an occasional artisan, established links between the diocese of Pola, other localities in Istria, Dalmatia, and the other archducal lands, "thus permitting at the popular level a modest circulation of ideas that otherwise would have been impossible in these desolate areas."[24]

The Lutherans came to light through a dispute between two Franciscans, one, a Catholic, belonging to the Observants, and the other, a Conventual, a follower of Bartolomeo Fonzio. What took place, specifically, was an oratorical duel from the pulpits of Pirano. P. P. Vergerio, who was then papal legate, got wind of it and wrote in consternation to P. Carnesecchi on 30 August 1534:

> I have heard that in Trieste, a city in our Italy on the shores of our Adriatic, Lutheranism is germinating, brought by commerce with Germany. I have taken harsh measures, joining royal authority to that of my nunciature, and I hope, Monsignor, to root out those evil plants most severely and thoroughly, as is necessary.... Furthermore, I hear that this plague has gone out from Trieste and attacked a castle [fortified town] called Pirano, where a number of ribald people are going about in the open contaminating the souls of simple people. Monsignor, I know the nature of that country, for it is my native land. If the Lutheran sect takes hold among such simplicity of

[22]Cf. E. Comba, *I nostri protestanti*, 288–95.

[23]E. Zille, *Gli eretici*, 127–40.

[24]A. Pitassio, "Diffusione e tramonto della Riforma in Istria: La diocesi di Pola nel '500," *Annali della Facoltà di Scienze Politiche dell'Università di Perugia* 10 (1968–70): 26–27.

intellect, if that section of Italy is bitten, Your Reverence will soon see (but God avert it!) all the contiguous provinces and regions infected and corrupted. Hence I pray through Jesus Christ that you immediately and fervently communicate this information to His Holiness as a most important matter, so that the menace can be stopped in the beginning.... I know perfectly well that some of those wicked Piranese have been summoned to Venice for this reason, but I know, too, that greater severity should be employed than is in fact being used. I say, Monsignor, that nothing is more important today than this, and if such people go unpunished, all Istria, all of Italy, will be imperiled.[25]

Aleandro lost no time assigning to Giacomo Pesaro, bishop of Pafo, responsibility for the prosecution as heretics of the humanist Giovanni Antonio Petronio, the teacher of Giovanni Battista Goineo, author of *De situ Histriae*, who would later become a leader of the heretical movement in Istria and an exile in Germany; Marco Antonio Venier, a patron of scholars in Pirano, and Marco Caldana. The group, many of whom cannot be clearly identified, may have included the physician Colantuono of Monopoli in Puglia (*Nicolaus de Apulia phisicus*), a town not too distant from Ceglie Messapico, which had a colony of Waldensian peasants who sent their own representative to the assembly at Chanforan in 1532. We do not know with certainty how the Venetian trial of the Pirano Lutherans concluded, but since some of them were accused again by Annibale Grisonio at the time of his 1549 inquest, they must have abjured their erroneous opinions and been absolved.

It is against this background of searching for religious enlightenment by the Istrian educated classes and of the changes taking place in the ecclesiastical establishment in the bordering Austrian lands, that we should place the impetuous and passionate proselytizing activity of one of the leaders of the Minor Conventuals, Fra Baldo Lupatino. Lupatino was born at Albona in 1492 or 1493, and educated in Venice, Padua, and perhaps even Cittadella, where he met Speciale. He entered his religious order at about thirty years of age and quickly achieved renown as a preacher fluent in both the Italian and Slavic languages. He traveled around Istria, including the island of Cherso, where he created great scandal by his sermons founded on Sacred Scripture, denying the efficacy of indulgences, rejecting purgatory, free will, the cult of the Madonna and the saints. His accuser, Iacopo Curzula, went so far as to assert that the monk by his preaching "has turned this land upside down and there are few persons left who have not become heretics."[26] One of the witnesses who were summoned in corroboration, a rather reticent shoemaker, voiced the common view of Lupatino's listeners: "I cannot tell you anything else except that people say that he preaches the Gospel.... I myself do not know about such things because I fix shoes."[27]

---

[25]F. Gaeta, "Documenti," 16. [The translation is taken from A. J. Schutte, *Pier Paolo Vergerio, the Making of an Italian Reformer* (Geneva: Droz, 1977), 76. [Trans. note.]

[26]A. Pitassio, "Diffusione," 36.

[27]E. Comba, *I nostri protestanti*, 328.

In view of the abundant evidence gathered against him, Lupatino was finally arrested and brought to a Venetian prison. It was a Saturday, 4 November 1542, when he was thirty-nine years of age, as Lupatino himself recalled in some Latin verses. He underwent a long and vexing trial, during which he never wavered, despite the harshness of his ordeal and the punishments meted out for the proselytizing activity he continued to carry on even from his cell. His replies to the interrogations on 22 September 1547, which he set to paper, somehow reached Pietro Speciale who himself was in prison. Speciale copied them and had a young girl bring them to a friend, a certain Michele Catalicchio of Albona, to have them printed. But this had already been done at Cherso and the document was circulating throughout Istria. Inquisitors confiscated a copy of the work that enunciated a definite Lutheran position. Though the text proceeds from an identical Augustinian base, subterfuges such as those used by Galateo are dropped. Lupatino no longer adduces the teachings of the church fathers, not even of Augustine, but founds his opinions exclusively on Scripture, although it is obvious that he knows Luther's three great writings of 1520 and other of the reformer's works.

The second trial concluded on 27 October 1547 with a death sentence, signed by the nuncio Giovanni Della Casa, but was commuted by the doge to life imprisonment. During the five years roughly, from the death of Galateo and the publication of his *Apologia*, to Lupatino's condemnation, a series of momentous events mark the first phase of the Protestant movement in the Veneto.

The number of Venetian evangelicals, who had taken advantage of a certain tolerance and indecision on the part of the *Signoria* in the various lands it controlled, grew considerably. Repression intensified with countless arrests, trials and harsh sentences. Appeals to the Republic from Galateo, Speciale, and Lupatino were rejected and the attempts of a few senators to align Venice with the Schmalkaldic League also failed. Contemporaneously, Baldassarre Altieri, secretary to the English ambassador Edmond Harwell, wrote a long fervent letter to Luther, in the name of the religious dissenters in Venice, Vicenza, and Treviso, informing him about their conventicles and the organizational difficulties they faced due to the lack of pastors and catechists: "we have no public churches, every person is a church within himself, according to the judgment and caprice of each."[28] He asked for clarification on the thorny question of the Lord's Supper, and closed by beseeching aid for the prisoners in Venice under sentence of death, among whom was Baldo Lupatino. This brief correspondence with the German reformer, who entrusted to Matthias Flacius, Lupatino's nephew, the task of seeking the intervention of the princes of the Schmalkaldic League, is significant as confirmation that Protestants at the time thought of Luther as "God's chosen," to carry to completion the great work of reforming the Church. Although Altieri succeeded in entering the service of Elector Johann Frederick of Saxony and of Landgrave Philip of Hesse, and at the Diet of Speyer in February 1544 was named representative to the *Serenissima* of the Protestant league, he failed to

---

[28]E. Comba, *I nostri protestanti*, 193.

improve the miserable conditions of Baldo Lupatino and the other Venetian prisoners.

With Luther's death in 1546 and the defeat of the Schmalkaldic forces at Mühlberg in 1547, the possibility now vanished forever of influencing the ecclesiastical policies of the only Italian state that could have stood up to the Church of Rome.

Baldo Lupatino, dead as far as the outside world was concerned, provided vital support for his fellow inmates, among whom he carried out a fervent ministry. As one witness for the prosecution declared at his trial, "He often sticks his head out of the hole of his cell and preaches in a loud voice to the prisoners." He also wrote messages of exhortation and theological controversy that must have affected even the common criminals, some of whom refused to confess themselves, "declaring that God by his own blood has saved everyone." The wealthy German merchants in Venice sustained Lupatino financially, while his evangelical brethren circulated his writings.

Lupatino had even thought he might try to write books. The inquisitors grew increasingly uneasy to have as one of their charges a person who was a witness to his faith both within and without prison. In 1552 he had composed a dialogue in honor of Duchess Renée of Ferrara. Evidently he must have heard of the protection she was extending to the many suspects who had sought refuge at her court. On 17 September 1556, at the conclusion of the third trial, at which Lupatino declared, among other things, that the pope had sold out Christ to gain sovereignty over this world, he was finally sentenced to death. It was ordered that he should be drowned "deep in the sea," silently and secretly, "*sine sonitu et sine strepitu.*"[29]

The echoes of the martyrdom of Galateo, of Speciale, of Lupatino, of Spiera's awe-inspiring death reported by Vergerio, were probably much greater than what the surviving documents suggest, and contributed to the growth of the Protestant movement in Italy.

MARTIN BUCER AND THE ITALIAN BRETHREN

The sojourn of a small group of Italians in Strasbourg for a few months sometime before 1526 was a channel for the diffusion in the peninsula of Lutheran doctrines that has remained somewhat neglected, partly because it is linked to Erasmian ideas. The information comes down to us from the reformer of the city, Martin Bucer (Butzer), who dedicated to his "Italian brethren" his Latin translation of the fourth volume of Luther's *Postils*, the previous installments of which had been well received in Italy. Without identifying them in the prefatory letter, Bucer stated that he had learned of the existence in Italy of true believers in Jesus Christ from some of those of fervent piety who had visited him in Strasbourg.

It should not be supposed, as Tommaso Bozza stated recently, that the letter was written to an actual Italian Protestant community.[30] It seems more likely that Bucer

---

[29]Ibid., 349, 356.
[30]Cf. T. Bozza, "Lutero nel Cinquecento italiano," *La Scuola Cattolica* 3 (1983): 245–46.

was addressing educated persons interested in learning more about the Reformation and its doctrinal and liturgical developments. The document, in fact, is a small treatise on Lutheran theology, and would read almost like a catechism, if it were not for the angry words reserved for the Peasants' War and the Anabaptists.[31] In his letter, Bucer, alongside all other theologians enunciating the basic Protestant message, reduced evangelical faith to its essentials: justification by divine grace alone and love of one's neighbor. Christ established only two sacraments: baptism, the tangible sign of God's covenant and pardon, and the Holy Eucharist, the visible sign of our communion with him.

Bucer's only divergence from Luther is in his interpretation of the nature of Christ's presence in the Eucharistic celebration. In sympathy with the views of Oecolampadius and Zwingli, Bucer proposes a spiritual presence in the moment of communion, rejecting the notion of any sort of transformation of the bread and the wine. Similarly, when the risen Christ breathed down on his disciples, saying: "Receive the Holy Spirit," the Spirit was not restricted to the breath, which was only a tangible sign of a spiritual phenomenon. The letter closes with an exhortation to study, to prayer, to modesty, to understanding, and with the hope for tolerant rulers and princes who would permit the free preaching of the Gospel.

Bucer's missive, dated 27 July 1526, at the outset of ecclesiastical reform in the imperial city of Strasbourg, where the mass celebrated in German was not abolished until 1529, was directed to humanists and professional men, readers who would have been familiar with Erasmus and Luther. The diffusion of the Bucerian form of Lutheranism in the next decade and a half intersected and overlapped the extensive circulation of the works and thought of Erasmus. The story of Bucer's importance for Italian history, still largely to be told, owes much to the humanism of the former Dominican. When at a young age, during the disputation at Heidelberg in 1518, Bucer aligned himself with Luther, he was a dedicated follower of Erasmus. Even later he remained an admirer of the great Dutchman, whose irenic and ecumenical sentiments he inherited. Bucer worked tirelessly for the unification of all German and Swiss evangelicals and supported, until the failure of the religious colloquy at Ratisbon, the attempt being made to bring about a reconciliation between Catholics and Protestants. Bucer's links to Italian sympathizers with the Reformation and his correspondence with them, which endured almost two decades, can be explained by his tenacious belief in the essential oneness of true believers in Christ.

Thus far it has not been possible to identify the Italians who visited Strasbourg about 1526. Bucer's letters written after 1541 and 1544 offer no clues outside of the indication of a few geographical locations. Emilia, Veneto, and Sicily and some of the cities, Bologna, Modena, and Ferrara, are named as cultural centers where Erasmian circles flourished.

Silvana Seidel Menchi has recently traced the course of the Italian acceptance of Erasmus as precursor and theoretician of the Reformation, a "Lutheran" Erasmus

---

[31] Repr. in *Correspondance de Martin Bucer*, publiée par J. Rott, vol. 2 (1524–26) (Leiden: Brill, 1989), n. 135, 146–64.

adopted by a vast network of people possessing modest educational attainments, both lay and ecclesiastic, schoolteachers, notaries, lawyers, physicians, and through them, even merchants and artisans. The diffusion of Erasmian ideas in the ranks of the evangelicals clearly emerges from the rich documentation assembled by the author: the freedom of the Christian, the boundless mercy of God, conjugal love, and so on. The success of Erasmus was undoubtedly due to his extraordinary powers of communication, more attuned to the taste, mentality, and literary traditions of Italians than were Luther's "paradoxes." According to the contemporary account of Alberto Pio da Carpi, it was much more diverting, as fascinating as listening to the songs of the Sirens, to read the *Colloquia* or the *Encomium Moriae* rather than the three great Lutheran manifestos of 1520, of which anonymous and generally flat and unappealing translations circulated in Italy. From her judicious examination of inquisitorial trials, Seidel Menchi has gathered a convincing mass of evidence from which, setting aside discrepancies of a geographical, social, and chronological nature, a unifying theme emerges: Erasmus is the teacher of a spiritual form of Christianity and an opponent of a piety immersed in objects and ceremonies. The *Enchiridion militis Christiani*, reprinted at Venice in 1523, achieved five editions of the Italian translation between 1531 and 1543. It was the manual par excellence for Christian humanists.[32]

The transition from Erasmus to Bucer on the part of many educated and professional people is illustrated most aptly by the cases of Eusebio Renato, Giovanni Angelo Odoni, and Fileno Lunardi. The three were members of a small Bolognese group of "fervent Erasmians," active, though not continuously, from 1530 to 1540, whose aim was the diffusion of the "*restitutio Christianismi*" in Italy, in the Erasmian-Bucerian direction, which according to Seidel Menchi, was part of a tactical and strategic approach: "…because the theology of Erasmus and Bucer does not proceed by way of antitheses and by exclusion, as does Luther's (you either stand with the law or with the Gospel, you are either a Christian or a pharisee), but foresees and permits the coexistence of various stages, progressively ever more perfect, of Revelation, adducing as a model the higher stage without condemning the lower."[33]

To put their program into effect, the two Bolognese students, Odoni and Lunardi, decided they would try to visit the northern reformers, first to meet Erasmus personally in Freiburg, and then moving on to Strasbourg. The two Italians remained there for almost three years, from the autumn of 1534 to the summer of 1537, residing as boarders in Bucer's home and attending his lectures, participating in what was "probably an actual course in evangelical specialization."[34] What the two youths got out of their Strasbourg experience and from their two visits with Erasmus at Freiburg is not obvious. Odoni entered the service of Agostino Gonzaga, bishop of Reggio

---

[32]S. Seidel Menchi, *Erasmo in Italia, 1520–1580* (Turin: Bollati Boringhieri, 1987). Available also in German translation: *Erasmus als Ketzer…*(Leiden: Brill, 1993). [Trans. note.]

[33]Idem, "Sulla fortuna di Erasmo in Italia: Ortensio Lando e altri eterodossi della prima metà del Cinquecento," *Schweizerische Zeitschrift für Geschichte* 24 (1974): 542.

[34]Ibid., 554.

Calabria, in the capacity of theological advisor hoping, in vain, that he would gradually be able to introduce the new theology. In 1544 he returned to his studies, obtained a medical degree from Bologna, and disappeared from the scene. About Fileno Lunardi and Eusebio Renato we know nothing more.

And yet Bucer's contacts with the Italian "brethren" continued, at least until 1544. It can be surmised that the recipients of the letters addressed to the evangelicals of Bologna, Modena, Ferrara, and Venezia were among the educated classes of these cities, where Giovanni Angelo Odoni had many contacts. Unfortunately, no name has as yet come to light. The key year in Bucer's correspondence with these Christian humanists is 1541, the year of the colloquy at Ratisbon, desired by Charles V in the hope of healing Germany's political and religious divisions.

Bucer had worked tirelessly to achieve doctrinal unity between the German and Swiss Protestants and succeeded in obtaining their signatures to a confession of faith, the Concord of Wittenberg, 1536. Together with Melanchthon, he was one of the leading participants in discussions attempting the reunification of all Christians. It was in 1541, to mark the failure of his grand and noble dream, that Bucer wrote three letters to the Italian "brethren." The first, dated 17 August, is a bitter acknowledgment of the failed Ratisbon negotiations;[35] the other two are dated 19 September and 23 December.

The addressees, members of unknown conventicles, were acquainted with the new doctrines but needed clarification on the more sensitive points. Two in particular were discussed: predestination and the Lord's Supper. On the first question, which had risen to the fore once again with the publication of the second edition of Calvin's *Institutes*, Bucer referred to Paul's Epistle to the Romans, warning about the difficulty in explaining these mysteries to simple believers. But everyone, he cautioned, educated and ignorant alike, had to accept the certainty that everything depended upon God's free will. A second certainty was the election of those persons who had been called through the Word, selected by God's immutable destiny before the beginning of the world. There remained the mystery of the damnation of the wicked, but the believer must hold firmly that "God's judgments are inscrutable and always just and equitable. There can be no iniquity in God, who rules the world with justice."[36] As for the Lord's Supper, Bucer reaffirmed the concept of the spiritual presence of Christ during the celebration and its significance as a remembrance of the expiation of sins and as a bond of love and unity among all believers.[37] But there remained the vexing question of the objective value of the sacrament, in which the body and blood of Christ might be "exhibited" even to nonbelievers. Bucer resolved it by denying any value to communion with the body and blood of Christ for anyone who did not believe in the promise of the Lord's words.

---

[35]Partially reprinted in M. Bucer, *Scripta anglicana fere omnia* (Basel, 1557), 685–86.

[36]"Iudicia Dei inscrutabilia sunt, et iusta semper, equissima, non potest esse apud Deum iniquitas, qui iudicat in equitate orbem." Letter dated 23 December 1541, pub. in P. Simoncelli, "Inquisizione romana e Riforma in Italia," *RSI* 120 (1988), app. 1, 108–12, and esp. 110.

[37]Letter dated 10 September 1541, in *Calvini Opera*, 11:276–79, n. 353.

These letters from the 1540s should be read together with Bucer's *Memorandum*, totaling no less than 802 articles. A copy of the first part of this document, consisting of forty-three theses, is preserved in the Biblioteca Comunale, Bologna, among the records of the inquisitorial trial against the Sicilian Minorite, Paolo Ricci, alias Lisia Fileno, alias Camillo Renato. The *Memorandum* is directed to persons who, even though they may have accepted the evangelical truth, are compelled to live under the Church of Rome. The author proposed a plan for reforming the church from within, suggesting participation in its liturgical life but interpreting the rites subjectively. This was not a Nicodemite stratagem, but the search for a via media based on the principle that there are true believers even in the Church of Rome, shoulder to shoulder with false believers, about whom is said: "non est cibus sumendus cum iis."[38]

The last known letter, sent from Speyer (1 April 1544), to the brethren in Italy and Sicily, poses an even more difficult problem in attempting to identify the addressees, since nothing is known about Sicilians who might have been in contact with Strasbourg.[39] Nevertheless, Bucer's letters and *Memorandum* confirm the reformer's links to that small group of Italians who resided for a time in Strasbourg and of whom he requested Hebrew, Greek, and Latin books printed in Italy, the purchase of which he had entrusted to the Englishman D. Richard Hillis. Bucer maintained a network of friendships that extended even to Baldassarre Altieri and to persons who sent him funds for the Italian exiles. He clung desperately to the Erasmian conviction of the need to restore the unity of the church. But his plan to establish in the Church of Rome *"ecclesiolae in Ecclesia"* was never to be. He realized it in his own person when in 1549 he had to abandon Strasbourg to avoid having to accept the *Interim* of Augsburg, which reestablished Catholicism in the Empire.

A recent important discovery by Paolo Simoncelli casts new light on Bucer's connections to Italian religious dissent during the 1540s, confirming the acceptance of certain basic elements in the Lutheran credo on the part of a sector of pre-Tridentine Catholicism. The arrest in 1551 of Vittore Soranzo, bishop of Bergamo, after an investigation conducted personally by Michele Ghislieri, did not follow merely from unfounded accusations on the part of his enemies, or by malevolent rumors, but from the confiscation of a "notebook," the contents of which were wholly unambiguous. The bishop had copied in it the Augsburg *Confession*, Luther's preface to the New Testament, the letter from Justus Jonas to Johann Frederick of Saxony on the *Doctoris Martini Lutheri Christianus recessus et mors*, the *Genealogia Papae*, and Bucer's letters to the Italian "brethren." The volume also contained copies of Luther's letters to B. Altieri, a letter to a "Pr. Romanae Curiae" (perhaps the protonotary P. Carnesecchi), the *Confessio totius territorii Electoris Saxoniae contra Interim* (1548), and a letter of B. Ochino. The presence of Bucer's two letters and Luther's to Altieri,

---

[38]"Food [the Supper] should not be consumed with them." See P. Fraenkel, "Bucer's Memorandum of 1541 and a 'Lettera Nicodemitica' of Capito's," *BHR* 36 (1974): 575–87.

[39]Published by P. Simoncelli, "Inquisizione romana," app. 2, 113.

suggests "an area of diffusion of Bucer in Italy politically and doctrinally both vast and unforeseen."[40]

Carnesecchi, who had already been accused at the time of his first trial in 1546 (in which he was absolved), of having had "dealings" with B. Altieri in Venice and of having written a letter to Bucer, an accusation made at the time of his third trial in 1566, thus explained the origins of his erroneous opinions: "I believe that it was in Naples in 1540 that I began to have doubts about purgatory and confession.... This seed grew in me as I began to read books by Luther and others of his persuasion, which I first saw at Viterbo, when I was with the cardinal of England, and in the company of Flaminio. One of these books was Bucer on the Gospel of Saint Matthew, and I believe that I also saw certain discourses of Luther on the Psalms, although they did not discuss these doctrines."[41] During the session of his trial held on 21 August 1566, Carnesecchi acknowledged that while he was residing at the court of Cardinal Pole at Viterbo in 1541, he had read Bucer's commentary on the Epistle to the Romans, loaned to him by Flaminio. These very works were also the preferred readings of G. A. Odoni and the Bolognese group.

The "Brood" of Franciscan Conventuals

Bucer's plan had been to link up the Lutheran groups of Emilia and the Veneto, and extend the network as far south as Sicily. But his moderate message began to run up against obstacles. The Venetian group guided by Altieri and by a person only identified as Seraph, facing an intensified propaganda effort by Zwinglians, Calvinists, and Anabaptists, appealed directly to Luther, himself seldom inclined to compromise, hoping for clarification on the vexing question of the Lord's Supper. At the same time, the proselytizing efforts in Bologna and Modena of Paolo Ricci, alias Camillo Renato, impugning the objective value of the sacraments, brought further disorder and confusion to the situation.

Contemporaneously, after Agostino Mainardo, Giulio della Rovere, Francesco Negri, and Pier Paolo Vergerio threw in their lot with the reformed churches in the Grisons, Switzerland and Calvinism exerted an ever stronger appeal. If the arrest of Bishop Soranzo demonstrated the impracticality of the via media articulated in Bucer's *Memorandum*, the tragic epilogue to the preaching of the doctrine of justification by numerous Franciscans, marked its permanent demise. Today we can no longer tell if the impassioned and tenacious propaganda carried on by Benedetto Locarno, Giovanni Buzio da Montalcino, Cornelio Giancardo da Nicosia, and Giovan Battista Vinci da Palermo was worked out in concert, nor to what point they were influenced by Bucer, as was certainly true in the case of Bartolomeo Fonzio. But certain factors lead one to suppose they may have been. All five were Franciscan Conventuals and followed the teachings of Girolamo Galateo and Baldo Lupatino. As masters in theology and celebrated preachers they were also in contact with one

---

[40]P. Simoncelli, "Inquisizione romana," 33 ff.
[41]Ibid., 60.

another because of their assignments and standing in the hierarchy of their order. Except for Locarno they were all tried and condemned as Lutherans. Their brother-member, Girolamo Mariano, guardian of the convent in Milan, who found refuge at Zurich in 1544 under the protection of the ex-Franciscan Conrad Pellikan, then a professor of Hebrew and Greek, lumped Locarno and Buzio with other leading Franciscans in Italy who were proclaiming the *"evangelium Christi fideliter et solide."*[42]

After Benedetto Locarno had preached with great success at Venice, Palermo, Genoa, Milan, Florence, and Mantua, he returned to his home at Locarno. On 15 July 1544, the schoolteacher Giovanni Beccaria, who had introduced the Reformation in that city, wrote warmly to Pellikan about Benedetto's arrival, hailing him as the leader of Franciscan preachers, "marvelously knowledgeable and versed in Holy Scripture," who for five years, from 1549 to 1553, had brought comfort cautiously to the people of the city who were being pressed by both ecclesiastical and political authorities to return to Roman obedience. Benedetto may indeed have been one of them, able to take decisive action at last, after a period of uncertainty. His name, however, does not appear among those who were forced to abandon the city and go into exile in Zurich after refusing to return to Catholic obedience. We do not know whether he was among those who bowed to the pressure and espoused the old orthodoxy, emigrated elsewhere, or simply died before the mass exodus of his fellow citizens.

Quite different was the fate of Giovanni Buzio, dubbed Mollio, from Montalcino, near Siena. After a first trial about 1540, mentioned by Pellikan in his *Chronicon*, he was transferred to the convent of San Lorenzo in Naples, and from there to Ravenna where he met Pietro Manelfi. At the beginning of 1552, Buzio was arrested on the Adriatic coast. In spite of the efforts made on his behalf by the government of Siena, Buzio was executed as an unrepentant heretic at Rome in the Campo dei Fiori on 4 September 1553. Before dying he proclaimed his faith in Christ before the cardinal inquisitors and the Roman people. The event was reported in a letter written by an eyewitness, printed at Strasbourg in the same year. News of the martyrdom was communicated to Calvin by the humanist Gaudenzio Merula from Turin on 27 April 1554: *"Montalcinum qui libere praedicabat evangelium…Romae fuisse combustum."*[43] Buzio would be followed in death sometime later by Cornelio Giancardo and Bartolomeo Fonzio for their activities during these same years between 1540 and 1550.

Fra Cornelio Giancardo, from his convent in Nicosia, went to Lugano to preach the Advent season of 1546.[44] How had this summons from an old Franciscan establishment in Sicily to a city beyond the Alps, neighboring the famous monastery of

---

[42]For this quotation and on Locarno in general, see S. Caponetto, "Una sconosciuta predica fiorentina del minorita Benedetto Locarno," *NRS* 57 (1973): 410–21, repr. in the author's *Studi sulla Riforma*, 205–13.

[43]See the entry by J. Tedeschi, *DBI*, 15:634.

[44]On Cornelio da Nicosia, cf. F. Meyer, *Die evangelische Gemeinde in Locarno, ihre Auswanderung nach Zürich und ihre weitern Schicksale*, 2 vols. (Zurich, 1836), 1:162ff.; T. von Liebenau, "I primordi della Riforma religiosa nel Ticino," *Bollettino Storico della svizzera italiana* 2 (1880).

Santa Maria del Sasso at Locarno, come about? A fellow brother in the order, Benedetto Locarno, had preached in Sicily, and perhaps it was from him that Cornelio
had learned of the situation in the Swiss cantons, some of which had gone over to the
Reformation. Cornelio's sermons created a scandal and divided the population,
which heard him expound the fundamental points of Protestant theology, with
emphasis on predestination in line with the teachings of Bucer and Calvin. The
monk also attacked "hypocrites," who feigned to be Christians so that they could
empty the pockets of the poor. He was accused of heresy but made an able defense
presented before the twelve regents of Lugano in which he claimed that his words
had been misrepresented. Giancardo was arrested at the order of Bishop Melchiorre
Crivelli, inquisitor over Lombardy (Lugano was part of the diocese of Milan), and
admitted that he had denied free will and the intercession of the saints, as well as having affirmed justification by grace and predestination. He astonished his judges with
shrewd reasoning: prayer to the saints is idolatry and a fiction since the believer is
appealing to saints, even though he knows that Christ is the only bestower of grace.
The defendant made a full retraction, and was ordered to return to Lugano as a penitent, with a cord about his neck, to ask the people for pardon.

A few months after his sentence (25 January 1547), Giancardo resumed his
preaching with the permission of the provincial of his order. But his reputation was
greatly diminished and Protestantism never took hold in Lugano, as opposed to
Locarno, where the reformer of the city, Giovanni Beccaria, won over populace and
nobility alike by his fortitude during prosecution and incarceration. On 3 March
1555, somewhat more than a hundred of Beccaria's converts abandoned the canton
and found refuge in Zurich, where they established an Italian language community
with Bernardino Ochino as pastor.

Cornelio Giancardo returned to his convent at Nicosia, became reconciled to
the church and renounced his Lutheran doctrines at the auto da fé held at Palermo
on 18 June 1553.[45] But even on this occasion he could not fully persuade himself to
remain silent. Some years later, in 1560, he was arrested again, and after an imprisonment of just under a year, was condemned to the stake at Palermo as a *relapsus* on 8
June 1561. The list of persons released to the secular arm for execution (*Serie dei
rilasciati al Braccio secolare*) gives a confusing summation of the reasons for the condemnation. But the conclusion leaves no doubt about the Lutheran faith which the
victim had managed to conceal for almost two decades. The Augustinians, Giovanni
Gigliuto of Noto and Andrea Lanza of Buscemi, shared Giancardo's fate, joined by a
Paduan merchant, Francesco Vicino, all condemned as "obstinate" and "relapsed"
Lutherans.

Was Giovanni Battista Vinci of Palermo, a master in theology, one of the
addressees of Bucer's letter, dated April 1544, to the Sicilian "brethren"? There is no
conclusive evidence for this supposition, but a reading of the trial conducted against
him at Palermo in 1546 or 1547 does not exclude it. His attitude towards the

---

[45]The identification of Fra Cornelio da Nicosia with the Franciscan Fra Cornelio Giancardo is my
own. Cf. S. Caponetto, *Studi sulla Riforma*, 111.

ecclesiastical life, his disapproval of its rites and ceremonies and the themes of his sermons, resemble closely the ideas contained in Bucer's *Memorandum*. Vinci admitted that he had doubted the existence of purgatory for about a decade, thus dating his own initiation into heterodoxy to about the year 1536, namely the period of most intense diffusion of Lutheran currents in the peninsula. He was accused, among other charges, of having stated "that Lutherans were good Christians enlightened by the Holy Spirit and followers of the Gospel...who spoke badly of cardinals, of the pope and of the other prelates."

Vinci abjured his belief in justification by faith alone, his rejection of purgatory, the efficacy of religious images, auricular confession and the cult of relics (once when he had been asked if he was fatigued after a long procession, he replied that he was tired of honoring "a piece of bone").[46] At the time of his reconciliation to the church (13 February 1547) Vinci was suspended from teaching and preaching, and compelled to wear the garment of the penitent heretic. But he relapsed into his old errors and was condemned to death as a recidivist at the Palermo auto da fé of 18 June 1553. The inquisitor, however, had to content himself with burning a straw effigy, because the monk had broken out of prison in April of the previous year, making his way north across the entire peninsula, finding refuge in the Franciscan convent at Udine. He may have thought that in a city controlled by Venice he would be out of reach of the Spanish Inquisition, as some other Sicilians had succeeded in doing. But it was not to be. Vinci was denounced to the *rettore* in Udine, the official representing the Venetian government there, and arrested on 26 October 1552. He was transported to Venice and locked up in the prison of San Giovanni in Bragora, where he was still languishing on 22 December when he sought permission to confess himself and receive communion that Christmas season.[47] His name does not appear among those executed by the *Serenissima*. It may be that the Sicilian, now convinced that the via media had failed, made his peace once and for all with the Church of Rome.

Bartolomeo Fonzio definitely was influenced by Martin Bucer. After wandering from city to city, Fonzio settled at Cittadella in 1551 where he was appointed schoolmaster and taught for seven years, deeply appreciated by his students. He fell under suspicion after an altercation with the archpriest Camillo Cauzio, and a catechism Fonzio had written for the "instruction of the young" was subjected to rigorous scrutiny. He was arrested on 27 May 1558 and brought to Venice. After four years of interrogations and imprisonment, on 16 June 1562 he was asked to abjure a number of equivocal and unorthodox propositions. Afraid that he would betray his conscience and sin against the Holy Spirit, he replied to his judges that he did not feel he had fallen into error, and had nothing to abjure, "holding in greater esteem honor and one's soul before God, true and just judge, than this miserable life, as duty

---

[46]"so that they may not seem ungrateful for such a grand benefit of creation, redemption and salvation." This definition is taken from Galateo's *Apologia*, 91.

[47]ASV, Sant'Uffizio, b. 10. The quotations come from the copy of Vinci's trial held at Palermo in 1547 that concluded with his reconciliation. It was forwarded to the Venetian tribunal after the monk's arrest in Udine. Cf. *Serie*, n. 324.

requires."[48] On 4 August 1562 he was "cast into the sea" and "drowned" "with a rock tied around his neck," as was the Venetian custom.

During the final week of his imprisonment, Fonzio wrote the *Fidei et doctrinae...ratio*, which he entrusted at the last moment to his judges. It contained 284 Latin theses that expound a concept of Christianity, based on the Bible and Augustine, from whose doctrine of predestination it borrows. Although Fonzio had accepted some of the basic teachings of the Reformation, from justification by faith to the sacraments as signs of grace, he continued to hope in the convocation of a universal council that would restore unity and concord in the light of Scripture.[49] This was a final echo of the Erasmian and Bucerian utopia.

BIBLIOGRAPHICAL NOTE

For the history of the diffusion of Lutheranism in Italy, the older treatments on the subject are still useful for the mass of information they contain, rather than for their interpretations. They are listed in the bibliography attached to F. Lemmi, *La Riforma in Italia e i riformatori italiani all'estero nel secolo XVI* (Milan: Istituto per gli studi di politica internazionale, 1939), 15. Additional references can be gleaned in the general histories by Achille Olivieri, *La Riforma in Italia: Strutture e simboli, classi e poteri* (Milan: Mursia, 1979), 162–75, Manfred Welti, *Breve storia della Riforma italiana* (Casale Monferrato: Marietti, 1985), and Massimo Firpo, *Riforma protestante ed eresie nell'Italia del '500* (Bari: Laterza, 1993).

With Federico Chabod's *Per la storia religiosa dello Stato di Milano durante il dominio di Carlo V,* first published in 1938, a new phase began in Italian Reformation studies. This magisterial reconstruction of events destroyed the old legend that the Protestant movement in Italy was a "party of literati," unsuited to the needs of the common people (C. Cantù, *Gli eretici d'Italia: Discorsi storici* [Turin, 1865], 1:386). The classic book by Delio Cantimori, *Eretici italiani del Cinquecento: Ricerche storiche* (Florence: Sansoni, 1939; 4th ed. Turin: Einaudi, 1992) appeared almost contemporaneously with Chabod's work. The *Eretici* inaugurated a current of studies that has flourished to this day, modifying our perspective on the Italian Reformation, enlarging the parameters of the movement, and highlighting its complexity.

For comprehensive surveys of Italian religious history, cf. Carlo Ginzburg, "Folklore, magia, religione," in *Storia d'Italia: I caratteri generali* (Turin: Einaudi, 1972), 1:603–70; Giovanni Miccoli, "La storia religiosa," in *Storia d'Italia*, 2:430–1079; and Antonio Rotondò, "Atteggiamenti della vita morale italiana del Cinquecento: La pratica nicodemitica," *RSI* 79 (1967): 991–1030. See also Susanna Peyronel, "Per una storia delle donne nella Riforma," in her edition of R. H. Bainton, *Donne della Riforma I.* (Turin: Claudiana, 1992).

---

[48]E. Comba, *I nostri protestanti*, 104; E. Zille, *Gli eretici*, 145–221.
[49]See A. Olivieri, "Il 'Catechismo' e la 'Fidei et doctrinae […] ratio' di Bartolomeo Fonzio, eretico veneziano del Cinquecento," *Studi veneziani* 9 (1967): 339–452.

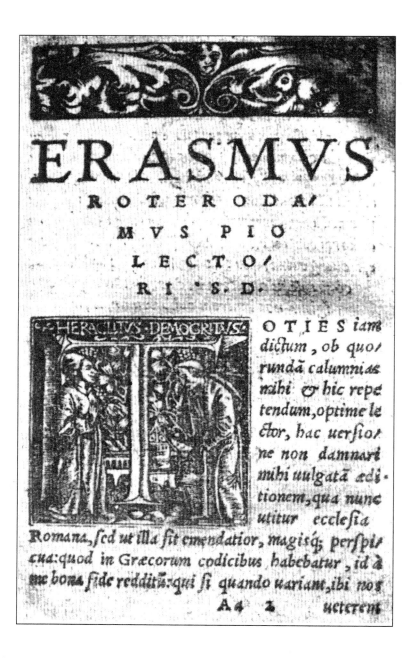

Preface to Erasmus's edition of the New Testament, original Greek text with new Latin translation (Basel, 1523). The author defends himself from the charge that he had undervalued the Latin Vulgate.

5

JUAN ᴰᴱ VALDÉS ᴬᴺᴰ VALDESIANISM

VALDÉS, "KNIGHT OF CHRIST"

IN 1535 A NEW AND ORIGINAL element made its appearance on the stage of the Italian Reformation. In that year a Spanish gentleman by the name of Juan de Valdés, the brother of one of the secretaries of Charles V, came to live in Naples, where he remained until his death, as imperial agent.

Juan de Valdés (1509?–41) was one of the most important Christian thinkers of the sixteenth century and one of the greatest writers in the Castilian language prior to Miguel de Cervantes. A fervent admirer of Erasmus, Juan contributed, together with his brother, to the diffusion of the Dutch humanist's thought in Spain. Juan was still a young man when he was received at Escalona as a member of the household of the marquis of Villena, where he was able to hear the *alumbrado* Pedro Ruiz de Alcaraz, the marquis's lay preacher, whose teachings can be summed up as "You will be lost, if you do not surrender yourself to God's love." When in his sovereign freedom God grants his love to humankind, the latter will be saved, despite the persistence of sin. From this freely given justification ensue the rejection of meritorious works and devotions, the denial of the ecclesiastical state, and even the real presence of Christ in the Eucharist.

The youthful Valdés left Escalona in February 1524, after the arrest of Alcaraz. At home, Valdés passed a period of intense study of Holy Scripture, reflecting on the spiritual crisis of European society by meditating upon his master's teaching and reading works by Erasmus and Luther. In 1526 Valdés attended the celebrated University of Alcalá de Henáres. He remained there roughly four years immersed in the study of Greek, Hebrew, Latin, and Italian and Spanish literatures. But in 1529, after the publication of his *Diálogo de doctrina cristiana*, a first inquisitorial trial was mounted against him, followed by a second early in 1531, on the charge of Lutheranism.

In August of that year Juan went to Rome as imperial agent accredited to the court of Clement VII. On 3 October the pope granted him safe-conduct so he could be reunited with his brother Alfonso at the court of Charles V. Apparently the peace

concluded between the emperor and the Medici pope, after the horrors of the Sack of
Rome, had erased the Spanish Inquisition's proceedings against Valdés. But Juan was
not to be reunited with his brother, who had moved with the imperial retinue from
Ratisbon to Bologna and died from the plague in Vienna on 6 October 1532.

The short time Juan de Valdés spent in Naples, where from a knight of Caesar,
he became a "splendid knight of Christ," is a brief moment in the span of a century
that saw the currents of religious protest spread throughout the peninsula. But it was
a crucial time in an intense period of sowing, the years of his greatest creative ener-
gies. Valdés commented on the Psalms, wrote the *Alfabeto cristiano*, that enchanting
dialogue with Giulia Gonzaga, commentaries on Paul's Epistles to the Romans and
Corinthians, and finally, the Gospel commentaries, of which only the one on Matthew has survived.

Even though Valdés's correspondence with Cardinal Ercole Gonzaga demonstrates his interest in imperial politics and in the widespread longing for peace in the
world and in religion, actually during these years he assumed the duties of "doctor
and pastor of noble and illustrious persons," as he was described by Celio Secondo
Curione.[1] In the manner of an *alumbrado*, just as his teacher Pedro Ruiz de Alcaraz
had done, Valdés received in his house at Chiaia groups of listeners and followers
from every corner of Italy, attracted by his fame as exegete and spiritual guide. His
portrait, as composed by Jacopo Bonfadio in the famous letter he wrote immediately
after the master's death to two of his most loyal disciples, Marcantonio Flaminio and
Pietro Carnesecchi, remains still today the most telling evidence of the admiration he
aroused for his learning and as a person:

> This has been, to be sure, a great loss for us and for the world, because
> *signor* Valdés was one of the rare men of Europe, and those writings he has
> left to us on the Epistles of Paul and the Psalms of David, will testify to it
> fully. He was without doubt, in deed as well as in words and in all his coun-
> sel a whole man. He sustained with a particle of his soul that feeble and
> slender body of his; and with the greater part of it and with his pure intel-
> lect, almost as if it resided outside the body, he always directed his thoughts
> to the contemplation of the truth and of things divine. I convey my condo-
> lences to *messer* Marcantonio, because he, more than any other, loved and
> admired him.[2]

But what was it that Valdés taught? Today we are in a position to state with certainty that the Valdesian teaching was one of the decisive channels, though a less
obvious one since he avoided any sort of anti-Roman polemic, for the diffusion of
the central doctrine in Lutheran theology: justification by faith alone, frequently
summed up by the Spaniard in the Melanchthonian formula, "the benefit of Christ."
Delio Cantimori, discarding ancient, opposed interpretations, suggested as far back

[1] *Considerazioni*, 567.
[2] Jacopo Bonfadio to Pietro Carnesecchi (undated, but 1541), in *Opuscoli e lettere di riformatori italiani del Cinquecento*, a cura di G. Paladino (Bari: Laterza, 1913), 1:95–96.

as 1961, that Juan de Valdés "succeeded in introducing his rejection of the Catholic dogmatic tradition and his proselytization for Lutheran doctrines into that movement of return to the practice and faith of the Biblical and apostolic age, which is called evangelism and has nothing heterodox about it."[3] This view was recently documented by Carlos Gilly in a definitive essay.[4] The *Diálogo de doctrina cristiana* literally translated or paraphrased countless passages from Luther's *Decem praecepta praedicata populo* (1518) and *Explanatio dominicae orationis pro simplicioribus* (1520).

Until a few years ago, on the basis of the comprehensive study by José C. Nieto, who, however, decisively rejected the notion of any Lutheran influence on Valdés,[5] it was possible to assert that the fundamental principles of Valdesian theology—the election of the justified person, justification by faith alone, namely the "benefit of Christ," regeneration and sanctification, the rule of the Holy Spirit—bore some resemblance to the teachings of Luther and Calvin. But now we have to conclude that their matrix was in large part Lutheran. The image of a mystical, unusually enlightened, and spiritualist Valdés, resembling, for example, a Sebastian Franck, was mistaken and now should be set aside.[6] The erroneous notion was based principally on three of Valdés's *Considerations* (3, 22, 63), where, in metaphorical language, the superiority of the Holy Spirit over Scripture was affirmed, the latter being compared to a beginner's alphabet, or to a candle that illuminates a dark place, which is no longer needed when the light from the sun, the Holy Spirit, appears. But Nieto did clarify, in some of the most felicitous pages of his book, that in the work of the Spanish reformer, the illuminating function of the Holy Spirit should be understood in the context of salvation and has nothing in common with the Neoplatonic religion of the universal Spirit.[7]

To view the *Considerations* as a work of Valdés's maturity and the culmination of his thought was a serious error in dating and methodology. Quite the contrary, in the *Proemio de los Evangelios*, the reformer advised the reader that his Gospel commentaries were the consummation of his reflection on Scripture. A reading of the proemium and commentary on the Gospel of Matthew, the only one to have reached us, is crucial to understanding the teachings and spirituality of the Spaniard. There he asserted unambiguously the normative and exclusive function of Scripture, denying any significance, for the purpose of Christian knowledge and perfection, to any sort of direct and particular revelation.[8] With this premise, it is no longer an easy

---

[3]D. Cantimori, "Il circolo di Valdés e gli altri gruppi evangelici," in *Umanesimo e religione nel Rinascimento* (Turin: Einaudi, 1975), 197.

[4]Cf. C. Gilly, "Juan de Valdés: Übersetzer und Bearbeiter von Luthers Schriften in seinem "Diálogo de Doctrina Christiana,'" *Archiv für Reformationsgeschichte* 74 (1983): 257–305.

[5]Cf. J. C. Nieto, *Juan de Valdés and the Origins of the Spanish and Italian Reformation* (Geneva: Droz, 1970) (rev. Spanish trans., *Juan de Valdés y los origines de la Reforma en España y Italia*, [Mexico, Madrid, Buenos Aires, 1979]). All citations are to the Spanish version.

[6]E. Cione, *Juan de Valdés: La sua vita e il suo pensiero religioso* (Bari: Laterza, 1938, 103ff.; 2d ed., Naples: F. Fiorentino, 1963).

[7]J. C. Nieto, *Juan de Valdés*, 372–82.

matter to pinpoint the originality in the Spanish reformer's thought and explain, aside from his personal charm and ability to communicate, the tremendous success of his message. The concept of faith as an existential experience of the believer "incorporated in Christ" and the description of the dramatic journey from regeneration to sanctification, together with his uncommon capacity for the introspection of the mind, were among the most successful contributions of Valdés to the rich and varied religious panorama of the sixteenth century.[9]

Another special feature in the Spaniard's thought, one that has not received the attention it deserves, was his loyalty to Erasmian irenicism. Valdés's consciousness of the human inability to know truth, enveloped within infinite divine wisdom, and his need to respect all opinions, allowed him reflections of incomparable value and significance in that epoch of deep divisions in the church and in society and of theological animosity and fierce repression. Apropos the words of Jesus in John 16:2, "the hour is coming when whoever kills you will think he is offering service to God," Valdés commented: "In this statement I learn this, that every man must be careful never to become passionate about things which pertain to religion—I mean defend this or attack that with passion—so that passion should not blind him in such a way that he should come to err against God out of ignorance born of malice."[10]

The aim of Valdés was to lead towards knowledge of the central doctrines of the Christian faith based on Scripture and to the consequent knowledge of the book of one's own soul. He was never concerned about citing his sources, and did not hearken back to the church fathers or to ecclesiastical institutions. The words "Roman church" appear nowhere in his writings. For him, it sufficed to go back to Augustine, followed by Luther, Melanchthon, and Calvin, who held that the true church is the church of the elect and justified of God, of whom Jesus Christ is the head. Valdés disregarded the Church of Rome, but he equally failed to mention Wittenberg and Geneva. Whoever accepted the "benefit of Christ," that is, the remission of sins and freely given salvation, renouncing the possibility of winning one's own justification and trusting in the justice of God accomplished in Jesus Christ, is one of the elect and has entered the Kingdom of God.[11]

The Neapolitan *alumbrado* was a Nicodemite. Well aware that he stood outside the Church of Rome, he nevertheless did not urge the abandonment of its rites and of its sacraments, but instead their refashioning, assigning a higher place to inner religiosity over external forms and devotions. In this sense, Valdés was a conveyor of Erasmian spirituality. He quickly became a point of reference for persons who were experiencing profound religious restlessness and were not finding the way in their difficult spiritual search after the schism in Christendom and the emergence of dis-

---

[8]"El proemio de los Evangelios," in *El Evangelio según San Mateo, declarado por Juan de Valdés* (Madrid: Librería Nacional, 1880), 1–14.
[9]Cf. J. C. Nieto, *Juan de Valdés*, 409–61.
[10]*Considerazioni*, CV, 477.
[11]*Considerazioni*, LXXV, 311–14.

cord among the nascent Protestant churches. A spiritual master who abhorred polemic, who was a guide to the study of Scripture for comprehending the road to salvation, Valdés had a major vehicle for the diffusion of his ideas in his links to powerful noble families in Italy and in Spain.

From the very beginning of his Italian sojourn, Valdés had attached himself to the influential family of the marquises of Mantua, allied to the empire, whose network of relatives extended throughout Italy. Cardinal Ercole Gonzaga ruled in Mantua, his sister Eleonora was the duchess of Urbino, his brother Ferrante was viceroy in Sicily from 1535, and their cousin Giulia was countess of Fondi and a personage of the first rank in her culture and spirituality among Italian nobility. It suffices to scan the roster of Valdés's disciples to discern that most of them came from the ranks of the patriciate and the wealthy, from persons of culture, both ecclesiastics and laymen: Mario Galeota; Marcantonio Flaminio; Don Benedetto Fontanini; Apollonio Merenda; Vittore Soranzo, bishop of Bergamo; Pietro Carnesecchi; Andrea Sbarra; Ferrante Trotta; Giovan Tommaso Minadois; Ferrante Brancaccio; Antonio Imparato; Antonio d'Alessio; Giovan Tommaso Blanco; Baron Consalvo de Bernaudo; Cesare Carduino; Gian Francesco Alois; Pietro Cirillo; Simone Fiorillo; Scipione d'Afflitto; Sigismondo Mignoz; Piero Boccapianola; Giovan Vincenzo Abbate; Ambrogio de Apuzzo; Marcantonio Villamarino; Juan de Villafranca; the archbishop of Otranto Pietro Antonio di Capua; Lattanzio Ragnoni; Donato Antonio Altomari; Galeazzo Caracciolo, marquis of Vico; the abbot Girolamo Busale; Giovan Francesco Verdura, bishop of Cheronissa; Bartolomeo Spadafora; Bernardino Ochino; and Peter Martyr Vermigli. Among the women were Giulia Gonzaga, Donna Brianda and Isabella Bresegna, wife of Don Garcia Manrique, a noble Spanish captain who became governor of Piacenza.[12] Giulia Gonzaga, Mario Galeota, Marcantonio Flaminio, and Pietro Carnesecchi were the most sensitive, receptive, and faithful among the disciples of Valdés. It was they who saved the master's manuscripts and had them copied, translated, and printed.

Giulia Gonzaga

Giulia Gonzaga (1513–66) was one of the most celebrated women of Italy, renowned for her beauty and intelligence, her praises sung by Ariosto and Bernardo Tasso. At the age of sixteen she was widowed by the death of her husband Vespasiano Colonna, lord of Fondi. She rejected all subsequent marriage offers and dedicated herself to the careful administration of her small fief, where she was visited by F. M. Molza, Francesco Berni, Pier Paolo Vergerio, Annibal Caro, and many others who came to enjoy her conversation, and admire her wisdom, humor, and grace. Count Fortunato Martinengo, after a visit, thus summed up his impressions of her in a letter to Vergerio, written in June 1547: "About Lady Giulia there would be, indeed, much to say. Let it suffice that out of her friendship for you she received me willingly and

---

[12]E. Cione, *Juan de Valdés*, 111.

showed me much kindness. I shall say only that never have I been so timid in the presence of any woman, as I was in hers."[13]

From Giulia's encounter with Valdés at Naples in 1536, on the occasion of the much anticipated Lenten sermons of Ochino, a relationship was established based on esteem, reciprocal admiration, and friendship, to which she remained loyal until death. Valdés considered her his spiritual heir and entrusted the manuscripts of all his writings to her. It was she who, with Galeota, organized the diffusion of the master's thought within the limits imposed by inquisitorial vigilance and later by the persecutions of Valdesians at the hands of Paul IV. To Marco Antonio Magno she assigned the translation into Italian of the *Alfabeto cristiano*, to Flaminio, the translation of the *Considerazioni* and of the *Trattatelli*, which, even if they were not all from the pen of Valdés, expressed his ideas through the versions prepared by Flaminio or other persons.

Benedetto Croce wrote, apropos the *Alfabeto cristiano*, the first work of Valdés dedicated to Giulia, which reflects their conversations after attending the fiery sermons of the great preacher Ochino: "The dialogical development of the *Alfabeto cristiano* is moving and dramatic, in which we witness the progress of a soul, that another soul (rendered stronger and better) itself guides and leads upward. It is enlivened by images and parables, and here and there in certain passages recalls the lively style of Erasmus's colloquies. At times we catch a glimpse of Giulia Gonzaga, beyond her sorrows, anxieties, and religious fervor, with her gracious and witty manner of speaking, which was one of her attractions. Serious as she might have been in certain things, she had been gay and festive as an adolescent and as a young bride, and always fond of jesting...."[14]

The portrait of Giulia painted at Fondi in the summer of 1532 by Sebastiano del Piombo, the disciple and colleague of Michelangelo, offers not only the image of fascinating beauty and grace, but evokes for us the girl of nineteen who renounced remarriage and the pleasures of life at court to which her noble lineage and beauty called her. Del Piombo, the painter of Christ bearing the cross, who after the Sack of Rome shared with Michelangelo and Francesco Berni the distress of witnessing God's judgment on the Church of Rome, succeeded in portraying her lifestyle: the solemn widow's garments, the absence of all ornamentation or of rings on her slender fingers, a gentle melancholy in her eyes, "beautiful with a beauty to which pain is no stranger."[15] The best comment on del Piombo's masterpiece came from Giulia herself. Moved by the sermon they had just heard, she said to Valdés at the door of the church of San Giovanni Maggiore: "I want you to know that ordinarily I am so unhappy with myself, and also with all the things of this world, and am so indifferent, that, if you could see into my heart, I am certain that you would not refuse your com-

---

[13]*Delle lettere di diversi autori raccolte da V. Ruffinelli* (Mantua, 1547), xxv.

[14]Juan de Valdés, *Alfabeto cristiano*, a cura di B. Croce (Bari: Laterza, 1938), xxi-xxii of the introduction.

[15]Ibid., ix.

passion, because in it you would find nothing but confusion, perplexity and anxiety."[16]

Giulia's correspondence with Pietro Carnesecchi is a lofty expression of Valdesian spirituality and a valuable source for understanding how the master's teaching had been appropriated. Convinced that they belonged to the ranks of the elect because they had accepted the "benefit of Christ," the two, bound by a profound friendship and a fraternal love, exerted themselves to keep alive their master's teaching, summoning to faith in the Gospel of Christ those capable of receiving it, and standing in solidarity with those trapped in the great wave of persecutions unleashed by Gian Pietro Carafa, who became Paul IV: Spadafora, Verdura, Galeota, Soranzo, Morone, and so many others; or giving succor and support to those, who like Isabella Bresegna, drawing their own conclusions from Valdés's message, had gone over to the Reformation. In 1536 Giulia took up residence in the convent of San Francesco in Naples, where she continued to direct the movement, now extending over the entire peninsula. The goal was individual conversion, but also, although it was uncertain how much it was possible to modify the ecclesiastical institutions, to devise approaches that might influence the Council of Trent. Valdesians eventually experienced the dwindling of their aspirations. They came to realize that the ecclesiastics whom they had looked to as guides in the renewal of the church, from Pole to Seripando, from Cortese to Morone, were solidly bound to it and to the pope. Giovanni Morone and Ercole Gonzaga would be the last to preside over the Council that placed its definitive seal on the schism within Christianity.

Mario Galeota

Mario Galeota (1499?–1585) was Giulia Gonzaga's right hand in directing the Valdesian movement. He belonged to an illustrious Neapolitan family (his father, Giovan Bernardino, was the lord of Monasterace in Calabria) and studied mathematics and military engineering without neglecting literature. He had begun as a participant in the gatherings in the home of Valdés and became his follower and intimate friend. With the countess, Galeota dedicated himself, with enthusiasm and courage, to the diffusion of the master's thought and writings. First in Naples and later in Monasterace he organized a scriptorium for the copying of Valdés's manuscripts, arranged to have them translated into Italian and subsequently to have them printed. He was so taken by these works, that after their condemnation and prohibition, when asked how this would affect him, he replied: "It matters very little to me, because they are in my head, and no one can erase them from there, and even if they can prevent me from reading them, they cannot take them from my mind."[17]

Galeota was investigated in 1548, after the Neapolitan revolt against the intro-

[16]Ibid., 7–8.

and, finally in 1565–66. He ended by abjuring his Valdesian and Lutheran doctrines, namely that the pope had no other authority than to preach; that "faith alone justifies and saves man"; that works are not meritorious since "Jesus Christ made atonement with his own blood"; that neither purgatory nor free will exists; that in the sacrament, the substance of the bread remains in the consecrated host; that saints cannot intercede for us; that indulgences, jubilees, and monastic vows are without efficacy. The sentence against Galeota closes with the words: "You must abjure, damn and detest the aforementioned heresies and errors of which you are gravely suspected, including those contained in the book called the *Beneficio di Cristo* and those contained in the books and writings of Valdés, and any and all other heresy, of which you have been gravely suspected, thus before your sworn absolution, as well as after."[18] His sentence, dated 12 June 1567, took into consideration that in 1559 he had not taken advantage of the popular revolt following the news of the death of Paul IV to flee from Rome. He was sentenced to a term of five years in prison, but as early as May 1571 he was once again in Naples and had resumed his normal life. If we reflect on the different fate of Pietro Carnesecchi, sentenced only a few months after Galeota, and the fact that they were both accused of the same doctrinal errors,[19] we must accept Galeota's abjuration as sincere. By then he must have become convinced of the defeat of the movement in both the religious and political spheres.

IN SICILY

The opinion of one of the principal accusers of Valdesians and philo-Valdesians, the priest Ranieri Gualani, himself a former follower of Valdés, imprisoned by the Holy Office in Rome in 1551 on the suspicion of heresy, that Valdés had infected "all of Italy" had some merit. It can be documented that the movement spread to Sicily, Tuscany, and the Veneto, but when one thinks of the preaching activities of Ochino, Vermigli, and Buzio, the area extends much beyond.

Valdesianism penetrated Sicily before other regions, not only because of its relative geographical proximity to Naples, the center from which the proselytization began, and because of the daily contacts of a political, economic, and cultural nature between the two Spanish viceroyalties, but also because of the passage through the island of one of the principal followers of Valdés: Benedetto Fontanini, a Mantuan Benedictine, named by Carnesecchi at his trial as the primary author of the *Beneficio di Cristo*.[20]

---

[17]P. Lopez, *Il movimento valdesiano a Napoli: Mario Galeota e le sue vicende col Sant'Uffizio* (Naples: F. Fiorentino, 1976), 105.

[18]Ibid., 178.

[19]"Processo Carnesecchi," 551–73; O. Ortolani, *Pietro Carnesecchi* (Florence: Le Monnier, 1963), app. 248–60.

[20]For Benedetto da Mantova, see my biographical sketch in *DBI*, 7:437–41; *Beneficio*, "Nota critica," 467–96.

The Benedictine convent of San Giorgio Maggiore, Venice, in an engraving by Luca Carlevarijs (end of the seventeenth century).

Don Benedetto da Mantova had studied at San Benedetto Po, where he had taken his vows at the hands of Gregorio Cortese on 16 February 1511, together with Teofilo and Giambattista Folengo, Luciano degli Ottoni, and Dionisio Faucher. About 1533–34 he entered the monastery on the island of San Giorgio Maggiore where he would remain until August 1537. Don Benedetto had come to Venice after two decades of life in the Benedictine order where he associated with brothers of unusual humanistic and theological education. Under the leadership of its abbot, Cortese, San Giorgio Maggiore had one of the most illustrious periods in its history. From 1534 to 1537 its inhabitants had included Cardinal Reginald Pole, an exile from the persecutions of Henry VIII; the Hebraist Johann von Kampen, hailing from Nuremberg and Cracow, where he had tried in vain to obtain a hearing for a program to reunite Catholics and Protestants; and Marcantonio Flaminio, who had still not made his choice among Aristotle, the Muses, and Holy Scripture. It is here that the meeting must have taken place between Don Benedetto—who along with the two Folengo brothers had read Erasmus and Melanchthon—and the refined poet, Flaminio, who would become his collaborator in the final version of the *Beneficio di Cristo*.

In the spring of 1537 the general chapter of the order decided to transfer Don Benedetto to the monastery of San Nicolò l'Arena in Catania, where he arrived at the end of August. He interrupted his journey in Naples at the monastery of Saints Severino and Sossi, and the halt may have been longer than was customary. He came into contact with the circle of Valdés, perhaps through Giulia Gonzaga, to whom he was related, since his brother, Angelo Fontanini, was married to Margherita Gonzaga.[21] This channel is highly likely, not only because of the familial tie, but because at the time he was on his way to Sicily, its viceroy was Don Ferrante Gonzaga, Giulia's cousin.

In the monastery of San Nicolò, at the base of Mt. Aetna, Don Benedetto recalled his conversations with Teofilo Folengo and Juan de Valdés and his circle, and reflecting upon a sundered Christianity, he wrote the *Beneficio di Cristo*. That same year, Don Pietro da Piacenza, who had also taken his vows at San Benedetto Po, was sent to Sicily to direct the monastery of San Martino delle Scale. In 1538 he was named abbot of San Nicolò Arena, where he would remain until 1541. In that same year, 1538, Teofilo Folengo, who had returned to his order with his brother Giambattista, after a period of penance at San Benedetto di Monte Conero (Ancona) and at Punta Campanella in Campania, was sent to San Martino delle Scale, subsequently becoming regent of Santa Maria delle Ciambre, not far from Palermo. From the time when the Sicilian congregation had joined that of Cassino in 1506, to maintain harmony and unity, "two steady streams of monks ascended and descended each year between Sicily and the mainland."[22]

---

[21]Cf. E. Menegazzo, "Per la conoscenza della Riforma in Italia: Note d'Archivio," *Atti e Memorie dell'Accademia Patavina di Scienze, Lettere ed Arti* 90 (1977–78), pt. 3:193–210.

[22]G. Billanovich, *Fra don Teofilo Folengo e Merlin Cocai* (Naples: Pironti, 1948), 161–62.

The two Mantuans, Don Benedetto and Don Teofilo, brought to the Sicilian houses of their order the benefits of their studies and echoes of the learned discussions from Erasmian and evangelical circles in northern and central Italy. Emilio Menegazzo's intriguing suggestion that Teofilo Folengo (Merlin Cocai) was referring to his brother-member Benedetto in the following passage of the *Orlandino* (1526), seems ever more probable. After eulogizing Erasmus and the belief that "more than works, it is faith that counts," Teofilo asserted:

> I find much learning of every sort,
> but few good writers and even less judgment;
> however, with time doors will open
> for distinguishing virtue from vice;
> oh holy, oh blessed, oh worthy guides
> for knowing of Christ his benefit.[23]

Don Benedetto was one of the leading members of the chapter in the famous establishment of San Nicolò, occupying the fourth place in the hierarchy, after the abbot Pietro da Piacenza, the prior Bernardo da Aversa, and Innocenzo da Paternò, a dean (*decano*), as was he. Don Benedetto's numerous administrative responsibilities did not keep him from his meditations and from meeting persons who shared his deepest sentiments. In March 1539 he visited San Placido in Messina and from there it is not difficult to suppose that he pushed on to Naples to meet with Flaminio and his friends in the circle of Valdés.

Giulio Besalù, a Venetian lawyer who lived in Naples from the fall of 1542 to 1551 (with interruptions), mentioned our Benedictine among numerous people he met during these years with whom he discussed the issues of the day, and linked him, among others, with two jurists of Palermo, Filippo de Micheli and Giovanni Antonio Cannizu, tried on charges of Lutheranism in 1547, and with Giulio Cesare Pascali and Ludovico Manna, both of Messina, who would become exiles in Geneva. This piece of evidence is important, because the lawyer Besalù named Benedetto da Mantova among those who had accepted justification by faith alone and broken with the church's teachings concerning the mass and the sacraments.

Even if we do not know how Fontanini reacted to his experience of the Sicilian milieu, so different from the sociopolitical and religious point of view of the Mantuan and Venetian, and the influence he might have exercised on his monastic brothers in the Sicilian houses of the order, these years were decisive in his evolution towards Valdesianism and the claims of the Protestant Reformation.

BERNARDINO OCHINO IN SICILY

Bernardino Ochino, returning home along with Fontanini and the Sicilians after participating in the Neapolitan circle, should be mentioned among the channels by

---

[23]T. Folengo, *Orlandino*, 3:21, in *Opere di Teofilo Folengo*, a cura di C. Cordié (Milan, Naples: Ricciardi, 1977); cf. *Beneficio*, 473–74.

which Valdesian and Lutheran teachings reached the island. This general of the
Capuchins, one of the great preachers of the century, in 1536 in the church of the
monastery of San Giovanni Maggiore at Naples, gave a series of Lenten sermons that
even moved Charles V, homeward bound from his victorious Tunisian expedition.
Ochino returned to preach in Naples in 1539 and again in 1540. It was said, among
the followers of Valdés, that the master furnished him with the subjects the night
before that he would treat in his sermon the next day. Ochino's preaching, simply
couched and deeply felt, spread the great themes of grace, faith, and works among
the common people. They had an impact and were discussed in the street, and in the
marketplaces for days after. Ochino's fame spread to Sicily, and in 1537 Viceroy Don
Ferrante Gonzaga attempted in vain to invite him to Palermo. A second invitation
was extended to Ochino in 1539. On 2 May the baron of Burgio wrote to Cardinal
Alessandro Farnese in the hope of obtaining the preacher for the following Lenten
season, so that "each one of us by his life and example may become like a Capuchin
in his own person."[24]

When Bernardino finally visited Palermo and Messina in 1540, he was already
suspected of Lutheranism. Among Sicilians, easily moved to enthusiasm, obsessed
even when concealing it, with human destiny and the afterlife, the words of the great
proselytizer of the "benefit of Christ," of salvation as the gift of Christ, must have
provoked a profound impression.[25] Along with the preaching of the Augustinians
and the Minims of the order of San Francesco di Paola, Valdesians were among the
first to bring the teachings of Luther to Sicily.

BIBLIOGRAPHICAL NOTE

J. C. Nieto's cited work contains a vast bibliography on Valdés. A survey of the most
recent studies can be consulted in A. Aubert, "Valdesianesimo ed evangelismo italiano: Alcuni studi recenti," *RSCI* 41 (1987): 152–75. M. Firpo's *Tra Alumbrados e
"spirituali": Studi su Juan de Valdés e il valdesianesimo nella crisi religiosa del '500 italiano* (Florence: Olschki, 1990), is a comprehensive analysis of the influence exercised by the thought of Valdés. See also Juan de Valdés, *Alfabeto cristiano*, a cura di A.
Prosperi (Rome: Istituto storico italiano per l'età moderna e contemporanea, 1988);
idem, *Il dialogo della dottrina cristiana (1529)* a cura di T. Fanlo y Cortes (Turin:
Claudiana, 1991), containing in appendix an edition of the brief catechism, *Qual
maniera si devrebbe tenere a informare [...]* (1545?); and the new edition of the *Alfabeto cristiano*, a cura di Massimo Firpo (Turin: Einaudi, 1994).

For G. Gonzaga and the relevant bibliography, cf. B. Nicolini, "Giulia Gonzaga
e la crisi del Valdesianesimo," in Nicolini's *Ideali e passioni nell'Italia religiosa del
Cinquecento* (Bologna: Palmaverde, 1962), 79–102.

---

[24]See my biographical sketch in *DBI*, 15:19.
[25]For B. Ochino, see R. H. Bainton, *Bernardino Ochino, esule e riformatore del Cinquecento*
(Florence: Sansoni, 1940).

For Sebastiano del Piombo, cf. M. Calì, *Da Michelangelo al Escorial: Momenti del dibattito religioso nell'arte del Cinquecento* (Turin: Einaudi, 1980). Michelangelo's relationship with Francesco Berni is discussed by S. Caponetto, "Lutero nella letteratura italiana della prima metà del Cinquecento," in *Studi sulla Riforma*, 333–49.

On Benedetto Fontanini and the Folengo brothers, see C. F. Goffis, *L'eterodossia dei fratelli Folengo* (Genoa: Pagano, 1950).

Bernardino Ochino, general of the Capuchins; from the title page of his *Dialogi sette* (Venice, 1542).

6

THE *BENEFICIO DI GIESÙ CHRISTO* AND THE DIFFUSION OF VALDESIANISM IN TUSCANY AND THE VENETO

THE AUTHOR

A BOOKLET ENTITLED *Trattato utilissimo del beneficio di Giesù Christo crocifisso verso i christiani* appeared in Venice in 1543 from the presses of Bernardino de Bindonis (printers of Savonarola's *Prediche sopra Aggeo*), immediately "flying like a spark touching off other sparks throughout Italy."[1] This "dulcet booklet," as Pier Paolo Vergerio called it, presented itself to its readers in a modest typographical vestment without pretense to elegance, without the name of the writer, so that, as we read in the preface, "you may be moved more by the content than the authority of the author." The work enjoyed an extraordinary success, and even if it seems hard to believe the ex-bishop of Capodistria, who wrote that in the short span of about six years, forty thousand copies were printed and sold in Venice alone, it is certain that it enjoyed wide diffusion and was reprinted several times. The booklet appeared at a crucial time in European history: after the failure of the colloquies at Ratisbon and the repudiation of the chief negotiators, Melanchthon and Contarini, by Luther and his followers, as well as by the Roman Curia and intransigent Catholics. The break between the Church of Rome and the northern reformers was an accomplished fact. The death of Gasparo Contarini, the champion of reconciliation, in August 1542, was followed by the flight to Protestant lands of two famous and popular Tuscan preachers, Bernardino Ochino and Peter Martyr Vermigli, admirers and friends of Valdés. The Roman Inquisition, reconstituted by the bull *Licet ab initio* (21 July 1542), was being organized energetically by Cardinal Gian Pietro Carafa, to whom heresy was an evil greater than the plague, against which the church had to be on guard with all possible means. All those—and by now they were numerous in all social levels—who had been influenced by the preaching of justification by faith, and were sympathetic

---

[1]B. Croce, "Il 'Beneficio di Cristo,'" *La Critica* 38 (1940): 115–25, reprinted with corrections and additions in Croce's *Poeti e scrittori del pieno e del tardo Rinascimento* (Bari: Laterza, 1945), 1:211–28.

towards Luther and Calvin, or regretted what was occurring in Germany and Switzerland, found in the *Beneficio*, so imbued with a total love for Christ, a refuge, a consolation, a response to their all-consuming query: What must we do to be saved?[2]

The singular events surrounding the booklet are well known. It was appreciated and praised for its profound spirituality by such learned and pious prelates as the Benedictine Gregorio Cortese, the prince-bishop of Trent Cristoforo Madruzzo, and Cardinals Giovanni Morone, Tommaso Badia, and Reginald Pole. And yet it was quickly also branded as heretical by inquisitors and theologians. The Dominican Ambrogio Catarino wrote a violent diatribe against it: He was the first to understand how much the anonymous author owed to Luther, Bucer, Melanchthon, and Calvin.[3] On 21 July 1546, the Council of Trent condemned it, with the participation of Galeazzo Florimonte, bishop of Aquino and Sessa, an old friend of Marcantonio Flaminio. After it was placed in Giovanni Della Casa's *Index* of prohibited books issued in 1549, the pursuit of the *Beneficio* by inquisitors became so frenzied that in a decade or two almost all copies were destroyed. The booklet, precious to believers of all religious persuasions, would be consumed by the flames in Italian town squares together with the *Sommario della santa Scrittura* and books by Erasmus, Luther, and Melanchthon. Whoever possessed it was immediately suspected of harboring Lutheran sympathies, and prosecuted.

While French, English, Croatian, and Spanish translations circulated throughout Europe, the original Italian version was becoming increasingly rare. Someone succeeded in acquiring a copy as late as 1556, after which all trace of it was lost. In the eighteenth century it was a bibliographical rarity. In 1855, when Reverend Churchill Babington located an exemplar through the catalog of the library of St. John's College in Cambridge, the discovery proved to be a significant cultural event. A new chapter opened in the history of the *Beneficio di Cristo*. Centuries after the inquisitors' own investigations, scholars began a serious inquiry into the identity of the author. Only in 1870, through the labors of the Mazzinian bibliophile Giacomo Manzoni, the publication of the trial against Pietro Carnesecchi, who was tied by fraternal friendship to Valdés and to Flaminio, could one read the precise, informed opinion of one who was familiar with the facts: "The first author of this book was a black monk of Saint Benedict called Don Benedetto of Mantua, who said he had composed it while staying in the monastery of his order in Sicily near Mt. Etna; since this don Benedetto was a friend of M. Marcantonio Flaminio he gave him the said book, asking him to polish and clarify it with his beautiful style, so that it would be more readable and pleasing, and so Flaminio, while preserving the subject entire, corrected it as it seemed proper to him...."[4]

Persistent, concurrent scholarly investigations established the paternity of the Benedictine Benedetto Fontanini, whose life remains obscure after the Sicilian period when he traveled northward in the company of Teofilo Folengo and Pietro da

---

[2]I refer the reader to the "Nota critica" in my critical edition of the *Beneficio*, 469–519.
[3]See Ambrogio Catarino Politi, *Compendio d'errori e inganni luterani* (1544), in *Beneficio*, 371–72.
[4]Ibid., *Documenti*, n. 42, 459–60. [The English translation is quoted from "The 'Beneficio di Cristo,'" translated, with an introduction by R. Prelowski, in *Italian Reformation Studies in Honor of*

Piacenza at the end of 1542. After serving as rector during the years 1544 to 1546 at the abbey of Santa Maria di Pomposa, the abbot of which was Don Luciano degli Ottoni, an old friend from his youth, Benedetto was implicated with him in the trial against their brother-member Giorgio Rioli, known as Siculo. The latter had taken his vows at San Nicolò l'Arena on 24 February 1534, and remained there from the monastic years 1537–38 to 1539–40. For about three years this young monk from Catania completed his studies under the deanship of the Mantuan, by whom, in all probability, he was guided in the study of Holy Scripture and introduced to Valdesian doctrine. The bond between the two restless Benedictines began on the slopes of Etna and continued later in Ferrara, or in other cities in northern Italy, through which Siculo wandered.

Unfortunately we are still largely in the dark about the life of Don Benedetto, whose work achieved a leading place in Italian sixteenth-century religious history. It may not be presumptive to imagine him succumbing to the discipline of his superiors and of the Roman church, and yet, remaining intimately convinced, as was the case with Flaminio and all the other Valdesians, of belonging to the invisible church of the elect.

A "DULCET BOOKLET"

If a direct acquaintance with Valdés on the part of the first author of the *Beneficio di Cristo* is only a probable conjecture, there is no doubt about the intrinsic connections of the author's thought with Valdesian doctrine and spirituality. Marcel Bataillon wrote in 1937: the *Beneficio* "is without doubt the most important expression of Valdesianism, a book which succeeds in communicating its spirituality far beyond an intimate and aristocratic circle"; and he reaffirmed this opinion thirty years later.[5] Don Benedetto knew the *Alfabeto cristiano*, the *Cento e dieci divine considerazioni*, as well as the commentary to Saint Matthew that was circulating in manuscript form among the friends of Giulia Gonzaga, Mario Galeota, and Marcantonio Flaminio.

The purpose of the *Beneficio* is summed up in the conclusion of the work:

> to praise and exalt, in accordance with our limited ability, the stupendous benefit that the Christian has received from Jesus Christ crucified, and to demonstrate that faith itself justifies, meaning that God receives as just, all those who truly believe that Jesus Christ has satisfied for their sins. However, just as the light is not separable from the flame which burns of itself

Socinus, ed. John A. Tedeschi (Florence: Le Monnier, 1965), 21–102, at 26 (henceforth cited as R. Prelowski, "Beneficio"). Trans. note.]

[5]M. Bataillon, *Erasme et l'Espagne* (Paris: Droz, 1937), 550; idem, *Erasmo y España*, 509–10.

alone, so good works cannot be separated from faith, which justifies of itself alone.[6]

But justifying faith is not the "historic faith" that does not differ from knowing of the existence of Caesar or of Alexander the Great; it is the "living faith," namely "a work of God in us, through which our old man is crucified and we are all transformed in Christ, so that we become a new creature and very dear children of God."[7]

Chapters 3 and 4 are dedicated to demonstrating justification "by faith alone," based on Holy Scripture and corroborated by the authority of the church fathers: Augustine, Origen, Basil, Hilary, and Ambrose. Chapters 5 and 6 are a corollary of the preceding, with the first clarifying how the Christian clothes himself in Christ, and how he should imitate Him. The sixth presents the remedies against a weak faith and temptations: prayer, the remembrance of baptism, the frequent recourse to communion, the essence of the mass, and knowledge that the elect are predestined.

In his account the writer oscillates between the joy of the personal rediscovery of the "benefit of Christ" and the passionate desire to confute the opponents of the doctrine of justification by faith; between a hymn of gratitude so mystical in tone as to recall for us the *Imitation of Christ*, widely circulating among Benedictines, dear to Valdés and to Flaminio, and the pages where the polemic against "false Christians" is so biting and sarcastic. The institutional church is forgotten, and when he mentions the ecclesiastical hierarchies, he does so with hostility against their laws and precepts, with a sentiment of detachment from the historical church.

In contrast to Valdés who, except for Scripture, almost never indicates his sources, Don Benedetto does so carefully, but omits, for obvious reasons, at least four: Luther, Melanchthon, Valdés, and Calvin.

Giovanni Miegge, followed by others, precociously juxtaposed the *Beneficio* with Luther's *Liberty of the Christian Man*. From the latter derived the doctrine of a gratuitous justification with its insinuating and forensic emphasis. The doctrine of double justification, developed by Gropper, supported by Contarini at Ratisbon in 1541, accepted by Melanchthon, and later defended, but in vain, at Trent by Seripando, is rejected in the *Beneficio*, if not with Luther's scathing hostility, at least with equal firmness.

If ongoing philological research has added instances of the *Beneficio's* indebtedness to Luther, this is no less the case in certain respects, with Melanchthon's *Loci*. The *Beneficio* has the same doctrinal framework as the 1521 edition of the *Loci*, based on the triad: sin-law-grace, as well as concepts, exegesis, admonishments, and Biblical images common to both works. But, despite the many points of similarity with the theology of Luther and Melanchthon, the *Beneficio* is unmistakably Valdesian in its emphasis on the imitation of Christ, the role it assigns to the Holy Spirit and its terminology. Don Benedetto da Mantova and M. A. Flaminio were not intending to write an anti-Roman work, at least not openly, but an edificatory one,

---

[6]*Beneficio*, 83; R. Prelowski, "Beneficio," 94.
[7]*Beneficio*, 42; R. Prelowski, "Beneficio," 67. The two statements come directly from Luther. See *Praefatio in epistulam Pauli ad Romanos*, WA DB 5, 622 and 624.

an exhortation for justification by faith alone, overflowing with the certainty of divine election, to console and support the doubting and undecided. The element of polemic against false Christians is overshadowed by the song of love and gratitude of the justified person.

Moreover, the *Beneficio di Cristo* possesses an originality all its own, which has been overlooked by scholars preoccupied with assigning it to a preestablished scheme. It appeals to all Christians not to contaminate the sacrament of communion by rejecting the Biblical promise of gratuitous salvation or by shattering the unity of the body of Christ, "separated by hate from our brethren." The Eucharist is the symbol of the unity of the body of Christ. Borrowing and paraphrasing this theme from Augustine as well as from Calvin, the two authors affirm a solemn Biblical truth, that remains to this day the most serious obstacle to ecumenism. If this is the meaning of the sacrament, two sins of unfaithfulness weigh upon Christians: the sin of "villainous hypocrisy" on the part of those who receive the signs of the passion of Christ without believing in its power to justify; and the sin of those who receive the signs of charity and unity while lacerating the body of Christ through hate of their brethren, forgetful that the sacrament cautions us that "we should be joined and united with so much harmony of spirit, that the slightest division cannot intrude among us."[8] The recipients of this admonition, conveyed in somewhat disguised language ("let every Christian be cautioned") are Catholics who deny justification by faith alone and Protestants who reject unity and charity.

The booklet is historically significant because it helped to circulate in Italy and elsewhere in Europe, even among the less educated classes, the Lutheran and Melanchthonian concept of "the benefit of Christ." The differences among scholars concerning the author's purpose rise from the intentionally ambiguous and veiled language he employed.[9]

Benedetto da Mantova, meditating in the peace of his cloister under the shadow of Mt. Etna on the splintering of Christ's body and on the passions and controversy that the Reformation had unleashed in Europe, ended by considering justification by faith in divine grace the line that separated those who searched for the glory of God from those who intended to follow tradition and "human judgment." Don Benedetto brought to Valdesianism the notions about reconciliation and harmony held by Contarini and his companions, persuaded, like the cardinal, that justification was the true foundation of the Christian faith. For Valdés, whoever held the belief in justification within himself had to feel the certainty of his proper vocation. Consequently, his disciple, Don Benedetto, saw incorporated and joined to Christ, all those who were "justified," on both sides of the ecclesiastical divide, in patient expectation of God's work in the conversion of all those who had "Hebrew souls." This uninhibited eclecticism that associated the fathers of the church with Luther, Melanchthon, and Calvin was a deeply felt conviction.

---

[8] *Beneficio*, 66–68; R. Prelowski, "Beneficio," 83.
[9] *Beneficio*, "Nota critica," 479.

During his last trial in 1566 to 1567, Carnesecchi stated clearly and explicitly that Valdés and Flaminio had taught that the truth of justification by faith was "held by all true Christians if not *explicite, saltem implicite*, and that, if not earlier, at least *in articulo mortis*, it had been revealed to them by God, as the only way they could be saved."[10] In support of their belief they cited Augustine, John Chrysostom, Bernard, Origen, Hilary, Prosper, among many others. But Carnesecchi also revealed that he himself, along with Flaminio, Bishop Soranzo, Alvise Priuli, and others of the Viterbo circle, studied appreciatively the writings of the reformers who had restored that truth to the light of day after many centuries of oblivion. Carnesecchi singled out Luther, a great man sincere in his beliefs, "of whom, even if he had spoken well about many things, and interpreted many places in Scripture properly, one could not because of this conclude that he possessed the Spirit of God, except to the extent that God had bestowed it for the benefit and edification of his elect; and thus they drew ideas from him 'as if collecting gold from dung, and the rest (as the saying goes) they gave back to the cook.'"[11]

Thus for Valdesians, Luther was not only a Biblical exegete, whose interpretations could be useful for other investigators, but one of God's prophets sent to his elect. Carnesecchi specified who they might be: "All those who believed in the gift of faith following the opinion of Valdés and the others who agreed with him, and who demonstrated they possessed such a gift, not only by their words, but also by their life and works." [12]

The Augustinian vision of the church of the elect, generated in Don Benedetto, as it had done for Valdés, indifference and distrust in the human capacity to restore the unity of Christ's body. The *Beneficio* does not even make a passing mention of the imminent meeting of the Council, convoked at Trent for 1 November 1543. This loyalty to Valdesian thought distances the author from the struggle raging all over Europe to construct a new church in opposition to the Church of Rome, and deters him from making a commitment on the human and historical level. Don Benedetto holds that strife, even in the cause of truth, takes away from the imitation of Christ, as it is stated in 1 Peter (2:19–24), on which he comments:

> Since Christ was humble, meek and removed from contentions, we ought to make every effort towards humility and meekness and flee all fights and contentions, those that consist of words and disputes, just as much as those consisting of deeds. Just as Christ endured all the persecutions and disorders of the world for the glory of God, we should cheerfully undergo the ignominies and persecutions which false Christians impose on all those who want to live piously in Christ. Christ laid down his life for his enemies and prayed for them on the cross, and we should always pray for our

---

[10]"Processo Carnesecchi," 333.
[11]Ibid., 325: "…tamquam aurum ex stercore colligentes et cetera (ut aiunt) reddebant coquo."
[12]Ibid., 223.

enemies and willingly lay down our life for their salvation. This is how we follow the footsteps of Christ, as Saint Peter says.[13]

Imitation of Christ, model of gentleness and humility, and exaltation of the Eucharist as symbol of the unity among all believers, confirm the Valdesian stamp on the famous booklet.

The "Valdesian Manifesto"

One is left with the impression, however, that the *Beneficio* might have served a political purpose in view of the imminent opening of the long awaited Council at Trent. The possibility that it might have been intended to serve such a function is reinforced when we think that it was reprinted in 1546 and put on the market in the thick of the conciliar discussion, initiated in June, on the difficult and controversial question of justification.[14] This imprint had been preceded the previous year, shortly before the Council opened, by the publication of a considerable portion of the Valdesian corpus of writings: the *Alfabeto cristiano*, the *Sul principio della dottrina cristiana*, and probably, the first edition of the small catechism, mentioned by Vergerio with the title *In qual maniera si dovrebbono instituire i figliuoli de Christiani*. As J. C. Nieto points out, 1545 was not only the year of the Council of Trent, but also the year of the "Valdesian manifesto."[15] A missionary effort was launched by Galeota, Flaminio, and Carnesecchi, working in conjunction with Giulia Gonzaga, its goal being to persuade at least some of the conciliar participants about the need to reconsider the essential doctrines of the Christian faith without letting themselves be prejudiced against certain interpretations of Scripture merely because they might come from Luther, as Pole argued when the Council began its discussion of justification.

That there was a political objective behind the publication of the Valdesian corpus and the new edition of the *Beneficio* is confirmed by the contemporary Italian translation (1546) of the *Due dialoghi* by Juan's brother, Alfonso de Valdés, a member of the Erasmian-oriented imperial secretariat. Written on the day after the Sack of Rome as a justification for the war against Clement VII, the manuscript circulated in Spain and in the territories of the Empire. The dialogues were not printed at once since the emperor and pontiff made peace, with the reconciliation culminating in the coronation of Charles V at Bologna in 1530. The dialogues appeared in print in the original Spanish at Venice about 1543, when they became timely again thanks to the deterioration of the politico-religious situation. The Italian version, appearing at a crucial moment in the Tridentine debates, was "a practical and political translation in the broadest possible meaning of the term," as Alfonso De Gennaro noted twenty or

---

[13] *Beneficio*, 55; R. Prelowski, "Beneficio," 75.

[14] See M. Firpo, "Juan de Valdés e l'evangelismo italiano: Appunti e problemi per una ricerca in corso," *Studi storici* 25 (1985): 733–54 (repr. in *Tra alumbrados*, 127–53).

[15] See J. de Valdés, *Two Catechisms: "The Dialogue on Christian Doctrine" and "The Christian Instruction for Children,"* ed. J. C. Nieto (Lawrence, Kans.: Coronado Press, 1981), 24–25 of the introduction. [A "Second Enlarged Edition" appeared in 1993. Trans. note.]

so years ago in his critical edition.[16] There is no ambiguity about the work's purpose, a fact underscored by the many interpolations made to it by the anonymous translator, who was part of the campaign to disseminate Erasmian and Valdesian ideas, intended as critical barbs against the conservatives in the Council who obstinately opposed any conciliatory gestures towards the doctrines of the reformers and abetted a policy of repression and hostilities against Protestants.

Against this intransigence, we read in the *Dialogo delle cose accadute a Roma nel 1527* that God had aroused first Erasmus and then Luther to goad and scourge the Church of Rome, which had been deaf to the appeal that it return to the original mission of Christ's church. With the same stinging sarcasm of Erasmus's *Colloquies,* the dialogue denounces the tyranny of a pope who prohibits the "preaching of the pure, shining and sincere evangelical doctrine," abandons charity and the footsteps of Christ in pursuit of the dominion of this world by intrigue and war, and accumulates wealth for himself, his bishops and cardinals, while sanctioning daily disregard of the needs of the "poor," "living temples of God."[17] The dialogues thus joined the ranks of anti-Roman controversialist literature as the other face of Valdesianism. This was one of the "secrets" of the followers of Valdés. They did not intend to be assimilated into the ranks of those who manifested only superficial sympathy for the Augustinian doctrine of grace.

The political campaign of Valdesians and *"spirituali,"* linked in the aspiration for a doctrinal and disciplinary reformation of the church, was resoundingly defeated with the vote on the decree *De justificatione* on 13 January 1547, which peremptorily crushed any possibility of reaching agreement with the Protestants. From that moment on the *Beneficio* became the most effective vehicle of Lutheran propaganda, without referring to Luther's name, an element in the construction of an individual faith that permitted cohabitation, even though separated, with the Church of Rome, making use of that "dulcet booklet" as of a friend "which offers invincible charms against spiritual misery."[18]

In Florence and Tuscany

The *Beneficio* continued to circulate in Italy until late in the century, if we take into account the fourth edition in Italian that appeared at Tübingen in 1565 prepared by Stefan Consul and Antonio D'Alessandro for Italians in Dalmatia and Istria. The booklet's passage from Venice through Treviso, Modena, Bologna, Florence, Naples, and Catania is noted in many inquisitorial trials as the trail that led to the discovery of religious dissidents. Cardinal Morone had it circulated in Modena by the bookseller Antonio Gadaldino and distributed free of charge to the faithful in the diocese.

---

[16]Alfonso de Valdés, *Due dialoghi, traduzione italiana del sec. XVI,* a cura di G. De Gennaro (Naples: Istituto Universitario Orientale, 1968), xci.

[17]Ibid., 314, 333, 346, 383–85.

[18]M. Bataillon, *Erasmo y España,* 193. This was the judgment about the Spanish version of Erasmus's *Enchiridion militis christiani* in 1524. In my opinion it also fits the *Beneficio di Cristo.*

In the *Mezzogiorno* the *Beneficio* even came into the hands of the bishop of Catania, Nicola Maria Caracciolo, together with the *Prediche* of Bernardino Ochino and books by Valdés, despite the extreme vigilance of the Sicilian Inquisition. The ex-Augustinian Lorenzo Romano commented on the *Beneficio* and Melanchthon's *Loci* to his students in 1549 at Piedimonte in the Caserta area.

After their departure from Naples, Carnesecchi and Flaminio stopped in Florence. From May to October 1541 the refined Latin poet was a guest in the home of his Florentine friend, whose generous hospitality he praised in poem 17 of book 5 of his *Carmi*. For the two men it was an intense period of reflection about their Neapolitan experience, comparing it to the teachings of Calvin's *Christian Institutes*, which appeared in a second Latin edition in 1539 and was reprinted in French in 1541. Carnesecchi and Flaminio renewed their acquaintance with the Florentine cultural élite, the great humanist Pier Vettori, Lelio Torelli, first secretary to Cosimo I, and Cosimo's majordomo Pier Francesco Riccio, but especially with Caterina Cibo, an admirer of Ochino, who had instructed her in the new way.

Flaminio, fascinated and persuaded by the thought of Valdés, had arrived in that Florence where Neoplatonic philosophy was still represented by Francesco Verino and where the memory of Savonarola was not wholly extinguished. In 1540 Flaminio had written to the abbot Giovan Francesco Anisio, apropos the immortality of the soul, "that natural light is very obscure and gives little aid in knowing the truth." Thus, he had laid aside Plato and Aristotle and wanted "no other master than Jesus Christ, who is a scandal to the Jews and foolishness to the wise men of the world; but to the elect he is the power and wisdom of God, and the eternal salvation of all the faithful."[19]

For Flaminio these were months of important contacts with Ochino in the convent of Montuchi, perhaps with Vermigli in the *Badia* at Fiesole, and with others tormented by concern for their own salvation and by the condition of the Church of Rome. These conversations could not ignore the mission and martyrdom of Savonarola. Then, or not long after, as evidence that persons influenced by the Reformation still clung to the legacy of the prophet of San Marco, in that world transformed by the discovery of justification by faith, Flaminio composed the following epigram that appeared in print for the first time at Lyons in 1548 thanks to the efforts of his cousin, Cesare Flaminio:

Dum fera flamma tuos, Hieronime pascitur artus
Religio, sanctas dilaniata comas,
Flevit, et o, dixit, crudeles parcite flammae,
Parcite; sunt isto viscera nostra rogo.

As soon as the piece became known in Florence, perhaps after the first edition of Flaminio's poetic collection, the *Carmi* published by Torrentino in 1549, Benedetto Varchi turned it into Italian, though somewhat freely and with a variant or two of

---

[19]S. Caponetto, *Aonio Paleario*, chap. 5.

Baroque inspiration.[20] In his version Savonarola symbolized faith and pure religion, the victim of human cruelty, without the slightest allusion to his prophecies of the *renovatio ecclesiae*.

The Florentine man of letters Varchi, an ex-republican who had returned to Florence from Venetian exile in 1543 thanks to Pier Francesco Riccio who interceded with Cosimo on his behalf, was the only contemporary Italian writer who dared to praise Valdés openly, associating him with Vittoria Colonna and Pietro Bembo in the sonnet addressed to the Valdesian Caterina Cibo, written in 1547 or 1548.[21]

Varchi's transparent admission of Valdesian sympathies was corroborated recently by another, disguised, but nevertheless significant piece of evidence. A careful textual comparison by Paolo Simoncelli established that Varchi's *Sermone fatto alla Croce*, written for Good Friday 1549, was in large part lifted from the *Beneficio di Cristo*, virtually a clandestine reprinting of the famous booklet.[22] This episode, which reflects the author's possible intimate connections with the Company of San Domenico, where the *Sermone* was supposedly recited by Antonio Lenzi, is only one fragment of that widespread penetration of the teachings of Valdés occurring in Florence and Tuscany. This success of Valdesian ideas actually is not so surprising if we think of the expectations left by Savonarola, of his legacy, jealously preserved by his loyal disciples, based on a return to Sacred Scripture and the centrality of Christ in the plan of salvation, nor when we recall the flurry of Erasmian publications produced by the Giunti in 1518–1519. From their presses issued some of the most important of the great humanist's works, from the *Praise of Folly* to the *Complaint of Peace*, from the *Education of the Christian Prince* to the adage "The Sileni of Alcibiades."

Thus Valdesian ideas fell on well-tilled fields. There is firm documentation for the circulation of the *Beneficio* and of Valdesian writings in Florence, Siena, and Lucca. The only known manuscript copy of the *Beneficio*, older than the *editio princeps* of 1543, was owned by Pier Francesco Riccio, Cosimo's secretary, in a miscellaneous codex of writings on the subject of justification, which also contained Valdés's treatise *Della medesima giustificazione*. It is likely that Carnesecchi had given a copy of the manuscript of the book to Riccio, shortly after Flaminio had revised it. Whatever the case, it is certain that the work was known in Florence before its 1543 edition.[23]

Cosimo Bartoli, in the public reading held in the Florentine Academy on 17 December 1542 on the theme of faith, taking as his text canto XXIV: 64–66 of Dante's *Paradiso*, introduced into Ficino's and Pico's scheme of universal revelation the Valdesian concept of "the true and living faith," drawing his entire argument

---

[20]Ibid., 48–49. "Mentre le membra tue fiamma empia e fera / Girolamo, pascea sacrate e sante / piangea la Fede, e trista in vesta nera / dicea piangendo al mesto rogo avante: / Fiamme crudei, crudei fiamme restate / che non lui, no, ma me cenere fate."

[21]Ibid., 50.

[22]P. Simoncelli, *Evangelismo italiano nel Cinquecento: Questione religiosa e nicodemismo politico* (Rome: Istituto storico italiano per l'età moderna e contemporanea, 1979), 330–47.

[23]*Beneficio*, "Nota critica," 499–504.

The Roman "academy" of Baccio Bandinelli (1487–1559), sculptor, painter, and art theorist. Modest artists' studios such as this one were often the scene of lively discussions on the significance of works of art and their theological and philosophical premises. Engraving by Agostino Veneziano, 1531.

from the *Beneficio*, with textual interpolations from the first four chapters. Confirming Flaminio's known connections to the work, at the beginning of his lecture he spoke of him as "a man of rare literary ability who in theology has opened our eyes and made clear many sacred writings."[24] Flaminio, the Latin poet who had refused to accompany Cardinal Contarini to the colloquy at Ratisbon on the grounds that he was ignorant of the subjects under discussion, assumed, after his departure from Naples, a leading role as theologian and scriptural interpreter in Florentine academic and cultural circles.

Some years later, in 1546, Pompeo Florido, majordomo to the cardinal of Ravenna, Benedetto Accolti, intimate friend of Juan de Valdés and a correspondent of his brother, Alfonso, was considered by the cardinal's nephew "a most Christian and evangelical person" because he kept "in his chambers that *Beneficio di Cristo* which so arouses the ire of the monks."[25] From the Medici court to the great palaces of the Florentine nobility, from the Academy to the studies of the *literati*, the teachings of Valdés continued their progress without interruption for about a decade, even penetrating the lower strata of society.

Ochino's Advent and Lenten sermons from 1537 to 1540, in Florence, Siena, Lucca, and Pisa, years when his fame reached from one corner of Italy to the other, brought to the masses of artisans, laborers, and peasants the themes of sin and of redemption, of gratuitous grace and works, fruits of "the living faith." After the final series of Sienese sermons, Bernardino Buoninsegni, an intimate friend of Paleario and a great admirer of Ochino whose apostasy he saw as a calamity for Tuscany and for Italy as a whole, wrote a sonnet that began:

The great trumpet of Christ calls Father Ochino
Every day to the right path
The soul of his frail body made restive
To lead him to this good, exalted and divine....[26]

After Ochino fled into exile, his *Prediche*, printed at Geneva in 1542, and his epistle to the *Balìa* of Siena of November 1543 became the writings most pursued by inquisitors, fully cognizant of their dangerous propaganda value.

The author of the *Diario di Firenze*, a Savonarolan of modest culture, anti-Medicean and an enemy of clerical corruption, but loyal to the Church of Rome and opposed to the Reformation, noted in his diary for the years preceding the arrival of the Jesuits in Florence in 1546, the bitterness of the controversies between those who, "for the sake of their freedom scorned the good order of Holy Mother Church and every sacred rite and said that it sufficed to believe in God," and those who were faithful to the church of their fathers.[27] Among the former we should include certain Augustinians of Florence and of Colle Valdelsa, and perhaps even of Fivizzano, if

---

[24]S. Caponetto, *Aonio Paleario*, 49.
[25]B. Accolti to B. Florido (Pisa, 27 October 1546), in *Beneficio*, "Documenti," n. 22, 440.
[26]L. Kosuta, "Aonio Paleario et son groupe humaniste et réformateur à Sienne (1530–1546)," *Lias* 7 (1980): 35.
[27]S. Caponetto, *Aonio Paleario*, app. 3, 236.

only out of a spirit of solidarity towards a celebrated brother-member of theirs, a great theologian, unjustly expelled from the church.

When the Jesuits arrived in the city of Savonarola they had a difficult time penetrating the various civic milieux. For the Lenten sermons of 1547 they summoned Diego Lainez and the next year Peter Canisius, the famous and learned German missionary. It was essential to oppose the "Lutheran" preaching of Giuliano da Colle Valdelsa, discussed previously. The apparent indifference of the Florentines to the Jesuits was their response to the rigid orthodoxy on the subject of justification engineered victoriously by the Jesuit Salmerón against Girolamo Seripando, general of the Augustinians, at the Council of Trent.

A Sermon for the Academicians?

Even after the flight to Protestant lands in 1542 of the celebrated Tuscan pulpit orators, Ochino and Vermigli, the Florentine philo-Protestants did not concede defeat and persuaded the civic authorities to invite Lenten preachers sympathetic to the Reformation. In 1543 when he was a professor of theology at Bologna, Benedetto Locarno, famous for his sermons at Palermo, Genoa, and Milan, preached at Santa Croce. The Franciscan delivered a sermon with scholastic overtones, not one for popular consumption, in which he attempted to inject justification by faith alone into the philosophy of Nicholas Cusanus. The symbol of the sea, Christ, and of the rivers that flow into him, are reminiscent of the symbolism in Cusanus and especially of his sermon "*Cum venerit Paracletus*" (Brunecg, 1 June 1545). Believers find justification flowing into Christ, savior and redeemer, like rivers into the sea, and—being reborn in him—assume the saltiness of his wisdom and justice: "by participating in it are we justified and become new creatures, reborn of water and spirit, *expoliantes veterum hominem induimus novum hominem, qui renovatur in agnitionem Dei.*"[28] Benedetto da Locarno must have had an uncommon audience before him, perhaps even members of the Academy and among them Riccio, owner of the codex that contained someone's transcription of Benedetto's 1542 or 1543 sermon. His words on this occasion must have been the subject of discussion and even have met with a warm reception if Riccio thought it appropriate to include them, just after the *Beneficio*, with which they have points in common, in the manuscript anthology of famous writings on the justification controversy.

The Valdesian Frescoes of San Lorenzo

During those years of oratorical duels from the pulpit, of lively discussions in patrician homes, artisans' shops, as well as in the Florentine Academy, which according to the anonymous diarist, harbored a conventicle of "Lutherans" with Benedetto Varchi

---

[28]S. Caponetto, "Una sconosciuta predica," in *Studi sulla Riforma*, 205–18.

at its head, the Valdesians concocted a scheme of transporting to the visual arts the Biblical plan of salvation along their own and Lutheran lines.

Pier Francesco Riccio obtained Duke Cosimo's consent for entrusting the frescoes in the principal chapel of the church of San Lorenzo, of which he was canon, to Jacopo Pontormo. The artist of the fascinating and original "Deposition of Christ" in the church of Santa Felicità, began his work on the San Lorenzo frescoes in 1547 and completed them eleven years later. Many contemporaries must have been astonished at the sight of this magnificent history of salvation from the creation of Eve to the sin of Cain, from the universal flood to the victory of Christ, which dominated the center of the chapel above God the Creator. This anomaly did not escape Vasari, who thus wrote about it: "But I have never been able to understand the meaning of this story, although I know that Jacopo [Pontormo] was intelligent and knew learned and literate persons, except that it was meant to signify in that part where Christ is on high resuscitating the dead, and beneath him God the Father who creates Adam and Eve."[29] Unfortunately, restorations on the church of San Lorenzo in 1742 led to the destruction of Pontormo's last work.

In 1950 Charles De Tolnay broached a plan to reconstruct the iconographic complex by using the surviving drawings of it. He was the first to intuit that the program of the fresco cycle was "the triumph of grace over sin, predicted by the Evangelists and the Old Testament Law," in line with the teachings of Valdés and of the Italian Reformation.[30] This intelligent, incisive interpretation found corroboration in recent years through the research of Kurt W. Forster[31] and Raffaella Corti. The latter juxtaposed the fresco cycle with the *Beneficio di Cristo*, underlining the identical appropriation of the Biblical scheme of human salvation.[32] It seems probable that someone among the disciples of Valdés furnished the artist with an outline of the master's teachings outstanding for its clarity and simplicity, possibly the catechism for children, perhaps printed at Venice in 1545, with the title: *Qual maniera si devrebbe tenere a informare infino dalla Fanciullezza i figliuoli de Christiani delle cose della Religione*, and many times reprinted with the title *Latte spirituale, con il quale si debbono nutrire e allevare i figliuoli de Christiani in gloria di Dio*.[33] The pictorial cycle can be read, following as directions for the individual frescoes, numbers 1 to 18 of this brief set of Christian precepts written down for children.

Pontormo was a secretive and solitary man who left nothing in his diary to help us penetrate the world of his ideas. But, through his friends and acquaintances, it is

---

[29]Quoted from the interesting article by R. Corti, "Pontormo a San Lorenzo: Un episodio figurativo dello 'spiritualismo italiano,'" *Ricerche di storia dell'Arte* 6 (1977): 21. Cf. the remarks by P. Simoncelli, "Jacopo da Pontormo e Pierfrancesco Riccio: Due appunti," *Critica storica* 17 (1980): 331–48. Cf. plate 5.

[30]C. De Tolnay, "Les fresques de Pontormo dans le choeur de San Lorenzo à Florence: Essai de reconstruction," *La Critica d'Arte*, ser. 3, 9 (1950), fasc. 33:49.

[31]K. W. Forster, *Pontormo* (Munich: Bruckmann, 1966), 93–98.

[32]Cf. R. Corti, "Pontormo a San Lorenzo," 14–23.

[33]Published by E. Boehmer in *La Rivista Cristiana* 10 (1882): 3–15. This valuable text can now be read in a more correct edition in Juan de Valdés, *Il dialogo della dottrina cristiana*, app. 187–200, and in M. Firpo's edition of the *Alfabeto cristiano*.

not difficult to identify the channel by which he came to know Valdesian ideas. To the Benedictine Vincenzo Borghini, a close friend of the painter, Benedetto Varchi addressed a sonnet in which he proclaimed the sovereignty of divine grace:

> But they are many and so great the merits
> Of Jesus, who was crucified for us,
> That there is no one who does not merit heaven because of him.[34]

Moreover, in Varchi's *Sonetti spirituali*, as Marcel Bataillon noted, we discern a sincere religiosity in a man conscious of his wretchedness, bound to the spirituality of the "benefit of Christ."[35] Several of these poems were dedicated to the protagonists of the religious dissent: Pietro Carnesecchi, Caterina Cibo, Fra Andrea da Volterra, among others. Riccio, who had obtained the San Lorenzo frescoes' commission for Pontormo, rather than for Vasari, was a Valdesian who read and admired Luther. He was portrayed as ignorant and factious by the malevolent pen of Benvenuto Cellini, and some men of letters and artists were resentful and unhappy with the quality of his intercession for them before the duke. But Riccio's role in Cosimo's education from a tender age, shrewdly assigned to him by Maria Salviati, and the expressions of esteem, some of high praise, from such men as Aonio Paleario, Anton Francesco Doni, and Francesco Robortello, convey a quite different opinion.[36] Born at Prato in 1501, Riccio was a priest of upright habits, honest, tolerably well educated, totally dedicated to Cosimo, for whom he was first tutor at home and in exile, and during the duke's reign, his secretary and majordomo. His ownership of codex 1785 of the Riccardiana Library, which along with the *Beneficio di Cristo* contains some of the fundamental writings on justification, the most debated religious question of the first half of the century, could be evidence simply of Riccio's curiosity regarding the theological controversies of the day. However, for the years to which these texts pertain we have positive evidence of his interest in the reformation of the church.

On 2 August 1541 from Colle Valdelsa Paleario conveyed to Riccio his whole-hearted gratitude for having defended him before the duke and the ecclesiastical hierarchy from the accusations made against him by the master in theology, the Dominican Vittorio da Firenze, a bitter enemy of justification by faith, with whom Paleario had argued after the monk's Lenten sermons at Colle. Moreover Paleario confided in him the hope of seeing an ecumenical council of the learned, *"quasi censura episcoporum, vindices veritatis,"* come to pass.[37] Cosimo's secretary, along with Francesco Campana, Francesco Verino, and Pier Vettori who were among Paleario's closest friends, was thus cognizant of the latter's religious evolution if he was made the recipient of such imprudent confessions.

But we have more than this piece of evidence, in itself quite telling, of Riccio's previously unknown religious sentiments and interests. His correspondence contains

---

[34] K. W. Forster, *Pontormo*, 94.

[35] See M. Bataillon, "Benedetto Varchi et le cardinal de Burgos, D. Francisco de Mendoza y Bobadilla," *Les Lettres Romanes* 23 (1969): 59–60.

[36] See S. Caponetto, *Aonio Paleario*, 53–55.

[37] Ibid., 72.

a letter, lacking the signature, written from Venice on 28 July 1544, responding to his anxious wait for the imminent appearance of Luther's *Hauspostille*. The epistle states that the book had not yet appeared, but that the bookseller, or perhaps Antonio Brucioli who previously had often been asked to procure books, could send "all the works of Melanchthon." "And command of me as you will, so that you may learn with what goodwill I serve the faithful of Christ. May the Lord cause us to grow along the path of his truth with the assistance of his Spirit."[38]

The letter does not leave any doubt about the search for a new spirituality on the part of the two correspondents, precisely during the crucial years of the diffusion of Lutheran and Valdesian ideas and of the efforts being made by the "*spirituali*" to reestablish the unity of the Christian church through the Council assembled at Trent to achieve this very goal.

In February 1550, Riccio received the provostship in the cathedral of Prato. That same year he invited as preacher the Augustinian Alessio Casani who already had been tried as a Lutheran in 1529, and accused anew in 1548 by brother-members in the convent of Santo Spirito in Florence. Joined by some Dominicans, they accused him "of nourishing himself and nourishing others with the flour of Egypt," meaning the heresies of Luther.[39] Casani, a master in theology and celebrated preacher, succeeded in evading the arrest ordered by the inquisitor, through appeals made to the duke by the dean of the Faculty of Theology, Andrea Ghetti, himself a suspect. Cosimo, even though it meant irritating the ecclesiastical authorities, ordered the Inquisition to desist from its inquest.

In 1551 Riccio was struck by a serious illness and, it seems, lost the use of his mind. Some years later, on a codex containing the *Breve esposizione* by Guglielmo Perlano da Bibbiena to John Chrysostom's commentary on the Gospel of Matthew, Riccio wrote a strange note in which he lamented having been accused by numerous enemies "de falso crimine."[40] Since the onset of his illness coincided with the arrival of the Jesuits in Florence, and the beginning of the repression of religious dissent involving some of his friends, it is quite plausible to imagine insinuations also being made against Riccio, a person linked to Paleario, Carnesecchi, Brucioli, and such Augustinian preachers of the doctrine of grace as Andrea Ghetti and Alessio Casani. The duke, by stepping in to suggest to his old faithful servant that he should withdraw from the scene and care for his health, undoubtedly cut short any inquisitorial attempt to investigate him.

Recently doubts have been expressed about Riccio's Valdesianism and the depth of his religious sentiments, interpreted as a reflection of the sovereign's ecclesiastical politics.[41] It is certainly difficult to evaluate the personal convictions of a person who was bound by such strong affection and devotion to Cosimo, whom he had even exalted as a divine emissary for the prosperity of Florence and of Tuscany. However,

[38]Ibid., 54.
[39]S. Bondi, "Alessio Casani" (cited at chap. 2, note 9), 28.
[40]See below note 44.
[41]Cf. G. Fragnito, "Un pratese alla corte di Cosimo I: Riflessioni e materiali per un profilo di Pierfrancesco Riccio," *Archivio storico pratese* 62 (1986): 31–83.

one should not ignore—as has been done up to now—the fact that he had been recommended to the latter's mother, to his uncle Jacopo and to Clement VII himself, as
preceptor for the young Cosimo by Girolamo Benivieni, just as ardent a Savonarolan
as Maria and Jacopo Salviati.[42] In 1524 the choice of a young priest of good habits,
well versed in Greek, Latin, and music, but lacking religious sensibilities in that age
of searing theological debate, seems unthinkable. Perhaps the note indicating Riccio's
possession of the Riccardi Library codex merely suggests a reading of Savonarola's
prophecies. But, apart from this conjecture, the perusal of this splendid codex may
shed some light on the meditations of the now elderly priest, then recovering from a
long illness.

Bibiena's *Breve esposizione* is a summary, a paraphrase, and a partial translation of
the homilies by John Chrysostom on the Gospel of Matthew. Chrysostom was one of
the church fathers often held up by Valdesians in support of justification by faith
alone. In 1545 the French translation of the *Beneficio di Cristo* was printed together
with the sermon "On the woman of Canaan" and Clément Marot's translation of
Psalm 33.[43] The compiler of this collection intended underlining the exegesis of that
episode narrated in Matt. 15:21–28, in which the Canaanite woman obtained a miracle by praying directly to Jesus, without the mediation of the apostles. In the *Breve
esposizione* the homily on the Canaanite woman is reduced to the essential part, but
the translation of the explanation regarding the inefficacy of the apostles' intercession
is literal: "Because he would rather be prayed to by us sinners, than by someone else
for us." The exegesis of Matt. 16:16 is similarly translated: "And on this rock, that is
on this faith, on the confession of this belief *will I build my church*. By these words he
refers to the multitude of those who were to believe in him. Beyond this he raises the
mind of Peter and establishes him pastor over the church." Thus the rock on which
the church is built is not Peter, but Peter's profession of faith. The interpretation
adopted by Luther, Valdés, and Calvin can be traced back to Chrysostom. Nor
should we neglect the translation of the exegesis of Matt. 28:20. The promise of
Christ's presence cannot be applied to the apostles, who are not immortal, "but he
speaks to all the faithful as one body" (fol. 128v).[44]

Like all Valdesians, like the authors of the *Beneficio di Cristo*, Pier Francesco Riccio
enjoyed finding confirmation for his ideas in the ancient scriptural exegetes. As the end
of his life approached, he thought it opportune to pencil in on the cover of the codex
testimony of his faith that the divine promises would be fulfilled, within which he had
found a guide and comfort in his difficult, complex, and hidden religious journey. It is
emblematic that a short section from the beginning of Chrysostom's commentary

---

[42]Cf. C. Re, *Girolamo Benivieni fiorentino* (Città di Castello: Tipografica editrice, 1906), 132ff.; O.
Zorzi Pugliese, "G. Benivieni umanista e riformatore," *La Bibliofilia* 72 (1970): 255; C. Vasoli, *DBI*
8:554.

[43]E. Droz, *Chemins de l'hérésie: Textes et documents* (Geneva: Slatkine, 1974), 3:115ff. and 185ff.

[44]Florence, Biblioteca Riccardiana, cod. 1259: *Breve esposizione di Giovanni Crisostomo, arcivescovo
di Constantinopoli, nello Evangelio di S.to Matteo dalla lingua greca nella latina da Cristofano Serrarighi da
Foiano et da quella in questa nuovamente tradotta da Guglielmo Perlano da Bibbiena*, fols. 66v, 69v, 70r,
128v.

opened Bibbiena's *Breve esposizione*: "The present Gospel is that book, because it contains the cancellation and revocation of the penalties and payment for our sins and because it announces equally to each person their sanctification, their adoption as children and their inheritance of the Kingdom of God" (fol. 2r).[45]

BIBLIOGRAPHICAL NOTE

On the religious literature of the sixteenth century, cf. D. Cantimori, "Le idee religiose del Cinquecento: La storiografia," in *Storia della letteratura italiana, V: Il Seicento*, a cura di E. Cecchi and N. Sapegno (Milan: Garzanti, 1967), 7–87; N. Badaloni, "Vita religiosa e letteraria tra Riforma e Controriforma," in *Cultura e vita civile tra Riforma e Controriforma di Nicola Badaloni, Renato Barilli e Walter Moretti* (Bari: Laterza, 1973), 87–114.

For an updated bibliography on the *Beneficio*, see Benedetto da Mantova and Marcantonio Flaminio, *Il Beneficio di Cristo*, a cura di S. Caponetto (Turin: Claudiana, 1991).

On the reign of Cosimo I and the Florentine cultural milieu, cf. G. Spini, *Cosimo I e l'indipendenza del principato mediceo* (Florence: Vallecchi, 1980; R. von Albertini, *Das florentinische Staatsbewusstsein im Übergang von der Republik zum Prinzipat* (Bern: Francke, 1955); M. Plaisance, "Culture et politique à Florence du 1542 à 1551: Lasca et les Humidi aux prises avec l'Académie Florentine," in *Les écrivains et le pouvoir en Italie à l'époque de la Renaissance*, deuxième série (Paris: Université de la Sorbonne nouvelle, 1974), 149–242.

On the influence of Savonarola, cf. S. Caponetto, *Aonio Paleario*, 41–57.

For Flaminio, cf. A. Pastore, *Marcantonio Flaminio: Fortune e sfortune di un chierico nell'Italia del Cinquecento* (Milan: F. Angeli, 1981).

For C. Bartoli and the Florentine Academy, cf. Judith Bryce, *Cosimo Bartoli (1503–1572): The Career of a Florentine Polymath* (Geneva: Droz, 1983).

On P. F. Riccio, the most complete information has been collected by C. Guasti, "Alcuni fatti della prima giovinezza di Cosimo I," *Giornale Storico degli Archivi Toscani* 2 (1858): 13–64, 295–320.

The Spirit and the Word. Engraving by H. Sebald Beham (1536).

---

[45]Ibid., fol. 2r. Cf. *Chrysostomi Commentarius in S. Mattheum Evangelistam*, in *Opera omnia*, MPG, vol. 58, 7:2, coll. 518ff.

RESOLV:
TIONE SOMMARIA CON-
tra le conclusioni Luterane, estratte d'un
Libretto senza nome de l'Autore, in-
titolato, Il Sommario de la sacra
scrittura; Libretto scismatico,
heretico, & pestilente.
FRATE AMBROSIO CATHA-
rino Polito Senese de l'Ordine de
Predicatori Autore,

IN ROMA
Ne la Contrada del Pellegrino.
M. D. XLIIII.

⸔TRATTATO⸕
VTILISSIMO

DEL BENEFICIO DI
GIESV CHRISTO
CROCIFISSO,
VERSO I
CHRI-
STIANI.

Venetiis Apud Bernardinum
de Bindonis. Anno Do,
M.D. XXXXIII.

The *Beneficio di Cristo* (Venice, 1543) and the confutation (1544) by the Dominican Ambrogio Catarino (Lancillotto de' Politi) of the *Sommario della santa Scrittura.*

7

THE END OF AN ILLUSION

THE COLLOQUY OF RATISBON (1541)

THE RELIGIOUS COLLOQUY of Ratisbon (4 April–29 July 1541), which had been sought by Charles V in the hope of reestablishing the political unity of Germany in the face of the looming Turkish threat, failed to achieve a reconciliation between Catholics and Protestants, sealing the tragic reality of the schism within the Christian church: As Hubert Jedin has observed:

> It was precisely the negotiations for reunion at Augsburg and Ratisbon that made it perfectly clear that the ultimate and quite irreconcilable opposition between the Protestant ecclesiastical communities and Catholicism was due to a wholly different conception of the sacramental system and the juridical structure of the Church. The sacrificial character of the Mass, transubstantiation, the seven sacraments on the one hand, and the hierarchical structure of the Church and the Pope's primacy of jurisdiction on the other, constituted a chasm between the two parties which no amount of good-will and no political advantage could bridge over. When they discussed the Eucharist, the sacrifice of the Mass and the papal primacy more often and more fully than any other controversial question, Catholic apologists gave evident proof that they did not fasten on mere externals but were fully aware of the depth of the divergences.[1]

This lucid analysis of the "chasm" embraces all the components of the Catholic reform movement, the current of the "*spirituali*," comprising Cardinals Giberti, Cortese, Fregoso, Pole, and Contarini, as well as the current of the conservatives and intransigents. In 1532 the Benedictine Gregorio Cortese, replying to a Protestant polemicist, had already affirmed that without papal authority, the church would be like a headless body.[2] Twenty years later, even though he had become an enthusiastic

---

[1] H. Jedin, *A History of the Council of Trent*. Trans. Dom Ernest Graf (St. Louis: Herder, 1957), 1:409.

[2] Cf. G. Fragnito, "Il cardinal Gregorio Cortese nella crisi religiosa del Cinquecento," *Benedictina* 30 (1983): 38–39.

reader of the *Beneficio di Cristo*, he was of the same opinion. The authors of the *Libellus ad Leonem X*, Pole in his *Pro ecclesiasticae unitatis defensione*, and Contarini in his *De potestate pontificis* (1538), were just as emphatic on the subject. At Ratisbon, Contarini proposed this formula on the question of papal primacy: "That Christ established this hierarchy placing bishops in their dioceses, archbishops, patriarchs and primates, over all of which to preserve the unity of the Church he constituted the Roman pontiff, bestowing upon him universal jurisdiction over the entire Church."[3] The failure of Ratisbon, in spite of the irenic spirit of Bucer and Melanchthon, Gropper and Contarini, revealed the irreconcilability of the two theologies.

Once it became clear that it was impossible to build any sort of bridge between the two sides, the road was open for the Counter-Reformation, that program for the reform of the church in opposition to the Protestant Reformation, comprising disciplinary reform as well as a clarification of dogma in the light of traditional theology. But the paramount objective was the repression of the Lutheran heresy, which was making ever larger strides in the Catholic states and in Italy itself. The recomposition of the reforming party took place during this vast program of defense and restoration to which Paul III dedicated himself with intelligence, energy, and measure in the closing years of his pontificate.

THE "ECCLESIA VITERBIENSIS"

It was misleading, as Dermot Fenlon pointed out in 1972, to reconstruct artificially the milieu of Viterbo, of the *ecclesia Viterbiensis* by commencing with the examination of a few of Cardinal Pole's doctrinal formulations and by assuming the *Beneficio di Cristo* to be the manifesto of a reformed church. Doing so meant forgetting the complexity of the cardinal's situation and that of the Valdesians who flocked to become part of his "family" after he was appointed governor of Viterbo.[4] Many followers of Valdés found refuge there between the autumn of 1541 and spring 1542: Donato Rullo, Apollonio Merenda, Vittore Soranzo, Flaminio, and Carnesecchi. The latter two arrived after they had spent six months in Florence during which time they engaged in active intercourse with Tuscan *literati*, as well as with Ochino, Vermigli, and Caterina Cibo.

Massimo Firpo's recent explanation of the origins of the *ecclesia Viterbiensis* is much more plausible. He puts it into the context of the Valdesians' propaganda campaign, devised some months prior to their master's death, perhaps at the onset of his illness. Certainly, Valdés gave consideration to the diffusion of his beliefs, entrusting his writings to Giulia Gonzaga and Mario Galeota, and concentrating his thought into his marvelous brief catechism for children, which in this final formulation seemed in great part identical to Lutheranism.

---

[3]H. Jedin, *A History*, 1:384.
[4]D. Fenlon, *Heresy and Obedience in Tridentine Italy: Cardinal Pole and the Counterreformation* (Cambridge: University Press, 1972), chap. 6.

The spread of Valdesians to Rome, Florence, Padua, Venice, and elsewhere joined the need for a program of witnessing with another, less noble and more modest, of finding an outlet suitable to the experience of conversion to the truth of "Sacred Scripture," in reshaping ecclesiastical and social behavior. After Contarini, unjustly accused of Lutheranism and confined to Bologna, died disheartened in August 1542, Pole remained the only hope of protection for Valdesians from the growing power of the Roman Inquisition. He was also available for discourse, understanding, and to lend an ear to their secret belief: that the acceptance of justification was the sign of divine election, of the true and living faith through which we had already entered the Kingdom of God. Massimo Firpo, by exploiting the vast documentation collected in the trial against Morone, has overturned the older image of the *ecclesia Viterbiensis*, namely that of a "holy company" living in the quiet and tranquillity of its studies.[5] On the contrary, Viterbo was the scene of dramatic exchanges of views, of serried dialogue between Cardinal Pole and his Valdesian entourage. Flaminio and Carnesecchi, who possessed a deep and admiring understanding of the message and work of Valdés, convinced the English prelate that justification by faith alone was the revelation of "the mystery of the Christian faith," which "according to the teachings of Valdés" they held to be "true and catholic even though that other [view] was the one called catholic, because it was believed in more universally."[6]

Instead of resurrecting a "stereotypical image" of a small group of aristocratic prelates, refined intellectuals, sensitive noblewomen, and delicate protonotaries, tenaciously attached to their ecclesiastical benefices and to their social privileges, Firpo has thrown a wholly new light on the English cardinal's "family." At Viterbo they busied themselves, according to this theory, with a plan intended to influence the imminent Council of Trent to accept the doctrine of justification by faith. The works of Valdés and the *Beneficio di Cristo*, with their appeal to the unity of true Christians, were to serve as the concealed persuaders in this ambitious program, with which Vittoria Colonna and Cardinal Morone became associated.

It is difficult to say to what point Pole was also involved since the ambiguities in his position are well known. We know about his concern for the inferences drawn from the doctrine of justification, his aversion to the reading of heretical books and towards Colonna's inquisitiveness. The advice given by Pole to the poetess on the question of a Christian's ethical behavior was certainly ambiguous: "She should believe as if she could be saved only by faith, but on the other hand, she should act as if her salvation would depend upon her good works."[7] Actually, just as Contarini, Morone, Fregoso, and Seripando among the "*spirituali*" were favoring the Lutheran doctrine of gratuitous salvation without being able to measure its ecclesiological consequences, Pole was demanding that Lutherans return to the bosom of the church of Rome. Between March and April 1545, with the convocation of the Council

---

[5]Cf. M. Firpo, "Valdesianesimo ed evangelismo alle origini dell'ecclesia Viterbiensis (1541)," *Schifanoia* 1 (1986): 152–68, reprinted in Firpo's *Tra alumbrados e "spirituali,"* 155–84.
[6]"Processo Carnesecchi," 296.
[7]Ibid., 269.

imminent, he wrote the treatise *De concilio*, in which he founds the authority of the Church on Christ's promise to Peter (Matt. 16:16).[8]

The very year that the Valdesians managed to have the *corpus* of Valdés's writings published at Venice, in a last attempt to influence the doctrinal reformation of the church, the papal legate was restating the traditional interpretation of the primacy of Peter and of his vicar the pope, from whom the authority of the church descended, dispenser and administrator of divine grace. This was a view that contrasted profoundly with the Reformation position, lucidly expressed by Melanchthon in his *De Ecclesia autoritate* (1539):

> Now, when I mention the Church, I do not mean principally popes, bishops, or the others who approve their opinions. Because they are enemies of the true Church, in part Epicureans, in part worshippers of manifest idols. But what I call the Church is the gathering of those, who truly believe, who hold to the Gospel and the sacraments and are sanctified by the Holy Spirit, as the Church is portrayed in the fifth chapter of the Epistle to the Ephesians, and in John, chapter ten where it is stated: "My sheep hear my voice."[9]

A tone of ambiguity seems to be present in the famous letter to Carnesecchi from Flaminio, who had become the preceptor of the *ecclesia Viterbiensis*, written from Trent where he had accompanied Pole for the opening of the Council, which had been moved back to 1 January 1543. Superficially, the epistle might appear to be a disavowal of Valdesian ideas, a painful return to the bosom of the church, a consequence of the English cardinal's work of persuasion. But, after a closer reading, Flaminio's preoccupation with Carnesecchi's inclination towards the Zwinglian conception of the Lord's Supper as a simple commemoration of the death of Jesus Christ, denying his real presence in the elements of the Eucharist, is the same as Luther's. Against the Zwinglians, Flaminio affirmed the reality of the "exhibition" of the body and blood of Christ under the species of bread and wine, but he does not say that transubstantiation had taken place. In fact, at the end of the discussion he cites the example of Bucer and of the other Protestants assembled at Ratisbon, "who agreed with us that in the sacrament of the Eucharist there is exhibited to the communicant the true body and the true blood of Christ our Lord."[10] But the text formulated by Bucer and Melanchthon decisively excludes transubstantiation and thus could not be accepted by the Catholic side. Thus, Flaminio was articulating a concept of the Lord's Supper opposed to Roman doctrine.

Flaminio's letter should be read from the same perspective as the *Beneficio di Cristo*. The three purposes of the Lord's Supper formulated in the Ratisbon article just alluded to above—commemoration of the death and resurrection of Jesus Christ; rendering of thanks and praise; sign of reciprocal love of believers and witness

---

[8]Cf. D. Fenlon, *Heresy and Obedience*, chap. 7.

[9]P. Melanchthon, *Opera*, CR 23:597; S. Caponetto, "Due opere," in *Studi sulla Riforma*, 365.

[10]M. Flaminio to P. Carnesecchi (Trent, 1 January 1543), Marcantonio Flaminio, *Lettere*, ed. A. Pastore (Rome: Edizioni dell'Ateneo e Bizzarri, 1978), 133–38, epistle n. 47.

of their unity—can also be found, fervently expressed, in chapter 6 of the *Beneficio*, which would be published a few months later.[11] The letter makes no mention of the opening of the Council, that event which by now everybody believed was indispensable for the life of the church, to heal its wounds and reestablish unity. Silence on this point is symptomatic of distrust on the historical level of a true general reformation of the church that would reestablish the unity of the body of Christ, so profoundly and irremediably sundered. Thus, Flaminio took refuge in the "catholic" church, which was not the same as "the holy Roman Church," as Carnesecchi felt constrained to point out to inquisitors at his trial from 1566 to 1567, but the one that Valdesians call "catholic," namely the "church of God's elect," that Melanchthon called "the Catholic Church of Christ," living within and beyond the boundaries of the institutional churches. Thus, it was useless for Flaminio, as for many other Valdesians, to break with the old ecclesiastical structure and risk his "honor, his property, his life."

Carnesecchi's reply to Flaminio, with its appeal to scriptural sources, against which tradition had to be measured, was also tied to the *Beneficio*. It returned to the theme of the profanation of the sacrament of the Eucharist by those who did not receive it with feelings of unity and love towards all their brethren, and lamented that the Eucharist, once a sign of unity, had become the symbol of separation and hate.[12]

Some years after this exchange, Francesco Negri, the ex-Benedictine, schoolmaster at Chiavenna, and collaborator with Agostino Mainardi, pastor of the town's reformed community, in the preface to his *Tragedia del libero arbitrio*, gave a pitiless analysis of the reform notions of the *"spirituali"* and of the Valdesians, which despite the rigid schematically dualistic vision, still rings true today as a precise historical judgment:

> I cannot but be amazed at Cardinal Pole of England with his Priuli and Flaminio, at Cardinal Morone, at Signor Ascanio Colonna, at *Signor* Camillo Orsini, and at the many other men of great authority both in the world of letters, and other mundane dignities, who seem to have created a new school of Christianity fashioned to suit themselves, where, true, they do not deny that the justification of man is accomplished by Jesus Christ but then do not want to admit the consequences which necessarily flow from them. Because they want just the same to have the pope, they want to have Masses, they want to observe a thousand other papist superstitions and impieties, all wholly contrary to truly Christian piety. They imagine, I do not know how, that these things can coexist together. But pray tell how light can coexist with the shadows? And Christ with Belial? Is it possible to serve at the same time at the table of Christ and of the Devil? By now these people, who are not blind in everything, should be able to see that this mixing of Christian and papist things is done only so that they can sit (as we

---

[11]*Beneficio* (Ital. ed.), 68. On this interpretation of Flaminio's letter, see my review to the Pastore edition of the correspondence, in *RSCI* 36 (1982): 497–501.

[12]Cf. J. G. Schelhorn, *Amoenitates historiae ecclesiasticae et literariae*, 2:155ff.

say) astride two saddles and thus flee Christ's cross, which they would see before their eyes, if they were to actually reveal things as they truly are. Oh, with what great difficulty the rich enter the heavens! Oh, how difficult it is for those who search for glory in each other to really believe in Christ! But let them beware of the sentence of God those who in order to preserve their state and their greatness in the world will not freely confess the known truth, inasmuch as Jesus Christ is not about to confess himself or to acknowledge them before God.[13]

THE SPIRITUAL JOURNEY OF BERNARDINO OCHINO

But not all Valdesians dreamed of using Pole to influence the conciliar fathers gathered at Trent, nor did they all seek refuge in the individualistic and inner remedy of tasting "how sweet our Jesus Christ is, and how sweet it is to think and speak about him, and to imitate his most holy life."[14] For them this was not the hour for contemplation and obedience to the ecclesiastical hierarchies, but the hour of painful decision. In 1542 shortly after the reconstitution of the Roman Holy Office, three of the greatest and most popular Italian preachers fled to Protestant lands: Bernardino Ochino, Pietro Martire Vermigli, and in 1543 from a Venetian prison, Giulio della Rovere.

Bernardino Tommasini (1487–1563) of Siena, called Ochino from the name of the *contrada dell'oca*, in which he was born, was at the moment of his flight one of the most enthralling preachers in Europe, the Savonarola of the sixteenth century, in Roland Bainton's words.[15] He had entered the Franciscan order as a young man, passing from the Observants to the Capuchins in 1534, imagining that he could find the straight path to salvation through obedience to the Rule of Saint Francis. From 1534 to 1542 he preached in the major Italian cities, arousing popular enthusiasm and provoking lively discussions on the great issues of the day, to the great scandal of the professional theologians. But in spite of his intense activity as preacher and guardian of souls, of his intercessions with civil authorities in favor of the poor and the downtrodden, he failed to find peace of mind. Proceeding in his difficult religious journey, he became aware of the contradiction between the simplicity of the evangelical message and the immense, age-old ecclesiastical superstructure of traditions, devotions, dogmas, and valueless ceremonies.

The insistence on the crucified Christ in Ochino's preaching had its source in the Augustinianism of Saint Bonaventure, but he soon became conversant with Luther's and Melanchthon's theology of the cross. Nevertheless, the decisive impulse to move into a new dimension, the world of gratuitous justification, came after Ochino's meeting with Valdés, by whom he was deeply influenced. Ochino's ser-

[13]F. Negri, *Della tragedia intitolata Libero Arbitrio*, 2d ed., 1550.
[14]*Beneficio*, 19–20; R. Prelowski, *Beneficio*, 51.
[15]Cf. B. Nicolini, "Il pensiero di Bernardino Ochino," *Atti della R. Accademia Pontaniana di scienze morali e politiche* 59 (1938); R. H. Bainton, *Bernardino Ochino*, 3.

mons, after their meeting in Naples, practically "seem to be a popular translation of Valdés's *Alfabeto cristiano* and *Cento e dieci divine considerazioni.*"[16]

Ochino's emphasis in his preaching on the Lutheran themes of *sola gratia* and *sola fides* and the absence of references to the cult of saints and to purgatory, began to arouse suspicion against him, even though he was admired by Vittoria Colonna and the *spirituali*, and protected by highly placed ecclesiastics. The matter came to a head during his Lenten sermons in 1542 when he directed his message to the government of the *Serenissima*, which had incarcerated Giulio della Rovere: "Oh Venice, whoever tells you the truth, you imprison; therefore, one cannot tell the truth, but if one could, then you would know how dear is the truth."[17]

Ochino was summoned to Rome to exculpate himself, well aware of the risks that a full inquiry into his preaching might bring. He interrupted his journey at Bologna where he met a gravely ill Cardinal Contarini. Proceeding to Florence, in the home of Duchess Caterina Cibo, he made the fateful decision to divest himself of his cassock. He fled on horseback in layman's garb towards Switzerland, finding refuge first in Morbegno in the Valtellina and then in Geneva, where he was greeted warmly by Calvin. The Italian was fifty-six years old and had spent about forty of them in the Franciscan order.

The apostasy from the Church of Rome of the Sienese, considered from one tip of the peninsula to the other a shining spiritual guide, provoked an uproar in the multifaceted Italian religious world of the 1540s. The *"spirituali"* viewed it as the end of their hopes, and retreated into obedience to the pope as Christ's vicar. To them Ochino had separated himself from the church, outside of which there was no salvation. The death, a few days later, of Cardinal Contarini, the most resolute champion of reconciliation with Protestants, signaled the end of an era.

The Valdesians were thrown into confusion, not by the espousal of the Gospel and of Saint Paul in Ochino's preaching, since they recognized the Valdesian origins, but by the decision to break with the Church of Rome on the very eve of the convocation of the Council of Trent, fixed for the Feast of All Saints (1 November 1542), on which many of them had pinned hopes of reaching agreement with their friends among the *"spirituali."* Very different was the reaction of others, among the followers of Valdés, admirers of Luther, Melanchthon, and now also of Calvin, whose thought had become more accessible thanks to the appearance of the third edition of his *Institutes*, published in French in 1541.

Ochino's flight, followed by the no less clamorous departures of Peter Martyr Vermigli, Prior of the Lateran Canons of San Frediano in Lucca, and of Giulio della Rovere, reinforced in this second group the conviction that it was necessary to separate from the Church of Rome, deaf to the appeal that it should reform itself *in capite et in membris*: it had not heeded Savonarola, nor had it heeded the recommendations contained in the reform commission *De emendanda Ecclesia*. It had allowed a quarter of a century to pass from the posting of Luther's Theses without assembling that

---

[16]C. Cargnoni, "Ochino," in *Dictionnaire de spiritualité ascétique et mystique* 11:col. 588.

[17]B. Ochino, *I "dialoghi sette,"* 13.

council earnestly desired by all parties—the emperor, Protestants, and Catholics alike—to resolve the disputed questions.

The humanist Aonio Paleario, Latin poet and orator, after experiencing a trial in Siena in 1542 on the charge of Lutheranism, in his oration *Pro se ipso* written a year later but only published at Lyons in 1552, pronounced the flight of the ex-Capuchin a misfortune for Tuscany and for Italy. He courageously laid the blame at the feet of the new tribunal of the Inquisition, which he called a dagger poised against learning and the freedom of conscience. The following year, 1543, Paleario, the long-standing Erasmian and admirer of Ochino, whose sermons he had attended in Siena, aligned himself without hesitation with the reformers, Luther, Melanchthon, Bucer, and Calvin. He addressed to them a famous letter exhorting them to participate, united against canny adversaries, in a free and general council to be assembled by political authorities in defense of Apostolic institutions and of the Gospel. He closed this letter, dated 20 December 1544, on a plaintive note, with a prayer to Calvin, "good and faithful minister of Jesus Christ," to watch over Bernardino Ochino: "In whatever way you assist him, you will be assisting Christ. Farewell, oh my brother."[18]

Ochino's involvement with Italy did not end with his arrival in Geneva where he became preacher to the small group of Italian exiles. He plunged into a frenetic publication program directed to the peninsula. His *Prediche*, *I dialoghi sette*, and the *Imagine di Antecristo* all appeared in the fall of 1542. In the preface to his sermons, he wrote: "From now on, oh my Italy, since I cannot any longer preach to you with my voice, I will compel myself to write and in the vulgar tongue, so that it will be more familiar, and I shall deem it that Christ has so willed it that I should have no other concern than to the truth."[19] Henceforth he would be able to preach Christ "naked," and not "veiled" as he had been forced to do for years. Ochino's writings, together with those of Valdés translated into Italian, the *Beneficio di Cristo*, the *Sommario della santa Scrittura*, Curione's *Pasquino in estasi*, and Negri's *Tragedia del libero arbitrio*, circulated throughout the peninsula among persons of all social levels. Readers sought out Ochino's printed sermons as the continuation of his preaching.

These literary efforts contributed decisively, together with the accounts about the reforms taking place in Switzerland and Germany brought to Italy by merchants, students, and monks, to the formation at midcentury of small clandestine conventicles. Ochino's *Prediche* were read alongside Sacred Scripture as a guide in the search for evangelical truth. For these groups, he helped make acceptable the belief that it was proper to flee from one's homeland in the face of persecution, exalting Geneva as the *cité-refuge*, where the preaching of the Gospel went hand in hand with high moral behavior. The severe Calvinist discipline that had turned Geneva into a city of "monks" filled the former Franciscan with enthusiasm.

The case of the Valdesian Ludovico Manna, the friend of Carnesecchi, seems emblematic. With the connivance of a merchant of Pisa, he brought into Florence the *Prediche* of Ochino and the *Cento e dieci divine considerazioni* of Valdés. In 1552

---

[18]Reprinted in S. Caponetto, *Aonio Paleario*, 217–22, app. 3.
[19]*Prediche*, G. Paladin, *Opuscoli e lettere* 1:120.

Manna turns up in Geneva as a member of the Italian community, where he would be joined later by arrivals from Siena, Florence, and especially Lucca. Before fleeing north, Manna had asked Ludovico Domenichi to translate into Italian Calvin's *Excuse à messieurs les Nicodémites*. The pamphlet was full of sarcasm and cutting logic against those who argued that compromise was possible between the Gospel and papist doctrines. This was the Sicilian Manna's last exhortation, directed to Florentine and Tuscan Valdesians, to follow Ochino's example.

Ochino, through his agonizing over the faith, had grasped the essence of the Christian message: the *fides fiducialis* in the crucified Christ, Savior, and Redeemer of humanity. Like Erasmus and Valdés he was impatient with theological subtleties and interminable discussions. Salvation for him did not come from belief in a set of doctrines, not even the much-discussed ones of the Trinity and Christ's presence in the Eucharist, but only from believing in the infinite love of God and in the promises of the Savior. He held up as an example God's promise to the good thief, ignorant of catechisms and doctrines. Ochino advanced a shining truth, grasped by Christians of every persuasion, and one of the foundations of modern ecumenical discourse, namely that the Christian faith is summed up in the Apostles Creed. No one can be obliged to believe what it does not contain. These were the conclusions that he reached after an agonizing theological search. They would lead him, after experiencing the rigidity of the new Protestant dogmatics, to rebel against the "new popery" in the name of freedom of conscience and charity. We read, in the final volume of Ochino's *Prediche*, printed at Basel in 1562, bitter, unsparing words about the divisions and dissensions afflicting the Protestant churches:

> one church is Zwinglian, another Lutheran, some are Anabaptists and others libertines, thus there are many sects; and among them there are great differences and contrasts, from which come murmuring, discord, slanders, infamies, calumnies, hate, persecutions, and endless ills, since each church believes the other to be heretical. So that one is forced to conclude: they do not have the truth of the Gospel, or the Gospel is a diabolical doctrine, since as Paul wrote, God is not a God of dissension, but of peace....[20]

The following year, thanks to Ochino's harsh critique, and the publication of his *XXX Dialogi*, in which he condemned the burning of Servetus and the execution of Anabaptists in Zurich, an inquest was opened against him, which concluded with his expulsion from Zurich where he was serving at the time as pastor to the evangelical exiles from Locarno. This Italian Odysseus, in the dead of winter, once again was forced into exile to resume his wanderings. He was "seventy years old, weak and infirm, with four little children to care for."[21] Ochino would die at Schlakau in Moravia in 1564 in the house of a Venetian Anabaptist, Niccolò Paruta, after losing three of his offspring to the plague.

---

[20]R. H. Bainton, *Bernardino Ochino*, 125.
[21]Cited from B. Nicolini, "Bernardino Ochino e la Polonia," *Ideali e passioni*, 119.

BIBLIOGRAPHICAL NOTE

For this chapter in general, cf. H. Jedin, *A History of the Council of Trent*, 1, bk. 2.

For the *ecclesia Viterbiensis*, M. Firpo's, "Valdesianesimo ed evangelismo" cited at note 5, is the most complete and persuasive treatment. A different perspective is offered by T. Bozza, *La Riforma cattolica* (Rome, 1972) and *Nuovi studi sulla Riforma*.

On Pole, see P. Simoncelli, *Il caso di Reginald Pole* (Rome: Edizioni di Storia e Letteratura, 1977).

Martin Bucer, from *Bilder aus der Lutherzeit,* by George Hirth (1883) and Peter Martyr Vermigli, from *Icones, id est, Verae imagines virorvm doctrina simvl et pietate illvstrivm,* by Theodore Beza (1580)

8

POLITICS AND RELIGION

Luther and the Venetian Brethren

THE PROTESTANT REFORMATION sank roots in those European countries where the interaction of religious, social, and economic factors provided it with the political support that in spite of profound conflicts, permitted it to construct a new church separate from the Church of Rome.

All the great reformers—Luther, Zwingli, Melanchthon, Bucer, Calvin—realized, from the experience of their struggle for the affirmation of "Christian freedom," that it was impossible to carry on a war on three fronts, against pope, emperor, and Sorbonne, representing respectively religious and political authority, and the authority of traditional theology. For success, secular rulers had to be convinced that not only the clergy but even individual believers had the right to interpret Scripture, and that the pope was not endowed with the divine right of absolute sovereignty over the civic and social life of their states.

With a high sense of realism and exquisite political instinct remarkable for a man who had lived previously between a monastic cell and a university classroom, Luther addressed himself "to the Christian nobility of the German nation," with the first of the three great works he published in 1520. Similarly, Calvin prefaced the first edition of his *Institutio Christianae religionis* (1536) with an appeal to Francis I of France to force an end to the ecclesiastical persecution against the preachers of the Gospel in his country. Zwingli's approach to the Zurich City Council was not substantially different.

But for the Italian states, barring the appeals to the *Signoria* of Venice by the martyrs Galateo, Fonzio, and Lupatino, it was not clear who might dare attempt such an initiative without risking reprisal from the pope who could bring to bear the full weight of his spiritual and temporal authority, built on a closely knit network linked by the economic interests of the great noble families, bankers, and merchants of the peninsula.

Conscious of this fact, even if somewhat imprecisely, on 7 September 1523 Luther wrote to Duke Charles III of Savoy. The letter is striking for the writer's profound conviction of the truth of his message and for the extraordinary clarity and simplicity of his exposition, prepared for a distant Italian ruler who had been mentioned as a supporter of the ecclesiastical Reformation by Ennemond de Coct, a gentleman from Dauphinée. The rumor was unfounded. During his long reign the duke became the scourge of Waldensians and Lutherans. Nevertheless, the letter remains a solemn clarification by the reformer of the essential points of his doctrines:

> First of all, we are taught, and ourselves teach that the beginning of our salvation, the crux of Christianity, is faith in Christ who, with his blood alone and not by means of our good works, freed us from sin and destroyed the empire and power of death, and, as the prophet David said, "He freed those who had been chained" (Psalm 68:9). Another principal point is that we who are justified through the Word of God and have entered into communion with our Lord Jesus Christ, we whose faults and infirmities are annulled by Christ, have nothing else to do than to live well and do good. Not for the purpose of becoming so pleasing to God, nor of doing expiation for our sins (which can only happen through faith in Christ) but to produce good fruits like good trees, sanctifying ourselves....

Luther's programmatic letter went on to attack papal tyranny and the innovations concocted by the ecclesiastical tradition. "These inventions (as I said above) have to be eradicated, because Christians must not be governed by other than the Word of God, through which they become Christians, that is, free of all sin, by means of the pure Gospel of God alone, without layers of councils, ancient teachers and ancient fathers." The reformer closed by auguring that "the spark which has already begun to shed light" may generate a conflagration that "from the house of Savoy, just as from the house of Joseph," will spread throughout France.[1]

The appeal was as useless as it was eloquent, as far as Luther's hopes were concerned, but helpful in informing us about the early spread of his teachings in Italy. The letter, with a preface by de Coct himself, was published at Zurich in 1524, clearly intended for distribution in Italy and France. How widely it circulated is unknown, but the ideas it expressed recur in the first north Italian heresy trials. Approximately twenty years later, Luther launched an appeal to the Venetian civic authorities at the urgent request of a diplomat from Aquila who had been converted to the Reformation, Baldassarre Altieri (d. 1550), secretary to Edmund Harwell, the English ambassador at Venice.

Altieri had written a long letter to Luther on 26 November 1542 in the name of the evangelical churches of Venice, Vicenza, and Treviso to beseech the Protestant princes of the Schmalkaldic League to intercede with the Venetian Senate to end its persecution against their members. Wrote Altieri, "Many among us have been banished or have had to flee to Switzerland, while a host of others have been thrown into

---

[1]G. Jalla, *Storia della Riforma,* 1:15 ff.

prison where they languish their lives away. There is no one to free the innocent and to see that justice be done for the poor and orphaned. There is no one to intercede for the honor of God."[2]

Under these conditions the communities were disintegrating out of fear of persecution and from a lack of organization:

> We do not have public churches, and every person is a church unto himself, in accordance with his or her judgment and whim. The weakest raise themselves up against the strong beyond the measure of their faith; the latter do not tolerate the former with a spirit of kindness and mercy. Almost unaware that they share in the same weaknesses and the same temptations, they swell up with pride, and are quick to neglect and even despise them. All of them prefer to pass as teachers rather than pupils, even though they know nothing and are not guided by the Spirit of God.[3]

The dissension described in the letter had been provoked by the Zwinglians' interpretation of the Lord's Supper, and Luther's opinion on this controversial point was now being sought out. Some ten or so days later Altieri wrote to Geneva to express his thanks for its reception of the exiles, who have lost their "precious goods, but have found refuge in a secure port from the great tempest and are now content." It is clear, thus, that the doctrinal difficulties were not with the Calvinists. In any case, flight to Geneva offered many more possibilities for settlement than did Germany, where, among other factors, there was the problem of the language.

Luther's response, delayed by illness, did not come until 13 June 1543. It opened with words of humility and gratitude towards God: "I am a sinner, but by the Lord I have been plucked from the shadows into his marvelous light, and called, though unworthy, to so great a ministry." He rejoiced that the salutary mystery of Jesus Christ had been revealed even in the land of the Antichrist.[4] As for the Eucharistic question, he inveighed against the Swiss, especially the people of Zurich, whom he esteemed enemies of the sacrament. On the contrary, at Basel, Strasbourg, Ulm, Cologne, and the rest of Germany, a unified interpretation had been reached. Unfortunately the Protestant princes had not intervened with the Venetian *Signoria*, but he still hoped that it could happen. The elector of Saxony, John Frederick, in the name of the Schmalkaldic League, wrote movingly to the Doge Pietro Lando in favor of "the pious, good men, lovers of pure religion," who were being persecuted only "because they had embraced the Gospel of Christ and because they desire to exalt its glory and see it become known." Specifically, he asked for the senators to intervene to snatch "from the grip of the Roman pontiff Baldo Lupatino, a man of singular piety and learning."[5] The *Signoria* adroitly evaded the request by adducing the incompetence of civic authorities in matters of religion.

---

[2]For this and the following references, cf. E. Comba, *I nostri protestanti*, 192–208.
[3]Ibid., 193.
[4]Ibid., 198.
[5]Ibid., 329. Comba always gave the name as "Lupetino."

The indefatigable Altieri turned to Luther anew, insisting, like the importuning friend of the scriptural parable, on a renewed intervention on the part of the Protestant princes to prevent the complete destruction of believers and the spread of the Nicodemite practice and further defections. There is an ingenuous hope that evangelical truth will triumph: "It is true to some extent, and we must admit it, that a certain glimmer of light can be found among us, which properly supported, and especially by you as we hope, could set off such a conflagration throughout Italy as to empty the kingdom of the Antichrist and bring you no little joy."

Luther allowed months to pass before he replied, waiting until 12 November 1544 to express his joy at learning that "the Venetian brethren were enriched by the gifts of divine grace." He also communicated that he had asked Lupatino's nephew, Matthias Flacius Illyricus, to make every effort to secure his uncle's freedom from prison. Meanwhile, Altieri, during the Diet at Speyer (February 1544) succeeded in having himself named as the Schmalkaldic League's representative to the Republic of Venice. But events rushed on. Luther died in 1546 and in the spring of 1547 the League was defeated at Mühlberg. The Elector of Saxony and other Protestant princes were captured.

Thus vanished the dream of winning Venice over to a policy of toleration towards the movement for religious reform, despite a few sympathizers among the governing classes. But Altieri did not give in. He traveled to Zurich, with a recommendation from the pastor at Chiavenna, Agostino Mainardi, to argue the cause of the Italian evangelicals, asking to be named Zurich's agent in Venice, even without stipend, so that he could remain in his homeland and not have to abandon the evangelical communities beset by renewed persecution. The Swiss city turned him down. After a vain attempt to enter the service of Cosimo I in Florence, Altieri, one of the few Italian reformers convinced of the need to give a political base to the movement, ended his days at Bergamo in August 1550.

MELANCHTHON AND VENICE

For many years Venice remained a fixture in the plans for political action of both German reformers and Italian evangelicals. In 1539 Melanchthon wrote to the Venetian Senate. He had become acquainted with and come to like, for his intelligence and sensitivity to the religious situation of the day, a Venetian priest, Michele Brazetto, who had arrived in Wittenberg to study the year before. From him Melanchthon had heard that certain members of the Venetian governing class were interested in learning more about the Reformation occurring in Germany. Melanchthon cogently explained that the movement had tried to restore the faith to the purity "of the primitive church," rejecting human means for attaining satisfaction "in order to make a place for the benefit of Christ and the true conditions for the remission of sins."[6]

Melanchthon thus appealed to Venetians as a people among whom for centuries a true aristocracy had been preserved so the freedom to teach and believe might be fostered and the unjust cruelty exercised elsewhere against dissidents opposed. Luther's great collaborator plays upon the Venetian penchant for independence from the Roman Curia, suggesting, for an objective overview of the Reformation, his own *Loci communes,* where Catholic abuses in the cult of saints and in the liturgy are shown to be virtually indistinguishable from the pagan cults. Very early John Gerson and St. Augustine had criticized the church's neglect of divine precepts in favor of human traditions. Melanchthon intended his letter to be serene in tone and reassuring for the Venetian nobility, "which has always been hostile to tyranny," among whom one could even find supporters of the Reformation, reluctant to accept ecclesiastical control over the cultural and religious life of the Republic.

Bernardino Ochino was another who hoped that Venice might become "Italy's doorway" to the introduction of the Reformation. The letter that he wrote to the *Signoria* on 7 December 1542 immediately after his apostasy, does not attempt to justify or explain his beliefs as he did in the one addressed to the magistrates of Siena a month earlier. But it is a fervent exhortation to seek freedom from the "diabolical yoke," "to seek to understand the pure Gospel," and to support those who preached God's Word. It closed on this note:

> Let us then accept Christ as our Lord, because, even if he establishes a reign of grace, he does not thereby destroy republics; rather it is not strange that he should magnify and establish them since the Gospel states: *non eripit mortalia qui regna dat celestia.* Christ has already begun to enter Italy, but I should like him to enter in glory, openly, and I believe that Venice will be the way, and blessed will you be if you accept it, and woe to those who with Herod out of human fear persecute them. The time of the Kingdom of Christ has arrived, and already he begins to reign in various parts of the world and the great Babylon to crumble, just as is written in the Apocalypse. The works of God cannot be dissolved, as Gamaliel said, but let us accept them gladly, which I pray to the Lord he may grant to everyone, but especially to my Venice.[7]

This hope was taken up three years later by Pier Paolo Vergerio, bishop of Capodistria, in his congratulatory oration at the election as doge of Francesco Donà (Donato), 24 November 1545. It was published at Florence in 1547 by Anton Francesco Doni in his *Raccolta di orazioni diverse,* dedicated to P. F. Riccio. The speech clearly bears an Erasmian and Melanchthonian stamp, but even more obvious is the Lutheran concept of the prince as external bishop. The reformation of the

---

[6]Ibid., 186–88. Notice the syntagma "benefit of Christ," which becomes the title of the famous work.

[7]B. Ochino, *I "dialogi sette,"* dialogues 2, 8:128–29.

church is his responsibility since its ills and abuses, the superstitions and caprices of the clergy, the persecution as heretics of innocent persons, even while the corruption of priests continues unabated, encroach upon the civic sphere and justice.[8] Vergerio, former law professor and rich in political experience from his years as papal legate to Germany, proposed to the newly elected doge intervention by the secular power to resolve religious questions, following the example of the Swiss cantons and the free cities of south Germany. Vergerio hoped that he would see his friend Donato, well known for his opposition to the Curia, support those anticlerical and philo-Protestant elements among the Venetian nobility who aspired to an alignment with the Protestant princes of the Schmalkaldic League, triumphant at the time, rather than capitulate to the power of Spain and the influence of the papacy. The appeal to the new doge expressed one more hope that the Italian Reformation might begin from the Republic of Venice, in which many Italians saw represented "the living image of the ancient greatness and liberty of Italy," as the bishop of Verona, Matteo Giberti, stated in 1534.

The "Capo finto" of Johann Sleidan

Contemporaneously, Italian evangelicals were attempting, through the powerful medium of the press, to implement an audacious political scheme: to persuade Italian rulers of the imminent end of the temporal authority of the Roman church, the Babylon of the Apocalypse, usurped by the pope over the centuries. With the title, *Il Capo finto (False Chief)*, they printed clandestinely and anonymously, with misleading typographical information, the translation of the *Oration an alle Stende des Reichs vom Römischen Nebenhaupt, im Keyserthumb erwachsen* (1542) by Johann Sleidan (1506–56), the German humanist and diplomat who settled in Strasbourg and wrote the first history of the Reformation. The extremely rare Italian imprint is dated 1544, the same year as the publication at Strasbourg of the Latin translation by the author, to which is joined an oration to Charles V on the same subject.[9]

This vigorously polemical work, addressed to the German princes, denounces the ancient usurpation of power by the bishop of Rome who assumed for himself the right to spiritual and temporal supremacy, as alleged heir to the authority of Rome, *caput mundi*. With this pretext the pope obtained the privilege of confirming imperial elections, thus usurping the ancient rights of the Roman people, transmitted to councils and to princely electors: "...he has become lord not only over the property

---

[8]See A. Stella, "L'orazione di Pier Paolo Vergerio al doge Francesco Donà sulla riforma della Chiesa (1545)," *Atti dell'Istituto veneto di Scienze, Lettere ed Arti* 128 (1969–1970): 1–39, and my review in *RSI* 83 (1971): 466–68.

[9]*Il Capo finto, nuovamente dalla lingua tedesca nella italiana tradotto et con somma diligenza corretto, et rivisto, stampato nella inclita città di Roma per gli heredi di Marco Antonio di Prati, Barolitano*. Nell'anno del Signore MDXLIIII. Unnumbered pages. (Preserved in BNF, Guicciardiniana, 16.4.28.) Cf. F. H. Reusch, *Der Index der verbotenen Bücher* (Bonn, 1885) 1:122. The work turns up in the *Index* of Della Casa and of Paul IV, the French translation in the Paris 1551 *Index*. It was printed at Strasbourg under the pseudonym of Battista Lasdeno.

of men, but also over their hearts and consciences, and all this for the sake of greediness." The pope believes that he alone can interpret Holy Scripture, "enlarging or reducing it as he pleases." The false chief has revealed himself to be the abomination placed in a holy place (Matt. 24:15) and the son of perdition of 2 Thess. 2. But against a false god, God has produced "his Holy Gospel." Twenty years ago "this *Capo finto* began to be exposed on paper." From this stemmed his excessive response in which he sought to exterminate his adversaries, "The greater part of whom for no other reason than this: they believe that Christ is the only head of us all and of his church, the sole mediator between the Father and ourselves, and that no one can be saved by his own efforts."

The booklet goes on to state that the tyranny of the pope was now being contested everywhere, even if the prudent and the circumspect, though acknowledging the corruption of the church, refuse to seek the truth in Scripture. The cardinals, who have their earthly paradise, show concern not for the needs of the church but for the greatness of their families. They do not want reform because they fear losing enormous privileges of power and wealth. Paul III is considering holding a council, but no one will any longer tolerate the ecclesiastical hierarchy sitting in judgment over itself: "The time has passed, and you are accused before the Supreme Being." Germany is on the brink of destruction due to the discord introduced by the Church of Rome that has been deaf to all appeals for justice. Italians are a powerful nation, torn by the wars fomented by the pope. They have not yet experienced persecutions as have Germans, French, and Hungarians, who have been burned and chased out of their countries because they read the Scriptures, in spite of being prohibited by the Antichrist, backed up by his henchmen, the inquisitors. The hour has come to break with the false chief, to whom the emperor has now become an adversary, because in Germany the arts are flourishing and the pure doctrine of the Word of God has been made manifest. The greatest virtue today is to accept with reverence and thanksgiving "the Word of God, and not allow it to be deprived of anything in this world." Sleidan's work is a hardheaded and cutting evaluation of the *status Ecclesiae* at the dawn of the convocation of the Council of Trent, formed from historical readings by a recent convert to the Reformation, after the experience and the delusions of Hagenau and Ratisbon.

In his oration Sleidan fused the anticlericalism of the humanists with the essential principles of the Reformation, originating not from Luther's personal drama—he is never mentioned in the work—but from the new culture, which had inculcated the necessity of a return to the sources, and thus to Scripture, to learn the founding principles of Christianity. It is difficult to say how widely such an explosive work might have circulated, since it was undoubtedly hunted down and suppressed. We find it in the *Index* of Della Casa of 1549, the Parisian of 1551, and Paul IV's of 1557. A copy was confiscated at Padua in the home of Pietro Cocco in 1551. It is even more important to ask the question: Who was behind this politically inspired translation and for which Italian princes was it intended?

Two circumstances, one political, the other cultural, turn our attention towards Florence and Tuscany. The date of publication of the *Capo finto*, if it is not fictitious, is almost contemporary to a year of serious preoccupations for Cosimo I, brought about by the unexpected rapprochement of the emperor and the Farnese pope, despite the imperial alliance in February 1543 with the schismatic Henry VIII. Thus vanished the duke's hope of a break with his implacable papal enemy. When the rumor began to circulate that the emperor, in need of funds for his Flemish campaigns, would sell Siena to the Farnese, Cosimo's vexation reached its limit, barely soothed by the Spaniards' return of fortresses in accordance with an agreement made on 12 June.

But the danger from papal machinations against the Medici state was not over. Already by the end of 1539, over the question of the collection of papal tithes, refused by Cosimo because of the terrible famine under which Tuscany, along with the entire peninsula, suffered, the papal collector laid an interdict over the Florentine dominion. In the instructions given by Cosimo to his ambassador in Rome over the protest he was to lodge with the pope, Cosimo added, with a touch of malice (as Giorgio Spini perceptively observed), that the "populace could take heart and lose the habit and in the future place in surety what pertained to the divine cult, and that…already there were some who were saying, just as we can go without bread, we can go without Masses!"[10]

At the height of the Schmalkaldic War, on 6 February 1547, the duke wrote to the emperor, echoing discussions among his ministers, followers of the anticurial Erasmian orientation of Charles V's secretariat, from Mercurino da Gattinara to Alfonso de Valdés. Cosimo stated that the only means to eliminate heresy in Germany and purge Christianity "from the evil and strange habits of priests" was "by way of the council to deprive the Pope of his reputation, and bring about reform, so that priests will cease their past and present tyranny, restoring everything to the sacred laws, without touching a single hair of theirs naturally, but not allowing him further usurpations, which are nothing less than tyranny.…" In the event that the pope should stupidly throw himself on the side of France, they should "give him a good cudgeling," so that during the lives of his majesty and his children, popes will cease "to daily torment the world."[11]

In those years of bitter conflict with the Farnese pope, the subjects of papal tyranny and of the reformation of the church, the preoccupations of Sleidan's two orations were at the heart of the thoughts and discussions of Cosimo's ministers and Florentine intellectuals, who after 1542 gathered together as members of the Florentine Academy, which had become an organ of the state, an instrument of the duke's cultural policies.

THE POLITICAL THOUGHT OF AONIO PALEARIO

To further clarify the coincidence of these themes of antipapal struggles and longings for reform of the church, with Florentine concerns during the 1540s, namely in the

---

[10]G. Spini, *Cosimo I*, 176.
[11]A. Desjardins, *Négociations diplomatiques de la France avec la Toscane* (Paris, 1865) 3:171–175.

years during which Cosimo was building his state and Erasmian and Valdesian ideas were circulating, it might be useful to dwell briefly on the humanist and religious reformer Aonio Paleario (1503–70) and on his relationship to the Florentine governing class and cultural elite.[12]

Paleario was born at Veroli in a family of small landholders and went as a young man to Rome to complete his humanistic studies under the patronage of Veroli's bishop, Ennio Filonardi. After attending the philosophy lessons of Ludovico Boccadiferro and the lectures on eloquence of Pierio Valeriano, Paleario abandoned Rome disgusted at the anti-Erasmian crusade being waged by Pietro Corsi and the Roman Academy, following the uproar caused in 1529 by the publication of Erasmus's *Ciceronianus*. Between the two sects of *literati*, "one Ciceronian and the other dubbed Erasmian," Paleario sided with the latter, in spite of his great admiration for the Ciceronian style. He confessed this choice to Erasmus himself in a letter written in 1534 with which he hoped to persuade the great humanist to form a common front with Luther against papal tyranny in the forthcoming ecclesiastical council.

Paleario moved about between Perugia, Siena, and Padua, where "Pallas Athene" teaches all the arts. Here he attended with great pleasure the lectures on Greek literature of Benedetto Lampridio, renowned classicist and poet, linked to the Benedictine milieu and to the abbot of San Giorgio Maggiore, Gregorio Cortese. Paleario became a member of Pietro Bembo's circle, frequented by such fervent Erasmians as Emilio degli Emigli, the translator of the *Enchiridion militis Christiani* (1531) and the philosopher Vincenzo Maggi. Paleario's anti-Lucretian poem, *De animorum immortalitate*, printed at Lyons in 1536 by Sebastian Gryphius, came out of his Paduan period. That same year he returned to Siena, settling in Colle Valdelsa in 1537 where he married Maria Guidotti with whom he had five children.

The success of Paleario's *De animorum immortalitate* opened the way for him to come into contact with the cultural and political leaders of Florentine society: the great philologist Pier Vettori, Pier Francesco Riccio, Francesco Campana, the philosopher Francesco Verino, and Bartolomeo Panciatichi, who was consul of the Florentine Academy in 1546. These friendships and the intercession of Cardinal Sadoleto who was passing through, saved Paleario in 1542 from being condemned as a Lutheran following his bitter exchanges with the Dominican Vittorio da Firenze, a member of the Florentine theological faculty. From the moment that he was absolved for lack of evidence, Paleario's life vacillated between outward adherence to Catholicism, and imprudent gestures, dictated by an irrepressible need to participate in some way in the religious battle being waged throughout Europe.

In 1543, the year following his accusation, Paleario wrote an apology, *Pro se ipso*, in a Ciceronian vein, vigorous, emotional, and elegant. It championed freedom of conscience and free cultural exchanges and dialogue, reaffirming the values of humanism and of the Christian faith. One should not be censured, he claimed, for following the teachings of Oecolampadius, Erasmus, Luther, Melanchthon, Pomeranus (Bugenhagen), and Bucer, if they are founded on Holy Scripture and on the

[12]I refer the reader to my *Aonio Paleario*, 37–76.

church fathers. This statement in his own defense, printed at Lyons in 1552 with Paleario's other orations, would be used against him years later.

At this point the confluence of factors seems to suggest that Paleario and his Florentine and Sienese friends were behind the Italian translation of Sleidan's oration. At the news that the Council of Trent was scheduled to open the following year, Paleario addressed a letter to Luther, Melanchthon, Bucer, and Calvin on 20 December 1544 exhorting them to set aside their theological differences, judged to be of secondary importance, so that they could participate in the Council forming a common front against the "execrable tyranny" of the pope and his Curia.

Paleario proposed—at the suggestion of certain "brethren"—a revolutionary plan for the convocation of a truly free and general council. Its participants were to be persons expert in divine things, untouched by papal corruption, elected by the *plebs sancta*, by the people of God, without confessional, hierarchical, or social distinctions of any sort. But who were these "brethren" whom Paleario mentioned in his letter? We do not have sufficient positive evidence to identify them, and yet the idea of a free council, summoned by secular authorities, is broached in a letter to Cosimo's majordomo in August 1541. Therefore it is not impossible that the project to translate Sleidan's orations was the fruit of discussions held by Paleario with his Florentine and Sienese friends, and given the legal character of the document, that one of the participants was Lelio Torelli. Unfortunately, we still lack a modern biography of this celebrated jurist and statesman that might help us to understand him more completely than what we know from his public life, from his celebrated edition of the *Pandects* (1761), and from his well-known stands against ecclesiastical encroachment in the secular sphere. The anonymous eighteenth-century author of the *Memorie per servire alla vita del senator Lelio Torelli* indicated that Torelli, the friend of Campana, Flaminio, Doni, Bartoli, Varchi, and Vincenzo Borghini, "disliked monks and showed this openly." He considered them idlers capable only of causing harm to the state, to which they should not have been exempted from paying taxes:

> Malicious ravagers of the sacred laws, traitors to their vows of chastity, they think only of stuffing themselves; and those who have a better reputation possess no other merit than that of having compiled many volumes to hinder the progress of religion with their endless citations of passages from Scripture, the holy Fathers and the Councils. Important assignments for them are those that concern the administration of their patrimonies obtained by despoiling the best citizens, who now by their own efforts must earn their necessary sustenance and pay with their own sweat the Prince's levies.[13]

Torelli, agreeing with what reformers had done in Germany and Switzerland, favored the abolition of the monastic orders, because they no longer expressed the original scriptural rules, but rather the accumulation of enormous wealth and privileges.

We should not exclude, moreover, the possible contribution to the Sleidan translation project of another great jurist, Mariano Sozzini, at the time professor at

---

[13]FBN, ms. Palatino, 976, fols. 4v–5r.

Bologna, who had met Paleario in Padua and become his intimate friend. But the most substantial lead is offered by Paleario himself, one of the more original among the Italian reformers, a political theorist convinced that only a change in the European situation would allow Italy to join the nations who had freed themselves from the secular and religious yoke of the papacy.

In his *Actio in pontifices Romanos*, begun in 1536, but written between 1544 and 1545 on the eve of the opening of the Council of Trent, Paleario took up many of the arguments in the two orations of Sleidan, who like him had come to the Reformation from an Erasmian position. So similar is the congruence of ideals between the two humanists and their mutual involvement in the political controversies of the day, that it is difficult to imagine how Paleario could not have been acquainted with Sleidan's work, published a few years before the final version of his own celebrated "act" of accusation against the Roman pontiffs. We might even speculate that the translation of the *Capo finto* from the Latin into Italian might be Paleario's own.

The *Actio*, addressed to "Christian princes and to the prefects of the council," consists of twenty depositions. It is preceded by a testamentary letter and by an exhortation to the heads "of the holy churches of the Helvetians and of the Germans," who are assigned the task of reading the "Act of accusation" on the inevitable day of the convening of the solemn, free, and universal court, when "after the equity of the judgment shall have been established, abuses will be ended by the sword of the Word of God, religious controversies will be eliminated, the churches will be purged and healed, so that they may reunite in a single body...."[14] In the opening remarks, the writer turns directly to the princes asking them to stamp out an erroneous opinion that had become second nature for many men concerning the infallibility of the pope in religious matters, and to become new apostles to defend and reestablish the truth of the Gospel.

Taking its cue from the "De gratia et iustificatione" of Melanchthon's *Loci communes* (which is not cited, just as there is no mention of Erasmus, Luther, or Calvin), the *Actio* argues that false prophets who have substituted human works and laws for the perfect works of Christ as means to obtain salvation, "conceal the benefits of the blood of Christ, cover up sanctification through the Spirit of God, and announce a different gospel."[15] It is impossible to set the tradition of the church against the teachings of the apostles and Scripture, because no tradition can be considered valid if it is not corroborated by the Word of God: "God's holy church has always rested on the Word of God."[16] All believers and every church, Luther as well as the pope, must submit before Holy Scripture.[17] Human traditions have had nefarious consequences

---

[14]*Aonii Palearii Verulani Actio in pontifices Romanos*, in G. Paladino, *Opuscoli e lettere di riformatori italiani* 2:4: "Constituta aequitate iudicii, gladio verbi Dei rescindantur abusus, dirimantur controversiae de religione, purgentur et sanentur ecclesiae, ut cohaereant in unum corpus...." The *Actio* remained in manuscript until 1600, when it was published at Heidelberg by the physician of Locarno, Taddeo Duno. It was translated into Italian by Luigi De Sanctis: *Atto di accusa contro i papi di Roma e i loro seguaci, formulato da Aonio Paleario* (Turin: Claudiana, 1861). Facsimile repr. (Livorno: U. Bastogi, 1973).

[15]*Actio* (in Paladino), 2:28–29 (chap. 2).

[16]Ibid., 98 (chap. 10).

[17]Ibid., 96 (chap. 9).

for the church: its unity has been shredded because of the just rebellion of Luther and of his followers, and the spirituality of believers destroyed by such superstitions as vows and relics, belief in purgatory, priestly celibacy, and the dogma of transubstantiation.

One of the basic reasons given by Paleario for the current depravation was the abandonment of the evangelical and apostolic teaching that Christ is the cornerstone, and its substitution with the doctrine of the primacy of Peter. The *Actio's* conclusion was identical to Luther's, but also to Sleidan's and Ochino's, namely that the papacy was a manifestation of the Antichrist. The booklet's adherence to the essential principles of the Reformation was full and explicit, even if the author, citing only Scripture, the fathers and doctors of the church, went out of his way to demonstrate that his credo was that of the apostles and the early church. Paleario's was not a position of sectarian exclusiveness, since he expressed the conviction that in all churches there are sincere believers, desirous of being enlightened by the Word of God. The responsibility of princes is to be receptive to the ardent desires of the people, convening a free and universal council to judge the abuses of popes and bishops, establish sound doctrine, and restore the unity of believers under the authority of the Gospel.

The last section of the work is everywhere pervaded by ethico-political passion. Echoing Machiavelli, it affirmed (the same argument can also be found in Sleidan's oration) the responsibility of the pope for Italy's misfortunes, thanks to his avidity for wealth and power. In Rome shameful corruption was permitted at all levels and persecution and death were the lot of those who asked that respect be shown to the Gospel and to the truth. Prostitutes, panderers, and simoniacs lived freely, but witnesses to the Gospel were being imprisoned, tortured, and condemned to death. The peroration, addressed to Emperor Charles V, vigorously but concisely summarized Paleario's thought and closed with a doleful premonition of his death. In the context of the Italian Reformation, the humanist of Veroli was neither a theologian like P. M. Vermigli and B. Ochino, nor was he a popular proselytizer. But what he tried to be was a teacher, an organizer of public opinion, a political theorist. In a word, he could very well have been the translator of Sleidan's two orations.

BIBLIOGRAPHICAL NOTE

On Luther's political thought, see the introduction and bibliography by L. Firpo in M. Lutero, *Scritti politici,* tr. G. Panzieri Saja (Turin: UTET, 1959); and A. E. McGrath, *Reformation Thought: An Introduction,* 2d ed. (Oxford: Blackwell, 1993). For the intrinsic link between religious revolution and social reform, see the first part of A. Bielèr, *La pensée économique et sociale de Calvin* (Geneva: Georg, 1961), 3–135. Valuable insights are contained in B. Moeller, *Imperial Cities and the Reformation: Three Essays,* ed. and trans. H. C. Erik Midelfort and Mark U. Edwards, Jr. (Philadelphia: Fortress Press, 1972).

On Melanchthon's dealings with the *Signoria* of Venice, the older study by K. Benrath, *Geschichte der Reformation in Venedig* (Halle: Niemeyer, 1887), is still fundamental.

On Vergerio, cf. A. J. Schutte, *Pier Paolo Vergerio*, chaps. 7–9.

On Sleidan, cf. W. Friedensburg, *Johannes Sleidanus: Der Geschichtsschreiber und die Schicksalsmächte der Reformationszeit* (Leipzig: M. Heinsius, 1935). Sleidan's two orations can be read in the edition by E. Böhmer, *Zwei Reden an Kaiser und Reich von Johannes Sleidanus* (Tübingen, 1879). Cf. S. Caponetto, "'Il Capo Finto.' Una traduzione cinquecentesca della 'Oration an alle Stende des Reichs, von Römischen Nebenhaupt im Keyserthum erwachsen,'" in *Studi in onore di Arnaldo D'Addario* (Lecce: Conte Editore, 1995), 2:625–33.

On Paleario, one can now consult the massive study by E. Gallina, *Aonio Paleario*, 3 vols. (Sora: Centro di Studi Sorani "Vincenzo Patriarca," 1989). On Paleario's political thought, cf. G. Morpurgo, *Un umanista martire: Aonio Paleario e la Riforma teorica italiana* (Città di Castello: I. Lapi, 1912). For a different interpretation, see my *Aonio Paleario e la Riforma protestante in Toscana*.

John Frederick of Saxony (contemporary engraving) and Philipp Melanchthon, from *Icones, id est, Verae imagines virorvm doctrina simvl et pietate illvstrivm,* by Theodore Beza (1580).

In the Duchy of Savoy, Marquisate of Saluzzo and Republic of Genoa.

9

THE WALDENSIANS JOIN THE REFORMATION: CALVINISM IN THE PIEDMONT

THE WALDENSIANS ON THE EVE OF THE REFORMATION

THE ACCEPTANCE OF THE SWISS REFORMATION by the Waldensians of the Dauphinée, Provence, Piedmont, Calabria, and Puglia was an event of capital importance for the spread of the Protestant movement in the peninsula. The efforts of the Church of Rome and of the dukes of Savoy to prevent the valleys of the Pellice, the Chisone, and the Germanasca, along with the marquisate of Saluzzo, from becoming the Italian gateway for the introduction of heresy, suggests the real danger represented by this Protestant bridgehead on the soil of Catholic Italy.

The preoccupation was well founded and from the 1530s on began to alarm the papal Curia even more than was the case for Istria and Venice as entry points into Italy for the northern heresies. The transit of men and ideas, of heretical books, of broadsides decorated with blasphemous drawings, was a common occurrence in all the border areas—in the Trentino, Istria, Lombardy, and Piedmont—which enjoyed daily commercial contacts with Switzerland, Austria, and Germany where the Protestant doctrines of Zwingli, Luther, and Melanchthon circulated freely. Here and there in the Italian border areas small groups of sympathizers were occasionally discovered, but the situation was very different in Piedmont where eight thousand or so inhabitants of the Waldensian valleys threatened to pass en bloc to the Reformation.

Ecclesiastical and political authorities knew that sizable family groups existed in Piedmont, linked by an underground organization with centuries-long experience in religious dissimulation. At the dawn of the sixteenth century, the Waldensian movement, which in the *Quattrocento* had achieved a diaspora of European dimensions and together with the Bohemian brethren, had become an integral part of the "Waldensian-Hussite international," was greatly reduced after a century of persecutions. The missionary efforts had diminished the itinerant ministry of the "barbs," elders, so called from a designation common throughout northern Italy identifying an uncle as the most elderly and knowledgeable person. They limited themselves now to preserving the continuity of their teaching and attending to the religious needs of the initiated. In their clandestine existence, the resistance of the Waldensians, constrained to live the public life of the broader community in which they were situated, was reduced to the refusal of military service and office holding. They had very little leeway as far as religious behavior was concerned. To avoid detection they participated in the rites of the Roman church, including confession and communion. It would have been impossible to separate themselves from the spiritual life of the majority of the population without risking discovery by the ever vigilant Inquisition. Social and religious life were indissolubly bound by the law and age-old traditions and customs. Nevertheless, in spite of this facade, Waldensians succeeded in maintaining a second identity, under the guidance and periodic visits of their "barbs." Above all, as Gabriel Audisio has demonstrated for the Luberon, to which many Waldensians from Piedmont and the Dauphinée fled at the end of the fifteenth century to escape persecution at home, many old beliefs had survived. The appreciation for the scriptural value of poverty, understood as moderation in the use of money and earthly goods, was demonstrated by the modesty of dowries among Waldensians compared to the rest of the population. They also had books, both printed and in manuscript, of Sacred Scripture and manuals compiled by the "barbs." The level of literacy and the quality of religious instruction were superior to those of other rural populations of the fifteenth and sixteenth centuries. The Waldensians' Christocentric piety, founded on a reading of the Gospels, constituted the most enduring bond of Waldensian religiosity, "even before it became the chief appeal in the Protestant Reformation."[1] The Waldensians' absolute faith that "Jesus Christ alone was the perfect redemption and justification of the entire human race,"[2] and that Scripture contained the entire truth were the existential links between the only surviving medieval heretical movement and the teachings of Luther and the Swiss and Rhenish reformers.

Guillaume Farel and the Waldensians

A number of the better-educated "barbs," readers of Erasmus and Luther, began to feel an urgency to become directly acquainted not only with the doctrines of Luther, Oecolampadius, and Bucer, but also with the great ensuing social upheavals. Travelers from Germany, Switzerland, and Strasbourg, where the movement of protest had sunk deep roots, despite conflicts, excommunications, and the first condemnations, enthusiastically reported the great changes that had followed the preaching of the Gospel of grace and of "the liberty of the Christian." As early as 1526, Waldensian leaders gathered at Laus (Laux) in the high valley of the Chisone, understood that a new era had dawned and that the significance of these events needed to be explored.

---

[1] G. Audisio, *Les Vaudois du Luberon: Une minorité en Provence (1460–1560)* (Lourmarin: Ass. d'Études Vaudoises, 1984), 240, 270 ff.
    [2] Ibid., 167.

Perhaps the time had come to practice their faith publicly in spite of intensified persecutions at papal insistence in Piedmont, Savoy, and the Dauphinée. It was thus decided to send an exploratory delegation to Oecolampadius in Basel made up of the "barbs" Guido of Calabria and Martin Gonin of Angrogna.

At Aigle in the Vaud the two men made contact with Guillaume Farel (1480–1565), who was involved in a vigorous effort to introduce ecclesiastical reform in the town. This French gentleman, born at Gap in the Dauphinée, eventually became the chief intermediary between Waldensians, with whom his ancestors might have once had close ties, and the Reformation. For a number of reasons—he came from a part of France where there had long been a Waldensian presence; his language and culture were French; he possessed a decisive and impetuous character—he played a crucial role in persuading the sect to break with its medieval traditions. Farel, formerly a follower of Lefèvre d'Étaples and of Bishop Briçonnet, had gone beyond their Christian humanism. In Basel, Berne, and Neuchâtel he carried on a frequently violent anticlerical campaign, persuading the populace towards a doctrinal and liturgical reformation of a Zwinglian type. From 1536 until his death, he was Calvin's greatest ally. The encounter with Farel was decisive for Gonin, who returned to Angrogna enthusiastic, loaded down with books in French and Latin.

The general assembly at Mérindol in Luberon (1530) decided to send a mission northward to seek clarification on certain doctrinal and ethical points of Waldensian tradition that appeared to differ from Protestant teachings. The "barbs" Georges Morel of Freyssinière (Dauphinée) and Pierre Masson from Burgundy, after a visit with Farel in early October 1530, reached Basel, where Oecolampadius, a disciple of Erasmus, had achieved the reformation of the church with the cooperation of the magistracy. Oecolampadius received them with understanding and kindness and resolved their doubts on two fundamental questions: the relationship between justification by grace through faith and works, and the acceptance of the state, as an organism instituted by God in accordance with Paul's insistence in the Epistle to the Romans, chapter 13. For centuries, Waldensians had accepted as normative the teachings of the Sermon on the Mount, attributing preeminent authority to works, while their religious leaders took an oath of poverty, celibacy, and chastity.

In the letter-questionnaire, probably compiled by Morel, for Oecolampadius, the Waldensians humbly declared: "Therefore, to be sure, in all matters we are of the same opinion as you, and from the time of the apostles, believing always as you do, have been in agreement concerning the faith. We have differed only in this, that due to the fault and laziness of our nature we have absolutely not comprehended Scripture correctly, as you have. We have thus come to you to be guided, instructed, edified, and taught. The same God belongs to all."[3]

The reformer of Basel, and, shortly after, Bucer at Strasbourg, offered some simple explanations founded on Scripture. It was not difficult to persuade the two delegates on the point of *sola gratia* and *sola fides*, emphasizing that the fruits of good

---

[3]Cited by V. Vinay, *Le confessioni di fede dei Valdesi riformati, con documenti del dialogo fra "prima" e "seconda" Riforma* (Turin: Claudiana, 1975), 51.

works stem from a living, not a dead faith. But it was more difficult to get people to accept the laws of the state when they experienced its hostility and persecution on a daily basis. On this point the delegates found greater comprehension in Martin Bucer, who was in contact with Erasmians in Bologna and various Italian evangelicals and knew from them that it was impossible to openly preach the Gospel in that country.

After two years of readings, discussions, reflection, and conflict with the defenders of the ancient traditions, the *consilium generale*, composed of "barbs" from Piedmont, Dauphinée, Provence, and even from as far away as Puglia and Calabria, joined by all the family heads of the Piedmontese Waldensians, met at Chanforan in the valley of Angrogna from 12 to 18 September 1532. A recently published source informs us that two unidentified Italian monks also attended the assembly, probably, according to the descriptions of their garb, an Augustinian and a Dominican. It is thought that they participated in the discussions supporting the doctrine of justification by faith alone. When it became time to take a definitive decision over the Reformation doctrine, Guillaume Farel and the pastor Antoine Saunier were invited to attend. Martin Gonin of Angrogna was the promoter and organizer of the meeting. Except for the final declaration of the assembly of Chanforan (which does not discuss justification), very little has survived of the discussions over the replies given by Oecolampadius and Bucer to the questions posed by the two emissaries. We have Morel's account of the encounter, and from it we gather the great difficulty experienced by the "barbs," recruited from a rural population and possessing a modest and literally oriented Biblical education, in the face of the great body of doctrine elaborated by the reformers in the course of two decades and the formidable Biblical exegesis of Luther and Zwingli.

Reformation teachings basically clashed with the traditional Waldensian-Hussite view that one could conduct ethical and legalistic opposition within the Roman church. Farel's strong personality must have exerted a decisive role in pointing out the contradiction under which the Waldensian movement labored with its acceptance of the structure and rites of the Constantinian church, the "church of the malignant," opposed since the days of Valdus. In spite of differences, the assembly overwhelmingly accepted the recommendations urging association with the Swiss Reformation propounded by the more forward-looking "barbs," a decision ratified at Prali in 1533. In the following years, the Waldensians formed a special bond with Geneva, where Farel had settled, reluctantly joined in 1536 by Calvin, whose intended destination had been Strasbourg.

When the Waldensian leaders commenced their transformation of the ancient medieval movement into a reformed church, they demonstrated not only spiritual sensibility, having grasped the essential principles of the Lutheran message, but also political astuteness in interpreting the signs of the times. By throwing in their lot with the Reformation, the Waldensians avoided the destiny of a sect and of being absorbed by the Roman church, the fate of all other medieval apostolic movements. It also meant that they would not remain isolated in the ghettoes of the Alpine valleys and the peasant colonies of Calabria and Puglia, but would have direct access to the dynamics of the new European culture. After the assembly at Chanforan, Waldensian history ceased to be merely the story of a determined but isolated resistance of a small minority, but joined the course of European Protestantism.

The French translation of the Bible from the Hebrew and the Greek by Louis Olivier, known as Pierre Robert Olivétan, Calvin's cousin, carried out in the valleys and commissioned and paid for by Waldensians between 1533 and 1535, was the symbol and tangible reality of this confluence. Its printing at Neuchâtel was completed on 4 June 1535 and the translator concluded his labors on this massive tome, weighing well over ten pounds, with this verse: "The Waldensians, evangelical people,/ have made this treasure public." Olivétan's Bible became the symbol of the encounter between the Waldensian protest and the Reformation: the conviction of the superiority of scriptural teaching over every other.

WALDENSIANS AND THE SWISS REFORMATION

The enthusiastic report made by the "barb" Pietro Gonin concerning the new religious and social world he had observed at Basel, Berne, and Neuchâtel influenced the peasants in the valleys towards a better understanding of the Gospel and of the Waldensian tradition than the explication of the Pauline Epistles. Fascination with the descriptions of life beyond the Alps told by returning travelers was not limited to the Waldensian valleys, but extended to all the border areas. The inhabitants in these regions, where merchants, soldiers, laborers, artisans, coachmen, as well as students and ecclesiastics, tramped daily through the Alpine passes, listened with astonishment to the reports of the great changes taking place. In the collective imagination, these revolutionary events to the north became distorted, perhaps magnified and idealized, or under the lash of Catholic controversialists, assumed the sinister aspect of the demoniacal.

Such an episode from the years of the first Waldensian contacts with the world of the Reformation occurred at a border area at the other extreme of the peninsula. In 1535 Cristoforo de' Cavalli of Trent, a courier by profession, was accused of spreading Lutheran teachings. The suspect had described what he had seen during his trips to Bolzano, Merano, and Bruneck to friends gathered in a druggist's shop. In Austrian taverns he had heard merchants lately come from Germany say that the religion of Luther was superior to the Catholic; where German princes had embraced it, one lived better than in imperial lands, because priests no longer commanded. Cavalli acknowledged that he would have preferred to live there, where the Gospel was heeded, instead of among Italians for whom sermons went in one ear and out the other. He hoped that Philip of Hesse and John Zápolya would be victorious in their war against the emperor, whom he disdainfully dubbed "Carletto," "little Charles."[4]

One can discern in the minds of modest and poorly educated persons the collapse of the twin pillars of medieval authority, emperor, and pope, accompanied by

[4]V. Zanolini, "Appunti e documenti per una storia dell'eresia luterana," *Annuario del Ginnasio pareggiato della diocesi di Trento* 8 (1909): 25–27.

the beginning of the construction of the myth of the ideal city, where a better justice would be established. While many persons were undoubtedly shocked by the news of Luther's marriage to the ex-nun Caterina von Bora, others approved, juxtaposing it to the disgraceful situation of parish priests with their concubines and bastard children. Incomprehensible even for observant Catholics, was the raging of the pontiffs against this new Lutheran impiety, since everyone knew of the scandalous life of ecclesiastics, from pope to lower clergy. Heeded much more readily were those who said that the prohibition of marriage was a violation of divine law, foretold by the apostle Paul as a sign of the last days (1 Tim. 4:1–3).

The subject became even more alluring and fascinating when the discussion turned to the abolition of the mass, which would be replaced by preaching in the vernacular about the Gospel of Christ, Savior, and Redeemer of Christianity; to clearing away from the altars the relics of saints that until recently were the object of commercial trafficking, superstition, and lucre; or to the giving of the chalice to the faithful, previously excluded from this privilege. There was animated talk about the monasteries' being emptied of the many parasites who would now be compelled to work like everyone else and of the flight of nuns from their convents, where as young girls they had often been enclosed for life against their will by their parents. Corruption had reached such an unbearable point behind these cloister walls, that the patrician G. Priuli noted in his *Diarii* in 1509 the Venetian scandal of "prostituting nuns" (*monache meretrici*)[5] and, thirty years later, the baron of Burgio, apostolic nuncio to the viceroyalty of Sicily, writing to Cardinal Alessandro Farnese, delivered a harsh judgment about the Sicilian establishments: "more like houses and refuges for women unable to marry, than convents...."[6] Such matters were discussed everywhere, in the church square after the Sunday sermon, in the taverns, where merchants and drivers rested from their travels, sometimes in the company of *colporteurs* transporting Bibles and heretical books; in the artisans' shops, in the universities of Padua, Siena, Pavia, and Bologna, to which hundreds of foreign students flocked; and in the many academies and religious houses.

During the 1540s events had gone well beyond the suggestion of the innovators' preaching, or the reading of the Bible and prohibited books by the literate public. A consciousness of a new world and a new church was taking hold, whose members were being called "new Christians." Their communities, organized into reformed churches and linked from the mid-1530s to Farel's and Calvin's Geneva, became important channels for the discovery of this new world beyond the Alps. After the publication of the French edition of Calvin's *Institutes* (1541), Calvinism spread throughout France and much of southern Europe, and Waldensians became fully conscious of their ties to European Protestantism and no longer felt themselves isolated in their valleys. This undoubtedly influenced the development of Protestantism in Italy much more heavily than the surviving documentation can tell us. As far as Piedmont

---

[5]D. Hay, *The Church in Italy in the Fifteenth Century*, 62.
[6]G. A. Buglio to Cardinal A. Farnese (9 August 1538), in P. Tacchi Venturi, *Storia della Compagnia di Gesù*, I, pt. 1, 82. Cf. my entry, "Leotta Buglio," son of G. A. Buglio, in *DBI*, 15:19.

was concerned, in the traditionally Waldensian areas such as the valleys of the Pellice, Chisone, and Germanasca, the cities of Chieri and Cuneo, and the marquisate of Saluzzo, there was no difficulty in establishing continuity from Waldensianism to the Reformation. The sect, cautiously perhaps, and with concern for the consequences of the abandonment of their traditional Nicodemite practices, clearly demonstrated their intentions to learn the new doctrines. Pastor Saunier, back in Switzerland after the assembly at Chanforan, wrote to Farel on 5 November 1532, that some of the inhabitants of the valleys "simply to hear the Word of Truth traveled on foot for two days."[7] Olivétan busied himself organizing a school to prepare children for reading Scriptures.

Despite the urging of Waldensians to be prudent in openly proclaiming their new faith, even by emissaries from Geneva, it was the consensus that the time had come to cease hiding their light under the proverbial bushel. Catelano Girardet, native of San Giovanni di Luserna, accused of traveling the valley of Paesana and neighboring areas preaching the new doctrine, was one of the first to openly give witness. Arrested at Revello and sentenced to death in the autumn of 1535, he gave a shining example of courage and fortitude, according to the account gathered from among the older Waldensians by Girolamo Miolo, pastor at Pragelato and then at Angrogna from 1579 until his death in 1593: "An example of living faith and constancy is told about a person called Catelano Girardo of San Giovanni di Luserna, who was imprisoned at Revello, in the Marquisate of Saluzzo, and burned because of it. And already bound to the stake he asked to be given a rock in each hand and then said: 'When I shall have eaten these two rocks, you'll have abolished the Waldensian faith,' signifying that it is invincible and will live forever."[8]

During the decade from 1550 to 1560 the Reformation sank deep roots in the Waldensian valleys and throughout Piedmont. The communities of the old sect provided the framework of an organization dependent on Geneva from which came pastors and teachers, Bibles and religious books. The martyrs who faced death in this period publicly protesting their faith in Christ and in the scriptural message, appeared in the trial records and in bits of other scattered evidence, convicted of having been elected and predestined to salvation according to Calvinist teachings.

The sequence of executions is the crowning evidence of the maturity attained by the evangelical communities, the consequence of the devoted reading of Scripture by the people and of the fiery preaching of such highly educated converts as the former Franciscans Paolo della Riva and Gioffredo Varaglia. In June 1550, Maria Cupina della Torre of Luserna, accused of having preached in the valleys of San Martino (Germanasca) and Perosa, and Iacopo Macelli (Massel) of Pomareto di Perosa, were in prison at Pinerolo. Maria Cupina, who had revived the Waldensian tradition of feminine ministry, remained unshakable during the inquisitorial interrogation. The Parliament in Turin ratified her death sentence, which probably was carried out in Pinerolo. At the end of the year Paolo della Riva of Fenile was condemned to be

---

[7] G. Jalla, *Storia della Riforma*, 1:34.
[8] G. Miolo, *Historia breve e vera degl'affari dei Valdesi delle Valli*, a cura di E. Balmas (Turin: Claudiana, 1971), 89.

burned alive in Pinerolo, the sentence to be carried out on a market day so that the spectacle could be viewed by the largest possible public. This former Franciscan, scion of one of the great families of Vigone, had been condemned to the galleys on an earlier occasion, but after abjuring, had returned home to find that the Protestant ideas he had once professed were now widely diffused. This swayed him to begin preaching again in the Val Luserna, where he was arrested, and as a *relapsus*, now could not escape his fate.

The construction of a bridgehead for the Reformation in Piedmont was facilitated by the centuries-old Waldensian presence in a geographical complex of contiguous territory, consisting in the south of the marquisate of Saluzzo bordering the Dauphinée and Provence, and in the north of Savoy and the Val d'Aosta adjoining Lausanne and Geneva. But credit should also be given to the political upheaval brought about by French domination of the area from 1536 to 1559. Francis I snatched a large part of the duchy of Savoy from his uncle Charles III, who was allied to France's enemy, Spain, leaving him only Vercelli, Niece, Cuneo, and the Val d'Aosta, garrisoned by Spanish troops. The population and the land suffered during the conflict as a consequence of pillaging by the military of both sides. To the territories already conquered, in 1548 Francis I added the Marquisate of Saluzzo and annexed it to the Dauphinée. In 1538 he had established at Turin a *Parlement* or supreme court endowed with political, judicial, and administrative responsibilities, including jurisdiction over the crime of heresy, which it adjudicated together with the inquisitorial court.

During the French occupation notable changes affecting the population took place. For example, in the Waldensian valleys where peasants were subject to their masters, even though they had succeeded between the end of the fifteenth century and the beginning of the sixteenth in organizing themselves into communities and had obtained certain rights and exemptions, the French rulers eliminated or redefined the powers of the feudal lords who had opposed them in the war. When, in 1549, Giovanni Caracciolo, prince of Melfi, ordered the demolition of the ancestral towers at Torre, Luserna, Perrero, and Bricherasio, the population hailed the event as "the ruin of the ancient lords."[9]

A number of highly placed officers among the occupying French troops openly favored the Reformation. The governor of Turin, William de Bellay, protected his Protestant subjects until his death in 1543. In the Waldensian valleys, William of Fürstemberg, who was governor after the conquest, commanded six thousand Germans in French service, many of whom were Protestants. His second in command was Gauchier Farel, brother of the reformer, who labored to convert the entire population of Angrogna to the Reformation, even going so far as to enter a Catholic church, sword in hand, demanding explanations of doctrine from a surprised and embarrassed priest.[10]

---

[9]A. Armand Hugon, "Popolo e chiesa alle Valli dal 1532 al 1561," *BSSV* 81 (1961), n. 110: 14.

[10]On this point and what follows, cf. G. Jalla, "Il Parlamento francese di Torino e la Riforma in Piemonte," *Rivista Cristiana* 39 (1912): 361–78, 425–42.

In 1537, a year after the beginning of the French occupation, the situation changed and Waldensians experienced a period of persecution. This was the revenge taken by the commander of the French army, Anne de Montmorency, against Fürstemberg, who, at the meeting in Nice of Francis I, Charles V, and Paul III, had refused to kiss the pope's slipper. Marguerite of Navarre, under similar circumstances, did not show the same constancy. Although she too sympathized with the reformers, she was always ready to sacrifice herself for her beloved brother, Henry. Returning to the Waldensian valleys in 1539, Fürstemberg freed Montmorency's prisoners.

This was not an isolated incident of support for evangelicals. Marguerite de Cardé, the wife of Paul de la Barthe, marquis of Thermes, governor from 1545, was a fervent Huguenot and attended the reformed church at Val Luserna. With her brother Giacomo Saluzzo-Cardé and her sister-in-law, Anna di Tenda, she turned her small fiefdom of Cardé into "a sturdy outpost of the reformed faith."[11]

The marquis of Thermes was succeeded by Giovanni Caracciolo, the prince of Melfi, mentioned above, a Neapolitan exile whose son, Giovanni Antonio, abandoned the bishopric of Troyes to embrace Calvinism. The senior Caracciolo, who governed from 1548 to 1550, shielded Waldensians from persecution. The multinational garrison composed of French, German, and Swiss helped to spread the new ideas to the most humble levels of the population, a phenomenon thus described by a modern authority: "at Turin, Savigliano, Busca, Chieri, and Carmagnola...officers, soldiers and evangelizers among the foreign troops, occasionally proselytized so brazenly and provocatively as to force clergy and civic officials to react, or sometimes even bring about direct royal intervention."[12] Thus, thanks to a sequence of concomitant circumstances, by midcentury the Reformation had infiltrated everywhere in the area.

As Waldensians more and more openly professed their faith, taking advantage of favorable local situations, they constructed "temples" in the valleys of Angrogna (1555) and Germanasca (1556). In the villages of San Martino, Massello, and Rodoretto, the abandoned Catholic edifices were appropriated for use by the Protestant cult; and pastors from Lausanne and Geneva organized formal communities conforming to Calvinist theology and discipline.

THE REFORMED CHURCHES OF PIEDMONT

Waldensians and evangelicals, under the leadership of their pastors, expended great efforts creating a solid base for the Reformation in Piedmont. A reformed conventicle was established even in Turin where it was much more difficult to elude the

---

[11]A. Pascal, *Il marchesato di Saluzzo e la Riforma protestante* (Florence: Sansoni, 1960), 118–19.
[12]Ibid., 33, 106.

repressive measures of the president of the Parliament, the Milanese exile Renato Birago, who now was serving France and had earned the title of *malleus hereticorum*.

Gaudenzio Merula (1500–55) of Borgolavezzaro (Novara), a renowned humanist, an elegant writer in Latin, the author of works of history, geography, folklore, and a volume of *Memorabili* dedicated to Birago and printed at Turin in 1551, came into contact with these reformed groups. Merula's *De Gallorum antiquitate*, first printed at Lyons by Sebastian Gryphius in 1536, enjoyed three other editions later in the century. Ortensio Lando considered the humanist of Novara one of his friends and mentioned him in the *Cicero relegatus* as well as in the *Forcianae Quaestiones*, among the guests of Ludovico Buonvisi at Forci, his villa in Lucca.

Merula's interest in the religious questions of the day and the vexing Erasmian proposition, *Ciceronianus es, christianus non es*, began in the mid-1530s. After almost two decades in Milan, in 1545 he was appointed by the town of Vigevano as a teacher of grammar and moral philosophy. In Milan he had met a number of Erasmians and the great jurist Andrea Alciati, and in 1541 listened avidly to the Lenten sermons of Bernardino Ochino. But what decided Merula's conversion to the Reformation was the friendship he struck up with a lawyer from Locarno, Martino Muralto, one of the first to organize the evangelical community in the city. At the time Muralto was serving as *podestà* of Vigevano during the biennium from 1548 to 1549 when he met Merula. Towards the end of 1550 when the latter, under the patronage of Renato Birago, was invited to Turin to lecture publicly, he was already a critic of the Church of Rome. Merula became more bold in his beliefs after meeting with evangelicals and reading works by Calvin. He urged his pupils to become acquainted with the Scriptures, conversed freely with soldiers of the garrison about the Christian faith, and finally decided to abandon teaching and return home, from where he would set out for Geneva hoping to meet Calvin, whose follower he professed himself to be.

Merula tells us this in a letter dated 27 April 1554 to the Genevan reformer. The document might be defined as the confession of a Nicodemite, convinced that up to that time he had been a "base" servant, in bondage to the purple-garbed prostitute, that "Circe who seduces men with her horn of plenty," from which God up to now had spared him. He hoped that grace would make him worthy to be snatched from that "Babylonic mist."[13] Old age makes him avaricious, but Christ would make him munificent and cause him to abandon his honest labors that did not permit him "to serve Christ freely." Through Calvin's teachings he felt that he was walking in the warming light of the Truth and desired nothing more than to meet and converse with him and with Bernardino Ochino, who was the first to bring him to Christ. This was the hope shared by many Italian evangelicals, conscience stricken and eager to shed the mask of Nicodemism, but one never fulfilled by Merula who, as a teacher and Latinist, could have professed his faith openly and found employment in Protestant Switzerland. The return to his native city was not a happy one due to disagreements with his wife, who opposed undertaking such an adventurous journey and probably

---

[13] *Calvini Opera omnia*, 15:121–23, n. 1946.

even her husband's ideas. Moreover, his talk about the failings of the Roman church caused him to be investigated on suspicion of heresy first in Novara and later in Milan. He was absolved in the first case, thanks to the intercession of his friend Bonaventura Castiglioni, historian and philologist, and also, perhaps, of Cardinal Giovanni Morone, then bishop of Novara. Merula went back to his Nicodemite ways and died, anguished, at the conclusion of his Milanese trial, on 22 March 1555. His friend Simone Del Pozzo thus marked the day: "He died at Borgolavezzaro and I worry about the fate of his soul, because he passed away in the grip of the Lutheran perfidy."[14]

A prayer written by Merula accompanying a gift to the confraternity of San Rocco di Borgolavezzaro of a coin presumed to have belonged to Judas, is suggested by his biographer (who didn't know of Merula's letter to Calvin) to be an expression of Catholic orthodoxy. It is, instead, a clear acknowledgment of that *certitudo fidei* that was considered, during the Tridentine deliberations on justification, to be the unfailing proof of Protestant belief.[15] Merula's conversion testifies to the effectiveness of the clandestine work carried out by the evangelicals of Turin, who were in contact with the Waldensians in their valleys, and who acquired from them as pastor Alexander Guyotin, a well-known jurist and man of letters, and as his collaborator, Girolamo Selvaggio of Pinerolo. The two organized the French- and Italian-speaking Protestants of Turin into two communities, both of which grew in membership.

Guyotin was betrayed by antitrinitarian followers of G. Paolo Alciati, but succeeded in fleeing. In the course of his journey to Geneva he passed through Castiglione d'Asti, Villanova, Poirino, Moncalieri, Carignano, Pancalieri, and Villafranca, where he mobilized the philo-Protestants into small congregations, which then turned to Geneva for ministers of the faith. In the letter written early in June 1556 by Pastor Domenico Vignaux to his colleagues in Geneva, there is an enthusiastic, perhaps exaggerated, account of his first contacts with the evangelicals of the valleys, who now numbered in the thousands:

> These people differ from almost all others in their piety and moral behavior. They possess an exceedingly rare simplicity and docility, and it would be difficult to find, as we do here, men transformed into lambs, so that, from the first day of my arrival, I felt I was transported to another world. And if you could see how they yearn to hear the Word of God! They travel great distances over horrible roads to every place where there is preaching. They shun luxuries, blaspheming and scandals and place all their happiness in knowing the will of God.... I could never have believed that the Celestial Father had concealed such incomparable treasures

---

[14]Quoted from C. Ramponi, "L'umanista Gaudenzio Merula di Borgolavezzaro e la Controriforma cattolica," *R. Deputazione subalpina di Storia patria, Bollettino della Sezione di Novara* 32 (1938): 15.

[15]Ibid., 96: "Now, oh merciful Christ, Son of God, who has freed me with your most precious blood from eternal damnation, direct, while I am still on earth, my steps along the path that is pleasing to you. And when my vital forces begin to fail me, pull a merciful veil over the ignorance of my pilgrimage, and say to my soul: this blood which I spilled over the altar of the cross all for you, let it be a pledge of your salvation and redemption."

among these mountains.... Meanwhile, we are totally like sheep destined
for slaughter whose lives hang by a thread; all the violence of our enemies
is directed against us, and it is as if we were being attacked by lions and
bears thirsting for our blood. We teach publicly and even the papists
come freely to hear us. The Gospel has been spread widely and the harvest
is plentiful, but the workers are few.[16]

Some days later, Calvin, Beza, and Viret, cognizant of the importance of establishing
a solid ecclesiastical structure in the valleys, if the movement in Piedmont was to
grow, sent two ministers, Pierre Guérin and Stefano Favonio. In this climate of
enthusiastic proselytization, organizational fervor, and massive attendance at the sermons and rites (according to one piece of information reaching Switzerland six thousand persons partook of the Lord's Supper at Angrogna), the martyrdom of the
colporteur Bartolomeo Hector, the student Niccolò Sartoris, and Gioffredo Varaglia
occurred.

Hector, a Frenchman of Poitiers, traversed the Waldensian valleys selling Bibles
and other religious books that he brought from Geneva. He was executed on 20 June
1556 in Piazza Castello in Turin, after three months of interrogations and torture,
which he endured with courage and fortitude.

Niccolò Sartoris was a twenty-six-year-old student, born at Chieri, the oldest
child of the notary to Duke Charles III of Savoy, G. Leonardo Sartoris. Leonardo, a
convert to the Reformation, settled four of his children in Geneva and allowed Niccolò to study theology in Lausanne. While preparing to move to Geneva with his
wife and two other children, Leonardo was arrested in Savoy and had his books and
documents confiscated. He was brought to Chieri, where he abjured his errors, but
without convincing his judges. "In 1556," a contemporary noted, "Leonardo Sartoris of Chieri, noble, learned and elderly, laden down with heavy chains, in the dead
of winter, perished in his cell from the cold and piously fell asleep in the Lord."[17]
Leonardo's son, Niccolò, who had gone to Aosta on business, was betrayed by his too
public efforts to shake the evangelicals there out of their Nicodemite torpor. After his
capture and three months of interrogations and torture, he was condemned to the
stake in the square of Aosta on 4 May 1557. News of his death flew throughout the
duchy, driving Emanuel Philibert to complain to the bishop of Aosta that "it was
scandalous and dangerous to openly kill those who stand firm in their error, such as
the person who was recently burned there, because the constancy that they display in
death more often persuades their supporters to obstinacy than to repentance...."[18]
The exemplary end of two of their fellow citizens strengthened the still-lethargic people of Chieri in the new faith. The city, one of the richest and most populous of Piedmont, came to be called the "little Geneva" because of the large number of

---

[16]G. Jalla, *Storia* 1:85–86.

[17]Ibid., 99. His nephew, Jacopo Sartoris, was a pastor in Geneva from 1619 to 1650. See V. Burlamacchi, *Libro di ricordi degnissimi delle nostre famiglie*, a cura di S. Adorni-Braccesi (Rome: Istituto
storico italiano per l'età moderna e contemporanea, 1993), 204.

[18]G. Jalla, *Storia* 1:91–92.

evangelicals it produced, and in fact, in the half century after 1555, forty of its citizens found refuge in the actual Geneva.

The most famous of the three martyrdoms, and the best known because the trial records were published by a contemporary, Scipione Lentolo, was that of the pastor of Angrogna, Gioffredo Varaglia. A former Franciscan, he had been born at Busca, at the extremity of the marquisate of Saluzzo, about the year 1507. At the age of forty, he laid down his cassock and entered the service of the papal legate to the court of France. There, the doubts that had tormented him for years evolved into the wish to learn more about the doctrines of the Reformation. From Lyons he set out for Geneva, where he was consecrated a minister of God's Word in 1557 and sent to the valley of Angrogna, where a minister was urgently needed to instruct the new converts. Varaglia labored among them for five months and they came from all over Piedmont to hear him preach. He was called by Bernardino Guarino of Dronero to Busca to debate the monk Angelo Malerba and accepted the invitation, happy to be returning to his birthplace to testify to the truth of the Gospel. The disputation aroused great interest among populace and nobility alike. But during the journey home Varaglia was arrested at Barge, where a preliminary interrogation took place. He was taken to Turin, locked up in the prison of the Parliament, where he was questioned and pressed at length about his faith by members of the higher clergy. The learned former Franciscan fearlessly held up his end of the discussions focusing on the great disputed themes of the day, from justification to the invocation of saints, from the cult of images to the authority of the pope, resting his arguments on Holy Scripture. He was defrocked in that very same cathedral in Turin where he had been ordained priest thirty years before, and on 29 March 1558, he ascended the scaffold in Piazza Castello. An eyewitness, the physician of Busca, Girolamo Raffaele Alosiano, described the event in a celebrated letter he wrote to Protestant princes in Germany on 13 April 1559: "Thanks to pressure exerted by the pope on the king of France, he [Varaglia] was condemned by the Senate in Turin to be first hung and then burned. With such great fortitude, serene countenance, and comforting words, did he march from prison to the stake, that I do not believe apostles and martyrs ever confronted more willingly the cross and death itself, all the time instructing and exhorting to read the Holy Scriptures. And when he had climbed the scaffold in the presence of ten thousand bystanders, he expounded the reasons for his death, confessed his faith and justification, and affirmed his hope for eternal life through Jesus Christ."[19]

The letter from the physician of Busca is precious also for the information it imparts on the entire Protestant movement in Piedmont and for the allusions to its infiltration in various Italian cities,

> where there are large numbers of Christians, who due to the proximity of the Roman Antichrist and surrounded by their enemies proceed much more secretly than we do, except for the duchess of Ferrara, who has a minister who preaches the Christian truth to her and to her people, although

---

[19]Ibid., 100.

the duke himself is opposed to the Word.… In the valleys of the province of Piedmont, and in the mountains, where, without fear of the enemies of Christ all the profane traditions and blasphemies of the papists have been rejected and abolished, the Sacred Gospel of our Savior is purely preached and the sacraments are administered as they were instituted by Christ and the apostles. These are the churches of the valley of the *contado* of Luserna, of the valley of Angrogna, of the valley of San Martino, of the valleys of Perosa and Pragelato, and in the marquisate of Saluzzo there are two Christian churches in the mountains at Praguglielmo, Bioleto and Botoneto. In these valleys thirty ministers of the church of God preach openly, without fearing the enemies of Christ, the Word of God purified of all filth, and they administer the other things necessary in the church of Christ, which numbers about forty thousand faithful.

There were also many faithful in the plain, including in Turin, "and there is hardly a village in which one does not find a church of Christ, whether hidden or revealed. And even when they are unable to have ministers, at least they pray, and those among them who are literate and more educated read the Sacred Scriptures in their own homes."[20]

THE ECCLESIASTICAL POLICY OF EMANUEL PHILIBERT: THE TREATY OF CAVOUR (1561)

The letter by the physician of Busca was intended to convey to the duke of Württemberg, Landgrave Philip of Hesse, and Count George of Montbéliard, as well as to the ministers of "the loyal churches" the gratitude of the "churches and pastors of Piedmont." Thanks were being given to them for having received an embassy composed of Bernese and Genevans, including Guillaume Farel, Pierre Viret, and Theodore Beza, who had fulfilled their assignment of pleading before Henry II the cause of obtaining freedom of the cult for the churches in the Waldensian valleys. Unfortunately the situation, favorable to the consolidation of the evangelical communities, which were by now solidly structured within the sphere of the Swiss Reformation, suddenly changed with the treaty of Cateau-Cambrésis (3 April 1559), which restored almost the entire territory of the duchy of Savoy to Emanuel Philibert.

Thanks to the splendid victory that he won against the French at San Quintino, Emanuel Philibert, commander of the imperial troops in Flanders, obtained the full support of Philip II to regain possession of his dominions and to marry Marguerite of Valois, the daughter of Francis I and sister of Henry II. The duke now faced the difficult task of securing the full independence of his state and proceeding to its reorganization. At this level, ecclesiastical policy of necessity assumed great importance in view of the increasingly bitter conflict in much of Europe between Catholics and Protestants, which the duke as a former combatant against the Schmalkaldic League knew from personal experience.

[20]Ibid., 98–99.

Emanuel Philibert, raised at the court of Charles V, was a Spaniard for life, having promised loyalty and devotion to Spain and to Philip II. Consequently, out of conviction, as well as for reasons of politics, the duke was a proponent of the principle, *cuius regio eius religio*, who had to pluck from his side the thorn of the Calvinist Waldensians, closely linked to their co-religionaries in Geneva, Lausanne, and France itself. Political unity was strictly tied to religious uniformity, especially since the French continued to occupy Turin, Pinerolo, Chieri, Chivasso, and Villanova d'Asti. Even before setting out on his homeward journey, the duke wrote from Gand on 12 August 1559 to his ambassador at the Holy See: "As soon as we reach Nice, we shall begin to tend to the matters of religion in our domain. It is a thing that weighs upon us and we wish to accomplish the most, as it concerns us. When we shall find persons who harbor evil opinions, we are resolved, with the help of God, to extirpate them, certain that besides rendering a service to Our Glorious God, we shall also be doing something pleasing for His Holiness and the Holy See."[21]

Nevertheless, the duke understood that, after twenty-five years of French dominion, he had to obtain the consensus of his subjects. Not realizing the extent to which Protestantism had taken root in the region, he asked the episcopate to begin converting Waldensians and evangelicals, while implementing a series of provisions for improving the cure of souls in their dioceses and greater discipline in the monasteries and convents. From the information he received, and from the suggestions made by bishops and his counselors, the duke decided to issue from Nice, on 16 February 1560, an edict abolishing freedom of religion. It imposed a fine of a hundred golden ducats for the first offense, and a sentence to the galleys for the second against any of his subjects, regardless of their rank, who went to hear "the Lutheran ministers" in the valley of Luserna, or in other places, granting the authority to incarcerate to his ministers of justice and the mayors of the communities, accompanied by the promise that they could pocket a third of the fines levied. The persecutions had begun.

The duke's commissioners proceeded rigorously, thinking that they could frighten the populace with exemplary condemnations. At Carignano, where the Protestant presence went back several years, the Frenchman Mathurin (or Maturino), together with his wife, and Giovanni di Cartignano, also called Giovanni delle Spinelle because he manufactured tubing for barrels and tubs, who lived in the valley of Luserna, were sentenced to be burned alive. According to Scipione Lentolo, who witnessed these events, this humble artisan, for "his invincible constancy" and for "the pure and free confession he made of the doctrine of salvation," was a shining example of loyalty for all (14 March 1560).[22]

When Emanuel Philibert saw that edicts, threats, and harsh sentences were not working, he sent Giorgio Costa, count della Trinità, on a punitive expedition against the Waldensians of Luserna for the purpose of reducing them to complete submission to the laws of the state and the Church of Rome. In October 1560, the intended

---

[21]Ibid., 111.
[22]Ibid., 130.

victims, at the urging of their French pastors, convinced of the lawfulness of taking up arms in self-defense following the Huguenot example in France, withdrew with their families to the mountains, resolved to defend their right to obey God, rather than man. The fervor that animated their struggle against the pope, who called for their destruction through the mouths of the Jesuit Antonio Possevino and other ecclesiastics, their absolute familiarity with the topography and the courage of pastors and peasants alike, thwarted the campaign of Trinità and his troops. Due to the intercession of his wife, Duchess Marguerite, and of Count Filippo of Racconigi, the duke was compelled to pardon his rebellious subjects and to sign a treaty of peace at Cavour on 5 June 1561 with their chiefs and pastors as well as with laymen selected by the valley dwellers. The pact recognized a Protestant minority's right to exist, "the first act of religious toleration in Europe," the "Magna Charta" of the reformed Waldensians' juridical existence.[23]

The available records, greatly enriched by the appearance in the last few years of previously unpublished sources, confirms the decisive role played by Duchess Marguerite of Savoy in arranging the peace settlement. A recent, splendid study by Jean-Claude Margolin reveals a woman educated by her aunt Marguerite, queen of Navarre, as a princess of Erasmian inspiration. The French scholar makes clear, better than any previous attempt, that her defense of the "barbettes" against the intransigents at court and even against her own consort was not motivated by political considerations alone but was based on the conviction that every sincerely professed faith deserved respect. Even in her difficult role as wife of a prince whose laws had been violated by the Waldensian rebels, Marguerite was able to save them from destruction. A spiritual daughter of Erasmus and of Michel de l'Hospital, her influential counselor before he became chancellor of France, she evenhandedly extended her protection to the Catholics who had been driven out of Lyons after its capture by the Huguenots, as well as the Huguenots themselves who were well represented at her court.[24]

After the treaty of Cavour, the communities of the valleys were exhilarated by their perception that they had received divine assistance in their unequal struggle against the ducal troops. Under the steady leadership of their pastors, among whom the Neapolitan Scipione Lentolo was the guiding force, sent from Geneva to replace Gioffredo Varaglia, they reorganized and extended their influence over all the evangelical communities in Piedmont, including the numerous conventicles in the marquisate of Saluzzo. The latter groups had grown during the intervals of French toleration towards the Huguenots, to the point that after receiving complaints from the duke of Savoy as well as the pope, French sovereigns had to exclude their subjects in Saluzzo from privileges they had granted to Protestants at home. During the periods of recurring persecution, evangelicals of the marquisate found refuge in the Waldensian valleys, and vice versa, when oppression fell on them. The unity of faith

[23]A. Armand Hugon, *Storia dei Valdesi*, 2:30–31.

[24]Cf. J. C. Margolin, "Une princesse d'inspiration érasmienne: Marguerite de France, duchesse de Berry, puis de Savoie," in *Culture et pouvoir en temps de l'Humanisme et de la Renaissance: Actes du Congrès de Marguerite de Savoie*, ed. Louis Terreaux (Geneva: Slatkine, 1978), 156–83.

between the churches of the marquisate and the Waldensian churches in the valleys of the Pellice and the Chisone, was sealed at the synods of Angrogna and of Villar Pellice in 1563. Their union was regulated by the *"Ordonnances Ecclésiastiques faicts par nos très honorés Pères et frères ministres de la Parolle de Dieu aux Vallées de Luzerne, St. Martin, Pérouse, Cluson et Marquisat [de Saluces], là devant faictes au synode d'Angrogne, 15 septembre 1563…."* On 18 April 1564, a general assembly of the faithful from all of Piedmont met, joined by many of their co-religionaries from Saluzzo, Cuneo, Caraglio, Demonte, and other places in the plains.[25]

The Protestant movement, despite the persecutions it had endured, extended through the entire region, with the marquisate of Saluzzo and the Waldensian valleys its major centers. In Saluzzo in 1567 there were twenty regularly constituted religious communities served by nine pastors; although they were administratively independent of the Waldensian churches, they remained linked to them spiritually. Similarly in Caraglio, Busca, Villafalletto, and Cuneo, bordering the marquisate of Saluzzo, the movement had achieved significant successes. In Caraglio, for example, the majority of the population was Protestant and controlled the reins of government. This situation vexed the duke, his court in Turin, and Pope Pius V who, having once been bishop at Mondovì, feared that Piedmontese heresy might spread to contaminate all of Italy.

The danger was real, and not, as has often been believed, a fabrication of the higher clergy. The Protestant menace had even penetrated the religious houses, such as the abbey of Casanova where the prioress was suspected by the inquisitor of harboring Calvinist beliefs (1567). In Saluzzo itself, not far from the governor's castle, at the inn of the "Selvaggio," the proprietress and her Huguenot sons openly kept prohibited books in various languages, including Pierre Viret's *Anatomy of the Mass* for the use of the guests who came in large numbers because of the good treatment they received.[26]

In 1576, the Venetian ambassador Molino gave the following report to the Senate of the *Serenissima* on the situation in the duchy of Savoy:

> The duke's subjects are Catholic except for some who dwell in certain valleys, and especially Lucerna, which includes Angrogna, and some others neighboring the Dauphinée which are highly infected. There are about thirty or more different domains and twenty-eight castles in which sermons in the Huguenot fashion are held, and in these places in a few churches the Mass is celebrated for Catholics who I do not believe are even 5 percent of the population.
>
> The duke is extremely anxious to separate these people from that religion. But they, professing not to have had any other for thirty years, to preserve their faith do not hesitate to sacrifice their property, their children and life itself. In addition, they are so situated that they can be reached only with great difficulty, and in the valleys bordering the Dauphinée, the Huguenots

[25]A. Pascal, *Il Marchesato di Saluzzo*, 228 ff.
[26]Ibid., 195.

living there would not hesitate to help them in times of need. They have frequently shown the duke how he, who is so zealous for the cause of religion, must support this plague in his states, however unwillingly....

Since previous attempts to bring the Waldensians to reason by force had failed, the duke had decided, the dispatch continued, that

it is good counsel to keep them as content as possible, and not furnish them with the occasion since they are in Italy and on this side of the mountains, of inundating and infecting it, which is what they have always greatly wanted. And with the peace and truces that have occurred in France, they contrived that the marquisate of Saluzzo should not be exempted from the free exercise of religion. But the duke has always opposed himself to this to the infinite benefit of Italy. However, many persons succeed in passing through, and large groups gather together secretly. Thus, despite the diligent inquiries that have been made and are regularly conducted, it has been impossible to obtain definite information about any. And yet it is absolutely certain that from many places in Piedmont, Lombardy, the dominions of your serenity and from the states of the Church these people gather at least once a year for their suppers, nor do they return home without bringing with them books and other sorts of ceremonies of this false religion, to distribute them where they hope to obtain some fruit.[27]

Molino's report confirmed that Waldensians, after the treaty of Cavour, had turned their area into a center for the diffusion of Calvinism and the Genevan Reformation. The allusion to an annual gathering of brethren from the neighboring Italian regions referred to the annual synods held in the valleys. The inclusion of representatives from the states of the church, Lombardy and the Veneto, comes from reliable sources. A detailed denunciation to the Inquisition by Salvatore Panettino concerning three secret conventicles held by Calvinists in Faenza in 1566 mentioned the name of a certain Girolamo Bertani, who each year went to Geneva to purchase books and occasionally returned with a "reader," a catechist. It would have been possible for Girolamo, who was called "bishop of the sect,"[28] or others among the roughly fifty citizens of Faenza who professed themselves to be Calvinists, to travel to the Waldensian valleys for the synods and other important gatherings.

Our discussion of the penetration and impact of the Reformation in Piedmont would be incomplete without a glance at the entourage of Marguerite de Valois, the duke's consort. Fortunately, Arturo Pascal left a precise description based on a close examination of the correspondence of the papal nuncios to Turin between 1560 and 1580.[29] Among those mentioned in the dispatches are the treasurer Jean de Brosses,

---

[27]G. Jalla, *Storia* 1:354–56.

[28]F. Lanzoni, "I nuovi documenti sui 'Luterani faentini,'" *Bollettino diocesano di Faenza* 14 (1927), n. 4:85.

[29]Cf. A. Pascal, "La lotta contro la Riforma in Piemonte al tempo di Emanuele Filiberto, studiata nelle relazioni diplomatiche tra la Corte sabauda e la Santa Sede (1559–80)," *Bulletin de la Société d'Histoire Vaudoise*, n. 53 (1939): 10–12 (document 47).

seigneur of Tournay, who later found refuge with his wife in Geneva; the lady-in-waiting Claudia Boratto of Caraglio; Marguerite's personal physician, Charles de Rochefort, the baron of St. Angel, who also repaired to Geneva with his wife; Moreille de Châteauneuf, lady of Théobon; Mons. de Boivin, agent of the king of France; Mons. de la Forea, Huguenot exile; Antonio Berscetto, lord of Montigny, who, if the nuncio had not intervened against him, would have become the tutor to the duke's young heir, Charles Emanuel; the jurist Della Maddalena and Captain Salviano Marsigliano, both Huguenots; Mons. Di Giolì, the duchess's secretary; the *seigneurs* of Senantes and of Contrelor, suspected of being Protestant ministers masquerading as merchants; the *seigneur* Carboneraro, of whom it was insinuated that he had been sent by Beza to console Jacqueline de Coligny, the widow of admiral Gaspar de Coligny, the first illustrious victim of the St. Bartholomew's Day Massacre (1572), whose arrest the duke ordered as she was on her way home to reclaim her paternal inheritance.

A number of proud, resolute women populated the court in Turin. Despite their apparent Calvinism, the duke, even though spurred by the reiterated protests of the pope, did not succeed in expelling them out of respect to his wife and to the court of France. The countess of Tenda, Margherita di Saluzzo-Cardé, known as the lady of Thermes since she had married Paul de la Barthe, *seigneur* of Thermes, was a fervent Huguenot who had joined the Waldensian church and attended its ceremonies in the Val Luserna. Her retinue included Anne of Cardé, the wife of Giacomo di Saluzzo-Cardé, a Huguenot captain, and their daughters; Lady Liptof, the wife of one of the lords of Montafia; *mademoiselle* de Péguigny and Jacqueline d'Entremont, who later married Coligny. The entire time that they were at court in Turin and in Piedmont, despite their promise to conceal their true evangelical sentiments, the entourage of the duchess took advantage of their intimacy with her to forge links with French and Swiss Protestantism, to the Huguenot party, and to those families of the Piedmontese nobility, such as the Solaro of Moretta and the Solaro of Villanova, who sympathized with or actively supported the Reformation. These courtiers were bound by a network of family relationships and a communality of interests that helped them to ward off repressive action on the part of the duke, of which confiscation of property was one of the most feared measures. As members of the nobility and persons of great prestige, they played a significant role in the diffusion of Reformation doctrines, much greater than what can be deduced from the dispatches known to us, namely the letters of the papal nuncios. Vincenzo Lauro, the bishop of Mantua, who served as papal legate to Savoy from 1568 to 30 March 1569, thus wrote to Cardinal Alessandrino in Rome:

> I have also discovered that with the Countess of Tenda there is a French doctor of jurisprudence called Mons. della Maddalena, who practices the law and serves as minister; and there must also be some others with madame of Montafia and madame of Termes. Although these persons are frequently very ignorant, nevertheless, once they have read the catechism of Calvin, they become unrestrained preachers, and for them it suffices to

upbraid and calumniate Catholics and the truth. As long as those women remain here, I for one will never believe that they can restrain themselves from having their secret suppers and sermons. And as I recently told the duke, who had persuaded himself that they were observing the faith and that no performance of the new cult was taking place, when people take up with this sect, you cannot believe anything that they promise, since the Devil keeps them bound in such a guise that they do not even want to practice their false religion, but persuade themselves *"se obsequium praestare Deo"* to deceive his highness so as to bring about the ruin of the Catholic religion. We have already before our eyes the example of Flanders, and even worse of France....[30]

The nuncio did his utmost to have these courtiers expelled. He also placed high hopes in the fall of Geneva, breeding ground of heresy, from which pernicious doctrines emanated and spread throughout Christianity, together with books supporting these beliefs, which circulated in large numbers and had even penetrated the convents. During the time of its greatest success in Piedmont, children's education assumed a high priority, evidence of the consolidation and institutionalization of the reformed movement. Three Italian versions of the *Catechism*, Calvin's religious primer appeared in print. The first one, translated by Giulio Domenico Gallo of Caramagna (Cuneo) and printed at Geneva in 1545, was anonymous and lacked typographical information to facilitate its circulation in Italy. The second edition, printed in 1551, is identical to the first, but reveals the name of the translator. It is dedicated to Countess Maria Valperga di Montevé (or Montué) de' Gabbi. She should be identified as Maria Provana di Leinì, daughter of Giacomo, married to George II, count of Valperga and Montué, who was governor of Ivrea in 1544. This dedication, omitted in the first edition, is significant because it suggests that the noblewoman was sympathetic to the Genevan version of the Reformation. She was probably also a friend of the Calvinist noble ladies at court, and the translator, who knew her well, could write enthusiastically that the small book "contained the sum of celestial wisdom" and whoever received it entered "in the holy Catholic church."[31] The third edition was seen through the press by the Lucchese Niccolò Balbani, pastor of the Italian exiles' church in Geneva, who prefaced the volume with an epistle (dated Geneva, 1 August 1566), "To the Faithful of Italy." The nuncio almost certainly was referring to this version. Balbani's missive evokes the precarious state of the Reformation movement in the peninsula, afflicted by persecutions and the refusal of

---

[30]Ibid., 75–76.

[31]*Catechismo, cio è formulario per amaestrare i fanciulli nella Christiana religione: Fatto in modo di dialogo, ove il Ministro della chiesa dimanda, e 'l fanciullo risponde. Composto in latino e francese per M. Gioanni Calvino e tradotto fedelmente in italiano per G. Domenico Gallo Caramagnese* (N.P.: Per Adamo e Giovanni Riveriz frategli, 1551), 8. We know very little about the translator, who must have enjoyed the confidence of the Genevan Consistory since he was permitted to translate, in addition to the *Catechismo*, Calvin's *La forma delle preghiere ecclesiastiche* (Geneva: Per Adamo e Giovanni Riveriz frategli, 1551). Scholars have only paid attention to the first edition of the *Catechismo*, where one can read in the preface interpolations

princes to allow the establishment of regularly constituted communities where the Word of God could be freely preached, the sacraments administered, and children and converts educated.

Balbani's experiences in his native Lucca, at Bologna, and at Ferrara, where he graduated with a degree in both canon and civil law, at Lyons, and in his daily dealings with exiles, provided him with a realistic picture of the situation in Italy. He made several suggestions in his epistle for ways to keep the faith alive: organize secret congregations, where he who has received the gift "purely expounds the Word of God, administers the sacraments according to the ordination of Jesus Christ, and in the name of the entire company offers public prayers to God." But, he cautions, princes would be suspicious of these secret congregations and consider them a danger to the state. The best solution would be freedom of conscience and freedom to preach, as was the case in many parts of Europe. Unfortunately this was impossible in Italy, since "the Antichrist reigns whose power and tyranny fills the Princes of this earth with fear."[32] Thus Balbani ended his remarks by reiterating Sleidan's judgment about the indispensable role of politics in the Reformation.

In the Ghetto of the Waldensian Valleys

On 14 December 1562, the duke of Savoy reentered Turin, after almost thirty years of French occupation, and finally received the total restitution of his duchy, with the exception of Pinerolo. By this date the Protestant movement had touched all levels of society, from the nobility to the peasants in the valleys, from professional people to merchants and laborers. Including the marquisate of Saluzzo, which would remain under French sovereignty until 1601, the physician of Busca suggested in his letter mentioned earlier that the number of faithful in Piedmont might total forty thousand. This figure cannot be too far off the mark. We know of the organized communities and prominent personages, whose independence and rebellion against the levies of the ecclesiastical hierarchy frequently met with the approval, not untainted by considerations of an economic nature, of their subordinates. Moreover, an anonymous mass, fluctuating between dissent and conformity, made up of schoolteachers, booksellers, students, monks, merchants, foresters, patrician ladies, and common folk existed in Turin and in other large urban centers. Whether consciously or inadvertently, either out of sympathy or aversion, during their moves from one place to another, many of them brought news of the successes of the Reformation in

---

from the preface by Juan de Valdés to his own children's religious primer, perhaps printed in the same year, 1545 (see J. C. Nieto, "The Christian Instruction for Children," in *Two Catechisms*, 24–25). In the 1551 edition these interpolations disappeared from the preface and were replaced by the dedication to Countess Maria Valperga, about whom cf. G. Vernazza, "Genealogia patria," vol. 30, plate 11, Turin, Biblioteca Reale, MS 80.

[32]Quoted from C. Ginzburg in *DBI*, 5:339.

neighboring states, of the civil wars in France and Huguenot victories, and of the flourishing Waldensian communities closely associated with Geneva.

A few of the most daring among them were caught by the Inquisition. One was a schoolteacher of Biella, Giorgio Olivetta, who was tried at Vercelli in 1564 and burned alive as a *relapsus* three years later—a consequence of pressure exerted by Pius V. He rejected the commutation of Olivetta's punishment to a galley sentence as requested by the duke and pressed by many of his subjects and moderate elements at court.[33] Another victim was the ex-Franciscan, the Sicilian Gian Tommaso Sirleto, the teacher of the young Bernardino Bonifacio, marquis of Oria, whom he accompanied to Switzerland when, *religionis causa*, Bonifacio had to take leave of his lands in Puglia. Sirleto matriculated at the University of Basel in 1557–58, where he may have been the secretary of Boniface Amerbach, as well as of Bonifacio. Later he returned to Italy and opened a school in Venice. It is not certain if he remained in that city from 1561 until 1570, the year he was arrested in Turin and extradited to Rome. At the conclusion of his trial, he seems to have evaded a death sentence by abjuring.[34]

In the two decades from 1560 to 1580, Emanuel Philibert, with the ability, shrewdness, force, and cruelty of a true Renaissance prince, largely accomplished the plan he had nurtured from the day he had regained possession of his lands, the systematic destruction of the Protestant communities, a story that has been told with a wealth of detail by Giovanni Jalla and Arturo Pascal. Even the marquisate of Saluzzo, where the application of the older laws favoring evangelicals was continually being disregarded through ducal and papal intervention, had all its reformed churches thrown into disarray by the edicts issued by the duke of Nevers on 10 and 19 October 1567. The new provisions called for the banishment of all the pastors since they were not natives of the area and of any of the faithful who had not been born in the marquisate, or were the subjects of foreign rulers. These dispositions resulted in the serious reduction of persons committed to the pursuit of their freedom of conscience, as a notable increase in the flow of Piedmontese emigrés to Geneva developed from the 1550s forward, including twenty-one heads of families from Chieri alone arriving between 1568 and 1597. The Piedmontese population who had expatriated to the redoubt of Calvinism by the end of the century would total two thousand souls.

A sizable residue of Waldensian peasants, the "Israel of the Alps," with their pastors and schoolteachers, remained confined to their valleys. They continued to be conscious of their ideological bond with the Protestant churches of Europe, and their institutional ties to Geneva and Lausanne, despite the hostility of the dukes of Savoy, whose attempts to reconquer Geneva at the beginning of the next century concluded with the miserable failure of the celebrated *Escalade* in 1602.

[33]G. Jalla, *Storia* 1:259–60.
[34]Ibid., 293–94.

BIBLIOGRAPHICAL NOTE

For the encounter of Waldensians with the Reformation, in addition to the works cited in the notes, the following offer a rich bibliography: J. Gonnet–A. Molnár, *Les Vaudois au Moyen âge* (Turin: Claudiana, 1974); A. Molnár, *Storia dei Valdesi, I: Dalle origini all'adesione alla Riforma* (Turin: Claudiana, 1974); A. Armand Hugon, *Storia dei Valdesi, II: Dal sinodo di Chanforan all'Emancipazione* (Turin: Claudiana, 1974).

For G. Farel and the Waldensians, cf. G. Audisio, *Les Vaudois, ad indicem.*

For the presence of the two, probably Italian, monks at the assembly of Chanforan, cf. G. Audisio, *Le barbe et l'inquisiteur: Procès du barbe Vaudois Pierre Griot par l'inquisiteur Jean de Roma (Apt. 1532)* (Aix-en-Provence: Edisud, 1979), 183–86.

The mission to convert Waldensians entrusted to the Jesuits by Emanuel Philibert is well documented by R. De Simone, *Tre anni decisivi di storia valdese: Missioni, repressione e tolleranza nelle valli piemontesi dal 1559 al 1561*; Analecta Gregoriana, 97, Sectio B, n. 19 (Rome, 1958).

On the final decades of existence of the evangelical churches in Saluzzo, cf. D. Bouteroue, *Discorso breve delle persecuzioni occorse in questo tempo alle Chiese del Marchesato di Saluzzo (1620)*, a cura di E. Balmas e G. Zardini Lana (Turin: Claudiana, 1978)

Theodore Beza's homage to Waldensian martyrs in his *Icones* (1580).

IO

ITALY'S OTHER GATEWAY: THE ISTRIA OF THE VERGERIO BROTHERS

THE REFORM EFFORTS OF BISHOPS GIOVAN BATTISTA AND PIER PAOLO VERGERIO

IF THE WALDENSIAN VALLEYS were Calvinism's gateway into Italy, Istria was a great open door for the penetration of Lutheran doctrines. Venetian Istria bordered several Habsburg dominions, Styria, Carniola, and Carinthia, favorable to the Lutheran Reformation, supported by members of the nobility and bourgeoisie. At Lubiana a Lutheran conventicle had formed as early as 1527. The *Confessio Augustana* had spread so widely that in 1578, Duke Charles of Habsburg, faced by the tenacious resistance of the population, made the commitment to respect its freedom of belief (religious pacification of Bruck). During the entire century, this strip of Venetian territory experienced a period of grave economic depression, a consequence of the war between Venice and the Empire that concluded with the Treaty of Worms in 1521. The plague, malaria, loss of population, conflicts among the clergy over benefices that constituted a major source of income, and the abandonment of many dioceses by their bishops created a desolate situation. The spiritual needs of the people were tended by a few parish priests, who shared their miserable lives and administered the sacraments with some regularity, and by the many confraternities dispersed in the four dioceses of Capodistria, Pola, Parenzo, and Cittanova.

The Roman Curia was preoccupied with the looming threat from the very first appearances of the religious dissent. The Venetian nuncio, Girolamo Aleandro, in a dispatch to the papal secretary in Rome, Pietro Carnesecchi, dated 28 January 1534, described the spread of the Protestant penetration, and confirmed the proselytizing of Bartolomeo Fonzio and his followers:

> We have recently discovered that in a territory of this [Venetian] state called Pirano, the majority of the population and its leading citizens are Lutheran. And we fear that the same is true for the neighboring areas bordering Germany and Hungary, where the heresy was born more than four years ago

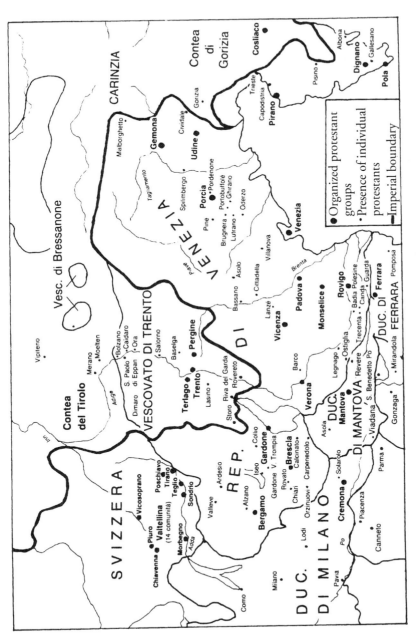

Northeastern Italy, Switzerland, and Imperial Territories

and grows more and more each day. Finally this past Christmas, the situation became even more public thanks to the preaching of two Minorite monks, one a Catholic Observant and the other a Conventual, the latter a disciple of that Bartolomeo Fonzio who fled to Germany as a consequence of this heresy....[1]

The nuncio's worries were primarily political and focused on the hesitation of the Venetian *Signoria* to take rigorous measures: only yesterday it had been forbearing in the case of Girolamo Galateo, not realizing that heresy could provoke an uprising by a populace always ready to seize one occasion or the other to incite a tumult and to loot under its cover. Some months later, Pier Paolo Vergerio, papal legate in Germany, after hearing what was happening in his native Istria, wrote in alarm to Carnesecchi:

> I have learned that in Trieste, a city in our Italy situated on the shores of our Adriatic, Lutheranism is germinating, brought by commerce with Germany.... Furthermore, I hear that this plague has gone out from Trieste and attacked a castle [fortified town] called Pirano, where a number of ribald people are going about in the open contaminating the souls of simple people. Monsignor, I know the nature of that country, for it is my native land. If the Lutheran sect takes hold among such simplicity of intellect.... Your Reverence will soon see (but God avert it!) all the contiguous provinces and regions infected and corrupted.... I say, Monsignor, that nothing is more important today than this, and if such people go unpunished, all Istria, all of Italy will be imperilled....[2]

Due to the unceasing traffic of persons coming from adjacent areas where the liturgical reforms and the renewal of preaching were becoming established under the impetus of events in Germany and the diffusion of books by Luther and his associates, especially Melanchthon, it was indeed difficult to prevent comparisons from being made with local conditions. It was obvious that discussions would ensue about the need to reform the Church of Rome. The urgency of this responsibility was recognized as their pastoral duty by two brothers, Giovan Battista Vergerio (d. 1548), bishop of Pola from 1532, and Pier Paolo Vergerio (1498–1565), named bishop of Capodistria after his return from his German nunciature. The two belonged to a distinguished family of Capodistria, who numbered among their ancestors the humanist Pier Paolo Vergerio, the Elder (1370–1444). Their ecclesiastical careers were advanced by their brother, Aurelio, a secretary in Clement VII's Curia.

The bishop of Pola dedicated himself to bringing order to his diocese, striving energetically to reform the deplorable condition of the clergy and restore discipline to the religious houses. If the acts of the diocesan synod he held in 1536 were extant, scholars would be in a better position to weigh whether the reforming program was limited to the morality of ecclesiastics and disorder in worship, or if it also touched

---

[1] F. Gaeta, "Documenti da codici Vaticani," 14 (cited at chap. 4, note 15).
[2] Ibid., 17. The English translation is from A. J. Schutte, *Pier Paolo Vergerio*, 76–77.

preaching and the liturgy. In his lifetime, despite the controversies surrounding his brother, Giovan Battista was never accused of heresy. But it is certain that he favored the preaching of Baldo Lupatino, who from 1539 to 1541 was active in the diocese and on the island of Cherso. The canon of Dignano, Pasquale Velico, tried as a suspected Lutheran in 1548, stated that Lupatino's ideas did not differ much from the bishop's. There is little doubt that Giovan Battista had become convinced along with his brother, and many other ecclesiastics in the diocese, of the scriptural basis for justification by faith alone. And in 1572, after two decades of unceasing accusations against his memory from Girolamo Muzio, he was disinterred and his bones cast into the sea.

The personality of Pier Paolo, one of the leading figures in the Italian Reformation, was much more complicated. He was not a theologian of the stature of Peter Martyr Vermigli, nor a preacher with the appeal of a Bernardino Ochino, but a great popularizer, a "journalist," capable of grasping facets of daily life and exploiting their propaganda value. Vergerio did not write for educated persons, but addressed himself to the more humble and yet literate spheres in the population. To those who reprimanded him for his superficiality and for the vulgarity of his attacks, he replied unperturbed that his "little books" were not the solid food of doctrine, but "milk to nourish and instruct those who were still weak and rough."[3]

Pier Paolo obtained a law degree at age twenty, and was called to teach civil law at the University of Padua, where he had studied. His decision to dedicate himself to the ecclesiastical life came after the death of his wife, Diana Contarini. Thanks to the influence of his brothers Aurelio and Giovan Battista, he was sent by Clement VII as nuncio to Ferdinand, archduke of Austria. Word of the favorable impression he made at the Viennese court spread widely, inducing the humanist Aonio Paleario to preface his *De animorum immortalitate* (Lyons, 1536) with a letter addressed to Vergerio, beseeching him to present his poem to Ferdinand, king of the Romans, Hungary and Bohemia, to whom it was dedicated.

Following this assignment, Vergerio was appointed nuncio to Germany by Paul III with the mission of communicating to the German princes the convening of a council at Mantua, and obtaining their consent to the choice of the site. From this vantage point he became personally acquainted with the country where the Reformation had originated and become established. He began to realize that the movement of protest had not simply originated with "monkish quarrels," but from the profound longing for the renewal of the entire Christian church.

When Vergerio returned to Capodistria in 1540, of which he had been named bishop in 1536, and embarked, along with his brother, on the reform of his diocese, he undoubtedly shared with Gasparo Contarini and the "*spirituali*" a vision of a rejuvenated church and of reconciliation with the Protestants. Vergerio's contacts in these years with Vittoria Colonna, Renée of France, Eleonora Gonzaga, and Marguerite de Navarre impelled him to seek out in the Scriptures the sources for the doctrine of justification by faith and the election of believers. He thus began to cultivate the

---

[3]E. Comba, *I nostri protestanti*, 459.

Erasmian dream of the reunification of the body of Christ by means of a universal council, and gave his support to the Lutheran aspiration of representing the Augsburg Confession at this gathering. Vergerio, in his treatise *De unitate et pace Ecclesiae*, which circulated in manuscript at the Diet of Worms in 1541, and was printed at Venice the following year, invited Catholics and Protestants alike to remain united in Christ as head of the church, "who is our reconciliation and our peace."[4]

When Vergerio took possession of his diocese, he labored to eradicate the brambles from the vineyard that the Lord had entrusted to him. The bishop viewed the prevalent abuses, popular superstitions, cultic excesses, and corrupt morals as the clear consequence of the absence of preaching based on the Scriptures. Influenced by his reading of Erasmus and the works of the reformers, with the zeal and occasional verbal indiscretions that came naturally to his impetuous character, he embarked on a program to edify his flock founded on the Bible, directed especially against the cult of saints which he perceived overshadowed the person of Jesus Christ. Vergerio, in line with his catechetical instruction directed towards a return to the teachings of the apostolic church, found it useful to promote the circulation of the *Beneficio di Cristo* and the *Sommario della santa Scrittura*. His efforts met with favor from the more enlightened clergy and schoolteachers, as well as among humbler segments of society, downtrodden by poverty and spiritual abandonment, but it provoked hostility from those who felt they were singled out as ignorant, swindlers, or concubinaries.

The accusations of heresy made against Vergerio, the "Lutheran bishop," interrupted a reforming campaign that might have given a different physiognomy to the church in Istria, without causing it to break with Rome. The Vergerio brothers were attempting to institute in their dioceses, which included the more progressive cities of the area such as Capodistria, Pirano, Pola, and Albona, the basic aspects of the Catholic reform being promoted by Cardinals Contarini, Pole, and Fregoso, complemented by the central demands of the Lutheran Reformation: the return to Holy Scripture and justification by faith alone.

Thus, it appears that between the years 1546 and 1548, the bishop of Capodistria nurtured a project to reform the church in Istria and Friuli, separating these regions, if necessary, from Roman obedience. He could harbor such hopes because he knew that the people, including the parish clergy, had welcomed the Lutheran protest. The two brothers Vergerio, seeing in the Austrian dominions of Carniola, Carinthia, and Styria, where the Augsburg Confession had spread widely, freedom from tithes and payment for performance of the sacraments, the abolition of clerical celibacy, and the forced reclusion of women in convents must have thought that the time was ripe for reform.

The Vergerian program implied the acceptance of principles that were strenuously opposed by the Catholic controversialists and by the hierarchy. On 2 January 1546, the nuncio to Venice Giovanni Della Casa ordered judicial proceedings to begin against the bishop of Capodistria, and he, in fact, presented himself before the Inquisition in Venice on 10 June of that year. Unfortunately, the records of this first

---

[4]E. Comba, *I nostri protestanti*, 412.

appearance are not extant. In the following months Vergerio submitted his first defenses in writing, but did not succeed in being received by the conciliar fathers who had been meeting in Trent since December 1545. Having abandoned all hope of being absolved, and convinced by now, after having witnessed the death throes of Francesco Spiera, that compromise between his convictions and obedience to the pope meant to reject Christ, in May 1549 Vergerio took flight and found refuge first in Poschiavo, in the Valtellina, where a part of the population had espoused the Reformation.

Anyone wishing to penetrate Vergerio's thought two months after his apostasy, instead of turning to his *Otto defensioni*, which reproduce the defense he prepared at his trial, should read his *Il Catalogo de libri…condannati et scomunicati per heretici, da M. Giovan Della Casa*, well known for the rich information it contains on the Italian diffusion of heretical literature. The booklet was completed on 3 July 1549 and dedicated: "To the Christian brethren, elect and children of God."

The polemical themes of this small work rest on four main arguments: (1) The Augsburg *Interim* of 1548, with which Charles V had made only exceedingly modest concessions to the Lutherans (the chalice to the faithful in the Lord's Supper and the permission of marriage to priests) while awaiting the decisions of the Council, recognized certain errors in the Church of Rome; (2) by denouncing Pope Hadrian VI, the church itself had recognized its errors; (3) the church had condemned the writings of those who, from Erasmus to Luther, wanted to reform it; and (4) the truth of the Gospel would triumph because God would not abandon his elect. From the observations Vergerio interspersed between his clarifications of the significance of the condemned works, it can be deduced that he accepted fully the two fundamental principles of the Reformation, the supreme authority of Holy Scripture, and justification by faith alone: "If they should take everything from us," he writes, "the Gospel suffices, and if they should take even this from us, at least they cannot deprive us of the Gospel engraved in our hearts by the Holy Spirit." Justification by faith alone must be "pure" and it must be preached purely and not, as some would have it, "mingling the worth of our own works with freely given reconciliation."

This had become the line of demarcation separating the Catholic evangelism of Contarini and Pole from the positions of all Protestant theologians, including the most irenic of all, Melanchthon. In his booklet Vergerio repeatedly demonstrated an unconditional admiration, both for his *Loci communes* as well as for the *Confessio Augustana*, a copy of which had been personally given to Vergerio by the German reformer. With the eye of the seasoned diplomat and statesman Vergerio sought to evaluate the forces at work, and despite Germany's precarious situation after the defeat of the Schmalkaldic League and the about-face of Maurice of Saxony, was convinced that there could be no turning back. The goals of the Reformation were being pursued by many valiant writers: "It is no longer possible for these books to be banned; the thing has gone too far; let them think of something else, such as giving in to the truth, and begin to correct errors and superstitions." The "true Christian" will not give in now, just as Pietro Cittadella (Speciale) and Baldo Lupatino of Albona also had never given in. The churches of the Reformation had the future before them. The innovators quite opportunely were dedicating themselves to compiling catechisms for children so that they might be educated in scriptural truth, rejecting "lies, idolatry, and priestly impiety." [5]

It was clear by now, continued Vergerio, that pope and bishops wanted neither reform nor councils. The church, by consenting to and maintaining abuses that had already been condemned on so many occasions, including by the *De emendanda Ecclesia*, by not providing the sacraments and even burial to the poor who could not pay for them, was no longer a catholic church. The true catholic church had remained faithful to the truth of the Gospels and of the apostolic credo. In this situation, it was up to the Italian princes "to provide for the health, safety and tranquillity of their people without further waiting for a council, or reform, or any provision from the pope, and they were held to this and obliged to it by both divine and human laws."[6] Vergerio, with his gaze fixed towards his homeland, dreamed that the Venetian senate would convene "a council and begin a reformation of its churches." He repeated now, more explicitly, what he had augured in his oration at the time of the election of Doge Francesco Donato (December 1545), that Italian rulers, with Venetians in the lead, would assume responsibility for a Reformation, as had happened in Germany and elsewhere in Europe. Italian reformers, especially Venetians and Istrians, clung to this illusion tenaciously to the end of the century.

THE "BISHOP OF CHRIST"

Vergerio became convinced, because of the persecutions he had experienced, that he was one of the elect, and conceived of himself as a "bishop of Christ," summoned to the arduous task of converting his fellow Italians and destroying the power of the Antichrist.

At Poschiavo, where Vergerio found an organized Protestant parish under the ministry of Giulio della Rovere who received him warmly, he lent his support through preaching and through his polemical writings. When Vergerio learned that the community of Vicosoprano, founded in 1529 by the ex-Dominican Bartolomeo Maturo, was searching for a pastor, the ambitious former papal nuncio, who had been the guest of Ferdinand at the Viennese court, and honored by German princes as well as by Marguerite of Navarre, the sister of Francis I, did not hesitate for an instant before accepting this modest post in a tiny village nestled in the Rhetian Alps. Vergerio was received kindly by the people, honored to have as their pastor a former bishop who had renounced his exalted position for the sake of the Gospel.

For four years this "exile for Christ" carried on a frenetic activity as preacher and polemicist. He wrote some forty pamphlets and booklets to denounce the spiritual

---

[5] *Il Catalogo de libri, li quali nuovamente nel mese di Maggio nell'anno presente MDXLVIIII sono stati condannati et scomunicati per heretici, da M. Giovan Della Casa legato di Vinetia, et d'alcuni frati: È aggiunto sopra il medesimo Catalogo un iudicio et discorso del Vergerio* (N.P., 1549). The last sentence refers (chap. 6, note 33) to Valdés's brief catechism for children, which Vergerio translated into Latin in 1554.
[6] Ibid.

dangers and injurious political consequences of dissimulation and of Nicodemism, taking his message from the tragic end of Francesco Spiera, punished by God for having defected from the truth. Through the press of Dolfino Landolfi in Poschiavo Vergerio hurled his missiles against the Council of Trent and those bishops who, although they had found the truth in Scripture, lacked the courage to proclaim it publicly. Despite some ambiguity on his part concerning the possibilities of a "free" council in which all the Reformation churches would participate, in view of the imminent reconvening of the Council of Trent, the ex-bishop of Capodistria's break with the Church of Rome and with the party of the *"spirituali"* was by now irreversible.

Vergerio preached the length and breadth of the Val Bregaglia, assailing superstition by a simple but forceful attack directed against the cult of saints and images. It is difficult to say whether he himself participated in acts of iconoclasm, but certain actions taken by the populace were undoubtedly the consequence of his sermons against the "idolatry" of the Roman church, fomenter of the commerce in relics and pilgrimages to shrines. After a year of activity, he could write to Bullinger on 6 May 1551 that five entire villages now had their own evangelical minister. Even if Vergerio's stay was relatively brief and interrupted by summer travel to Basel, Zurich, and St. Gall, he contributed enormously to the transformation of the Val Bregaglia into a Protestant enclave.

Vergerio's pride and authoritarian ways brought him into occasional conflict with the pastors at Chür, who doubted his willingness to enter into dialogue even with persons unsympathetic to the increasingly rigid evangelical confessions of faith; but the synod of Chür, which supervised the reformed communities of the Val Bregaglia, acknowledged his zeal, sincerity, and upright morality. Together with the majority of Italian Protestants who wanted to establish the Reformation at home, Vergerio was hostile to theological debates over subtle points of doctrine because he sensed that they might lead to the further splintering of the movement. He was convinced that there had to be a united front against the Antichrist and his acolytes, while he himself was drawing ever closer to Melanchthonian irenicism. In 1553 his brief but intense pastorate in the Valtellina came to an end. Vergerio accepted the invitation from Duke Christoph of Württemberg to come to Tübingen as his theological counselor, thereby realizing his dream of laboring for the Reformation in the service of a Protestant prince. He was thus returning to his political vocation, but with the spirit of the evangelical missionary. Lutheran doctrines had been introduced in the duchy by Johann Brenz, Luther's friend and disciple, and Vergerio found himself comfortable with the climate of religious moderation created by Brenz and the duke.

Vergerio, now fifty-five years old, but still a source of inexhaustible energy, made the University of Tübingen the center of his political and publicistic activity. He returned to the highways which he had traveled as a young diplomat in the service of the Church of Rome, now to forge an alliance among the enemies of the papacy. He journeyed throughout Germany, Austria, and Poland, where he labored to consolidate the Reformation in vain, attempting to unite Calvinists, Lutherans, and Czech brethren on the basis of the *Augsburg Confession*. In the spring of 1558, returning from Vienna, where he had been received amicably by Maximilian of Austria, he surreptitiously attended a reunion of family and old friends near Trieste, not far from his own Capodistria.

Vergerio's activity as publicist and polemicist drew renewed vigor from an unexpected source. The Slovenian priest Primus Trubar (1508–86), who had studied at Fiume and later served the reform-minded Bishop Bonomo at Trieste, settled at Nuremberg in 1548. Twelve years before, in 1536, as a preacher in the cathedral at Lubiana in 1536, he had been accused of heresy because of his attacks on popular superstitions. After he found refuge in Germany he began to translate religious works into the Slovenian language. Vergerio, whom he might have met years earlier in Trieste, persuaded him to include the New Testament in his translation program, and also introduced him to Baron Johannes Ungnad von Sonneck (1493–1564), former governor of Styria and Carinthia. After becoming a convert to the Reformation, Ungnad had settled at Urach, near Tübingen, determined to dedicate his life and his resources to the diffusion of the Scriptures in his old homelands. For this purpose, he set up a printing press and a Biblical institute. With the collaboration of Vergerio, Trubar, the Istrian Stefan Konsul, and the Dalmatian Antonio D'Alessandro, the Urach establishment became a vital missionary center. In three years alone, from 1561 to 1564, it published thirty-seven books, six in Italian, for a total of more than twenty-five thousand copies.

Luther's short *Catechism*, the *Confessio Augustana*, Johann Brenz's *Postils* were printed in Croatian and Slovenian. The first two works, together with the *Apology* for the *Augsburg Confession*, as well as the *Beneficio di Cristo* appeared in Italian. This famous little booklet seemed the most appropriate for the purpose of proselytization, and was printed also in Croatian with Latin and Glagolitic characters. Vergerio's promotion of the *Beneficio* and the *Catechism* of Valdés, which he translated into Latin, as well as of the latter's *Considerations*, which he had printed in Basel, expressed his great admiration for the Spaniard, whose thought he viewed as an original contribution to the Reformation.

The Diffusion of the Reformation in Istria

The endurance of Vergerio's legacy in Istria came out at the inquest conducted by Annibale Grisonio, the papal commissioner assigned inquisitorial powers over all of Istria as a continuation of the trial against the former bishop of Capodistria. Grisonio, a canon in the city, denounced from the pulpit of the cathedral those foolhardy readers of the Scriptures lacking the necessary understanding, who had been led astray by the nefarious bishop. For Grisonio, this unlawful reading of the vernacular Bible was the root of the present evil. As Vergerio would later write, "In one of his sermons, not only did he [Grisonio] try to dissuade us from reading the Gospels, but he showed so much fear of the Word of God as to counsel our womenfolk that it was better for them to read the *Cento novelle*, Ariosto, and Petrarch; these books, he added, may make you licentious, but the Gospel will turn you into heretics."[7]

The early results of Grisonio's investigation, begun in December 1548, brought out the gravity of the situation. A Milanese salesman of varnishes, a certain Ambrogio, testified that in Dignano and Pola the majority of the population was "Lutheran." Even shepherds and peasants openly discussed these scathing topics. In the diocese of Pola, several canons were accused: Michele Parenzani, Marino de Marini, Giovanni Poteto, Michele Schiomena, Biagio Tesser, parish priest of Gallesano, and the priests Pasqualino of Momarano and Pasqualino Velico of Dignano. All were tried and abjured their errors between March and August 1549. Their statements furnished an unvarnished picture of their Lutheran beliefs. Marino declared, without hesitation, "I have believed and stated that we are saved by the blood of Christ, not by our works, but by Christ."[8]

All the accused were opposed to pilgrimages to the Madonna of Loreto, to the cult of images, to ex-voto offerings and to prayers for the dead, just as their bishop, Vergerio, had been. In the spirit of Luther's forty-third thesis, he had proclaimed to a poverty-stricken population that it was better to assist the indigent than squander money on indulgences. In general, they all believed in the presence of Christ in the elements of the Eucharist, also the position of the *Augsburg Confession*. At that embryonic stage of the movement, differences of opinion were not lacking. In a group of Dignano, for example, it is known that one Giovanni de Paolis, known as Pellizzaro (furrier), possessed a copy of Calvin's *Institutes*. Their leader, Biagio Tesser, "priest Biasio," one morning proclaimed at the celebration of the mass: "Up to now, we have all been deceived in believing that here is the body of Christ. I want you to understand that it is not, but that it is in the heavens, and this host is nothing but a piece of blessed bread that Christ left to his disciples...."[9]

The trial instituted by Grisonio concluded with a few sentences to exile or the galleys, but did not eradicate the dissent at the root. In April 1554, Albona, in the diocese of Pola, received the close scrutiny of the inquisitor for Istria and Dalmatia, and despite the efforts of the people and many eminent families to shield their heretical fellow citizens, great lapses on the part of the clergy came to light. Of the four priests who had ceased celebrating mass, two had fled the city and the others responded evasively. But one of them, Giovanni Pagovic, could not resist mocking the inquisitor. When asked about the existence of Purgatory, "the place where souls go to be purged," he replied, "I do not know because I have never been there." He was more explicit about justification and the intercession of the saints, with this fine rejoinder: "I do not see anyone else as our advocate except Christ crucified...."[10] On twenty-five occasions he refused to answer whether he believed that Christ was

---

[7]L. A. Ferrai, "Gli eretici di Capodistria," in *Studi storici* (Padua & Verona: Drucker, 1892), 184.
[8]A. Pitassio, "Diffusione e tramonto della Riforma in Istria," 41 (cited chap. 4, note 24).
[9]Ibid., 43.
[10]Ibid., 47–49.

present in the consecrated host. On 20, May failing to appear before the tribunal in Pola, he was sentenced contumaciously.

Apart from Anabaptist infiltrations in the castle of Cosliaco, in that part of Istria under Austrian domination, the feudal holding of Francesco Barbo who became Vergerio's collaborator in 1563 in the diffusion of heretical literature, the tenacious hold of Lutheranism in Istria was demonstrated by a new trial begun in January 1580 by the Apostolic Visitor, Agostino Valier, bishop of Verona. The defendant was an Albanian shoemaker, a member of the Cosliaco community, which had been organized and was guided by its pastor, Matthew Zivcic. The judicial proceeding was the vehicle for recapturing the thread of the movement at Dignano, in which Biagio Tesser and Pasqualino Velico reappear at a distance of thirty years. The latter, after his first trial, had organized a clandestine group with the connivance of the local priest, Paolo de Paolis, winning over to his ideas a family of Greek origin, Marco, called Callegher (or Callegaro), because he was a shoemaker (*calzolaio*), and his sons, Andrea, Francesco, Santo, and all his relatives. Many of the accused, part of the Dignano group, responded fully during their interrogations, thereby hoping for a full pardon or at least milder sentences. From their testimony, we can reconstruct their beliefs and how they were passed on to scantily educated or illiterate persons such as Marco Callegaro. The latter, however, thanks to his cobbler's trade, traveled about widely with his sons, visiting Albona, Pola, Pisino, Fiume, Cosliaco, and Lubiana, expanding his views to the point where he could instruct his family.

Thus contacts were established with heterodox groups in these localities, and Bibles and other books were purchased. To the humble artisans who gathered around the Callegaro family, Priest Pasqualino Velico read the Bible, Vergerio's pamphlets, Luther's easier writings, and perhaps, as Armando Pitassio believes, also taught the first rudiments of reading. Marco Callegaro, in the evening, after his work, at the table, or before the warmth of the hearth, tried to explain to his family and neighbors what he had learned from Velico. Despite the intervention of the inquisitor of Pola in 1569 which concluded with the abjuration of Andrea Callegaro and flight to the Grisons of a certain Gambaletta, the Dignano group continued to grow in the decade of the 1570s, adding such adepts as the furrier Giovanni de Paolis and the Cinei family. De Paolis had been to Gallesano on business, to sew linings in fur coats in the home of a *Messer* Annibale, a Sicilian, who ran an inn frequented by guests of many nationalities. Here he learned Calvinist doctrines. The innkeeper's son possessed a work of Calvin's against the mass; a passing miner, Piero Tenis, had Calvin's *Institutes of the Christian Religion* and a *Summario della vita e della dottrina cristiana della chiesa di Ginevra*. The Dignano evangelical community reached a total of forty members, who annually elected a leader from their midst. Most of them were adroit Nicodemites who attended Catholic services, although almost all were reasonably well acquainted with Protestant doctrine.

The long trial lasting six years reveals, through the testimony of defendants and witnesses, the life of a clandestine community of Lutherans and Calvinists, bound by their fervent anticlericalism and by their conviction that they could judge the doctrines and rites of the Roman church. All were convinced believers in justification by faith alone. The priest Biagio Tesser had taught them that Christ atoned for us on the cross and that Christians are the elect of God. Even more explicitly he affirmed that "only Christ's blood" is the true jubilee, and that the money used to purchase indulgences was used by priests to strut around with their concubines and impoverish the gullible. The cult of saints was of no avail because wooden images cannot intercede. In a milieu of artisans, stone cutters, and peasants, Protestant doctrine was translated into highly efficacious images of daily life.

Marco and Andrea Callegaro for nine or ten years had been instructing Andreolo Cinei, Berto's brother, telling him that "the Mass is a jumble like a salad made up of many sorts of herbs."[11] In his turn, Berto Cinei entertained his friends after the evening meal by reading to them from a Bible he kept hidden in his garden, which he pulled out at opportune moments, and also from a book that he called "Martino" or "Vergerio," probably the Italian translation of Luther's *Small Catechism*. Topics of discussion included the pope, whom they considered the Antichrist, Catholic ceremonies, deemed to be a betrayal of Christ and of the Christian religion, and they read the prophecies of the Old Testament. The book of Baruch was specifically mentioned. After having read the Holy Scriptures, Berto Cinei was quoted as saying: "Now the time has come, as this book states, that the omens will be transformed and will exhibit Christ throughout the earth."[12] He was referring to priestly processions as examples of travestied persons, signifying the rejection of an outward religion and the search for a personal faith.

Priest Pasqualino Velico taught that the host "is a figure of Christ."[13] From the trial records we can deduce that all the accused interpreted the Eucharist spiritually and symbolically. Giovanni de Paolis translated this teaching into popular language, chiding, "Do you believe that the body of Christ is in that host? You are ignoramuses if you believe such a thing!"[14] Nevertheless, the trial succeeded in eradicating heresy from the diocese of Pola. It concluded on 13 March 1584 with the conviction of Andrea Callegaro as a relapsed heretic, sentenced to death by drowning in a Venetian lagoon. Marco and Francesco Callegaro, Giovanni de Paolis, and Andreolo and Berto Cinei received prison terms. A few defendants escaped with simple abjurations. The priest Velico died before he could be tried, and the priest Biagio Tesser went into exile, eventually followed by Giovanni de Paolis.

From abroad, through his unflagging efforts, Vergerio had managed to convert many of his relatives in Capodistria. From Tübingen he bombarded them and their most trusted friends with letters and treatises. On 14 January 1555, for example, he thus exhorted them: "Pray for me, all of you, because I pray for you. Seize the occasions God has offered you, and let one of you every day read from the Scriptures, daily pray together, especially beseeching that our blessed knowledge of God may

---

[11]"Processi di Luteranismo in Istria," *Atti e Memorie della Società Istriana di Archeologia e Storia Patria* 17 (1901–1905): 248.

[12]Ibid., 60.

[13]Ibid., 20 (1904), the trial session of 20 March 1586 involving Francesco Cerdone. The image comes from Calvin's *Institutes* 1:11–13.

[14]"Processi di Luteranismo in Istria," 17 (1901): 285.

grow."[15] Vergerio's nephew, Aurelio, who had served as a *colporteur* of propaganda pamphlets from Germany to Istria, Dalmatia, and the Veneto, abjured solemnly before the Inquisition on 16 May 1557. This defection led to the identification of many leading citizens among the evangelicals, who in turn were compelled to abjure their errors: Ottonello Vida, Giuliano and Dorigo del Bello, Niccolò and Antonio Sabini, Cristoforo and Antonio Apollonio, Giovanni de' Vettori, Girolamo Vergerio, Girolamo Zarotto, Odorico Tofani, and Agostino Sereni. From the Venetian Holy Office records emerge the names of more than one hundred and sixty suspects in Istria, drawn from all ranks in society, but the majority humble working people, of whom many were identified as Lutherans and Calvinists. That writer may be correct who stated that proportionally the Reformation won more followers in Istria than in any other Italian region, when one thinks how small its population was.[16]

As for the rest, this success is explainable, considering the region's proximity to Austrian territories already won to the Protestant cause, and from the fact, unique in Italy, that Luther's basic teachings were preached from the pulpit of the episcopal cathedral. The Vergerio brothers, whose spiritual authority lasted long after their deaths, were the two great missionaries of the movement. The persecutions they had endured seemed to the victims themselves and to their followers a gift from God and a sign of their election.

GIOVANNI BATTISTA GOINEO AND MATTHIAS FLACIUS ILLYRICUS

Giovanni Battista Goineo (1514–78) and Matthias Vlacich (Flacius) (1520–75), two other illustrious sons of this border region, continued to think longingly of Istria and Italy, dreaming of the day when their homeland would be free from the yoke of the Antichrist.

The humanist Goineo's *De Situ Istriae*, finished in exile after 1550, expresses sadness and nostalgia for his beloved homeland. Born at Pirano in a family of means, Goineo studied at Bologna in the Arts Faculty under Romolo Amaseo c. 1530, and had as his companions Arnoldo Arlenio, the future printer to Cosimo I de' Medici, Pier Angeli of Barga, and Francesco Robortello. Here Goineo encountered works by Erasmus, Guillaume Budé, and Étienne Dolet. This was a time, the 1530s, when an Erasmian circle had formed at the university and among the members of Achille Bocchi's Academy. Giovanni Angelo Odoni and his friends were formulating a program of religious reform and were in contact with Martin Bucer. The young Goineo participated in the controversy between Ciceronians and anti-Ciceronians and defended his great teacher Amaseo from the attacks of Sebastiano Corrado. Goineo's *Defensio* was published in 1537. This work, alongside references to Aristotle, Plato, Pico della Mirandola, and Poliziano, emphasizes the guiding value of the Scriptures

[15]Quoted from E. Comba, *I nostri protestanti*, 684.
[16]"Processi di Luteranismo in Istria," 2 (1886): 180.

with a statement that does not seem to be purely rhetorical: *"sine Christo nulla via, nulla veritas est ad salutem."*[17]

After Bologna Goineo moved to the University of Padua, where he received a medical degree in 1543 and was appointed physician for the city of Pirano. He promptly showed himself to be a follower of the new ideas, which he had first acquired in the university milieux at Bologna and Padua, and saw in practice during a long journey to Germany, Austria, and the Low Countries. In Pirano, a city of ancient humanistic traditions, Goineo found himself at the center of a cultural circle composed of Antonio Petronio, known as Caldana, Marco Antonio Venier, and Giovanni Antonio Petronio, a schoolteacher. Together with a physician from Puglia, they had all been tried by the Inquisition on the suspicion of Lutheranism at Venice in 1534, after they had been denounced by the nuncio Girolamo Aleandro. Caldana, in his deposition, clearly stated how he believed that "the Lutheran sect is the true religion" and that good works are not necessary for eternal life, since the passion of Christ sufficed.[18] They abjured their errors and escaped with light penances. In spite of the fact that Goineo had aligned himself with Vergerio during the latter's trial and had gone to hear him preach at Zucole, six kilometers from Pirano, to which the bishop had withdrawn after being suspended from his bishopric, Goineo was not implicated in the affair. But in 1549 after Grisonio's investigation, Goineo was accused of having made heretical utterances in public, in the convents, among his friends, and of having circulated the *Beneficio di Cristo*, the *Dialogo tra Mercurio e Caronte* by Alfonso de Valdés and the *Medicina dell'anima* by Urbanus Rhegius.

Goineo was tried in Venice in May 1550. He defended himself by invoking for his cause the Gospels and St. Augustine, as Girolamo Galateo had done before him. But in the end, he preferred flight to house arrest in the home of his brother Niccolò and to the humiliation of a public abjuration and condemnation, with all their dire consequences for his practice as a physician. At first he may have found a haven at Lubiana in Carniola, where it would not have been difficult to obtain the protection of prominent Lutheran families, into which his medical profession would have opened doors. According to late evidence, Goineo died about the year 1579, "in Germany where, after his banishment, he had lived a long time among the heretics."[19]

Matthias Flacius Illyricus (1520–75) of Albona, the nephew of Baldo Lupatino, was considerably more famous. After studying in Venice, Basel, and Wittenberg, Flacius became an ally of Luther's and a doctrinaire champion of his teachings. His bitter, intransigent, fanatical views directed against Melanchthon's irenic position weakened the Lutheran camp. But they also prevented Luther's genial and original theological labors from being compromised with Romanism for reasons of political expediency. Flacius denounced the acceptance of the Augsburg *Interim* (1548) as an impoverishment of the essential principles of the Reformation. Especially in the

---

[17]S. Cavazza, "Profilo di Giovanni Battista Goineo, umanista piranese," *Atti del Centro di ricerche storiche di Rovigno* 11 (1980–81): 143.

[18]Ibid., 154.

[19]Ibid., 159.

bitter days following the defeat of the Schmalkaldic League after the imperial victory at Mühlberg (1547), and during the siege of Magdeburg, Matthias Flacius steeled the will to resist of ministers and people.

Thoroughly educated in both theology and history, Flacius conceived the idea of a history of the church by century. The result was the famous *Magdeburg Centuries*, published in thirteen volumes, the fruit of the labors of a team of scholars working under his guidance at great personal cost, without financial support from German cities or rulers. Building on the scheme of Flacius's *Catalogus testium veritatis, qui ante nostram aetatem reclamarunt papae* (Basel, 1556), the history sets out to demonstrate how the primitive evangelical message had become distorted, but at the same time showed the persistence of a minority of faithful witnesses to the truth, from the church fathers up to the Reformation. It was a pioneering work, an original and fruitful conception, for its time.

Flacius, like Vergerio, never forgot his native Istria or the Venetian Republic. In 1570 he published a *Christian exhortation to the most serene prince and to the glorious Venetian Senate, in the midst of the present religious controversies and in the face of the manifestations of the Antichrist, to search for and investigate the truth in the celestial oracles of Holy Scripture*. It was a letter that he had sent to the *Signoria* five years earlier, and to which he did not receive a reply; in it he urged consideration of the serious degeneration in Christianity caused by the deceptions, superstitions, and idolatry tolerated and fomented by the Church of Rome.[20] Flacius was still tenaciously clinging to this hope of political intervention at the height of the Counter-Reformation offensive. Highly esteemed by Luther in his lifetime for his loyalty and intransigence, Flacius died poor and alone at Frankfurt in 1575.

BIBLIOGRAPHICAL NOTE

The most detailed examination of the diffusion of the Reformation in Istria is A. Pitassio's, cited in the notes.

The best study on Vergerio's career before his apostasy is A. J. Schutte, *Pier Paolo Vergerio, the Making of an Italian Reformer* (Geneva: Droz, 1977). But E. Comba's biographical sketch in *I nostri protestanti*, 395–476, is still useful. The novelist Fulvio Tomizza has reconstructed Vergerio's entire career in his *Il male viene dal Nord: Il romanzo del vescovo Vergerio* (Milan: Mondadori, 1984). For Vergerio's work as publicist during his sojourn in the Valtellina, cf. S. Cavazza, "Pier Paolo Vergerio nei Grigioni e in Valtellina (1549–53): Attività editoriale e polemica religiosa," in *Riforma e società nei Grigioni, Valtellina e Valchiavenna tra '500 e '600*. Ed. A. Pastore (Milan: F. Angeli, 1991), 33–62.

On G. B. Goineo, besides the sketch by Cavazza cited in the notes, see also Cavazza, "Umanesimo e Riforma in Istria: Giovanni Battista Goineo e i gruppi

---

[20]*Esortazione cristiana al serenissimo principe e all'inclito senato di Venezia, a volere, in mezzo alle presenti controversie religiose e di fronte alle manifestazioni dell'Anticristo, scrutare e investigare la verità nei celesti oracoli delle Sacre Scritture.* Cf. E. Comba, *I nostri protestanti*, 383–86.

eterodossi di Pirano," in *Umanesimo in Istria* (Florence: Olschki, 1983), 91–117, and in the same volume, see also A. Miculian, "Fonti inedite per la storia della Riforma in Istria," 204–13.

   On Matthias Flacius, see the relevant chapter in E. Comba, *I nostri protestanti*, 359–94.

Matthias Flacich Illyricus. Contemporary engraving.

II

IN THE ARC OF THE THREE VENICES

THE CIRCULATION OF HERETICAL BOOKS IN FRIULI AND GORIZIA

BEGINNING IN THE 1520S, the entire area encompassed by the "Three Venices"[1]
(*Triveneto*), from Trent to Trieste, was inundated by Lutheran propaganda imported
by persons of every social class, ecclesiastics, schoolteachers, merchants, and artisans,
both Italian and German.

Immediately after the Edict of Worms (16 May 1521) outlawed Luther, Archduke Ferdinand of Augsburg ordered the confiscation of heretical books in Trent, a
principate of the Empire. Some years later Clement VII sent briefs to the prince-
bishop of the city and to the nuncio in Venice, ordering the rooting out of Lutheran
books in Trent, Brescia, and Verona, and granting authority to punish vendors and
buyers. But in the next few years, from Germany, Switzerland, and Austria, a verita-
ble flood of German and Latin Bibles, and works by Erasmus, Luther, and the principal reformers spilled over into all the border areas. In the 1540s other books were
added to them, among which were Brucioli's *Bible*, the *Prediche* of Ochino, Vergerio's
pamphlets, the *Sommario della Santa Scrittura*, the *Beneficio di Cristo*, and the *Tragedia del libero arbitrio* by Francesco Negri.

The role played by the printing press in the spread of Lutheran teachings
assumed impressive proportions in the eastern zone of the *Triveneto*, Friuli, and Gorizia, where in noble palaces and in the homes of professional people large hordes of
prohibited literature were discovered. These readings and the accompanying work of
proselytization carried on by the new converts, who were able to confirm through
actual visits to Germany or the bordering Austrian dominions, the liturgical and disciplinary changes introduced by the Lutherans, probably had a more lasting effect
than the preaching from the pulpit about the salvation of the sinner through divine
grace. As Luigi De Biasio has argued, to understand the gulf separating the people

---

[1]Comprising Venezia Euganea, Venezia Tridentina, Venezia Giulia. See *Enciclopedia Italiana* 35:78.
[Trans. note.]

from the traditional faith, we must first consider the geographical and political conditions of the diocese of Aquileia, the largest in Europe in the sixteenth century, comprising three nationalities (Italian, German, and Slovenian) dispersed over five areas:
Friuli, Cadore, Carinthia, Carniola, and Styria.[2] The proximity of Carinthia and
Styria where the Lutheran Reformation met with a warm reception among the clergy
and in the population as a whole, under the aegis of the nobility, explains the reception of the new ideas by ecclesiastics and educated laypeople in Friuli and in Gorizia.
Paolo Bisanti, episcopal vicar for the diocese of Aquileia, wrote a truly illuminating
report on 25 October 1581 to Duke Charles of Habsburg after his visit to Carniola
and the fiefdom of Cilli. Bisanti had discovered that parish priests, completely ignorant of Latin, to gain a little familiarity with the Bible, for years had been using the
Catechisms by Luther and by Primus Trubar, Vergerio's collaborator at Tübingen.
Bisanti claimed that in a short time he had destroyed two thousand of these books,
and was happy "to have set free the minds of those poor little ones, who day and
night were doing their exercises reading these versions and interpretations without
regard to papal excommunication."[3]

Towards the end of the century, in 1592, after fifty years of confiscations and
book burnings, fifty-six heretical works, of which twenty-eight were by Martin
Luther in German, together with writings by Melanchthon, Erasmus, and Brenz,
were still found in the library of Count Giorgio Della Torre, governor of Gorizia, at
his death. The valuable collection was set to the torch on the very day of their discovery in the castle square, before the widow's helpless gaze.[4] In 1558, thanks to accusations by a Venetian goldsmith, a Lutheran community was uncovered at Gemona. Its
members included Antonio de Pinguento, a chaplain in the town, who evaded capture by fleeing to Lubiana; the schoolteacher Giovanni Spica, owner of a printed
copy of the *Confessio Augustana*; and two noblemen, active proselytizers, Marco
Antonio Pichissino and Dionisio Rizardi. Pichissino, the more committed of the
two, had already been convicted on an earlier occasion, and would be tried again in
1574, but actually taken into custody only seven years later. In 1583 he broke out of
jail and found refuge at Malborghetto with a Lutheran family but continued his violently anti-Catholic campaign. Rizardi had been going back and forth between
Gemona and Germany, engaged in the book trade. At his inquest, he made a full
confession of his errors. Several German merchants were tried together with the two
men.

In addition to Gemona, there was a large Lutheran presence in the more impor-
tant centers of Friuli, at Cividale, Udine, Spilimbergo, Pordenone, and Gorizia.
Almost all those who were eventually convicted had become acquainted with the
Reformation in Germany. One of the most audacious among them was Daniele

---

[2]L. De Biasio, "L'eresia protestante in Friuli nella seconda metà del secolo XVI," *Memorie Storiche Forogiuliesi* 52 (1972): 71–81.

[3]S. Cavazza, "Inquisizione e libri proibiti in Friuli e a Gorizia tra Cinquecento e Seicento," *Studi Goriziani* 43 (1976): 38–39.

[4]L. De Biasio, "L'eresia protestante," 79–81.

Dionisi, called "Cargnello," a native of a village in Carnia, who settled in Carinthia where he became a Lutheran. He was arrested at Graz while actively proselytizing both Italians and Austrians, and was condemned to death at Udine in 1588.

Two artisans were arrested at Cividale in 1558: the carpenter Domenico and the tailor Floreano Filippi. The former succeeded in fleeing to Germany, but when, almost a quarter century later, he returned to Cividale, he was arrested by the Inquisition and condemned to death as a relapsed heretic. He died in prison the day before the scheduled execution. In his abjuration Filippi filled out the events of his career: "I learned these opinions and errors from the books of the heretics which I had read and from conversations in Germany and in other places with heretics, where I lived for many years and I discussed them with many who were Catholics in Italy and outside, believing them and holding them to be true and laboring to persuade others that they were true." He disclosed the names of his accomplices, almost all of whom belonged to patrician families, and admitted having circulated the *Augsburg Confession.* There were also a few priests, three canons of the cathedral, and several professional men among the participants. They all mounted an able defense, denied every charge, and were absolved.

A long trial was held at Udine ten years later against the priest Giovan Battista Clario, a private tutor in a villa near Cividale. He was jailed and accused of teaching Lutheran doctrines to his students. A search of his private residence turned up copies of works by Brucioli and Peter Martyr Vermigli. He ended up confessing that he had corresponded with many persons, some of whom, such as Floreano Filippi, had already been tried for heresy. He made a full abjuration of his errors, from which one gathers his "profound knowledge of and full adherence to Lutheran teachings."[5]

In 1565 in Gorizia the consequences of the missionary activity of Primus Trubar, the Slovenian reformer, who had returned to his homeland from Urach-Tübingen in 1563, came to light. Under the protection of Count Giorgio Della Torre he had preached in German, Slovenian, and Italian, making converts to the Reformation from among both nobility and populace, performing his pastoral ministry, baptizing, and administering the sacraments. The patriarch of Aquileia, Giovanni Grimani, informed Duke Charles about these activities on 20 January 1565. Trubar had baptized the son of the nobleman Hannibal d'Eck, to whom another son was born at the end of 1564. Trubar was being hunted at the time and sent another pastor in his stead, who managed to obtain an annual stipend as a preacher from the population. The patriarch then added the most scandalous piece of news of all: the minister had dared to celebrate the Eucharist at San Pietro di Gorizia, "giving to some drovers the sacrosanct relics of the Blood of Christ." To put the chalice into the hands of these miserable wretches was the last straw, even for the patriarch of Aquileia, himself suspected of Lutheran sympathies![6]

[5]Ibid., 93 ff., esp. 95, 101.
[6]P. Paschini, *Eresia e Riforma cattolica al confine orientale d'Italia.* Lateranum, n.s. 17, nos. 1–4 (Rome, 1951), 47–48.

More evidence of Trubar's proselytizing mission turned up in 1567 during the trial of Giulio Passavolanti of Gemona, in whose house were discovered almost all the Italian works produced by the Urach/Tübingen press, together with works by Vergerio. Passavolanti was absolved after he informed his judges, who were rather lenient in these border areas, that the books belonged to students who had left them in his house. In 1571, a couple dozen volumes were found in the possession of Giovanni Battista Godessa, a notary of Gonars, including writings by Luther, Erasmus, Brucioli, and the two dialogues by Alfonso de Valdés. Godessa too denied ownership, and since he was known as a good Catholic, was absolved also.

To better understand the wholehearted acceptance of the new faith on the part of the popular classes, rather than evaluate the vacillations, excuses, and recantations of the educated, it is useful to consider the trial against a smith of Lubiana, Ambrogio Castenario, an Austrian who had been residing in Udine for five years. Castenario had been raised on the German Bible and Luther's *Catechism*, so that his replies to the questions posed by the Udine inquisitors constitute a notable example of the acquisition of a new culture and a new spirituality. In the interrogation session of 28 July 1568 at the first question about his beliefs, he replied, "And my faith is in Christ and in Christ I want to die." And he went on in this vein, unwavering, on the value of works, purgatory, the cult of saints, the Eucharist, and papal authority. Clearly and precisely he expounded the theology of Luther, whose catechism, together with other German books, had been confiscated from him. When he was asked why he possessed a portrait of the German reformer who had been excommunicated by the pope, he objected: "You may have excommunicated him, God did not." As to what he understood by the term Catholic church, he replied: "It means the Church of the apostles, and I am now in that Church and it has always been persecuted, as I am because of the Word of God." The smith, as a "pertinacious and impenitent" heretic, was strangled to death in prison on 6 September 1568.[7] Finding such a highly developed faith in a humble artisan naturally presupposes that he had participated actively in a clandestine community.

Jacob Strauss and Urbanus Rhegius (Urban König)

For about a year, from early in 1521 until 4 May 1522, Jacob Strauss of Basel (1480/1485–1533) preached and conducted his reforming activity at Hall on the Inntal near Bressanone. He had come from Schwaz as a young doctor in theology, where he had ministered to the miners. His great popularity had won him the protection of the local authorities. When the principal church edifice could no longer

[7]S. Cavazza, "Inquisizione," 42–46. See the trial against Ambrogio Castenario published in L. De Biasio, *1000 processi dell'Inquisizione in Friuli (1551–1647)*. Regione Autonoma Friuli-Venezia Giulia, Quaderni del Centro di Catalogazione dei Beni Culturali, 4 (Udine, 1976), 105–30. The quotation is at 120.

accommodate his horde of listeners, who came even from the outlying areas, he spoke to them in the fields and in the public square.

Strauss was an impetuous preacher, sensitive to the needs of the poor, but ended up making enemies of the ecclesiastical authorities through his harsh criticism of abuses in the administration of confession. The parish priest of Hall, a canon in Bressanone, preached against Strauss's sermons on the subject of confession delivered at Lent in 1522. Bishop Sebastian Speranzio also stepped in, forcing the authorities to expel Strauss amidst the loud lamentations of a large crowd that gathered to bid him farewell and to voice their indignation against the clergy. Strauss eventually settled in Saxony, where with Luther's recommendation, he was taken on as preacher by Count George of Wertheim, who became annoyed with his arrogant ways. Eventually, due to his vacillations and intemperance, Strauss even lost the confidence of Luther and Brenz. It appears that he may have returned to the Catholic church about 1533, but at least it can be said that his youthful ministry at Hall and his energetic attacks against Roman teachings, had large popular repercussions.

After Strauss's departure, Hall called as its preacher another champion of "evangelical truth." He too was a doctor of theology, Urbanus Rhegius (1489–1541), a Basel graduate already famous for his oratorical skills. He hailed from Augsburg, where his views on reform had aroused the hostility of the cathedral canons. In the short time he spent at Hall, during which he did not drop his contacts with Augsburg, he attacked the privileges of the high clergy from the pulpit, the use of Latin in the mass, and the cult of saints. In addition to preaching, he also wrote pamphlets and broadsides in which he tellingly reproached the exploitation of country folks: "If the great bells sound, the peasants come running, as if something new had appeared.... The money worshippers say, 'peasant bring your money here.'"[8] Until 1523 Rhegius was a Zwinglian, but after witnessing scenes of sectarian radicalism, he threw in his lot with Luther, to whom he remained faithful his entire life. Rhegius, the author of a famous work translated into Italian as the *Dottrina vecchia e dottrina nuova*, which we discussed earlier, went on to become the reformer of Augsburg and Lüneburg after he was forced to abandon Hall, due to the hostility of the bishop of Bressanone in the summer of 1524.

THE PEASANTS' WAR AND MICHAEL GAISMAYR

All of the German-speaking northern Tyrol was caught up in the Peasants' War in 1525, which had broken out in Germany the year before. The revolt spread to the miners and to the lower classes, vexed by the grievous taxes, extraordinary imposts, low wages, and long hours of work. The inhabitants of the area who had at first been influenced by the Lutheran preaching of Strauss and Rhegius, gradually turned to the

---

[8]J. Macek, *Der Tiroler Bauernkrieg und Michael Gaismair* (Berlin: VEB Deutscher Verlag der Wissenschaften, 1965), 80: "Wenn da die grossen Glocken läuten laufen die Bauern herzu, als sei etwas Neues erschienen.... Es sprechen die Geldgötzen: Bauer, gib Geld her."

social and religious radicalism championed by Thomas Müntzer, who had visited Hall in 1522.

At the beginning of 1525, rebellions broke out at Schwaz, Vipiteno, and Chiusa among the miners exploited by the German bankers Wesel and Fugger, whose mining concessions dated back to 1487. The peasants of Bressanone, Bolzano, and Merano rose up under the skilled political and military leadership of a native Tyrolian, Michael Gaismayr. In the "peasant diet" held at Merano from 30 May to 8 June, the delegates from the Trentino area and from the southern Tyrol approved a "Magna Charta for the common people." They asked to be relieved from burdensome tributes and to be taxed more equitably, but also for a radical reform of the religious life, the suppression of convents, and their transformation into hospitals and hospices "for the needy and shameful poor." Moreover, the communities were to be permitted "to choose their own priests," who were to be honest and versed in the Holy Scriptures.

It was an ephemeral victory. The moderates among the rebels permitted themselves to be persuaded by the promises of Archduke Ferdinand of Austria and abandoned the peasant cause. In the Val Sugana the revolt was crushed by the mercenaries of George of Frundsberg. Gaismayr was captured and taken to Innsbruck. A ferocious repression, accompanied by death, torture, and mutilations ended the peasants' and workers' dreams of freedom. To prevent arson and pillaging by the rabble, heavy fines fell upon them. Gaismayr fled from prison and made a desperate attempt to link up with the peasant army at Salzburg, but failed miserably to unite against Ferdinand all the rebels occupying the Tridentine Tyrol.

Gaismayr, the champion of an evangelical communism, took refuge with a retinue of a few hundred in Venetian territory, and succeeded in entering the service of the Republic, given his reputation as a brave captain with a large following among Tyrolian and German peasants. In 1527 he withdrew to Padua, without abandoning his dream of a war against the Habsburgs. He tried to persuade Venice to join a coalition, being organized by Zwingli, comprising Zurich and the German Protestant princes. Zwingli's death on the field of battle at Kappel in 1531 was followed the next year by the assassination of Gaismayr, possibly at the hands of Ferdinand's henchmen.[9]

In 1527 a certain Wolfgang, a pastor in the Val Sarentina, was imprisoned at Bressanone. He admitted that for a year he had been preaching the new doctrines in that city, as well as at Egna, Bolzano, and in neighboring places. This humble man of the fields, who may have been influenced by the preaching of Strauss and Rhegius against those authorities who had usurped the rights of the people, attacked priests, monks, and the pope, whom he called minions of the Antichrist, declaring also that the mass was of no avail since Christ was not really present in the sacrament of the altar, that the cult of saints was superstitious and human laws worthless.[10]

---

[9]A. Stella, *La rivoluzione contadina del 1525 e l'utopia di Michael Gaismayr* (Padua: Liviana, 1975).
[10]See V. Zanolini, "Spigolature d'Archivio: Appunti," 22.

In 1529 the milliner Jacob Hutter, one of the leaders of early Swiss Anabaptism, left his native soil in the Val Pusteria, and after being rebaptized at Klagenfurt, dedicated himself to proselytizing in the Tyrol. After emigrating to Moravia he came into contact with the Anabaptist colonies that had become established there, thanks to the toleration of the local lords who needed laborers for their abandoned fields. Hutter became attracted to evangelical communism, which offered a life of sharing for the faithful until the day of Christ's return. He arranged for the clandestine exodus of many Tiroleans towards Moravia and concurrently dispatched missionaries from there to the Tyrol. In his two years in Moravia, Hutter showed notable organizational skills, grouping his followers into agricultural cooperatives geared to production and consumption.

Meanwhile Anabaptism was spreading quickly among peasants, laborers, and artisans throughout the Tyrol. Between 1529 and 1532 representatives of the sect were discovered at Vipiteno, Bressanone, Gudon, Chiusa, Bolzano, Caldaro, and Egna. Ferdinand of Habsburg's ferocious repression fell upon all of them. Almost seven hundred were sentenced to death, but many others were banished or succeeded in fleeing to Moravia where they found a fraternal welcome, work, and the freedom to practice their faith under Hutter's leadership. But in 1535, while the revolutionary Anabaptists were being defeated at Münster in Westphalia, persecution also fell upon the peaceful Hutterite colonists in Moravia. Their communities were dispersed, and Hutter, unable to withstand "that terrible tyrant and enemy of the faith in God, Ferdinand," returned to the mountains of the Tyrol. He was arrested at Chiusa in the home of Hans Steiner, together with his wife and his hosts. After vain attempts to draw out of him by torture the names of his accomplices, he was publicly burned to death at Innsbruck on 25 February 1536. His wife managed to flee but was recaptured two years later and executed at Schöneck. The Hutterite communities in Moravia, which reorganized after their founder's death, experienced bitter travails until they were finally expelled in 1622.

The gallows of Bolzano, Egna, and Caldaro on the Ritten failed to crush the movement of religious and political protest, which counted among its members the countess of Oettingen, the judge Bartolus Schöpfer, Baldassarr Schegg, and Sigismund of Wolgenstein. For a few months in 1526, George of Frundsberg was in the Tyrol recruiting troops for Charles V's war against Clement VII, the ally of Francis I, which would culminate in the Sack of Rome. Frundsberg, bitterly opposed to the pope and to the Church of Rome, favored the religious innovators in every way he could.[11]

LUTHERANS AND CALVINISTS IN TRENT

The attempts made by the prince-bishop of Trent, Bernard Clesius, to reform the clergy and reclaim the dissidents was largely a wasted effort. He had initiated the program with the diocesan synod of 1537, which called a halt to the oral and written

---

[11]A. Stella, *Dall'Anabattismo al Socinianesimo nel Cinquecento veneto* (Padua: Liviana, 1967), 19–23.

Bird's-eye view of Trent. *Above left:* The castle. Engraving, 1580.

propaganda flowing into the areas bordering Germany and Austria, which were largely Italian speaking but under the sovereignty of the Empire. In the opinion of the Czech scholar Josef Macek, the common people listened to Luther and the other reformers, not so much because they fully understood their teachings, but because, in their courageous denunciation of the evils of the church, they saw the way to "a pure Gospel" and the end of daily misery.[12] Meanwhile unsettling news reached Rome from the nuncio to Venice, Girolamo Aleandro. Bolzano, he wrote on 7 September 1538, was "badly infected with Lutheranism" due to its commercial contacts with Germany. Several years later, the Venetian ambassador Alvise Mocenigo, a future doge, in his report to the Senate in 1546 after returning from the court of Charles V, disclosed what he perceived to be the sentiments of the Tyrolian people towards the pope and the Church of Rome:

> It was clear to him [Charles V] that the *contado* of the Tyrol, and almost all the other states of the king, his brother, were infected with this heresy, even though out of fear of the king they proceeded with caution in this matter, but not so much that many manifest signs were not seen of these opinions; among other things, I can recall that in the course of my mission, passing through a place that belongs to the king, Chiusa, or Covolo, as some call it, I saw written over a doorway: "Long live Christ and death to the Pope."[13]

During the episcopate of the prince-bishop of Trent, Cristoforo Madruzzo, a cardinal of the imperial party, admirer of the *Beneficio di Cristo*, protector of such religiously suspect persons as Carnesecchi, Bartolomeo Spadafora, Niccolò da Verona, the restive ex-Augustinian Ortensio Lando, Fra Andrea da Volterra, and Jacopo Nacchianti, the city became a haven for the persecuted. The most famous case is that of Filippo Valentini, prominent in Modenese literary circles, who for many years participated in the philo-Protestant movement centered around that city's Academy. After he left Modena, under the threat of arrest, he became *podestà* of Trent in 1548. Because of its status as imperial principate, it was only after the closing of the Council of Trent that Madruzzo had to establish a tribunal of the Inquisition in April 1564.

The Reformation thus was able to grow, even if in clandestine and Nicodemite form, until the end of the century, especially in the German-speaking areas. It should be borne in mind that even the local Italians knew German. Cristoforo Madruzzo, who had learned it from his mother, considered himself more German than Italian. The city had from six to seven thousand inhabitants and its many fairs attracted merchants from Augsburg, Verona, Ferrara, Venice, and Mantua. The situation is described aptly by Achille Olivieri: "Trent takes on the twofold aspect of an important urban center, a point of transit for intellectuals and merchants, but a city participating in the great movement, European in scope, unleashed by Martin Luther."[14]

---

[12]See J. Macek, *Der Tiroler Bauernkrieg*, 78.

[13]V. Zanolini, "Spigolature d'Archivio: Appunti," 28.

[14]A. Olivieri, "Trento e l'Alto Adige: La circolazione della Riforma e delle eresie," in *Presenze ebraico-cristiane nelle Venezie* (Vicenza, 1993), 174.

One of the Inquisition's first acts, after its establishment, was to institute a trial against a citizen of Trent, well known as a notary and as a poet and passionate reader of Ariosto and Dante. The proceedings in 1564 against Leonardo Colombino (1524–80), despite the fencing and vacillations of the defendant, ended with the discovery of a clandestine group of committed Protestants. The three who were most seriously implicated saved themselves through flight: a shoemaker, Giovanni Bertignollo; a rich merchant, Giovanni Antonio Zurletta; and the schoolteacher for the city, the Sienese, Vincenzo Bezzi, who had resided in Trent since 1557.

Bertignollo, who had been consul twice, fled after a search of his house turned up an Italian Bible and Lutheran writings against the mass. One of the witnesses at Colombino's trial remembered him speaking despairingly about the Council: "The Council of Trent is a monastery for monks, a congregation of priests and the fathers are scribes and pharisees."[15] This vehement anticlericalism helps to explain why the group, of which the artisan was one of the leaders, consisted exclusively of laypeople.

About twelve years earlier, Giovanni Antonio Zurletta, a rich merchant and citizen of Trent, but a member of a family originally from Dimaro, was forced to flee. His name could be found in the heraldic roll of honor because he had funded the splendid choir in Santa Maria Maggiore. But neither Zurletta's devotion manifested in the beautification of the church where the Council held its closing sessions, nor his love for religious art, so intimately tied to the Catholic tradition, preserved him for the orthodox faith. He had been tried for the first time in 1548, again in 1551, and a final time in 1552 as a *relapsus*. He evaded judgment by fleeing the city and finding refuge in Tirano in the Valtellina. From there he corresponded with his wife, his sister-in-law Caterina, and her brothers Giambattista, Osvaldo, and Girolamo Sizo. He exhorted them to remain firm in the faith and to read Scripture daily, as well as the books that he would send them. He hoped that his wife "would want to extricate herself from the things of this world and follow her husband, as God commands; and if she did otherwise, let her know that she would incur the judgment of God for certain."[16] At Tirano, Zurletta was joined by Vincenzo Bezzi, the only member of the Tridentine conventicle to have possessed a copy of Calvin's *Institutes*, which he circulated among his fellows.

The second trial against Leonardo Colombino (the first had concluded with his abjuration and reconciliation to the church on 15 May 1564) began on 21 September 1579, following a visitation of the diocese by Cardinal Ludovico Madruzzo, Cristoforo's nephew. It concluded on 14 April 1580 with Colombino's abjuration and reconciliation. The chief piece of evidence against him was incontrovertible: a letter from Zurletta in Tirano dated 13 April 1566 in which the writer expressed his happiness at the news of Colombino's conversion, and in which he exhorted him to persevere in the faith of Jesus Christ and read Scriptures daily: "Because now our salvation is closer than we had believed. The night has already passed, and day is drawing near. Let us thus put aside the works of darkness and don the arms of light;

[15]V. Zanolini, "Spigolature d'Archivio: Appunti," 52, 55–58.
[16]Ibid., 37–41.

the rest you may read for yourself."[17] The books requested by Colombino would soon be on their way to him: Calvin's *Institutes* and Johann Sleidan's *Commentaries*, both in Italian translation, which would be purchased in Chiavenna, as well as the *Dialogo* of *messer* Jacopo Riccamati, a pseudonymous work by the Tridentine engineer Giacomo Aconcio, who had converted to Protestantism in 1557. The letter closed with the wish that all of the Valtellina might espouse the Reformation, because there "every day the papacy is gradually being struck down so that one may hope that soon the governors of the Grisons will send that diabolical Mass packing," just as had happened in Scotland, England, and also in France where freedom of worship had been achieved. The same was hoped for Poland and other reigns in Europe.[18]

Zurletta closed with a salutation "for all those who walk in the truth," for his wife, who had chosen not to follow him into exile, and for the notary Nicodemus. The letter reveals, thirty years after his flight, the continuing existence of a conventicle in Trent, but we know that there were others because at his second trial Colombino was accused of being the leader of groups at Terlago and Pergine.

The able defense mounted by Colombino, his knowledge of legal procedure, his appeal to enactments of Ferdinand I and Maximilian II granting freedom of worship to Lutherans, and his insistence on being represented by a skilled advocate did not wholly succeed in neutralizing testimony by several witnesses about the insincerity of his first abjuration. He had been nicknamed "Luther," by persons of Terlago, because of his anticlerical utterances. Doctor Odorico Paurinfaint testified that he had received from Colombino a book against the Eucharist that stated that Catholics worshipped a piece of dough. At Pergine, where Colombino resided in 1579, he had associated with a certain Martin, lute maker, well known as a Lutheran who never went to mass.

With the evidence against him mounting, on 5 October 1579 Colombino was finally taken into custody. The accusations became increasingly serious. Vincenzo Bordogna testified that one day he chanced to be in church with him, and when Colombino saw him genuflect before "the most holy Sacrament," exclaimed: "Oh how crazy you are. God is in the heavens! What you see there is dough, and as for that lamp burning there, it would be better to give the oil to the poor."[19] In his first trial Colombino had admitted reading heretical books, including the *Beneficio di Cristo*, the *Pasquino in estasi*, Ochino's commentary to the Epistle to the Galatians, and works by Vergerio and Viret. But the most damning evidence was the letter from his old friend Zurletta and its information about Bezzi, the Calvinist schoolteacher.

And yet, in spite of six months of questioning and the threat of torture, the defense attorney Odorico Costede succeeded in fending off all the accusations. He

[17]Ibid., 43.

[18]Ibid., 42–44. The letter contains information on the printing of religious books: G. C. Pascali's Italian translation of Calvin's *Institutes* (1557) and the translation of Sleidan's *Commentaries* (1556), both from Genevan presses.

[19]V. Zanolini, "Spigolature d'Archivio: Appunti," 100. For the trial against Colombino, cf. 58 ff., 97–115.

cast doubt on the veracity of the prosecution witnesses and on the authenticity of Zurletta's letter. On his client's behalf he called thirty-two witnesses from Terlago, Lasino, Baselga, Pinè, and Trent. They all vouched for the poor, deaf, and bizarre notary's full obedience to all the precepts of the church. Furthermore, the attorney argued, the proceedings were illegal, since thanks to a privilege granted to the city of Trent, trials over questions of the faith came under the jurisdiction of the archduke of Austria and not of the ecclesiastical authorities. Colombino was released on 14 April 1580. Cardinal Ludovico Madruzzo, who had succeeded his uncle in the government of the principate, may have prompted the judges to accept as valid Colombino's profession of faith, which if not fully Tridentine, agreed substantially with the apostolic credo.

Thus concluded the trial against a man, a student of the Latin classics and Italian literature, as well as Scripture, who had eagerly immersed himself in the study of Calvin's *Institutes* and the works of Jacob Wimpfeling, the Strasbourg humanist, which had been found concealed in a chest. In certain respects these proceedings are emblematic of the contradictions experienced by many Italian intellectuals in that century, wavering between the desire for the liberty of the Christian and reluctance to break with their families, their friends, and their professions.

As a young man Colombino had come into the good graces of Cristoforo Madruzzo. On 3 May 1547, when the cardinal gave a magnificent feast to celebrate the imperial victory over the Protestants, Colombino participated by acting the part of the Madman in the game of tarots, an event he described in a poem entitled "The Tridentine Triumph." The central feature of the celebration, enlivened by the dancing of maidens from Trent, Rovereto, and Riva, was a Triumph representing the symbolic figures of heavenly bodies, the devil, death, love, and fame impersonated by the most beautiful ladies from the nobility of Trent. The annoying conciliar discussions on justification, which after dividing Christianity and perturbing consciences all over Europe, had terminated in January of that same year, seemed far removed from that enchanted world of refined elegance. In spite of his persisting anticlericalism and his Protestant leanings and friends, the old notary Colombino did not succeed in detaching himself from this world of his youth and perhaps did not wish to.

At the conclusion of Ludovico Madruzzo's first visitation of Trent and its *contado* (1579–80), evidence of the religious dissent was no longer apparent, and perhaps, since we have no information that heretics were executed, had been wholly eliminated without recourse to harsh condemnations.[20] The archdukes of Austria, eager to annex the principate, and the bishops, defenders of their proper autonomy, had no intention of turning the population against them.

Two sensational cases were resolved when the protagonists chose exile voluntarily. In 1568, during the struggle between Archduke Ferdinand II, supported by the citizenry, and the bishop, Ascanio Schrattemberg, illustrious philosopher and physician, who was serving as consul that year, was imprisoned. As a follower of Pomponazzi, he

[20]Ibid., 87 ff. Cf. L. Colombino, "Il Trionfo Tridentino," in F. Ambrosi, *Scrittori e artisti Trentini* (Trent, 1894; repr. Bologna: Forni, 1972).

did not believe in the immortality of the soul, nor in the divinity of Jesus Christ. Tyrolian authorities succeeded in obtaining his release. A decade later he was in Brescia, where he published a medical work, *De indicationibus curativis libri X.*

The decision by Hildebrand, lord of the castle at Sporo, to proclaim himself a Lutheran in 1571 achieved greater notoriety. The nobleman refused to yield before the arguments of the Jesuits of Innsbruck or to accept the conciliar decisions on the Eucharist. He might have retained his castle at Flavon if he had been willing to guarantee that he would bring his children up as Catholics, but he preferred to sell his worldly goods and go into exile. At Flavon and in all the Italian-speaking areas, Madruzzo's visitation unearthed some residues of dissent scattered among all social levels. The most dangerous were the two teachers of humane letters at Storo, Bortolo Maleotti and Ambrogio degli Schiavi, quick to burn their prohibited books as soon as they were warned by their friends. The notary Benvenuto di Tenno surrendered his copy of a Biblical commentary by Bucer.

In the German-speaking areas the visitation turned up quite a different situation: many Anabaptists at Villanders and numerous other heretics were living clandestinely at Bolzano, receiving prohibited books during the various fairs from Augsburg merchants. It was useless to try to confiscate them because they kept on coming. Even the parish priest possessed such books as Erasmus's *Colloquia.* Five years later, during a second visitation, more than a thousand prohibited books were destroyed, with Bolzano still the center of activity. There, a Bavarian knife-grinder gave up his Luther Bible, but was probably not willing to admit his error, since the notary jotted down on the margin of the inquest record, "*Is suspectus et pertinax.*" The two schoolmasters of Bolzano were philo-Lutheran. One, Christian Pfanner of Hall, abjured; the other, Cyprian Heller, refused to accept a Catholic confession of faith, and was probably banished from the city. When the visitors came to his house he was in the act of teaching about a hundred pupils. Luther's *Postills*, his translation of the Psalter, Bugenhagen's *De passione Christi,* and Savonarola's *Miserere*, translated by Cyriakus Spangenberg, were among the books confiscated.

Other writings were seized in the neighboring villages of Ora, Mais, and Moelten, works by Luther (his Catechism, Psalter, New Testament), Bucer, and Spangenberg. The parish priest Gaspar Lechner was a Lutheran and covertly tried to convert his flock and celebrated mass administering the Eucharist under both species. He tried to excuse his behavior by claiming he did not know that he had erred. At Montan, Egna, San Paolo di Eppan, Caldaro, Ora, and Salorno, the dissidents held out until the end of the century, concealing their Bibles and prohibited books, which eventually they had to surrender. The library confiscated from Elia Oler of Egna, who may have led a conventicle but managed to evade arrest, provides a measure of the liturgical and practical use of these books: Luther's *Postills, Catechism, Hymns,* and a work of his on the sacrament of the Eucharist, and then the Gospels, more hymnals and summaries of doctrine, including the writings of Christopher Lasius.

From an examination of the trial records and of the lists of confiscated books spanning more than a half century, the links with the Lutheran Reformation and

German culture are obvious. Rarely do the names of Zwingli and Calvin turn up and Erasmus appears only twice in connection with his *Colloquia, Enchiridion militis Christiani*, and *De libero arbitrio*.

VERONA AND BRESCIA

Verona and Brescia were the two northern cities where German and Lutheran influences were most visible. Located at the mouths of the Adige River and of Lake Garda, both navigable at the time, they were also on communication routes leading to Trent and the Brenner. Although Verona and Brescia were under the suzerainty of the Republic of Venice, they had almost daily commercial contacts with the principate of Trent and with Bolzano, where eight daylong fairs were held three times yearly, and with the great trading center of Augsburg. In both Verona and Brescia, the many Germans who worked there and in the outlying areas were the principal go-betweens with German culture. From the fifteenth century on, German industrialists and merchants had established themselves in the Val Trompia and Valcamonica to work the iron mines. Verona, an important center for textile production and export, had many Germans working in this trade.

Another channel for the penetration of the new ideas originated in the Valtellina. At midcentury, the printer Dolfin Landolfi of Poschiavo, with the pretext of purchasing paper there for his press, had made Brescia, across Lake Iseo, the center of distribution for books intended for Mantua, Brescia, Verona, and Venice. P. P. Vergerio, and Giulio della Rovere, the founder of an evangelical community in Poschiavo, were among Landolfi's most active collaborators, supplying material for the books he printed.

The 1550 trial against a group of Veronese suspects, recently brought to light by Lorenzo Tacchella, corroborates, through their testimony, what we have stated concerning the incidence of both oral transmission and the importation of the printed word, as well as the possibility in these border areas of knowing the new religious situation unfolding beyond the Alps. On this last aspect, Veronese dissidents did not rely only on the tales told by Italian emigrants returning to their native land, nor on what was recounted by German students, merchants, innkeepers, and laborers. Some of the conventicle's members had traveled to "German lands" to have their confessions heard by Lutheran pastors, and thus saw the situation with their own eyes.

When the inquisitor asked who had instructed him in his heretical doctrines, Bartolomeo della Barba, the son of a silk merchant, himself an agent for a group of merchants whose goods he transported to Germany, answered: "Zuan Batioro, a German, who has a business, and other Germans as well who do as they please, and his house might be called an academy of Germans."[21] As elsewhere, a shop of a German goldsmith had become a place for meeting and proselytization.

---

[21]L. Tacchella, *Il processo agli eretici veronesi nel 1550: S. Ignazio di Loyola e Luigi Lippomano (carteggio)* (Brescia: Morcelliana, 1979), 101, note 15: Testimony of Paola Vicentini against Bartolomeo della Barba.

As early as 25 January 1524 Clement VII had ordered his nuncio in Venice to investigate the sale of Lutheran books in Verona and Brescia, and a few days before had written to the bishop of Trent to apprehend and punish vendors and buyers.[22] In Verona the heretical infiltration was contained by the energetic pastoral activity of Bishop Matteo Giberti, who presided vigilantly over his see from 1527 until his death in 1543, work continued later by his successors Agostino Valier and Luigi Lippomano. But in spite of their collective efforts, the trial at midcentury brought to light a large conventicle of Lutherans and their sympathizers.

The first to have proselytized for the new views was the Augustinian, Niccolò da Verona, a master in theology, who in 1530 arranged for the reprinting of Urbanus Rhegius's *Doctrinae novae ad veterem collatio*, a useful manual to buttress his preaching. In 1537–38 he was prior of the convent of San Eufemia, but expelled from the order by its general, Girolamo Seripando, on 22 June 1540 because of his association with Agostino Mainardi and other brother-members suspected of Lutheran sympathies. A year later, the marquis Del Vasto ordered his arrest, together with Mainardi and the Conventual Francesco da Cocconato. Niccolò evaded capture and found a temporary haven in Trent at the court of Cardinal Madruzzo, until the latter was compelled by papal intervention to withdraw his hospitality. Niccolò may have rejoined Mainardi, by now an emigré in Chiavenna. Many of the defendants in the 1550 trial admitted that about a decade earlier they had learned the doctrine of justification in the convent of Santa Eufemia from Niccolò. From that time they had believed "that there was no other purgatory than the blood of Christ who had purged and canceled out our deficiencies, and thus it was madness to believe that there was another purgatory...."[23] The other great proselytizer had been Bernardino Ochino. The famous general of the Capuchins gave his final sermons before his apostasy in Verona in the church of Santa Maria Vecchia, near the convent of his order, where for several months both ecclesiastics and laymen heard him expound the Pauline Epistles.

The Verona heresy trial was held from 22 February to 27 August 1550. The many detailed depositions by both defendants and witnesses provide an unadulterated view of life in a Lutheran conventicle, immersed in a social context of artisans' shops and mercantile establishments, which were great channels of communication due to the mobility of the workers and the constant contact with the northern centers of production of raw materials. The nucleus of the group was composed of artisans and tradesmen encompassing a myriad of occupations, as well as two priests and a schoolteacher. The only patrician was a doctor of law, Tiberio de Oliveto, a convinced Lutheran, in whose home the members met to discuss Scriptures and seek to clarify the new doctrines. Oliveto arranged for the purchase of Latin religious books from Pandolf Ferlegur in Nuremberg and Italian texts from Venice. His home became a repository, housing works from the *Beneficio di Cristo* to the *Sommario della*

[22]Ibid., 97, note 7.
[23]B. Fontana, "Documenti vaticani contro l'eresia luterana," *Archivio della R. Società di Storia Patria* 15 (1892): 77, 81.

Sacra Scrittura, from Brucioli's translation of the New Testament to the *Prediche* by Ochino and Giulio della Rovere.

Because of the prestige of his house and his educational attainments, Oliveto was treated as the leader of the conventicle. He was forty-four years old at the time of the trial, married to the noble lady Cecilia de Montagna who bore him six children, four of whom, a boy and three girls, would later erase the stain of the paternal heresy by taking ecclesiastical vows. Although everyone considered him the principal figure in the group, he succeeded in avoiding interrogation, because the trial concluded a few days before his scheduled appearance set for 9 September. The reason is unclear, as is the fact that lay representatives of the government did not participate in the trial, as had been required by Venetian law since 1548. Verona henceforth would have to adhere to this norm also.

De Oliveto was the person to whom members of the conventicle turned to have clarifications on the more controversial points of doctrine: free will, predestination, purgatory, and the presence of Christ in the Eucharist. The jurist's role was important especially because many of these artisans and laborers attended mass to hear sermons by preachers sympathetic to the new teachings, who obviously would have had to employ language that was not readily comprehensible, disguised, ambiguous, and perhaps even contradictory, out of fear of discovery. The most frequently discussed question within the conventicle remained the presence of Christ in the Eucharistic elements, since some of its members who were merchants or carters traveled to Ferrara where Calvinism had many adepts. A priest in the group, Omobono degli Asperti, who was widely read, declared himself a Zwinglian. On the thorny issue of this sacrament, which had produced a severe cleavage in the ranks of the Reformation after the Colloquy of Marburg in 1529, Oliveto would reply, in agreement with the Lutheran exegesis: "How can we have any doubts on this score, if Martin Luther himself believes that the body of Christ is in the host, as I tell you."[24] Not everyone agreed with this view, as we deduce from a joking remark attributed to the priest Vincenzo Cicogna, himself a Protestant sympathizer, that "if the body of Christ is in the host in the same way that it was put on the cross, then the host would have to be as large as the bottom of a big vat...."[25] On all the other questions there was complete agreement with de Oliveto, who had taught over and over that "the true purgatory was the blood of our Lord Jesus Christ in whom all our defects have been purged, and when someone died, as long as he died truly believing, immediately through the grace of God and the shedding of his blood, he went to Paradise."[26] Among the artisans, there were some who considered themselves sufficiently well versed to be able to gather their fellow workers together in various parts of the city "to speak with them about Scripture." One of them, Annibale de Lombardis, possessed the works of Giulio della Rovere; another, Girolamo de Floris of Santa Croce in Cittadella, in the home of a friend once pulled a Bible out of his pocket and

[24]L. Tacchella, *Il processo agli eretici veronesi*, 125.
[25]Ibid., 117.
[26]Ibid., 136.

proceeded to read passages from a Pauline Epistle, exclaiming: "Look at all these good and saintly things…," concluding, "if you should come with us to where we usually meet to read, you would learn good and beautiful things, things for Christians…."[27]

Annibale "marangone," a carpenter of the *contrada* of San Paolo, made admissions to the court that were detailed, precise, and included the names of all his evangelical friends. His statements permit us to enter into this world of working people, where the new teachings were discussed, appropriated, and passed on, prohibited books were borrowed or purchased, and links forged with co-religionists in Vicenza, Padua, and Venice. Annibale stated the source of his beliefs, which he now was about to repudiate. On the Lord's Supper he had allowed himself to be persuaded by the *Prediche* of Giulio della Rovere, recapitulating sermons 43 and 44, with the words:

> He [della Rovere] does not believe that the sacrament of the Eucharist was
> a simple sign, as some would have it, but neither did he believe that the
> body of Christ was really there, as Holy Mother Church believes. And
> because he saw that it is not given under one or the other species, namely
> the bread and the wine, from this my conscience was troubled when I
> received this sacrament, and I always felt that I should receive it in the way
> that Our Lord had instituted it.[28]

Lucidly, he explained the doctrine of works as a sign of the justification that had occurred. He could recite the titles of almost all the books of vernacular literature, in addition to the *Trattato sull'orazione* of Cardinal Fregoso and a "Monarchia del Mondo" (perhaps Giulio Camillo Delminio's *Teatro del Mondo*). With his friends, the tailors Brontola and Niccolò, the dyer Zuanpier, and Bernardino "coltraro" (plowman), he recruited "evangelical" preachers, such as Don Vincenzo Cicogna at San Zeno and Don Albert Lino, archpriest of San Sebastiano. People gathered to read the Gospels and Ochino's *Prediche,* sometimes in his house, and sometimes in that of the hatmaker Tommaso.

All the artisans who abjured at the conclusion of the 1550 trial, had hungered for the preaching of God's Word, and flocked to hear "that angel and spirit of God," as they described Don Vincenzo Cicogna. In their own homes they would say that the pope was the Antichrist, "who has his feet kissed and whose followers are cardinals and other prelates…."[29] About a certain "Maistrella," the only woman mentioned in the trial, the rector of the church of San Rustico stated quite unambiguously: "I know her, and by public reputation she is Lutheran to the core, so much so that she scandalizes all that *contrada* and even beyond it." She publicly scoffed at the mass and the priesthood, rejected purgatory, prayer, fasting, and the other precepts of the church, and carried about with her the Epistles of Saint Paul,

[27]Ibid., 116.
[28]Ibid., 123.
[29]Ibid., 153.

with which she tried to convert Don Antonio de Ticholis, curate of San Pietro in Cornario.

According to Pietro Manelfi, the Anabaptist "bishop" who returned to the Catholic fold and betrayed all his brethren in the sect, Bartolomeo della Barba, one of the best educated, thanks to his readings and travels, was an Anabaptist. But Bartolomeo failed to convert the others to the sect when he suggested a natural birth for Christ. The most disconcerting figure to emerge from the trial was undoubtedly the priest Omobono degli Asperti of Cremona, formerly curate at Correzzo, a restless adventurer with some education, who owned books by Bullinger, Brenz, and Erasmus, all of which were confiscated from him. He professed himself a follower of Zwingli, Oecolampadius, and Bucer, and opposed the Lutheran interpretation of the Lord's Supper. He harshly criticized the church of the Antichrist, and his steadfastness showed that he did not fear martyrdom. But nothing came of it.[30]

Turning now to Brescia, that other city not too distant from Trent and the eastern shore of Lake Garda, it is surprising to discover the bourgeois-aristocratic character of the heterodox movement there, as opposed to its primarily lower class composition in neighboring Verona. This is a qualified opinion, of course, based on the surviving records, which concern primarily persons from the ecclesiastical sphere who had responsibilities for preaching and instruction, for whom maintaining a Nicodemite posture was becoming ever more difficult. The seeming absence from the records of artisans and laborers can be explained, perhaps, by lingering memories of the terror sown among the more humble classes in the city and outlying areas by the massacre of alleged witches and sorcerers in the Valcamonica in 1518. Bishop Paolo Zane, "corrupt and concubinary," in less than a month had condemned to the flames and to confiscation of their property some eighty persons, mostly ignorant and superstitious women. At Pisogne, Darfo, Breno, Cemmo, and Edolo the repression had been so ferocious that Venice became alarmed at the reports that already by 14 July, "Seventy witches had been burned…and their property seized and given to the churches."[31] At Pisogne, "a certain misser Pasino," a notary of the *Signoria*, also ended by being executed. The government, shocked by the laments of the valley dwellers paralyzed by the continuing slaughter, intervened to restore its authority, decreeing, on 21 March 1521, that henceforth all trials in Brescia had to occur in the presence of two lay jurists. The pitiless persecutions of Bishop Zane, added to the many condemnations for witchcraft and heresy in the second half of the fifteenth century, must largely have rid the lower classes of any desire to immerse themselves in such questions as that of the *libero* or *servo arbitrio*. The only religious reality was now the unlimited power of inquisitors and of the governing classes.

It was an easier matter for the populace, and much less risky, to observe from a safe distance the parody of a procession, such as one organized by youths of good families, who in May 1527 carried aloft through the streets of the quarter of San Alessandro a crucifix turned upside down, all the while reciting blasphemous litanies.

---

[30]Ibid., 152–55.
[31]E. A. Rivoire, "Eresia e Riforma a Brescia," *BSSV* 78, n. 105 (1959): 36–37.

Some years later in May 1542, manifestos against the idolatrous cult of the Holy Crosses were hung from the city walls. The reward of a thousand ducats offered by authorities for the discovery of the culprits was to no avail. The people were fed up with inquisitions, condemnations, and the immorality of the clergy. Once again, in 1527, the people had to witness in the city square the beheading of an elderly monk from Bergamo, Benedetto della Costa, accused of magical practices and witchcraft. As for the attitude of educated persons, ecclesiastical or lay, many of whom belonged to the patriciate, although they generally shared the prevailing views about witchcraft, they opposed the merciless application of justice and the overbearing power of the church.

The new bishop, Domenico Bollani, previously *podestà* of Brescia, received from Paul IV the authority to absolve repentant heretics. If our sources are reliable, in 1559–60, some fifty apostate monks appeared before him to be pardoned, almost all of whom had belonged to convents in the city and surrounding areas. Brescia could claim a goodly number of eminent persons in the intellectual and the religious life, some of whom became protagonists in the Protestant movement. In 1526 a young Augustinian who had won a degree in theology at Padua, preached in the church of Sant'Afra. Peter Martyr Vermigli, who was destined to become one of the leading figures among Protestant reformers, exercised great influence over the movement in Lucca and later still on the English Reformation. The Carmelite Giambattista Pallavicino preached some scandalous Lenten sermons in 1528, taking a different tone from the previous year when he had condemned the blasphemous youthful procession.

In 1530 we encounter four figures important for the Italian Reformation, of whom the first, Francesco Negri, was the future author of the *Tragedia del libero arbitrio*. Negri had fled abroad after leaving his monastery years before, and now had returned to Italy from Strasbourg to urge members of his old order to abandon the Church of Rome. At San Faustino Maggiore for an entire day he worked on the Benedictine Vincenzo Maggi, but failed to persuade him. Sixteen years later, however, Maggi would finally leave his monastery and enter the diplomatic service of France.

Two other personages who will appear again later are equally well known: the Florentine Michelangelo Florio and Giovanni Buzio da Montalcino, both Minor Conventuals. In all likelihood they had contacts with Brescia's Erasmian circle, composed of both laypeople and clergy, which persuaded the notary Milio de' Migli to translate into the Tuscan vernacular Erasmus's *Enchiridion militis Christiani*. In the course of asking the Dutch humanist for permission to publish the celebrated manual, Migli professed himself his devoted disciple, placing him on a level with Origen, Jerome, Augustine, and Chrysostom. He also informed Erasmus that Dominicans and Franciscans had been spreading false reports of his death. The Aristotelian philosopher Vincenzo Maggi, not to be confused with the homonymous Benedictine, served as intermediary between Migli and Erasmus.[32]

The latter replied from Freiburg on 1 June 1529, giving his permission for the translation, but urging Migli to omit the preface to Paul Volz, dated 1518, a manifesto of an antilegalistic and antidogmatic religiosity, and to soften the sharpest barbs against the monastic orders so as to minimize the hostile reaction the book would receive, but holding up St. Paul as the example of one who was all things to all men and could gain their conversion. In the letter, Erasmus reconfirmed his ideal of peace and the imitation of Christ.[33] The Italian translation of the *Enchiridion* appeared at Brescia in 1531 and was reprinted there by Ludovico Britannico in 1540. At least three editions of the work were published at Venice between 1539 and 1543.

Migli's letter to Erasmus sheds light on the cultural life of Brescia in the 1530s, while emphasizing the importance of a vernacular translation of such a crucial text as the *Enchiridion* for persons who did not know Latin, thereby signifying that it would be important to contrast it with Erasmus's great adversary, the Luther of the *Liberty of a Christian Man* and *Bondage of the Will*. Brescia, the scene of the translation and publication of the most significant work of Christian philosophy written by the great Dutch humanist, joined Venice and Padua as a center for the diffusion of his reforming message. In 1542 the printer Britannico brought out another work in an Erasmian vein, one emphasizing the vast number of those who would be saved in the last days, the Carmelite Marsilio Andreasi's *De immensa Dei misericordia*.

Emilio de' Migli, with the philosopher Vincenzo Maggi, Aonio Paleario, Benedetto Lampridio, and others had participated in the Paduan circle clustered around Cardinal Pietro Bembo, to whom he was tied by a close friendship. Migli was a man of culture as well as piety. As a high official in the Brescian government, he had won the esteem of the nuncio to Venice, Altobello Averoldi, bishop of Pola, his fellow citizen, to whom he dedicated the translation of the *Enchiridion*. Migli died the year of its publication and thus did not live to see the success of his version, intended not for erudites alone, but for a larger audience of young and old, men and women alike, so that they might become aware of "how distant we are from Christ, while our vain appetites and immoderate desires remain immersed in the waves of this stormy sea of mundane matters."[34]

The destiny of a number of noble youths, some of the most cultivated and thoughtful in the Christian church, was being played out in many a convent during these years. We find among them some who would become teachers of the laity, such as the Lateran canon Don Celso Martinengo, who spent a period of his life at Sant'Afra and would become Vermigli's collaborator at Lucca; don Ippolito Chizzola, who would be forced to abjure alleged doctrinal errors at Rome in 1551 after his Lenten sermons at Cremona and Venice; Gian Pietro Gozi, who fled to Chiari, where he doffed his religious habit, only to return to the bosom of the church a decade later. Chizzola became a zealous champion of the Counter-Reformation and in 1562

---

[32]Emilio de' Migli to Erasmus (Brescia, 4 May 1529), in *Opus epistolarum Erasmi*, ed. P. S. Allen, 7:143, n. 2154: "…vir profecto minime superstitiosus sed Evangelicae libertatis ac pietatis professor."

[33]Ibid., 8:176, n. 2165.

[34]*Enchiridion di Erasmo Rotherodamo, dalla lingua latina nella volgare tradotto per M. Emilio di Emilii bresciano, con una sua canzone di penitenza in fine*. In Brescia, 1531, 44–54.

published a diatribe against Vergerio, whom he described as a "vile and abject worm," and a "rabid dog."[35]

The innovators' long clandestine efforts were finally exposed in 1543. The discovery was made by the canon Annibale Grisonio of Capodistria, who as episcopal vicar general, was responsible for rooting out heresy. Rumors had been circulating of meetings in the castle at Barco belonging to Gian Francesco Martinengo, attended by his brothers Ercole, Alessandro, and Ludovico; of a group at Orzinuovi that gathered in the home of Bonamente Donzellino and included his sons Cornelio, Fra Teodoro, a Dominican, Girolamo, a physician, and Piero, a student, together with the priests, Calimerio and Agostino Agostini, and Francesco Moneta, the physician Agazzi, and a druggist named Valerio. The most worrisome case consisted of the return to Brescia from Bologna of the crossbow maker Ludovico Medigini, a man in his fifties who took up residence with his son-in-law, Giovan Battista Vertua. Here, in the evenings after work, armorers and merchants met to read the Bible. Medigini was discovered and faced serious charges, including the possession of the *Pasquino in estasi*, but he got off by making a simple abjuration.

Grisonio, whose new superior, Bishop Andrea Cornaro, resided in Rome, was left with full freedom of action. Fully aware of the danger posed by conversions to the Reformation of masters of theology and highly placed men of culture, Grisonio asked for the assistance of the Jesuit Diego Lainez. But there must have been minimal improvement in the situation because, when in 1545 Grisonio left Brescia to begin, as was mentioned earlier, his inquest in Istria, his successor, Gian Pietro Ferretti, bishop of Milo, found the population of the diocese still gripped "by the perversity and ignorance of Lutheran errors."[36]

Even while the exodus of religious men and women from convents was continuing, Pier Paolo Vergerio, the controversial bishop of Capodistria, made a brief appearance in Brescia, stopping for a week from 9 to 15 December 1545, as a guest of the leading families, including Counts Gerolamo and Fortunato Martinengo. On his way back to Mantua, Vergerio halted his journey at Calcinato where he stayed with the doctor of laws and man of letters, Giovan Andrea Ugoni (1507–71), the son of the nobleman Antonio Ugoni.

In 1546 the younger Ugoni was put on trial, accused of associating with Lutherans and of discussing with them free will, purgatory, and the authority of the pope. Curiously, his teacher in matters of the faith was not one of the many learned preachers who passed through, such as the Augustinians Tommaso da Carpenedolo and Angelico da Parma, both themselves suspects, but the rich farmer of Asola, Paolo Veronici. The most serious accusation against Ugoni, confirmed by a search of his house, was the possession of prohibited books: the *Beneficio di Cristo*, works by Zwingli, and the *Dottrina vecchia e dottrina nuova* by Urban Rhegius. Clever lawyer that he was, Ugoni succeeded in having the trial annulled since the proceedings had not adhered to dispositions laid down by the Council of Ten in 1521.

[35] E. A. Rivoire, "Eresia e Riforma a Brescia," n. 106, app. XV; note on I. Chizzola, 85.
[36] Rivoire, "Eresia e Riforma," n. 105, 50.

The Inquisition again arraigned Ugoni in the summer of 1552, and this time was constrained to abjure his errors and to repeat the ceremony publicly in the church of Calcinato before all the parishioners. The peasants who labored on his large farms must have enjoyed the spectacle! Ugoni was sentenced to various penalties, including having to put up a bond of two thousand ducats, pay thirty ducats in charity for the poor, and be confined to the city of Brescia. After returning to Calcinato, he refused to present himself when the tribunal summoned him and was condemned as a contumacious heretic to perpetual banishment and the confiscation of his property. His wife, Laura Maggi, continued to be allowed access to it, but under the administration of her brother, Ottavio Maggi. Ugoni fled to Venice where he rented the house of the painter Titian and lived undisturbed for a time.

One day many years later, in February 1565, Ugoni was recognized and arrested. Two letters were confiscated from him, one to Maximilian II, king of Bohemia, and the other to Catherine de' Medici. He admitted to his judges that he had hoped to persuade the two rulers to grant freedom of religion to their Calvinist subjects, in the hope of seeing a future Huguenot majority in these realms. Incarcerated in a cell in the doge's palace in Venice, Ugoni realized that his cause was lost and confessed that he had been seduced by the works of Calvin and Bullinger. He spilled the names of the "Lutherans" he had known in Venice, many of whom attended the sermons at San Matteo di Rialto, "where the Gospel is preached in an extraordinary way." He mentioned Giovanni Donà; Francesco Spinola; Alessandro Citolini; Agostino Curione (the son of C. S. Curione); Michele Basilio, a Slovene of Curzola, who is "like the beadle of all the heretics"; Francesco Stella; Gerolamo Crato; Ludovico Abbioso; Giovanni Sanser; *messer* Cesare, a schoolmaster who married the widow of Pomponio Algieri, "burned in Rome as a pertinacious heretic"; the Neapolitan Traiano Cioffo, a teacher of letters; and his brother Rinaldo; the butcher Girolamo; Venturino delle Madonne; Antonio Marangon; and Andrea da Ponte, who fled to Geneva. Among the Brescian heretics, Ugoni mentioned the bookseller Piasentin, don Paolo da Lodi, and Paolo Veronici, "the beginning, the poison that got me going down this crooked path." Ugoni seemed to be fully repentant, especially since he had furnished the Inquisition with the names of his companions in the faith. Thus, he was freed from the excommunication laid upon him earlier and banished to his home at San Canciano. But three years later, in January 1568, the Inquisition ended his house arrest and gave him permission "to move freely throughout the whole city of Venice."[37]

Gian Battista da Gardone met a very different fate. At the conclusion of his trial in Venice on 15 July 1553, his judges offered him the opportunity to avoid death if he abjured his errors. But he came from a lower social class than the poet and jurist Ugoni, from Gardone in Val Trompia where there were many smithies for the working of metal. Quite likely Gian Battista was a laborer or an artisan, who had engaged in his trade side by side with Germans. Ten years earlier, the Conventual Gomezio Lovisello had preached not far from there at Collio, and then had quickly to decamp

---

[37] Ibid., n. 106, 59–61, 79–82.

to avoid prosecution for his audacious doctrinal statements. Gian Battista may have been in his audience and swayed by his ideas.

At his Venetian trial, Gian Battista had responded proudly to the inquisitors: "I do not want to go back on these opinions, because I heard them from God…I would be cutting myself off from the truth. Even if my body should die, I shall not die, but I shall live, and whoever loses his life for Christ, finds it." To the question whether he felt himself "united to the Catholic, Roman and apostolic Church," Gian Battista replied, "I do not belong to the Roman church, but I hold the church to be the union of the faithful; and we do not recognize anyone on earth as head of the church, except Christ, and all are equal and servants; and where two or three persons are gathered in the name of Christ, the church is there."[38]

The *podestà* Caterino Zeri wrote to the Venetian Senate on 9 September 1553 apropos the inhabitants of Val Trompia: "All here carry arquebuses, and those of Gardone are not content with one, and even the women carry two, one in the hand and the other stuck through a belt; it is a wicked race, presumptuous, Lutheran, almost impossible to control…."[39] Most likely the stalwart Gian Battista belonged to the evangelical community of Gardone, about which, unfortunately, we have precious little information. We only know of it through the career of the minister Girolamo Allegretti, an ex-Dominican who, after having been in the Valtellina at Poschiavo where he had struck up a friendship with Giulio della Rovere, and at Chiavenna, was appointed head of the large Calvinist congregation of Cremona. In 1550 when dissension broke out in the community of Gardone after it was infiltrated by Anabaptist and antitrinitarian elements, Allegretti paid a visit there to seek clarification of the situation. But after he became caught up in the internecine quarrels and himself was accused of Anabaptism, he returned to Catholicism and to his old convent.[40]

The congregation at Gardone, now solidly Anabaptist, was a cause of concern for both Venetian civic and religious authorities, who feared rebellion in the Val Trompia, which was proud of its administrative autonomy. On 14 October 1563 the Council of Ten ordered that "those villainous heretics of Gardone should be brought to justice." But four years later in 1567, Pius V still had to be informed that the Anabaptist menace persisted there, and he urged the Venetian government to intervene, cautioning them that "those people who rebel against Our Lord God that much more easily will rebel against their temporal lords."[41]

Small nests of dissenters existed elsewhere in Brescian territory at Chiari, Rovato, and Iseo. We know virtually nothing about them except for a few isolated names of persons who were tried and abjured, such as the priest Giovanni Menoni da Rovato, who, swayed by the teachings of the preacher Lovisello, protested against the authority of the Roman church, and died in 1548 without admitting his errors. Another disciple of Lovisello's, Fra Marco Oldofredi, expressed his penance, abjured, and was reconciled.

---

[38]Rivoire, "Eresia e Riforma," 67–68.
[39]Ibid., 68, note 2.
[40]Ibid., 64.
[41]A. Stella, *Dall'Anabattismo*, 136.

Looking at the many Brescian heresy trials that took place from 1564 until the end of the century, an intense and widely felt need for a direct contact with the Scriptures and a search for a more personal piety is apparent. Except in a few cases, we do not find a will to break with Rome and the pope; and it may be the fragmentary nature of the documentation that explains the lack of information about the seizure of books by Protestant authors, as has been noted for neighboring cities. The case of Fra Daniele Baratta of the Minor Conventuals, who are almost as numerous in the ranks of the religious dissent in northern Italy as Augustinians, may provide some notion of the nature of the protest, inspired more by Erasmus than by Luther.

Fra Daniele, who had taken his vows in the convent of San Francesco, came from Montichiari. He had gained a reputation as a preacher beginning in 1546 at Camarana (Modena) and at Chiari. In 1550 at Rovato, during his Lenten sermons, he declared passionately that "there is no other mediator than Jesus Christ, and whoever says that the Madonna is a mediator, commits an abominable sin."[42] During the inquest into his preaching, six priests of Rovato attested to the sympathy that his Pauline message had aroused in the people. From 1551 until 1553, with growing success, he was heard in Brescia, Carpenedolo, Asola, and Legnago. He was arrested in Venice and confined in the prison of San Giovanni in Bragora for three years, finally abjuring on 30 March 1557. The chief accusation against him was having said that "the entire matter of our salvation consists in nothing other than in believing."[43] Daniele Baratta's faith in the justifying God and in Jesus Christ, the only mediator, and his tempered criticism of ecclesiastical institutions resemble positions associated with the "*spirituali.*"

We can conclude that much of the religious unrest experienced by Brescians, whether it took the form of anticlerical utterances on the one hand, or rancor towards the innovators on the other (culminating in the assassination of the gentleman Giacomo Colino, "a rotten heretic"), was founded on the desire for the rebirth of the church and the purification of its institutions. Its result would be a magnificent flowering of charitable establishments, created by celebrated figures in the Catholic reformation, of whom the most illustrious was Saint Angela Merici.

BERGAMO

Among all the cities then under Venetian dominion, Bergamo appears to be the least affected by the Protestant movement, if compared to its neighbors and omitting Venice, which might be considered the focal point of the entire movement. Luigi Chiodi, most recently, summarizing previous research, asserted that the known cases of religious dissent connected with Bergamo totaled roughly no more than a dozen.[44]

---

[42]E. A. Rivoire, "Eresia e Riforma a Brescia," n. 106, p. 163.

[43]Ibid., app. 20, 88, abjuration of Fra Daniele Baratta, 30 March 1557.

[44]Cf. L. Chiodi, "Eresia protestante a Bergamo nella prima metà del '500 e il vescovo Vittore Soranzo: Appunti per una riconsiderazione storica," *RSCI* 35 (1981): 462–63; G. D. Bravi, "Note e documenti per la storia della Riforma a Bergamo (1536–1544)," *Archivio Storico Bergamasco* 6 (1986): 185–228.

However, the total lack of trial records makes it impossible to determine the true extent of the city's participation in the religious dissent. In weighing the situation, one need only look at the rather considerable number of evangelical *Bergamaschi* who found refuge in Chiavenna and in Geneva, and the ease with which one could expatriate to the Grisons, thereby avoiding prosecution. The alleged low penetration of the new ideas into Bergamo should be viewed in the context of the city's less active cultural life, in the fewer institutions of higher education, and the limited number of printing establishments.

There were certainly some German and Swiss Protestant mercenaries who carried on a violent and crude anticlerical propaganda and engaged in vulgar manifestations of iconoclasm against such popular devotions as the cult of the Madonna and of the saints. In 1525 foreign troops led by Count Caiazzo set fire to churches and occupied the cathedral of San Alessandro, causing great damage. Some years later in 1529, they affixed placards against the pope, purgatory and the cult of saints to the cathedral door and elsewhere in the city. The local population was enraged by these wanton acts, made worse by the fact that Venice, sorely in need of mercenaries after the military reverses of the last twenty years, chose not to punish the soldiers who continued their vandalism, defiling painted images of Christ, the Madonna, and the saints. On 8 September 1531, a mob lynched a soldier caught in the act at Borgo San Leonardo.[45]

Bergamo is remembered for the unjust oppression suffered by its bishop, Vittore Soranzo (1500–58), twice imprisoned by the Holy Office, in 1551 and 1557, during the great wave of persecution against the Valdesians. Only the severity of the grand inquisitor, Michele Ghislieri (the future Pius V), who went to Bergamo to investigate the bishop's supposed transgressions firsthand, and the rigid Paul IV could bestow a bad reputation on a pious prelate who was the friend of Pole, Flaminio, and Carnesecchi. There are no known documents to suggest that the bishop ever acted contrary to church discipline. Granted, Soranzo had experienced some of the attractions of Valdesian and Lutheran spirituality, but without ever wishing to separate from Rome, unlike some other followers of Valdés. Soranzo's only fault was to have permitted the preaching of justification by faith in his diocese, such as that of the Franciscan Bartolomeo della Pergola; or of having invited Benedetto Locarno and Girolamo da Piacenza to preach in Bergamo, with the approval of the communal council. They shared the beliefs of the "*spirituali*," although neither man separated from the Church of Rome.

The first famous case of religious dissent in Bergamo concerned the jurist and notary, Giorgio Vavassori Medolago, who belonged to one of the leading families in the city, arrested in 1536. He was a man about fifty years of age who clung to his beliefs, Lutheran in inspiration, on confession, the authority of pope and councils. His friends succeeded in arranging his flight from the convent of Santo Stefano where he was being held. Apprehended anew and imprisoned in Venice, he is

---

[45]Cf. P. Rivoire, "Notizie intorno alla Riforma in Italia nei secoli XVI e XVII," *Bulletin de la Société d'Histoire Vaudoise*, n. 54 (1929): 15.

thought to have died in the course of his trial sometime before July 1539. Giulio della Rovere, who must have had firsthand information, recalls his "marvelous constancy" in the second edition of his *Esortazione al martirio* (1552). The priest Pietro Pesenti of Gerosa abjured the same year, but he was arrested again in 1544 and later would die in prison.

It is difficult to know if there is a connection between the warnings delivered to the booksellers Pasino Canelli of Brescia and the poorly identified Gallo over the sale of prohibited books, the first time before 1537 and then in 1547 and 1549, and the discovery of the library belonging to the ex-Benedictine Giovanni Giacomo Terzo, after his house in Borgo Pignolo was searched. It contained works by Oecolampadius, Bugenhagen, Zwingli, Melanchthon, and Bullinger, beautifully bound and a few even annotated. It came out during Terzo's trial that they had been brought from Germany and Basel by a certain Bartolomeo Stampa and that Terzo himself had rebound them under cover of night. He confessed having read books by Luther, including his *De servo arbitrio* and *A Prelude concerning the Babylonian Captivity of the Church*. Terzo was not a solitary reader and admitted having circulated and sold Luther's books.[46]

Cristino del Botto of Ardesio was probably the most important figure among Bergamo's religious dissidents, given his profound knowledge of Reformation doctrines. He was first accused in 1547 in the company of Lazzarino de' Becchi and Simeone de' Coltanei. During his interrogations, he confessed his disbelief in the ecclesiastical prohibition of food on fast days, masses for the dead, auricular confession, the cult of saints, and purgatory. He asserted as well, "that our works are of no avail for justification and salvation because Our Lord Jesus Christ has satisfied for all; that the sacrament of the altar is only the sign and commemoration of the Passion of Christ, but not a transubstantiated body." He also condemned "the ceremonies of that sacrifice because they are of no value." And almost as a way of summing up his evangelical beliefs, he asserted "faith alone saves us," and therefore, there is no need to obey the teachings and institutions of the Roman church because it is "false and Babylonic."[47]

Since the judges discovered that Botto and his friends had propagated these ideas in the neighboring areas of Ardesio and Valleve, it is highly likely that it was this activity being referred to in a letter, dated 14 June 1550, to Doge Donato from the Venetian ambassador in Rome, Mattia Dandolo. The document reported that Julius III had been informed that in the environs of Bergamo, on feast days the artisans went about "the villages and climbed trees preaching the Lutheran sect to the populace and to the peasants...."[48] Cristino del Botto was condemned to death on 8 November 1550. But the sentence of capital punishment might have met with popular protest unwelcome to the Venetian government, and so banishment from the city was substituted for it.

[46]Ibid., 12–16.
[47]L. Chiodi, "Eresia protestante a Bergamo," 462–63.
[48]P. Paschini, *Venezia e l'Inquisizione romana da Giulio III a Pio V* (Padua: Antenore, 1959), 42.

The very different fate that awaited Marco Zobia of Brescia, who had been residing at Chiavenna since 1563 and was arrested at Bergamo in 1572, opens a window on a virtually ignored phenomenon, emigration from Bergamo to the Valtellina. Through the Brembana and Seriana valleys communications were easy and frequent. Zobia was a merchant, a member of the evangelical church of Chiavenna, who had formed a friendship with exiles from Bergamo, Francesco Bellinchetti, an elder in the refugee community, and the minister Girolamo Zanchi. Bellinchetti was a rich merchant who owned iron mines at Bergün in the Grisons. In 1556, with his brother Alessandro, he had been captured by guards of the Inquisition in Italian territory, but succeeded in obtaining his release thanks to the intervention of the powerful family of Frederick von Salis. Zobia, married to Caterina Bazardi of Chiavenna, resided in a house owned by the children of Battista Pestalozzi. In 1570 he had rented a room to Ludovico Castelvetro when he arrived from Vienna.

Castelvetro, the great Modenese literary critic who had been wandering about Europe as a religious exile for a decade, a few hours before his death added a codicil to the testament he had drawn up in 1553. He wanted to attest to his affection for Marco and Caterina Zobia, who had offered him their hospitality and had served and assisted him during his months in Chiavenna. He bequeathed to them his clothing and few possessions, outside of his books and manuscripts which were to be consigned to his brother, Gian Maria, to whom he recommended them warmly. It was a deserved testimonial for this good and tolerant man who sided with the pastor Zanchi at the time of his conflict with the intransigent, narrowly orthodox first pastor of the community, the Neapolitan Simone Fiorillo.

Zobia was arrested in Bergamo in 1572, where he had probably gone for reasons not connected with business alone because the government of the Grisons failed to get him released. The Venetian authorities ordered their representative in Bergamo to secretly carry out the Inquisition's death sentence against Zobia, either by hanging or drowning. On 27 August he was strangled in prison and buried at night in the embankment of the *Rocca*. Marco Zobia, refusing to abjure and to be reconciled to the church "because of his obstinate desire to continue in his grievous opinions,"[49] remained true to his faith in the evangelical message. Francesco and Costantino Zobia, as well as the latter's son Marco, who found refuge in Geneva in 1579, were related to Bergamo's only victim of inquisitorial justice. From 1551 to 1586 several persons from the city emigrated to Geneva: Cosimo Montano, Giovanni Antonio del Vian, Vincenzo Venturino, Battista Pavese, Bartolomeo Bolla, Bernardino and Francesco Lonagella, and Raimondo Longhino.

At midcentury several others succeeded in evading punishment. Among them were Gian Giacomo Galuppi, Antonio Laner, and the grocer Francesco Medichello, whose shop was at the sign of the *Giustizia Nuova* in San Pancrazio. Medichello,

---

[49] P. Rivoire, "Notizie intorno alla Riforma," 33. Cf. G. Zucchini, *Riforma e società nei Grigioni: G. Zanchi, S. Florillo, S. Lentulo e i conflitti dottrinari e socio-politici a Chiavenna (1563–1567)* (Coira: Archivio di Stato e Biblioteca Cantonale dei Grigioni, 1978), 15; G. Giorgetta, "Le ultime volontà di Ludovico Castelvetro," *Clavenna* 14 (1975): 372–73.

whose place of business was probably, as was often the case, the site of the clandestine meetings, and who was tried in absentia, suffered confiscation of his property and perpetual banishment from the Venetian state. A reward of six hundred ducats was offered in vain, for his capture.[50]

The repression eventually ended by getting the better of the persecuted, even of those who could not easily resign themselves to desist from discussing questions of the faith. As the priest Simone de' Borsetti burst forth spontaneously before his judges in 1545: "It's true that the monk Zaccaria de' Carmini said that I believe the true body of Christ is in the sacrament of the altar; but not the same body born from the Virgin."[51] He also confessed that he had read the *Sommario della santa Scrittura* and a work by Zwingli loaned by a colleague, Sebastiano, parish priest of Pascante. The latter kept a school for boys on the road between the Brembana and Seriana valleys, but he must have taught them more than to read and write because in the classroom, out in the open, he had a copy of Luther's commentary on Galatians.

On 19 May 1576 the *podestà*, Iacopo Contarini, wrote to the doge in these reassuring terms:

> I have little to tell your lordship on the matter of the Inquisition, except to give you pleasure by reporting a great marvel, which hardly anyone can believe is true. Even though this city is beset by constant traffic and borders on Lutheran countries, we have not discovered a single instance of heresy. And in the twenty-four months that I have been in Bergamo, despite the diligence I have shown, I have not found a single case even deserving the slightest mention. Your lordship should be aware that monsignor the bishop, the Inquisition, and I myself have all investigated thoroughly, since it did not seem possible, even to us who are on the spot, that either openly or secretly there should not be some taint of infection. But truly there is none, for which infinite thanks must be rendered to our Lord God from whom this miracle proceeds, and about which your lordship should be well pleased.[52]

Even if the greater part of their lives and careers took place outside Italy, a few words need to be said about two natives of Bergamo who attained great notoriety in the world of European Protestantism: the theologian Girolamo Zanchi (1516–90) and the physician Guglielmo Gratarolo (1516–58). The former, at the age of fifteen, had entered the Augustinian convent of Santo Spirito, where he was preceded by three cousins, Giancrisostomo, Basilio, and Dionigi. In the 1530s this establishment was beginning to attain an important cultural position as a center for humanistic and patristic studies. Basilio Zanchi published a volume of *Poëmata* in Vienna while his cousin, Giancrisostomo, was investigating Bergamo's ancient history. The prior of Santo Spirito, Valeriano Olmo, who had met P. M. Vermigli in the convent of San

[50]P. Rivoire, "Notizie intorno alla Riforma," 31.
[51]Ibid., 24–25.
[52]Ibid., 34.

Giovanni Verdara at Padua, translated into Italian "The Divine Names" of Dionysus the Areopagite.

Girolamo Zanchi's education, which began in this milieu of classical and scriptural studies and of reflection and prayer, was completed at Padua. After he was elected preacher in the Lateran order, he was transferred in 1541 to the convent of San Frediano in Lucca. Here he met his brother-member, Celso Martinengo of Brescia (in the world Count Massimiliano Martinengo). Both, along with others, were converted to the evangelical faith by the prior P. M. Vermigli. Neither Zanchi nor Martinengo immediately followed their leader when he went into exile in 1542. But when Martinengo was accused by Girolamo Muzio of having preached justification by faith alone during his Lenten sermons in Milan in 1551, he fled the country, followed by Zanchi. Many of the latter's friends were under investigation in Bergamo, including Gratarolo. From his birthplace of Alzano, through the pass of San Marco, Zanchi made his way to Chiavenna. It was the beginning of a life of wandering: Geneva, Basel, Strasbourg, and Heidelberg.

In February 1553, on the recommendation of C. S. Curione, whose daughter Violante he married the same year, Zanchi became professor of Sacred Scripture in the school at Strasbourg founded by the humanist Johannes Sturm, where Calvin and Vermigli had also taught. Though he had gone from his cell at San Frediano to a key European center, where the Reformation, under the impetus of Martin Bucer, had gradually won over the entire population, the former Augustinian was at ease and quickly gave proof of his solid theological and philological background. In a time of hardening confessional positions, in the face of the rigid definitions assumed in Strasbourg by the Lutheran Johannes Marbach, a champion of the *Augsburg Confession* imposed by the emperor after the *Interim* of 1548, Zanchi displayed his generous and charitable spirit, trusting that it was possible to enter into dialogue even with Anabaptists, Spiritualists, Zwinglians, and others who opposed Lutheran orthodoxy.

Zanchi was similarly open-minded during the time when he served in Chiavenna from 1563 to 1567 as only the second pastor to be appointed there. It was a period marked by disagreements with Simone Fiorillo, the first to have served in the post, who resented his successor's cultural superiority, sometimes flaunted perhaps, and his attitude favoring the "foreign brethren," who were in Zanchi's opinion eligible to serve on the council of Chiavenna's church even if they were not full citizens. In 1568 Zanchi accepted an invitation from the elector Palatine, Frederick III, to teach at Heidelberg, which had become the center of Calvinism in Germany. Here Zanchi died on 19 November 1590. His *opera omnia* was collected and published in eight stout volumes at Geneva in 1619. According to J. Moltmann as cited by G. D. Bravi, he was the first reformed theologian to place the problem of the people of Israel on an eschatological plane.[53]

Guglielmo Gratarolo, born at Bergamo on 16 May 1516, was a contemporary of Zanchi. After graduating from the University of Padua, he practiced medicine in

---

[53]See G. D. Bravi, "Girolamo Zanchi: Da Lucca a Strasburgo," *Archivio Storico Bergamasco* 1 (1981): 35–64.

his native city with great success. When he was accused of heresy, he crossed the Valcamonica into Rhaetia, eventually reaching Strasbourg where he was well received by his friend Zanchi, who recommended him to Theodore Beza. Gratarolo taught medicine at Marburg and at Basel, where he became dean of the Faculty of Medicine. He died on 16 April 1568, leaving behind sixteen original works and an edition of Pomponazzi's *De incantationibus*. He is one of the many Italian reformers who deserve a critical biography because of his undoubted achievements in the medical field, his gifts as a writer and his place in the world of contemporary culture. Liberal in orientation, opposed to the persecution of dissidents, and disturbed by the execution of Servetus and the posthumous trial of the Anabaptist David Joris, Gratarolo nevertheless supported the severe Calvinist discipline for reasons perhaps more political than ideological. After his flight, Gratarolo was condemned as a contumacious heretic, *"professor haereticae pravitatis,"* on 4 July 1551 by Bishop Soranzo and the Bergamo Inquisition. His property was confiscated and he was to be brought to justice should he ever be apprehended. His wife, Barbara Nicosia, who had followed him into exile, lost her dowry. Gratarolo asked that the epitaph on his tomb should state: *"Guglielmo Gratarolo ob religionem exuli."*[54]

---

[54]P. Rivoire, "Notizie intorno alla Riforma," 20–21.

Bibliographical Note

For the first section, see S. Cavazza, "Un' eresia di frontiera: Propaganda luterana e dissenso religioso sul confine austro-veneto nel Cinquecento," *Annali di storia isontina* 4 (1991).

For the Friuli, see A. Del Col, "La storia religiosa del Friuli nel Cinquecento: Orientamenti e fonti," *Metodi e Ricerche*, n.s. 1 (1982), n.1:69–87; n.s. 2 (1983), n. 2:39–56.

For Jacob Hutter and the Hutterite communities, see U. Gastaldi, *Storia dell'Anabattismo dalle origini a Münster, 1525–1535*, 2 vols. (Turin: Claudiana, 1972; 2d ed. 1992), 1:339–40, 370–76.

For the Brescian cultural milieu and Emilio de' Migli, see S. Seidel Menchi, *Erasmo in Italia, 1520–1580* (Turin: Bollati Boringhieri, 1987), pp. 116, 388; S. Caponetto, "Fisionomia del Nicodemismo italiano," in *Movimenti ereticali in Italia e in Polonia*. Atti del Convegno italo-polacco (Firenze, 22–24 settembre 1971) (Florence, 1974), and now also in Caponetto, *Studi sulla Riforma*, 227–35.

A biographical sketch of Gratarolo, with much new information, is published in F. C. Church, *The Italian Reformers, 1534–1564* (New York: Columbia University Press, 1932), *ad indicem*.

On Zanchi, see J. Burchill, "Girolamo Zanchi: Portrait of a Reformed Theologian and his Work," *Sixteenth Century Journal* 15 (1984): 185–207.

Allegory of the victory of Charles V over the League of Schmalkald in the form of an imperial seal (engraving by Michael Ostendorfer, 1547). *Center*: The two-headed eagle of the Habsburgs, holding in its beaks a cross (faith and religion) and a column (strength), has vanquished and dispersed the wicked. *Left*: The victorious imperial army. *Right*: The conquered Protestant cities.

12

VENICE: A REVOLUTIONARY
CLEARINGHOUSE

POLITICS AND CULTURE

IN THE VAST AND COMPLEX PROTESTANT MOVEMENT in the Three Venices, the inter-
acting political, social, and religious factors at work cannot always be separated, and
often differ from one place to another even in the same state, with the Republic of
Venice a clear case in point. The documentation to help illuminate the religious life
and the activities of the inquisitorial tribunals in the cities of the *Terraferma* is much
harder to come by than for Venice itself. All the trials initiated in the provincial tribunals not actually transferred to the capital have in large part remained buried in
the local episcopal archives. Consequently, many pieces of a vast mosaic still need to
be fitted together. When a scholar does finally succeed in gaining access to one of
these repositories, much light is shed on events of great interest for the life of a small
city in the Venetian dominion.

If our knowledge of the activity of these provincial courts is still fragmentary, the
sources for the Holy Office in Venice are abundant. On 22 April 1547, the tribunal
was reconstituted to include the papal legate, the inquisitor, the patriarch, and, at
government insistence, three lay assistants known as the *Savii all'eresia*. Thousands of
trials were generated by this court, which despite assiduous work upon them since
the last century, have not yet been properly catalogued and inventoried, as noted
recently by Andrea Del Col who is conducting a systematic investigation of the
material.[1]

Venice was more than the meeting ground for the entire movement of anti-
Roman dissent in the territory of the Republic; it took in almost the entire area

---

[1] A. Del Col, "Organizzazione, composizione e giurisdizione dei tribunali dell'Inquisizione romana
nella repubblica di Venezia (1550–1588)," *Critica Storica* 25 (1988): 244–94; idem, "L'Inquisizione
romana e il potere politico nella repubblica di Venezia (1540–1560)," ibid. 28 (1991): 189–250.

spanned by the Three Venices. From the 1540s until roughly 1570, Venice was the center from which the new ideas spread throughout the peninsula, as far south as Sicily. After the Sack of Rome and the fall of the Florentine Republic in 1530, Venice and the University of Padua became the leading Italian cultural centers, channels for the diffusion of European intellectual life. In Venice flourished famous printing establishments, academies, schools, and private gatherings in the homes of patrician families where no subject was off limits, from Holy Scripture to the works of Machiavelli, from astrology to prophecies, from the works of Erasmus and Savonarola to those of Luther, Melanchthon, Zwingli, and Calvin. All the excitement generated by the great religious upheaval of the first half century could be found at Padua's University, no less than in the schools of the monastic orders, enlivened by the constant arrival of books from Germany, Switzerland, and France. The Benedictine establishments of Santa Giustina in Padua and San Giorgio Maggiore in Venice became places for meetings and discussions, as Antonio Brucioli recalled in his *Dialogues*. The *Serenissima*, with its hundreds of printers, typographers, and booksellers, was the leading publishing center in Europe during the entire sixteenth century, and also one of the greatest commercial emporiums in the whole Mediterranean. It was much easier for heretics to infiltrate this immense manufacturing and trading complex than elsewhere.

Certainly, the contribution made by exiles from the states of the church and from Tuscany, anti-Mediceans, anticlericals, Savonarolans and philo-Protestants should not be overlooked. It was a Florentine, Francesco Strozzi, hailing from the Lutheran conventicle in Rome, who translated C. S. Curione's *Pasquillus extaticus* into Italian. Another Florentine, Antonio Brucioli, became the great popularizer of the Scriptures. The Bolognese exile, Ludovico dall'Armi, in the service of Henry VIII, conspired to foment a revolt in the *Romagna*, concerted with the Lutheran princes of the Schmalkaldic League, which would lead to war with the Habsburgs and prevent the linking up of papal and imperial forces. As part of this scheme, another exile in Venice, Guido Giannetti of Fano, in accord with Baldassarre Altieri of Aquila, was given the responsibility of establishing contacts with Johann Frederick of Saxony and with Philip of Hesse. In May 1546 Giannetti dangled before the duke of Saxony the hope of seeing "political liberty" and the freedom to preach "the genuine and just doctrine of the Holy Gospel joined on Italian soil." Many Italians, he suggested, were inclined towards the Gospel, "but suffer the cross and persecution," and cannot show their true faith because of the papal tyranny.[2] In the fall of the same year Piero Strozzi, whose father, Filippo, had committed suicide in prison after the unsuccessful attempt to bring down the rule of Cosimo I, negotiated an alliance between Francis I and the Schmalkaldic League. It was rumored that the Protestants would send Strozzi to Italy as their captain general. These were not projects wholly without foundation when one remembers the discontent over Spanish rule that came to a head at Genoa with the conspiracy of the Fieschi in 1547; at Lucca with the

---

[2] A. Stella, *Dall'anabattismo*, 52.

republican, anti-Medicean plot of Francesco Burlamacchi; and the possibilities available to the French after a decade of occupation in the duchy of Savoy.

But the Venetian governing class, although aware that it had to maintain good commercial and cultural relations with Germany and Switzerland, including the Protestant states, could not bring itself to support such a risky political alliance. The imperial victory at Mühlberg (24 April 1547) confirmed the soundness of the cautious Venetian policy. Dall'Armi was arrested by the governor of Milan, Ferrante Gonzaga, and turned over to the *Serenissima* where he was condemned to death for his part in the assassination of a Venetian nobleman on 14 May 1547.[3] The deaths of Henry VIII and Francis I, and the defeat of the Protestant princes the same year, 1547, marked the end of the political aspirations of Italian evangelicals, despite the recurrent hopes of a Huguenot victory in France, until these too ended with the tragic massacre of Saint Bartholomew in 1572.

THE WORK OF PIER PAOLO VERGERIO

After these events, with repercussions felt in the world of Protestants, philo-protestants, and exiles, Venice became the clandestine clearinghouse for the Reformation movement in the peninsula. Evangelicals flocked there and to neighboring Padua from every part of Italy, even from as far south as Messina. Laymen and clergy, some of them both socially and culturally prominent, settled there, without severing connections with their places of origin, and their families and friends. In fact, they served frequently as intermediaries in supplying them with information on recent publications, on the underground commerce in prohibited books, and on the conventicles organized by the "new Christians." This was the case with Vergerio, the priest Lucio Paolo Rosello, the jurist Francesco Stella of Portobuffolé, the physician Orazio Brunetto, originally from Porcìa, the Brescians Girolamo and Cornelio Donzellino, the Vicentine Alessandro Trissino, Vincenzo Maggi, a former Benedictine from Brescia, and the Sicilian Bartolomeo Spadafora, among many others.

In the three years preceding his flight into exile in the Grisons, the bishop of Capodistria, Pier Paolo Vergerio, was the most prominent member of this group. In spite of the judicial proceedings that had already been set in motion against him, he remained a figure of great prestige thanks to the positions he had held, his strong background in theology and the law, his oratorical skills, and extensive social connections. Wherever he went, he was received warmly and held in high esteem. After the deaths of cardinals Contarini and Fregoso, and the departures of Ochino, Vermigli, and Giulio della Rovere (Giulio da Milano) into exile, religious dissidents thought of Vergerio as the last surviving heir of Catholic evangelism and a champion of the evangelical cause. In Venice and Padua he came in contact with ecclesiastics, professional people, and students, all interested in his singular case, that of a bishop

---

[3]A. Stella, "Utopie e velleità insurrezionali dei filoprotestanti italiani (1545–1547)," *BHR* 27 (1965): 133–82; idem, "La società veneziana al tempo di Tiziano," in *Tiziano nel quarto centenario della sua morte (1576–1976)* (Venice: Edizioni dell'Ateneo, 1977), 103–21.

accused of having tried to reform the preaching and the care of souls in his diocese, the very things that had been longed for in vain for many years by the *"spirituali"* and by the commission *De emendanda Ecclesia*.

If we follow Vergerio's itinerary as traced by Andrea Del Col, we find him in the Venetian bookshop of Andrea Arrivabene, where he spoke freely about ideas condemned by the church which he shared with Arrivabene, the printer of many books on religious subjects and other questions of the moment.[4] Vergerio also became a close friend of the lawyer Francesco Stella, with whom he remained in touch even after he reached Poschiavo. The embattled bishop, experienced jurist, and diplomat that he was, defended himself ably against his accusers, and implicitly revealed his ideas on the question of reform, which daily resembled more and more those of the Protestants, especially Melanchthon's. He traveled incessantly, visiting Trieste, Udine, Portobuffolé, Oderzo, Mantua, Brescia, and Trent. It was easy for him to make contact with dissidents, who read his persecution as a divine sign of the spiritual obtuseness of the Church of Rome. Almost everywhere he went he could count on relatives, friends, and followers to hear him out and assist him. At Udine, Vergerio's sister Coletta, a Clarist nun in the convent of San Francesco, along with some of her fellow nuns, had espoused his views as Pietro Manelfi would testify in the detailed confession he made to the inquisitor of Bologna in 1551. A certain Nicola of Treviso, with the help of some "Lutherans," had managed to enter the convent to convert the sisters to Anabaptism. But when he first spoke to them about Reformation doctrines, he found them already "well instructed."[5]

Francesco Stella, in Venice, where he frequently hosted gatherings in the home of Arrivabene and was a friend of B. Altieri, directed his proselytizing efforts towards Portobuffolé, Villanova, Ghirano, Lutrano, Monsué, and Oderzo. The themes that he now broached, the *loci communes* of the Reformation, were far removed from Augustinianism and a generic sympathy for the Lutheran protest: the pope was the Antichrist, the Church of Rome was the devil's own congregation, the mass an abomination. There should be only two sacraments, baptism and the Eucharist, understood in the Calvinist sense. These were the notions professed in the 1540s at Oderzo, in the gatherings led by Stella and by Lucio Paolo Rosello, who had arrived there in January 1541.

The doctrines held by the conventicle not only resembled those of the Lutheran groups discussed previously, but even repeated their more typical expressions: "The blood of Christ is our purgatory," "the elect cannot die, even if they choose to," "faith alone can save me without works, but I also believe that nothing but good works can result from my faith," "the sacrament of the altar is bread and that signifies the body of our savior," the church is "the union of faithful Christians."[6] And the members in

---

[4]See A. Del Col, "Lucio Paolo Rosello e la vita religiosa veneziana verso la metà del secolo XVI," *RSCI* 33 (1978): 422–59.

[5]C. Ginzburg, *I costituti di don Pietro Manelfi* (De Kalb: Northern Illinois University Press; Chicago: The Newberry Library, 1970), 81–82.

[6]A. Del Col, "Lucio Paolo Rosello," 427.

attendance, such as the notary Francesco Pirochin, jurists, and churchmen, read works by Luther, Calvin, Rhegius, Vermigli, Valdés, the *Sommario della santa Scrittura*, and the *Beneficio di Cristo*.

In 1545 the Oderzo group hosted Vergerio in the home of Bernardino dei Melchiori, and in subsequent years it invited as a preacher the Augustinian Giuliano Brigantino, called "da Colle," because he hailed from Colle Valdelsa, whose run-ins with the Inquisition we have mentioned earlier. His presence in Venice at the same time as Ludovico Domenichi, both leading figures in the Florentine dissent, represents one of the many threads linking the *Serenissima* to the rest of the peninsula. The physician Orazio Brunetto of Porcía, once a student at Padua and later associated with literary figures who sympathized with the new ideas, was another of Vergerio's companions. Brunetto's contacts included the physician of Capodistria Leandro Zarotto, Domenichi, Alessandro Citolini, Paolo Crivello, Anton Giacomo Corso, and Malatesta Fiordiano. In 1548 Brunetto published a collection of letters dealing with a variety of subjects. Themes drawn from Catholic evangelism run through them, with the accent on the value of Scripture, the predestination of the elect and of the reprobate, and justification by faith alone, ideas heavily indebted to Augustinianism, but with Lutheran and Valdesian overtones. As Del Col correctly observed, "the questions and the themes that are expressly treated, at greater or lesser length, touch upon religious issues of a general nature: the world, life itself, human events guided by divine providence; fate, 'Fortune,' 'Nature' are all fables because it is God who directs all things and thus we must accept everything from his hands and follow his will."[7] Brunetto separated himself from the "*spirituali*" and reflected the influence of Reformation literature by stating more radically the need to abandon the old manner of preaching, to set aside rhetoric and return to the simplicity of the Gospel, since the Holy Spirit is over everything and makes eloquent even the rough apostles. There is close agreement between Brunetto and Vergerio on these themes, since the latter was himself addressing his spoken and written word to an audience of "*rudes*." Brunetto encouraged him to regard his travails before the Inquisition as a sign of his election.

Lucio Paolo Rosello and the Conventicle at Porcìa

After Vergerio went into exile, his place as proselytizer was taken by the priest Lucio Paolo Rosello (d. 1556). Rosello was born in Padua towards the close of the fifteenth century, became a doctor of both laws, and in 1525 published a manual of canon law, followed by other writings of jurisprudence. By 1530 he was already expressing interest in the Reformation, writing a letter of support to Melanchthon on the occasion of the Diet of Augsburg, and also corresponding with Francesco Negri. From 1532 to 1548, Rosello was parish priest at Maron della Brugnera, seat of the counts of Porcìa and Brugnera, a town of 1,300 inhabitants enriched by a small convent and

---

[7]Ibid., 429.

some professional people. This period witnessed the first manifestations of open dissent and rebellion there against the rites and precepts of the church.

The moving spirit behind them was Antonio Fachin who had married Caterina, Rosello's sister, a little before 1540. Fachin, who had a linen business, turned his shop into a place where laborers and artisans could discuss religious issues. He kept on hand Brucioli's translation of the Scriptures and made it available to anyone who cared to consult it. Like the authors of the *Sommario della santa Scrittura* and the *Beneficio di Cristo*, Fachin, who had a fairly good education and perhaps had even read these two extremely popular books, took a positive stance and did not directly attack the church and the pope. Although he had stopped going to mass and was not making a secret of his religious sympathies, he was left undisturbed. A number of people agreed with him and even the counts of Porcìa harbored some sympathy for Lutheranism, which was not a unique attitude among the Friulan lesser nobility. In 1527 Count Wenceslaus married Lucrezia Martinengo, whose brothers Massimiliano and Fortunato were working for church reform.

The small conventicle of Porcìa over which Fachin presided consisted of relatively affluent artisans, his brother Zan Hieronimo, Francesco Soldà, known as Cechon, a leather worker, Zulian della Massara and Ieronimo Massara, both shoemakers, Fiorì di Luchetta, a teamster, the German laborer Zorzi Stanfelder, and Alvise "Cinque dea," a weaver. They were later joined by a priest of Villanova, Polidoro Novello. When, almost a decade later, the entire group was put on trial, Antonio Fachin, simply and lucidly, explained the origin of his faith in Jesus Christ:

> Perusing and reading the Holy Gospel of our Lord and Savior, I became convinced that I was finding in it all the spiritual treasures and the great goodness and mercy of God towards Christianity through the incarnation, nativity, life, preaching and passion, resurrection, ascension of our Savior, and through such a fruit and faith in the Holy Gospel the human race was reconciled by this means with the majesty of God. And so, since the Gospel is the door through which we are led to heaven, believing in this, I have held firmly that the blood of our Lord, spilled for the remission of the sins of believers, has been abundantly sufficient for the remission of sins, without human inventions. And so because of this I trusted, as I have said, in fact wholly trusting, I am obliged to believe and observe what is commanded by that Sacred Gospel.[8]

The corollary of this profession of faith was the return to the teachings of the church of the apostles by the abolition of such human innovations as clerical celibacy, vows, indulgences, the cult of images, fasting, and so on. Fachin's was essentially a reformed profession of faith, as we note in his interpretation of the Lord's Supper.

---

[8]Trial session of 4 November 1557, in A. Del Col, "Eterodossia e cultura fra gli artigiani di Porcìa nel secolo XVI," *Il Noncello* 46 (1978): 59.

The Venetian trial against the conventicle had opened with a denunciation made on 22 April 1556, and concluded two years later with the abjuration of all the defendants. Felice Peretti, the future Sixtus V, was the inquisitor presiding over these proceedings. Antonio Fachin himself realized that he could not successfully use a defense based on the claim that a heretic is only one who does not believe in God and Jesus Christ and does not obey the scriptural injunction to love one's neighbor. In March 1558 he abjured with his companions. The spiritual journey of the artisan of Porcìa resembles his brother-in-law Rosello's, the leader of the Porcìa group. After leaving his parish at Maron, Rosello settled at Venice in 1548. Since he did not have financial worries, he dedicated himself to an intense career as writer and translator, and associated with persons who shared his religious views, among whom the Brescians stand out: Vincenzo Maggi, the ex-Benedictine; the physicians Girolamo Donzellino and Zuan Battista; the priest Paolo da Lodi, tutor in a patrician family; Gasparo Citolino, former secretary to the English ambassador; Gasparo Parma, steward to Andrea Pisani and his wife Pantasilea; and the Roman, Pietro de Meis.

Vincenzo Maggi and his friends were denounced to the Holy Office by Caterina Colbertardo, who had been in the service of Maggi's wife, Lucrezia Panza for three years. She testified: "They are new Christians, just like him, and they gather together and know each other's secrets."[9] When Maggi's house was searched in April 1553 he fled to Switzerland and found refuge at Chür, never again to return to Italy. In 1557 he matriculated at the University of Basel and by 1565 can be found in Geneva. Girolamo Donzellino left Venice shortly after Maggi. It is not too difficult to deduce the beliefs of the group, which were also Rosello's, from the trials against Maggi and the priest Paolo da Lodi: justification by faith alone, rejection of the notion that salvation can be obtained through works, denial of the existence of purgatory, of the efficacy of indulgences, of papal authority and of the real presence of Christ in the Eucharist.

CORNELIO AND GIROLAMO DONZELLINO

By the time Rosello moved finally to Venice, his religious beliefs had matured, as well as his intentions to communicate them to others in writing and by word of mouth. He came to know Girolamo Ruscelli, Pietro Lauro, the translator of the *Colloquia* of Erasmus, and Ludovico Dolce, but he also established true friendships and working relations with committed Protestants. One of them was the Brescian literary figure Cornelio Donzellino, brother of the physician Girolamo. Cornelio, who had come to Venice in the summer of 1550 with Count Ercole Martinengo of Barco, previously had been tutor to the nephews of P. P. Vergerio in Capodistria and was sympathetic to the latter's travails.[10] Once again we discern the threads linking the various strands of Venetian heterodoxy. Rosello and Donzellino worked for about a year on the translation of the *Philippics* of Demosthenes, helping to satisfy the growing demands

---

[9]A. Del Col, "Lucio Paolo Rosello," 439.
[10]Ibid., 447.

for vernacular versions of the classics. They also collaborated in producing an Italian translation of the sermons of Theodoret of Cyrrhus, *Della providenza di Dio*.

In 1551 almost contemporaneously, the two friends and co-religionaries independently published books that can be considered products of their mature theological positions. In spring, the printer Comin da Trino of Monferrato brought out Rosello's *Considerazioni devote intorno alla vita e Passione di Christo*; while in Lyons Cornelio Donzellino's *Le dotte e pie parafrasi sopra le pistole di Paolo a' Romani, Galati ed Ebrei* appeared. The two works, from different perspectives, propounded similar teachings along the lines of the Augsburg *Confession* and Calvin's *Institutes*, with Rosello standing in the tradition "of a tendency within Italian religiosity characterized by emotionalism and immediacy, responsive to contemporary exigencies."[11] Taking the approach of the *Beneficio di Cristo*, he presented his ideas about Jesus Christ, Savior, and Redeemer of humanity positively and without polemic. Donzellino, on the other hand, in his commentary on the Pauline Epistles, assumed the other face of Protestant theology, and took a harsh approach to Roman teachings, which he dubbed "the pestiferous doctrine of the devil" and of the Antichrist, whose spokesmen were false apostles and false prophets.

The two writers accepted the Calvinist doctrine of Communion and of double predestination. As Del Col correctly discerned, the intermingling of Lutheran and Calvinist elements is easily apparent,[12] in a formula that became the fundamental characteristic of the Italian Reformation for the rest of the century. The danger that the encroachments of radical Anabaptists would lead to its disintegration, precisely at the time when it was attempting to establish throughout north-central Italy a clandestine network linked to and assisted by the evangelical churches in the Grisons and Geneva, emerges from these writings by Rosello and Donzellino. Hoping to bring unity to the movement and dissipate the rancor generated by the theological disputes dividing Lutherans and Zwinglians, they translated into Italian Calvin's *Petit traicté de la saincte cène de notre Seigneur Jesus Christ*, originally published at Geneva in 1541. The *Treatise* is one of the most lucid of the reformer's writings. Based on a thorough study of Biblical texts, it affirms the real spiritual presence of Christ in the elements of the Supper through the work of the Holy Spirit, a teaching that resembles the Lutheran, but without its materialist residues. The Italian version was never printed and a manuscript copy of it was found among the papers confiscated in January 1550 from Zuane de Honestis, a friend of Donzellino and Rosello.[13]

In June of the next year, a search of Pietro Cocco's house, where Rosello lived, turned up prohibited books, and the latter was arrested. After several exhaustive interrogations in which, as a jurist, he defended himself skillfully, he ended up admitting and abjuring his errors. Rosello was condemned to house arrest and was

---

[11]Ibid., 456.

[12]Ibid., 451–57.

[13]The Italian translation of Calvin's *Petit traicté* was published anonymously at Geneva in 1561 with the title: *Breve e risoluto trattato de la Cena del Signore composto da M. Gio. Cal. e tradotto nuovamente in lingua volgare italiana*. Appresso Francesco Durone, 1561.

not heard from again. Cornelio Donzellino slipped out of Venice during the crisis. In February 1552, as we shall see, he was in prison in Florence.

The close ties between Brescian and Venetian reformers is evidenced also by the case of Girolamo Donzellino, Cornelio's physician brother. After graduating from the University of Padua, he went to Rome in 1543 and joined the Lutheran conventicle gathered about Diego de Enzinas, who would be condemned to the stake at the end of 1546. A letter written by Enzinas to Luther in which he called the reformer "angel of God," had fallen into the hands of inquisitors. The document conveys the perplexity of Enzinas over Luther's recent affirmation of the real presence of Christ in the Eucharistic elements, and asks whether even a person lacking faith could receive the body and blood of Christ. These queries testify to the continuing anxiety over these questions preoccupying Italian evangelicals.[14] Donzellino learned that under torture, Enzinas had divulged the names of his companions, among whom was Francesco Strozzi, the translator of C. S. Curione's *Pasquillus extaticus*, and Guido Giannetti. The news prompted Donzellino to return to his family in Brescia.[15] Subsequently he accepted an invitation from the senator Leonardo Mocenigo to establish his medical practice in Venice, where he quickly developed a flourishing clientele among the city's patrician families, such as the Bembo, Valier, Centanni, and Canal. Donzellino also ministered to women's convents, caring for such patients as Sister Febronica, formerly Cecilia Morosini, and Sister Paola, the daughter of Alvise Marcello. One night the two women disappeared, never to return to the convent. Many years later Donzellino was accused of having arranged their flight. When Paola was finally discovered at the age of seventy and questioned, she told her examiners that she had been forced to take the veil by her parents: "I was stuck in there forcefully when I was very young.... I did not want to go...and I was never happy."[16]

Donzellino joined clandestine groups, participated in university gatherings where the principal questions of the day were discussed, and met people of all religious persuasions: Valdesians, Lutherans, Calvinists, and Catholic reformers. The names that emerged from Donzellino's two trials in 1560 and 1574 mirror the development and spread of religious dissent in Venice. They range from the former Benedictine Vincenzo Maggi to Bishop Andrea Centanni, from the Counts Martinengo to the Augustinian Giuliano da Colle, from B. Altieri to Alessandro Citolini. And to these we could add L. Manna, B. Spadafora, M. Florio, G. Zanchi, F. Porto, to mention only the best known. Donzellino was wholly immersed in a vast movement of dissent, and when in 1553, Vincenzo Maggi and his wife were accused of heresy, Donzellino fled Venice, first stopping to visit the duchess Renée in Ferrara, and then proceeding to Germany where he met up with Vergerio in Tübingen. Serious family

---

[14]Letter of Diego de Enzinas to Luther, dated 24 December 1545, in P. Tacchi Venturi, *Storia della Compagnia di Gesù*, 1, pt. 2, 137–39.

[15]For G. Donzellino, see E. A. Rivoire, "Eresia e Riforma a Brescia," *BSSV*, n. 106 (1959): 70–74; L. Perini, "Ancora sul libraio Pietro Perna e su alcune figure di eretici italiani in rapporto con lui negli anni 1549–1555," *NRS* 51 (1967): 363–404; A. Del Col, "Lucio Paolo Rosello," 440–43; and the biographical sketch by A. J. Schutte in *DBI* 46: 238–43.

[16]E. A. Rivoire, "Eresia e Riforma a Brescia," 71, note 20.

matters brought him back to Brescia in 1560. He presented himself spontaneously before the Holy Office in Venice and abjured his errors on 1 February 1561.

ALESSANDRO TRISSINO

In 1558, Alessandro Trissino (1523–1609), the natural son of Giovanni Trissino, who would become one of the most influential representatives of Calvinism in the Veneto, came to Venice as legate from Vicenza.[17] Although his background differed from Rosello's, he took his place as leader of the evangelical movement. The careers of Trissino, of the notary Domenico Mazzarelli, and of the lawyer Domenico Roncalli of Rovigo reveal a network that encompassed Venice, Vicenza, Rovigo, Padua, and Monselice.

Alessandro, through the intercession of his cousin Giulio Trissino (1504–76), and son of the humanist Gian Giorgio, a prominent figure in the Calvinist movement, was accepted in the school run by Fulvio Pellegrino Morato, who served as "reader" in Vicenza for seven years (1532–39). During this time Morato, who was also the father of the poetess Olimpia Morato, was openly voicing his anticlerical views. His students included Niccolò and Marco Thiene, Giulio Trissino, and Count Carlos de Seso. After Morato moved to Ferrara, he continued to watch over their education, providing them with books and ideas until his death in 1548.[18] Another teacher of Alessandro's and of such youths as Giovan Battista Trento, whom we shall meet later, was Francesco Malchiavelli, public reader from 1545 to 1548, who explicated Calvin's *Institutio* to his students.

From his native Vicenza, a city rich in cultural initiatives and "innovative ferment," Alessandro enrolled in the Law Faculty at the University of Padua, attended by students from all parts of Italy and Europe, including hundreds of Germans, English, and Swiss (about six thousand in the half century 1550 to 1600), many of whom were Protestants. Here the young Trissino began to attend clandestine meetings organized by Federico Manusso of Candia where he met persons from nearer (Udine, Venice) and more distant (Cyprus) parts. They alternated gathering in various homes, Angelo da Treviso's, Zonetto Belecca's, or in Porciglia, at dame Angela's, where they read Lutheran books and discussed news from beyond the Alps. They became convinced that the great conflict in progress there might culminate in the demise of the papacy and the Church of Rome.

Setting his studies aside for three years from 1558 to 1561, Trissino served as Vicenza's representative in Venice, where he broadened his circle of acquaintances and deepened his relations with evangelicals in Padua, Vicenza, and Monselice. Monselice had become a center for Calvinist proselytization thanks to the activities of a merchant from Puglia, Oddo Quarto, who owned land there. Alessandro possessed an extraordinary capacity for socializing and made many friends. Under cover

---

[17]A. Olivieri, *Riforma ed eresia a Vicenza nel Cinquecento* (Rome: Herder, 1992), 300–14.
[18]Idem, "Alessandro Trissino e il movimento calvinista vicentino del Cinquecento," *RSCI* 21 (1967): 54–117.

of his political appointment, he brought together in the residence of Vincenzo Grimani members of the governing class and cultural elite, such names as Vittore Pisani, Vittore Correr, Giovanni Paolo Contarini, Girolamo Dolfin, Marino da Pesaro, Prassildo Volpe, and Fabio della Saona. He included fellow Vicentines, Francesco Squarzi, Giulio and Tiberio Piovene, and Ludovico Corte of Crema, an apostate Augustinian and jurist who had been living in Venice since 1545. The group ranged from such members of the nobility as Count Sforza Pallavicino and a number of professional people, to artisans such as the Veronese tailor Francesco Pignolo, who opened up his house in the "Salizzada" of San Lio for the gatherings.

These congregations, held in various locations throughout the city, did not concern themselves specifically with questions of Scripture, or at least this is what we deduce from the trials initiated against them, although we should remember that the accused persons would have tried to conceal incriminating matters. These gatherings were mini-academies where everything was open to discussion, from such lofty subjects as the freedom of man and the sovereignty of God with St. Augustine as a guide, to the question of the cult of saints and the efficacy of images; from Machiavelli, whose pessimism about man was seen as being akin to Luther's *De servo arbitrio*, to the authority of the pope and the church over secular authority. According to a recent study,[19] it appears that alchemical and magical notions figured in the animated discussions. Alessandro Trissino, with a certain delicacy, knew how to move the conversations to the theological realm.

The atmosphere was very different in the Vicentine gatherings held in the homes of Francesco and Ludovico Trissino, of Bernardo da Schio, or in the villa of "Lanzé" where the nobility of the city were accustomed to meet. At Lanzé, Alessandro Trissino's friend from student days, G. B. Trento, made secret appearances. He had become a furrier and settled in Geneva in the summer of 1557. As a member of the Italian exiles' church there, he served as the liaison with the Calvinist groups in Vicenza and Rovigo. He was closely bound, in fact, to Domenico Roncalli, founder of the Academy of the "Addormentati" in Rovigo and organizer of the city's evangelical community. Trento, an audacious proselytizer who was committed to the diffusion and sale of prohibited books, brought to the peninsula information about the progress being made by the Reformation elsewhere, the Wars of Religion in France, and life in Calvin's Geneva. He was called "the crazy and heretical Huguenot."[20]

The conventicle at Lanzé was made up primarily of Calvinists, but it had some Anabaptist members. There were long discussions over the person of Jesus, but the majority rejected the denial of his divinity, even if the absence of a pastor among them affected their theological development adversely. The Bible, the *Beneficio di Cristo* and Calvin's *Institutes* were the most widely circulated books. From Geneva, Trento shipped entire bales of Bibles, which through a certain Piero Torniero, reached the Pellizzari brothers, the largest representatives of the silk industry in Vicenza. The evangelical community made a serious effort to organize itself and tried

[19]Ibid.
[20]Ibid., 61.

to recruit members from the lower classes by paying for their daughters' dowries and dispensing charity for the needy. It was in contact with conventicles at Rovigo, Venice, and Monselice through Trissino and his friends, Oddo Quarto and the "knight of Lendinara," as the lawyer Domenico Roncalli was known after he was made a knight of St. Mark by Doge Francesco Venier in 1554, as well as the notary Domenico Mazzarelli, he too, a member of the Academy of the *Addormentati* in Rovigo.

The various groups did not restrict themselves to prayer, Bible readings, and the celebration of the Lord's Supper. They also passionately discussed the political situation, unable to conceal their admiration for the Huguenots, whose victory they ardently championed, since it would have great repercussions for Italy as well. Others longed for the unification of all Christian churches under the auspices of a council, "piously assembled and by the will of God," in which everybody would have to submit, pope included, to the Gospel truth. Their thinking resembled that of the humanist Aonio Paleario, as if someone among them knew the *Actio in pontifices Romanos*, although it would not be published until 1600.

An unforeseen event exposed the activities of Trissino and his friends. At Como, in early January 1563, during a routine customs inspection of goods being shipped by the Pellizzari brothers, letters were discovered from persons in Vicenza addressed to their "brethren" in Lyons and Geneva. A close examination of the documents revealed that the correspondence had been going on for years. Information was being exchanged about the Vicentine evangelical community and help requested especially for prosecuted and imprisoned brethren. One of these letters, dated 28 June 1562, signed by Alessandro Trissino, provided the irrefutable proof of his Calvinism and of his ties to the churches at Chiavenna and Lyons. This discovery provoked a scandal and was met with incredulity by those who thought him a good Catholic.[21]

The Roman Inquisition demanded exemplary punishment to throw fear into the many Vicentine and Venetian patricians who had inclined towards Calvinism and the Huguenot cause. The Curia sent an energetic warning that "if the Republic should not put out quickly this diabolical fire, it would spread greatly, but may God never permit it, that it would foment even larger fires as we see consuming other provinces and kingdoms."[22] The threat of political upheaval was always the most efficacious way to gain the cooperation of aristocratic Venice. Trissino attempted a desperate defense before his judges, declaring himself to be a good Catholic, but interrogated under torture he realized that dissimulation was impossible. He plotted his own escape from the house of Francesco Trissino, which had been assigned to him as his "prison," and wrote to his trusted friend Prassildo Volpe to track down the lawyer Roncalli. The latter hastened to Vicenza and began to organize the flight of his brother in the faith. At dawn on 31 May 1563, Alessandro fled Vicenza and eventually reached Chiavenna in the Valtellina. His family hoped, in vain, to persuade him

---

[21]A. Olivieri, *Riforma ed eresia a Vicenza nel Cinquecento*, 379–401.
[22]Idem, "Alessandro Trissino," 65.

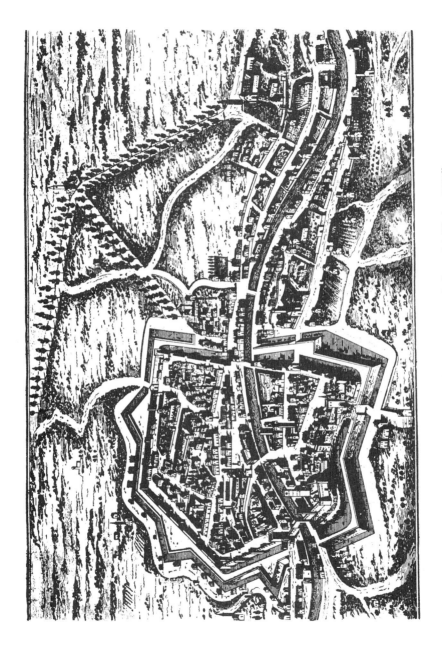

The city of Rovigo (from Salmon, *Descrizione di alcune città* [Venice, 1751]).

to return. On 7 March 1564 he was condemned as a heretic in absentia and burned in effigy.

The firmness with which the Council of Ten cooperated with the Vicentine tribunal of the Inquisition and acceded to Roman pressure was a consequence of its preoccupation with Vicenza, which went back almost three decades. As early as 1535, a traveling salesman, Giovanni Boselli of Brescia, known under the name of Zan Maria di Rozzo, had been going about from village to village slandering the church, accusing it of extortion. The next year a certain Sigismund, a German, was taken into custody.[23] His work was continued by other German artisans and merchants, as well as by two men identified only as Giovan Battista of the Valtellina and Giovanni of Poschiavo.

The "bad seed" had germinated so successfully that Paul III, in 1546, felt compelled to intervene directly with the Venetian government. Several suspects were arrested the following year as a consequence of accusations made by a Spanish Franciscan, but there was not enough evidence to convict them. The only defendant to confess was Giandomenico Gastaldi of Monza, in whose pharmacy, the "Colombina," clandestine gatherings had been held. But he said only that the participants denied the authority of the pope and the existence of purgatory. He did add that the membership was large, perhaps as many as five hundred, and that there were some "big chiefs" among them. [24] When these suspects left their Venetian prison, they smuggled out a work by Baldo Lupatino, incarcerated there, and passed it on to an Istrian printer, Michele Catalicchio. Among those implicated in the proceedings, the names of Counts Giuseppe and Manfredo da Porto, Adriano and Ottavio Thiene, Giulio Capra, and Alessandro and Giulio Trissino were mentioned. Suspicions were also cast against members of various noble Vicentine families, the Pigafetta, Pasini, and Pagello. Even if this was still in the realm of hearsay, it was natural that Vicenza, already chafing under Venetian domination, should fear that these allegations might provide the Republic a pretext to seize even greater control.

The Calvinist Community of Rovigo

The discovery of Alessandro Trissino's intrigues, fifteen years after the arrest and condemnation of numerous Anabaptists, was a hard blow and a timely warning for Venice's governing class. Trissino's absolute confidence that he would be assisted by the solicitor, Giovanni Domenico Roncalli, sets the stage for one of Italy's most important Calvinist communities. The significance of the group is not based so much on their number, as on their unity, their organizational ability, and their bond to the ideals of Bernardino Ochino and Peter Martyr Vermigli. One of the more prominent members, Cesare Aldiverti, was reported to have told the faithful assembled at Canda

---

[23]M. Spagnolo, "Prodromi della Riforma a Vicenza nel secolo XVI," *Regnum Dei* 5 (1949): 95–96.
[24]A. Stella, *Dall'Anabattismo*, 57.

that he possessed a copy of Ochino's *Prediche* that was so "very dear to him that at night he kept it like a pillow by his head."[25]

The short history of Rovigo's evangelical community is of much interest. The first missionaries came from outside the city, and two of them, Antonio da Torino and a teacher of French, Guglielmo Dolceti (Dulcet?) were Protestants from the Turin area, Waldensians perhaps. At first Antonio, Roncalli's voice teacher, was critical of his pupil's idle and dissolute existence: "The whole night he leads the insolent life of a youth lacking moderation." But he succeeded in converting him, "and in but a short time, the knight was transformed in everything and for everything from one type of life to another."[26] Antonio instructed Roncalli in the new faith between 1551 and 1552 and the latter, in turn converted his mother, Margherita Casalini, and also Cesare Aldiverti, who owned lands in Canda.

The links to Piedmontese evangelicals were not limited to this first encounter. Domenico Mazzarelli, one of the leaders of the embryonic community, gave his sister Giovanna in marriage to Francesco Serralonga of Turin. The latter, after being condemned in absentia by the Holy Office in Venice, emigrated to France and then to Geneva where he appeared on the rolls of the bookseller-printers by January of 1560. His brother, Giovanni Bernardino, became a deacon in the Italian exiles' church and Francesco's son, its pastor. But there is more. When on 4 April 1562, the wife of the notary Mazzarelli, Laura, gave birth to her first son, Teofrasto, the godfather would be another Piedmontese Calvinist, Cesare Boniparte of Novara, a solicitor in Venice and later a merchant in Geneva, after 1572. Thus a deep bond of faith existed between Piedmont and Rovigo, which resulted in the creation of a homogeneous family group.

The conventicle, initially small, grew as it made conversions in educated and professional circles, winning over such persons as the physician Giovanni Battista Minadois, the teacher Antonio Riccoboni, the notary Girolamo Bicaccia, the landowner Ottaviano Giglioli of Ferrara, and the notary Domenico Mazzarelli. The latter had studied law at Padua where he first came into contact with Reformation doctrines. During 1548–49 he taught in Rovigo and it appears that two sonnets exalting salvation by divine grace and the priesthood of all believers date from this period. They were a response to "mendacious and useless" polemical remarks made by a preacher in the church of San Francesco. The sonnets circulated among Mazzarelli's friends and Girolamo Biscaccia recited them from memory. Mazzarelli and Roncalli became impassioned proselytizers, "doctors of Lutheran doctrine."[27] The two realized the importance of the domestic "church" since they could not meet publicly for the reading of Scripture and for prayer. Mazzarelli went to Venice to take a wife, Laura, the sister of the Protestant, Giacomo Pellegrino.

---

[25]G. Marchi, *La riforma tridentina in diocesi di Adria nel secolo XVI, descritta con il sussidio di fonti inedite* (Cittadella: Rebellato, 1969), 189.

[26]Ibid., 168, 171.

[27]Ibid., 172–73.

Cesare Aldiverti converted his relatives, including his uncle, Benedetto, and proselytized in the area of Canda, where the family had owned or rented land since 1555. In 1546 Cesare's cousin, Aristotele, had scandalized his friends one day in a Venetian church where he had gone to listen to a Franciscan preacher. When the priest began the mass, he hid behind a column so that he would not have to see the altar and thereby commit idolatry. During his youth he had traveled on business to the Orient, and in Venice he had been in contact with merchants from the German quarter (*Fondaco dei Tedeschi*), where it was easy to acquire prohibited books, and where he had heard speak about Lutheran doctrines and the new Christian church. Listeners frequently clustered around Cesare Aldiverti in Rovigo, one of them a player of the lyre, Giovanni Panciera, called "Orbo," because he was blind. Thanks to the patient efforts of a person who read to him from the Bible and various prohibited books, he had become so expert on the subject that in 1569 the Lenten preacher had to alert the bishop that he could not match Panciera when it came to quoting from the Scriptures.

An evangelical community had formed at Canda that included the blind man's reader, Marco Fichente, whose own relatives, as well as those on the Buoni di Badia side of his family were suspected of harboring heretical notions. The conventicle was closely associated with Rovigo's and professed the same doctrines. When inquisitors issued an arrest warrant for Panciera, the latter received advance warning and managed to flee to Ferrara. After the blind man was condemned in absentia in June 1568, for a year or two he moved about the countryside of Val Alta (Trecenta), where he found refuge among peasants. Word reached Fichente, his old reader of the Scriptures, that the fugitive was tired of his vagabond existence and had decided to turn himself in and try to save himself by accusing his religious brethren. Before long his cadaver was fished out of the river Tartaro. Someone insinuated that Fichente was behind the deed, whereupon a cousin of Panciera, a certain Guido, killed him. This tragic episode caused the demise of the Canda conventicle. On 20 November 1573 an inquest against Fichente concluded with his condemnation and his bones were disinterred and burned.[28]

Meanwhile persecution raged about the heads of these Calvinists who were anxiously following events in France and praying for a Huguenot victory. Roncalli was compelled to abandon Rovigo, settling first in Padua and then in Venice. In both cities his home was a gathering place for the reading of Scripture and discussions. Among the participants was Cosimo I de' Medici's agent in Venice, Piero Gelido, the future pastor of Acceglio in the Val Maira, near Cuneo. The dissenters of Canda had been closely associated with those of neighboring Badia. A certain Giovanni Ludovico Bronziero, who traveled to France and Germany, supplied them with books. Bronziero's ideas were shared by his nephew Lauro Simeoni, a druggist, and Carlo Moscone.

On 12 August 1564 the bishop ordered Moscone's arrest at the request of the Venetian doge. He was eventually apprehended on 3 May 1566, and after

[28]Ibid., 176–77, 222–24.

equivocating for more than a year, confessed his evangelical views: Jesus Christ is only spiritually present in the consecrated host; Christ is the true purgatory; the pope does not have the authority to grant indulgences; vows and devotions are useless; the predestined person is already saved; our works are not meritorious; man's will without grace is not free. After making his abjuration, Moscone fled from the convent of San Francesco where he was being held, rented a carriage, and abandoned Rovigo and Italy, settling at Morbegno in the Valtellina with his wife Violante, and his sons Aurelio and Giambattista. Upon fleeing, he sent the monks of San Francesco who had been his jailers the key to his cell, with the message: "This is yours; take good care of it, you may need it again."[29]

As the domestic "church" of Rovigo continued to grow, it began to feel that it needed a more solid theological grounding and a life of worship closer to the Genevan model as it was described to them by Francesco Serralonga, who went there to purchase books for the Venetian trade. The instruction was placed in the hands of a former monk from Brescia, Giovanni Antonio Manara, a schoolmaster who at Easter in 1560 administered the Holy Supper to the Roncalli, Mazzarelli and Aldiverti families. Two years later he baptized Mazzarelli's son in the house of the Giglioli, where at Pentecost the Lord's Supper was once again celebrated. In December 1561 at Padua, Roncalli dictated his testament to his friend Cesare Aldiverti, in the presence of seven witnesses:

> I know that it is not necessary for me to speak of my soul, because I had, have now, and shall always have this faith, which God, from eternity, loved so much that he sent his only begotten Son Jesus Christ just to save it and to assume upon himself all its sins. Thus I shall die with this vivid hope and consolation, that God through his grace and mercy, looking at the merits of his Son, and not to my vile acts, which are all sinful, will bestow upon my soul eternal and glorious life. May his divine Majesty always be honored and praised through Jesus Christ our Savior.[30]

A few months later, on 14 March 1562, Roncalli died and the Venetian group broke up. The Giglioli returned to Papozze; Antonio Maria Mazzarelli, with his sister-in-law, Laura, settled at Arioste, a few kilometers from Argenta, as steward for a property rented by his brother, Domenico. The bonds among the friends were not totally dissolved, but Roncalli's death deprived them of his leadership and great organizational skills.

The Rovigo conventicle continued to proselytize and grow under the direction and driving force of Mazzarelli and of the Frenchman Guglielmo Dolcetti, public schoolteacher in 1561–62. As one of the members of the Academy put it, "Dolcetto and Mazzarelli were the ones who tried to seduce everyone." And the fellowship itself was closed down by the *podestà* of Rovigo, because "it was a refuge for heresy and

[29]Ibid., 225–29.
[30]Ibid., 183.

perhaps for other evil activities...."[31] Dolcetti, a prominent figure in that assemblage, was banished from the city and the entire Po delta. Mazzarelli did not concede defeat and continued his efforts clandestinely, as did Oddo Quarto at Monselice, with whom he had been in contact, using Roncalli as a go-between. The work of evangelization through the printed word proved to be the most successful.

When the Inquisition took its investigation into the homes of Mazzarelli in Rovigo, of Giovanni Giacomo Beato in Venice, and of Giovanni Ludovico Bronziero at Badia, prohibited books were discovered in the most unlikely places. In the latter residence, Brucioli's *New Testament* was found "jammed under the eaves of the roof in a basket filled with many other books."[32] There were works by Erasmus and Ochino, Negri's *Tragedia,* and writings by Calvin and Vermigli, Francesco Betti's *Lettera...al Signor Marchese di Pescara,* and as already noted, Brucioli's vernacular New Testament.

A letter from Domenico Mazzarelli's brother, Antonio Maria, to Roncalli's widow, Margherita, which announced the imminent end of the papacy and "of the wretched papist church," fell into the hands of her paternal uncle, who transmitted a copy to the bishop. This set the machine of repression in motion. Even though Antonio Maria Mazzarelli was banished for ten years, in October 1564 he ended up in the prisons of the Inquisition in Ferrara. Under torture, he admitted his errors and abjured. The bishop of Adria, who had the responsibility of confirming the sentence, commuted it into something much milder but carrying shame: during eight feast days Mazzarelli had to stand before the cathedral of Rovigo, a candle in hand, garbed in the vestment of the penitent heretic.

Mazzarelli's confession implicated the Giglioli family. Ottaviano Giglioli, a member of the Rovigo group, had moved his family to Venice, to the home of his brother-in-law, G. D. Roncalli. In October 1564, several of its members, Ottaviano, his wife Barbara, the mother Margherita, as well as Roncalli's widow were compelled to abjure. As salutary penances they were made to go on pilgrimage to the convent of San Domenico in Bologna and each of them had to pay a fine of one hundred ducats. Meanwhile in Rovigo, the Mazzarelli family and their group went on trial. The notary Domenico, seeing that defense was futile, abjured. His wife was conceded a private abjuration. Contemporaneously the law struck against the Aldiverti family, with the arrest of Cesare and his cousin Aristotele. On 24 February 1564, Aldiverti and Domenico Mazzarelli abjured in the church of San Francesco before a large crowd. With the arrest and humiliation of its leaders, the choices remaining for the small community were flight, dissimulation, or return to the old beliefs. From a careful reading of the trials G. Marchi has reconstructed the Calvinist faith of all the defendants.

Almost all (and later Ludovico Biscaccia joined them) courageously declared, defying the judges, that for them the only true church, "the congregation of the

[31]S. Ferlin Malavasi, "Intorno alla figura e all'opera di Domenico Mazzarelli, eterodosso rodigino del Cinquecento," *Archivio Veneto,* ser. 5, 109 (1977): 68.
[32]G. Marchi, *La riforma tridentina,* 189.

elect," was that of Geneva, founded by Calvin: the pope was the Antichrist, the mass idolatry, Christ the only purgatory, and Holy Scripture "the only rule of faith." To this reformed profession of their beliefs, the Giglioli added a statement on the freedom of conscience as an inalienable right of man: "Heretics are not to be tortured, nor burned, and no one should be compelled to embrace any faith."[33] To relapse at this point into the errors that one had abjured meant facing an atrocious death. Thus the academicians, A. Riccoboni, G. B. Minadois, and Girolamo Biscaccia, humbly asked for forgiveness. But since Biscaccia had failed to denounce his heterodox brother and Giovanni Giacomo Beato, and since he had continued to possess prohibited books, he was declared to be a *relapsus* and condemned to the stake on 1 April 1570.

Domenico Mazzarelli, prosecuted anew as someone who had feigned conversion, was condemned to death as a contumacious heretic. When he saw that the appeals on his behalf to the Council of Ten being made by his friends and relatives were of no avail, he escaped, stopping first in Piedmont where he knew that he would find like-minded brethren. On 3 November 1571 he was burned in effigy. His enrollment in the Italian exiles' church at Geneva is recorded under the year 1573, and his acceptance as a *habitant* of the city in April of the following year. He had been preceded by his brother-in-law Francesco Serralonga and his godfather Cesare Boniparte of Novara.[34]

Flight was not a possibility for the mercenary captain Alfonso Ariano (1516–71), a native of Ferrara. He had fought in Flanders, Hungary, and France where he had sided with the Huguenots. He returned to Italy in 1562, visiting several northern cities, finally settling at Guarda Ferrarese, where he lived as a Lutheran. When he was investigated by the Holy Office of Rovigo in 1569 (Guarda belonged to that diocese), he fled, only to be captured two years later at Chioggia and brought to Venice. Although he was questioned under torture, he refused to recant or to name his accomplices. On 4 September 1571, the secular authorities of Rovigo executed the inquisitorial sentence. Ariano was first strangled and then burned in the night, "*sine strepitu*."[35]

Venetian Anabaptism

This picture of Rovigo's heresy is incomplete without an account of its Anabaptist component, which should be discussed within the general context of the intense and heroic struggle of Italian Anabaptism, concentrated, as Ugo Gastaldi informs us, in

---

[33]Ibid., 200–210.
[34]Cf. S. Ferlin Malavasi, "Intorno alla figura," 70–76. The information given here that Mazzarelli had become minister of the Italian exiles' church in Geneva is incorrect. In the document published by P. F. Geisendorf, *Les livres des habitants de Genève* (Geneva: Droz, 1963), 2:100, we read that the minister of the Italian church had stood as a witness for the three new *habitants*, "A. Trissino, Cesare di Teodoro, and D. Muzzarello."
[35]G. Marchi, *La riforma tridentina*, 238–42.

Above: The interrogation of an Anabaptist in prison. *Below:* The execution by drowning of an Anabaptist woman. Engravings by Jan Luyken (1649–1712) from Tilleman Van Braght, *Het Blodig Toneel* (Amsterdam, 1685), pt. 2. The splendid engravings by the Dutch artist were also reproduced in Italy, but without historical explanations, in the *Teatro della crudeltà*, published in Venice in 1696 by Girolamo Albrizzi (Venice, Biblioteca Marciana).

two and a half years, from 1549 to 1551.[36] We lack precise information about the origins of the sect in the peninsula. The doctrines circulated, beginning in August 1549, by an enigmatic personage identified in the sources as "Tiziano," have nothing in common with the revolutionary Anabaptism of Thomas Müntzer that in turn influenced the peasants of the Tirol and the followers of Michael Gaismayr. Tiziano, according to testimony submitted by Bruno Busale, "said that he had received his authority from Germany." Our mysterious figure, even though he had ties to Camillo Renato, the fractious Sicilian intellectual who championed a rational Christianity, advocated Anabaptist doctrines of Swiss origin. To the essential principles of the Reformation, the Zurich circle of Conrad Grebel, Simon Stumpf, and Felix Manz, which separated from Zwingli, added the concept of the local community constituted only of true believers, rebaptized, separated from the world, and all equal among themselves. Tiziano belonged to this moderate doctrinal current and at Asolo he established a conventicle, which was joined by such prominent citizens of the town as the notary Benedetto del Borgo, Marcantonio del Bon, and Giuseppe Sartori, together with Nicola d'Alessandria of Treviso, who generously financed the missionary work of the group. From the Veneto, Tiziano went to Finale, near Villa d'Este, in the Ferrara area, and from there traveled to spread the ideas of his movement around central Italy, as far south as Florence.

Tiziano took advantage of the ground that had been prepared for two decades before him by Lutherans and Calvinists, and organized small Anabaptist communities in Vicenza, Rovigo, Cittadella, Gardone, and Padua. The largest of these was the Vicentine, which attained a membership of about sixty. The sect grew quickly because its message was simple, based solely on the announcement of the forgiveness of sins through the redemptive work of Jesus Christ. Adult baptism was the sign that one's past life had been purified and of a commitment to a new life in the faith. The autonomy of each local "church," even if composed of only a few members, and the active proselytization of the itinerant "bishops," gave a flexible organizational structure to a movement that recruited its members among artisans, laborers, and professional men.

In the spring of 1550 an event that would have dire consequences for the future took place. Benedetto del Borgo and Nicola d'Alessandria met in Padua the abbot Girolamo Busale at the head of a group of Neapolitan exiles, previously affiliated with Valdesian circles, who had allowed themselves to be rebaptized as Anabaptists. But they quickly brought dissension into the movement by affirming the humanity of Christ and the mortality of the soul. These views were adopted by Benedetto del Borgo, the person who enjoyed the highest prestige in Venetian Anabaptism, and most of the leading members: Nicola d'Alessandria, Marcantonio del Bon, Giuseppe

---

[36]Cf. U. Gastaldi, *Storia dell' Anabattismo*, vol. 2, chap. 12, "L'anabattismo in Italia," 531–90. At Cinto Caomaggiore (Venice), almost the entire town became Anabaptist, centering about a group of peasants oppressed by a grave famine. In 1557 many emigrated to Moravia, but not all managed to make the adjustment. Cf. G. Paolin, "I contadini anabattisti di Cinto," *Il Noncello*, n. 50 (1980): 91–124

Sartori, Giacometto "stringaro" (lace salesman), Pietro Manelfi, Giulio Gherlandi, and Francesco Della Sega.

The doctrine of a human Christ—poor, weak, elevated by God to be his Son— was received warmly by artisans who, surprisingly perhaps, succeeded in casting off the traditional Christian message based on John 1:1–14 even before their better-educated brethren. Tiziano refused to accept this antitrinitarian view and assembled representatives of the sect to discuss the doctrine that was taking Anabaptism out of the Reformation, rigidly Christocentric. The "council" that met at Venice in October 1550, thoroughly studied by Gastaldi, who exposed the exaggerations and untruths in the account left by the renegade Manelfi, boiled down to a confrontation between the views of Tiziano and Busale. It did not result in a break between the two factions, but in a compromise, the precise terms of which are unknown. It would appear that the radical position of the Neapolitan abbot prevailed among all the communities, with the exception of Cittadella's, which did not attend the Venetian "council."

On 17 October 1551, Pietro Manelfi, one of the leaders of the movement, an ex-priest about thirty-two years of age from San Vito (Senigallia), presented himself spontaneously before the inquisitor of Bologna, Leandro de Albertis. He declared that "he wanted to return to the bosom of the Holy Roman Church," abandon the Lutheran heresy and the "Anabaptist perfidy." Since he had been "touched by the Holy Spirit," he now regretted his errors and was ready to accuse all the Lutherans and Anabaptists he had known or heard talked about during his traveling ministry in central and north Italy. Manelfi was transferred to Rome where he completed his revelations, thus putting at the disposal of the Inquisition everything that it needed to destroy Anabaptism in Italy and inflict further damage on what remained of Italian Protestantism.

The transcripts of Manelfi's depositions were brought to Venice by the Dominican Girolamo Muzzarelli, who had conducted the interrogations. They were accompanied by a letter from the Roman Curia that voiced alarm over the dangers threatening the church and the Italian states: "Throughout Italy, the infinite goodness of the Lord has brought to light the existence of a multitude of Anabaptists who have conspired against magistrates, against the faith and against Christ our redeemer...." The sect "first of all considers all Christian magistrates to be enemies of God, and insists that no Christian may be an emperor, king, duke, or hold any office whatsoever, and the people are not obliged to obey them...."[37]

Even before Manelfi's betrayal, the *Signoria* must have had some inkling of the infiltration into its territories of these subversive doctrines. In February 1551 Benedetto del Borgo, one of the outstanding figures of Italian Anabaptism, was arrested in Rovigo and executed after only a month (17 March 1551). In May, Francesco Sartori of Asolo met the same fate. Later in the same year, Giovanni Maria Beato, also of Rovigo, who had been one of the participants in the Venetian "council," along with Francesco Della Sega, Gerolamo Venezze, and Giovanni Ludovico Bronziero, fell into the inquisitorial net. Beato had a presentiment of the imminent persecution and

---

[37]U. Gastaldi, *Storia dell'Anabattismo* 2:538.

had arranged for his mother, wife, and two sisters to set out for Austerlitz in Moravia, where Jacob Hutter, from the Tirol, had established numerous colonies. Somehow, Beato managed to escape and be reunited with his family, living with them there for about a decade. His brother, Giovanni Giacomo, who had been asked to administer their property, moved to Venice where he resided in the home of Giovanni Ludovico Bronziero, whose daughter Costanza he married. When he returned to Rovigo with his bride in 1569 he was tried and compelled to abjure.[38]

Four Italians who became members of the Hutterite brotherhood would have their martyrdoms recorded in the annals of European Anabaptism. They were Giulio Gherlandi of Spaziano, near Treviso (1520–62), Francesco Della Sega of Rovigo (1528–65), Antonio Rizzetto of Vicenza (d. 1565), and Gian Giorgio Patrizi of Cherso (1524–70), all Venetian citizens who paid for their fearlessness. The four had left Italy after 1557 and found their ideals exemplified by the Hutterites, who persuaded them to abandon the radicalism of their original communities. The four Italians were so convinced that they had discovered the true church of Christ that they asked permission to return home to convince their old brethren to declare openly their evangelical faith and follow them into exile.

In September 1562 three of the Anabaptists were incarcerated in the Venetian prison of San Giovanni in Bragora. Giulio Gherlandi, the first one captured, gave witness to the depth of his faith by facing his martyrdom with equanimity. Francesco Della Sega and Antonio Rizzetto, after grueling physical and mental tortures, were no less ready to confront their deaths in February 1565. In early January 1563 Della Sega had written a letter to the Hutterite brethren. It is an important source for understanding the prisoner's religious views, which were based wholly on Scripture.[39] Gian Giorgio Patrizi belonged to a noble family of Cherso. He had married Anna, the sister of Francesco Barbo, lord of Cosliaco in Istria, whom we have already met as a sympathizer of the Reformation. Patrizi, an avowed Anabaptist and antitrinitarian, helped to arrange the exodus to Saloniki of persecuted Venetian evangelicals. Following a trial at Cherso, he lived as a Nicodemite, but finally in 1558 shed his reserve and resumed his missionary activities. When he heard of the Hutterite communities, he set out for Moravia in 1567 with his son Matteo. He returned to Cherso in 1570, where he was denounced to the authorities by a man who had become the lover of his wife, who had refused to follow Patrizi into exile. Patrizi was executed at Venice at year's end.

The Venetian Network

The conventicles that have been mentioned thus far, offshoots of the evangelical communities in Brescia, Vicenza, Rovigo, and Monselice, did not comprise the whole of Venetian religious dissidence. The doctrinal message became somewhat dissipated in the course of its transmission, since the groups were in flux, and a few

[38]G. Marchi, *La riforma tridentina,* 178-80.
[39]A. Stella, *Dall'Anabattismo,* 114.

indoctrinated Protestants conscious of the significance of their alternative Christian church, were cautiously attempting to instruct their brethren. Only fragmentary and imprecise information emerged from the trials because the defendants attempted at all costs to suppress the most compromising information. But from other sources, we are told of the existence of clandestine groups so well organized that they almost escaped detection. An example is provided by the arrest at Padua in May 1555 of the student Pomponio Algieri of Nola (1531–56). The documents confiscated in his residence do not yield up any names and the fifteen letters found among his papers are unsigned. But their content is clear enough, consisting of requests for clarification of various doctrinal points. In a letter addressed to the "brethren" that Algieri sent from prison, the names are fictitious and offer no clues. We do not even know why he was arrested. It may be that the flight to Geneva of the famous professor of law Matteo Gribaldi Mofa led to an investigation of his students and acquaintances.

But one thing is certain: Algieri's friendship with Francesco Scudieri of Cremona. When the latter was arrested in 1560, among the confiscated books, two letters were found "written to him from prison by that Pomponio, who was extradited to Rome to be burned."[40] Scudieri had abandoned the order of Canon Regulars in 1552 and traveled between Venice and Ferrara before settling in Padua as a teacher. He had remained in his order even after don Celso Martinengo had apostatized from it in 1551, and was in contact with the evangelical communities in the Grisons (one of his friends was Niccolò Pastalot of Chiavenna). Although Scudieri held reformed views, he did not agree with Calvin and the Genevan Company of Pastors on all points and disapproved of the killing of Servetus.

Algieri, with his intelligence and youthful ardor, succeeded in confounding his judges, by presenting his faith in an exclusively New Testament light, but his views did not differ from Scudieri's, with whom he trustingly communicated from prison. Algieri's strategy was to refrain from mentioning Luther and Calvin but to base his beliefs (salvation by grace through faith alone, rejection of the cult of saints, purgatory, transubstantiation, and the Church of Rome) on Biblical and Augustinian foundations. His definition of the church, "*Credo sanctam ecclesiam catholicam, communionem sanctorum* and I hold Christ to be its head," is that of the apostolic credo, but can also be read verbatim in P. M. Vermigli's catechism, published at Basel in 1544, which circulated widely in Venice (copies were confiscated in the homes of Francesco Stella [1549] and Pietro Cocco [1551]),[41] and is probably the source of Algieri's views on the sacrament: "I say that in the Eucharist and Lord's Supper we really do receive the body and blood of Christ, but in spirit, and that in the bread we find not only the accidents, but also the substance of that bread."[42]

---

[40]L. Perini, "Ancora sul libraio Pietro Perna," 396.

[41]Ibid., 390, 392.

[42]Cited from C. De Frede, *Pomponio Algieri nella riforma religiosa del Cinquecento* (Naples: F. Fiorentino, 1972), 225, note 28; idem, "Una notizia postuma su Pomponio Algieri e i costituti del suo processo padovano," *Campania sacra* 25 (1994): 27–46.

Algieri's judges, despite the gravity of his position, were reluctant to pronounce sentence, considering his youth and the turmoil his arrest had provoked among the students in the university, where many northern Protestants were enrolled. The tribunal preferred, for the time being, to let him suffer "the torment of prison" in the hope that "perhaps he might abandon his obstinacy and melancholy humors."[43] Between his second and third interrogation Algieri sent a letter from prison addressed to "my beloved brethren, fellow servants of Christ, who emigrated from Babylon to Mt. Zion." The text, dated 21 July 1555, was printed for the first time in 1563 by Henry Pantaléon, who had received the original from C. S. Curione, editor of Valdés's *Considerations*. As we said, it is impossible to identify precisely the addressees of Algieri's letters, but the pseudonyms employed suggest evangelicals residing in Venetian territory, or in a neighboring state, who were in contact with Curione in Basel, whose student, Basil Amerbach, had been enrolled at the University of Padua from 1553. The letter is a noble expression of Protestant spirituality, expressing confidence in the divine presence as the fulfillment of the scriptural promise (Matt. 10:16–21) and the experience of faith. A distant and inscrutable God had drawn closer and made himself more familiar through the person of Jesus: "Experience, oh my beloved, how sweet is the Lord, how mild and merciful, he who visits his servants in their temptations and deigns to abide with us in a rough and vile cell, offering a serene mind and placated heart."[44] From the first interrogation the youth experienced neither doubt nor vacillation about confessing his faith. He must have been familiar with the case of Francesco Spiera, and had no intention of avoiding punishment by making a hypocritical abjuration. Certain other readings must have inspired him along the same lines. A likely candidate is Giulio della Rovere's exhortation to martyrdom, *Esortazione al martirio*, published in a second edition in 1552, which held up as examples the martyrs Fanino Fanini of Faenza, Domenico Cabianca of Bassano, and Galeazzo da Trezzo of Lodi. Algieri would follow their shining example as confirmation of his election to eternal life.

After negotiations dragged out for almost a year, the Supreme Congregation of the Inquisition obtained Algieri's extradition for the completion of his trial in Rome. During the brief proceedings, lasting from April to June 1556, the student, then twenty-five years of age, gave proof of his full adherence to reformed doctrines. On 19 August he was taken to Piazza Navona, immersed in a vat filled with oil and pitch, and burned alive. Eyewitnesses, astonished by his courage and constancy, reported his last words shouted in a loud voice: "*Suscipe, Deus meus, famulum et martyrem tuum*" (Sustain, my God your servant and martyr). The Venetian ambassador wrote to the Senate that the judges had reported to him Algieri's words at the reading of the sentence: "This is what I have always asked from my God. *Vivat Dominus meus in aeternum*" (May my Lord live in eternity).[45] Algieri's tragic life reveals the existence

---

[43]Idem, *Pomponio Algerio*, 114.
[44]Ibid., 123.
[45]Ibid., 200–202.

Heretic burned alive in a cauldron with oil, pitch, and turpentine. English engraving from John Foxe, *Actes and Monuments* (London, 1684), vol. 1.

of this clandestine evangelical community in Padua, about which we know nothing except the spiritual heights it inspired, measured by the martyr's message.

Another community, made up of Calvinists and their sympathizers, which remained hidden from Venetian authorities, both secular and ecclesiastical, until 1565, but organized in Venice before 1560, was discovered at the time of the arrest of a grocer from the neighborhood of San Fantin. His gatherings were attended by Pietro Carnesecchi, Piero Gelido, Andrea da Ponte (the brother of the future doge, Niccolò), the lawyer Alvise Malipiero and his brother Paolo. A casket of money had been deposited at the shop to assist the needy and brethren who had decided to flee. Among the largest contributors were the Malipiero brothers and Andrea da Ponte, at whose home another group met, among whom were the priest Faustino di Zanone, the brothers Corneretti, drapers, the Venetian patrician, Niccolò Paruta, a Neapolitan teacher of grammar, "*messer* Piero," namely Gelido, and the gentlemen Agostino Tiepolo, Marcantonio Canal, Francesco Emo, Vincenzo Sanudo, the Venetian patricians Giovanni Antonio Maffei and Giovanni Francesco Labia, and the lawyer Carlo Cornaro. Da Ponte had loaned Cornaro Calvin's *Institutes* and to the Malipiero brothers the *Beneficio di Cristo*. Links were maintained between the two groups through Piero Gelido, who probably served as preacher to both. The second of the two conventicles numbered about sixty members, who shared a common desire for religious change, a decided aversion against the repression of freedom of conscience, and a conviction that inquisitorial persecution was a token of being blessed, rather than a sign of infamy. When the Florentine Carnesecchi was summoned to Rome for his third trial, Gelido sent this message to the secretary of Cosimo de' Medici in June 1558:

> It can be said that the monsignor has been abandoned by everyone except myself, who could no more abandon him than a mother could her child. I love him as one can love a true friend. Certainly this is not because of the benefices that I have received, or hope to receive from him, but because I have always known him as an upright man and a good Christian. And I am more than ever convinced that in this affliction, which is one of the gravest that can befall a man because it entails the loss of property, honor and life almost, God is with him, who guides and consoles him and strengthens him. Because otherwise he could not tolerate this mortal blow with such a constant heart, almost joyfully, as he does in effect tolerate it.[46]

The ever more frequent reports about condemnations to death; the permissions granted by the Venetian government for the extradition of suspects to Rome, as in the case of Algieri, followed by that of Bartolomeo Spadafora, Sicilian landholder and Venetian nobleman (thanks to a privilege granted to his ancestors); and the condemnation *in contumacia* of Carnesecchi confronted religious dissenters ever more forcefully with the choice between Nicodemite dissimulation and flight. The

---

[46]G. Jalla, "Pietro Gelido, riformato italiano del secolo XVI, segretario papale, residente fiorentino a Venezia, ministro evangelico in Piemonte," *Rivista Cristiana* 1 (1899): 217.

dilemma was one faced by the entire Italian evangelical movement, but was more thoroughly discussed in the mid-1550s in Lombardy and the Veneto, partly because from these areas passage over into the Protestant Grisons was much easier. But there was another reason, too: the energetic intervention of two celebrated pastors, known throughout central and north Italy: Giulio della Rovere and Peter Martyr Vermigli. The former, in his *Esortazione al martirio* urged his readers to fearlessly face the supreme sacrifice: "The Christian in the cross finds his contentment, in exile awaits the long looked for Jerusalem and in death rediscovers life."[47]

Vermigli proposed something different in his *De fuga*, which took the form of an epistle sent to a friend not long after his apostasy. Although he was aware from his own experience of the difficulties and risks in flight, he was convinced that there was no alternative for a people under papal domination denied freedom of conscience. To dissimulate one's true faith was to extinguish the light of truth. Martyrdom did not provide the possibility of giving witness, because the victim was not permitted to address the populace. To turn down exile in the hope "of opening the way to the Gospel in our Italy" was an illusion, a vain hope. To this could be added the impossibility of organizing evangelical communities led by qualified pastors, ministers of the Word of God, administrators of the sacraments. When the continuous nourishment of Scripture was missing, factionalism and mistaken ideas could take over, which then lead to the community's demise.[48] Opposed to this view, there were those who maintained that they should go on as they were while awaiting better times, because the church would be reformed when God willed it. Meanwhile, the essential was to pursue inner renewal and a life true to Scriptural teachings. This is what a father wrote to his son, a student who had espoused the new faith, in fear that he would flee to Protestant lands:

> therefore let us content ourselves and abide living like Christians, and doing so we can live just as well here as there…and by doing so we fulfill the will of God, without going about vagabonding as do some who go about looking for the Lord God more in one place than in another. They fool themselves because God is everywhere, and in any place the Christian can live in a Christian way by the grace of his Majesty.[49]

The question was long debated in dissident circles. It anguished Carnesecchi after the death of Pole (18 November 1558) and the flight to Geneva of such companions in the faith as Galeazzo Caracciolo, Isabella Bresegna, and Apollonio Merenda. In accord with his close confidante, Countess Giulia Gonzaga, who was determined not to leave Naples in spite of the rumors of an inquisitorial investigation against her, Carnesecchi, a former protonotary of Clement VII, trusting in the help of God and in the protection of Cosimo de' Medici, resolved to remain in Venice, secluded in his residence as if it had been a prison. Many, such as Piero Gelido,

---

[47]E. Comba, *I nostri protestanti*, 170.
[48]Cf. L. Santini, "La tesi della fuga nella persecuzione nella teologia di P. M. Vermigli," *BSSV* 80, n. 108 (1960): 37–49.
[49]E. Pommier, "La société venitienne," 26.

Fabrizio Brancuti, Andrea da Ponte, and Niccolò Paruta, made a different decision and chose exile, followed by others less well known; Antonio Marangon, for example, who may be the same as the carpenter condemned in 1534 as a "Lutheran" preacher. Their destination was Geneva where they became members of the Italian refugees' church, the pastor of which since 1561 was the Lucchese Niccolò Balbani. To his judges, Alvise Malipiero confessed how he had been urged by Andrea da Ponte: "He used to tell me that one had to go forward.... Whoever wanted to be saved had to take the next step." But Agostino Tiepolo and Marcantonio Canal, who belonged to da Ponte's conventicle, commented bitterly: "This is how Christians resolve things, in the way *Messer* Andrea did, leaving their homeland to go and serve God."[50]

The exiles, in turn, felt that they had woken from a nightmare and had been freed from the fear of death. The solicitor Paolo Moscardo from Geneva, *cité-refuge*, wrote to his fellows in Italy that he had lacked the courage to face the fate of a Jan Hus, nor did he feel that he was out of his mind for having left behind his wife and small children:

> And you, dearest brethren, do not be angry because I place my faith in my Lord God and in my Christ, who if they aided me back in Venice, will do so elsewhere as well. And if my family has been left without me, the Lord will look after them and perhaps will be so graceful as to reunite us, and he will console you since he is true and does not go back on his promises.[51]

On 24 March 1562, Piero Gelido wrote to Duke Cosimo a letter of confession, informing him that he had met with the reformed ministers at Montargis, where Renée, duchess of Ferrara, now resided, and that he was now in Geneva. There "even if I may have to beg for my bread, I live most happily, because the spiritual bread is plentiful, and that is the food that never perishes."[52] The letter from the former Medici diplomat dwells on such subjects as the growing strength of the Huguenot party in France, and his hope that the duke will be inspired to persuade the pope to convene "a legitimate council in the heart of Germany which he would attend in person, and proceed to a true reform of the church." But the *leitmotif* of the letter is Gelido's inexhaustible hunger to hear the Word of God preached. He who had contacts with the Waldensians, and had seen at first hand their slaughter at Luberon in Provence in 1545, concluded his long spiritual journey as pastor of the reformed community at Acceglio in Val Maira, near Cuneo in Piedmont.

Protestants may have been a minority in the Venetian dominions, but one to reckon with. The rumor circulating at Frankfurt and Heidelberg, and reported back to Doge Niccolò da Ponte in 1580 by a German priest, that Venice possessed four Calvinist communities each with its minister, may have been an exaggeration, as was the information brought back to the Waldensian valleys by the minister, Gille de Gilles, heading home after a missionary tour in Calabria (1556). He had been told

---

[50]Ibid., 10.
[51]E. Comba, *I nostri protestanti*, 639.
[52]G. Jalla, "Pietro Gelido," 293.

by evangelicals in Venice that the faithful in the city totaled almost six thousand![53] Judicial proceedings there brought to light a number of clandestine groups. In 1548 artisans and small merchants in the neighborhood of San Moisé used to gather in a shop to read the Bible, scriptural commentaries by Brucioli, the *Beneficio di Cristo*, and Ochino's *Prediche*. They discussed justification, predestination, the sacraments, and indulgences. In 1553 two conventicles of artisans were discovered at San Barnaba and at San Pietro, followed by three more in 1557 and 1558. The group that gathered at San Felice, totaling about twenty-five members, used to meet with the approval of the parish priest. They may not all have been Protestants, but quite a few were or wanted to be.

In Venice, Padua, Vicenza, Rovigo, and Brescia, for religious dissenters, the time for preaching from the pulpit and for clerical acts of reform had passed. The movement was now in the hands of members of the mercantile and aristocratic classes, although in addition to the brief success of Anabaptism with the populace, Lutheranism and Calvinism made inroads in the lower spheres of society to a larger degree than is evinced by the trial records. Nor should the transmission of the new ideas at a popular level through the efforts of its own members be underestimated. The boatman Stefano Ongari, who had been converted at Mantua by a woman of the people, was led to believe by a carter, whom he had met in a tavern in the Brianza (1555), that the mass and prayers for the dead were diabolical inventions.[54] Andrea delle Gambarare, an itinerant peddler, was persuaded by a woman of Sarceo to buy himself a *Beneficio di Cristo* from a bookseller in Venice: "And so I read that book…which I liked very much" (1568).[55] A certain Franceschina, from the quarter of San Pantaleon, was heard to tell her neighbors, Angela and Elisabetta:

> It is a bad thing to go to Mass, because Christ did not establish it. It is written in the Old Testament that when the golden calf was raised up, everybody ran to worship it and lost themselves in that idol. It is the same with us; when the consecrated host is lifted up, we run to adore it as if we believed in that calf, and we lose ourselves, because it is an idol…. And we should pray to God, because he is the principal one…. And we must worship Christ in spirit and in truth, not in that piece of dough…. He is our purgatory, and when we die we shall either go to heaven or to hell.[56]

Even if Franceschina had never read Calvin's *Piccolo trattato sulla santa Cena*, she had repeated its ideas, almost verbatim: "In fact, to prostrate ourselves before the bread of the Supper is to adore it, almost as if Jesus Christ were contained in it. This is making an idol of it, not a sacrament."[57] Someone had taught her this!

[53]T. Elze, *Geschichte der protestantischen Bewegungen*, 31–32; E. Comba, *I nostri protestanti*, 637; P. Gilles, *Histoire ecclésiastique des Églises Réformées* (Geneva, 1644), 81.

[54]ASV, Sant' Uffizio, b. 12 (5), trial against Stefano Ongari.

[55]*Beneficio*, 461 (document, n. 44).

[56]E. Comba, *I nostri protestanti*, 635–36, Cf. Ex. 32:8.

[57]*Giovanni Calvino, Il "Piccolo Trattato sulla Santa Cena" nel dibattito sacramentale della Riforma*, a cura di G. Tourn (Turin: Claudiana, 1987), 91.

Such evidence is hard to come by, since simple people did not catch the attention of the law as easily as did more socially or professionally prominent persons. Moreover, trials against the poor, from whom there was nothing to confiscate, were dispatched with haste. If defendants did not cling to their beliefs obstinately, they would generally get off with abjurations and light salutary penances. Nevertheless, for Venice, as well as for Verona and, as we shall see, other Italian cities, we have scraps of information about popular reactions, such as those just examined, that are truly symptomatic of the radical changes in mentality.

Bibliographical Note

The sources for this complex chapter and the more recent pertinent literature have been mentioned in the notes. To these we can add the old work by K. Benrath, *Geschichte der Reformation in Venedig* (cited at p. 116). Useful data is contained in P. Paschini, *Venezia e l'Inquisizione romana da Giulio III a Pio V* (Padua: Antenore, 1959); C. De Frede, "L'estradizione degli eretici dal dominio veneziano nel Cinquecento," *Atti dell'Accademia Pontaniana*, n.s. 20 (1970–71): 256–86; C. Vasoli, "Il processo per eresia di Oddo Quarto da Monopoli," in *Monopoli nell'età del Rinascimento*. Atti del convegno internazionale di studio (Monopoli, 1988), 2:569–624; S. Oswald, *Die Inquisition, die Lebenden und die Toten: Venedigs deutsche Protestanten* (Sigmaringen: Thorbecke, 1989); L. Calò, *Giulio Gherlandi "heretico ostinatissimo": Un predicatore eterodosso del Cinquecento tra il veneto e la Moravia* (Venice: Il Cardo, 1996); F. Ambrosini, "Tendenze filoprotestanti nel patriarcato veneto," and S. Seidel Menchi, "Protestantesimo a Venezia," in *La Chiesa di Venezia fra Riforma protestante e Riforma cattolica*, a cura di G. Gullino (Venice: Studium Cattolico Veneziano, 1990), 155–81, 131–54.

2.

BREVE E RI-

SOLVTO TRAT-

tato de la Cena del Signore com
poſto da M. Gio. Cal. e tradotto
nuouamente in lingua volgare
Italiana.

1. COR XI.

Proui l'huomo ſe ſteſſo, e coſi mangi di
queſto Pane, & beua di que-
ſto Calice.

Appreſſo Franceſco Durone.

M. D. LXI.

Title page of the Italian translation of Calvin's *Petit traicté de la saincte Cène*, published at Geneva in 1561.

13

CALVINISM IN LOMBARDY AND THE VALTELLINA

CALVIN'S MAGISTERIUM

IN AUGUST 1557, urged on by his brethren in the Italian exiles' church in Geneva, Giulio Cesare Pascali, a refugee from Messina, published his Italian translation, the first into that language, of Calvin's *Institutes of the Christian religion.*[1] In his dedication to Gian Galeazzo Caracciolo, the translator claimed that his effort was the earliest and principal instrument "for understanding the renascent Gospel message," which after Scripture, would be as eternal "as the ink with which it is written." The work had been fervently requested by his fellow evangelicals so that they might "see the kingdon of Jesus Christ progress in our Italy."[2]

From the 1550s forward the list of Calvinist titles confiscated in the peninsula from individuals and booksellers grew dramatically. The *Institutes*, in the Latin editions of 1536 and 1539, as well as in the French versions of 1541 and later years, was the reformer's most widely circulated work and enjoyed a large readership. After 1557 these earlier imprints would be joined by Pascali's beautiful and lucid translation, based on the French text. The Genevan reformer's *magnum opus* played a crucial role in the religious education of Protestants in Italy and became the preferred guide to Scripture for new converts. A group of evangelicals at Grosseto and Siena, brought together in 1544 by the physician Achille Benvoglienti, possessed a copy of the *Instituzione*, and at least one other work by Calvin. "That book was kept in a room, and each person could borrow it in turn." "I do not believe I am wrong," continued the

---

[1] Pascali's remained the only Italian translation until the recent one by G. Tourn, based on the 1559–1560 edition: *Istituzione della religione cristiana...*, 2 vols. (Turin: UTET, 1971; 2d ed., 1983).

[2] *Instituzione della religion christiana di messer Giovanni Calvino: In volgare italiano tradotta per Giulio Cesar P[aschali]*, Geneva, Appresso J. Burgese, A. Davodeo e F. Iacchì [Bourgeois, Davodeau et Jaquy], 1557. It is dedicated to Galeazzo Caracciolo.

notary Fabio Cioni in his testimony, "I think, as I remember, that it was an Explication by John Calvin on the New Testament."

At the conclusion of the trial against this Tuscan conventicle, of which Cioni had been one of the principal figures, the judges concluded: "He [Cioni] believed in all the abominable ideas of that impious heresiarch John Calvin. Not only did he hold them, but he discussed them with many of his accomplices who had fallen into the same errors, and together had read the works of the aforesaid Calvin."[3]

As has been noted, the evangelical conventicles discovered between 1550 and 1580 were the consequence of the teaching imparted by zealous and tenacious followers of Calvin. Editions of Giulio Domenico Gallo's translation of the reformer's *Catechism* were published in 1545 and in 1551.[4] They were joined by Ludovico Domenichi's Italian version of Calvin's *Excuse à messieurs les Nicodemites*, which appeared at Florence in 1548 with the title of *Nicomediana*, followed in 1553 by the *Del fuggir le superstizioni*. In 1561 the Genevan printer François Duron (Francesco Durone) brought out an anonymous translation of the *Petit traicté de la saincte cène*, entitled: *Breve e risoluto trattato de la cena del Signore composto da M. Gio. Cal. e tradotto nuovamente in lingua volgare Italiana.*

A year later in 1562, the same printer produced an Italian Bible, which according to the anonymous translators was intended to correct and improve Brucioli's version with more down-to-earth and clearer language. "In translating Holy Scripture we should use simple and current words and sentences so that they can be easily understood by ordinary people, as we have tried to do, without distinguishing greatly between high style and low and mediocre style, leaving affectation and Tuscanisms to those who want to turn their books into the vernacular language of Boccaccio."[5] According to Tommaso Bozza, this was the Italian Calvinist Bible *par excellence*, since it depended closely on the French version published by François Jaquy at Geneva that same year. From this version, corrected and revised by Geneva's pastors, even the apparatus and notes were translated, and included together with the illustrations.[6]

With these weapons in missionary hands, Calvinist teachings penetrated everywhere, in the universities, convent schools, academies, princely courts, artisans' shops, and among the peasants and laborers of the Garfagnana. With extraordinary clarity and force of persuasion they worked an unbelievable transformation in religious thought. To be able to destroy in the sixteenth century the mysterious and sacral conception of the Eucharistic host, which the believer approached with a sentiment of adoration mingled with fear and trembling, seems an incredible achievement. The reception by the lower classes of the Calvinist conception of the Lord's Supper was the result of spiritual and cultural indoctrination.

Almost contemporaneously, between 1548 and 1550, from Dignano in Istria to Lucca in Tuscany, when it was time to explain the symbolism of the Lord's Supper,

---

[3]V. Marchetti, *Gruppi ereticali*, 77.
[4]See chap. 9, 138–39.
[5]T. Bozza, "La Bibbia calvinista e il caso Brucioli," *Il Bibliotecario* 9 (1986): 46.
[6]Ibid., 46 ff.

the same definition was offered, taken directly from the *Institutes*. When the canon of Dignano, Pasqualino Velico, instructed a group of laborers and artisans, some of whom were illiterate, he told them that the host "is a representation of Christ."[7] Calvin, discussing the idolatry of sacred images, had written that only two images could be admitted in houses of worship: "it seems to me unworthy…to take on images other than those living and symbolical ones which the Lord consecrated by his Word. I mean Baptism and the Lord's Supper, together with other rites by which our eyes must be too intensely gripped and too sharply affected to seek other images forged by human ingenuity."[8]

The transmission and reception of Calvinist doctrine, whether in the context of queries as to why revered images and spectacular liturgies must be rejected, or in seeking clarification on the significance of the host, reveal heartfelt searching for the truth. The evidence that emerges in the inquisitorial inquests of a ubiquitous effort at proselytization that could even penetrate women's convents is especially striking. There is documentation for this concerning Siena, Bagnacavallo, Venice, and Udine. The most explicit in this regard is the confession uttered by Sister Prudenzia Corona of the convent of San Girolamo in Venice, an establishment frequently visited by Piero Gelido. From a Neapolitan notary the nun had received "a Genevan Catechism and certain other works." She had thus educated herself and succeeded in converting several other sisters.[9]

Persons who became persuaded of the truth and efficacy in the Calvinist exposition of the Christian message resorted to every imaginable device to proselytize for it, from anonymous writings to plagiarism. The most notorious case known to us concerns the *Pia esposizione di Antonio Brucioli ne' dieci precetti, nel simbolo apostolico et nella orazione Dominica*, first printed at Venice in 1542 by the Brucioli brothers, and then again in 1543 and 1547. Through this work, which is the translation, or summary of chapters 3, 4, and 9 of Calvin's *Institutes*, Calvin's message reached even the celebrated Renaissance court of the duchess of Urbino, Eleonora Gonzaga, the sister of Cardinal Ercole Gonzaga who had been Ochino's and Vergerio's protector.[10]

The widespread diffusion of Calvin's writings and of reformed efforts at evangelization was accompanied from 1550 to 1570 by attempts to establish clandestine communities on the Genevan model. Calvin's Geneva assumed a mythical aspect for all members of society who aspired to settle in a republic, where in addition to freedom of worship, they also would find a helping hand extended to the needy. Geneva, a returning traveler reported, was a city regulated by the Word of God, where the

[7]See the trial against Francesco Cerdone Callegaro, in *Atti e Memorie della Società Istriana di Archeologia e Storia Patria* 20 (1904): 291–312.

[8]John Calvin, *Institutes of the Christian Religion.* Ed. John T. McNeill. Trans. Ford Lewis Battles. 2 vols. (Philadelphia: Westminster, 1960), 1:113–14. [Trans. note.]

[9]E. A. Rivoire, "Eresia e Riforma a Brescia," app. 23, 90.

[10]Cf. T. Bozza, *Calvino in Italia* (Rome, 1966), 3–10. The abjuration of Hieronimo "Calligaro," actually written for him by Pietro Percoto, is another instance of the diffusion of Calvinist doctrines through plagiarism. Cf. A. Del Col, "L'abiura trasformata in propaganda ereticale nel duomo di Udine (15 aprile 1544)," *Metodi e Ricerche*, n.s. 2 (1981): 57–72.

mighty did not command. There, nobles and merchants, artisans and laborers, rich and poor participated together at the Lord's table. This idealized image caused a needy Venetian to exclaim in 1566: "There is no longer any charity, nor faith here; faith serves those in Geneva better, and if I could, I would find in that land one who would advance me fifty *scudi* and more, if I needed it."[11] Geneva had become "the capital of the militant Reformation."[12] In Italy, where the Counter-Reformation, allied to secular rulers and assisted by the Society of Jesus, would crush any attempt to overturn the institutions and traditions belonging to the papacy, persons of the reformed faith turned to Calvin's Geneva, "the holy city," as their brethren in France, Scotland, Bohemia, Hungary, and Flanders were also doing.

Confirmation is demonstrated by the tragic end of six evangelical leaders of north-central Italy at midcentury: Fanino Fanini of Faenza (22 August 1550), Domenico Cabianca of Bassano, condemned at Piacenza (10 September 1550), Galeazzo da Trezzo of Sant'Angelo Lodigiano (November 1551), Giovanni Buzio da Montalcino (1553), Francesco Gamba of Brescia (21 July 1554), and Ambrogio Cavalli of Milan (15 June 1556). With the exception of Buzio, all had either been influenced by the Calvinist message, or by sojourns in the Valtellina or in Geneva. The case of Francesco Gamba, who used to periodically visit that city to learn more about the faith and to receive the Lord's Supper, is especially tragic. He was apprehended at Como, returning from one of these journeys, and condemned to the stake. A friend wrote a long letter to his brother describing the martyr's profound faith in divine election. His tongue was pierced before the execution to prevent him from addressing the populace that had flocked to witness the spectacle.[13]

No less eloquent is the account of the death at the stake in the public square of Lodi of the gentleman Galeazzo da Trezzo, administrator of the property of Counts Attendolo Bolognini, whose case provoked a sensation. Da Trezzo had been accused of not believing in purgatory, the cult of the saints, and transubstantiation. Although he succumbed to the threats and exhortations of his judges and declared himself repentant, he in fact refused to fulfill his penances or read his abjuration publicly. He was declared to be relapsed and condemned to death, but the governor commuted the sentence to the confiscation of his property. However, on the scaffold, during the auto da fé, da Trezzo, who had been the friend of Curione, began to shout at the populace that he had not been allowed to express his convictions and support them from Holy Scripture. He argued with the inquisitor, insisting that "it is idolatry to adore the host and I shall prove it from the Acts of the Apostles." He barely escaped the wrath of the populace, but not the stake that awaited him a few days later.[14] These are not isolated instances. A faith so mature that it would not bend in the face of

[11]E. Pommier, "La société venitienne," 21.

[12]H. Hauser & A. Renaudet, *Les débuts de l'âge moderne*, 246.

[13]Cf. P. D. Rosio De Porta, *Historia reformationis ecclesiarum Raeticarum* (Curiae Raetorum [Chür], 1771), 1:257–63.

[14]Cf. L. Fumi, "L'Inquisizione romana e lo Stato di Milano: Saggio di ricerche nell'Archivio di Stato," *ASL*, ser. 4, 13 (1910): 370ff.; 14 (1910), documents 10, 11: sentence against Galeazzo da Trezzo and report to Charles V. Cf. F. Chabod, *Per la storia religiosa*, 311 & 356.

death would thrive in a climate of spiritual fervor and solidarity among those convinced of the predestination of the elect.

Solidarity, enthusiasm, and support were popular reactions elicited by Domenico Cabianca (c. 1520–50), a furrier of modest means, who halted his itinerant ministry spreading evangelical teachings at Piacenza. According to the dispatch sent to Duke Ercole II of Ferrara by his ambassador, Alfonso Trotti, "it was discovered that a number of citizens had given him [Cabianca] money and the will to speak freely."[15] Some had assured him of their protection, and that they would defend him, even with arms if necessary. At night, before a large audience, he preached in the public square against priests, auricular confession, and the sacrament of communion. After his arrest, the inquisitors hoped to get Cabianca to abjure, but the governor, Ferrante Gonzaga, Cardinal Ercole's brother, demanded that he be turned over at once to the secular authorities and had him promptly hanged, as a lesson to the many followers of the new ideas in the Piacenza area. Gonzaga's exemplary gesture may have had its effect on the fainthearted, but not on those deeply convinced of the justice of their protest, such as the notary Alessandro da Caverzago, sentenced to the stake "as a relapsed heretic, in fact as preacher, teacher and leader of heretics," on 2 June 1564.[16]

LOMBARDY

If we leave out Fanino Fanini, who worked to convert the *Romagna*, all the other evangelical leaders mentioned were either Lombards or were active in Lombardy. Brescia and Bergamo, since the eighteenth century integral components of present-day Lombardy, were then cities subject to the Republic of Venice. Their geographical position resulted in intensive commercial contacts, meetings at the fairs, exchanges of laborers, and the transit of preachers and teachers with the State of Milan. The links between dissidents in Milan and the Veneto are confirmed by the fact that persons from Milan, Piacenza, and Pavia are mentioned in Venetian inquisitorial trials. The most striking examples are those of Giulio della Rovere of Milan, who was tried in Venice, whence he fled to Poschiavo in 1543, and of C. S. Curione, a professor at Pavia, who moved to Venice in 1539 to avoid being arrested as a "Lutheran," where he remained for two years and established a friendship with della Rovere.

Federico Chabod has reconstructed the course of the Reformation in the State of Milan, describing its salient characteristics through a wealth of documentation. Milan constitutes a great laboratory for the investigation of the early spread of Protestant currents. From as early as 1519 it was one of the centers for the distribution of Luther's works throughout the state and beyond. Francesco Calvi of Pavia and later his brother, Andrea, were frenetically active booksellers. If the information is reliable, Michele Ghislieri, sent to Como in 1549 to settle serious conflicts between the local inquisitor and the canons of the cathedral, caused twelve cases of heretical books to

---

[15]Quoted from D. Caccamo, *DBI*, 15:689.
[16]L. Mensi, "Alessandro da Caverzago," *Bollettino Storico Piacentino* 1 (1906): 56.

The perforation of a condemned man's tongue to prevent him from addressing the crowd at his execution. Death through suffocation in casks. Engravings by Jan Luyken from Tilleman Van Braght, *Het Bloodig Toneel* (Amsterdam, 1685), pt. 2.

be confiscated. They had been shipped to a merchant from Poschiavo for further distribution in Cremona, Vicenza, Modena, Faenza, and Cosenza. This failed operation is evidence of the existence of the nascent evangelical communities and their dire need for Bibles and other religious books for use in controversy and edification.

Milan was the hub that provided the thrust to the Augustinians who favored Luther. Following arrangements taken by the general of the order, Girolamo Seripando, to resolve the internal problems provoked by the flight of Agostino Mainardi, the discovery of a clandestine conventicle of his supporters in the *Studium* of the convent of San Marco, one of the principal schools of the order, came as a rude shock. Five monks were accused at the end of 1547 of having remained in contact with their apostate brother member. Francesco da Rimini was seized at Como while making his way to Chiavenna to be reunited with Mainardo, now a pastor there. Francesco was a bearer of letters from other Augustinians, Stefano da Sestino, a distinguished theologian who headed the school at San Marco, and Francesco da Asti. Benedetto da Rimini and Aurelio da Corinaldo were implicated with them as followers of Mainardi. They received light punishment. They were transferred to other religious houses and, after a few years, resumed their places in the hierarchy of the order.[17]

The intense toil of Augustinian preachers over two decades, in which they were joined by Franciscans and Capuchins, the wide diffusion of the heretical press, and continuous contacts with dissidents in the *Veneto* and Valtellina, fomented anticlerical sentiments among all levels of society. Inquisitors, by their intransigence and executions of witches and heretics going back to the 1480s, came in for special opprobrium. In addition to scattered anticlerical gestures evidenced by blasphemous verses and other ephemeral compositions, Protestant communities, generally Calvinist in their orientation, were discovered in Milan, Pavia, Lodi, Como, and Cremona. This theological propensity is verified by the fact that in the course of the sixteenth century over eighty people from the State of Milan sought refuge in Geneva, of whom fifty-two were from Cremona alone. Other family groups headed for the Valtellina, most of whom were members of the bourgeois class or of the lower nobility, professional people, landowners, merchants, and artisans.

The patrician, Guarnerio Castiglione of Cuvio, was one of the first to abandon his homeland out of fear that his evangelizing activities would be exposed. After arranging to sell his property, he settled at Locarno with his wife Bona Ronchi, where he came into contact with the prominent Protestant family of the Muralto. Paolo Camillo Balsamo of Liscate (b. 1540) went to study in Geneva at the age of seventeen and never returned home, thereby abandoning his family for the sake of his faith. Many years later, when his case came to the attention of Cardinal Federico Borromeo, the prelate had him condemned *in contumacia* and his property confiscated (3 April 1571).

---

[17]F. Chabod, *Per la storia religiosa*, 349–54.

But it was not these isolated cases—such as that of the "humble saddle maker," Battista Terzaghi condemned to the stake as a heretic in 1559—that concerned the civil and ecclesiastical authorities.[18] Much more vexing was the discovery of a clandestine reformed community in the city of Cremona, brought to light by the arrest of two Benedictines who had fled from the monastery of San Benedetto di Polirone at Mantua, where between 1545 and 1546, Vergerio, Don Valeriano da Gazzo, and Don Sereno di Pontremoli had resided. In September 1550, the three, behind false beards and disguised as soldiers, armed and in coats of mail, had hidden in the home of Giuseppe Fossa, the son-in-law of Bartolomeo Maggi, whose *"domus"* was one of the wealthiest and most powerful in the city. The trials mounted against the two Benedictines, one of whom, Don Valeriano, had enjoyed a long association with the Maggi family, permits us to learn the doctrines they had preached to the peasants of Giuseppe Fossa and to the various persons who used to gather in the home of Bartolomeo and Tommaso Maggi.

If the confession made at his trial by Don Valeriano, known as Giampietro da Cremona before he became a monk, appears to be substantially Lutheran, Don Sereno's comes from Calvin's *Institutes*. In fact, it seems to follow closely the chapter order of the 1541 edition. Don Sereno, then in his thirties, was an educated young man who mentioned neither Calvin nor Luther among his readings, and cited only Francesco Negri's *Tragedia* and Sleidan's *Capo finto*. He stated that he believed, first of all, in justification by faith alone in the merits of Christ (*sola fides est ad salutem necessaria*) and that he had received the Spirit of God after having reflected on the Holy Scriptures. He no longer accepted the Church of Rome because it coerced adherence to its teachings and opposed the truth of the Gospel. For him the church was the congregation of those who had not turned their backs on the Scriptures but followed its teachings. He affirmed: "Christ alone" is the head of the church and we are its members. He is not in the consecrated host, because the Scriptures tell us that he is at God's right hand. Christ is only to be found in spirit in the consecrated host and the adoration of the host is idolatry. Purgatory is "Christ himself," and what the priests call purgatory "is a humbug intended to deceive poor Christians." Finally one should not pray to saints because *"solus Christus rogandus est."* Both men declared that they were certain about their own predestination and thus of their salvation. Don Sereno added that he was not convinced about infant baptism, preferring to see the sacrament postponed to a time when the recipient was able to believe in Jesus Christ.[19]

The interrogations of the two monks yielded up the names of twenty-two lay suspects, against whom an inquest began that dragged on for two years from the end of 1550 to the end of 1552. They constituted only a small part of the *"ecclesia Cremonensis."* The evidence of this is the presence in Geneva of people from Cremona

---

[18] For all these cases, see P. Rivoire, "Contributo alla storia della Riforma in Italia," *BSSV* 55 (1936): 57–62.

[19] See L. Fumi, "L'Inquisizione romana," 13 (1910): 352–59 and 14 (1910): 205–10, documents 8, 9.

who had already fled before the trial began, a number that would grow to fifty-two, the largest Italian colony after the Lucchese. Others followed them to Geneva and to the Valtellina at the termination of the judicial proceedings. The twenty-two defendants came from every social level and included the physician Girolamo Maccagno and the jurist Pietro Comendulo; the goldsmith Giovanni Battista Bombarda; the merchant Giovanni Battista Gaspari; the bookseller Girolamo da Brescia; and the shoemaker Nicolò Picenardi. The authorities were astonished to discover among them members of the city's leading families, the Sommi and the Maggi, and not a few rich landowners: Agostino and Mauro Sommi, Giuseppe Fossa, Francesco and Giovanni Niccolò Fogliata, Francesco Adamonti, Giuseppe Bondiolo, Giacomo Antonio Baruffini, Andrea Roncadello, Giovanni Battista Guazzoni, to cite only those about whom there is some information.

Almost all the suspects between 1551 and 1555 found refuge in Geneva with their wives, where they were reunited with members of their conventicle who had fled before being incriminated. Among them the name of Tommaso Puerari stands out. He had been asked to write, in the name of the entire evangelical community of Cremona, to their former pastor, Girolamo Allegretti, now directing the new church at Gardone, to express their solidarity with him after he was accused of Anabaptism by the church at Poschiavo.

The Valtellina

A significant segment of the *"ecclesia Cremonensis"* settled in the mountainous commune of Teglio in the Valtellina, an important center which was home to the wealthy Protestant families of the Besta and the Guicciardi. The pastor of the town, from 1554 until his death twenty years later, was Paolo Gaddi, who had succeeded Allegretti as pastor in Cremona. Gaddi had gone into exile with some of his parishioners during the prosecutions of 1550 to 1552, heading for Geneva where he spent two tranquil years. He next turned up at the court of Duchess Renée in Ferrara, and later at Zurich. During his ministry he enjoyed good relations with Calvin and with Heinrich Bullinger, Zwingli's successor as *antistes* of Zurich.

Teglio had become the new home of the wealthy Roncadello family headed by the two brothers Alfonso and Alessandro. Here they pursued their commercial activity as landowners and merchants and continued to prosper. As Alessandro Pastore justly observed, to whom we are indebted for this information on the Cremona exiles that complements the research begun by Chabod, Alessandro Roncadello's will, drawn up by the notary Martino Pozzi, is highly useful for the light it sheds on his social position and ideas, as well as for the names of the witnesses to the document, Italian exiles and native evangelicals of the Valtellina. His nephew Filiberto, Alfonso's son, is named as his universal heir, described as "living and abiding in the Christian and not papist church."[20] The first bequests are assigned as dowries for the daughters

---

[20]A. Pastore, *Nella Valtellina del tardo Cinquecento: Fede, cultura, società* (Milan: Sugar, 1975), 101 ff. & 128–29.

of poor peasants of Teglio, or of other evangelical communities, if they will take Protestant husbands.

Demonstrating the close family and business relationship maintained by the testator with the former members of the Cremona church, is a bequest of a dowry of six hundred *lire* made to the daughters of Tommaso Aimo and Margherita Roncadello, now refugees in Geneva. In addition, Alessandro named as executors of his will Francesco and Giovanni Niccolò Fogliata, and Giuseppe Fossa. Gathered about the testator and his notary as witnesses on that day in February 1563 were Paolo Gaddi, the jurists Gilberto Salis and Martino Pergola of Tirano, Count Ulisse Martinengo from Brescia, the physician Niccolò Guicciardi of Teglio, and Curzio del Puono of Cremona. As confirmation of the guidance he had received from Calvin's teachings during his spiritual journey, Alessandro Roncadello, who chose to end his days in Geneva, was the proud owner of the *Institutes*, Theodore Beza's *Confessio*, and various works by Pierre Viret.

As Chabod observed, the persecutions of 1551 and 1552 and the condemnations of 1558 failed to "break up the organism created by the secret efforts of people well rooted in their ideas, so well rooted, in fact, as to prefer exile to abjuration."[21] Further evidence of the firm foothold achieved by Protestantism in Lombardy is provided by the large number of preachers and pastors from the region who settled in the Valtellina. Besides Giulio della Rovere, whose long ministry left profound traces, there were Leonardo Borletti and Bartolomeo Silvio, both from Cremona, Giovanni Antonio Gala of Milan, Lorenzo da Soncino, Antonio di Piacenza, and Girolamo Turriano.

The Valtellina, an area Italian in culture and language, conquered in 1512 by the Swiss League of the Grisons after almost two centuries of Milanese domination, at midcentury enjoyed religious toleration that had been established by the "articles" of Ilanz on 7 January 1526. This was indeed an anomalous situation for a region included in the diocese of Como, bordering the State of Milan. Thus the Valtellina was destined to become the first place of refuge for the Italian religious exiles, both the closest and the most convenient in terms of the great routes of transit to Switzerland and northern Europe. Among those who paused in the Valtellina for a time were many of the principal Italian reformers, Bernardino Ochino, Pier Paolo Vergerio, and Peter Martyr Vermigli.

Life in the Valtellina was the austere and rugged existence of mountainous places far removed from the centers of culture and civilization. The Jesuits sent there to try to roll back the great advances made by Protestantism under the aegis of the Grisons, acknowledged the difficulty of communicating with a rough and "sheep-like" population. The arrival of the religious exiles meant, for the inhabitants of the region, to encounter a culture, descended from the Italian Renaissance, which had succeeded in pervading all social classes. Even the brigands of the Garfagnana restored his freedom to Ludovico Ariosto when they learned that he was the author of the *Orlando Furioso*! Throughout the Valtellina, a religious debate was being

---

[21] F. Chabod, *Per la storia religiosa*, 361.

waged that favored the Reformation cause, the bearer of a simple and comprehensible message for villagers who had been abandoned by a neglectful clergy. The local reformers, now assisted by eager and cultivated exiles from Italy, founded evangelical communities in all the major centers and adjacent villages.

In certain respects, these communities were, along with the Waldensian valleys and the valleys in the Saluzzo and Turin regions, a great organizational laboratory of Protestant life for both the exiles and the local inhabitants. It was not an easy task to inculcate the basic principles of the Reformation and their social consequences, and not made easier by the controversies fomented by Camillo Renato and the Anabaptists. Nevertheless, the religious refugees made an enormous contribution. It is enough to see who were the pastors in Sondrio, Chiavenna, Poschivao, Teglio, and Piur, persons who came from almost every region of Italy. The names of the Neapolitan Scipione Lentolo and of the two Lucchese, Scipione Calandrini and Ottavio Mei, stand out. But notable efforts were also made by laypeople, such as Ulisse Martinengo and his mother Laura Gavardi, the widow of Count Alessandro Martinengo. Laura, dubbed "a rotten heretic," scandalized the Catholic population of Sondrio by "holding forth in the public square, a vernacular Bible in her hand…reading from it like a doctor." Such behavior "was totally foreign to the mental universe" of the exasperated archpriest Scotti, who wrote about it in June 1570 to Charles Borromeo. He expressed the hope that the countess could be forced to go away, "to where everybody is a Lutheran."[22] Ulisse Martinengo lived in various places in the Valtellina, including Chiavenna and Sondrio, where he gave both spiritual and economic support to new converts. His faith had matured in Geneva where he had lived for a time, perhaps in Beza's own house.

It is impossible to consider the history of the Italian Reformation without taking into account its more-than-half-century association with the Valtellina, a bond that would be smashed only by the "Holy Slaughter" (*Sacro Macello)* of 1620.

BIBLIOGRAPHICAL NOTE

The works by F. Chabod and A. Pastore cited in the notes encompass the bibliography on the subject.

---

[22]A. Pastore, *Nella Valtellina*, 105.

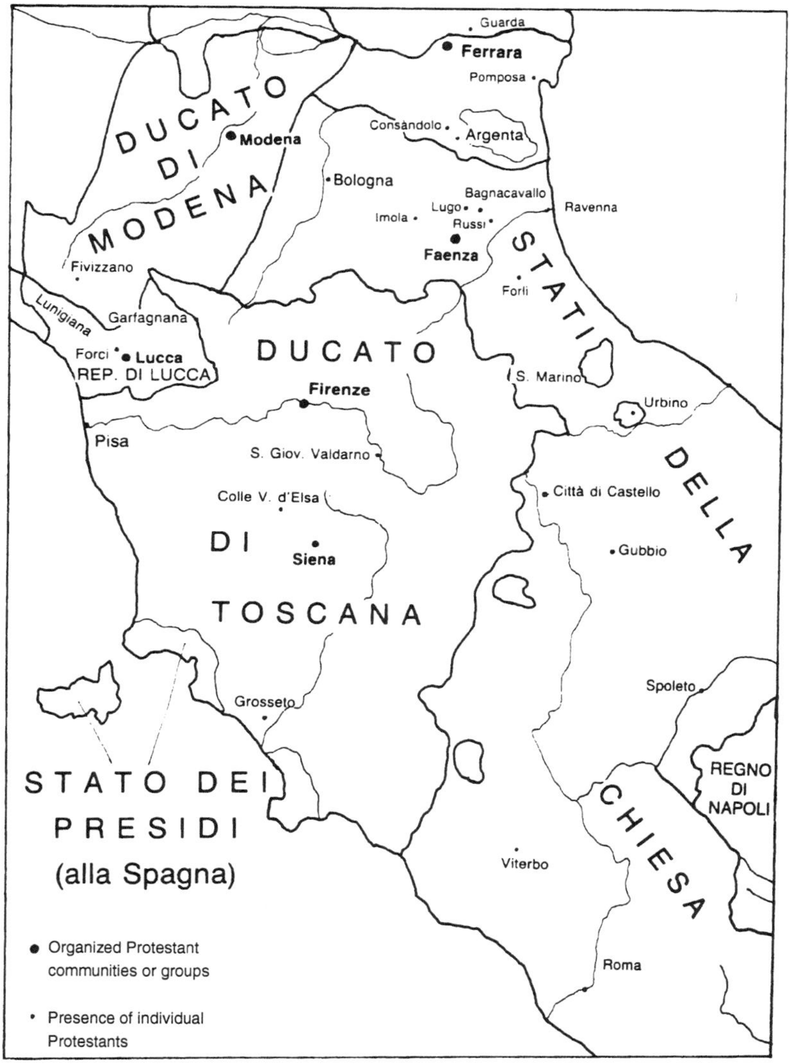
Guarda
Ferrara
Pomposa
DUCATO DI MODENA
Modena
Consandolo
Argenta
Bologna
Bagnacavallo
Lugo
Imola
Russi
Ravenna
Faenza
Forli
STATI DELLA CHIESA
Fivizzano
Lunigiana
Garfagnana
Forci
Lucca
REP. DI LUCCA
DUCATO DI TOSCANA
Firenze
S. Marino
Urbino
Pisa
S. Giov. Valdarno
Colle V. d'Elsa
Città di Castello
Siena
Gubbio
Grosseto
Spoleto
STATO DEI PRESIDI
(alla Spagna)
REGNO DI NAPOLI
Viterbo
Roma
Organized Protestant communities or groups
Presence of individual Protestants

Central Italy

14

RENÉE DE FRANCE AND CALVINISM AT FERRARA AND FAENZA

AT THE COURT OF RENÉE DE FRANCE

THE INTRIGUING LIFE of Renée de France (1510–76), the daughter of Louis XII and Anne of Brittany, who became the duchess of Ferrara in 1528 when she married Ercole II d'Este, a French ally, has not been treated equitably by her principal biographer, Bartolommeo Fontana. Fontana, attempting every way he could to diminish Renée's contacts with John Calvin and the church of Geneva in the vain effort to demonstrate that she was neither a Protestant nor a Catholic,[1] avoided drawing a full picture of Ferrarese Calvinism and its diffusion to neighboring towns.

Renée had been orphaned as a child and was brought up at the court of Francis I, who had married her sister Claude. These early years of the reign of Francis, before his defeat at Pavia in 1525, were a high point of humanistic culture in France and of the diffusion of the works of Erasmus and Luther. The young king, with the connivance of his mother, Louise of Savoy, and of his sister Marguerite, queen of Navarre, protected the reforming efforts of Guillaume Briçonnet, bishop of Meaux, and of his disciple Jacques Lefèvre d'Étaples, humanist, mathematician, and theologian.

Under their direction, Marguerite, cultivated and sensitive, had come to a personal faith, founded on the conviction of the centrality of Scripture and that the salvation of the believer was a gift from God. At court echoes were heard of the bitter attacks of the Sorbonne against the perceived errors of Erasmus and Luther, and at Paris heretics were being sent to the stake, beginning with the Augustinian Jean Vallière on 8 August 1523. During these years Renée received spiritual guidance from Marguerite, the king's sister, a devoted follower of Lefèvre d'Étaples. When the eighteen-year-old Renée came to Ferrara in 1528 as Ercole's bride, she joined one of the most famous of Italian Renaissance courts, one still under the spell of the great

---

[1] B. Fontana, *Renata di Francia, Duchessa di Ferrara* (Rome: Forzani, 1898), 3:361.

poetry of Ariosto. The young princess brought with her a painful nostalgia for France and Marguerite, and the remembrance of the religious discussions at court. Renée had already accepted the essential principle of the Reformation, the priority of the Gospel message over any other teaching of the Church. The existential significance of this faith would accompany her for her entire life. In the testament that she signed on 22 October 1573, she thanked God for having allowed her to be instructed in the Scriptures' "pure words and truth, which are a singular benefice, exceeding all others which we can have in this world...."[2]

Renée's meeting with John Calvin in Ferrara was decisive for her religious development. The future reformer had just published at Basel in 1536 the first edition of his theological manual, the *Institutio Christianae religionis*. He had also contributed to the French translation of the Bible published in 1535, executed by his cousin, Louis Olivier, known as Pierre Robert Olivétan, at the behest of Waldensians. Calvin wrote a preface for it that contained "a marvelous exhortation to be constant in faith:" "What can separate us and take us away from this holy Gospel?... We know that Jesus Christ has walked along the path that we must now follow...."[3]

Neither Calvin nor Renée ever disclosed the nature of their discussions during the weeks that he passed at the court of Ferrara in the summer of 1536, which coincided with the period of the first inquisitorial investigations. Just a short time before, the duke had expelled from court the duchess's governess, Michelle de Soubise, an avid reader of the Scriptures, to whom she was closely attached. Renée's secretary, the poet Clément Marot, a translator of the Psalms into French, the version that would become the first hymnal of French Protestants, was also chased away. Calvin was convinced of the political importance of converting princes and members of the ruling classes if the Gospel was to be successfully propagated among the people. Thus, he clarified the basic doctrines of the Reformation for this daughter of Louis XII and sister-in-law of Francis I, to whom he had dedicated the *Institutes* in the hope of obtaining protection for the persecuted evangelicals of France. With Calvin's first letter to Renée in November 1541, in which he attacked the mass as blasphemy when it was conceived as a sacrifice to Jesus Christ, he became her spiritual guide during her difficult relationship with Ercole II. In spite of her turbulent marriage, her court became transformed into a refuge for the persecuted.

Celio Secondo Curione, who had to leave Venice during the trial against Giulio della Rovere, in whose house he had been living, was Renée's guest for a few months in 1541. The author of the *Pasquillus extaticus* brought to her his experience of the evangelical life, thereby contributing to the conversion of his friend, Fulvio Pellegrino Morato. At court, Curione met the poet Olimpia, Fulvio's daughter, the tutor of Renée's daughters, and the two German Lutheran physicians, Johann and Chilian Sinapius. It was Renée who urged Curione to take a position with the family of Niccolò Arnolfini in Lucca. Curione paid a second visit to Ferrara in the autumn of

---

[2]Ibid., 326–27: "en sa pure parolle et vérité, qui est ung bénéfice singulier, excédant tous aultres qui se peulvent avoir en ce monde…"
[3]Quoted from H. Hauser & A. Renaudet, *Les débuts de l'âge moderne*, 293.

1542 on his way to retrieve his wife and children whom he had left behind in Tuscany at the time of his precipitous flight from Lucca when Cardinal Bartolomeo Guidiccioni had ordered his arrest. During his brief halt in Ferrara, Curione left a copy of Bullinger's *Commentarii in Mattheum* with the duchess.[4]

The small Protestant group gathered about Renée grew with the arrival of several former Augustinians who had already been tried and condemned and were now convinced Lutherans: Gabriele da Bergamo, alias Dionysus, Don Stefano da Mantova, and Ambrogio Cavalli, whose adventurous life we have already noted. Also at court were masters of theology and preachers, the professor of classics Francesco Porto, and the schoolteacher Franceschino di Lucca. They were all in the service of the duchess in various capacities, who in addition to her correspondence with Calvin, communicated with the ministers at Chiavenna and Poschiavo. Since she wanted to educate her daughters Lucrezia and Anna in the new faith, she felt the need for strong spiritual guidance to help her withstand her husband's growing opposition. Renée managed to receive a clandestine visit from the pastor at Poschiavo, Giulio della Rovere, who stayed with Francesco Porto at neighboring Consandolo during the Lenten season of 1550 which saw the election of Julius III to the papacy. della Rovere, the author of the *Exhortation to Martyrdom* examined earlier and an intransigent Protestant, preached fifteen sermons to the evangelicals at court that gave an impetus to the creation of a clandestine conventicle, defying the anger of the duke, and the spying eyes of hostile servants.

In 1551 or a little before, the Lord's Supper began to be celebrated with the participation of the duchess. About twenty persons joined in, including her two daughters, Madame de' Grari, and her husband, though some members of the household refused to take part in this reformed rite. Isabella Breseña, who had been a member of the Valdesian circle in Naples, the wife of the governor of Piacenza, with her son Pietro and his wife, Elisabetta Confalonieri, attended one of these gatherings.[5] This intelligent and accomplished Spanish lady went into exile for her religious views, first visiting Vergerio at Tübingen, later settling at Chiavenna where she joined the church guided by Agostino Mainardi. She would never return home, despite the hardships of her new life and the pleas of her children.

Renée's reputation as protectress of dissidents and as an instrument for the propagation of Calvinist doctrines spread throughout Italy and abroad. Persons who had been condemned to prison or to the galleys sought her assistance, among whom we find Baldo Lupatino, Cornelio Donzellino, Ludovico Domenichi, Fanino Fanini, the Anabaptist Antonio Pagani, Pietro Bresciani of Casalmaggiore, and the Augustinian Andrea Ghetti of Volterra. Renée was in correspondence with the ex-Benedictine Vincenzo Maggi who had emigrated to Basel; with Juan de Enzinas, the brother of the Lutheran Diego de Enzinas condemned to the stake at Rome in 1545, who wrote

---

[4]See the biographical sketch by A. Biondi, in *DBI*, 31:443–49.
[5]B. Nicolini, "Una Calvinista napoletana: Isabella Bresegna," in *Ideali e passioni*, 4–23, and *DBI* 14:189–90.

to her from Wittenberg seeking a subsidy for his Spanish translation of the Bible; and with Bartolomeo Panciatichi, sentenced in Florence in 1551, as we shall see below.[6]

The efforts of the duchess, skillfully conducted, and exploiting her position in the French royal family, were not restricted to assisting the prosecuted. At her villa of Consandolo, where she resided for part of the year, she created a beehive of evangelical activities, including storing and distributing prohibited books, and organizing a type of underground railroad that made possible the clandestine expatriation of evangelicals to the Grisons and other Protestant lands. A merchant of Imola, a certain Innocenzo Magnani of Tossignano, who had gone to Lugo and Ferrara to buy grain, struck up a friendship with Renée's steward at Consandolo, where he was astonished by the fact that even the farm boys knew their Scriptures and could converse about them intelligently. Magnani learned that each year Bibles were brought down from Germany by messengers who then "visited the various Christian congregations and churches in turn." He also ran into a shoemaker "who offered hospitality to the persecuted, sent them on to Ferrara and then from place to place until they reached Lutheran lands."[7]

THE MARTYRDOM OF FANINO FANINI

From Ferrara and Consandolo, Calvinism spread to all the neighboring localities: Argenta, Lugo, Faenza, Imola, Forlì, Modena, and Ravenna. The trial in 1550 against a baker of Faenza was a memorable event for the Este duchy. At its conclusion, the baker was sent to the stake. Fanino Fanini (1520–50) was prosecuted in Ferrara after he was apprehended preaching heretical doctrines at Bagnacavallo, a fiefdom of the Este. We do not know where the young baker learned the new doctrines, nor how he had mastered so effectively the art of preaching. He might have heard Bernardino Ochino in Faenza and certainly, in his travels to buy grains for his ovens, he would have had ample opportunities to push as far as Ferrara and neighboring localities.

The new, enthusiastic prophets of the Reformation preached everywhere, from workplaces to churchyards after mass, and even in religious houses. Fanino, with his friends Barbone Morisi and Giovan Matteo Bulgarelli, Alessandro Bianchi, Nicola Passerino, and a certain Nicoletto, had succeeded in getting into the convent of Santa Chiara in Bagnacavallo to instruct the nuns, who had begun to read prohibited books, to cease believing in the intercession of priests, and to recognize one pastor only, Jesus Christ. The nuns were now asserting that "to go to the Divine offices and to the Mass is blasphemy, and the consecrated host is only a piece of dough." In short, they seemed to have accepted Calvinist beliefs.

---

[6]See the list of letters confiscated during the 1554 trial, in ASM, Archivio Fiaschi, b. 42, fasc. 2, fols. 74–79.

[7]G. F. Cortini, "La Riforma e l'Inquisizione in Imola (1551–1578) e Marco Antonio Flaminio, luterano," *La Romagna* 16 (1927): 465–83; 17 (1928): 74–92, at 19 of the offprint.

The trial against "poor Fanin" caused a sensation in Ferrara, where he was imprisoned, at Faenza, and in every place he had visited. His message, simple and persuasive, but uncompromising had met with much success. After his first arrest in 1547, he abjured and was banished from Faenza. But a year later at Lugo he returned to his ministry, going from house to house. According to his accuser, Master Giovan Pietro Delfino of the Minor Conventuals, many women who were impulsive creatures had been charmed by him.[8] Fanini remained incarcerated at Lugo for eighteen months, while his case became a *casus belli* between the duke, wholly subservient to the church but keen to preserve his jurisdictional prerogatives, the pope, and the Inquisition. The sovereign upheld the principle that the trial should take place where the crime had been committed, namely at Lugo, in Este territory. But the ecclesiastical authorities argued that Lugo fell under the diocese of Imola, a papal state. During the controversy, which dragged on until the election of Julius III (February 1550), energetic efforts were being made behind the scenes to save the young preacher.

Renée wrote twice to her husband imploring mercy for the prisoner, and persuaded the famous Captain Camillo Orsini, whose son had married Lavinia della Rovere, a friend of the duchess and of Olimpia Morato, to appeal to the duke to turn Fanini over to him. Orsini promised to tame him by making a soldier out of him. Olimpia and Lavinia visited Fanini in prison and may have brought him the duchess's charity, to whom he wrote in thanks. But Ercole II, pressed by inquisitors in Ferrara and Rome, one of whom, Cardinal Marcello Cervini, was in Bologna where the Council was sitting, could only obtain from the new pope the right to execute the sentence against the relapsed heretic in Ferrara. On 22 August 1550 Fanini was first hung and then burned at the stake, with his ashes cast into the Po. Reports of the courage, steadfastness, and fervor of the young baker of Faenza, unswayed by the entreaties of his wife and children and convinced that he had been chosen for martyrdom as a witness for Christ, circulated far and wide in Italy and abroad.

Francesco Negri in his *Tragedia del libero arbitrio*, a work that was very well known in Romagna, the second edition of which appeared in that same year, 1550, was the first to extol Fanini's name. The former Benedictine from Bassano, only two months after the execution, corrected the proofs from Chiavenna of a small Latin booklet in which he provided a detailed description, undoubtedly relayed by Italian eyewitnesses, of the supreme sacrifice made by Fanini and by Negri's fellow townsman Domenico Cabianca.[9] Giulio della Rovere, who had followed events closely during his clandestine visit to Ferrara at Lent in 1550, also wrote about Fanini. His account of the life and death of the martyr is rich with details, including the information that the baker had left many writings—letters and sermons—which he had used to propagate the new faith.[10]

---

[8]See A. Casadei, "Fanino Fanini da Faenza: Episodio della Riforma protestante in Italia," *NRS* 18 (1934): 170, 196–97.

[9]*De Fanini faventini ac Dominici bassanensis morte, qui nuper ob Christum in Italia, romani pontifici iussu, impie occisi sunt, brevis historia, Franc. Nigro, bassanensi auctore,* Tiguri [Zürich], 1550. Cf. G. Zonta, "Francesco Negri," 315.

[10]A. Casadei, "Fanino Fanini," 187–88.

THE VISIONARY FROM CATANIA: GIORGIO SICULO

A year later, another sensational trial shook the Benedictine order and disrupted the tranquillity of Ferrara. On 23 May 1551 the Sicilian Giorgio Rioli, known as Siculo, succumbed to his fate. This mysterious personage, whose early years at the Benedictine convent of San Nicolò l'Arena in Catania have already been mentioned, continued into later life the friendship forged at that time with Don Benedetto da Mantova. The latter lived for many years among brother members of his order in Sicily and the peasants who worked the lands owned by the convents of Santa Maria di Licodia and of San Nicolò l'Arena. Don Benedetto translated a number of Giorgio's works from the Sicilian dialect, and while he was rector of Santa Maria di Pomposa, the abbot, Luciano degli Ottoni, also translated Siculo's *Libro della verità christiana* into Latin. Among all Siculo's writings, until recently only his *Epistola di Giorgio Siculo* was known, having been studied by Delio Cantimori, who underlined its radical spiritualism and its rejection of the Protestant doctrines of predestination and justification by faith alone.[11] But now Carlo Ginzburg and Adriano Prosperi have furnished us with a fuller portrait of the astonishing Sicilian visionary.[12] During the first phase of the Council of Trent, Siculo aspired to appear before the assembled members to reveal the teachings he claimed that he had received directly from Jesus Christ. This secret truth may have been what was contained in the so-called "greater book" (*libro maggiore*) or *Libro della verità christiana*, of which no copy is known.

This Benedictine, unlettered, not expressing himself easily in the vernacular, ignorant of Latin according to the contemporary scholar Nascimbene Nascimbeni, nevertheless communicated his message that Christ by his death on the cross had bestowed salvation on the entirety of humanity and not only on the predestined. Siculo also prophesied the coming of the age of the Holy Spirit and of regeneration for all believers in the divine promise. Meanwhile, the Christian church and its rites, including the sacraments, had lost their significance. It was this destructive doctrine that brought Siculo his death sentence. Luciano degli Ottoni in vain tried to persuade Cardinal Ercole Gonzaga, protector of the Benedictine order, to save him. Benedetto da Mantova and Luciano himself, incarcerated at Verona in March 1549 for possessing and proclaiming the "*libro maggiore*," were tried and convicted. As part of their sentence they were relegated to the small monastery of Santa Croce di Campese near Bassano del Grappa (1552). The two Benedictines, thanks to the protection of Cardinal Gonzaga, who was also governor of the marquisate of Mantua, and because they had made a complete confession and abjuration of their errors, got off with light punishment.[13]

---

[11]Cf. D. Cantimori, *Eretici italiani del Cinquecento*, chap. 8, 57–70.
[12]C. Ginzburg, "Due note sul profetismo cinquecentesco," *RSI* 78 (1966): 184–227; A. Prosperi, "Un gruppo ereticale italo-spagnolo: La setta di Giorgio Siculo," *Critica Storica* 19 (1982): 335–51; idem, "Opere inedite e sconosciute di Giorgio Siculo," *Bibliofilia* 87 (1985): 137–57.
[13]G. Fragnito, "Ercole Gonzaga, Reginaldo Pole e il monastero di San Benedetto di Polirone: Nuovi documenti su Luciano degli Ottoni e Benedetto Fontanini (1549–1551)," *Benedictina* 34 (1987): 253–71.

Twenty years or so after the execution of Giorgio Siculo, a new investigation was launched in Ferrara against his sect. It turned out that his prophecies had spread to Benedictine convents in the city and to San Benedetto Po in Brescia. The abjuration in 1568 of Don Antonio da Bozzolo, dean and cellarer from 1555 at San Benedetto Po, contained startling revelations, including the extent of involvement in the sect of Benedetto Fontanini and Luciano degli Ottoni. In 1570, preoccupied by the arrests taking place in Ferrara, Nascimbene Nascimbeni, who was at the time teaching in Ragusa, presented himself voluntarily before the Inquisition in Venice. The names of the two Benedictines, together with a large number of Ferrarese men of letters, academics, and physicians, are mentioned in the memorandum that he submitted to the tribunal. The latter category is of some significance: it was composed of Francesco Severi of Argenta, Antonio Florio, Pietro Giudice, Pietro Bresciani of Casalmaggiore, and Francesco Severi of Argenta, a humanist and professor at the University of Ferrara who was himself arrested in 1567 and condemned to death in 1570. It appears that the appeal of the Sicilian seer, prophet of a rebirth in which all men would be redeemed, saved, and made perfect, was felt more by educated persons than by artisans and laborers. Siculo's followers, in fact, included students at the Spanish College in Bologna who were tried (and pardoned) in 1553 and 1554.

Nascimbeni spent eight years in confinement at San Giovanni in Bragora, and then, to be treated for ailments contracted during his incarceration, was assigned to house arrest in the home of his fellow physician, the Brescian Girolamo Donzellino, his companion in prison during the years of the second trial against the latter, 1574 to 1577. In July 1578 Nascimbeni slipped away from his friend's home and is thought to have found refuge in Padua, where he dropped out of sight, causing problems for Donzellino, suspected of complicity in his flight. The former was detained but released after putting up a bond of two thousand ducats.

THE TRIAL AGAINST RENÉE DE FRANCE

The condemnation of Fanini and Giorgio Siculo signaled for the champions of the new ideas in Ferrara, Modena, Faenza, and the regions of Emilia and Romagna as well, the end of the illusion that dialogue with Rome was still possible and that a posture of clear dissent from the doctrines of the church could be maintained. The Inquisition, under the energetic direction of Cardinal Gian Pietro Carafa and of Fra Michele Ghislieri, now had the upper hand and was turning Rome in an intransigent direction. The storm was quick to break over the Calvinist group at the court of Ferrara. In 1551 Ignatius Loyola sent the rector of the Jesuit College in Rome, Jean Pelletier, to the city with the assignment of establishing a school there under the aegis of the duke, but with the secret mission of investigating the extent to which Calvinism had spread in the entourage of the duchess. Pelletier devised a plan with the sovereign to purify the ecclesiastical rites performed at court, add to the devotions, and expel suspect persons.

But the sermons of Ambrogio Cavalli and Giulio della Rovere had stiffened Renée in her adherence to reformed teachings. For twelve years she had been

The city of Ferrara. *Center:* The castle of the Este family. Engraving of the mid–eighteenth century from Salmon, *Descrizione di alcune città.*

dispensed from the obligation of participating at mass. In March 1554 when Ercole asked that his daughters attend the celebration of Easter, Renée replied that the mass was idolatry and taking part in it was blasphemy.[14] The duke was obsessed by the fear that after the failure of the Jesuit effort, the Inquisition would launch a direct investigation of his family and of his court. He wrote to Henry II of France asking for a theologian who might succeed in making his wife see reason. She seemed incapable of grasping the political repercussions of a possible heresy accusation, at a moment when Spanish power had been further strengthened by the marriage of Philip II with Mary, queen of England. Henry acquiesced, and dispatched to Ferrara Matthieu Ory, prior of the Paris Dominicans, and inquisitor general of France. In turn, Calvin, who heard of this from Lion Jamet, one of the French suspects expelled from court by Ercole, sent the pastor François Morel to lend support to Renée, torn between obedience to the Gospel and obedience to the king of France and her husband, and to aid her in her disputations with the expert Catholic theologians.

Duke Ercole became exasperated when he heard of Morel's arrival, and on the night of 7 September 1554, had his wife summoned from her country residence at Consandolo and confined in the castle. He ordered her to receive no one and accompanied this with the threat that she would not lay her eyes on her daughters who were presently in a convent, until the day when she decided to return to the church and its teachings. After some days of resistance, but faced with the threat of being pronounced a heretic, which would mean the confiscation of her property in France and scandal for the royal family, she yielded, promising to attend mass on the next holy day. But obtaining Renée's acquiescence to confession and communion was more difficult. In the account of a bystander to the drama, the ambassador of Cosimo de' Medici, it appeared that Renée had declared that she believed in the Catholic Church, but not in the Church of Rome.

The following year, 1555, Ambrogio Cavalli returned to Italy from Geneva, perhaps sent by Calvin himself to regain contact with the duchess. But he was spotted, arrested, and taken to Rome where, after a short trial, he was executed on 15 June 1556, declaring that he was dying "for the glory of God." In the course of the judicial proceedings, Cavalli revealed many details about the clandestine life of the Ferrarese conventicle, its links to groups in the Romagna, the loyalty of Renée to her most sacred beliefs, even after she had reverted to the Catholic rite, her continuing correspondence with Calvin, and the protection she was still offering to evangelicals, as best she could.[15] Reports of the vaunted Jesuit triumph at Ferrara spread throughout Europe and distressed Protestant ranks, especially Calvin, not so much for the duchess's lack of constancy, whose extremely delicate political situation was recognized, but because of the concern that the news would have an adverse impact on the Protestant movements in Italy and in France at a moment when the Counter-Reformation was

---

[14]This is what Ercole II wrote to the king of France, 27 March 1554. Cf. B. Fontana, *Renata di Francia*, 2:347.

[15]See a copy of the interrogations from the Roman trial in ASM, Archivio Fiaschi, b. 42, fasc. 2, n. 16, and the sketch by U. Rozzo, in *DBI*, 22:712–17.

marshaling its forces.[16] Nevertheless, Renée, until she left Ferrara to return to France at the death of her husband (1560), remained a figure to be reckoned with for all Italian dissidents, a model of the wise and liberal sovereign, a lover of culture, thirsting for knowledge of the truth. This is how Paleario depicted her in a letter to Bartolomeo Ricci, the preceptor of Alfonso II, the Este heir, in October 1548.[17]

When the Waldensians and the other evangelicals in the duchy of Savoy were compelled by Emanuel Philibert to choose between abjuration and exile, it was to Renée that they turned beseeching her to intervene on their behalf with the duke and his wife, Renée's niece, Marguerite. On her journey back to France, Renée visited the ducal court at Savigliano (7 October). But her intercession failed in the face of Emanuel Philibert's resolve to extirpate "the evil plant" of heresy, in which he was spurred on by Pope Pius IV and seconded by the Jesuits, who sent Antonio Possevino to pursue "the holy enterprise."[18] After Renée returned to her domains at Montargis, where she was finally free to profess her faith, she gave her consent to the celebration of the reformed cult, and continued to give succor to the persecuted. As a seal of her former ties to the Italian Protestant movement, in November 1567, she opened the gates of her residence to a group of Lucchese exiles who had left behind "the abominations of the papacy so that they could enter the church of the Lord." They were fleeing from Luzarches, where they had been received by the prince of Condé, who was retreating with his army in disarray. The Italians consisted of Michele Burlamacchi with his wife Chiara Calandrini, her father Giuliano Calandrini, and her sister Laura with her husband Pompeo Diodati. Michele was the son of the unfortunate Francesco Burlamacchi, executed in 1548, who had dreamed of freeing Tuscany from the Medici and turning it into a federation of free cities under the protection of the emperor, from whom he beseeched the reform of the church "from the many abuses that afflicted her."

Renea Burlamacchi, born at Montargis on 25 March 1568, where she was held at baptism by Duchess Renée, whose name she received, reconstructed a half century later from accounts narrated by her parents, Michele Burlamacchi and Chiara Calandrini, the hardships endured on their journey and the special suffering of her mother and Aunt Laura, who were pregnant and reduced to weakness by cold and hunger: "They made it to Montargis with the help of the Lord, where they were received by the Duchess of Ferrara, Mistress of the place, in her castle, and treated with great kindness even though she did not know us. But the special compassion she felt for those two young expecting women, because they were Italians, prompted her to bring them into her own residence, and as long as they remained there she showed them all the courtesies and pleasantries that one could desire."[19]

---

[16]See C. Jenkins Blaisdell, "Renée de France between Reform and Counter-Reform," *Archive for Reformation History* 63 (1972): 217–25.

[17]See S. Caponetto, *Aonio Paleario*, 106–7.

[18]G. Jalla, *Storia della Riforma*, 1:137–42.

[19]*Descrittione della Vita et Morte del sig.r Michele Burlamacchi Gentilhuomo lucchese, missa in luce dalla Sig.ra Renea Burlamacchi, sua fig.a nel mese di Gen.ro del 1623 in Genevra*, fol. 61rv, Geneva, Bibliothèque publique et universitaire, MS suppl. 438. I am pleased to thank Lorenza Giorgi for a photocopy

Calvin's last letter from his deathbed, dictated to his brother Antoine, since he could no longer write himself, was addressed to Renée beseeching her to intercede with her niece, Marguerite, duchess of Savoy, still timid and undecided whether to proclaim her faith openly. By this letter the Genevan reformer was offering his positive judgment on the loyalty of Renée to Protestant principles, however hostile to fanaticism and violence towards adversaries she might have been. The fact that she was the mother-in-law of François de Guise, the leader of the Catholic League who was killed by a Protestant in 1563, had not deterred her, Calvin wrote, "from making a proper and pure profession of Christianity, and not with the mouth only, but through notable deeds. As for me, I protest to you that this has prompted me to hold your virtues in so much greater admiration."[20]

FANINI'S LEGACY IN FAENZA

Fanino Fanini was not soon forgotten. The successes achieved subsequently by Calvinism in Faenza, Imola, and in neighboring places cannot be explained except through the seeds sown by his ardent and courageous preaching, sealed by the sacrifice of his life. Many years later, small children still knew the tragic story of "poor Fanin...a great upright man, who was treated cruelly."[21] In the early days of September 1568, the pastor of the reformed church at Morbegno, Francesco Cellario, a former Minorite monk, who had been tried at Pavia and then fled to the Valtellina where he had married, came through Faenza in chains. He allowed a compromising thought to escape from his lips: "this is their dear city." A dispatch from the Venetian ambassador in Rome to the doge, dated 25 September, referred to admissions extracted from Cellario at his trial before the Supreme Congregation of the Inquisition. He was reported to have testified that "there was no city in the States of the Church reputed to harbor more heretics than Faenza. Thus, His Holiness stated that, if this was the case, he would destroy it totally, remove all its inhabitants and provide you with another colony. In these days many persons from that city have been brought here as prisoners of the Holy Office."[22] The anger of Pius V, who just the year before had established a tribunal of the Inquisition under the aegis of the Dominicans of Faenza to oversee all of the Romagna, was provoked by the bitter discovery of a clandestine organization that had been operating for almost two decades.

As early as the spring of 1545, the Jesuit Pascasio Broët had written to Francesco Severi that many men and women were covered with the stain of "evil Lutheran doctrine," no longer believing in purgatory or the intercession of saints. Broët dated the beginnings back to the preaching of Ochino in Faenza during the Lenten seasons of

---

of the MS. [The text is now printed by S. Adorni-Braccesi in *Critica Storica* 28 (1991: 31–76, in app. Trans. note.] See the sketch of Francesco Burlamacchi by M. Luzzati, in *DBI*, 15:440–46.

[20]Letter dated 4 April 1564 in *Calvini Opera*, 20:278–79, n. 4090.

[21]F. Lanzoni, *La Controriforma nella città e diocesi di Faenza* (Faenza: F. Lega, 1925), 100.

[22]Ibid., 223–24.

1534 and 1538. To be sure, there were other preachers as well who had cast doubts and aspersions on the ancient traditions of the church. Augustinians and Conventuals, such as Pellegrino Fontaguzzi of Cesena, are identified as among the first in Faenza to spread the teachings of the "new Christians," described by some, with greater accuracy, as "good Lutherans."[23] The first prosecutions were aimed against persons of some standing in the community to better throw fear into the humbler classes, who were beginning to discuss indulgences, purgatory, grace, and free will in their shops and in public places.

Paul IV's campaign of repression involved a rigorous investigation of religious conditions in the States of the Church, with provisions taken in regard to Jews, prostitutes, gambling, and, of course, heretics. Persons who had kept prohibited books hidden in their homes were ordered to turn them over to the authorities, as was the case with the doctor of law, Giovanni Evangelista Calderoni, who surrendered writings by M. A. Flaminio, Erasmus's New Testament and commentary on the Epistles of St. Jerome, and a large vernacular Bible, perhaps the Brucioli translation. Francesco Negri's *Tragedia del libero arbitrio*, from its very first edition in 1549, was among the books circulating. Negri's works were all in great demand by evangelicals after the publication of his account of Fanini's martyrdom. Calderoni himself admitted to a friend that he had read Negri's *Tragedy* when he had been a student at the University of Siena, and enjoyed it so much that he had it copied.[24] Another of those prosecuted was the well-known physician Giovanni Evangelista Nicoluzzi, who was reconciled to the church in 1548 after confessing that he had possessed and read prohibited books. He had allowed himself to be "deceived by the devil," in the person of the celebrated engraver, Giovanni Bernardi, who somehow was not molested. Except for the case of Fanini which ended tragically, the trials conducted during the decade from 1547 to 1558 concluded with the abjurations of the defendants. Authorities hoped that the city's unsavory reputation, which had spread throughout the Romagna and beyond, had finally been cleansed, but almost two hundred people were denounced before the Inquisition in the years 1567 to 1569 alone.

The records turned up by Cardinal Angelo Mercati and communicated to Mons. Francesco Lanzoni truly have "immense historical value" since they are housed in the still generally inaccessible Archive of the Roman Holy Office, and "cast much light on one of the most important periods in the history of Faenza."[25] The first of the nine documents in question is entitled "Names of those suspected of heresy tried in Faenza in 1550." It contains a list of persons actually prosecuted between 1547 and 1551, a total of 155 names, of whom 126 were men and 39 were women. It provides an almost complete picture (Fanini's name is not there because he was tried in Ferrara) of the vastness of the evangelical movement in a city of only fifteen thousand inhabitants. All social categories are represented: nine ecclesiastics,

---

[23]Ibid., 74.
[24]Ibid., 68, 111–12.
[25]F. Lanzoni, "Nuovi documenti sui 'luterani' faentini del XVI secolo," *Bollettino diocesano di Faenza* 13 (1926), n. 9:145–48; n. 11, 176–80.

including the prior of the convent of St. Augustine, two Franciscans, a number of parish priests, and two of the leaders of the entire movement, who will be discussed in more detail later because they were prosecuted again in 1567 and 1568, Don Luca Bertoni and Don Girolamo Dal Pozzo. Among the laymen, there is a tailor, a smith, painters and several ceramicists as well as three notaries and three physicians. There follows a long list of names belonging to the city's most prominent families, several of whom would be tried again two decades later and punished severely. What strikes one about this long roster is the frequent presence of entire family groups, wives, children, nephews, cousins, and even servants. There is a prevalence of professional men, merchants, and artisans, many of whom were members of the government and city councils. Peasants and laborers were almost totally absent. The documents inform us that some of the defendants made public abjurations in 1551 before Cesare della Nave, commissioner of the inquisition. Many others, taking advantage of a concession from Julius III on 29 April 1550 were permitted to abjure privately. But this general pardon did not eradicate the seeds Fanini had sown.

More than a decade and a half later, a certain Salvatore Panettino, a Faentine Familiar of the Inquisition, certainly a professional spy, after conducting a protracted and meticulous investigation, dispatched a truly explosive exposé either to the inquisitor of Faenza or directly to the Holy Office in Rome.[26] He reported the existence of two heretical conventicles, which he dubbed "sects" or "redoubts," accustomed to gathering at night. The persons who met in the home of Camillo Regnoli, a member of the city council since 1540, were his wife, Camilla Caccianemici, his brother Antonio, *Ser* Matteo dalle Tombe, Don Girolamo Bertoni, Bernardino Viani and Melchiorre Biasini, Enea Utili, Pier Paolo Stanchi, Battista Molesi, Matteo Rondinini, Alessandro Mondini, Don Girolamo Dal Pozzo, Domenico Simiante, Girolamo della Castellina, a tailor, Pier Maria Torello, Don Taddeo Bicchi, Silvestro Spada, Iacopo Bertuzzi, painter, Annibale and Jacopo Zanelli, the community's treasurer, Battista Molesi, druggist, with his brother Girolamo and his son Giambattista, Fabio Marchetti, Paolo Romani, Camillo Laderchi, and Eutropio Gulmanelli. The first fourteen named were "ancient" heretics, who had been tried and pardoned after their abjurations years before, the rest were recent converts. The spy had seen them slip out of Regnoli's house long after midnight in December 1566 "all muffled up in their cloaks." Camillo and Antonio Regnoli were the "captains of these conventicles," *Ser* Matteo delle Tombe, the secretary. The second conventicle, formed out of the first, had come into being only recently and met in the home of Federico Gucci. After the departure of the two Regnoli, some members of the older conventicle joined the newer, organized on a Calvinist model. The pastor was Girolamo Bertoni, identified in the documents as the "bishop of the sect," the direct liaison with Geneva, to which he traveled yearly to purchase new books and would return with a "reader" to interpret Scripture, or a catechist. The community had two beadles who were used "to keep peace among the others," deacons who collaborated with the ministers of the Word and helped with conversions. All the conventicle members

---

[26]Ibid., 14 (1927), n. 2:54–56; n. 4, 80–86.

read prohibited books, which included writings by Luther and B. Ochino, according to the accuser, but obviously, works coming from Geneva must have borne a Calvinist stamp. In the general gatherings, as well as in their homes, they condemned the church's precepts and the authority of pope and bishops.

Since the spy had never sat in on any of the clandestine meetings, he was uncertain about their doctrines. Nevertheless, in addition to the information passed on about their contacts with Geneva, where such persons as Melchiorre Biasini and Sforza Ferri found sanctuary, the sentences against many of the condemned unequivocally demonstrate their Calvinist beliefs. Don Girolamo Dal Pozzo, for example, an educated priest who was tried twice and who had been a member of the "sect" for more than twenty years, admitted to belief in a variety of Calvinist teachings: "the consecrated host is not really the body of Our Lord Jesus Christ; we do not have free will except to choose evil; we are certain of salvation; our works are not necessary for salvation because Christ satisfied for us in everything; we must not take vows, and works are of no avail; the pope lacks authority; there is no purgatory after the present life; indulgences and jubilees serve no purpose; prayers for the souls of the dead are of no help to them; images of the saints are not to be venerated; so many of the Church's ceremonies are superfluous." Dal Pozzo had read Negri's *Tragedia del libero arbitrio*, a heretical catechism, and other prohibited books.[27]

The members of the conventicle had tried to disguise their true beliefs. As elsewhere, they flocked to the sermons, regularly attended mass in the church of Sant' Agostino, and then lingered to discuss various issues with the priest. They frequently strolled in small groups in the periphery behind the city walls near the river Lamone. It would appear, according to the Latin inventory in the hand of the accuser, appended to his report, that two other "sects" or groups need to be added to the first two. In all, there were about fifty followers of the Reformation at Faenza in 1567. The exclamation that escaped the prisoner Francesco Cellario had not been idle boasting but was intended perhaps to frighten his jailers by intimating that he had many brethren in the city who would be able to help him escape. But events transpired very differently.

Faenza was terrified by the denunciations, arrests, and transport of prisoners to the dreaded Supreme Congregation of the Inquisition in Rome. Meanwhile, ecclesiastical authorities redoubled their efforts through preaching, processions, and pilgrimages, hoping to lead the population back to obedience and thus cause it to forget the transgressions of the many priests and monks who had helped to alienate the people of Faenza from the Church of Rome. On 2 August 1567 an event that everyone considered miraculous occurred. A house neighboring the convent of the Dominican sisters of Santa Cecilia was destroyed by fire, but a small painting of the Virgin Mary and child remained undamaged to the great amazement and joy of the people. A contemporary writer, Fra Giovanni Capalla of Saluzzo recorded the reaction of a woman to the wonderful event: "Where are those traitorous Lutherans now who would teach us not to revere saints and honor their images? How they must be

[27]F. Lanzoni, *La Controriforma*, 174–75.

angry that the fire respected what they do not want to honor!"[28] But a much greater purificatory blaze would be needed if Faenza and much of the Romagna was to rid itself of the Lutheran and Calvinist menace.

According to an anonymous contemporary chronicler, under Pius V, beginning about 1567, after denunciations from Panettino and others, 150 Faentines were arrested. The figure cannot be too far off the mark because another chronicler of the time, Alessandro Grazioli of Biagio (1524–75), who was usually well informed, compiled from memory a list of one hundred and fifteen persons imprisoned, to which at least another thirteen can be added from another source. According to Grazioli nine persons were condemned to death, forty-two to the galleys, and twenty-seven to prison sentences. Others were assigned to house arrest, monastic confinement, or charitable service in a hospital. The remainder were released for lack of evidence. Fines, the confiscation of property, and the obligation to wear the penitential garment effectively contributed to the uprooting of heresy.

Rather than repeat the names published by Monsignor Lanzoni,[29] the discussion should center on the nine who were sentenced to death, since they were the leaders of the movement. The priest Don Luca Bertoni, who had been tried in 1551 and was thus now relapsed, remained inflexible before the prayers of the Capuchins who beseeched him to repent and be reconciled to the church, and was hung at Rome on 28 February 1569. The influential Regnoli family was destroyed the same year. Camillo Regnoli, identified as the "captain" in the conventicle that had met in his home with the participation of his brother and his wife, belonged to a wealthy family which in the previous century had built a palace and the church of San Michele. A prominent lawyer, he was a member of the city council and a prior of the ruling body, the *Anziani*, on several occasions between 1556 and 1566. His case exemplifies the support for the Reformation and lack of confidence in the work of the Council of Trent felt by some members of the ruling classes. On 25 May 1569, after having protested in vain that he was not a recidivist, despite the earlier trial in 1549, he was hung in the square before the Castel Sant'Angelo in Rome and then his body burned. The pastor Francesco Cellario, also laboring under a previous conviction, met a similar fate in the same auto da fé. Antonio Regnoli, Camillo's brother, was sent to the galleys, where he died.

Neither belonging to the ancient and noble house of the Regnoli, nor her reputation as a wise and prudent matron saved Camilla Caccianemici, Camillo's wife, from a cruel death in the sight of the populace of Faenza. In the *auto* celebrated before the church of Sant'Andrea on 21 August 1569, sentences were read against her and against the painter Giambattista Bertuzzi. The latter was condemned to "life imprisonment" (*carcere perpetuo*), but the sentence was commuted. The woman was first hung and then burned, and in lowering her body from the scaffold, her head separated from her torso.[30] The severe sentence and the macabre spectacle probably

---

[28]Ibid., 196–97.
[29]Ibid., 161–69.
[30]Ibid., 247, 236–39; D. Orano, *Liberi pensatori bruciati in Roma* (Rome: Unione Cooperativa Editrice, 1904), 30–33, nn. 24, 32, 43.

suggested to the many Protestant sympathizers in the conventicles the wisdom of abjuration and repentance.

The year before on 10 May, during the great auto da fé in the church of the Minerva in Rome with sixteen cardinals in attendance, six Faentines were sentenced. Giovan Paolo Spiga, or Bucci, was condemned to the galleys; Giambattista Mengolini to a prison term and fined a thousand *scudi*. Eventually, the sentences of the two were commuted. But it was a different situation for the five sentenced to be handed over to the secular arm: *Ser* Matteo dalle Tombe, Don Francesco Stanchi, and *Messer* Francesco della Castellina, or Castellini, condemned to the galleys, pleaded in vain for pardon. Matteo Rondinini and Girolamo Bertini, "the bishop of the sect," "were led to the stake without the cross, and with yellow miters and vestments on which were painted devils, their lords and protectors, and, since they persisted in their false opinions, were burned alive."[31]

The repression did not cease with the many condemnations and the terror sown among the families and friends of the victims, and those who leaned towards their ideas. Many who had regained their freedom by repudiating their errors began to return to Faenza and be reinstated in their public offices. This reversal in their fortunes caused unease among those who had accused them from pulpits and in the schools or who had collaborated with the Inquisition in their prosecution. They now feared retaliation from the governing class, especially when the papal seat should become vacant and the reins of the city would be in the hands of the *Anziani*. In February 1570, a man of letters, Giulio Castellani, wrote to Cardinal Scipione Rebiba of the Roman Holy Office to pass on to the Holy Father that the time had come to purge the city, reform the entire general council, and establish new procedures for the election of its members and other officials. Two months later, the new papal legate for Bologna and the Romagna, Cardinal Alessandro Sforza, came to Faenza at the behest of the pope, canceled twenty-eight names from the roster of the council and an additional thirty-two from various positions. He replaced them with others and rewrote the medieval statutes, charging the magistracy of the "Hundred Peacekeepers" (*Cento Pacifici*), who served as a form of police to keep the peace, to lend their support to the inquisitor and his ministers.[32]

DISSENT IN THE ROMAGNA

A vast network radiated out from Ferrara and Faenza to religious dissidents in neighboring towns and cities, Argenta, Bagnacavallo, Imola, Forlì, Lugo, Russi, Ravenna, and Modena. The trial against Alessandro Ressa, a bookseller and clock maker of Imola, arrested in early March 1551, brought to light a group of persons of a certain education who met in his shop to hear the Scriptures read and explained. Ressa had been arrested when a compromising letter that he had written to a goldsmith, Pier Gentile, languishing in prison at Faenza on the charge of heresy, was intercepted. For

[31]F. Lanzoni, *La Controriforma*, 214–20; D. Orano, *Liberi pensatori*, 25–30, nn. 24, 25, 26.
[32]Idem, "I nuovi documenti," 14 (1927), n. 6:117–19.

a number of years Ressa and his brethren had been reading the *Enchiridion* of Erasmus, Brucioli's *Bible*, the *Prediche* of Ochino and of Giulio della Rovere. Although he was in contact with evangelicals of the Ferrara region, it would seem that Ressa's group had not gone beyond Erasmian positions and a general sort of criticism of current ecclesiastical practices. The most serious accusation against Ressa, who was extremely able in parrying the charges against him and in protesting his allegiance to the Roman church, were the reproaches he had hurled at some boys noisily accompanying a procession for the Madonna of Valverde as it passed by his house: "What sort of an abuse is this, parading around with a piece of wood! It is God, who does everything, it is he whom we should adore and none other."[33]

Ressa, as well as the brethren who came to his shop, Vincenzo Zoppi, Giovanni Zaccone, and the merchant Nocente Magnani of Tossignano, who served as go-betweens with the evangelicals of Consandolo, got off with a mere abjuration, perhaps because the local inquisitor was inclined to be indulgent towards defendants of some social standing. One of the group, a certain Giulio Cicognola who was tried a year later, made much more detailed statements. He revealed that meetings had taken place at his house and at that of a *"Messer* Bandino," attended by a priest from out of town, a certain Taddeo, and other visitors. During these gatherings they discussed "purgatory, prayer, the images of saints…and that our purgatory was Jesus Christ, and there was no other purgatory, because Christ himself had purged all our sins."[34] Cicognola abjured these errors and died repentant, but the inquisitors had him buried with the yellow penitential garment of the reconciled heretic to throw fear into the other conspirators. Ressa himself moved to Bologna, where he was tried anew (1559) for slanders against the pope and for asserting that he did not attend mass because it was not celebrated in the vernacular!

Bibliographical Note

For Ferrara, one can add: R. Horne, "Reformation and Counter-Reformation at Ferrara: Antonio Musa Brasavola and Giambattista Cinthio Giraldi," *Italian Studies* 13 (1958): 62–82; R. Raffaelli, "Notizie intorno a Francesco Severi, il medico di Argenta," *Studi Urbinati* B3, 56 (1983): 91–136.

For Faenza, see Maria Grazia Tre Re, "Gli avvenimenti del sedicesimo secolo nella città di Faenza, con particolare riguardo ai processi e alle condanne per eresia," *Studi Romagnoli* 8 (1957): 279–97, largely based on Lanzoni (cited in notes).

---

[33]G. F. Cortini, "La Riforma," 10, 17.
[34]Ibid., 22–23.

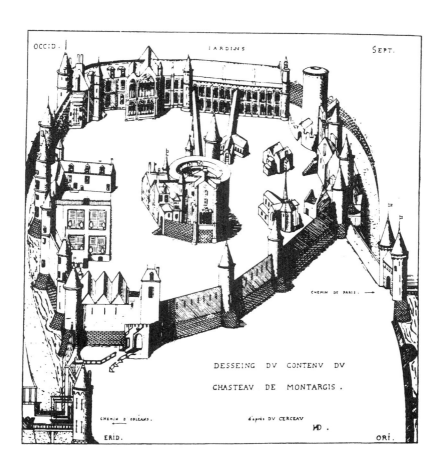

The castle of Montargis, near Orléans; from E. Doumergue, *Iconographie calvinienne* (Lausanne, 1917), 75.

15

THE SCANDAL OF MODENA AND MANTUA

THE BOLOGNA-FERRARA-MODENA TRIANGLE

THE IMPORTANCE OF MARTIN BUCER'S LETTERS of 1541 addressed to the Italian "brethren" of Bologna, Modena, Ferrara and Venice, which circulated among them clandestinely, has been mentioned (chap. 4). Present-day Emilia was the center from which the Strasbourg reformer's program radiated. It received a hearing in the universities, at Bologna in the circle of Achille Bocchi; in Ferrara in the company of the Erasmian philosopher Vincenzo Maggi; and at Modena among the *literati* of the academy headed by Giovanni Grillenzoni. It was not Giovanni Angelo Odoni and Bartolomeo Fonzio alone, two who returned to Italy after a long sojourn in Strasbourg, who took the lead in the discussions and controversies that disturbed the religious peace in these central Italian cities. The circulation of evangelical ideas between these centers depended on their geographical proximity and on the activities of certain key figures: the Minorites Fonzio, Fra Paolo Ricci, alias Camillo Renato, Giovanni Buzio of Montalcino, and the Augustinian Giulio della Rovere, tried after Lent 1538. In spite of the suspicions they had aroused and the inquests initiated against them by ecclesiastical authorities, they moved easily among the convents of their orders or found protection and friendship in influential families, as was the case with della Rovere, who, after the scandal provoked by his sermons, hid in the Bolognese home of the physician Prospero Calani, personally above reproach.

In these cities belonging to the states of the church or to the Este family, a variety of messages of religious protest can be identified, from Bucer's in the 1530s to the Valdesian of Bartolomeo della Pergola, from the original and corrosive program of Fonzio, which departed from the teachings of Luther and Bucer and aspired to the creation of a church of the poor, to the radical doctrines of Paolo Ricci (Renato). Alongside these subversive currents, the prophecies of Giorgio Siculo made inroads at Bologna in the Spanish College, and at Ferrara in the convent of the Benedictines. They would persist long after the death of the seer himself. In this climate of competing and intersecting theological currents it is difficult to identify a common thread, despite the passage from one city to another of itinerant preachers who left groups of "new Christians" in their wake. These attempts to establish a united network of "brethren" ran up against borders between states, and within a single state, the ancient, entrenched traditions of individual cities. Take as an example Modena, whose large conventicle of "brethren" (*fratelli*) was not in contact with the Calvinists of Ferrara and Faenza, except perhaps sporadically, in spite of the fact that Fanino Fanini's attempts to proselytize touched every corner of the Este dominions.

Tommaso Bavellino is a quite typical case of a layman who used his trading in silk to disseminate his religious message as he traveled between Bologna, Modena, and Ferrara.[1] He was tried at Ferrara in 1542, abjured his errors, and moved to Bologna where he joined a heterodox group drawn from the lower classes composed of weavers, tailors, schoolteachers, shopkeepers, merchants, and itinerant peddlers. They read the Bible in Brucioli's vernacular translation, with a preference for the book of Revelation, and Curione's *Pasquino in estasi*. When authorities discovered the existence of the conventicle, Bavellino again abjured his errors and saved himself from the fate of the relapsed because the Bolognese inquisitor was unaware of his previous conviction in Ferrara. Bavellino turned up next in Modena, where he met Bartolomeo Fonzio and participated in the activities of Grillenzoni's academy. Here he resumed his active proselytization, under Fonzio's influence, among weavers and tradesmen, working to create a "church of the poor."

In 1545 judicial proceedings opened in Ferrara against Bavellino and Fonzio, and the two took flight. Fonzio moved about restlessly between Rome and Ancona for several years, and eventually settled at Cittadella as schoolteacher in 1551. Bavellino returned to Bologna where he joined a conventicle led by a druggist named Girolamo Rinaldi, made up in large part of weavers such as the Modenese Francesco Tavani, Antonio Amadei, Antonio Bianchi of Cento, Giacomo da Montecalvo, and later the tailor Marco Magnavacca, the shoemaker Sforza Ferri of Faenza, who visited Geneva and then returned (only to be prosecuted), and a few cloth merchants. The Bolognese group was loosely linked to the Brescian conventicle of Ludovico Medigini, somewhat of a gossip, who would be tried in March 1543. He was heard to utter that "in Bologna there were four thousand persons who kept their faith in Christ according to the Gospels and not according to the modern priesthood."[2] To be sure, this was idle boasting, but dissidence in Bologna had indeed spread much further than what is revealed by the documents. We know almost nothing, for example, about the countess Diamante, the daughter of Girolamo Pepoli, who had married the Vicentine Odoardo Thiene, and, in second nuptials in Geneva, the Lucchese Manfredo Balbani.[3] After returning to Modena, Bavellino was arrested for a third time on 5 March 1549.

---

[1] See the biographical sketch by A. Rotondò in *DBI*, 7:206.
[2] A. Rotondò, "Per la storia dell'eresia a Bologna nel secolo XVI," *Rinascimento*, ser. 2, 2 (1962): 107–54, at 138–39.

The case of this daring Emilian proselytizer was not unique; there were many other men of letters in the area, influenced by Erasmus and Bucer, who kept in close contact with each other. One needs only to think of Giovanni Angelo Odoni, Francesco Bolognetti, Francesco Porto, Johannes Sinapius, Agostino Fogliata, Celio Calcagnini, and Arnoldo Arlenio Perassilo (the Italianate form of a Dutch name) who ran the German bookshop in Bologna and served as the intermediary between Italians and Bucer and German printers.

ANTI-ROMAN DISSENT IN MODENA

After the 1540s Modena became the chief center of religious dissent in Emilia, with a following approaching the numbers we saw for Calvinism in Faenza and Romagna. The Modenese movement, thanks to the prominence of its adherents, such figures as Ludovico Castelvetro, Giovanni Bertari, Francesco Porto, and Filippo Valentini; the role played in the controversies by the bishop of the city, Cardinal Giovanni Morone; and the establishment there of a clandestine community intended to be an alternative to the official church, has received critical scholarly attention in the last few years,[4] on which the following discussion is based. The variety of reform currents circulating in Modena can be compared to a laboratory of ideas in which the ingredients being tested were theological themes drawn from the larger European debate. They range from the connection between humanism and the Reformation to the radical views of Camillo Renato rejecting the objective value of the sacraments. The younger Modenese who gathered in the Grillenzoni academy were eager to examine the underlying sources of their secular culture and to read the Greek and Latin classics; but stimulated by the writings of Erasmus, Luther, Melanchthon, and Bucer, they also wanted to evaluate the scriptural foundations of Protestant teachings.

From the home of the physician Grillenzoni, the gatherings moved to his brother's druggist shop, where as many as fifty persons of all social classes might assemble. It was not a narrow circle of humanists drawn from the upper spheres of society, but a meeting place open to all, men and women alike, spurred on by the great issues of the day, strictly linked, nevertheless, to the traditions, customs, and economic interests of their city. If we were to reflect for a moment on the enormous social implications of the Lutheran doctrines of the priesthood of all believers and the worthlessness of monastic vows, we would grasp the significance of these discus-

---

[3]Cf. A. Pascal, "Da Lucca a Ginevra: Studi sulla emigrazione religiosa lucchese nel secolo XVI," *RSI* 49–52 (1932–35). See especially vol. 50 (1933): 56–57. The article, which appeared in several installments, was reprinted separately (Pinerolo: Unitipografica Pinerolese, 1935).

[4]S. Peyronel Rambaldi, *Speranze e crisi nel Cinquecento modenese: Tensioni religiose e vita cittadina ai tempi di Giovanni Morone* (Milan: F. Angeli, 1979); C. Bianco, "La comunità dei 'fratelli' nel movimento ereticale modenese del '500," *RSI* 92 (1980): 621–79; idem, "Bartolomeo della Pergola e la sua predicazione eterodossa a Modena nel 1544," *BSSV,* n. 151 (1982): 3–49; M. Firpo, "Gli 'spirituali,' l'Accademia di Modena e il formulario di fede del 1542: Controllo del dissenso religioso e nicodemismo," *RSLR* 20 (1984): 40–111. The contribution by A. Rotondò is cited at note 2.

sions in a society of merchants, professional men, and artisans, coexisting with large numbers of clergy with whom there was no lack of controversy.

Prominent roles were played in the academy by literary men endowed with strong humanistic educations such as Ludovico Castelvetro, Filippo Valentini, Giovanni Bertari, and the Greek scholar Francesco Porto, who would become a professor at the University of Ferrara and participate in the gatherings of the city's Calvinist conventicle. The public reading and explication of Scripture was an activity carried on even by laymen such as Filippo Valentini, who openly commented on the Gospel of Matthew to the great dismay of the religious orders. These activities, joined to the reading of works by Erasmus and Luther, Melanchthon's *Loci communes,* and the *Sommario della santa Scrittura,* steered the academicians and their followers towards the basic principles of Lutheran doctrine and persuaded them to criticize harshly the ignorance of preachers and Lenten orators who were still firmly rooted in scholastic theology.

As long as Renato and Fonzio remained in Modena, the academy served as the clearinghouse for their ideas, but it was not the only channel in the city for voicing doubts about traditional beliefs. A young churchman, Giovanni Bertari, a tutor for the children of F. M. Molza, commented on the Pauline Epistles in Molza's home to a large and interested audience of professional men and clergy. From October to June 1541, the episcopal vicar, Domenico Sigibaldi, sent alarming reports about the spread of heresy to the absent bishop, Giovanni Morone. The followers of the academicians and of Bertari coalesced into one compact group, in which both sexes were well represented. The feminine presence in the movement of religious dissent, underscored by our sources, in the Faenza and Modena areas, quite unlike what is known of the situation elsewhere, in Cremona for example, may be explainable by the large number of young women forced into convents to spare their family from the expense of a marriage dowry. We have evidence of this forced entry into the religious life from testaments drawn up by numerous Modenese parents.

It was now Morone's turn to be dismayed at the inroads which heresy had made in the city, where Latin books imported from Germany and works by Fonzio circulated freely, "and many women and children have already soaked them up."[5] The successes achieved by the academicians, and their ever sharper confrontations with traditionally minded preachers led Morone to ask Cardinals Jacopo Sadoleto and Gasparo Contarini for assistance in drawing up a confession of faith to be signed by the members of the academy and other civic leaders. A few of the academicians, such as Bertari and Girolamo Teggia, who were consulted on the text, expressed dissatisfaction that an open discussion had not preceded the actual writing, and limited their participation to a formal suggestion or two. The chief author of the creed, Contarini, after his failure at Ratisbon and the suspicions of Lutheran sympathies under which he now labored, made a valiant effort to draw up a Catholic formulary, but one purified of scholastic verbiage that emphasized the fundamental principle of faith in Jesus Christ but avoided the question of the gratuitousness of salvation. As

[5]M. Firpo, "Gli 'spirituali,'" 96, note 167.

for the soteriological role of works, this too was left in abeyance, though they were linked to the Passion of Christ. The creed was signed in September 1542 by almost all the academicians, including Castelvetro, but not by Valentini and Porto, who had left the city. By this device, Modena's reputation was cleansed of the stain of heresy and the intervention of the Inquisition was avoided, along with the crisis in the life of the city that such a measure would have provoked. On the other hand, the academy was compelled to abandon its role as driving force of the religious dissent.

But the movement, as M. Firpo remarked, "had welcomed the world of the artisans' shops,"[6] and "plebeians...seduced by those of the Academy," were not about to revert to the superstitions of the cult of saints and relics, or the old beliefs in indulgences, prayers for the dead, and the existence of purgatory, or give respect to monks, who were not distinguished either for their learning or morals. Placing their trust in Christ, the people had entered the world of justification by faith. As early as November 1540, the episcopal vicar had written to Morone that the city was infected by the contagion of many heresies. And a year later, he explained how the beliefs of the followers of Camillo Renato differed from other Protestant teachings: "As far as I have been able to fathom, these persons of [Renato's] sect are worse than the Lutherans, because it appears that they have embraced all the Germanic heresies."[7] As Peyronel has observed, this was a distinction that betrayed "unsuspected perspicacity" in the vicar, since "the Modenese reform movement varied as much in its social composition as in the doctrines it professed, [and] had moved by then outside the traditional pattern of the Lutheran protest, combining diverse elements originating in northern Protestantism with the mystical spiritualism of the Italian heretics, in a theological mix that is extremely difficult to classify as a single system."

Bartolomeo della Pergola

The activities of the Minorite Bartolomeo della Pergola, sent by Morone to preach the series of Lenten sermons for 1544, constitutes a crucial moment in the spread of heretical ideas. Pergola, who had been deeply influenced by his reading of the *Beneficio di Cristo*, replied implicitly to three sermons delivered some years earlier by the Jesuit Diego Lainez on the themes of grace, predestination, and free will. So great was Pergola's success with the artisans and laborers in his audience, that the ecclesiastical authorities compelled him to make a retraction from the same pulpit the following June. Many among those who heard him connected the Franciscan's preaching on divine election and gratuitous salvation to Lutheran doctrine.

Some of them would become the leaders of a vast community called the "brethren," which created a network reaching throughout the city, and continued to grow in the 1550s thanks to the influence of another Franciscan, Bartolomeo Fonzio. Giacomo Graziani, Giovanni Rangoni, Marco Caula, Giovanni Bergomozzi, Giovanni Maria Maranello, and Piergiovanni Biancolini were among the principal figures in

---

[6]Ibid., 107.
[7]S. Peyronel Rambaldi, *Speranze e crisi*, 244.

the movement. They achieved this status thanks to their learning and their social position, which permitted them to assist their more needy fellows, sharing their leadership roles with a number of merchants and artisans who were considered among the first proselytizers. At least this was the testimony in inquisitorial trials held some twenty years later. The wool-carder Geminiano Callegari, for example, named as his "first instructor and accomplice" a certain Francesco Camorana, from whom he learned, going back to 1544,

> that the body of our Lord Jesus Christ is not really contained in the consecrated host, which is only a commemoration of his passion and death, in the same way that a ring given by the bridegroom to his spouse is a constant reminder that she is his wife; and, moreover, that the pope and other priests have no authority to give absolution for sins, but only to preach and proclaim the Gospel, and this is what was meant by that Scriptural saying *'accipite Spiritum Sanctum quorum remiseritis….'*; and that confirmation was not a sacrament instituted by Christ, but devised by the Church as a validation for baptism, and that our works done with grace are not meritorious of paradise, however necessary it is that a true Christian should do good works.[8]

Camorana, married to the daughter of the heterodox physician Nicolò Machella, had been a member of the academy and possessed a rich library containing books by Calvin, Luther, Erasmus, Francesco Negri, Antonio Brucioli, and Agostino Mainardi, as well as the writings of his brother Girolamo, who had been Francesco Guicciardini's chief notary when he was governor of Modena and Reggio. Camorana's home was a gathering place for men of letters such as Castelvetro and Machella, but also for schoolteachers and weavers, such as Tommaso Bavellino and Cristoforo Bogazzano. The doctrines attributed to Camorana seem to suggest a reformed faith, but in the community gathered about him totaling some thirty or more persons, other views are discernible as well. In spite of his three decades of activity and the trial mounted against him sometime before 1564, perhaps because of the office he had occupied in the city government, it was not until after his death (28 September 1565) that the inquisitor ordered his cadaver to be exhumed and burned at the stake. Camorana's group included some influential persons who "represented the link between the academy and that movement from which came the community of 'brethren'(*Fratelli*)."[9]

The activity of the academy had ceased by the second half of the 1540s and Nicodemite preaching, of the kind made famous by Bartolomeo della Pergola, had become impossible, although his words lived on and would be recalled and used to settle arguments. Textile shops where wool, silk, and velvet were worked served as the principal locales for the transmission of the new religious message. The *Sommario*

---

[8]C. Bianco, "La comunità," 661. See the biographical sketch by A. Rotondò in *DBI*, 17: 204–5. Cf. S. Caponetto, "La metafora dell'anello nella dottrina della Santa Cena di Huldrych Zwingli," *Protestantesimo* 48 (1993): 318–20.

[9]C. Bianco, "La comunità," 627.

della santa Scrittura became the most popular and widely circulated book among laborers and artisans, who read with pleasure its praise of manual labor and its condemnation of parasitical priests and monks. Camorana combined study and business. In his wool working establishment he tried to convert his laborers "on questions of heresy." Nicolò Castelvetro did the same with his employees, one of whom, Francesco Bordiga, told a companion, Cosmo Guidoni, that he possessed

> a book which he [Castelvetro] recommended so highly to me, saying that even an ignorant person, by reading it would become educated. I asked him for it and he gave it to me; it was the *Summario della Sacra Scrittura*, which I read and from it I picked up many errors, which were confirmed when I was instructed by a certain Geminiano Callegaro, a wool worker in the shop of *Messer* Nicolò Fontana, who taught me and others, by persuading me and teaching me about heretical things.[10]

As the years passed, the anti-Roman protest continued to grow throughout the city, with meeting places changing from time to time to put spies off the track. At these gatherings in private homes, "teachers" read from the Holy Scriptures and Brucioli's commentaries, or from books that helped to explain them, such as the *Sommario* and the *Beneficio di Cristo*. In the residence of Giacomo Graziani, a wealthy landowner, readings consisted of the Italian translation of Calvin's *Institutes*, Ochino's *Prediche*, Curione's *Pasquino in estasi*, the *Dialogo di Mercurio e Caronte* by Alfonso de Valdés, and writings by Osiander and Luther. The Lord's Supper was celebrated at some of these conventicles, but not everybody was admitted to them.

The testimony and confessions elicited by the Modenese inquisitorial trials suggest that most of the defendants adhered to the reformed faith, although Anabaptist sympathizers such as the schoolteacher Giovanni Maria Tagliadi, "Maranello," turn up. There is evidence also of a prevailing spirit of toleration and understanding, a residue undoubtedly from Fonzio's teachings, hostile to confessional divisions. The ideal of a church of the poor did not lead to either social or doctrinal demarcations in this community where people from every walk of life gathered together peacefully. What distinctions existed among them resulted from their differing abilities to grasp the Scriptures, an endeavor in which even persons of modest education excelled. This large community could only survive clandestinely by adopting a Nicodemite posture, participating in the rites of the Catholic Church and dissimulating their true beliefs, in Valdesian fashion, by walking out of the mass after the reading of the Gospel. The mobility of both merchants and artisans favored the exchange of ideas, books, and information about the European progress of the Reformation. Great interest was aroused by the French Wars of Religion, and the struggles of the Huguenots and of the prince of Condé were followed with rapt attention. On one occasion, Count Giovanni Rangoni declared openly to a French monk: "You must be a good Christian, I do not say papist, but Huguenot, because Huguenots are true Christians and evangelists of Christian truth."[11]

---

[10]Ibid., 629.

During the biennium from 1566 to 1568, the repression unleashed by Pius V disrupted the evangelical movement, leading to the flight of some and the imprisonment of others. A brief, dated 10 February 1568, promised pardon to anyone who presented himself spontaneously before the inquisitor to confess his or her errors. Although many took advantage of the offer, considerable numbers were tried and convicted, and one, a certain Marco Magnavacca, about whom we know nothing else since he did not belong to the evangelical community, was executed. The physician Pietro Curioni reproached those who dared to jest about this unfortunate person, telling them that "he went straight to heaven just like the thief on the cross."[12] Curioni's pharmaceutical studio was a gathering place for evangelicals from all walks of life where discussions under his guidance took on a strong anticlerical tone and the pope was identified with the Antichrist. Not only did Curioni read from such standard fare as the *Sommario* and the *Beneficio*, but he also delighted in the anticlerical sonnets of Petrarch.

Pietro Antonio da Cervia, another victim of inquisitorial prosecution, was condemned to the stake at Bologna in 1567 as a relapsed heretic, after fleeing from Modena and moving about searching for work between Parma, Reggio, Borgo, and Fiorenzuola. His trial testimony constitutes one of our fullest sources for the Reformation movement in Modena and provides many details on the organization of the "*Fratelli*:

> As for the church, we used to say and hold that the church was the congregation of the faithful and of believers; that is, of those who trust that they are saved through the death and passion of Christ. That was the true church; but those who thought they were saved by indulgences, pardons, vows, pilgrimages, and other similar works did not have a true belief and therefore were not of the church.[13]

He added the interesting detail that they tried to make new converts even during their visits to the sick and needy.

At the beginning of the repression, several wanted persons hid in the homes of friends before fleeing the city. Count Giovanni Rangoni found refuge in the Valtellina and died at Sondrio, but not before asking to be reconciled with the church, probably to avoid repercussions for his family in Modena. The schoolteacher, Giovanni Maria Maranello, and Marco Caula, who had also made good their escape, returned to Modena and abjured. Others, such as Giacomo Graziani, Pier Giovanni Biancolini, and Giovanni Bergomozzi, took the road into exile for good, following the example of the academicians Francesco Porto, Ludovico Castelvetro, and Filippo Valentini. All those who remained behind were tried and sentenced to penalties vary-

---

[11]C. Bianco, "La comunità," 666–67.

[12]Ibid., 671–72.

[13]Ibid., 625. [J. Tedeschi and J. von Henneberg have produced an English translation of the trial, "'*Contra Petrum Antonium a Cervia relapsum et Bononiae concrematum,*'" in *Italian Reformation Studies in Honor of Laelius Socinus.* Ed. J. Tedeschi (Florence: Le Monnier, 1965), 243–68. The passage is quoted from 257. [Trans. note.]

ing in severity, lighter for those who presented themselves spontaneously and heavier for those who waited to be prosecuted. Magnavacca was the only person sentenced to death. The large Modenese evangelical community had been well integrated into the civic fabric and claimed among its members elements drawn from the cultural, mercantile, and wage-earning spheres including some representatives of the governing class. All this was overturned. Once again, the lack of independence of the Italian states showed the impossibility of organizing an alternative church, as had successfully occurred in much of Europe and even in Catholic France. In Italy no ruler was in a position to oppose Spain and the Empire, closely allied in the fight against Protestantism. In the words of the anonymous Italian translator of Calvin's *De vitandis superstitionibus*, "Italian princes do not have the freedom or the authority to introduce the Gospel and true religion in the dominions where they are sovereign, more than any other private person, even though this should be the prerogative of the absolute prince."[14]

The Road to Exile

This is not the place to treat in detail the fortunes of the few Modenese who chose to go into exile. There is no further information about Graziani and Biancolini who went to the Grisons. Giulio Sadoleto, the astute and enterprising merchant, settled first at Chiavenna and later at Morbegno, where he was still living in solid financial circumstances in 1589 with his wife Giulia and nine children. His descendants remained members of the reformed faith and could be found in Geneva until 1632.[15] The outcome differed considerably for Filippo Valentini and Giovanni Bergomozzi. Because they had shown Anabaptist leanings, they were not accepted by the communities at Chiavenna and Piur where they tried to settle. Valentini ended up an outsider to any Christian confession and Bergomozzi, who was banned from participation in the Lord's Supper in 1568, ended up accusing the local pastors of acting like papists and inquisitors. He was finally readmitted to fellowship, without having had to betray his ideas, thanks to the intercession of the Vicentine Alessandro Trissino.[16]

But the complex case of Ludovico Castelvetro (1505–71) deserves greater attention since he was the most prominent member of the entire Modenese evangelical movement. Despite his hesitation and wavering, he broke with Rome, his life emblematic of the travails experienced by a sixteenth-century Italian humanist who espoused the Reformation.[17] Castelvetro belonged to one of Modena's most influential families. The son of a rich merchant and banker, Giacomo Castelvetro senior, he took a law degree at the University of Siena and participated there in the activities of the cele-

---

[14]Quoted from D. Cantimori, *Prospettive di storia ereticale italiana del Cinquecento* (Bari: Laterza, 1960), 44–45.

[15]A. Pastore, *Nella Valtellina del tardo Cinquecento*, 114–15.

[16]See the sketch by A. Rotondò, in *DBI* 9: 96–98.

[17]For L. Castelvetro, see the sketch by V. Marchetti & G. Patrizi, in *DBI* 22: 8–21; S. Caponetto, "Due opere di Melantone," now reprinted in the author's *Studi sulla Riforma*, 353–74.

brated *Accademia Grande* which later became the academy of the *Intronati*. In 1532 he was appointed to the Law Faculty in Modena, but he soon abandoned jurisprudence for the world of letters. He became one of the active members in Giovanni Grillenzoni's academy and soon was being suspected publicly of being a Protestant sympathizer. There was substance behind the charge, because as previously noted, he was the translator of the 1521 edition of Melanchthon's *Loci communes* into Italian. For a committed reader of Erasmus like Castelvetro, the ingenious synthesis of Lutheran thought compiled by the young German humanist provided a bridge to critical reflections about humanism and the Catholic tradition.

But even more significant for understanding the background to the signing of the 1542 formulary of faith by the members of the academy and other supporters of the Reformation, is the attribution to Castelvetro of another vernacular translation, a second work by Melanchthon, the *De Ecclesiae autoritate et de veterum scriptis libellus*. When the autograph of the translation fell into the hands of Roman inquisitors it provided the evidence they needed to accuse the Modenese of heresy.

Duke Alfonso II made every effort to have Castelvetro tried in Ferrara, but in vain, and the suspect was compelled to present himself before the Holy Office in Rome, which assigned the convent of Santa Maria in Via as his place of confinement during the legal proceedings. From the very first interrogations, which began on 11 October 1560, Castelvetro understood that his judges had full knowledge of his second Melanchthon translation, which had been removed from his home in Modena. Fearful of the consequences, he fled on 17 October with the connivance of his loyal brother, Gian Maria. He hid temporarily in his villa at Verdeda, and proceeded to the Grisons in spring 1561. Then began a wandering existence that took him from Chiavenna to Geneva, where he lingered from 1562 to 1564, moving on to Lyons and then Vienna, finally returning to Chiavenna where he died on 21 February 1571. In the garden of the residence in Chiavenna of Colonel Rudolph von Salis, an epitaph recalled the peregrinations of the celebrated man of letters, translator, and editor of Aristotle's *Poetics*: "*Tandem in libero solo, liber moriens, libere quiescit.*"[18]

We only have a few scattered bits of information about Castelvetro's early religious beliefs. The noblewoman Dalinda Carandini, conversing with the rector of the Jesuit college in Modena, Bonfo de' Bonfi, her confidant during the years of the definitive defeat of the evangelical movement in the city, recalled the scriptural instruction that she had received from Castelvetro as a young woman, and his enthusiasm for the works of Erasmus, especially for his *Treatise on Preparation for Death*, which reaffirms the essential principles of the *Enchiridion militis Christiani*: "We are assured of victory over death, victory over the flesh, victory over the world and Satan. Christ promises us remission of sins, fruits in this life a hundredfold, and thereafter life eternal. And for what reason? For the sake of our merit? No indeed, but through the grace of faith which is in Jesus Christ. We are the more secure because he is first our doctor."[19] To the objections of the Jesuit that the works of Erasmus were prohibited (the conversation dates to February 1574), the lady's reply, even though at a dis-

---

[18]"Finally on free soil, dying a free man, reposes freely."

tance of many years, reflects the teachings she had received in her youth: the church had acted badly outlawing those "good works" and prohibiting the reading of the Scriptures in the vernacular, "since Christ had come to save every one, every one had to be instructed in the teachings of Christ."[20]

Mindful of this, Castelvetro translated Melanchthon's two works, excellent guides in his opinion, to the study of Sacred Scripture and Christian doctrine. The *Dell'autorità della Chiesa e degli scritti degli antichi* is of historical significance, aside from its value as a literary text, in that it helps to clarify, as was just noted, the discussions engaging the Modenese academy before its dissolution and Castelvetro's religious sentiments about 1540. First published at Wittenberg in 1539, it is one of Melanchthon's least studied works, as observed by Peter Fraenkel. But it is a text of great importance for determining the reformer's ecclesiological teachings, his unwavering interest in history, and his unceasing search for the *Primum et Verum.*[21]

The *De Ecclesiae autoritate* underscored the deep and unbridgeable chasm between Lutheran and Roman ecclesiology. The fundamental argument of Catholic polemicists against Luther and other Protestant reformers consisted then and remains today the affirmation of the superiority of the church's magisterium, the sole authorized interpreter of Scripture. In opposition to this age-old teaching of Augustinian provenance, Melanchthon began from the axiom of his *Disputatio de autoritate Ecclesiae*: "It is totally wrong to imagine that the church existed before the Word of God. The contrary is true, that men were called from the beginning of the world and reborn from the Word of God, just as Adam was called, when he heard the promise.... The church is born around the Word of God and is reborn where God lays down doctrine and bestows the Holy Spirit."[22]

The papist church is juxtaposed to the church of the Gospel:

> Now, when I mention the church, I do not mean primarily popes, or bishops, and the others who approve their beliefs, because they are enemies of the true church, part Epicureans, part adorers of manifest idols. What I call the true church is the gathering of those who really believe, who hold to the Gospel and the sacraments and are sanctified by the Holy Spirit, just as the church is portrayed in chapter 5 of Ephesians, and John states at chapter 10, "My sheep hear my voice."[23]

Castelvetro's translation of the *De Ecclesiae autoritate* probably should be dated about 1541, the crucial year when tension between the academy and the ecclesiastical authorities came to a head, and Lutheran and Calvinist currents were successfully infiltrating Modena and its *contado*. Castelvetro's translation, appearing at a time

---

[19]Quoted from R. H. Bainton, *Erasmus of Christendom* (New York: Scribner's Sons, 1969), 269.

[20]S. Seidel Menchi, *Erasmo in Italia*, 320. Cf. A. Rotondò, *Forme e destinazione del messaggio religioso*, 133–35.

[21]P. Fraenkel, *Testimonia Patrum: The Function of the Patristic Argument in the Theology of Philipp Melanchthon* (Geneva: Droz, 1961), 52–109.

[22]Ibid., 56–57.

[23]Quoted from S. Caponetto, "Due opere," in *Studi sulla Riforma*, 365.

when Bishop Morone was striving to bring the academicians and their supporters back into the bosom of the Roman church, was clearly intended to influence them to accept Melanchthon's impassioned appeal: break with the Church of Rome and enter the "company" of the followers of the Gospel by receiving the message of the Lutheran Reformation. This translation went beyond the vague, indeterminate citation of ambiguous texts where justification by faith was more Augustinian than Lutheran. It made a clear-cut distinction between the Catholic reformism of Gropper, Contarini, Pole, Sadoleto, Cortese, and Giberti, who were certainly receptive to some tenets of the Reformation and eager for a reunification of the body of Christ under the aegis of the papacy, and the convinced believers in the painful but unavoidable necessity that they had to separate from "papal dominion" if they were to enter "the Catholic Church of Christ" and accept "the pure doctrine of the benefits of Christ and of the faith."[24]

Castelvetro died in exile in the home of the Brescian merchant Marco Zobia, remembered in the literary critic's testament for the fraternal love and steadfast faith which would lead to his martyrdom at Bergamo two years later. The document contains the ritual allusion to divine grace. And then Castelvetro, as he was accustomed to do in conversation, entrusted to a proverb the expression of his most heartfelt sentiments: "Every day is to be so ordered as if it is the last" (*Omnis dies velut ultimus ordinandus est*). It was his idealistic motto during the years of persecution and exile.[25]

Mantua

The legend of Calvin's flight from Ferrara in 1536 through the duchy of Mantua, sowing his teachings as he went, was created by inquisitors in Ferrara and Mantua to explain the spread of Protestant doctrines in the townships of Viadana, Ostiglia, and Gonzaga at the beginning of the 1540s. Actually, heretical infiltration even at popular levels, among the "*rudes*" who dared to converse about the mysteries of the faith, began very differently.[26] Sergio Pagano's fortunate discovery of the trial against Endimio Calandra, the secretary of Duke Guglielmo Gonzaga, has filled many of the lacunae left by documents unearthed by Stefano Davari, valuable as they are, more than a century ago. Pagano's researches have now demonstrated the widespread sympathy for the Reformation in Mantua among artisans as well as professional men, a sentiment that even affected some of the duke's courtiers.[27]

Calandra made a long and detailed confession spontaneously to the inquisitor on 17 March 1568, in which he maintained that the seeds of religious doubt had been sown in Mantua by the famous Franciscan and Augustinian preachers with their talk of gratuitous justification: Benedetto Locarno, Bernardino Ochino, Andrea

---

[24]Ibid., 370.

[25]Ibid., 372.

[26]S. Davari, "Cenni storici intorno al Tribunale dell'Inquisizione in Mantova," *ASL* 6 (1879): 557, and doc. 11, 563.

[27]S. Pagano, *Il processo di Endimio Calandra e l'Inquisizione a Mantova nel 1567–1568* (Vatican City: Biblioteca Apostolica Vaticana, 1991).

Ghetti, and Costantino da Carrara. Their message conveying the essential principle of the Reformation was thought to agree with Pauline teachings, and Cardinal Ercole Gonzaga, steeped in humanistic culture and philosophy, familiar with Valdesian teachings, and a friend of Valdés, Vermigli, and Ochino (whom he helped to flee to Protestant lands), allowed matters to run their course until a time when the Council of Trent should pronounce itself. Moreover, the cardinal's library contained a large number of prohibited books, some brought from Germany, since he had permission to read them from Clement VII and Paul III. Persons such as Calandra, who had access to Ercole's collection, seized the opportunity. It was one thing as long as the theological discussions were restricted to educated persons and centered on different interpretations of the Pauline texts, but quite another when artisans and laborers, male and female, and even children, began to attack the doctrines and precepts of the church. At this point, the cardinal, regent of the duchy during the minority of his nephew, Francesco I, intervened energetically.

The edict published 24 March 1541 denounced the scandal at Viadana, where publicly and privately "many disputed and argued over the authority of the pope, images of saints, fasting, confession, free will, predestination, purgatory, and many other things it is not their place to discuss, since it is their duty to remain silent over the precepts, commandments and declarations of the Most Holy Roman Church."[28] This spread of Lutheran ideas at a popular level must not have been episodic and superficial if, at the end of 1543, another manifesto still had to refer to "certain reckless ones" of Gonzaga, who dared "to argue freely as if they were great theologians," about religious subjects. It was ordered that within ten days "scandalous books in the vernacular" had to be surrendered. Although they are not identified, it is possible that they included Ochino's *Prediche*, the *Sommario della santa Scrittura*, and the *Beneficio di Cristo*.[29]

Investigations carried out by Gonzaga's commissioner discovered that at an inn a visiting priest had been attacking such precepts of the church as fasting, prayers for the dead, and indulgences, buttressing his arguments with a work by "brother Bernardino," naturally to be identified with Bernardino Ochino. The book may have been his *Prediche*, printed at Geneva in 1542. It also became known that meetings had been organized in the house of the tailor, Antonio Catello, to hear the Scriptures expounded in the vein of Ochino's preaching.[30] The latter's fame in Mantua had endured long after his apostasy. Prince Ascanio Colonna, who had found refuge in the city after the "salt war," remarked that Endimio Calandra believed in "Bernardino Ochino as much as he did in Christ."[31]

Authorities could no longer ignore the reading of prohibited books at court, but the temerity of the popular classes in this respect was especially objectionable. From 1545 to 1550 Cardinal Gonzaga issued a series of severe measures for the inquisitor

---

[28]S. Davari, "Cenni storici," doc. 10, 562–63.

[29]Ibid., 556–57, doc. 11, 563.

[30]S. Pagano, *Il processo*, 120.

[31]S. Davari, "Cenni storici," 557; L. N. Bertuzzi, "Infiltrazioni protestanti nel Ducato di Mantova (1530–1563)," *Bollettino Storico Mantovano* 1 (1956): 129.

and government officials to enforce. At Viadana, the apothecary Viano de' Viani was arrested with his accomplices, and in Mantua itself, the notary Giulio Cipada was stripped of his office and banished, together with the tailor, Giulio Leali. The tailors' guild, which was in daily contact with the rulers at court and with merchants and their employees, was charged as a whole. An illiterate tailor confessed that he did not believe in the authority of the church, confession, the cult of images, and fasting.

The large percentage of artisans and laborers among the religious dissenters can be explained in terms of the large numbers in which they could be found in the duchy and the active roles played by their guilds. Mantua, centrally located in the plain of the Po and on the great traffic routes leading to northern Lombardy and beyond it to Germany through Verona, maintained commercial relations with Cremona, Bologna, Ferrara, and Modena, centers where the Reformation had made headway. The extraordinary mobility of the labor force provided the channel for the infiltration of heresy into the shops, which provided ideal venues for the efforts of Protestant proselytizers. The documentation on the missionary activity of Modenese workers is quite full and detailed. For example, in the 1550s the wool weavers Geminiano Callegari, considered a confirmed Lutheran, and Cristoforo Bagazzano sowed the seeds of heresy among their fellow workers in Cremona where they were residing at the time. There were many possibilities for such contacts between Modena and Mantua.

Gaspare Canossa left precious evidence concerning these efforts. At a Modenese inn he had met a certain Cataldo Buzzale and in the course of conversation discovered that they both considered themselves Lutheran. The latter introduced him to other Protestant sympathizers, including a certain Aloise, an itinerant salesman who lived in both Modena and Mantua. Subsequently, Cataldo visited him in Mantua and was welcomed warmly by him and his wife, "who belonged to the same sect of Lutherans, and he introduced me to two or three friends of the same faith, who were merchants in Mantua." Every time Cataldo visited Aloise's family in Mantua he met others "of the Lutheran sect, all of whom were upright persons."[32]

The extent of Mantuan religious dissent, fed in part by the anticlericalism of some of the bourgeoisie, came out in the open when Pius V ascended the papal throne. The city became, along with Ferrara, Modena, and Faenza, a principal target of his antiheretical campaign. The year 1567 was filled with important trials. On 31 May the pontiff protested vigorously to Duke Guglielmo Gonzaga, because one of his high officials, Count Francesco Gonzaga of Novellara, had obstructed the inquisitor from arresting some prominent citizens, among whom were a number of courtiers, without the duke's authorization. Pius deposed the old inquisitor, whose "lack of zeal" was unacceptable given the great dangers perceived to be threatening the duchy, and replaced him with Camillo Campeggi, a doctor of theology, who was then inquisitor at Ferrara. Even before the latter arrived to take up his post, numerous arrests were ordered from Rome that threw Mantua into turmoil. Among those incarcerated was the apothecary Giovan Francesco Anselmini, nicknamed "Scartoc-

---

[32]C. Bianco, "La comunità," 637–38.

cio." His shop in the *Piazza delle Erbe* was a place where people met to discuss the
news of the day, digest reports coming from every part of Europe, and also ponder
questions connected with religion, magic, and witchcraft. Anselmini, with his
brother Ludovico, abjured in the auto da fé of 16 May 1568.[33] The "Academy of the
Scartocci" had been much talked about in the city, and there were rumors that Rome
would even bring accusations of heresy against such noble ladies as Isabella Mai-
nolda, Lucrezia Manfrona, and Vittoria Gonzaga, who were related to the duke.
Count Carlo Maffei, writing about these events on 10 June to Pietro Martire Cor-
nacchia, remarked: "These are great events, because we can see that this is an Inquisition like the one in Spain."[34]

The new inquisitor, Campeggi, arrived with precise instructions from Rome and
a long list of suspected persons from every class of society. Tension continued to
mount in the city, finally erupting in a conflict over jurisdiction because the duke felt
that his authority was being totally subverted. There were more arrests, including
that of Giulio Bonamico, overseer of the ducal stables, the superintendent Cesare
Pedemonti, and his brother Pompeo. At Mirandola, it was the turn of the nobleman
Silvio Lanzoni, who was later extradited to Bologna where "he was burned alive as a
most obdurate unrepentant Lutheran." This was followed by the imprisonment of
the tailors, Girolamo Longino and Giulio Bagnoli, who were joined in the inquisitorial jail, now filled beyond its capacity, "by bakers, wine haulers and other ignorant
plebeians."[35]

The duke, hoping to find a middle ground, dispatched to Rome Count Teodoro
Sangiorgio to try to obtain at least one concession, namely that the abjurations of his
courtiers should take place privately, which would also spare them the shame of having to wear the garish penitential garment, a symbol of infamy and dishonor that
affected the families of the condemned as well. But the pope was inflexible. During
the drawn-out controversy, the duke, in addition to defending the prerogatives of his
state, gave signs of open-mindedness unusual among his contemporaries. On one
occasion, unwittingly citing the champion of religious toleration, the Savoyard
Sebastian Castellio, he questioned, before a shocked inquisitor, the legality of sentencing a heretic to death, a blasphemy that he later retracted.

The exasperation of Mantuans, gripped by what they viewed as an unmitigated
reign of terror, resulted in the murder of two Dominican monks on Christmas Day
in 1567. The duke tried to use the episode to place a brake on the inquisitor
Campeggi, but only received a rebuke from the pope instead.[36] Without mincing
words the pontiff informed the Mantuan ambassador in Rome:

[33]S. Pagano, *Il processo*, 286–87, note 2.
[34]Ibid., 7. In the decree, dated 4 August 1568 (ibid., 200, note 25) against the fugitives, one of
those named is the Vicentine weaver Simeone Simeoni who practiced his trade at Vicenza and Mantua
between 1550 and 1570. He was sentenced to death at Vicenza in 1570 as a "rebel" and "heresiarch." See
A. Olivieri, "Simeone Simeoni 'filatorio' di Vicenza (1570): Il dibattito su *charitas* e *pauperes*," in *Religiones
novae, Quaderni di storia religiosa* (Verona, 1995), 225–43.
[35]S. Pagano, *Il processo*, 8.
[36]Ibid., 101.

Write to your lord duke that as far as we are concerned we do not doubt that in the future His Excellency will see other similar and even more atrocious cases in his states because he does not choose to be as zealous as he should be in matters concerning the Inquisition, and therefore scoundrels take heart. But even if we should see all the monks of St. Dominic cut to pieces, we would not be afraid at all, nor would we desist from vigorously pursuing the course we have taken for the destruction of the heretics.[37]

The gravity and delicacy of the situation persuaded Pius to send Cardinal Charles Borromeo to Mantua to bring to a conclusion all the trials that Campeggi had initiated, and preside over the public abjurations and reading of sentences. His presence was intended to help persuade the duke to support the inquisitorial effort without giving in to the appeals for clemency. Members of the citizenry who had been most hostile to the ecclesiastical repression took immediate note. On the night of 15 March 1568, a writing was pinned to the portal of the church of Sant'Andrea: "Oh Mantuans, are you such cowards that you will not assassinate Cardinal Borromeo and that rogue bishop [Girolamo de Federicis] and all the monks of St. Dominic? Do so, and do it quickly and you will achieve glory in the world and the paradise of the omnipotent God. People, people, wake and take up arms!"[38] The authors of the manifesto were rumored to be relatives of the duke, Cesare, Vespasiano, and Massimiliano Gonzaga.

A great auto da fé took place on 4 April 1568, attended by large numbers of people. Of the condemned persons who ascended the platform, six abjured, clothed in the penitential garment: Pompeo Pedemonti, Roberto Campagnola, Girolamo Longino, Giulio Leali, Luigi Padovani, and Francesco Pinetti. Three, Francesco Volpati of Verona, an eyeglass salesman, the furrier Vincenzo da Treviso, and the Anabaptist physician from San Benedetto Polirone, Pietro Giudice of Rivoltella, were condemned to death. Their sentence was carried out on 12 April by beheading, the inquisitor Campeggi reported to his superiors in Rome, "without even wanting to look at a crucifix, but raising their eyes toward heaven, they invoked God's name, never mentioning a saint."[39] On 16 May another "spectacle of the faith" was held, this time involving fifteen people, of whom two were represented in effigy because they had fled, and one, a relapsed, the schoolteacher of Guastalla, Francesco da Bertinoro, condemned to the stake. Several of the victims were persons of prominence, including the fiscal officer Antonio Valerio, who was not spared a public abjuration with penitential garment, despite the duke's efforts. At the conclusion of some forty or more trials, Cardinal Borromeo returned to his diocese confident that, with the inquisitor Campeggi, he had fulfilled his mission and cleansed the city where the heretical contagion had not turned out to be as severe as once feared. On 5 September another auto da fé received the final defendants, among whom was the goldsmith Ettore Donato. Endimio Calandra, one of the principal figures in the retinue of the

[37]Ibid., 56.
[38]Ibid., 58, 101, 108, note 12.
[39]S. Pagano, *Il processo*, 162.

Gonzaga family, was still in prison. Despite the fact that he had made a full confession, it was hoped that he would assist the Inquisition in its great design of gathering more incriminating evidence against such members of the College of Cardinals as Giovanni Morone and the deceased Reginald Pole. Calandra had lived in Venice for thirteen years where he had made many friends in heterodox circles, Pietro Carnesecchi, Piero Gelido, Alessandro Trissino, Andrea Da Ponte, Fabrizio Brancuti, Ascanio Colonna, Giulio da Thiene, Francesco Porto, Guido Giannetti, and Turchetto, among others. In Padua Calandra had been present at gatherings in the home of Caterina Sauli da Passano, attended by prominent evangelicals from Venice, Rovigo, and Mantua. Calandra told all he knew, in the hope of reducing his sentence. On 12 September he abjured publicly and bore his humiliation with patience.

No attempt at intercession, no humble entreaty by the Mantuan ambassador to the Holy See could bend the pope from his inflexible design to destroy heresy with exemplary sentences. The strategy succeeded ultimately, and yet, from 1570 to 1583, during the entire reign of Guglielmo Gonzaga, trials and convictions continued. But now the social scenario was very different. In the list of thirty-seven sentences published by Davari, there are no artisans or laborers. Their dissidence had been crushed.[40] The severe punishments meted out earlier to many of the duke's courtiers similarly had decisively ended the participation of the governing class in the movement. The protagonists were now physicians, painters, and affluent tailors such as Cesare Brancaccio and Vincenzo Terzano, who were forced to build with their own funds the jail that would house them! The first name on Davari's list is that Count Giulio da Thiene of Vicenza, who was burned in effigy and had his property confiscated. He had been a refugee in Württemberg since 1555.[41]

In 1572, the apothecary Pietro Maria Salco was condemned to pay a fine of two hundred gold *scudi*, the same as his brother-in-law. But large financial penalties did not always spare defendants from prison and galley sentences. Other names belong to persons living in neighboring localities, Mirandola, San Benedetto Polirone, Canneto, Revere, etc., evidence of the spread of evangelical sentiments. In 1576 Gerolamo Tamara was condemned to death posthumously, but his cadaver was not exhumed for reasons of hygiene. In 1581 there was still one more auto da fé to burn the straw effigies of Giacomo Strada, a celebrated antiquarian dealer in the service of the emperor, of his son, the canon Paolo, and of Don Valeriano da Cremona. From these random references to condemnations and abjurations the extent of the evangelical movement in the duchy of Mantua during a forty-year period can be surmised.

The Venetian weaver Marcantonio Varotta, who had returned to Italy from Geneva where he had been a member of the Italian exiles' church, settled at Mantua in 1565 after visits to Turin and Milan. He worked in the shop of a good Catholic and had to conceal his religious sentiments. In the long statement Varotta made to inquisitors at Udine (21 January 1567), he stated that in no other place had he been as afraid as in Mantua, where he had heard that there were many Protestants, even

---

[40]S. Davari, "Cenni storici," 782–84.
[41]S. Pagano, *Il processo*, 372, note 49.

among the nobility, but no one dared to reveal himself for fear of the inquisitor.[42] Only a very few left their homeland before being compelled by circumstances to do so. Girolamo Ferone, wool-carder; Vincenzo Montaldo; Alessandro Lanzoni, the nephew of the noblemen Silvio Lanzoni, whose ideas he shared; and a certain Fenice (Fenis de Pierre), became members of the Italian church at Geneva in 1559. They were joined, from 1570 to 1587, by the apothecary Francesco Sordo, Agostino and Giovan Battista Cardo, and Raimondo di Chanares(?).[43]

BIBLIOGRAPHICAL NOTE

The recent edition of Calandra's trial, edited and richly documented by S. Pagano, cited in the notes, is now the fundamental work for the study of the Reformation in Mantua. It can be supplemented by M. Mazzocchi, "Aspetti di vita religiosa a Mantova nel carteggio fra il cardinale Ercole Gonzaga e il vescovo ausiliare (1561–1563)," *Aevum* 33 (1959): 382–403.

The church of Sant'Andrea in Mantua, the Renaissance portal (actual state).

---

[42]See M. Varotta's confession in D. Caccamo, *Eretici italiani in Moravia, Polonia, Transilvania (1558–1611* (Florence & Chicago: Sansoni–The Newberry Library, 1970), doc. 8, 202–3.

[43]J.-B.-G. Galiffe, *Le refuge italien de Genève aux XVIme et XVIIme siècles* (Geneva: H. Georg, 1881), 147; P. F. Geisendorf, *Le Livre des habitants de Genève*, 2 vols. (Geneva: Droz, 1957–63), 1:162, 213; 2:19, 89.

16

FROM ERASMUS TO CALVIN: LUCCA, FLORENCE, AND SIENA

ERASMIANISM IN TUSCANY

PAST STUDIES OF TUSCANY'S RECEPTION of Protestant ideas neglected the preparatory role of Erasmianism, although Silvana Seidel Menchi has done much recently to correct this omission. The "Lutheran" Erasmus was appropriated in this region, which was the cradle of Renaissance culture, more warmly than anywhere else in Italy. It was not difficult to discern the influence of Florentine humanism in the Dutchman's works. The spiritual Christianity of the *Enchiridion militis Christiani* bears its unmistakable stamp.

From 1518 to 1520 the Florentine printing establishment of the Giunti turned out the writings of Erasmus, producing ten different pieces collected in five volumes. Almost a half century later, in November 1564 at Siena, an inquisitorial search of the bookshop owned by Antonio Zenoli turned up 119 prohibited books, of which 27 were Erasmian titles, including the *Praise of Folly*, the *Paraphrase* of the Pauline epistles, the *Treatise on Preparation for Death*, the *Querela Pacis*, together with two copies of the pseudo-Erasmian *Declaration* on the Ten Commandments. A further search of other booksellers in the city, two years later, brought to light other Erasmian works, including the *Adages*.[1]

One of the more curious attempts to juxtapose Erasmus to Luther occurred in Bartolomeo Cerretani's *Storia in dialogo della mutatione di Firenze*. The author imagined a meeting in Modena of the governor, Francesco Guicciardini, in his residence, with Giovanni Rucellai and two young Florentine Savonarolans (*Piagnoni*), Lorenzo and Girolamo, who had just returned from a trip around Europe. They had visited Erasmus, of whom they sketched a brief profile, which might have served as the epigraph for Hans Holbein's famous portrait:

> He lives happily in the tranquillity of his studies…scorning property, ambition, temporal and spiritual greatness…. He is a man of great intellect and

---

[1] S. Seidel Menchi, *Erasmo in Italia*, 34, 343.

learning...his sustenance and dress are extremely simple and no more than he requires...solitary, he is constantly thinking and reflecting and holds to an upright religion alien to superstitions of any sort.

The youths now were planning a trip to Germany to visit Luther, some of whose writings they had read in Bologna,

> first the one against indulgences, as admirable as it is full of true and stable doctrine.... We are going to Germany, attracted by the fame of a revered religious man, who is called brother Martin Luther, whose writings, which have begun to appear in Italy and especially in Rome, suggest that he must be, thanks to his habits, learning, and religion, an excellent man.[2]

This episode, dreamed up about 1520 by a partisan of the Medici, who is also at the same time an admirer of the long-departed Savonarola, is extremely significant.[3] Some of the monk's followers, disappointed in the hope of a collective *renovatio* of society and in the coming of the Millennium, had fallen back on the need for immediate personal renewal through justification by faith alone in the Passion of Christ, as preached by Erasmus and Luther. Additional evidence of the breadth of the debate in Tuscany over the two great protagonists on the European religious stage is provided in a work by the Florentine Carthusian Giovanni Bernardo Gualandi, a follower of Ficino and of Pico della Mirandola, in his treatise *In Lutherum haereticum* (1525). Gualandi had read Erasmus's *Enchiridion, Adagia,* and *Duplice copia verborum ac rerum* and realized the differences between the Dutch humanist and Luther on the question of merit and works, and was concerned that the reform of the church in that age of tremendous changes would be "violent medicine."[4] Gualandi feared that the battle against superstition and those precepts of the church that were not founded on Scripture, and the emphasis being given to inner piety rather than ceremonies and rites, were leading to the sundering of obedience to the ecclesiastical magisterium. The Carthusian had accurately grasped the dangers of Erasmianism.

Ortensio Lando and the "Forcianae Quaestiones"

The circulation of Erasmus's ideas in Tuscany is well documented. We know about it from the diffusion of his books by his numerous followers and translators, and from their confiscation. Except for an occasional allusion, insufficient attention has been paid to the sojourn of a month and a half in Lucca and in the villa of the Buonvisi family at nearby Forci of the Augustinian Fra Geremia da Milano, alias Ortensio Lando. Lando had met Vincenzo Buonvisi in Lyons, where the latter was the most prominent member of the Lucchese mercantile colony, and had been invited by him to visit Lucca in May 1534. From 1531 to 1533 Lando had resided in the convent of San Giacomo in Bologna at a time when Giulio della Rovere was serving as "reader"

---

[2]S. Caponetto, *Aonio Paleario*, 42–43.
[3]For B. Cerretani, see the biographical sketch by P. Malanima, in *DBI*, 23:806–9.
[4]See S. Seidel Menchi, *Erasmo in Italia*, 65–67.

and the Erasmian circle composed of Eusebio Renato, Giovanni Angelo Odoni, and Fileno Lunardi was coming into being. Lando had formed close friendships with the group, which, filled with enthusiasm by its reading of Martin Bucer's Gospel commentary, was planning to travel to Strasbourg to meet him.

The Buonvisi were one of the richest and most influential Lucchese families. Vincenzo's brother, Antonio, an important banker, spent much of his time in England, and since he was a friend and protector of Thomas More, may have been the one to introduce Lando to the *Utopia*. The other Buonvisi brother, Ludovico, also a rich banker and merchant as well as patron of culture, would be remembered after his death in 1551 by Aonio Paleario as the most generous of his Lucchese benefactors.[5]

In his *Forcianae Quaestiones*, published in 1535, Lando described his Lucchese sojourn in the spring of the previous year and the magnificent hospitality of the Buonvisi in their villa at Forci. Visitors were received from the other great ruling families of the city: Girolamo Arnolfini, Giovanni Guidiccioni, Martino Gigli, Nicolao Turchi, Bernardino Cenami, who had been adopted by his maternal uncle Nicolao Buonvisi, and Vincenzo Guinigi. They were all members of the oligarchy, which under the leadership of the Buonvisi, had suppressed the popular revolt of the Lucchese poor, the *Straccioni*, in 1531. While Lando was at the Buonvisi villa at Forci, the company was joined by friends of the family who had been visiting the spa at Bagni di Lucca, such churchmen as Girolamo Seripando and Lorenzo Toscano, the humanists Gaudenzio Merula, Giulio Camillo Delminio, Étienne Dolet, and Paolo Seripando; and men of state such as Pomponio Trivulzio, governor of Lyons, Nicola Brittonio, Tommaso Sertinio, Albicio Beni, Monico Compargnano, and Ranieri Dejo. Other Milanese guests, besides Lando, were Giulio della Rovere and Annibale Della Croce.[6] The frivolity and superficiality of the discussions, as reported by Lando in the *Forcianae Questiones,* has obscured the fact that some of the most vocal participants in the debate raging about Erasmus, for and against, were present at these gatherings.

Lando had recently completed his first book, *Cicero relegatus et Cicero revocatus* (1534), written in response to Erasmus's *Ciceronianus*, published at Basel in 1528. Between sumptuous dinners and strolls in the magnificent gardens of the Buonvisi villa, discussions must certainly have ensued among the many partisans of Erasmus's Christian philosophy, foremost being the masters of the house, and the Ciceronians. Lando rediscovered at Forci, assuming that his recollections of these serene days were not at least partly invented, some of his intimate friends, della Rovere, Merula, and Trivulzio, to whom he dedicated his *Cicero relegatus et Cicero revocatus*, in which the first two appeared as interlocutors.[7] The gathering at Forci took place in the mid-

---

[5]For Ludovico, Antonio, and Vincenzo Buonvisi, see the entries by M. Luzzati in *DBI*, 15:295–98, 340–44, 356–59.

[6]See [O. Lando], *Forcianae Quaestiones, in quibus varia Italorum ingenia explicantur, multaque alia scitu non indigna,* Naples: Autore Philalethe Polytopiensi Cive, 1535. Excudebat Martinus de Ragusia [false imprint according to C. Fahy].

The city of Lucca. Engraving of the seventeenth century.

1530s, critical years for the diffusion of Lutheran ideas and the earnest search for evangelical truths in monastic circles, especially in the Augustinian order. It has been persuasively argued that in Lando there existed two souls, one Erasmian, the other Ciceronian. In the *Cicero relegatus et Cicero revocatus*, we have "the successful image of a Ciceronian, put into a state of crisis by Erasmus."[8]

Four renowned Augustinians, besides the author, appear in the *Forcianae Quaestiones*: Giulio della Rovere, who engaged the ladies at Forci in conversations about the feminine sex, Girolamo Seripando, Agostino da Fivizzano, and Francesco da Gambassi. It is a well-known fact that a common interest and concern for the reformation of the church was shared by the first two and that they chose completely different roads to achieve it. As for Gaudenzio Merula and his own religious development, we know that he was living in Milan at the time. It may be after the colloquies at Forci, that he wrote his *Bellum civile inter Ciceronianos et Erasmicos*, now lost, which prompted Erasmus to write a letter of protest to the duke of Milan in October 1535.[9] Twenty years later, having exorcised his youthful furies, Merula turned to Calvin asking to be raised from the darkness of Babylon.

Another protagonist in the controversy, "Tully or Christ," was Étienne Dolet (1508–46), the young French humanist, fanatical admirer of the Ciceronian language, who had been scandalized by Erasmus's *Ciceronianus*. He wound up writing a violent attack on Erasmus, but in 1542 at his celebrated printing establishment in Lyons, he produced a French version of the *Enchiridion militis Christiani* in the translation by Louis de Berquin, as well as works by J. Lefèvre d'Étaples. Dolet would die as a heretic at the stake in Paris on 3 August 1546.[10] Lando's encounter with the two other members of his order occurs on the way back to Milan, and is placed at the end of his *Forcianae Quaestiones*, providing a glimpse of the cultural and religious interests of the writer and of his Milanese friends, della Rovere, Merula, and Annibale Della Croce, the secretary of the Senate in Milan, who was a friend and protector of Paleario.

Agostino da Fivizzano, the teacher of Alessio Casani (to whom, as was mentioned, he would bequeath a library of "Lutheran" books), director of studies in the Roman convent of Sant'Agostino and a collaborator of Egidio da Viterbo, had been sent to France in 1519 to govern the Augustinian province, which was seriously troubled by the winds of innovation blowing from the north. After returning to Italy, the learned theologian was ordered, along with his fellow member, Agostino Mainardi, "not to speak Lutheran heresies." Sometime after 1527 Fivizzano had withdrawn to the small convent of Lupocavo, near Lucca, where Lando went to visit him. The old master rekindled in his brothers of the order and in his friends a desire for divine things, proclaiming the grace of God to them and urging them to meet with

---

[7]Cf. C. Fahy, "The Composition of Ortensio Lando's Dialogue 'Cicero relegatus et Cicero revocatus,'" *Italian Studies* 30 (1975): 30–41; idem, "Landiana," *Italia Medievale e Umanistica* 19 (1976): 325–87.

[8]S. Seidel Menchi, "Sulla fortuna di Erasmo," 574.

[9]Idem, *Erasmo in Italia*, 60, 369.

[10]On E. Dolet, see the rich note in *Erasmi Opus epistularum* 11:108–10.

Francesco da Gambassi. The latter, who was well known to his visitors, since by 1530 he was vicar general of his order for Lombardy, was more explicit still in his Erasmian lesson, founded on a Christocentric spirituality and on the necessity for scriptural study, sole revelation of divine truth.[11]

This meeting with Agostino Fivizzano provides a flashback to the conversations at Forci. Erasmus's message of Christian renewal must have been avidly discussed, even if Lando makes no mention of it then. But a few days later, in his dialogue *In Des. Erasmi Roterodami funus* (Basel, 1540), he identifies as enthusiastic readers of Erasmus Ludovico Buonvisi and Martino Gigli who hoped to see some of his works translated into the vernacular for people who did not read Latin. The *Dialogo erasmico di due donne maritate…*(Venice, 1542), dedicated to Ludovico Buonvisi, was a consequence of this project. At a slightly earlier date, the Augustinian Don Niccolò da Fivizzano had translated the *Paraphrases* of the Gospels, perhaps at the behest of these two Lucchese admirers of Erasmus.[12]

LUCCA AND THE CONVENT OF SAN FREDIANO

The fiery sermons of Bernardino Ochino in May 1538 at Lucca, which focused on charity towards the downtrodden after the revolt of the *Straccioni*, and of his brother-member Giambattista da Venezia, followed two years later by the Augustinian Raffaello Narbonese, must be reckoned among the foundations of the movement of religious dissent in Lucca. But the acceptance of the Erasmian program calling for a return to the study and meditation of Scripture was equally influential. The urge to rediscover the Christian sources was first felt in the circle of the wealthy merchants, who had resided for long periods of the year in northern commercial centers or were in contact with them, as was the case with Vincenzo and Ludovico Buonvisi. Moreover, Marino Berengo has underscored the Lucchese tradition of devotion to the Holy Countenance, the recollection of the crucified Christ, Redeemer and Savior.[13] But a reading of the *Enchiridion*, reprinted in Venice in 1523 and translated into Italian in 1531, must have been received as divine illumination: "You honor a statue of Christ in wood or stone and adorned with colors. You would do better to honor the image of his mind which through the Holy Spirit is expressed in the Gospels. Are you excited over the seamless robe and the shroud of Christ and yet doze over the oracles of his law? Far better that you should believe than that you should treasure at

---

[11]Cf. U. Rozzo, "Incontri di Giulio da Milano: Ortensio Lando," *BSSV* 97, n. 140 (1976): 94–101.
[12]S. Seidel Menchi, *Erasmo in Italia*, 189, 273.
[13]Cf. M. Berengo, *Nobili e mercanti nella Lucca del Cinquecento* (Turin: Einaudi, 1965), 359ff.

home a piece of the wood of the cross. Otherwise you are no better than Judas, who with his lips touched the divine mouth."[14]

Reflection on these themes took on even greater weight with the reading of works by Luther, Melanchthon, and Oecolampadius, brought into the country by merchants even before 1525. So extensive was the circulation of these writings that it gave pause to Morone, who, as a legate at Prague in 1537, heard reports about the many "Lutheran" books making their way to Lucca through commercial channels. He viewed this as a great danger, "considering the importance of that city, which, because of its site and many amenities, could open the door to all of Italy for those sects."[15] The successful diffusion of heretical printing was corroborated by Giovanni Guidiccioni in his *Orazione alla repubblica di Lucca* (Oration to the Republic of Lucca). But the proselytizing activities of three eminent Erasmians, Celio Secondo Curione, Pietro Martire Vermigli, and Aonio Paleario, constituted an even more powerful force determining the conversion of many Lucchese to the Reformation.

Curione (1503–69), was one of the greatest European humanists of the sixteenth century.[16] Born at Ciriè, in Piedmont, of a noble family, he had already begun to read Protestant authors by 1523, at the urging of the Augustinian Girolamo Negri, while he was studying letters and the law at the University of Turin. Giacomo Bonello and Francesco Guarino, who would go on to become pastors of the Italian exiles' church in Geneva and leading figures in Italian Protestantism, were Curione's companions at the university and in his early escapades. After Curione succeeded in escaping from the monastery of San Benigno di Fruttuaria in Milan where he had been confined by the bishop of Ivrea, he stayed at Casale Monferrato where he enjoyed the protection of the marquis Gian Giorgio Paleologo until 1534, and learned about the Waldensians' espousal of the Reformation. Curione next traveled in northern Italy until he was invited to join the faculty at the University of Pavia as *"publicus professor"* for a triennium where he taught to great acclaim. In 1539 while he was being investigated by the Holy Office, he fled to Venice where he met Giulio della Rovere and other evangelicals. Finding himself implicated during della Rovere's trial before the Venetian Inquisition, Curione moved on once more, settling in Ferrara and joining the circle around Duchess Renée. Here he resumed his contacts with his friend Fulvio Pellegrino Morato and met his daughter, Olimpia, whose writings he would publish in Basel many years later. Renée, who was aware of the inroads made by the Reformation in Lucca, recommended Curione to the Arnolfini family, and he began his duties as tutor in the home of Niccolò Arnolfini in October 1541.

By now Curione had moved from Erasmian positions to a full espousal of the Reformation. Pellegrino Morato wrote to thank him for having strengthened him in the new faith. In Lucca the brilliant humanist proselytized for his evangelical views and formed fast friendships with the learned Augustinians of San Frediano, P. M.

---

[14]Cited from R. H. Bainton, *Erasmus of Christendom*, 70.

[15]M. Berengo, *Nobili e mercanti*, 402.

[16]For C. S. Curione, see the sketch by A. Biondi in *DBI*, 31:442–49, and M. Kutter, *Celio Secondo Curione: Sein Leben und sein Werk (1503–1569)* (Basel & Stuttgart: Helbing & Lichtenhahn, 1955).

Vermigli, Paolo Lazise, Celso Martinengo, and Girolamo Zanchi. But his efforts were soon cut short. On 22 July 1542 Lucca's ruling body, the *Anziani*, received a request for Curione's arrest from Cardinal Bartolomeo Guidiccioni:

> That Celio who resides in the home of *Messer* Niccolò Arnolfini, who is said to have translated into the vernacular some of Martin's works, so as to give that wonderful nourishment to the simple women of our city, and who has had those precepts printed to his fantasy; moreover, from Venice and Ferrara, we have reports of his poor odor.[17]

Some weeks later, on 26 August, Cardinal Alessandro Farnese asked Pisa's governing authorities to track down "a terrible person called Celio from Turin" who "under the guise of being a schoolteacher...has professed Lutheran views publicly and in many places." But by now Curione, assisted by Vincenzo Castrucci and other friends, was safely across the Alps. He first resided in Lausanne, from 1542 to 1546, and then in Basel for another twenty-three years where he would achieve great prestige and a European reputation. But Curione did not turn his back on his Lucchese friends. In 1552 he was in touch with Paleario, who gave him information about his daughter Dorotea, who was being raised lovingly in the home of the Arnolfini. The bearer of these letters and of the girl's portrait was the merchant Francesco Micheli, who brought back information to the evangelicals in Lucca that they would later find useful in their Genevan exile home.[18]

The labors of P. M. Vermigli (1499–1562) in Lucca during the fifteen months that he was prior in the convent of Lateran canons at San Frediano were nearly contemporary to Curione's.[19] Vermigli had studied in Padua at the university and in the important *Studium* attached to the convent of San Giovanni Verdara, graduating in 1526. As time passed, he occupied important positions in the Augustinian order and as visitor came away with a clear notion of the urgent need to reform its establishments. After three years in Bologna, from 1530 to 1533, a time when some of the Erasmian members of Achille Bocchi's cultural circle were corresponding with Martin Bucer, he was assigned to Spoleto for another triennium lasting until 1536. Known within the hierarchy of the church as a dedicated reformer and highly esteemed by Cardinal Contarini, Vermigli was transferred to Naples in 1537 as abbot of the convent of San Pietro ad Aram. He remained in the city during the years of Juan de Valdés's greatest activity and became his fast friend and follower. So close was the consonance of views between the two that several of Vermigli's sermons and his commentary on Paul's First Epistle to the Corinthians bore a close resemblance to Valdés's contemporary commentary. It was in Naples that Vermigli fully appropriated the doctrine of justification by faith, which became the key to his interpretation of Scripture.

---

[17]A. Pascal, "Da Lucca a Ginevra," *RSI* 59 (1932): 153.

[18]S. Caponetto, *Aonio Paleario*, 109.

[19]I follow the account in P. McNair, *Peter Martyr in Italy: An Anatomy of an Apostasy* (Oxford: Clarendon, 1967).

When Vermigli arrived in Lucca to assume the priorate of the convent of San Frediano in June 1541, he had behind him a distinguished record as man of culture and renowned preacher. As its director, he restored the convent, to which the great aristocratic families such as the Buonvisi and Arnolfini were closely affiliated, to its former prestige. According to Philip McNair, the leading authority on Vermigli's Italian career, "like a good humanist and Erasmian reformer" he worked hard to reestablish discipline and high-quality education for the youths of the school. He turned San Frediano into a "miniature but brilliant university" with himself as its rector.[20] Vermigli employed some of the most learned brothers in the order, such as Paolo Lazise of Verona to teach Latin and Count Maximilian Martinengo of Brescia (Don Celso) to teach Greek. He also recruited the Ferrarese Jew, Emanuele Tremellio, who had converted to Catholicism under the aegis of Cardinal Pole. Education at San Frediano was not restricted to members of the religious house, but available to Lucchese youths who did not wish to be confined forever to a life in commerce. The program had a precise objective: to impart instruction in Hebrew and the classical languages so that the Holy Scriptures could be read in its original tongues. Vermigli himself set the example by publicly expounding the Psalms and the Epistle to the Romans, and preaching before large audiences drawn from every sphere of society.

Vermigli's unceasing labors as pastor and teacher gradually created a concept of the Christian faith far removed from rites and doctrines that were not based on the Scriptures. What might be termed an *ecclesiola in ecclesia* standing on clearly evangelical foundations gradually began to take form. The names of some of its most devoted members, drawn from the ranks of the Lucchese citizenry, have come down to us: Cristofano Trenta, Niccolò Diodati, Francesco Micheli, Regolo Turrettini, Niccolò Arnolfini, Giovanni Battista Bernardini, Vincenzo Castrucci, Francesco Cattani, Stefano Trenta, Girolamo Liena, Bernardino Macchi, and Matteo Gigli. In the memories of the first exiles' descendants, passed on from parents to children or entrusted to their "Memoirs," the pastor of San Frediano was remembered as the person who brought the light of the Gospel to Lucca. In the reply written in 1681 by the descendants of the Lucchese refugees in Geneva to the invitation sent by Cardinal Giulio Spinola to return to the Roman church, the name of "Peter Martyr" looms as large as Calvin's.[21]

It was becoming daily more difficult to conceal one's acceptance of the doctrines being preached by the monks of San Frediano. According to Nino Sernini, the Gonzaga ambassador in Rome, about two hundred Lucchese citizens were thought to be professing the "Lutheran" faith, denying free will, the mass, the sacraments, the cult of images, and confession. It was rumored in Lucca that the conventicle met in the home of his friend Matteo Gigli, who had told him frankly that he no longer believed in free will, and who had shown himself to be fully persuaded by the new ideas. Placards ridiculing him had been affixed around the city, which read: "Give

[20]Ibid., 221.
[21]E. Campi, C. Sodini, *Gli oriundi lucchesi di Ginevra e il Cardinale Spinola* (Naples & Chicago: PRISMI–The Newberry Library, 1988), 180.

charity to Matteo Gigli, whose mind is somewhat deficient and wants to sing his first Mass. He is married with children."[22] This eminent member of the ruling class may, like Martino Gigli, not have gone beyond Erasmian positions. He read the Bible to his friends in his home, claiming that he had the right to do so in light of Vermigli's teaching. But, like the Buonvisi and Martino Gigli, he would not follow his many fellow citizens who went into exile. Nevertheless, Martino could not avoid the great persecution set in motion by Paul IV and was confined for several months in the prison of the Holy Office at Rome, the Tor di Nona, together with Michele Diodati.

Diodati, who had already served three terms as Gonfalonier, was compelled to interrupt his term as *Anziano* to go to Rome at the end of 1558 to erase the stain of heresy from his name. But, even after he was pardoned, he did not renounce certain of his ideas. He was the only Lucchese nobleman to prohibit in his testament the taking of religious vows by any of his daughters before they reached twenty years of age, thus defying the tradition of coerced taking of the veil. His second-born son, Carlo, would be banned from Lucca as a heretic on 3 March 1568, and in 1572 became a *habitant* of Geneva,[23] four years before the birth of his own son, Giovanni, who became the famous translator of the Bible into Italian, the official version for Italian Protestants until this day.

In the summer of 1542, after Cardinal Bartolomeo Guidiccioni's entreaties to the Lucchese authorities to take active measures against the further spread of heresy in the city, the situation came to a head. The prior of the Lateran canons of Fregionaia, Don Costantino da Carrara, accused of harboring heterodox beliefs, fled from his convent and went into hiding. Meanwhile, a search began for Curione.

It dawned on Vermigli that he would not be able to continue his pastoral work, nor recant the Reformation principles in which he had ended up believing with profound conviction. He abandoned his convent in the company of Paolo Lazise and Emanuele Tremellio, and headed for Switzerland, but ended up in Strasbourg, where he was joined by his two companions. At this very time, Fra Girolamo da Pluvio, vicar of the Augustinian Hermits, residing in the monastery of Sant'Agostino in Lucca, was arrested. But on 21 September 1542, Vincenzo Castrucci, a friend of Curione, Francesco Cattani, Stefano Trenta, and Girolamo Liena helped him to escape. With the rigorous measures being taken by the government against the champions of religious dissent, many of whom headed for Geneva, it would appear that the movement had weakened. But a series of concomitant events show the depth of the roots it had sunk and how the Erasmian prelude had paved the way for the transition to Calvinism. The convent of San Frediano jealously preserved Vermigli's teachings, and he, from exile, initiated a correspondence with the small clandestine community he had left behind. He began by explaining to them the reasons for his flight, urging them to remain faithful to God's Word: "Oh, my beloved brothers, do not fear or be saddened. Even if I have been taken from you, God will certainly not

---

[22]M. Berengo, *Nobili e mercanti*, 408.
[23]Ibid., 447–48; S. Adorni-Braccesi, "Giuliano da Dezza, caciaiuolo: Nuove prospettive sull'eresia a Lucca nel XVI secolo," *Actum Luce* 9 (1980): 116.

abandon you, our most merciful Father, who will raise up someone among you in every age to proclaim to you the Word of Truth." These comforting words were followed by a positive judgment on the clandestine Lucchese community, based on precise information he had received: "I can assure you, that despite the exiles and persecutions which daily afflict her, your church does not produce fruits inferior to the churches here, which, by the grace of God enjoy tranquillity and peace."[24] And the "fruits" were the new converts flocking to it.

San Frediano continued Vermigli's mission through the labors of one of his most accomplished disciples, Don Celso Martinengo. After he became prior in 1549, even when confronted by countless difficulties and compelled to disguise his views and activities under a Nicodemite veil, Martinengo directed many of the faithful towards Calvinism. He was in Milan preaching the Lenten sermons for 1551, when he was accused of heresy by Girolamo Muzio. He fled to Geneva where he became the pastor of the Italian exiles' church.

A recently discovered trial, held from the end of December 1554 until early in 1555, against a soldier of Lucca's city militia, a certain Rinaldo Turchi Marsili of Verona, offers a remarkably full picture of the beliefs held by the community of San Frediano, of their methods of proselytization, and of their success penetrating even the lowest spheres of society.[25] From Rinaldo's testimony, we learn that Don Valeriano da Verona had guided him towards belief in the justifying faith of Jesus Christ, beginning in 1548 with preaching and "instruction" in his cell. The cleric had led him to believe that the Roman church, by professing erroneous views, such as the intercession of saints, praying to images, and transubstantiation, was not the true church, "because it is full of abuses and filth since it is governed by the ministers of Baal." Don Valeriano had also taught Rinaldo that purgatory was "the blood of Jesus Christ for our sins," that the bread of the Lord's Supper was "a sign of the covenant," a commemoration of the Passion and death of Jesus Christ. As for "the catholic church...it was the union of the faithful, who are governed by the Holy Spirit, but the Roman church is neither catholic nor apostolic, because it is a human invention and the pope is an Antichrist."

Fra Valeriano's instruction followed Calvinist teachings point by point, as they had been transmitted by Vermigli and Martinengo. The proselytizing efforts of the Nicodemite brothers of San Frediano were abetted by an obscure French missionary, a certain Ludovico or Aloisio, who had come from Geneva where he had lived for many years, and who now attended the conventicles meeting in the homes of Francesco Cattani and Vincenzo Castrucci. In these gatherings the participants read the letters of St. Paul and the commentaries of John Chrysostom, to confirm, in the words of the defendant Rinaldo, "that we are justified by faith in Christ without benefit of our works." But the Frenchman was even more explicit, vigorously criticizing

---

[24]A. Pascal, "Da Lucca a Ginevra," 161.
[25]AAL, *Contenzioso B. Raynaldus Veronensis processus*, 1544. I am pleased to thank Prof. Simonetta Adorni-Braccesi, who graciously made this important document available to me.

the mass and communion, urging his listeners to go to Geneva "and to those places where the Gospel and Word of God are freely preached."

As the soldier, who had accepted these teachings, was about to succumb to this exhortation, his wife told him simply and frankly: "Rinaldo, this could mean our ruination; let us wait some more, as we have done in the past. My children are little, and their mother has always instructed them"—a wife's anxious supplication to her husband, reminding him that they lacked the financial resources to confront the difficulties of exile, but also of her desire to preserve evangelical truth in her heart and transmit it to her young. Moreover, Nicodemite ways of concealing one's true faith had been taught by Don Valeriano because the modern scribes and pharisees, fearing to lose their power, were opposing the preaching of the Gospel and still represented a force to contend with.

In his long confession made to the court, the defendant Rinaldo named the persons who frequented the conventicles meeting in the Cattani and Castrucci residences. They included Martino Gigli, Cristofano Trenta, Alò Venturini, Silvestro Trenta, Nicolao Liena, Girolamo Liena, Matteo Gigli, Angiola, wife of Vincenzo Arnolfini, Angiola Castrucci, Stefano Trenta, Baldassar Menafa, and Lodovico Pitorsi of Carrara. Rinaldo acknowledged that there had been much discussion concerning the new doctrines but not everyone was in agreement about accepting the Calvinist teaching of the spiritual presence of Christ in the elements of the Lord's Supper. Martino and Matteo Gigli, for example, had argued with him over this issue. Rinaldo, at this point, was as far advanced in his thinking as most of those in the conventicle who would feel compelled into exile in Geneva.

In these years, during his travels, Rinaldo came into contact with other brethren in the faith. In Venice he met a teacher from Calabria named Armenio, the tutor in the patrician home of Giovanni de' Micheli, and a Ferrarese, Annibale Gorino, formerly a monk in the order of Lateran Canons who went by the name of Don Evangelista and was about to flee to the north. At Ferrara, where he accompanied Nicolao Liena who had been assigned there as ambassador, Rinaldo met an "Ambrosio," who had been the prior of San Frediano in Lucca and was presently residing at "the court of *madama* where he had the title of preacher and dressed as a priest." The monk identified himself to the soldier, who remembered having seen him at San Frediano.[26]

In Florence, Rinaldo saw Cornelio Donzellino, two artisans, and Ludovico Manna, who will be discussed below. For almost six years Manna had accepted the teachings in which he had first been initiated by a Piedmontese man of arms, an apostate monk and a "Lutheran," who had himself been converted by Don Valeriano. But Manna could not take the final step and follow his companions into exile. He abjured and was reconciled with the church of his fathers.

---

[26]It may be possible to identify "Annibale ferrarese" with Annibale Gorino, mentioned in the trial against Ambrogio Cavalli, an exile in Geneva and enrolled among the *habitants* with the name Annibale Gormo (7 October 1555). Cf. ASM, b. 42, fasc. 16, and L. Perini, "Ancora sul libraio," 371.

Until the Counter-Reformation finally crushed all Italian religious dissent, San Frediano continued as a center of piety and the spread of Calvinist teachings, no longer, as we have just seen in the case of Rinaldo Turchi Marsili, solely among the noble families traditionally linked to the convent, but even among the lower classes. In the autumn of 1550 two carpenters of Fivizzano, Francesco da Moncigoli and Ulivo di Lebbia, while working on the loft of a house at Fivizzano, began to cast aspersions on the feast of John the Baptist, the intercession of saints, and confession. Warming themselves before the hearth one evening, they scandalized their hosts and the women present. Among other things, the two workmen said "that in the Lord's Supper Christ in the flesh is not present in the wafer, but portrayed, because if he was really there in the flesh, there would not be a bite left, since he would have been eaten in so many places." The two carpenters persuaded their judges that they had been jesting. But even if that was the case, they must have picked up these notions at San Frediano where they regularly went to confess.[27]

The Popular Movement in the Garfagnana

The spread of Calvinism among peasants, laborers, and the poor attained successes in the Lucchese Garfagnana not encountered elsewhere in Italy.[28] This was due to the zealousness of the populace who had accepted these ideas with surprising shrewdness from the sermons and instruction of the monks of San Frediano, or from members of the patrician and mercantile classes of Lucca. Our friend, the soldier Rinaldo Turchini, one day went to the hospital of San Nicolao in Lucca to comfort a dying woman. Contradicting two Franciscans who were also present, he announced that she would be saved through divine grace: "My sister, do not doubt, confess yourself to Jesus Christ faithfully, fix the eyes of faith on the heavens, and ignore this piece of wood," pointing to a crucifix she was holding, "because this figurine will not be of any use to you. Look to the one who is in heaven who was beaten and scourged and died on the wood of the cross for your sins. And if you are willing to believe this in your heart and will not allow yourself to be persuaded that anything else is your salvation, then you shall be saved...." When the two monks interjected that purgatory was necessary, Rinaldo replied that he knew no other purgatory "than the blood of Jesus Christ for our sins."[29]

Ugolino Grifoni, master general of the order of the knights of Altopascio, in a letter he wrote from Pisa dated 28 April 1546, informed the Medici official in Florence, Pier Francesco Riccio, about the spread of heresy in the Garfagnana and its links with Lucca. A hatmaker, who had been taken into custody because during services in the church of San Francesco he had contradicted the preacher about

---

[27]ASL, *Offizio di religione*, n. 1, trial sessions of 8–26 November 1550.
[28]For much of what follows, see my "Infiltrazioni protestanti nella Garfagnana e nella Lunigiana," in *Barga medicea e le "enclaves" fiorentine della Versilia e della Lunigiana* (Florence: Olschki, 1983), 187–202, now reprinted in Caponetto, *Studi sulla Riforma*, 315–32.
[29]See note 25.

purgatory, was interrogated under torture by the authorities and revealed the activities of two priests in the valley of the Serchio: "during this last Lent they behaved delinquently, so that as a result the majority of the peasants of that area did not observe Lent, or go to the usual devotions put on by the confraternities. And here in Pisa there is another priest, who keeps company with Bernardo de' Ricasoli of Cola della Magona, and with some other people, as well, who according to what the commissioner told me, are offensive and infect this city." Moreover, Fra Tommaso da San Miniato, who had come from Lucca, had informed Grifoni, the writer of the letter, "that in that city there are more than five hundred persons [suspected of heresy] who are from good families, and it is feared that this will be the cause of great scandal in the city...."[30]

Another piece of evidence, besides Grifoni's, concerning the spread of religious dissent in the Garfagnana, is the report written by a disciple of Ignatius Loyola, Father Silvestro Landini, a native of Malgrate in the Val di Magra, who was destined to become, after a period of uncertainty, a shining example for other missionaries in the European field. He was already in his mid-forties when he was sent home by the general of his order to restore his fragile health. He remained in the Garfagnana and Lunigiana from the summer of 1547 to the summer of 1550, with the exception of eight months he spent in Rome and Foligno. His mission field included the Val di Magra and the entire Val Serchio and reached as far as Modena, where he lingered for a time in 1551. He labored tirelessly in remote mountain areas of the Tusco-Emilian Apennines ministering to the poor who were suffering from famine as well as spiritual neglect. After visiting Castiglione del Terziere, Gragnana, Filattiera, and San Lorenzo, Landini wrote on 7 February 1548, from Malgrate to the Jesuit Giovanni Alfonso Polanco, Loyola's secretary: "Hunger makes tasty even bread made out of barley and millet. Barley and beans are sold together in weights of 70 pounds for 18 *giulii*. Water is drunk in the place of wine. Storms have destroyed everything, and the poor do not have a single coin among them, who are in great numbers and exist on black bread. The Lord is seeing to it that we are paying for our sins...."[31] At the end of his mission, Landini succeeded in erasing all the doubts the general might have had about him, and he was admitted into the Society of Jesus in full standing. On 27 July 1550 the neophyte drew up an almost complete list of the lands he had visited, Genoese, Florentine, Ferrarese, Lucchese, including property owned by the marquis of Malaspina, "where at his command we sowed the Word of God." At the beginning of this mission, accomplished with great personal sacrifice by Landini as penance for certain deficiencies of his as a student in the Jesuit *Collegio Romano*, he had been amazed to discover the almost total absence of religious life among the population, a combination of gross neglect by parish priests, and an almost constant concern of the impoverished, downtrodden population for their next piece of bread. But even more surprising for Landini was the discovery in these lands of open hostility towards the

---

[30] S. Caponetto, *Aonio Paleario*, 231–32, app. 2.

[31] [For the documentation on Landini's mission, see ibid., 188, notes 22 ff., as well as the work cited at note 28. Trans. note.]

pope and his church, motivated by the immorality of the local clergy, but especially by the evangelizing efforts of Protestant, especially Calvinist proselytizers. This corroborates fully the evidence provided in April 1546 by the Pisan hatmaker, which we noted above, on the diffusion of Reformation teachings in the valley of the Serchio.

After preaching his Lenten sermons in 1548 at Casola, Landini wrote a detailed report in Spanish to the Jesuit Father Polanco in Rome, who was very interested in the progress being made by the Society of Jesus in Tuscany since, in 1546 he had been involved in the founding of its Florentine College. The account provides a minute description of the erroneous views of the "modern heretics," of whom the land was full, as shown by the many prohibited books confiscated in Lucca in 1545 and also known to be circulating in the neighboring localities:

> They reject everything, bringing it all back to predestination and fate; they live like beasts, and even worse reject free will, claim that grace is not given to everyone…except for their carnality; they deny the existence of heaven and hell. Of two children baptized at the same moment, they say that, in the case they die, one will be saved and the other damned. They reject Masses for the dead, the veneration of saints, images of Our Lord and of all the saints, altars in the churches, and praying in church. They say that the recital of the Offices is not necessary, prohibit the rosary of Our Lady, and even dare to say that the law prescribing marriage comes from God, but virginity is from the devil and hell, and that priests are right to have their concubines. They say that all things should be in common and that God creates evil and man cannot resist God; that the laws of the holy Roman and apostolic Church are human traditions, and that it is permissible to eat meat on Good Friday, on fast days, during the Ember Days and all of Lent. They eat meat on Holy Friday, never fast nor observe Holy Days. They blaspheme saying that it is of great merit at all times to use marriage just to satisfy the urges of passion and without honor (*etiam in passione desiderii et sine honore*). They reject all the monastic orders, and detest their garments. These same [Protestant] preachers, who hold to things of the flesh, preach carnally and try to convert monks who are tempted to throw off their religious habits. They reject sacramental confession and the most holy sacrament of the altar saying that it is just a piece of bread. Some pretend to celebrate Mass and then to raise up the host, and this even on the day of the Lord's Supper. They reject all good works, and they preach and write on paper and on the marble at the entrance [to churches] in large letters: everything comes from grace and faith (*omnia gratiae et fidei*).
>
> They possess the *Sommario della santa Scrittura*, the *Beneficio di Cristo*, Fabro (Lefèvre d'Étaples], Bucer, Martin Luther, Oecolampadius and other heretical books like these. They have convinced priests to marry and preach *Jacob dilexit, Esau autem odi habuit; et non est volentis, neque currentis; et ut lutum in manu figuli*; and the command to "grow and multiply" (*crescite et multiplicami*) they now consider to be a general command that applies even

to religious. They say that to rejoice in this world and to have a good time is the Lord's pleasure, and that when the body suffers, the soul cannot praise God, and that man cannot be chaste and the pure blessed. They preach that faith alone justifies and that dispensation can be given to marry one's relatives without the authorization of His Holiness, because priests have Christ's authority. Others neither say nor hear Mass, and they try to drag both young and old into these errors, as the Lutherans ardently hope, who call themselves preachers of the manifest Gospel, which they no longer want to preach secretly.

They say that the glorious Mother is not the Mother of God, but a poor servant woman, and they call St. Peter disparagingly "*Petruccio*" and St. Paul "*Traverso*." They are of the opinion that it might be better for the Christian to cling to the Epistles of St. Paul and put aside the rest of Scripture. They reject the sacred Doctors with the exception of those who teach predestination and St. Augustine, who they say is the greatest authority and laid his stamp on all others. They also say that our good works place no obligation on God, that his commandments cannot be observed and that the true Church is not the Roman, but their own!

The report of the zealous Jesuit patently contains ideologically motivated exaggerations and misrepresentations, with added notions from the mouths of ignorant people and from discussions with priests and monks who were well informed about Lutheran and Calvinist teachings. But it is also an extraordinarily direct and personal statement, one of the few that have come down to us that tell how the lower classes appropriated the polemics and teachings of the Protestant reformers. In the people's simple but colorful language we discern their astonishment at the discovery of the human dimension in the Biblical narrative, such as where "the glorious Mother of God" does not appear bathed in glory as depicted in the images they had always venerated, but as the humble handmaid of the Lord; or where the Lord's Supper is not presented in terms of the consecrated host containing the body and blood of Christ, but only as a piece of bread; and St. Peter, from whom the pope claimed to have inherited his primacy as well as spiritual and political authority, is addressed merely as "Petruccio," a fragile, fickle man who thrice rejected his Lord!

The emphasis on double predestination, the references to the classical texts of the doctrine's principal defenders, beginning with St. Augustine, acquires an existential and class-conscious flavor. God had kept them under the oppression of the rich and the powerful, but now he was freeing them from sin by his grace and was electing them to eternal life, leaving the rest behind among the masses of the damned!

Landini attributed a crucial role in the dissemination of these ideas to books brought by Lucchese landowners to their properties in the Garfagnana. This seems impossible for a population of peasants, laborers, and petty merchants who were mostly illiterate. It is much more likely that as in Florence, Modena, Bologna, Venice, Naples, and in many other Italian urban centers, a literate few possessed the *Sommario della santa Scrittura* and the *Beneficio di Cristo*, books that in a straightforward way expounded the doctrines of justification by faith alone, the predestination of the elect, and the other essential points of the Protestant Reformation mentioned in Landini's report. Calvin's *Institutes*, which had already appeared in six Latin and French editions circulating about Tuscany, is not one of the books he mentioned. It is more probable that the diffusion of Calvin's ideas was accomplished by word of mouth by followers who openly proclaimed his message, in defiance of inquisitorial repression, tired of "preaching a disguised Christ," in the words of Bernardino Ochino's letter to Vittoria Colonna in 1542 in which he tried to justify his recent apostasy and flight from Italy.

Calvinist emissaries spoke to peasants, laborers, merchants, soldiers, parish priests, oppressed by poverty, famine, disease, and without spiritual sustenance. The evangelical message was conveyed in a simple, almost rough, language intended to persuade them to abandon the rites of the Roman church and to join together to listen to Bible readings, celebrate the Lord's Supper as a remembrance of his death and resurrection, and oppose the necessity of works and precepts as devices for obtaining the salvation of the soul, imparted only through a free divine election. Their message, that everything came from grace and faith, was even affixed to church doors.

Landini waged intense activity in the Lucchese Garfagnana and at Càsola, an advance post of the Florentine state on the border with the Republic of Lucca, a prominent commercial center that bustled with the passage of merchants with their goods and troops of soldiers. He then moved on to Fivizzano, where prohibited books circulated in abundance and Reformation currents had made inroads. In May 1548 Landini preached against the new doctrines for three days. Many among the heterodox had ended up recanting their errors, but others, as he wrote to Polanco, "by the grace of Our Lord, now no longer dare to appear publicly in these parts, although the rumor is that they are still numerous and of great importance and that one of them has written a *sommario* (summary). Apropos Fivizzano and the entire diocese of Luni and Sarzana, one of the principal men of the area, Raffaello Augustini, attributed the spread of "Lutheranism" to the proximity of Lucca, "seat of that cursed and viperous Lutheran sect," and he beseeched Jesuit intervention to obtain excommunication for readers of heretical literature. Unfortunately, it is impossible to verify these accusations and whether links indeed existed between the popular movement in the Garfagnana and neighboring lands, including the Calvinists of Lucca, who were almost all patricians and wealthy merchants and would begin heading for Genevan exile in the mid-1550s.

The relatively sizable movement in the Garfagnana and eastern Lunigiana soon lost its leaders through arrest and voluntary exile. It may not have been difficult, between the repressive measures of political and religious authorities and Landini's selfless labors, to bring the strayed sheep back to the bosom of the Roman church. The missionary returned to the Garfagnana in May 1549 after an absence of eight months spent between Spoleto and Foligno. He informed Loyola from Puglianella (25 June 1549) and from Careggine (4 July 1549) of his bountiful harvest of errant souls in the Lucchese and Ferrarese parts of the Garfagnana, and the year before in areas of the Florentine and Lucchese states. Landini attributed his successes to

Loyola's *Spiritual Exercises*: "But you should know that everything is the fruit of your exercises, most reverend father. Before that meditation of the three sins, of death, of the Judgment and of hell, all the people tremble, and who does not tremble must be crazy!"

THE SCHOOL OF AONIO PALEARIO

Paleario, renowned humanist and Latin poet, was invited to teach the humanities in Lucca in spite of the taint of heresy under which he labored and his Sienese trial of 1542.[32] The *Offizio sopra Le Scuole*, the magistracy responsible for the city's educational system at mid-century, was composed of jurists, notaries, and physicians who had themselves received sound instruction in the humanistic disciplines and enjoyed the confidence of the General Council. During the years of Paleario's appointment to teach the humane letters in Lucca from 1546 to 1555, the magistracy was composed of leaders of the Erasmian and philo-Protestant faction in the city, all of whom would become his friends: Cristofano Trenta, Matteo Gigli, Vincenzo Castrucci, Nicolao Liena, Girolamo Arnolfini, Martino Gigli, and Ludovico Buonvisi.

Paleario collaborated with this magistracy to transform the old school for instruction in grammar into an instrument capable of transmitting to all levels of the population what Christian humanism, from Vittorino da Feltre to Philipp Melanchthon had defined "*eloquens pietas*" (learned piety), in other words, instruction that would enable young people to critically read and interpret scriptural texts.[33] Paleario was assigned as colleagues Antonio Bendinelli and Sebastiano Monsagrati, who would later be in trouble with the Inquisition because of their associations with him. The heredity of Vermigli's pedagogical ideas are easily discernible in this restructuring of the educational system. In a little less than a decade of teaching, Paleario inculcated in his pupils, through the reading of classical texts and the Scriptures, a taste for the free and independent search for truth. After the flights of C. S. Curione and Vermigli eased tension between the government of Lucca and the Roman curia, which had become alarmed by the spread of heresy in the city, there was a decade of relative tranquillity in the religious situation until the exodus to Geneva of a number of prominent families began in 1555.

During his Lucchese sojourn, although Paleario associated himself with the Nicodemite posture maintained by evangelical and Erasmian circles, thus keeping his promise to the government that he would not propagate his ideas, he wrote nothing against his conscience. Paleario's role is obscure during these years in which the city's Protestants were laying plans and biding their time. Their decision to flee was not taken suddenly but was the consequence of long reflection and soul-searching that had begun with Vermigli's ministry among them. Nevertheless, in thinking of the

---

[32] S. Adorni-Braccesi, "Maestri e scuole nella Repubblica di Lucca tra Riforma e Controriforma," in *Società e storia* 33 (1986): 581.

[33] [This and the following section in this chapter are taken from S. Caponetto, *Aonio Paleario*, chaps. 8 and 9, where more specific documentation is provided. Trans. note.]

families with which Paleario associated closely as the teacher of their children but also because of ideals he shared with them, an occasional segment of that hidden thread can be glimpsed that would only come to the surface fully in 1555. Scanning the names of the families that would find refuge in Geneva the same year that Paleario left Lucca, we find members of the Arnolfini, Micheli, Liena, Cenami, Calandrini, and Bernardini clans, all of whom were his friends and patrons.

The merchant Girolamo Arnolfini, three times Gonfalonier, together with his son Francesco, who was also greatly devoted to the schoolteacher, had many times hosted Paleario in his villa at Pancraziano. In 1561 the elder Arnolfini left Lucca for Lyons, Paris, and Antwerp, eventually settling in Geneva and apparently followed by his son. Francesco Micheli, who served as intermediary between the Lucchese and Curione, arrived in Geneva on 19 October 1556. On the same day the *cité-refuge* received the jurist Nicolao Liena, the former Lucchese ambassador to Ferrara, who had been Paleario's go-between with the Este family tutor, Bartolomeo Ricci, and his other friends at court. Of the Calandrini family, Paleario's pupil Scipione studied at Heidelberg and later became pastor at Morbegno and Sondrio in the Valtellina. Calandrini's efforts there to achieve a measure of mutual toleration and coexistence between evangelicals and Catholics must certainly owe something to Paleario's irenic insistence on the value of dialogue and the common search for truth.

Even during his relatively quiescent interlude at Lucca, Paleario never broke with his political vocation. The image of the schoolteacher, withdrawn, ever more confined to Nicodemite positions, his activities confined to family life and to the classroom, is misleading. A careful reading of the letters he exchanged in this period with the Latin poet and orator Bartolomeo Ricci in Ferrara, his links to the Ferrarese Alberto Lollio and Giambattista Pigna, the brilliant interpreter of Ariosto who wrote a poem in praise of Paleario for the latter's *De animorum immortalitate*, and probably with other representatives of Ferrarese university and cultural life, such as Vincenzo Maggi, are evidence of Paleario's continuing interest in the outside world.

Ricci's letter to Paleario that he was well advanced in the writing of his treatise, *De gloria*, prompted the latter in reply, to pronounce judgment upon those princes who turned to violence and war to resolve religious controversies, thereby negating the humanists' hopes for universal peace. Paleario, striking a contrast to these enemies of the *studia humanitatis*, glorified the duchess Renée as a model of a wise sovereign who was respectful of people's longings for the freedom of conscience and who had turned her mind to matters theological.[34]

Even Paleario's orations, official speeches to be delivered twice yearly by a city's teacher of Latin letters when the office of Gonfalonier changed hands, as was observed by Augusto Mancini, should not be viewed as mere rhetorical exercises, but as "significant historical and biographical documents."[35] In the context of Paleario's exaltation of the virtues of the Lucchese Republic—harmony, prudence, justice, strength, temperance, happiness—and his heartfelt homage to a state that had

---

[34]Ibid., 194, notes 57 and 58. [Trans. note.]
[35]A. Mancini, "Note su Aonio Paleario," *ASI* 84 (1926): 113–24, at p. 114. [Trans. note.]

invited him to educate its young, despite the diffidence of clerical and conservative forces, personal themes linked to the political struggle can still be discerned. He made frequent allusions to the urgency of defending the Republic's ancient freedom, recommended that ambassadors be sent to Venice to study its constitution, and beseeched that the history of Lucca be written so that posterity could read how a small state preserved its liberty through wise and steadfast rule during the clash of great powers in the peninsula. Paleario's apparent allusion to the "myth" of a serene Venice contains the latent suggestion of new alliances, of new political spaces on the altered European scene as emperor and pope linked forces in the war against the Schmalkaldic League. The orator condemned the revolt of the "*Straccioni*," which some of his powerful friends, the Buonvisi and Arnolfini, as we mentioned earlier, had helped to crush. But he issued a forceful admonition to the rich not to violate the natural rights of workers and not to exacerbate the inequality in incomes by failing to recognize the harshness of manual labor. During the years of the first important phase of the Council of Trent, of the Schmalkaldic War, and the resulting Protestant defeat, the speaker intentionally ignored the role of the pope and of the Catholic Church in both Italian and European politics. As for their impact on the civic sphere, he made no mention of ecclesiastical holidays and devotions, which had assumed a greater prominence in the life of the Republic, and hoped to dispel the not unfounded ecclesiastical suspicions about the orthodoxy of its people.

In spring 1552, Sébastien Gryphe in Lyons published all the orations Paleario had written up to that point, together with his letters and a reprinting of the *De animorum immortalitate*. The work contains a dedication, dated 1 April [1552] to Ferrante Sanseverino, prince of Salerno, to whom the author paid homage both as lord of the city of Paleario's forebears and as a patron of culture. Some days later, Sanseverino, who had already been compelled to flee from Naples in November 1551 and find haven in Venice, was declared a rebel and accused of heresy, sodomy, and of having given refuge to bandits by Don Pedro of Toledo, viceroy of Naples and father-in-law of Cosimo I. Paleario had carefully weighed the political significance of his literary gesture, which may not have wholly displeased the Lucchese but must not have been to the liking of the Florentine ruler: this was his response to the delusion he felt at Cosimo's altered ecclesiastical politics after the election of the Aretine Julius III to the papacy.

For Paleario, as for Ortensio Lando, Sanseverino had become the symbol of the patriot, the defender of the freedom and independence of the Neapolitan state, now threatened by the attempt to introduce the feared and hated Spanish Inquisition. The misadventures of the prince of Salerno had commenced, in fact, with the rebellion of 1547, which had united nobility and populace. Representatives of the former selected Sanseverino and Placido di Sangro to go before the imperial court and plead Naples' cause. Sanseverino went, strengthened by the resolve of his secretary, Bernardo Tasso, father of the famous poet, Torquato. The envoy was able to obtain the emperor's word that the feared tribunal would not be introduced into the viceroyalty of Naples, and, upon his return he received an enthusiastic welcome. Thus defeated, the viceroy swore revenge against Sanseverino, compelling him to flee. Intelligent, haughty, gallant, until the events of 1547 the latter had been at the center of Neapolitan cultural and aristocratic life. As commander of the Italian infantry during Charles V's expedition against Tunis, Sanseverino had distinguished himself in the capture of Goletta. On the return from North Africa he had hosted the emperor in his Neapolitan palace, which was frequented, as was his other palatial residence in Salerno, by such scientists and men of letters as Scipione Capece, Bernardo Tasso, Agostino Nifo, whom he had invited to teach philosophy at Salerno, and the two Florentines Ludovico and Vincenzo Martelli. Sanseverino's wife, Isabella Villamarino, whose charm attracted the young emperor during his visit, and who was often left alone by her husband off campaigning or having affairs, had as her spiritual guide and counselor Girolamo Seripando, archbishop of Salerno, who comforted her even in her moments of greatest misfortune when she too fell under suspicion because of the defection of her husband. In fact, the lure of Valdesian Naples touched her too, and she read the works of Valdés, according to the testimony of the Dominican preacher Ambrogio Salvio of Bagnoli in the 1566 trial against Mario Galeota. According to this witness, in 1546 the princess had ordered the destruction of the trial records against a group of suspected Calvinists of Salerno, all of whom were absolved through her intercession, to prevent news of the matter from reaching Naples.

Even the prince, although not devout for an instant, was aware of the greatly debated religious questions of the day. In the late summer of 1539 he had asked Seripando to explain how divine foreknowledge could be reconciled with free will. He might have been prompted to make his inquiry from hearing about conversations Marcantonio Flaminio had been having with the archbishop, while the former was a guest at Caserta in the home of Gian Francesco Alois, apropos the Sienese sermons on predestination by Agostino Museo. At first, Seripando tried to reconcile the two positions, but failing, ended up advising Sanseverino to give up his vain speculations and dedicate himself to good works. And to this proud and free baron of the realm, a good work in 1547 seemed to be blocking the introduction into his homeland of that implacable instrument of political and ecclesiastical tyranny that went by the name of the Spanish Inquisition.

The prince's contacts with Paleario must have begun after this notorious episode. The intermediary was Vincenzo Martelli, who had joined Bernardo Tasso as Sanseverino's secretary. Martelli, a Florentine man of letters who was celebrated by Anton Francesco Doni in his *Libraria*, and who was a close friend of Benedetto Varchi, frequently traveled to Lucca where he was the guest of the Erasmian Martino Gigli. It was here that he met Paleario and urged him to get in touch with Sanseverino. Eventually, the latter wrote him a courteous letter thanking him for the dedication and inviting him to visit at court so that they might meet and Paleario might be honored "as citizen and nobleman of Salerno." The occasion was not long in coming. When the prince, accompanied by his secretaries Tasso and Martelli and the nobleman Pompeo delli Monti, was forced to flee Naples, en route to Venice in November 1551 he stopped in Lucca at the home of the wealthy merchant Bernardino Cenami. Alerted to his arrival, Paleario hastened to the Cenami residence, but found neither Martelli nor Tasso, who had promised to introduce him. The human-ist screwed up his courage and knelt at the nobleman's feet protesting his admiration and devotion.

The prince's plan was to enter French service and seek allies in Italy to help expel Spain from his homeland. His attempts to involve Venice, which did not want to become implicated in such a risky venture, foundered. Ferrante Sanseverino, in the Italian situation, which differed so markedly from the German, was not destined to play the role of a Maurice of Saxony, as Paleario perhaps had dreamed after the Prot-estant princes forged an alliance with Henry II of France. At Marburg on 3 February 1552, the French sovereign caused a manifesto to be printed bearing the symbol of the Phrygian cap and the motto: "*Libertas. Henricus II, Francorum rex, vindex liberta-tis Germanicae et principum captivorum*" ("Liberty. Henry II, King of the French, defender of German liberty and prince of enslaved people.")

Having failed to arrange with France and with the Ottomans for an invasion off the coasts of Naples, Sanseverino withdrew to France where he received the protec-tion of Catherine de' Medici. In 1560 he visited his compatriot Galeazzo Caracciolo, marquis of Vico, in exile in Geneva for his religious beliefs. We know nothing about this encounter, but approximately a year later the prince married a Huguenot woman in Avignon and converted to Calvinism. He died there in poverty in 1568.

Sanseverino had been accompanied to France by Giuseppe Giova, who had served as his intermediary with Lucchese circles and with Paleario. Born in Lucca, Giova had moved to Rome where he joined the Academy of the *Vignaioli*, the mem-bers of which included Giovanni Mauro, Francesco Berni, F. M. Molza, and Gio-vanni Della Casa. In order to support himself, Giova entered the service of Vittoria Colonna and became her secretary in 1541. His bonds to the poetess were both liter-ary and religious; he may also have been influenced by Valdés and Ochino. He cer-tainly knew such persons who sympathized with the Reformation as Paleario, Giovanni Michele Bruto, and Benedetto Varchi. He was an intimate friend of Anni-bale Caro and held in high esteem by men of letters as a student of antiquity and col-lector of coins and manuscripts. During a sojourn in his native Lucca at Christmas 1560, under suspicion of heresy, he left the city for Lyons where he knew that he would be welcomed by the Lucchese colony. On 1 August 1562, his good friend Annibale Caro wrote to him, asking with concern whether he had become a Hugue-not, that is if he had joined their party, "not as far as the faith is concerned, of course, because I'm certain that you will always believe wholesomely."[36] But Caro was fool-ing himself about his friend's innocence, because since Giova had never been tried before by the Inquisition, he could have returned to Lucca and the Catholic Church, if he had wished. When he did not, he was pronounced a heretic and rebel on 2 December 1567. In 1569 we find him in Geneva where he was welcomed by the Ital-ian exiles. Sanseverino's small entourage had dispersed. Tasso returned to Italy, was pardoned, and entered the service of the dukes of Urbino; Vincenzo Martelli went home to Florence where he became Cosimo's loyal courtier.

---

[36]A. Caro, *Lettere familiari*, a cura di A. Greco (Rome, 1957–61), 3:117, n. 665.

The rapid demise of the hopes that had rested briefly on the ambitious but valiant and generous prince of Salerno, added to Paleario's feelings of isolation and nostalgia for his Cecignano, not distant from Colle Valdelsa, where he had built a villa with savings from his Lucchese labors. After the death of his friends and patrons, Sadoleto, Bembo, Flaminio, and Sfondrato, Paleario was not only alone, but without protection from his ubiquitous detractors. Once again, in contrast to his early grand aspirations, he felt a strong yearning to abandon the struggle and find refuge in the peace of family life. But now his reasoning ran deeper. Hearing of the death of Flaminio (February 1550), he wrote a letter so moving as to touch profoundly Cardinals Bernardino Maffei and Reginald Pole. Paleario's lament was for the irreparable loss of an intimate friend but also for the end of an epoch. Such men as Bembo, Sadoleto, and Flaminio would not be born again: with their loss, the sun of the world had set. The "beautiful school" of these learned freedom-loving souls was dissolved and nothing good could come from fanaticism and war.

Farewell to Siena

After having fulfilled the period of his teaching contract in Lucca, Paleario had to delay his return to Colle de Valdelsa with his family until the successful completion of the siege of Siena by imperial and Medici forces, occurring on 17 April 1555. He came back to scenes of squalor and destruction left by the war and the end of independence for the Republic of Siena. In the few months Paleario spent at Colle he pondered with deep nostalgia the years of his youth in the splendid and flourishing city of the 1530s, where he had found freedom of thought and manners, in which even women of a certain rank could partake. No longer confined to their homes and to domestic activities, a number of them were playing important roles in civic life, inspiring much of the intellectual ferment in the academies. This, at least, is what Girolamo Bargagli wrote decades later of the social changes in Medicean Siena, then controlled by the Jesuits, vigilant custodians of orthodoxy and strict morality.

During this period of reflection, Paleario began or returned to a treatise in the vernacular, divided in two parts, entitled *Del governo della città e Dell'economia o vero del governo della casa*. The first section, which has never been found, might have been useful for its insights into the political thought of the writer. The second, lacking introductory material, remained in manuscript until recent years.[37] The work is clearly dictated by political passion, by a conviction of the connection between the reformation of the church and the reformation of society, between religion and politics. It consists of a dialogue among four Sienese ladies—Cassandra Spannocchi, the wife of Antonio Bellanti, Porzia Petrucci, the wife of Buoncompagno degli Agazzari, and Cassandra's two daughters: Aurelia, the wife of Giovan Battista Bogini, and Francesca, married to Ambrogio Spannocchi. Without benefit of male company (and

---

[37] See A. Paleario, *Dell'economia o vero governo della casa*. Ed. S. Caponetto (Florence: Olschki, 1985).

this is one of the original aspects of the piece), they discuss the place of the woman in the family and in society.

Influenced by Erasmus's *Institutio christiani matrimonii*, Paleario defends a woman's autonomy. Although she has to be obedient to her husband and try to please him, she is not subject to him, and must always remember that she is a woman, not a servant, that she has the right to participate in the administration of her home, the education of her children, her own cultural life, and to avoid her husband, if he should be affected by the "French disease." The two older interlocutors, Porzia and Cassandra, have harsh words for the Jesuits who reject the notion of education for a woman, and want to see her become a "lady sheep." If such monkish educational theories should prevail, "every good and civil order of good living" could be corrupted. Paleario's dialogue calmly portrays an inner piety lived within the family, conceived as a sort of domestic church but inspired by Erasmian and Valdesian ideas.

From 1531, the year in which the scenes discussed in the *Dell'economia...della casa* are said to have occurred, until 1555, many of Paleario's companions and patrons had died, or left for places of exile in Lyons, Paris, and Geneva. Of his Florentine friends, some like Carnesecchi were far away, others cautiously treated him with great circumspection because of the new turn in Medici politics: Pier Francesco Riccio, under observation for mental ailments that were either real or feigned; Bartolomeo Panciatichi, as we shall see later, reduced to silence after the humiliation of prison. Paleario's dialogue was in homage to the Bellanti, Bogini, Spannocchi, degli Agazzari, Malevolti, Francesconi, Buoninsegni, and Carli Piccolomini families. At the moment of the demise of Sienese liberty, the writer looked back longingly to a social and cultural world that had vanished.

The moment of Paleario's departure from his home near Siena for Milan, where he had been invited to fill the humanities chair left vacant by the death of Marcantonio Maioragio, coincided with the exodus from Lucca to Geneva of the first contingent of evangelicals. This dramatic demographic shift has been described expertly by Arturo Pascal, who has traced the stages, first the obligatory halt in Lyons for the merchants among them who had business dealings there, and finally Geneva.[38] Here it is only necessary to recall that in the biennium 1555–57, next to the names of Vermigli's previously mentioned disciples, should be added those of the two carpenters, Giovanni Domenichi and Giovanni Antonio; the taffeta workers Ventura Venturini and Geronimo Castello; Regolo Benedetti, a weaver of silk; the tailor Marco de' Lauvini, and the physician Giovanni Baroncini. Their presence in the first wave of exiles is further evidence that the Reformation in Italy had its converts even in the lower ranks of society. But the truly dramatic aspect of the Lucchese participation in the movement comes from the fact that there is not a single family among the great patrician houses—from the Arnolfini and Balbani to the Tronconi and Turrettini—that does not have its representative in Calvin's Geneva.

---

[38]A. Pascal, "Da Lucca a Ginevra," *RSI* 49 (1932): 451–70; 50 (1933): 30–68, 211–61.

Repression of the "Lutheran Plague"

The 1550s were the years in Tuscany that witnessed the beginning of the repression of the "Lutheran plague," which culminated during the reign of Paul IV and Pius V. At the death of the Farnese pope, Paul III, and the ascension to the papal throne of Julius III, Cosimo's ecclesiastical politics experienced a dramatic shift. As long as he had to endure Paul's vexatious intrigues, the duke tolerated the anticlerical views and behavior of his closest collaborators, from Campana to Lelio Torelli, from Riccio to Bartolomeo Panciatichi. Although Cosimo had transformed the free Academy of the *Umidi* into the Florentine Academy, an organ of the state under his control, he had allowed Valdesianism to spread among the members. Since nothing eluded him, he was well aware of Paleario's discussions in Florence with the philosopher Verino, with Pier Vettori, with Riccio, and perhaps with Torelli. These were supposedly theoretical conversations about the immortality of the soul, the philosophy of Pomponazzi, Platonism, and Aristotelianism. But in those days of heated religious controversy, of oratorical duels from the pulpit between supporters and opponents of justification by faith, the duke and his counselors were cognizant of the verbal missiles that had been hurled against the papacy and, of course, of Johann Sleidan's previously mentioned oration published in Italian as *Il Capo finto*. After the dangers of a forceful takeover of Florence by Paul III had passed, Cosimo determined that it would be opportune to seek a rapprochement with the papacy. Moreover, in building his absolutist state, there could be no place for religious dissent, which was openly anti-Roman, out of fear that it might upset the political settlement. "Lutherans" now began to be scrutinized as closely as the surviving Savonarolans.

Francesco Puccerelli, notary to the tribunal of the *Mercanzia*, was arrested in November 1549, a few days after the death of Paul III, for having openly slandered the pope.[39] Since the offense involved a public official, the duke was infuriated and actually asked that the culprit be sentenced to the stake, but had to be content with a ten-year sentence to the galleys. Puccerelli's trial is not known to be extant, but precious clues concerning his thought and readings have come down to us in a few notes on the last leaf of the second volume of his notarial register for the years 1540 to 1547. It includes passages from Augustine's *De gratia et libero arbitrio* (chap. 8) and from the prophet Daniel (9:26–7). The first fragment deals with one of the most debated questions of the day, one that was of universal concern, namely the dignity and sanctity of marriage, juxtaposed to the celibate state. The passage affirms the freedom of choice between the celibate and conjugal life, both gifts of God. The Old Testament fragment was repeated in part by Jesus in his prophetic sermon announcing "the desolating sacrilege…standing in the holy place" (Matt. 24:15). The connection between the apparently discordant passages is clarified by B. Ochino in his *Imagine di Antecristo*, where the abomination in the holy place is related to the prohibition of marriage by the Antichrist. The notary Puccerelli penned his comments in

---

[39]See my "Un 'luterano' fiorentino del Cinquecento: Il notaio ser Francesco Puccerelli," in *Studi sulla Riforma*, 295–313.

1547, the year of violent controversies between the dissidents, avid readers of Ochino, and the Jesuits.

The case of Puccerelli, about whom nothing later is known except the brief reference in the *Diario di Firenze*, which states that he did not have his children baptized and had created a religion to suit his own taste, takes us back to his early career when he had been a peripatetic notary traversing the vast territory of the Florentine state as assessor of the tribunal of the *Mercanzia*. After 1534 we find him, almost always for six-month stretches, at Castrocaro, Péccioli in Val d'Era, Radda, Subbiano, Figline Valdarno, and finally at Fivizzano, at the judicial bench (*ad bancum iuris*) of the captain of the area, from July to October 1538. It would not be surprising if the notary became acquainted with the new ideas at Fivizzano, a strategic and commercial center situated at the very borders of Genoa, Modena, Parma, and Lucca.

The arrest of the writer Lodovico Domenichi, a member of the Florentine Academy, occurred almost at the same time as Puccerelli's. The former was accused of having translated and published with the title of *Nicomediana*, and the false place of publication of Basel, Calvin's booklet, *Excuse à messieurs les Nicodemites*. Domenichi had been commissioned to do it by Ludovico Manna, an ex-Sicilian Dominican (Fra Angelo da Messina), a Valdesian who was a friend of Carnesecchi and of Pietro Antonio di Capua, archbishop of Otranto. For a few years Manna had been living at Pisa in the home of the merchant Bernardo de' Ricasoli, and in league with him, Cola della Magona, and Lionardo de' Medici, had dedicated himself body and soul to promote Calvinism in Tuscany. Manna had arranged to import into Florence, concealed among bales of goods belonging to the Ricasoli firm, the *Considerazioni* of Valdés, the *Prediche* of Ochino, and the *Excuse* of Calvin. It is likely that Manna is the same person as that Aloisio *de regno neapolitano*, an itinerant minister at Grosseto and Siena.[40] Shortly before fleeing to Geneva, where he arrived at the same time as Celso Martinengo, he decided to have published Calvin's strong condemnation of religious dissimulation. The time must have finally come when Manna felt he had to drop that ambiguous Valdesian stance that was so widely held in Florence.

It is difficult to say what might have really prompted the courtier Domenichi to break the laws of the state by secretly publishing a heretical work. Equally, it is important to know how much of an influence the Modenese captain, Camillo Caula, who with his brother the notary Marco, was a Calvinist, may have had when he urged Domenichi to dedicate himself to evangelical teachings rather than to the classics. Domenichi may have simply wanted to accommodate his Calvinist friends, such as Manna, without necessarily accepting the message of the *Excuse*. After enduring his prison sentence in the convent of Santa Maria Novella, cut short thanks to the intercession of Duchess Renée, Domenichi was free once again in 1553 to assist the ducal printer Torrentino in the publication of Paolo Giovio's *Historie*. The following

---

[40]On Domenichi, in addition to my *Aonio Paleario*, 86–88, see A. D'Alessandro, "Prime ricerche su Ludovico Domenichi," in *Le corti farnesiane di Parma e Piacenza, 1545–1622.* Ed. A. Quondam (Rome: Bulzoni, 1978), 171–200.

year, Torrentino published two Italian translations of Erasmus: *Il paragone della vergine e del martire* and *Il Sermone della grandissima misericordia di Dio*. A *Commento del Paternoster* by Pico della Mirandola and a sonnet by Benedetto Varchi were joined to the *Paragone*. For the second work, the *Sermone*, only two men of letters, Domenichi and Pompeo della Barba, who was himself prosecuted later, had the courage to add accompanying sonnets of their own. Domenichi's is wholly pervaded by sentiments concerning divine grace:

> If because of your grace, and not through my merit,
> From the earth, in fact from nothing, I now breathe and live,
> And through your gift attain such heights,
> To Christ I am brother, and to you I am a son....[41]

Even after his acts of repentance, abjurations, and vacillations, Domenichi clung tenaciously, as did so many other Valdesians and sympathizers with the Reformation, to his beliefs in human powerlessness and freely given salvation.

Domenichi's arrest was not an isolated case. Between the end of 1551 and early 1552, as a consequence of the detailed accusations made by Pietro Manelfi to the Bolognese inquisitor on 17 October 1551, thirty-five members of a clandestine conventicle were arrested. Among those denounced by the renegade Anabaptist, we find, besides Manna, who is described as the patron for the translation of Calvin's book, a certain Giovanni Battista, hatmaker, who possessed "Lutheran books and especially the Nicodominicana." This suggests the existence of Calvinist sympathizers among Florentine and Venetian workers and artisans. In the words of the contemporary Florentine *Diario*, "Mingled in the sect were artisans and wealthy noblemen [who] disparaged the order of the Holy Roman Church and every holy rite. And they used to say that it sufficed to believe in God, and among them was a certain Bartolomeo Panciatichi, with the wealth of thirty thousand *scudi*."[42]

Manelfi's denunciations also snared an unnamed "defrocked monk" who is probably to be identified with someone we have already met, Cornelio Donzellino. On 12 February 1552 he sent an appeal from prison to the Medici official Pier Francesco Riccio, throwing himself on his mercy and begging for his intervention with Duke Cosimo. Donzellino, a former Dominican, had been forced to take the cowl by his father, but subsequently received papal dispensation to leave his convent. To keep him company he had found a poor orphan whom he kept as a wife for a year. "As for my beliefs," he concludes his letter to Riccio, "I remit myself in everything to the Holy and Catholic Roman Church." Donzellino was an able dissimulator who had come to Florence because he had friends and protectors there such as Domenichi and Manna, whom he had met originally in Venice. According to the diarist, the trial was thought to have concluded with a sentence to "perpetual imprisonment with

[41]S. Seidel Menchi, *Erasmo in Italia*, 409.
[42]Quoted from the "Diario di Firenze dal 1536 al 1555," in S. Caponetto, *Aonio Paleario*, 236, app. 2, 3; C. Ginzburg, *I costituti*, 39.

many others like him in Florence."[43] This source usually complements the information furnished by Manelfi, who in addition to Manna, Panciatichi and "master Leone the surgeon," adds the names of Ottaviano of Forlì, "a collar maker," Francesco and Pietro, "stocking makers," Paolo, a weaver of Montopoli, Niccolò, the Ferrarese carpenter, Pietro Orso and his brother Girolamo, goldsmiths.

The merchant and man of letters, Bartolomeo Panciatichi, was the most prominent figure among them. He was born in France in 1507 and had lived at Lyons until 1538, where his father, Bartolomeo, directed the largest Florentine commercial enterprise.[44] The young Bartolomeo received his education in the "seductive Lyonnais milieu," where one found in the bookshops and printing establishments what was most vital and innovative in European thought. The education he received leaned more to literature than to business and commerce. Evidence of this are his Latin and Italian poems and the fact that after his father's death, he left the running of the business to relatives.

Though an indifferent poet, he was esteemed by Rabelais, Dolet, and Lando, and struck up a friendship with Jean de Vauzelles, who had studied in Italian universities. Like so many others who remained anonymous, de Vazuelles, abbot of Montrottier, was caught up in the great spiritual movement intent on returning to the Gospels and St. Paul, advocated by such reform- minded persons as Lefèvre d'Étaples, Bishop Briçonnet, and Louis de Berquin. It manifested itself in the devotion they felt for their protectress, Marguerite de Navarre, to whom de Vauzelles addressed these sentiments: "Que vous demeuries à toujour la bonne Marguerite, que l'Evangile veult sur toutes choses apprécier." Panciatichi was the Frenchman's intermediary in the latter's translation of Pietro Aretino's works: the *Umanità di Cristo*, dedicated to Marguerite and the *Passione di Cristo*, both published at Paris in 1539.

In 1534 Panciatichi married Lucrezia Pucci and settled down in Florence, where he was welcomed warmly by the *literati* anxious to break out of the cultural isolation that followed the demise of Savonarola's republic and the establishment of Alessandro de' Medici's principate. On 20 January 1541, Panciatichi was accepted in the Academy of the *Umidi*, where he became one of the chief vote counters (*arroti*). On the thirty-first of the same month he became a reformer of the statutes of the Florentine Academy, together with Cosimo Bartoli, Alessandro Del Caccia, and Lorenzo Benivieni, and finally, in 1545, one of the academy's consuls. Anton Francesco Doni, in dedicating to Panciatichi his *Lezioni di accademici fiorentini sopra Dante*, called his term of office one of the most splendid. Panciatichi came into the good graces of Cosimo and the members of his secretariat of state and was dispatched to the court of Henry II and Catherine de' Medici on the occasion of the birth of their fourth child. But the real reason for the mission was to reestablish relations with the French monarchy, which

---

[43]G. Fragnito, "Un pratese alla corte di Cosimo I," 42, app. 11, and the note on Donzellino at 43.

[44]S. Caponetto, *Aonio Paleario*, 88–94. There is evidence for his presence as a student at the University of Padua during the years 1529–31. See F. Piavan, "Gli studi padovani di Bartolomeo Panciatichi," *Quaderni per la Storia dell'Università di Padova* 20 (1987): 119–22.

had frayed thanks to its conflicts with the Empire. From these trips to France (he returned to Lyons in 1539 and 1547) Panciatichi brought back news of the successes of the Reformation and books (some for Paleario), which probably included Calvin's *Institutes*. But Florence was not Lyons and Panciatichi was accused of heresy, arrested, and put on trial.

In September 1567 Paolo da Montopoli, a weaver who had been denounced by Pietro Manelfi sixteen years earlier, was imprisoned once again following charges lodged by fellow workers. Weavers from the quarter of San Frediano recalled the auto da fé celebrated on 6 February 1552 when Montopoli was sentenced the first time:

> fifteen years ago one saw Pagolo di Bartolomeo da Montopoli, called "il Bello," in the *piazza* of San Giovanni wearing a yellow tunic with a red cross in its center, holding a lighted torch in his hand. And on that square a hutch had been constructed filled with books, and Pagolo, together with many other men and women garbed just like him, set fire to the hutch and then filed into the cathedral of Santa Maria del Fiore where they were made to sit on a platform. And here various ceremonies were performed and then they were marched around Florence in their yellow tunics holding their torches.[45]

Not all guilty parties, however, were compelled to participate in the humiliating spectacle. The duke, depriving the inquisitor of full satisfaction, only permitted "the most perfidious and ignoble by birth," the lowest and most wretched among the populace, to march in the procession. Patricians and the wealthy were spared. On 12 February, three women "who shared their husbands' madness," were brought to the church of San Simone and "in the presence of the congregation, were reconciled" to the church.[46]

Panciatichi was released from prison after paying a large indemnity, and a few days later, on 24 February 1552, was elected a consul of the academy. He was getting a new start in politics and in 1567 he became a senator, to the displeasure of clerical circles, followed by appointment as commissioner for Pisa, and in 1578, for Pistoia. Panciatichi's sympathies for Calvinism and the Huguenot party by now must have been a distant memory.

Agnolo Bronzino made two justly famous portraits of Bartolomeo and Lucrezia Panciatichi, which today hang in the gallery of the Uffizi in Florence: "they are so natural, that they truly appear alive, and all that they lack is the spirit." The blonde Lucrezia, that "noble daughter of silence," like a luminous presence shining through an opening in the darkness, delicately rests her hand on a Book of Hours, open to a section of *Laudes* where we read the conclusion of Psalm 149: "Laudate Dominum de coelis..." and on the right, legibly, the hymn to Mary:

O gloriosa Domina
Excelsa supra sidera
Qui te creavit provide

---

[45]A. Prosperi, "L'inquisizione fiorentina dopo il Concilio di Trento," *Annuario dell'Istituto Storico Italiano* 37–38 (1985–86): 107.

[46]S. Caponetto, *Aonio Paleario*, 236–37.

Lactasti sacro ubere.
Quod Eva tristis abstulit
Tu reddis almo germine....

The paintings were executed in the early 1540s, the very years that Valdesianism was spreading in Florence and Tuscany.

Some symptoms of resistance to inquisitorial repression appeared on the part of Protestant sympathizers in the upper ranks of society, joined in some measure by artisans and laborers. But the Holy Office and the indefatigable Jesuits joined forces to protect orthodoxy in preaching, teaching, the cure of souls, printing and the book trade, and in suffocating dissent in the Augustinians, dispersing the Lutheran and Calvinist conventicles, imprisoning the more tenacious believers, shutting down the furtive gatherings of Paleario and his companions, eliminating the minor religious rebellion within the Florentine Academy, and silencing Panciatichi, Domenichi, Riccio, Varchi, Bartoli, Doni, Del Caccia, and Gelli, whose *Capricci del Bottaio* were placed on the 1554 *Index of Prohibited Books*.

On 18 March 1559 and the days following, great bonfires of prohibited and heretical books, which obviously had been circulating in large numbers, were lit in the squares before the cathedral of San Giovanni and the church of Santa Croce. Intellectual and governing circles, with some reluctance (we know of the opposition of Cosimo's first Secretary, Lelio Torelli, who upheld the jurisdiction of the secular sphere, to the publication of the 1559 *Index*) had to adapt to the duke's new political orientation. Here and there a few relics lingered of a dissent that was now almost impossible to maintain. Some may have tried to hide a vernacular New Testament, the *Prediche* of Giulio della Rovere, or the *Unio dissidentium* of Hermannus Bodius. Ochino's *Prediche* in the 1562 edition were confiscated from a miller of Montelupo, a certain Lucantonio, who had drawn from them such clear and precise concepts as that Christ's blood had liberated him from hell and that the daily drudgery of his mill was his purgatory. An innkeeper, a priest, and a shoemaker used to meet with Lucantonio in his mill for readings and discussions.[47]

A French artisan, Andrea, a jewelry maker, with his wife, two daughters, a servant, and other family members, were considered to be "Lutherans," "because they never attend Mass and have been seen eating meat on Holy Thursday." At home they kept "French and Lutheran books, and finally live just as they please." On 25 August 1564, the archiepiscopal vicar asked secular authorities to proceed with their arrest so that they might be questioned and their accomplices identified.[48] The spies of the Inquisition were relentless, knowing that they could profit their pocketbooks as well as their souls.

---

[47]A. Prosperi, "L'Inquisizione fiorentina," 110–12.
[48]A. D'Addario, *Aspetti della Controriforma a Firenze* (Rome: Ministero dell'Interno, 1972), 489.

THE SIENESE OPPOSITION

There is no doubt that Tuscan dissidents, who aspired to an alternate church from the one of Rome, attempted to link up and create an embryonic organization. Its chief promoter was the dynamic Sicilian Ludovico Manna, who would become catechist in the Italian exiles' church in Geneva during the ministry of Celso Martinengo. The publication of the *Nicomediana* fits into this program. The same year that a hatmaker in Pisa astounded the congregation by assailing the preacher in the church of San Francesco, Anton Francesco Doni, who had set up a printing shop in Florence in collaboration with Domenichi, mailed off to Siena the confession of faith of a weaver made shortly before his death, 28 November 1546. The document conveys the religious sentiments of a person who, though uneducated, had carefully appropriated Calvinist teachings, which he expounded with a wealth of details, from the predestination of the elect to the concept of the church itself as "a gathering of all those elected through divine predestination, who have existed from the beginning of the world and will exist to the end." The head of this church was Jesus Christ "in whom dwells the fullness of divinity," as sole mediator and advocate.[49]

The addressee of Doni's missive was the barber of the *Balìa*, Siena's governing magistracy, Basilio Guerrieri, who was to distribute it among the brethren in the city. Guerrieri had become a sympathizer of the Reformation after having attentively studied the letter that Bernardino Ochino, whose fiery sermons he had listened to in 1539 and 1540, had written in 1543 to the *Balìa* to explain his flight to the Protestant north. The document made such an impression on Guerrieri that it prompted him to travel to Strasbourg and then to Augsburg, where the former general of the Capuchins was then residing. After returning to Siena, Guerrieri began to cautiously proselytize in artisan circles seeking to work through the existing ecclesiastical institutions while imparting a message of gradual spiritual renewal, which probably had been suggested to him by Ochino himself.

On the eve of the feast of All Saints in 1544, in the artisan confraternity of the Holy Trinity, Pietro Antonio, the son of a goldsmith, astonished everyone present by challenging the veneration of saints, who, he claimed, should be only imitated and not worshipped or adored, since "in no way can they pray for us in heaven.... We have only one mediator, Jesus Christ."[50] Interrogation of the young goldsmith yielded up precious information for the Inquisition. The inspiration for his heretical preaching had come from the master of the converts, Basilio Guerrieri, who was a member of a small group guided by Lelio Sozzini, composed of students from leading families such as Buonsignor Finetti, Orazio Ragnoni, Antonio Maria Rocchi, Giovan Battista Tolomei, Giovanni Scotti, as well as a few artisans, among whom were Pietro Antonio and Guerrieri. Finetti and Ragnoni, the brother of Lattanzio Ragnoni, future pastor of the Italian exiles' church in Geneva, and Scotti were

---

[49]V. Marchetti, *Gruppi ereticali*, 260–63, app. 4, letter of A. F. Doni to B. Guerrieri, Florence, 28 November 1546.
[50]Ibid., 51–61, esp. 51.

students at the University of Padua. Pietro Antonio retracted his heretical harangue publicly and was pardoned; the other suspects had all left Siena.

The episode marked the organizational beginnings of a clandestine movement of protest, destined to develop through the tenacious actions and clear vision of Guerrieri, together with the sons of Mariano Sozzini, returned from Bologna. The Erasmian and Valdesian phase of Sienese religious history, which Paleario had inaugurated when he arrived in 1530, had ended. It had begun when he opened his school for instruction in Latin and Greek, through which he won the esteem of Bartolomeo Carli Piccolomini, Bernardino Buoninsegni, and other youths of the nobility. Moreover, as tutor within the politically powerful family of Antonio Bellanti, Paleario was able to assert his claims in the defense of culture and freedom of thought, which incurred the wrath of Master Vittorio da Firenze, a member of the Florentine theological faculty. Through the 1530s, Paleario still nurtured hopes for a free council that would reform and reunify the church along Erasmian lines, but after his 1542 trial became withdrawn, contenting himself with the company of his students and their families.

Carli Piccolomini was influenced by his teacher, but in turn, as a man of letters and an elegant writer in Italian, pressured Paleario to employ the vernacular to promote the spread of the new ideas. It appears that a small work was produced in collaboration, one that remained in manuscript and does not seem to have survived, entitled "Della pienezza, satisfazione e sufficienza del sangue di Cristo," clearly a defense of the doctrine of justification by faith in Christ. Piccolomini had been won over to Valdesianism by Ochino's preaching in Siena. According to a recent scholarly opinion, Piccolomini's *Regola utile e necessaria a ciascuna persona che cerchi di vivere come fedele e buon Christiano*, published posthumously at Venice in 1542, draws heavily from the *Alfabeto cristiano* of Juan de Valdés.[51] The premature death (1539?) of the Sienese contributed to the close of the Valdesian phase in Tuscany. Ochino's apostasy, a few years later, compelled his followers to devise new strategies, and this was precisely what Girolamo Pieri and Basilio Guerrieri proposed to do.

Pieri (b. 1495, d. before 1568) came from a family of Grosseto, and in 1526 was entrusted with the position of supervisor (*provveditore*) of the territory's defenses. As he moved about, he freely publicized the themes of Ochino's 1543 letter to the government of Siena, reading it and commenting on it to friends, one of whom was the Sienese physician, Achille Benvoglienti, who had been transferred to Grosseto. On top of his medical duties, Benvoglienti discussed the philosophy of Aristotle with young men of the city, then moved on to Ochino's published sermons and Curione's fascinating, satirical *Pasquino in estasi*. With the addition of the Sienese Attilio Marsili, Leonardo Benvoglienti, and Cristoforo Turamini, who were embarking on their medical careers under Achille Benvoglienti's tutelage, and of a few other persons of Grosseto, an evangelical conventicle came into being. The 1568 trial against one of the most confirmed believers among them, the previously mentioned notary Fabio Cioni, sheds light on the ideas espoused by the members and on their social

---

[51] See the biographical sketch by V. Marchetti and R. Belladonna, in *DBI*, 20: 194–96.

background. They were followers of Calvin, whose works along with the Bible, were available to them. This mixed group of relatively affluent young men from the Siena-Grosseto area were joined by two Frenchmen, one of whom, the student Nicolas Felix de Champagne, had brought with him Erasmus's *De infinita misericordia Dei*. For a time, another previously encountered figure, the itinerant Neapolitan preacher Aloisio, also was a member, and perhaps even the Venetian Marcantonio Varotta. When Achille Benvoglienti and the other Sienese returned home, the conventicle broke up.

Larger significance and much longer life were enjoyed in Siena by the group gravitating around Basilio Guerrieri. It has been noted that after his meeting with Ochino at Augsburg in March 1546, he returned to Siena to begin his work of pros-elytization among the artisans of the city with whom he was in daily contact. To the home of the patrician Giovanni Battista Tolomei, he had invited a stonecutter, a sta-tioner, two tanners, and a shoemaker. They were joined by the elderly Girolamo Pieri and the preacher Aloisio. In this milieu, animated by a hostility against the elevated classes and provoked by economic hard times, the preacher portrayed priests as deceivers: "For every time that you went to confession or communion, you were defrauded, because they took your property and your honor. And they also want to take your souls because they want us to understand things their way. I tell you that Christ is not in that host."[52] These words, spoken to people whose ears were attuned to the needs of daily life, introduced concepts of gratuitous salvation, the uselessness of the cult of saints, culminating in the denial of the real presence of Christ in the Eucharist. The Church of Rome was rejected and the reformed communion offered as a possible alternative.

From the street, the new ideas entered the convent. One of the bearers was the gentleman Antonio Maria Rocchi and the recipient his sister Dionisia, a nun in the Augustinian convent of San Paolo. For months at a time he went to "the grate" explaining the evangelical teachings clearly and simply, from the uniqueness of Scrip-ture as the Word of God, to the rejection of monasticism as contrary to the divine plan of creation, culminating in the rejection of the Church of Rome, because "the faithful are the true church." The true church, he said, literally repeating the Calvin-ist creed, is the one where we find "the ministry of the Gospel properly exercised and the pure administration of the sacraments." Sister Dionisia had come to such a firm awareness of truth, that she could declare to the inquisitors sitting in judgment over her: "I believe and ratify as above placing my faith in the Evangelists and the apostles who cannot err."[53] Three fellow nuns from noble families were prosecuted with her and all abjured. They were Francesca Venturi, Giulia Forteguerri, and Eugenia Van-nini. Marcantonio Varotta, who was being tried in Venice, recalled that he had been told of these proceedings when he was still in Siena:

> There were some nuns within [that convent] who were Calvinist heretics,
> and a few days before a sister had been investigated because the abbess

---

[52] V. Marchetti, *Gruppi ereticali*, 97.
[53]Ibid., 102–4.

accused her with the others. But she was prosecuted for being the leader who taught the others. She said that they had been converted [to the church] easily, but not that sister [Dionisia], and it was expected that she would go to the stake.[54]

Even Dionisia Rocchi managed to save herself, by making a long abjuration of all her errors (1566), which may have been a sort of liberation for her from an absurd Nicodemite practice that had endured for twenty years! Her first trial and abjuration had taken place in 1546.

When Siena rebelled against Spanish domination on 27 July 1552, a new phase began in the diffusion of religious dissent. Basilio Guerrieri was one of the protagonists in the effort, "a skillful man and greatly enamored of his country." In spite of his modest social position he was entrusted with some delicate missions. Lelio Sozzini made a hasty return from Switzerland bringing with him the hopes of Vergerio and other exiles that freedom would be gained from the Spaniards, "but also from every other sort of slavery." Sozzini succeeded, during his short visit, in introducing the Scriptures in the version of Antonio Brucioli to the patrician Marcantonio Cinuzzi, secretary of the governing council, who was a man of letters and a poet, and to the farrier, Bartolomeo Nelli. The latter worked in a shop owned by Sozzini, who taught him that "our works do not merit anything…we are saved through Christ."[55] But the end of the republic and Cosimo's assumption of power may be said to conclude the growth phase of the Protestant movement in Siena. Guerrieri disappeared from circulation. During 1559 and for part of 1560, four pro-Medici and philo-Protestant members of the nobility—Niccolò Spannocchi, Francesco Buoninsegni, Cinuzzi, and Lelio Pecci—were assigned to important positions in the government of the "new state." Closely associated with the governor, Agnolo Niccolini, thanks to their loyalty to the duke, the four patricians were able to deflect any suspicions that might have been raised over their orthodoxy, but they made no conversions. Worries about the activity of "certain tiny sects" increased with the return from Bologna in the fall of 1557 of the children and nephews of Mariano Sozzini, who had died the previous year.

The Jesuits became quite concerned and informed their general in Rome about these developments. Lainez concurred and asked for the intervention of the Roman Inquisition. When the suspects in Siena, with Spannocchi at their head, discovered these machinations, they began a campaign against the presence of the Society of Jesus in their city. They were supported in their efforts by friends and family members drawn from their social class, preoccupied, even though they themselves were orthodox, with the stain that the accusation of heresy would cast on their families. At night they had placards hung at street corners with slogans attacking the Society. No trace has survived of some of the blasphemous verse employed, but priests knew they were accused of being "liars, sodomites, adulterers, adulators, spies, scourges of poor

[54]Ibid., 105–6.
[55]Ibid., 129–31.

widows." The author might have been Marcantonio Cinuzzi, who in his unpublished poem, the "Papeide," used similar attributes in his anti-Jesuit invective:

Now this is the unfrocked militia
These are those soldiers so brave
Who are in the pay of his saintliness.[56]

In August 1559, Michele Ghislieri, commissioner of the Supreme Congregation in Rome, appointed Fra Angelo da Pistoia, prior of the Dominican convent, as inquisitor over the entire Sienese dominion. Towards the end of 1559, Spannocchi, who had gone to Bologna on business, was arrested on suspicions of heresy. Cosimo de' Medici's immediate intervention brought his release within a matter of days. The vituperations of the accused against the Jesuits, whom he considered responsible for the inquisitorial presence, led the Society to draw up a memorandum identifying Sienese heretics, which was mailed off to Ghislieri, who was poorly disposed to heed the duke's recommendations.

In mid-1560, the Bolognese Paolo Cataldi, master of writing and arithmetic in the home of the noblewoman Porzia Venturi, and a guest of Cornelio and Camillo Sozzini, was accused through an anonymous denunciation of having denied the authority of the pope and the sacrament of the Eucharist. Cataldi's students, Giulio and Lucrezio Venturi, confirmed their teacher's heresy, reporting that he told them "it was madness to believe that Christ was in the consecrated host and that he would allow himself to be eaten by men." Cataldi admitted that he had possessed Brucioli's version of the Scriptures, a copy of Erasmus's *Enchiridion*, an unidentified Biblical treatise, and some books of magic. He concluded by admitting his doctrinal errors, which he said he had acquired from the two Sozzini who had wanted to make a proselytizer out of him:

First they converted me on the sacrament of the Eucharist, that I should believe that the true body and blood of Christ were not really present, but that they were only a sign and commemoration of the Passion. Concerning confession they used to say that it should be made only to God and not to priests. About the pope, they used to say that he did not have the authority to absolve nor remit sins and that his indulgences were not to be believed in. Also that we were not to possess images, either in churches or at home, and that we were not to doff our hats to them or pay them reverence.[57]

The proceedings against Cataldi led to a search for the Sozzini. Dario was arrested but Camillo and Fausto were warned in time and decamped from the family villa at Scopeto outside Siena. Cornelio, trusting in his good relations with Duke Cosimo, who was not inclined to harshness where his faithful nobility was concerned, allowed himself to be arrested. Despite a full abjuration, Cataldi was conducted to Rome to be held at the disposal of the Inquisition, followed by Cornelio

[56]Ibid., 148–64.
[57]Ibid., 212, 217.

Sozzini. The duke had sacrificed his subjects in exchange for the title of grand duke of Tuscany conferred on him by the pope.

In the meantime, investigations were continuing in Siena, with the interrogation and then imprisonment of Cornelio's wife, Francesca. She firmly denied all the accusations brought against her husband and brother-in-law, Camillo, and also tried to shield Fausto and Dario. A search of the villa at Scopeto yielded up little of consequence, except perhaps that there were no sacred images in the house. Due to her fragile health, Francesca was released without having given satisfaction to her husband's accusers. The group of the Sozzini was now dispersed and all its members left Siena between 1561 and 1563. Some of their friends went to study in Bologna, Padua, and Rome. Others returned to their usual routines and put their defeated hopes behind them. Cornelio eventually regained his freedom; Spannocchi died in 1563. Of the circle of the Sozzini, the elderly Marcantonio Cinuzzi paid most dearly for his prominence as man of letters and statesman. On 2 November 1578 he was arrested and transferred to Rome the following year to be at the disposal of the supreme tribunal. He was allowed to return to Siena four years later, perhaps after making an abjuration of his errors.[58]

The foregoing discussion, based largely on the results of Valerio Marchetti's archival discoveries, has highlighted only the most conspicuous aspects of Siena's flirtation with heresy. But less obvious currents of sympathy for the Reformation existed both at popular and educated levels of society. Among the latter, for example, it was only after his flight from Italy in 1569 that the evangelical sentiments of Mino Celsi (1541–75) came to be known.[59] As a friend of Cinuzzi, Paleario, Alessandro Bellanti and Claudio Tolomei, bishop of Curzola, he had been an active member of the Academy of the Intronati, serving on the city's governing magistracy, the *Balìa*, in 1546 and on four other occasions after the Medici conquest. Celsi fulfilled important embassies for Siena in 1545 (to Milan) and again from 1555 to 1556. In mid-July 1569 he left the city to avoid a summons from the Roman Inquisition. On the thirty-first of the month the governor, Federico Montaguto, informed Cosimo of the fact and set it in the context of the ongoing trial in Rome against Paleario that had been dragging on for two years. When Celsi reached Basel, he matriculated in the university by taking advantage of assistance available for religious exiles and there formed an attachment with the city's more liberal elements, from Boniface Amerbach to Theodore Zwinger. The fame of the Sienese rests on a work published posthumously by Pietro Perna in 1577: the *In haereticis coërcendis quatenus progredi liceat Mini Celsi Senensis disputatio*. It is one of the earlier toleration manifestos, condemning the coercion of consciences whether practiced by Catholics or Protestants; it was influenced by the teachings of both Erasmus, who is highly praised in the work, and Sebastian Castellio.[60]

---

[58]See the sketch by Marchetti in *DBI*, 25:650–54.
[59]See the sketch by P. Bietenholz, in *DBI*, 23:478–82.
[60]There is a critical edition of the work by P. Bietenholz in the *Corpus Reformatorum Italicorum* (Naples & Chicago: PRISMI–The Newberry Library, 1982).

BIBLIOGRAPHICAL NOTE

For Lucca, see R. Ristori, "Le origini della Riforma a Lucca," *Rinascimento*, 3 (1952): 269–92; S. Adorni-Braccesi, "Il dissenso religioso nel contesto urbano lucchese della Controriforma," in *Città italiane del '500* (Lucca: M. Pacini Fazzi, 1988), 225–39. On Lyons, "the French Florence," cosmopolitan cultural center and banking and commercial capital, see L. Romier, "Lyon et le cosmopolitisme au début de la Renaissance," *BHR* 11 (1949): 28–42. [The recent formal opening of the Holy Office in Rome reveals that it houses, virtually intact, the archive of the Sienese Inquisition, transferred to that repository in 1911. Trans. note.]

17

THE COUNTER-REFORMATION

A Resurgent Papacy

WE TURN NOW TO THE EVENTS that marked the religious struggle in the second half of the century, culminating in the tragedy of the Waldensian colonies of Calabria, the forced return to the Catholic faith of their co-religionaries in Puglia, the Neapolitan revolt against the introduction of the Spanish Inquisition, the martyrdom of the Calvinists Bartolomeo Bartoccio, Gian Luigi Pascale, Giacomo Bonello, of the Valdesians Gian Francesco Alois, Pietro Carnesecchi, Pompeo delli Monti, and of the reformed Erasmian, Aonio Paleario. First, it is essential to cast a glance at the historical background against which these events occurred, namely the formidable revival experienced by the papacy and Catholicism, and the doctrinal, disciplinary, and moral restoration of the Church of Rome in line with the decrees of the Council of Trent and the rigorous, reforming popes Paul IV and Pius V. With the election just a few years apart of two grand inquisitors to the summit of the hierarchy, the Counter-Reformation could unleash all its resources to halt the spread of the Protestant revolt and embark on a purification of ecclesiastical life.

By May 1555, when Gian Pietro Carafa, cofounder of the Theatines and organizer of the supreme tribunal of the Inquisition was elected pope, the Roman church had lost two-thirds of Germany, England, the Scandinavian countries, much of Switzerland and the Low Countries, a part of Austria, Poland, and Hungary. France was torn by the successes of Calvinism and of the Huguenots. Moreover, Calvin had turned Geneva into the capital of European Protestantism, a city of refuge for the persecuted of France, Spain, and Italy from which daring missionaries set out to evangelize the continent.

The "Lutheran plague" had become a mortal danger for the Church of Rome, its teachings impugned by a sea of books and pamphlets of controversy and Protestant propaganda. It had suffered disastrous financial losses through the confiscation of ecclesiastical property in Germany, England, and Scandinavia, and its cultural prestige was at an ebb because of its condemnation of the works of Erasmus and also the curtailing of the freedom of thought and expression. This was the historical situation when Paul IV ascended the papal throne. At the age of seventy-nine, he possessed an energy and zeal for governing that filled the entire College of Cardinals with fear. Haunted by the idea that his bishops and cardinals had been contaminated by Protestantism, he blocked the rise to the pinnacles of the hierarchy of Pole and Morone in every way he could, since he considered them heretical for their perceived willingness to compromise with the Reformation. In 1557, during his ill-conceived enterprise against the Spain of Philip II, Paul ordered the arrest and incarceration in Castel Sant'Angelo of Cardinal Morone, and recalled Cardinal Pole from England where he had collaborated with Catholic Mary to bring the island back to Roman obedience, without opposing her cruel repression of the Protestants.

An episode, which as well as any other evokes the pope's fanatical conviction that he had been called by God to eradicate heretical pravity whatever the cost, was a conversation he had with the Venetian ambassador Bernardo Navagero in October 1557. After hurling recriminations against Pole, Priuli, and Marcantonio Flaminio, regretting especially that he had not been able to send the last named to the stake, the octogenarian pontiff vented his ire against his own nephew, Galeazzo Caracciolo, marquis of Vico, who, abandoning his wife, children, and property had fled to Calvin's Geneva. At this point, the pontiff broke off the painful discussion with these searing words: "Honorable ambassador, let us speak no more of this matter, because if my very father had been a heretic, I would be the first to bring the faggots to burn him."[1]

The *Compendium processuum Sancti Officii Romae* is an "indispensable lens" through which to view "the mental attitudes" of the great protagonists of the Counter-Reformation, as Massimo Firpo has astutely observed. "No mere repertory of names and facts, the *Compendium* constitutes a historical document of the first order for the reconstruction of an important aspect of sixteenth-century history, since within it those rigid controversialist models take the form which would so profoundly characterize the institutions and cultural life of the Counter-Reformation."[2] The document, compiled from the testimony presented at Morone's trial, gives the impression of having been intended to purge the ecclesiastical hierarchy, so large were the numbers of highly placed churchmen suspected of "believing erroneously" in matters of the faith, many of whom would be prosecuted under Paul IV.

Carnesecchi, in a letter to Giulia Gonzaga dated June 1557, remarked ruefully that "the pope seems to be intending to fill his prisons with cardinals and bishops on behalf of the Inquisition."[3] In turn, Federico von Salis, a patrician of the Valtellina, wrote from Venice to Bullinger describing the Italian situation two years after Paul's elevation to the papacy:

> In this Republic and, generally, everywhere in Italy where the pope has spiritual jurisdiction, as we say, the faithful are subjected to extremely rigorous surveillance. Inquisitors have complete authority to make arrests even on

---

[1]Quoted from B. Croce, *Un calvinista italiano: Il marchese di Vico Galeazzo Caracciolo* (Bari: Laterza, 1973). Reprinted in Croce's *Vite di avventura, di fede e di passione* (Milan: Adelphi, 1989).

[2]M. Firpo & D. Marcatto, *Il processo inquisitoriale del cardinale Giovanni Morone, I: Il Compendium* (Rome: Istituto storico italiano per l'età moderna e contemporanea, 1981), 87–88.

[3]"Processo Carnesecchi," 216–18.

the most trivial evidence, to proceed to interrogation with torture, which is more terrible than death, and extradite the prisoner to Rome, which had been unheard of before the accession of the present pope.[4]

The Holy Office, personally directed by the pontiff, ended by breaking the resistance of the secular authorities, including the reluctant Venetian Republic, which was now obliged to execute the sentences of the ecclesiastical tribunals or despatch the prisoners to Rome. The Counter-Reformation succeeded in establishing close control over publishing, the printing presses, academies, and the universities. In 1559 a draconian *Index of Prohibited Books* was published over the objections of printers and booksellers whose establishments were subject to inspection.

As the Council of Trent proceeded with its work, by the conclusion of its early sessions (1545–47; 1551–52), the hierarchy possessed definitive dogmatic pronouncements on doctrines that been debated with Protestants over grace, faith and works, justification, Scripture, the sacraments, the significance of the mass, and so forth. It was no longer possible to take refuge in a lack of theological clarity or of official decrees on the part of the church's magisterium. Preachers now had to abandon the individual theological traditions of their various religious orders.

In this enormous effort of doctrinal reconstruction and of disciplinary and moral reform, the church found unforeseen help in the Society of Jesus. After it had received papal approval from Paul III with the bull *Regimini militantis* (27 September 1540), the new order fanned out with extraordinary rapidity throughout Europe, Africa, the Indies, and South America. The rigid discipline imposed by Ignatius Loyola, the high level of education of its members, their conviction that they were acting *ad maiorem Dei gloriam*, their personal piety, and their spirit of self-denial turned the Society in a few years into the church's most valuable instrument in its own reform and in its struggle with Protestantism. Contemporaneously, Jesuits dedicated themselves to the instruction of the children of the nobility and the governing classes, opening colleges in the principal Italian and European cities. They also dedicated themselves to teaching the common people, ably exploiting popular psychology and the collective imagination by reviving liturgical functions, processions, pilgrimages, and sacred representations. As the inquisitors' most effective collaborators, they were also active in the work of repression.

THE PERSECUTION OF THE "SPIRITUALI"

During the reigns of Paul IV and Pius V the most energetic suppression of religious dissent was directed against the *"spirituali"* among the Valdesians and in the entourage of Cardinal Pole. All preceding trials were now reexamined and in a brief span of time during the biennium from 1557 to 1558, the prisons of the Roman Inquisition filled with the likes of Pietro Antonio di Capua, archbishop of Otranto, Giovanni Tom-

---

[4]Quoted from A. Aubert, "Alle origini della Controriforma: Studi e problemi su Paolo IV," *RSLR* 22 (1986): 342–43.

maso Sanfelice, bishop of Cava, Giovanni Francesco Verdura, bishop of Cheronissa, Egidio Foscherari, bishop of Modena, the knight Mario Galeota, the nobleman of Messina Bartolomeo Spadafora, the Neapolitan abbot Marcantonio Villamarino, Cardinal Giovanni Morone, and his chaplain Domenico Morando, among others. The persecution of Valdesians would culminate under Pius V with the great trial against Pietro Carnesecchi.

The magnificent edition of the Morone trial published by Massimo Firpo and Dario Marcatto, and the several important related studies they have dedicated to it, enlighten us fully on the significance and purpose of these proceedings. The intransigents in the College of Cardinals, guided by Carafa, had succeeded in turning the Holy Office into

> a highly efficient instrument of political action…for the purpose of imposing their policies on the entire Church…. It is in this historical perspective, and in its complex religious and political manifestations that we should place the Morone affair as a decisive moment in the bitter struggle fought by inquisitors against their adversaries who represented an extreme danger because they occupied positions high in the hierarchy, had been entrusted with delicate responsibilities, in a few cases had attained the dignity of the cardinalate and had been only a step or two from elevation to the papal throne. With this in mind, the judicial proceedings were being conducted not so much against a single individual and his alleged doctrinal deviations, as against recent pernicious developments in their totality. It was a decisive moment among the crises and milestones through which the Church of the Counter-Reformation broke with the age of the Renaissance.[5]

The resulting fracture was profound and unbridgeable. Erasmian irenicism with its vision of a church of Christ united and reformed, a vision that had inspired the *"spirituali"* from Contarini to Morone, and in part also the Valdesians, now was but a failed, youthful dream to the survivors.

Very little is known about the trials conducted in this period, with the exception of the cases of Morone, Carnesecchi, and Paleario due to the well-known losses suffered by the archive of the Holy Office in Rome, first during the tumult following the death of Paul IV in 1559, and many centuries later at the hands of Napoleon. One wonders what precious information might have been revealed by the trial against the nobleman of Messina, Bartolomeo Spadafora, fought over by both the Sicilian and Roman tribunals of the Inquisition, and on whose behalf the Republic of Venice, Charles V, and Philip II exerted themselves. Was Spadafora incarcerated in Rome for three years as an "imperialist" and ally of Morone, or because he was a Valdesian, a friend of Vittoria Colonna and Michelangelo?

The trials against Morone, Carnesecchi, and Paleario constituted the climax of investigations initiated in the 1540s, of previous trials and absolutions, and of com-

---

[5]M. Firpo, "La fase [difensiva] del processo inquisitoriale del Cardinal Morone: Documenti e problemi," *Critica Storica* 23 (1986): 144–45.

mon spiritual journeys shared by the protagonists even if their ultimate fate differed profoundly among them. Morone was absolved in 1560 by Pius IV and crowned his dramatic career as the last president of the Council of Trent, once again providing a tremendous service to that Church of Rome, from which, like Pole, he had never conceived of separating.

THE LOYALTY OF CARNESECCHI

Carnesecchi's situation differed. Along with Giulia Gonzaga, he deemed inopportune, "scandalous in fact," the declaration of loyalty to the Church of Rome made by Pole before his death. While Carnesecchi was residing in Venice he had entered into contact with the Calvinist conventicle that included Piero Gelido and Andrea da Ponte. When Carnesecchi was put on trial for a second time in November 1557, he was "tempted" to follow his friends into exile in Switzerland. But he decided against such a fatal step, so as not to further prejudice the positions of companions languishing in inquisitorial prisons, but also not to sunder his warm relationship with Countess Giulia Gonzaga, who persuaded him against such a dramatic decision. Carnesecchi thus remained under cover in Venice until he was absolved by Pius IV.

At Gonzaga's death on 16 April 1566, the inquisitors confiscated her papers, and found among them her correspondence with Carnesecchi and other friends, thus providing the authorities a virtual map of the vast Valdesian movement. On 26 June Pius V obtained from Cosimo the extradition to Rome of the protonotary who had long been a loyal servant of the Medici family. Carnesecchi's trial, published in 1870 by the bibliophile Count Giacomo Manzoni, is one of our most important sources for many aspects of Italian religious life in the first half of the sixteenth century.

In a first phase of the proceedings, Carnesecchi vacillated and attempted to explain his erroneous beliefs by the doctrinal uncertainties that had prevailed before Trent. But after he was interrogated under torture, he ended up confessing that he had, in effect, "agreed not only with Valdés, but even with Luther on the article of justification" and "the other articles which followed from it." He also declared candidly how he had believed that every person who upheld justification by faith had discovered "the mystery of the Christian faith" and that those who accepted it were God's elect. They felt themselves to be "friends and brothers" in the knowledge of this secret. Carnesecchi's judges were not satisfied with his testimony. They had hoped for a fuller retraction of his errors and revelations that would compromise his former associates who were still living.[6] The sentence solemnly pronounced against him on 21 September 1567 concluded with the words: "And finally you believed in all the errors and heresies contained in the aforesaid book, the *Beneficio di Cristo*, and in the false doctrine and institutions of the above mentioned Juan de Valdés, your master."[7] The condemnation to capital punishment was carried out on the square of

---

[6]See Carnesecchi's memorial to the inquisitors, written 8 July 1567, now in O. Ortolani, *Pietro Carnesecchi*, 154–56. Cf. the sketch by A. Rotondò in *DBI*, 20:466–76.

[7]O. Ortolani, *Pietro Carnesecchi*, 164–65; 256–57.

the Castel Sant'Angelo on 1 October by beheading and subsequent burning of the cadaver. The victim faced his martyrdom serenely and elegantly, with "a white shirt, and a new pair of gloves clutching a white handkerchief."

THE INTEGRITY OF AN INTELLECTUAL

Paleario's decision to abandon the quiet of his Tuscan retreat at Cecignano for Milan was influenced by his desire to settle in a strategically located urban center that would provide a vantage point to observe Italian and European events, neighboring Geneva and other places in Switzerland where so many of his Lucchese and Tuscan friends had found refuge. These factors weighed more on Paleario than financial considerations and the need to provide for the education and dowries of his daughters. He was convinced that only sweeping political and religious changes in Europe would raise Italy from its servile attachment to the papacy. He interpreted the peace signed by the emperor with the Protestants at Augsburg on 25 September 1555 as the beginning of recognition for the Lutheran confession. He also understood it to mean that the deliberations of the Council of Trent were now superfluous, as was recourse to the force of arms to crush the religious protest.

Paleario's summons to Milan as professor of Latin and Greek literature had been determined by the senate, upon a motion made by its president, Francesco Grasso, eminent jurist and orator. But behind the invitation it is not difficult to discern the hidden machinations of the Erasmians, Luigi Annibale Della Croce and Primo Conte. We know the former as friend of Lucchese Erasmians, Ortensio Lando, Giulio della Rovere, and Celio Secondo Curione from Basel, who sent him his student, Basil Amerbach. As a young man, Primo Conte had been in correspondence with Erasmus and was a voracious reader of his writings. But there were many others, as well, from Milan's political and cultural milieu who were happy to receive in their midst such a highly esteemed teacher and famous orator as Paleario, admired even by the great jurist Andrea Alciato. The coterie consisted of Publio Francesco Spinola, a Latin teacher and poet of some renown, the lawyer Gian Battista Castiglione, Francesco Luvigini, the future preceptor to Duke Alessandro Farnese, Giovanni Tonso, later general superintendent at the University of Pisa, and Cardinal Cristoforo Madruzzo, governor of the city, a protector of Valdesians and "Lutherans."[8]

Bartolomeo Orelli, a merchant of Locarno who traveled frequently to Milan on business, served as Paleario's go-between when the latter corresponded with Basel's liberal wing: Boniface and Basil Amerbach, friends and protectors of the Italian exiles, and the physician Theodor Zwinger, rector of the university, a scholar of European fame. In spite of Paleario's links to Swiss Protestantism and the occasional murmurings about his suspect orthodoxy, he lived a tranquil life and enjoyed powerful patronage. This all changed in 1559, when Father Vittorio da Firenze, with whom Paleario had disputed at Colle Valdelsa twenty years earlier, suddenly appeared in Milan.

---

[8]Cf. S. Caponetto, *Aonio Paleario*, chap. 11, and the recent article by D. Sacré, "Some Remarks concerning Aonio Paleario's Milanese Years," *Humanistica Lovaniensia* 38 (1989): 200–208.

Rare engraving depicting the square before the Ponte Sant'Angelo at Rome, with the "place of justice" (before which the condemned were hung or burned at the stake), the "*Pescaria*" (fish market), and the chapel of the confraternity of San Giovanni Decollato, which comforted prisoners in their last hours. In this place some hundreds of "heretics" were executed, although there is no memorial to record it. Engraving of the mid–sixteenth century.

Paleario was tried for a second time on the accusation of holding Protestant views but absolved on 23 February 1560, thanks to his able defense and his powerful protectors.

The trial was a rude awakening from the dream he had nurtured, following the peace of Cateau-Cambrésis (1559), which had given birth to his final oration, *De pace*, a sort of synthesis of his political thought. Meditating on the immense possibilities for economic rebirth that the treaty opened for Europe's richest nations, and inspired by Christ, he confronted the burning issue of the day. The Christian Church was in extreme disarray. Now that political peace had been achieved, peace within the church should also be established. The turmoil stemmed from the variety of opinions it harbored, from England to Hungary, from Germany to Switzerland, from France to Bohemia, nothing but controversies, upheavals, and struggles, with persecution raging in Spain and Italy. The oration invited emperor and rulers to note that religion cannot be coerced, that it existed in a plurality of opinions and confessions; and it augured the elimination of divisions and schisms from Christian society by means of the summoning of a free council in which representatives of nations, people, and princes would freely dispute and be instructed. The pope, who would have accepted the settlement, would not be able to hinder this "ecumenical" gathering intended to eradicate controversy and consolidate the peace.

In other words, Paleario, addressing himself to Ferdinand of Habsburg, was restating the great themes of his 1544 letter to the reformers. This was not the isolated outburst of a solitary visionary, but a carefully weighed political gesture. In 1558 the humanist had begun to correspond with Andrea Rapicio, a Triestine who was an imperial counselor and would become Ferdinand's secretary in 1556. Through him Paleario came into contact with the scholar and statesman Antonio Veranzio (Verancsis Antal), a correspondent of Erasmus and Melanchthon, in the hope of conveying to the emperor the *De animorum immortalitate* that Paleario had dedicated to him in 1536. The latter felt a reawakening of the youthful ambition to be summoned to court, linked now to the hope of strengthening with his own contributions the party of irenicists and Erasmians, among whom the young Maximilian II could be counted. But the silence on the matter of Emperor Ferdinand was a sign that the Counter-Reformation had triumphed. By now, despite his attempts at dissimulation, the noose was tightening about Paleario. His friends were being arrested: Carnesecchi, Pompeo delli Monti, formerly in the service of the prince of Salerno, and Publio Francesco Spinola. The last named, incarcerated in a Venetian prison on the charge of Lutheranism since 1564, would be executed by drowning in the lagoon on 31 January 1567. The patrician delli Monti's turn came at Rome in June 1566.[9]

In the hope of preserving some of the fruits of his intellectual labors, since he was fiercely convinced that he had the ability to refute his adversaries, on 12 September 1566 Paleario wrote to Theodor Zwinger beseeching him to safeguard the text of his *Actio in pontifices romanos* and consign it to the "bishop" of the church of Basel on the day when the free and universal council would finally gather. This letter is

[9]Cf. P. Paschini, "Un umanista disgraziato nel Cinquecento: Publio Francesco Spinola," *Nuovo Archivio Veneto*, n.s. 37 (1919): 65–186.

Paleario's spiritual testament, written after long reflection, in full awareness of the actual state of affairs, after long experience and having made many difficult choices, just a year after the beginning of his third trial. The document is a shining example of his loyalty to the Erasmian ideal of a unified and reformed church, the dream that had consumed his entire existence: "I am old now, oh my Theodore, and I am meditating on my journey towards Christ. I am preparing everything for his pleasure to whom I vowed myself from my youth."[10]

On 9 August 1567, a direct order came from the pope and the Holy Office summoning Paleario to appear in Rome before the supreme tribunal. After Emperor Maximilian II interceded in vain to have the trial transferred to Milan, at the end of the month the elderly professor arrived in the city of his early studies and dreams of glory, and was promptly confined in the Tor di Nona. The long trial took some dramatic turns. On 18 March 1568, when Paleario's judges confronted him with the audacious ideas in his oration, *Pro se ipso*, he realized the uselessness of further defense in view of the weighty evidence marshaled against him. Summoning up his courage, he declared:

> If your lordships have so many witnesses arrayed against me, there is no point taking up more of my and your time. I have decided to follow the advice of the blessed apostle Peter, who said: "Christ suffered for us, leaving you an example, that you should follow him in his steps. He committed no sin, no guile was found on his lips. When he was reviled, he did not revile in return; when he was exhibited, he did not threaten, but consigned himself to him who judged him unjustly" (1 Peter 2:21–23, Vulgate). Judge, then, and condemn Aonio so that satisfaction may be given to my accusers and to your office.

When Paleario's judges tried to make him acknowledge the pope as vicar of Christ, he replied contemptuously: "He cannot be the vicar of Christ and Peter's successor who does not feel love for his neighbor and obedience towards God." He elaborated on the point clarifying the close link between faith and civic responsibility: "It is not right that he who functions as vicar of Christ and Peter's successor should so treat and punish heretics. Whoever behaves in this way is not acting like the vicar of Christ." Once again, as he had done two months before, Paleario asked for an end to the trial, appealing anew to *pietas* in the imitation of Christ, quoting from the passage in Isa. (42:2) dear to Erasmus as emblematic of Christ's mercy: "You have the power; judge me according to your law; thus I believe and shall believe as long as I live; I do not want to dispute, but want to imitate my God, of whom it is said: 'he will not oppose, nor cry out, nor will anyone hear his voice in the public squares.'" On 19 July 1569, Paleario stated that he would not defend himself further and recognized no wrongdoing on his part, "because in the love of one's neighbor and in

---

[10]Letter to Theodor Zwinger, Milan, 12 September 1566. The Latin text is published in S. Caponetto, *Aonio Paleario*, 227, app. 6. For Paleario's correspondence with Zwinger, see D. Sacré, "Some Remarks," 206–8.

bowing to the glory of Christ there can be no error."[11] The court, having failed to get Paleario to abjure his belief in the doctrine of justification by faith alone, or disavow his rejection of purgatory, papal authority, and the value of monastic orders, which with cutting sarcasm he viewed as propagators of pagan rites, let him sit in his cell for six months. At that point, the skilled Spanish Jesuit, Giacomo Ledesma, who had been charged by Paleario's judges to try to bring him back to reason and to the obedience of the Church of Rome, seemed to have succeeded (a fact that is not wholly verified) in breaking the resistance of this old man who had suffered so much, and was now ill and at the limit of his forces, anguished by thoughts of his wife and children.

There is no ambiguity, however, about the fact that when Paleario was summoned to make a formal abjuration before the assembled tribunal, over which Pius V personally presided, he refused to don the penitential garment that was the mark of infamy, the sign of recantation, and symbol of civic death. Gripped by remorse and an irrepressible urge, Paleario seized the moment to launch himself into an accusation against the papacy and to give witness to his faith in Christ and in his Word. This was indeed the great orator's last oration. Two days later, at dawn on Monday, 3 July 1570, the death sentence against Paleario was carried out. He was first hung and then burned, on the square before Castel Sant'Angelo, the same spot that had also seen the executions of Gian Luigi Pascale, Pompeo delli Monti, and Pietro Carnesecchi. Shortly before Paleario was led out of his cell for the last time, in a decisive but trembling hand, he penned two letters that would become famous, to his children Lampridio and Fedro, reconfirming his witness to evangelical truth, telling them that he was abandoning himself serenely to the "goodness and infinite liberality" of his Lord.[12]

[11]S. Caponetto, *Aonio Paleario*, 157–58.
[12]Ibid., 162–63.

Heretics sentenced by the Spanish Inquisition in the early seventeenth century. On some occasions the condemned person would be strangled while already tied to the stake before being burned. Engraving by Bernard Picart (1722) (Paris, Société d'Histoire du Protestantisme, photo Lauros-Giraudon).

18

MEDITERRANEAN CALVINISM

FROM LYONS TO GENOA

GIORGIO SPINI SUGGESTED YEARS AGO that it might be well to add a chapter devoted to Mediterranean Calvinism to Braudel's famous work.[1] More than four decades of research on religious dissent in the Italian peninsula have fully confirmed the correctness of his astute intuition.

Along the great commercial routes traveled by the trade in silk, wool, cotton, spices, and arms, which from Lyons reached the entire western Mediterranean, missionaries from Geneva or from France, merchants, schoolteachers, and simple laborers, who were either Calvinists or influenced by Calvinism, reached the coastal cities of Marseilles, Nice, Savona, Genoa, Cagliari, Venice, Naples, Palermo, Messina, Syracuse, and even the Waldensian colonies in Calabria and Puglia.

Lyons was the great commercial and banking hub for France, the Mediterranean, and in fact for western Europe. Italy occupied a central place in this vast circuit. Two-thirds of its production in weaponry, silk, wool, and glass was exported through Lyons, where Florentine, Lucchese, Genoese, Lombard, and Venetian merchants maintained flourishing businesses. This "second capital" of France was also a focal point of European culture with its many printing establishments, gathering places for the leading literary figures, from whose presses the writings of the great scholars and religious reformers of the day circulated throughout the continent; and in turn, it was a place where one could learn about the latest cultural advances occurring anywhere in Europe.

It is difficult to calculate the number of Italians directly or indirectly influenced by the seductive Lyonnais milieu. In addition to such men of letters as Ortensio Lando, Bartolomeo Panciatichi, Ludovico Castelvetro, or important men of affairs such as the Balbani, Arnolfini, Buonvisi, and Pellizzari, all of whom would play a notable role in the religious controversies of the day, many others, humbler and

---

[1] G. Spini, "Di Nicola Gallo e di alcune infiltrazioni in Sardegna della Riforma protestante," *Rinascimento* 2 (1951): 145–78, esp. 174–75; F. Braudel, *La Méditerranée et le monde méditerranéen à l'époque de Philippe II*, 2d ed., 2 vols. (Paris, 1966).

unknown, learned about the new ideas in Lyons, where its four annual fairs attracted merchants and tradesmen, many of whom hailed from places in Switzerland and Germany where the Reformation had triumphed. It has been customary to focus on the higher spheres of society, neglecting its more obscure members, who in the inns and taverns struck up acquaintance with others of their class, and listened with curiosity and amusement to invectives against parasitical priests and monks and a pope who fomented wars among Christians.

The travelers who returned to Italy touched by the new religious notions must have been more numerous than previously imagined. And often—even if not actual converts to the Reformation—they willingly transported, along with the bales of their merchandise, prohibited books printed at Lyons and Geneva, the latter for centuries closely linked to Lyons, since it lacked industrial activity until the second half of the century.

HERESY IN GENOA

Heretical activity in Genoa, especially in the triennium 1540–1543, and the life of the merchant Bartolomeo Bartoccio, who was arrested there in 1567 after travels in the peninsula as far south as Sicily, constitute important aspects of Mediterranean Calvinism.

The Genoese were the island's leading capitalists[2] and their colony outnumbered all others including the Lombard and Tuscan. The ancient mercantile activities of the Genoese were no longer confined to trade in linens, grains, and cheeses, but now included many other branches as well. These were the master silk manufacturers in Messina, booksellers in Palermo where they imported publications from Lyons, and manufacturers of paper for the printing industry. By mid–sixteenth century Genoese had achieved enormous power with their monopoly over marine insurance and their leases over the great feudal properties. In Palermo they constructed palaces and occupied an entire quarter.

To this account drawn from Trasselli, we can add that the second martyr to the Reformation in Sicily was a Genoese merchant from a prominent family, Giorgio Costa, arrested at Palermo in February 1548 and sentenced to the stake on 19 May 1549 as a "Lutheran."[3] Andrea Doria, moved by the plight of Costa's wife and three nubile daughters now alone in Genoa, interceded in the case, but the famous admiral's plea for clemency arrived three months too late, after the execution. We are not fully informed about Costa's doctrinal beliefs, but the harshness of the sentence, at a time when it was still the policy of the church to try to reclaim the wayward to the fold, suggests that the Sicilian inquisitors viewed his errors as extremely grave. It is probable that Giorgio Costa's tragic end and the contemporaneous reconciliation of another Genoese, the silk merchant Francesco Campisano living in Messina, are somehow connected to the trials against "Lutheranism" held at Genoa in the early

---

[2]C. Trasselli, "Genovesi in Sicilia," *Atti della Società ligure di Storia Patria* 9 (1969): 168–69.
[3]See S. Caponetto, "Bartolomeo Spadafora," in *Studi sulla Riforma*, 42.

1540s, about which we are largely in the dark. Our knowledge does not go much beyond the data gathered by Michele Rosi at the end of the last century.[4] This is a serious gap in any attempt to reconstruct Mediterranean Calvinism, since existing records show that at least sixty Genoese found refuge in Geneva, though we possess only a meager list of names.

In the spring of 1540 the Genoese inquisitor arrested Count Giacomo Fieschi, a certain Giorgio Vivaldo-Costa, the pharmacist Bartolomeo Alessio, the notary G. B. Ponti, who had read works by Luther and Melanchthon, and Nicolò Casero. The absence of trial records or other documentation, makes it impossible to shed light on their activities and beliefs. Nevertheless, the accusation that they constituted a conventicle which used to meet in the pharmacy of Alessio, who was treasurer for the funds collected to succor needy evangelicals, and Casero's assertion that in the sacrament of the altar the body of Christ was not present *"realiter sed tantum in signo,"* suggests that we are possibly dealing with Calvinists.[5]

The clandestine movement in the city, site of a Waldensian hospice from medieval times, endured to the end of the sixteenth century, and even reached the periphery of the Genoese state. Franco Posaggio, the governor in Corsica, who had heard heterodox preachers in both Genoa and Rome and had read and memorized Curione's *Pasquillus extaticus,* in 1551 at Bastia, enthusiastically received a French agent, Aurelio Cicuta di Veglia. Disguised as a schoolteacher, the latter used his position to spread the new ideas. But in January 1552, Cicuta, alias Bonaventura Cosmio, was imprisoned and tried as a heretic. Posaggio's intellectual adventure quickly came to an end with his resignation.[6]

The Republic collaborated with the inquisitor as long as he did not overstep his bounds, as he was thought to have done in the case of Giovanni Battista Burgo (1577–82), who was removed from office over the protests of citizens and even the bishop of Savona. But generally the state acted with extreme prudence so as not to jeopardize its political and commercial relations with both church and empire, as well as with the Swiss Protestant cantons.

In 1568 after Bartolomeo Bartoccio was extradited to Rome for trial, seven or eight persons were arrested in Genoa, charged with participation in a heretical celebration of the Lord's Supper. The government tried to downplay the episode, but Pius V, alarmed by the news that one of the chief suspects had been freed, dispatched to the city Angelo Bianchi, the bishop of Teano, as commissioner with extraordinary powers to examine all the heresy cases. Genoa, as an important gateway to the peninsula, represented a grave threat for the diffusion of heresy. C. Cicada, cardinal of San Clemente, expressed his dismay on 19 March 1568 at the mildness of the proceed-

---

[4]See M. Rosi, "La Riforma religiosa in Liguria e l'eretico umbro Bartolomeo Bartocci," *Atti della Società ligure di Storia Patria* 24 (1892): 555–726; idem, "Storia delle relazioni fra la Repubblica di Genova e la Chiesa Romana specialmente considerate in rapporto alla Riforma religiosa," *Reale Accademia dei Lincei: Memorie della Classe di Scienze Morali, Storiche e Filologiche,* ser. 5, 6 (1899): 169–231.

[5]Idem, "La Riforma," 593 ff.

[6]See S. Seidel Menchi, *Erasmo in Italia,* 240, 269.

ings against those "Calvinists who had celebrated the Supper in a heretical manner." Four or five were condemned to the galleys, while others were sentenced to abjure their errors and wear the penitential garment, a novelty in Genoa that provoked lively protests from the government. But the complaints were rebuffed by the pontiff, who announced that "rigor is the only remedy for this pestilence."[7]

The government yielded once again. In 1570 the pope pardoned the offenders, but prohibited G. Agostino Contardo and M. Luchino Boero from exercising their professions as physicians. A decade later more "heretics" were discovered at Genoa, Savona, Albenga, and San Remo. The civic authorities had lost the possibility of intervening in inquisitorial trials and their intercession for rich and prominent citizens was to no avail.[8] Numerous Protestants were brought to light in 1580: two notaries, Stefano Casino and Giovan Antonio Tivello; the two brothers, Imperiali and Domenico Ricci, natives of the city; as well as Francesco Fontana and Nicolò Odone Cristoforo, who were all compelled to abjure. Two of the group were sentenced to the galleys and the others to various punishments.[9] Perhaps as many as ten Genoese, men and women, ended up in prison.

Great consternation was provoked by the condemnation to death of Pier Battista Botto as a relapsed heretic. The Genoese government petitioned the pontiff on 20 May 1581 for a commutation of the sentence from one of "capital punishment to one of civic death," since the offender was well known for his exemplary moral life and charity to the needy. This may have been granted.

Although the papal court repeatedly expressed its satisfaction at the Republic's efforts in the repression of heresy, relations became increasingly tense. Two eminent citizens, Agostino Bianco and Agostino Moneglia, were arrested, and in spite of the government's efforts to impede it, were transferred to Rome for trial in 1582. Two years later Moneglia was permitted to return home after making a solemn abjuration and paying a heavy fine of three thousand *scudi* for the benefit of Genoese monasteries and foundling hospitals. This sketchy picture of heterodoxy in the Republic would certainly be more complete if we knew something about the twelve citizens of Savona, Genoese subjects, who emigrated to Geneva.

THE MARTYRDOM OF BARTOLOMEO BARTOCCIO

The life and martyrdom of Bartolomeo Bartoccio (1535–69) should be seen against the background of these relatively murky events occurring during roughly a half century along the Ligurian coast from Savona in the north to La Spezia in the south.[10] Bartoccio, born at Città del Castello, was in Siena during the imperial siege of the city in 1555 where he learned of the new religious ideas from a youth of Gub-

---

[7]M. Rosi, "La Riforma," 638, 642.
[8]See G. Bertora, S.J., "Il Tribunale inquisitoriale di Genova e l'Inquisizione romana nel Cinquecento," *Civiltà Cattolica* 104 (1953), 2:184.
[9]M. Rosi, "Storia delle relazioni," 198–201.
[10]On Bartoccio, see M. Rosi, "La riforma," chap. 3, 646ff., and the biographical entry by C. Ginzburg in *DBI* 6:547–49.

The church of Santa Maria sopra Minerva at Rome, where the ceremony of sentencing was usually held by the Roman Inquisition. *Left*: The Dominican convent. Engraving of the mid–seventeenth century.

bio, Fabrizio Tommasi. After returning to Città di Castello he refused to have his confession heard or to receive communion during a life-threatening illness. He fled to Siena and Venice, and then proceeded to Geneva to avoid having to present himself before the court of the bishop of Città di Castello which had summoned him. In 1556 he became a member of the Italian exiles' church in Geneva and the following year he was accepted as an *habitant*. There he traded in silk, married an Italian woman named Maddalena, and distinguished himself for his business acumen and religious zeal. Francesco Greco and Theodore Beza were godfathers to his children.

The destruction of the Waldensians in Calabria and the forced return to Catholicism of their brethren in Puglia made 1567 a difficult year for evangelicals in Italy. Bartoccio went to see for himself and traveled as far south as Sicily under the cover of his commercial affairs. From the Sicilian emigrés in Geneva he had heard about the advances made by Protestantism at Messina, Palermo, and Syracuse. From Sicily he journeyed northward, accompanied by a servant and by other persons, including a knight of Malta, all suspected religious dissidents. Bartoccio's stop in Rome may be connected to the presence there of French and Savoyard Calvinists. We know about them because in 1561 or 1562 the new papal nuncio to Venice, Ippolito Capilupo, bishop of Fano, wrote to the Roman Curia that he had learned from the agent of the duke of Florence that "many notaries and scribes from France, Savoy and neighboring places gather together at night, and live as Lutherans and Huguenots."[11]

There must have been some truth in the report because on 21 March 1562 twelve "Lutherans" abjured at Rome in the church of Santa Maria della Minerva. In June a Greek monk named Macarius, archbishop of Macedonia, was condemned to the stake. This was followed in 1563 by the execution of the Dutchman Cornelius as an impenitent heretic, followed in September by the Cypriot Francesco Segretuzzo.[12] If most of the populace applauded these "spectacles of the faith," some among them were struck by the courage and fortitude of the condemned.

Bartoccio was discovered when he attempted to make contact with the Roman evangelicals. Cardinal Scipione Rebiba informed the Venetian doge and the government in Genoa that Bartoccio had left Rome. On 20 October he was arrested in Genoa, in the company of the Maltese knight. The pope immediately requested that the two be extradited back to Rome. Long negotiations followed because Geneva and Bern had intervened in favor of Bartoccio *solo religionis nomine,* known to them for his probity, sincerity, and ability. The Swiss cities warned that if he was not released they could not guarantee the safety of Genoese traders in their territories who had never been molested on account of their Catholic beliefs. In vain, the Genoese doge and his government made known to the pope the threats of reprisals made by the "barbarians." In March 1568, Bartoccio appeared before the Roman Inquisition, determined not to abjure his faith.

---

[11] P. Paschini, "Episodi dell'Inquisizione a Roma nei suoi primi decenni," *Studi Romani* 5 (1957): 294.

[12] D. Orano, *Liberi pensatori,* 13–14, nn. xii, xiii, xiv.

The attempts made by the Genoese to save Bartoccio foundered in the face of the weighty evidence in the hands of his judges. Cardinal Cicada, who had served as the intermediary with Genoa, informed the city's authorities on 15 October that the inquisitors had told him "that they had found him to be a heresiarch who had traversed most of Italy proselytizing and infecting wherever he went. Moreover he has shown himself to be so obstinate and pertinacious in his errors, that they were considering the stake for him, and that this celebration will come before Christmas."[13] Bartolomeo Bartoccio was burned alive on 25 May 1569 because to the very end "he refused to be persuaded by theologians and doctors." In his martyrology, Crespin passed on the tradition that the victim, already being consumed by the flames, shouted out, "Victory! Victory!"

THE REPRESSION OF THE 1560S

The pyres lit on the same day in May, which consumed Bartoccio, the former Minorite Francesco Cellario of Chiarella, evangelical pastor at Morbegno in the Valtellina, and the doctor Camillo Regnoli of Faenza, marked the close of the cruel repression of the 1560s. It had been a decade of sentences to the galleys, a penal servitude much harsher than imprisonment, to incarceration and to the stake. Without counting the many condemnations emitted in Sicily, Sardinia, Naples, and Venice, thirty sentences to capital punishment were pronounced by the Roman Inquisition alone, the majority for heresy. If we then take into account the sentences issued between the years 1564 and 1567 that are now preserved at Trinity College, Dublin and the records of the Confraternity of San Giovanni Decollato that accompanied victims to their executions in Rome, we are impressed by the large numbers of persons who were accused of heresy, most of whom were Calvinists. Alongside the few foreigners from Antwerp, Geneva, Holland, and Germany, the majority were Italians, principally from Neapolitan dominions. But due to the dispersal of inquisitorial trials, the documentation is very fragmentary.

Among the persons condemned to death by the Roman Inquisition between 1567 and 1569 besides citizens of Faenza discussed earlier (chap. 14), the record shows the names of Pietro Gelosi and Giovanni Maria de Blasii, both of Spoleto, Paolo Veloccio of Spalato, known as "the Venetian," Francesco Castellani, Filippo Borghesi of Siena, and Marcantonio Varotta. The Burgundian Alberto di Cristiano Boccadoro was saved at the last moment when he abjured before the populace, which was moved by his youth and began to cry "mercy, mercy!"[14]

Among the martyrs to freedom of conscience, the life of Marcantonio Varotta (d. 1568) epitomizes the saga of Mediterranean Calvinism.[15] This Venetian weaver had gone to Lyons in 1564 where, urged on by a Lombard acquaintance, he then traveled to Geneva in order to get to know a city of "Lutherans." There he met such

---

[13]*DBI* 6:548 and D. Orano, *Liberi pensatori*, 34–35, n. xxxv.
[14]D. Orano, *Liberi pensatori*, 28–35, nn. xxvii, xxxi, xxxiv, xxxvi.

The sentence to be walled in a prison meant to lose all contact with the outside world and to receive a meager meal three or four times weekly, through a small opening in the wall. Engraving from F. Petrarch, *De remediis utriusque fortunae* (German ed. 1539).

noblemen as Andrea da Ponte, Jacopo Campagnola, and Gian Galeazzo Caracciolo who brought him to the pastor of the Italian church, Niccolò Balbani. The latter instructed him in the new doctrines and erased from his mind the notion that "Lutherans" were atheists. Varotta was touched by the warm welcome and ended up convinced that the pope and priests had betrayed Christ by teaching false doctrines. He was received in the Italian exiles' church and went to work in the shop of Fabio Todesco from Cosenza, where he perfected his knowledge of the weaver's art. After more than a year had passed he tired of Geneva because it lacked diversions. He returned to Italy, visiting Turin, Milan, and Mantua, concealing his beliefs. Even though there were many religious dissidents in Mantua, neither they nor he acknowledged their true faith. In Venice, his family tried to bring him back to his old religion. He resumed his wandering, traveling to Siena, Rome, Udine, Trieste, Vienna, Cracow, and Austerlitz in Moravia. Here he resided with Niccolò Paruta who told him how Bernardino Ochino had passed his last days before dying in his (Paruta's) house. The many Anabaptist sects Varotta encountered in Moravia filled him with confusion. He compared their disunity to the cohesion of the Church of Rome and its unwavering doctrinal certitude. On his return journey to Italy Varotta fell seriously ill near Vienna and, penniless, decided to confess his errors to the Dominicans. The monks urged him to present himself before the inquisitor at Udine and ask for pardon and absolution for his errors. On 21 January 1567 he drew up a long and detailed confession, citing among the sources from which he had imbibed the reformed faith the Italian translation of Calvin's *Catechism*, the five books of Ochino's *sermons* that he had read in Moravia, and both the Old and New Testaments. But this abjuration of his errors did not save Varotta. The supreme tribunal of the Inquisition demanded that his trial be transferred to Rome where it concluded with a death sentence on 6 December 1568.

Among the ten persons condemned on 25 May 1569 the worst was Guido Giannetti of Fano, according to a report from Francesco Babbi to Duke Cosimo. Giannetti was described as "one of the most notorious heretics and the greatest champion that Genevans have in Italy, and is known to heretics all over Europe, having dealt with them in Germany, Flanders, England, France, and in all Christendom where one finds those villains. He is old and highly educated." Although, in the opinion of the writer, Giannetti "deserves to be burned alive," since he was not a *relapsus*, "he was condemned to be incarcerated for seven years, and this is too good for him."[16] It is not possible to establish whether Giannetti, an enigmatic figure, was in fact at the time of his arrest at Venice in 1566, a Genevan agent—perhaps a spy.

---

[15]The principal source for Varotta's biography remains his long confession before the inquisitor of Udine on 21 January 1567, published in D. Caccamo, *Eretici italiani*, 194–216. See also C. Ginzburg in *DBI* 6:489–90 (Barotta). Marcantonio Verotti of Venice (D. Orano, *Liberi pensatori*, 29, n. xxviii) is the same person as the M. Varotta discussed by Caccamo. Cf. A. Del Col, "La storia religiosa del Friuli nel Cinquecento: Orientamenti e fonti," *Metodi e Ricerche* 1 (1981): 71, 85, note 19

[16]ASF, Rome, *Carteggio diplomatico*, file 3595, fol. 8. On G. Giannetti, see A. Stella, "Guido da Fano eretico del secolo XVI al servizio dei re d'Inghilterra," *RSCI* 13 (1959): 196–238.

He had been in the service of Henry VIII, passing on information to him concerning Cardinal Pole. At one point Giannetti had associated with such Valdesians as Pietro Antonio di Capua, Marcantonio Flaminio, Donato Rullo, and Lattanzio Ragnoni. Subsequently, he served Elizabeth of England. At his trial he abjured thirty-eight articles, but got off with a light sentence because of the incriminating evidence he passed on against Pietro Carnesecchi and Pietro Gelido.

THE VALDESIAN DIASPORA

As we saw, the ideas of Valdés continued to circulate widely after his death. His followers fanned out about the peninsula disseminating his teachings, but interpreting them variously, both because the master had couched them ambiguously and also because not all his writings were yet known. Anyone who had read the *Alfabeto cristiano* placed the Spaniard in the current of Catholic evangelism, while others who might have read his beautiful, brief catechism for children convinced themselves of his identity with Protestant beliefs. Thus Valdesians ventured doctrinally in many diverse directions, from Catholic reform to Calvinism and Anabaptism. As Massimo Firpo recently explained, "the unifying element" in Valdesian thought is "the ensnaring religious individualism which led to a spiritualistic interpretation of Christianity."[17]

The movement toward Calvinism of many Neapolitans and of others as well, was encouraged by the news of the conversion to the Reformation on the part of the great preachers of justification by faith: Ochino, Vermigli, and Buzio, all of whom were extremely popular in Naples. In 1551 it was the turn of Gian Galeazzo Caracciolo, marquis of Vico, to abandon the city for Geneva. His conversion had an enormous impact on the Valdesians, even if they did not follow his example.[18]

Looking at the sentences against Giovanni Micro (or Miero?) of Naples, Giovanni Battista Sasso, the physician Giacomo Sala of Caserta, and Annibale Salato of Amalfi, a former Benedictine schoolteacher in Naples, the great inroads made by reformed currents is obvious. All the above abjured belief in the predestination of the elect and in the spiritual presence alone of Christ in the Eucharist, in addition to the basic doctrines of the Reformation.

Among the accused, the physician Sala was the one who spoke most explicitly, as can be deduced from his sentence emitted at Rome on 6 June 1566. He had held his erroneous beliefs for about sixteen years; thus it is not difficult to surmise that he had imbibed them from the former Augustinian Lorenzo Romano, who had instructed many gentlemen at Capodimonte near Caserta beginning in 1549. Sala admitted that he had read several prohibited books and believed that "in the consecrated host

---

[17]M. Firpo, *Tra alumbrados e "spirituali:" Studi su Juan de Valdés e il Valdesianesimo nella crisi religiosa del '500 italiano* (Florence: Olschki, 1990), 103.

[18]According to N. Balbani (*Historia della vita di Galeazzo Caracciolo*, ed. E. Comba [Florence: Claudiana, 1875], 27), it was Caracciolo's meeting with Vermigli at Strasbourg that made him go beyond "the simple knowledge of justification" at which the Valdesians had halted. Cf. B. Croce, "Un Calvinista italiano," and the sketch by E. W. Monter in *DBI* 19:363–66.

there is not the real body of Our Lord Jesus Christ, and thus it is idolatry to hear Mass...[and] the predestined necessarily must be saved and those who are not predestined necessarily must go to hell and free will is of no avail."[19]

The notary Fabio Populo, a reader of the *Beneficio di Cristo*, confessed in Naples on 14 December 1564 that he had attended the "Lord's Supper performed in the heretical way." Naples too had its clandestine evangelical community.[20]

The diffusion of Valdesianism was accompanied by the circulation of quantities of books by Erasmus and Melanchthon, hurled on bonfires together with the *Beneficio di Cristo* and the *Sommario della santa Scrittura* in the auto da fé held in the cathedral square of Naples in 1543. The repression of all manifestations of religious and political dissent was a chief concern of the viceroy, Don Pedro of Toledo, in office from 1532 to 1553, who was convinced of the revolutionary character of the Lutheran heresy. The sentiment was shared by his successor, don Perafán de Ribera, duke of Alcalá, who reigned from 1559 to 1571. All forms of cultural activity were placed under government control and the doors of the celebrated *Accademia Pontaniana* were closed, compelling its president, Scipione Capece, to seek refuge with the prince of Salerno. Attempts were made by the authorities to crush the flourishing trade in prohibited books brought in on Venetian, French, and Dutch ships. The trial against G. B. Cappello, the Neapolitan agent for the publishing house of Gabriel Giolito, from whom two hundred books were confiscated, sheds much light on this activity. As a consequence, new and more severe measures were applied against the illicit book trade.

The massive book burnings that took place in 1572, 1587, and 1610 accelerated the decline of humanistic learning. To the end of the sixteenth century authorities issued warnings to persons possessing or selling any work, however trivial, impugning their faith and morality. Naples, in the second half of the century, witnessed a harsh repression of heretical ideas (two hundred trials for crimes against the faith are preserved in the Archivio Storico Diocesano) and rigid control of all aspects of the religious life, resulting in an end to intellectual exchanges and personal spiritual creativity, as noted by Pasquale Lopez. But these measures were accompanied by earnest attempts to reform the Neapolitan church and bring the faith to the people thanks to the efforts of the archbishops Mario Carafa (1565–76) and Paolo Burali of Arezzo (1576–78).

The majority of Neapolitans, after the enthusiasm of the 1540s had waned, tended to support the reforming efforts of their pastors, but they remained opposed to the tribunal of the Inquisition. In 1547 patricians and populace rose up as one to

---

[19]The sentence was published from the records of the Roman Inquisition preserved at Trinity College, Dublin (MS 1224), in *Rivista Cristiana* 7 (1879): 500–501. New documents have been published on G. B. Sasso and A. Salato by P. Lopez, *Inquisizione, stampa e censura nel regno di Napoli tra '500 e '600* (Naples: Edizioni del Delfino, 1974), 253–59 (app.).

The discussion that follows in the text concerning the kingdom of Naples is based on Lopez, who complements the still fundamental work by L. Amabile, *Il Santo Officio della Inquisizione in Napoli*, 2 vols. (Città di Castello: S. Lapi, 1892).

[20]P. Lopez, *Inquisizione, stampa e censura*, 20.

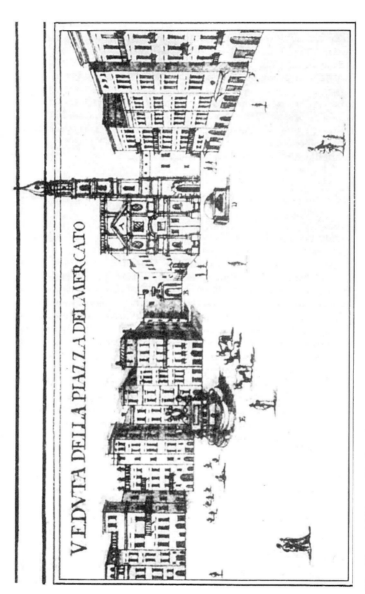

The *Piazza del Mercato*, Naples, where a number of heretics were burned on 4 March 1564, among whom were the former Valdesians Gian Francesco Alois and Gianbernardo Gargano. *Right* (letter D): the place where Conradin of Swabia was beheaded in 1268. Late-seventeenth-century engraving.

resist the viceroy's attempt to introduce it in its Spanish form, as had already occurred in Sicily and Sardinia. In the spring of 1564, just a few days after the execution in the Piazza del Mercato of Gian Francesco Alois (1510?–64) as a "relapsed" heretic, the masses vented their anger against both political and religious authorities who had collaborated in the execution of this esteemed man, whose brother Giambattista had died in the anti-inquisitorial tumult of 1547 fighting for the cause of religious freedom.

Gian Francesco Alois had been one of Valdés's most loyal followers. He was a friend of Scipione Capece, Paolo Giovio, Paolo Manuzio, and Marcantonio Flaminio, whom he hosted in 1539 in his villa at Caserta.[21] It was Alois who urged Caracciolo and Vittore Soranzo to lend an ear to Valdés. Alois did not follow Caracciolo and the others who fled to Geneva, perhaps because he hoped that imperial and Spanish dominion would soon end in Europe.

The testimony of the Dominican Ambrogio Salvio da Bagnoli, a famous preacher and master in theology, decisively an opponent of heterodox beliefs, sheds light on the penetration of Protestant and Calvinist teachings in the viceroyalty. On 16 July 1568 he made a deposition before the archbishop of Naples concerning the spread of heretical currents in the principate of Salerno. He had been called there in 1546 by the princess, Isabella Villamarino, a Valdesian, the wife of the ruler, Ferrante Sanseverino, who was concerned by the open proselytization being conducted at all social levels. In his report to the archbishop, Salvio stated that the canons of the cathedral in Salerno

> did not believe that the consecrated host in any way contained Our Lord Jesus Christ, but was only bread, and that even women talked about this heresy from their windows. And if one asked any of them if she wanted to go to Mass, she would reply that it was not necessary to go, because Christ was not to be found there, and the host was mere bread and that she had made it with her own hands at her uncle's....[22]

The trial instituted against the numerous suspects was held in the presence of the princess, the bishop's vicar, and the Dominican Salvio. It concluded with all the defendants' abjuring their errors precipitously and secretly out of fear that Don Pedro da Toledo, the viceroy in Naples, implacable enemy of the prince of Salerno and of his family, might step into the case. It was awkward securing the abjuration of a doctor of law from the University of Bologna "full of Lutheran heresy." If Salvio's recollections, twenty-two years after the fact are accurate, the map of heterodoxy in the principate of the first baron of the realm, who was both anti-Spanish and anti-clerical, and would eventually go over to the Huguenots, is much larger than previously imagined. The many foreigners passing through, English sailors, German merchants and mercenaries, contributed either consciously or just through their

---

[21]On G. F. Alois, see the entry by M. Rosa in the *DBI* 2:515–16.
[22]M. Miele, "La penetrazione protestante a Palermo verso la metà del Cinquecento secondo un documento dell'Inquisizione," in *Miscellanea Gilles Gerard Meersseman* (Padua, 1970), 2:846–47, app.

anticonformist attitudes and behavior, to this diffusion of heterodoxy, not without reformed overtones. Suspects almost always got off with a simple abjuration, but an obstinate Calvinist, a certain Goffredo Maymone, was turned over to the secular arm on 9 April 1573.[23]

THE DEATH OF THE WALDENSIAN COLONIES IN CALABRIA

The tragic events connected with the Waldensian colonies of Calabria and Puglia occupy a central place in any account of Mediterranean Calvinism. The annihilation of the ancient Calabrian settlements at San Sisto and Guardia, with their outposts at Fuscaldo, Montalto, San Vincenzo, and Vaccarizzo constituted an irreparable loss for the Italian Reformation as a whole. These Waldensians, presumably originating from the lower Val Pellice in Piedmont, had been invited to settle in the area about Cosenza by the local landowners to work in their fields, perhaps beginning as early as the thirteenth century. Although they were periodically visited by Barbs and secretly maintained the ancient traditions of their fathers, they had been integrated in part with the local populations and participated in the rites of the Roman church. They had been so successful in this that they managed to avoid the persecutions that fell upon their co-religionaries in northern Italy and southern France. We know nothing about that Guido di Calabria, whom the assembly of Barbs that gathered at Laux in Val Chisone (1526) sent to Switzerland and Germany, accompanied by Martin Gonin, to inquire about the new religious teachings. What is established instead is that Waldensians awakened from their quiet and withdrawn lives at the news, brought to them by the pastor Gille de Gilles in 1556, of the events taking place in the Piedmontese valleys where the first evangelical churches were opening their doors to the public. Fearful of the consequences for them if they followed this example and openly declared their faith, Gilles urged the Calabrian Waldensians to move elsewhere.[24] But it was difficult for a people who numbered more than six thousand peasants and small proprietors to abandon properties belonging to landholders who had been tolerant of them up to then, without other prospects of employment and settlement.

In 1557 when only Barb Stefano Negrin was left to care for the faithful, Marco Uscegli, known as Marchiotto, was dispatched to Geneva to seek aid and guidance for the organization of the communities in line with what was taking place in the Piedmontese valleys. Calvin and the Venerable Company of Pastors realized the importance of securing the full adherence of these peasants in the south of Italy to the Reformation. It would mean a new and firmer link with the Piedmontese

---

[23]P. Lopez, *Inquisizione, stampa e censura*, 93.

[24]On the tragic history of the Calabrian Waldensians, see A. Armand-Hugon, *Storia dei Valdesi*, vol. 2, chap. 4; E. Pontieri, "A proposito della 'crociata' contro i Valdesi di Calabria nel 1561," in *Nei tempi grigi della storia d'Italia: Saggi storici sul predominio straniero in Italia*, 3d ed. (Naples: E.S.I., 1966); G. Gonnet, "I Valdesi in Calabria (Secoli XIV–XVI). Ricerca storiografica," *Quaderni* 2 (1981–82) (Istituto di Scienze Storico-Politiche, Facoltà di Magistero, Università di Bari); E. Stancati, *Gli Ultramontani: Storia dei Valdesi di Calabria* (Cosenza: Aiello, 1984) (with bibliography).

Waldensians and with the reformed groups coming into being in Sicily and in other parts of Italy. The first missionary to be sent was Giacomo Bonello of Dronero, the companion of Curione's studies at Turin, assigned as pastor at San Sisto and Guardia. Bonello returned to Geneva in 1559 for consultations, and possibly through diplomatic channels directed to the king of Spain, to try to obtain freedom of conscience for his flock. He then returned to Calabria accompanied by Gian Luigi Pascale and teachers and catechists recruited from the Calabrian exiles in the *cité-refuge*.

The two youthful ministers were well prepared, courageous, and eager. Pascale had translated into Italian a work by Pierre Viret, *De fatti de veri successori di Giesù Christo et de suoi Apostoli et de gli Apostati della Chiesa Papale* (1556), and had produced a bilingual French and Italian edition of the New Testament based on an anonymous version published at Geneva in 1555. He took leave of his betrothed, Camilla Guarino, the sister of the brave missionary Francesco Guarino who was ministering at the time to the Waldensians in Piedmont, and placed his trust fully in divine providence, a confidence that he never abandoned even during the arduous trials encountered later.

Bonello and Pascale, together with their companions, and with Stefano Negrin now began a daring mission of evangelization among the Calabrian Waldensians, "demonstrating to them that it was preferable to die than to offend God by committing idolatry."[25] They were guileless and imprudent, and persuaded themselves into believing that they could obtain some measure of religious freedom while Paul IV sat on the papal throne and Michele Ghislieri was the head of the Inquisition, a man whose harshness in combatting heresy was proverbial.

It was an intense but brief ministry. Bonello was arrested at Battipaglia, probably after a visit to the brethren in Puglia. He was released from prison but apprehended anew at Messina where he had gone to establish contacts with Sicilian evangelicals, some of whose co-religionaries had found refuge in Geneva dating back as far as 1551. It is not unlikely that some Waldensian families from Guardia had moved to Sicily some time before. We know that a Michele Tundo of the town was arrested at Messina prior to 1572 at the request of the episcopal vicar of Cosenza. Tundo confessed that he had learned the heretical doctrines "from a teacher of Geneva who was preaching in a place called La Guardia."[26] On 18 February 1560 at the conclusion of a brief trial, the Waldensian pastor Giacomo Bonello was burned alive at Palermo in the Piazza dell'Ucciardone. Unfortunately, the only source surviving for this Sicilian mission is the *Serie dei rilasciati al Braccio secolare* (list of those turned over to the Secular Arm) where we read about him as: "a pertinacious heresiarch who had come from Geneva to preach the Lutheran sect."[27]

Pascale's ministry was also short-lived. He was apprehended just a few months after his arrival in Calabria and incarcerated in the castle belonging to Marquis Salvatore Spinelli of Fuscaldo. The nobleman wanted to proceed with moderation against

[25]S. Lentolo, *Historia delle grandi e crudeli persecuzioni*, a cura di Teofilo Gay (Torre Pellice: Alpina, 1906), 227.

[26]On Michele Tundo, perhaps to be identified with the person who, after daring escapades, found refuge in Geneva, see S. Caponetto, "Ginevra e la Riforma in Sicilia," in *Studi sulla Riforma*, 190–91.

[27]*Serie*, n. 274. Cf. S. Caponetto, "B. Spadafora," in *Studi sulla Riforma*, 55–56.

the Waldensian peasants, who were held in high regard for their industriousness and their strict morality. Pascale refused to heed the bishop of Cosenza and the inquisitors who urged him to abjure. He was thus taken from Cosenza to Naples on foot, reviled along the way by low elements among the populace who flocked to see the "convicts," and from there by sea to Rome. In the prison of the Tor di Nona, Pascale had to endure, in addition to the customary exhortations from his judges, also the vain pleas of his brother Bartolomeo, a Catholic, to abjure and be spared the final agony of the stake. On 16 September 1560, a few months after Bonello's death, Pascale was strangled and then burned in the square before Castel Sant'Angelo. Nothing more is known about his faithful companion Marco Uscegli.

The tragic end of the two ministers could have led the Calabrian Waldensians to return to their former Nicodemite practices. This course was urged on them by a few landowners who opposed a public cult. But the situation for those poor peasants became more complicated. From his prison cell in Cosenza Pascale had written them, on 7 April 1560, to stand firm in the faith, pray vigorously, read the "many books" they possessed, visit their brethren, and copy and circulate the letters he had sent them. In one, he had included the awesome admonition: "You may flee, but under penalty of eternal damnation you may not kneel before Baal."[28]

In November, the inquisitors Valerio Malvicino and Alfonso Urbino began their investigation of the "ultramontanes." They concluded from the statements they received that the Waldensians of Montalto, San Sisto, and Guardia were all heretics. At the beginning of these inquiries, many of the men of San Sisto had fled to the woods. Finally, after long hesitation, compelled by the endless vexations to defend themselves, they killed the Spanish governor Castagneto in a violent clash. The consequences were tragic. San Sisto, a town of six thousand inhabitants, was razed. Sixty men of Guardia, suspected of complicity in the killing of the official, were hung and their bodies hurled from towers to the ground far below. In June 1561 the viceroy of Naples, the duke of Alcalá, gave the order from Cosenza to root out the persons who had taken refuge in the forests. The mission was entrusted to about a thousand soldiers, including outlaws who were promised amnesty in exchange for their participation. The troops, assisted in the task by hounds, ferreted out the fugitive Waldensians and transported their prisoners, about fourteen hundred in number, to Montalto. Meanwhile, at Guardia, the marquis Spinelli, as evidence of his loyalty to Rome, ordered seventy-six houses to be razed and executed many of the inhabitants.

But the greatest massacre, the most fanatical application of a "terrible justice," occurred at Montalto. The event was described with words of sorrow for the fate of the "ultramontanes," as Waldensians were called, by an eyewitness writing on 11 June 1561, the very day of the executions:

> Up to now only the past events of these heretics have been written about. It is now time to tell how early today a terrible justice began to be done against these Lutherans. Only to think about it is frightening. Like animals

---

[28]Letter to Andrea Traverso from the Castle of Cosenza, in *Lettere d'un carcerato (1559–1560)*, a cura di A. Muston (Torre Pellice: "La Luce," 1926), 130.

about to be castrated they were locked up in a house and the executioner came and took them out one at a time. He tied a headband over the victim's eyes and took him to an open place some distance from the building, where he made him kneel and slit his throat. Then he left him lying there, took off the bloody headband and with his bloody knife in his hand went back for another, and repeated the operation. I watched this until they reached the number eighty-eight. I leave it to you to imagine how compassionate this spectacle was. The old people face their death serenely, and the younger men go more fearfully. The order has been given, and the carts have already arrived, that all the dead should be quartered and the pieces scattered along the road from here to the borders of Calabria....[29]

"In the history of barbarism and of man's inhumanity to man, the Waldensian martyrology" holds a prominent place, as was recently observed.[30] But the killing did not stop here. Another two thousand persons were exterminated in just eleven days and a hundred or so more killed in the countryside. The Barb Stefano Negrin died of hunger or from tortures received in a prison at Cosenza. Survivors were reduced to Roman obedience.

The massacre of the Calabrian evangelicals did not end in 1561. Even after years had passed, fugitives faced death wherever they were caught. A rather enlightening account has come down to us concerning Pietro Angelo Musco, a silversmith of Reggio Calabria, who was tried in his native city. He had been "dogmatizing," saying, among other things, that "the host is nothing more than a slice of bread." He had been apprehended at Messina where several Calvinist silver workers of Venetian origin plied their trade. Musco declared that Christianity consisted in refraining from evil and in giving charity. He told his judges that only Christ should be worshipped and that doing good and helping the poor was of greater value than attending mass. He also blurted out that pastors in Geneva were worthy people, while Roman priests were rapacious wolves. Under torture, he revealed the names of many accomplices in Reggio, but then repented doing so, retracted his confession, and died without doubts about the true faith on 26 June 1569.

At least five of Musco's co-religionaries met the same fate. Two men of San Lorenzo were also arrested in Sicily and consigned to the episcopal vicar of Reggio: the priest Antonio Micicheni and Crescente Sciglione. They were followed in 1568 by Antonino Nicolino of Guardia; in 1573 by Demetrio Madafar of Pentidattilo (Reggio Calabria); and in 1582 by Antonio Cavalcanti of Cosenza.[31] The actual number of those sentenced must certainly be much greater. More will be known after an exhaustive search of Calabrian ecclesiastical archives. At Squillace, for example, on 20 July 1570, an auto da fé was held before a great throng which had flocked to wit-

---

[29]A photocopy of the letter, preserved in the Archivio di Stato, Florence (Mediceo, filza 4148), has been reproduced in C. Ritacca, *San Sisto dei Valdesi: Note storiche* (Cosenza: Fasano, 1974), 97–98.
[30]A. Armand-Hugon, *Storia dei Valdesi*, 2:40.

[31]See S. Caponetto, "B. Spadafora," 68.

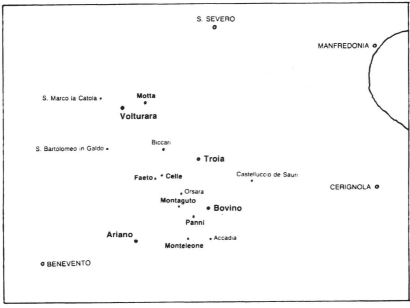

The Waldensian colonies of Calabria and Puglia in the sixteenth century.

ness an unusual spectacle and profit from the indulgences granted for such occasions. The barber Cesare Forese, condemned earlier at Messina to wear the penitential garment, asked to become a monk and thus saved himself from the stake. Not so for Cesare di Stalatti.[32] Only a very few from Montalto, Sant'Agata, San Lorenzo, and Reggio managed to make their way to Geneva and begin a new life. The "Italian St. Bartholomew Massacre" eradicated forever the Calabrian Waldensian colonies from that benighted area dubbed by Jesuit missionaries "the Italian Indies," and severed direct links with the brethren of the Piedmontese valleys and with Calvin's Geneva.

THE DEMISE OF THE COLONIES IN PUGLIA

The tragedy that befell the Calabrian Waldensians and shocked contemporaries overshadowed the fate of the Waldensian settlements in Puglia. Due to a lack of pertinent sources, their eradication towards midcentury is barely mentioned even by Waldensian historians.[33] We are indebted to the Jesuit Mario Scaduto for his diligent research resulting in the publication of new documents detailing the assimilation of the Waldensians of the Puglia into the Counter-Reformation Church. His fortunate discovery of a fascicle of letters written by the Jesuit Cristoforo Rodriguez to Inquisitor General Michele Ghislieri has contributed to the reconstruction of the facts behind the "holy enterprise."[34]

During the Angevin period, groups of Provençal peasants, welcomed by local proprietors eager for laborers to work their untilled fields as in Calabria, settled between Puglia and the Ultra principate, at Monteleone, Montaguto, Motta, Celle, and Faeto. In 1517 the lord of Ariano and Volturara received Provençal peasants on his lands, to whom he granted a statute in 1532. In 1561 Volturara totaled 115 households and was "almost wholly inhabited by Piedmontese and Provençals," as Rodriguez informed Father Francesco Borgia in a letter he wrote on 8 January 1564:

> This Volturara (where we were sent with a companion by the superiors of our order and by the most illustrious Inquisitors General) had been for about forty years deceived by the Waldensian and Lutheran heresies, seduced by false ministers who preached to them secretly in a private house, which the Holy Office ordered burned after learning about it. These here-

---

[32]See G. M. Monti, *Studi sulla Riforma cattolica e sul papato nei secoli XVI–XVII* (Trani: Vecchi & C., 1941), 251–52.

[33]See P. Rivoire, "Les colonies provençales et vaudoises de la Pouille," *Bulletin de la Société d'Histoire Vaudoise*, n. 19 (1902): 48–62.

[34]See M. Scaduto, "Tra inquisitori e riformati: Le missioni dei Gesuiti tra i Valdesi della Calabria e delle Puglie, con un carteggio inedito del Card. Alessandrino (S. Pio V)," *AHSJ* 15 (1946): 1–76; idem, "Cristoforo Rodriguez tra i Valdesi della Capitanata e dell'Irpinia, 1563–1564," *AHSJ* 35 (1966): 4–31, with appendix of unpublished documents, 31ff. My references are to this study, which is fuller than the preceding.

siarchs and preachers acted as physicians and surgeons the better to deal with and deceive the ignorant.[35]

These remarks by a Jesuit who had been sent on a special mission by the Roman Inquisition in 1563, corroborate the ancient tradition of links between Puglia and the Piedmontese valleys and explain why Barbs from Puglia were present at the Synod of Chanforan. The skillful practice of religious dissimulation, learned from the neighboring Calabrian colonies of fellow believers, permitted them to carry on their beliefs clandestinely until the onset of the persecutions. In the course of the trials mounted against the wretched survivors of the 1561 massacre, the relationship of the Calabrian Waldensians with their brethren in the Puglia came to light. The Dominican Valerio Malvicino, who had assisted the work of the Inquisition in Calabria, was immediately dispatched to Puglia to hunt down the heretics who had hidden behind the cloak of Catholicism. He promptly arrested many and had them shipped northward to Rome for trial. By the end of 1564, those who had not perished in prison were still awaiting judgment.

After the sorrowful impression left by the "terrible justice" meted out in Calabria and the work accomplished by the Jesuit fathers to bring back the survivors to the Catholic Church, the Roman Inquisition realized that it had to change its methods and seek the assistance of the Company of Jesus. The decision was reinforced by the abysmal ignorance of the clergy in the dioceses of Ariano, Bovino, Troia, and Volturara where the Provençal and Waldensian colonies were located. Father Rodriguez felt compelled to move thirty priests "especially deficient in grammar" into the episcopal residence at San Bartolomeo in Galdo for instruction. The Jesuit, who had arrived at Volturara on 14 August 1563 with his collaborators, determined to proceed with "gentleness" to eradicate the errors from the thinking of this good and simple people. The Waldensians, shocked by what happened to their Calabrian brethren, attempted to conceal their past leanings, proclaimed themselves good Catholics, and went to mass, as they had actually been doing for ages. But Ghislieri reminded the Jesuit that his flock were all heretics of long tradition, and should not to be permitted to participate in the mass without first purging themselves of their false beliefs. The Waldensians had to decide, the inquisitor wrote, "to come forward and openly and freely acknowledge the truth; or, otherwise, after we have employed gentle means and see that they do not work, we shall apply rigorous measures exterminating that city and the entire generation."[36] Rodriguez felt compelled to forward to Rome the names of 150 persons of Volturara who remained "negative." But the Jesuit, aware of the consequences for them, chose to question them again himself three, four, even six times, until he could write about those illiterate peasants, to whom pardon was promised for their relatives incarcerated in Rome, "they have been so fully convinced that...all have professed the truth."[37]

[35]*AHSJ* 35 (1966): 38–39, app. n. 6.
[36]Ibid., 14.
[37]Ibid., 15.

The return from Roman imprisonment of family members who had been arrested by the Dominican Malvicino served as the most efficacious instrument of persuasion. To return from Rome safe and sound seemed almost a miracle in itself! Another great tool had been the concession, obtained from the church reluctantly, to exonerate the reconciled from wearing the yellow penitential garment, a symbol of infamy. The penalties were reduced to freedom of movement under surveillance, fasting, prayer, and other salutary penances.

Alongside this work of spiritual reclamation, the Jesuits lovingly and conscientiously performed a great pastoral mission, instructing children between the ages of seven and fourteen and assisting the beleaguered peasants to appeal against onerous and unjust taxation. Waldensians released from Roman prisons who had converted to Catholic allegiance, such as Giovanni Ghigo, Giovanni Selvaggiato, and Lorenzo Mandone, expressed regret when Rodriguez left them. His mission brought 400 persons to espouse the Roman faith at Volturara, 270 at Montecorvino, 190 at Monteleone and Montaguto, 520 at Celle and Faeto. But all this was accomplished only with strenuous effort. A year and a half of intense activity concluded with about 1,500 conversions to the church. No one else was sent to Rome. The Catholicization of the Waldensians was accomplished skillfully through a policy of moderation, so moderate, in fact, that it has been forgotten even by historians of southern Italy.

BIBLIOGRAPHICAL NOTE

For the Inquisition in the Kingdom of Naples, the old work by L. Amabile, *Il Santo Officio della Inquisizione in Napoli*, 2 vols. (Città di Castello: S. Lapi, 1892), remains fundamental, usefully complemented by G. Coniglio, *Il regno di Napoli al tempo di Carlo V* (Naples: E.S.I., 1951).

19

MEDITERRANEAN CALVINISM: SPANISH SICILY AND SARDINIA

The Valdesian Backdrop

CALVINISM MADE SIGNIFICANT INROADS in the Spanish viceroyalty of Sicily from the mid–sixteenth century forward,[1] and Valdesianism appears to have paved the way. At present, research has not yielded the documents to verify the influence exercised by the sojourn there of Benedetto Fontanini, nor whether his *Beneficio di Cristo* circulated in manuscript in the Benedictine convents he visited. We have already mentioned that the bishop of Catania, Nicola Maria Caracciolo, possessed a copy of the printed edition, as well as Ochino's sermons and some works by Valdés. Discoursing about the Scriptures with Gian Francesco Alois, who had gone to see him sometime before 1547, he read some passages from it. We have also noted that Lorenzo Romano was accustomed, in the course of his lessons, to explicate the *Beneficio* as well as Melanchthon's *Loci communes*. But the great proselytizer of the doctrine of justification by faith alone, both Lutheran and Valdesian, was Bernardino Ochino. In a population that succumbed easily to enthusiastic fervor and was preoccupied, even when it did not allow anything to transpire, with human destiny and the afterlife, the words of the fiery Capuchin must have struck a profound chord during his 1540 Lenten preaching in Palermo. His flight to Geneva, barely two years later, reverberated broadly, especially among his fellow Franciscans.

In the early 1540s, perhaps as a consequence of these influences, a number of educated and well-born Sicilians crossed the straits of Messina to Naples, Rome, Ferrara, Modena, and Venice and entered into contact with groups sympathetic to the new ideas. Many returned home laden with prohibited books to report on what they had learned; others, who had become fully imbued with Protestant doctrines, actively proselytized their beliefs. The deposition made before the Inquisition by the

---

[1] For the Protestant Reformation in Sicily, I refer the reader to my "Bartolomeo Spadafora e la Riforma protestante in Sicilia." The page references are of its reprinting in my *Studi sulla Riforma*, 15–139.

Venetian jurist Giulio Besalù corroborates the close links between Sicily and Valdesian circles in Naples. Among the numerous persons with whom he discussed the
religious questions of the day in the decade from 1541 to 1551 when he had lived in
Naples, he mentioned Benedetto da Mantova; two lawyers of Palermo, Filippo de
Micheli and Giovanni Antonio Cannizu, prosecuted for Lutheranism in 1547; the
poet of Messina, Giulio Cesare Pascali, and Ludovico Manna, both exiles in Geneva;
and several Benedictines of San Giorgio Maggiore of Venice, where Benedetto da
Mantova had been dean in 1534 before being transferred to Catania. Besalù had conversed with them *"de iustificatione ex sola fide sine operibus."*

The Valdesian phase in Sicily, as in Naples, spanned the years roughly from
1539 to 1547. During this time, before the Council of Trent condemned the doctrine of justification by faith, numerous trials were instituted against schoolteachers,
Augustinian masters of theology, men of letters, jurists, merchants, and patricians
who belonged to that cultured elite among whom Valdés found a warm reception
and loyal followers.

In the second half of the century, from the 1560s on, the movement of religious
dissent assumed a pronounced Lutheran, and especially Calvinist cast under the
impulse of foreigners from Protestant Europe and Italians from the north, including
Calabria, so that here too that ideological and social parabola of the Italian Reformation to which Giorgio Spini alluded becomes evident.[2] In the hour of decision, the
humanistic circles, whether of Erasmian or Valdesian leanings, formed into evangelical conventicles composed of workers and artisans. The autos da fé were populated
with merchants, soldiers, and members of the lower classes, alongside ecclesiastics
and schoolteachers. In spite of the fragmentary nature of the sources and the indis-
criminate use by inquisitors of the term "Lutheran" to designate heretics in general,
there were few manifestations of autonomous religiosity or Anabaptist infiltrations.
Only the views of Antonio Caruso of Militello, a Franciscan tertiary residing in the
Oratory of Monte Scarpello (Catania), who was executed 5 July 1551 in Palermo,
seem to reflect a certain independence of thought. According to the confused
account by the author of the *Serie dei rilasciati*, he had maintained that "one should
not worship God, but only the humanity in Jesus Christ."[3]

However, we should not forget the highly original ideas of the Sicilians, Giorgio
Rioli, known as "Siculo," and Paolo Ricci, alias Camillo Renato, who initiated theological currents independent of both the Church of Rome and the Protestant
churches. In Cantimori's now classic formulation, they were "heretics" in the eyes of
both camps.[4] The doctrines of the two men, however, matured much later and did
not penetrate or have an impact on their native island. For sheer intelligence and
learning, for the modernity of some of his ideas, as well as for his outspoken defense
of freedom of conscience (he rose up with other Italian exiles to protest the execution
of Servetus in Geneva), Camillo Renato must be counted among the greatest Italian

[2] G. Spini, "Di Nicola Gallo," *Rinascimento* 2 (1951): 174–75.
[3] *Serie dei rilasciati*, n. 48.
[4] D. Cantimori, *Eretici*, chaps. 8, 9.

reformers.[5] The most interesting of his surviving works is undoubtedly the *Del Battesimo e della Santa Cena* (Concerning Baptism and the Lord's Supper). Here the author viewed the sacraments, not as rites objectively serving believers' consciences, but as "signs of faith," namely free and spontaneous manifestations of interior things. This rationalistic approach, as with Siculo, was coupled to a fervent mysticism and a vision of social equality and fraternal love, expressed tangibly in the Christian *agapé* for which he ardently longed.

It is not without significance that two Sicilians, emerging from a region where the most retrograde forms of feudal and ecclesiastical life still flourished, where citizens never fully tasted communal freedoms, and where all attempts at popular, republican, and anti-Spanish rebellion were ferociously crushed, should become the standard-bearers of theological independence and religious toleration, longing for a society transformed religiously and politically by the Spirit of God.

THE "ITALIAN INDIES"

The Jesuits engaged in missions to Calabria, Puglia, Abruzzi, and Sicily in 1548 and called these regions populated by a benighted clergy and people, the "Italian Indies." Girolamo Domenech in Palermo, Lainez in Monreale, and Diego Suarez, rector of the college in Messina, all wrote to their superiors that the ignorance of the clergy could not be believed if not witnessed at first hand. And as elsewhere, there was corruption to contend with as well. In 1536 the bishop of Catania in vain ordered his priests to rid themselves of their concubines. Certain customs, moreover, about which Ferrante Gonzaga complained in his report on the state of his dominions, especially irritated the people. According to the viceroy, parish priests in Palermo and in many other parts of the island, were accustomed to sell "the administration of the sacraments…, a pernicious and scandalous matter, and it has been reported to me that some poor people passed from this life without Communion and Extreme Unction, since they lacked the funds to pay for them." Another serious abuse required that a corpse could not be transported without the permission of the priest, a custom not abolished until 1781 during the reforms instituted by Marquis Domenico Caracciolo.[6]

If this was the state of the clergy, it is not difficult to imagine that of the people who confused the cults of the saints and of the Madonna with the pagan rite of hired mourners and other superstitions. Moral lassitude was widespread. According to the complaints voiced by contemporary writers, knifings, shootings, homicides, burglaries, rapes, and many other offenses were frequent occurrences. In marked contrast to this wanton behavior, were manifestations of fervently performed charitable work, attachment to the rites of the church, to holy days, and to the cult of relics and of

---

[5]S. Caponetto, "Bartolomeo Spadafora," 38–40. Cf. Camillo Renato, *Opere, documenti e testimonianze*, a cura di A. Rotondò (Florence: Sansoni; Chicago: The Newberry Library, 1968).
[6]S. Caponetto, "Bartolomeo Spadafora," 21–22.

saints. But on the whole, the Jesuits had to labor arduously to elevate the spiritual and moral levels of clergy and laity alike.

Thus in Sicily too, the church was in crisis, a situation that provided one of the principal motifs behind the European successes of the Lutheran protest. Francesco Maurolico, the humanist, scientist, and historian of Messina, in a letter to the Council of Trent on 1 October 1562, attributed the ills of the church to this looseness of morality and discipline, and recommended observance of the Gospel as the surest way to confute the Lutheran cause. This state of affairs had its repercussions in the higher spheres of society, especially in the cities of Palermo, Catania, Messina, and Syracuse, seats of an affluent citizenry where commerce flourished and foreigners were numerous. Preaching took on a previously unheard-of tone, prohibited books began to arrive, and numerous travelers brought news of events in Germany, Switzerland, and France. All this sparked curiosity in some more restless souls, and censure of ecclesiastical and political institutions took on a sharper edge. Moreover, in these southern people, their inquiring minds, love of argumentation and what is new helped form confused mixtures composed in part of fanaticism and supine acquiescence towards authority. Southern Italy, Gothein observed, is a land of extremes, especially where religion is concerned. In his famous *Avvertimenti a Marc'Antonio Colonna quando andò viceré di Sicilia* (Advice to M. A. Colonna on his becoming Viceroy of Sicily) (1577), Scipione di Castro had this to say about the character of the islanders:

> Sicilians in general are more astute than prudent, more shrewd than sincere, and they love innovations. They are quarrelsome, flattering, and invidious by nature, subtle critics of ministers' deeds, and they always suppose what they themselves would have done if they had been in the same circumstances to be the case.

Well before the first echoes of the Reformation reached Sicily, ill will, controversies, and protests had flared up over the Aragonese persecution of Jews and the founding of the tribunal of the Inquisition. Promulgated at Palermo on 18 June 1492, the new measures provoked a lively reaction, petitions, and requests for postponement from citizens and officials alike, with the result that the anti-Jewish measures were executed tardily and unwillingly. In addition to the economic interests threatened by the enactments, the protest was also animated by the ancient tradition of toleration, formed from the long cohabitation of many races pursuing different faiths and rites, which made Sicilians respectful of other religions. Authorities stridently exhorted the citizenry to attend the solemn "spectacles of the faith," which began in 1487 against those "neophytes" (Jews converted to Christianity) who had relapsed into their old faith. But the people always remained hostile to such forms of persecution and coercion and in the revolts of 1516 and 1522 showed their opposition to the Inquisition that Spain had imposed over them.

In 1513 the parliament courageously raised its voice against the procedures of the tribunal, which were much harsher than those of other magistracies of the kingdom, claiming that some of the condemned persons had admitted to confessing "either out of fear of torture or for other reasons, and were killed while manifesting wonderful signs of devotion and of being good Christians, to the very end of their lives, always retracting their confessions, saying that they were dying in atonement for their other sins."[7]

Three years later, at the death of Ferdinand the Catholic, a violent popular revolt in Palermo drove out the inquisitor, Melchiorre Cervera, who was barely saved by the Senate. Charles V was petitioned to restore the ancient customs by entrusting inquisitorial duties to bishops in their dioceses and to the Dominicans. But Spain could not renounce such a powerful instrument of control, and steered a course adroitly between concessions to parliament and a return to the former privileges of the tribunal, which ended up becoming the arbiter of government for the dominion, able to ruin any viceroy who dared to insist on respect for the law as Scipione di Castro had occasion to write, and as the endless jurisdictional battles amply demonstrate.[8]

Nevertheless, the emperor, with his Tunisian triumph behind him, found himself compelled to give in to the remonstrances of the parliament and suspended the privileges of the Inquisition for five years, a term extended to 1545. According to the inquisitor Antonio Franchini, the institution lost its entire authority during this period and Sicily became "a redoubt of iniquity and an asylum of heretics, with the danger that faith in God and loyalty to the monarch would be lost." But even before the second quinquennium expired, the emperor, concerned by the spread of Protestantism in Europe, restored total authority to the tribunal. The Inquisition, in spite of the determined opposition of the other magistracies, with the connivance of the viceroy who wanted nothing more than tranquillity for the dominion, attained such power that it appropriated cases pertaining to the feudal establishment, as well as cases of bigamy, thereby usurping both episcopal and viceregal prerogatives.

The rancorous jurisdictional squabbles were motivated by the desire of the senate and viceroys to safeguard the ancient rights of the kingdom, of which the Sicilians made full use in their opposition to Spain, against inquisitorial encroachments.[9] The tribunal fought back with such weapons as excommunication, accusations of heresy, and the humiliation of public penance, from which even Don Carlos of Aragon, duke of Terranova, president of the viceroyalty, could not exempt himself in 1568. Some members of society now began to feel their convictions shaken about the legitimacy of such provisions in religious as well as legal terms, and stimulated by the great theological debates, began to assume anticlerical and spiritually independent stances. This was the case with such judges of the Great Court as Giovanni Antonio Cannizu and Gian Guglielmo Boniscontro; the doctors in both civil and canon law, Filippo de Micheli and Giovan Domenico Briganti; the landowners Bartolomeo Spadafora and the baron of Burgio, Ludovico Buglio, "obstructor of the Holy Office," all tried for espousing the "Lutheran" heresy or for activities against the tribunal of the faith.

---

[7]Ibid., 22–23.
[8]Garufi III; V. Sciuti Russi, *Astrea in Sicilia: Il ministero togato nella società siciliana dei secoli XVI e XVII* (Naples: Jovene, 1983).
[9]Cf. F. De Stefano, *Storia della Sicilia* (Bari: Laterza, 1948), 120 ff.

Two of them, G. Boniscontro and B. Spadafora, tried to avenge themselves for the sufferings they had received at the hands of the Inquisition. The first of the two had taken his degree in jurisprudence at Ferrara in 1545, where he had Andrea Alciato as a teacher. It was here that he came into contact with reformed doctrines. Boniscontro, who had served as the lawyer for the indigent prisoners of the Holy Office from 1558 to 1561, was himself incarcerated by the tribunal in Palermo together with the knight, Don Francesco Bologna,[10] and sentenced to wear the penitential garment for ten years after being convicted "of having believed certain propositions held by the sect of Luther" against the intercession of saints, the veneration of images, the mass, and affirming that the Christian had only one prayer: the Lord's Prayer. In his *Capitolo in lode della Torta* (A Chapter in Praise of Cake), heavily laced with sarcasm, we read Boniscontro's lament for his life ruined by inquisitors and the horrors of his confinement:

> Of which to give you a true account
> It will suffice if I tell you in two words
> I am held a prisoner by the Holy Office.
>
> Now how will my voice, as it is accustomed
> Ever be able to compose soft sayings,
> If it is suffering when it should be rejoicing?
>
> That a cruel din of irons and keys,
> Of shackles, chains, a strange horror
> Aggravates my painful and heavy thoughts;
>
> The wonder is that one does not die
> Amidst so much sorrow, and how a man can bear
> So great a torment and not lose heart!

Boniscontro retired to the beautiful countryside outside Palermo to fulfill his salutary penances and to forget his past travails. In addition to the *Capitolo*, where he mocked ecclesiastical corruption and the empty formalism of the Familiars of the Holy Office, he wrote many fine poems in Italian and in Sicilian dialect.

Spadafora between Two Inquisitions

The case of Bartolomeo Spadafora, involving jurisdictional battles between the viceroy Don Giovanni Vega and the inquisitor Bartolomeo Sebastian, and between the Holy Offices of Rome and Spain, sheds light on the tensions within the ruling classes in sixteenth-century Spanish Sicily.

Bartolomeo Spadafora (1510?–66) was the second born to Francesco, baron of Mazzarrà, Venetico and San Martino, and to Melchiora Moncada, the daughter of Don Giovanni, baron of Ferra (or Ferla).[11] Spadafora had received a good humanistic education and aspired to a political career. Hoping to gain entrance into the court

---

[10]For Boniscontro, see Garufi II, 349–71.

of Charles V, after the sovereign's successful campaign in Tunis and brief halt in Sicily, he followed him to Naples. It was here that Spadafora came into contact with Valdesian circles, met Giulia Gonzaga, and perhaps heard Ochino preach. He formed what would become a close friendship with the countess and with Pietro Carnesecchi.

Early in 1546 Spadafora undertook a journey to Germany to meet the emperor at the next Diet in Ratisbon and present for judgment his family's ancient controversy over its ancestral lands with the city of Mistretta. On the return journey, he stopped in Rome to visit Vittoria Colonna, to whom he was related. Fourteen years later, writing from Messina to Michelangelo (15 March 1560) he recalled nostalgically his uplifting conversations with "that saintly soul," and recalled the hours passed with the aged artist, after her death, recalling her "holy memory."[12] This Roman sojourn, occurring after the failure of the second colloquy at Ratisbon between Catholics and Protestants and the enfeeblement of the current of so-called evangelism, was decisive in Spadafora's cultural and spiritual orientation.

While in Rome pursuing his claims to the barony of Ferla, formerly the property of his maternal grandfather, Don Giovanni Moncada, Spadafora received the disturbing news that he was being cited by the Sicilian Inquisition on charges of heresy and ordered to appear before it at once. It is uncertain what was behind the summons, a vendetta, perhaps, on the part of enemies who had opposed his ancestral rights to his lands, or the result of his imprudent words after the failure of the Ratisbon colloquy? Spadafora did not respond to the summons and was thereby declared contumacious and excommunicated and his property confiscated. The Sicilian inquisitors informed the Holy Office in Rome of the situation, but Paul III took charge of the case himself and absolved Spadafora. It was a strange situation. He had been convicted as a heretic in Sicily but exonerated by the supreme head of the church. The case opened a delicate question of jurisdiction between the two powerful tribunals of the faith.

It was the year 1547 and Charles V, to strengthen his hold over Sicily and tie it ever more closely to the crown of Spain, dispatched two inflexible officials to the island: the viceroy, Don Giovanni Vega, and Bartolomeo Sebastian, former head of the Inquisition in the Kingdom of Granada. On 3 July 1549 Vega responded to an inquiry from the emperor, reminding him of the autonomy of the Holy Office in Sicily and cautioning him about claims being advanced by the baron of Venetico, Spadafora's father, over the property confiscated from his son.

To avoid the dangers of a second trial, the humiliation of imprisonment, and the risk of torture, the only recourse for Bartolomeo was exile and the search for a safe haven and powerful patrons to help him obtain an imperial pardon. The Spadafora family had been bound to Venice for centuries and Bartolomeo's father-in-law was at the time the Republic's consul general in Sicily. Venice, still tolerant and

---

[11]See S. Caponetto, "Bartolomeo Spadafora," 79–139, for the account that follows and the accompanying quotations. [Trans. note.]
[12]Ibid., document n. 13, 137.

moderate even in religious matters, might be persuaded to receive someone condemned as a contumacious heretic. With the help of Cardinal Morone, Spadafora settled in Venice where he asserted his nobleman's rights as heir and descendant of Francesco Spadafora. On 17 May 1550 the authorities accepted his claims in full.

The gratitude of the guest, "poor, foreign gentleman, unknown, stripped of all honor, of every favor and of all support," was without limits. Spadafora felt that he owed a great debt to the republic and tried to transmit his gratitude to posterity. He wrote two beautiful orations, one at the death of doge Marcantonio Trevisan and the other at the election as doge of his friend and patron, Francesco Venier, in 1554. The two orations bore little resemblance to the run-of-the-mill speeches that constituted a popular and monotonous literary genre. In Spadafora's declamations, which contained their share of literary reminiscences, rhetorical flourishes, and commonplaces, one discerns a sincere admiration for republican liberties, all the more significant in an exile from that distant island of Sicily, now reduced to a Spanish province where the educated class and the aristocracy clung to ancient privileges and fought tenaciously to defend their autonomy, but could not prevent the consolidation of a foreign nobility and institutions directly linked to Spain.

Venice represented the ideal form of government in the eyes of Spadafora, whose city, Messina, possessed some aspects of an aristocratic, commercial republic tending towards autonomy in the sixteenth century. The myth of the *Serenissima* was not created by local poets and writers alone; such non-Venetians as Donato Giannotti and Spadafora contributed to it also. After the shocking Sack of Rome and the miserable end of the second Florentine republic, they viewed the queen of the Adriatic as a symbol of Italian honor and freedom.

In Spadafora this political ideal owed much to Erasmian and Valdesian notions, refined by constant meditation on the Sacred Scriptures, and nothing to Counter-Reformation thought. Venice is presented as a church-state, upon which God's protection descended vertically without the mediation of the Roman Curia. Spadafora, in his admiration for "the sacred and mysterious Republic," hyperbolically exalted as "hospice and asylum of safety, tranquillity and freedom placed by God on earth," oscillated between the utopian and the rationalist.

Spadafora's orations, as well as two others he delivered before the Academy of the *Uniti* which he joined in 1552, were published by Girolamo Ruscelli in 1554. The exile asked Ruscelli to eulogize in a preface both Charles V and Lady Isabella Vega, the daughter of the viceroy of Sicily who was married to Pietro di Luna, related to Spadafora on his mother's side. It was hoped that praise for Isabella's grace and beauty would touch the viceroy's heart and remind him of Spadafora's unfortunate predicament. Aggrieved by the separation from his wife and children and by the stain on his ancient name brought by the condemnation for heresy, Spadafora was effectively prevented from embarking on a promising political career in Venetian service.

In 1553 for the third time, Spadafora appealed to the emperor "to be restored to his grace and recognized as a faithful and devoted servant of God and vassal of His Majesty...,"[13] a petition that must have been supported by the Venetian Republic.

The emperor wrote directly to the Sicilian inquisitor, and the latter replied from Messina on 8 October coupling the case of Spadafora to a report about an auto da fé held on the previous 18 June. The inquisitor could not conceive separating the matter of the nobleman from the spread of Protestant currents on the island, and especially in the city of Messina. To pardon a contumacious heretic without going through the prescribed judicial processes would be a disservice both to God and to the imperial majesty.

But Venice did not let the issue drop and ordered its ambassador at the court of Charles V, Antonio de Mula, to seek grace for Spadafora or at least a safe conduct so he could return home to assist his family after the deaths of his father and oldest brother. It was the viceroy, Don Giovanni Vega, at odds with the all-powerful tribunal, who offered a solution: put the question to the Supreme Council of the Monarchy. It was a deft maneuver against his archenemy, the inquisitor.

On 13 May 1555 the emperor ordered that the exile be pardoned, invited to return home, and the confiscation of his property rescinded, and the viceroy from Messina sent Spadafora a letter of safe conduct. The emperor had come to his decision recognizing the importance of maintaining good relations with Venice, a matter of great urgency at a time when hostility to Spain was brewing throughout the peninsula. Moreover, he did not want to add his faithful vassal, Spadafora, to the growing ranks of hostile exiles.

News of Spadafora's impending rehabilitation raced among his friends. Carnesecchi wrote about it joyfully to Giulia Gonzaga at the end of April. The countess immediately acceded to his request to assist the poor Bartolomeo, always short of money and now about to face the long journey home, by having funds transferred to him from her Venetian holdings. But then came a stunning reversal of fortune. Just a few months after the emperor's favorable decision, the "magnificent Spadafora" was arrested in Venice at the order of Paul IV and brought as a prisoner to Rome. The new Sicilian inquisitor, Francesco Orosio, ready to take any steps to enhance his tribunal, had his revenge. To arouse the suspicions of the old inquisitor in Paul IV and push him to a review of the judicial proceedings, it sufficed to remind him that Paul III had shown clemency to Spadafora through the intercession of Cardinal Pole. The Carafa pope's opinion of the Sicilian patrician must have been akin to what he thought of Cardinal Morone, imperial and "heretical." Spadafora was caught up in the great persecution under way against the Valdesians. After having successfully eluded Sicilian inquisitors for a decade, Spadafora now began his imprisonment at the hands of the Holy Office in Rome. It was 8 September 1556.

After the peace of Cave resolved Paul IV's differences with Spain, to the great bitterness of the pope and the relief of the Romans fearful of another impending sack of their city, Carnesecchi's hopes for the release of the imperialists Morone, Spadafora, and Galeota were not fulfilled. Other supporters of the emperor and rebellious vassals were freed, but Morone remained incarcerated in Castel Sant'Angelo and Spadafora and Galeota were left to languish in their cells in the

---

[13]Ibid., document n. 3, 131.

prison of Ripetta, where in the summer they were "as cool as in a furnace." The true reason for Spadafora's confinement was his friendship with the English Cardinal Pole, whom the pope considered the head of a family of apostates and heretics.

In spite of the intercession of Venice and the efforts made by Carnesecchi and Giulia Gonzaga to have him relegated to house arrest, Spadafora's only consolation was to be able to share his confinement with the Augustinian Andrea Ghetti and Bishop G. Francesco Verdura. With the slow passage of the months, the hopes of the Valdesians that they could bring relief to the prisoners dissipated. On 20 May 1559 nothing more could be said than that "they are alive, which is quite a lot considering where they are."

The death of the old, ailing pope was now awaited by Carnesecchi as a release for himself as well as for his friends. And thus it must have appeared also to the Roman populace who erupted violently at the news of his passing on 18 August. The eighteenth and nineteenth were turbulent days filled with destructive excesses, during which the people, spurred on by the enemies of the Carafa family, vented their rage against everything that recalled the rule of the Neapolitan pontiff, while the powerful lords whom he had banished from the city made a triumphant reentry with the Colonna family at their head.

The seat of the Inquisition on Via Ripetta was besieged and its prisoners, some seventy in number, freed after being made to swear that they would live as good Catholics. A few such as Galeota, convinced that they were fully entitled to absolution, remained in the city, but most of the others saw that unexpected event as their salvation and took advantage of it without delay. Spadafora walked out of prison on 18 August and found refuge with Giulia Gonzaga, who was happy to announce the glad tidings to those who had suffered with her. "I rejoice greatly," Carnesecchi replied from Florence on 2 September, "that Don Bartolomeo has been freed, and every hour seems like a thousand years until I can see him and embrace him again, and the same for Signor Mario [Galeota], although I was able to rejoice about him even sooner."

Spadafora's return to Messina, after an absence of fourteen years, marked the beginning of a new life, one still filled with pitfalls and dangers, but which he confronted steadfastly and with renewed confidence. He succeeded in securing freedom and reconciliation to the church for his sister Mattia, the widow of Girolamo Moncada, baron of Ferla. We do not know precisely why she had been tried, but it is likely that her troubles were connected to her brother's, who had concerned himself with property matters connected with his brother-in-law's barony.

While Spadafora awaited final absolution from the new pope, he dedicated himself to restoring the prestige of his family and rebuilding his patrimony. In April 1560 he wrote to the Venetian ambassador in Rome requesting for himself and for his son confirmation as Venetian consul general in Messina, a position previously held by his father-in-law. The following year he was seated in the most important civic governing body, the Senate, where his family had long been represented. The scattered bits of information on Spadafora during this period show him eager to enhance his family's wealth and secure a solid future for his children. In the letter of

1560 to Michelangelo, mentioned above, the religious enthusiasm that had been aroused in Spadafora by Vittoria Colonna was a faded memory, crowded out by the pressing needs of daily life. Nevertheless, when he learned that his old acquaintance, the general of the Augustinians Girolamo Seripando had been made a cardinal and appointed to the Supreme Inquisition on 1 April 1561 Spadafora wrote him at Trent a long Latin letter of congratulations, expressing his great satisfaction at the well-deserved honors, and the wish that he would be effective in healing "the pernicious dissent among Christians."

In April 1566 the indefatigable countess of Fondi, Giulia Gonzaga, died and rumors began to circulate quickly that the Inquisition would find itself very busy now that it had come into possession of her correspondence with Carnesecchi. Spadafora's own death in July of that year freed him from the nightmare of renewed persecution after twenty years of struggling, suffering, and affronts, but all in the name of Christ, as he had written to Seripando in a moment of pride recalling his persecutions as a sign of grace.[14]

LEARNING AND THE PRINTING PRESS

Boniscontro's literary campaign remained an isolated affair, and Spadafora's victory an exceptional case. In Sicily, political, cultural, and religious conditions hindered the manifestation of any sort of serious dissent. At the close of the period of internecine conflict, which aggravated by foreign intervention had tormented the island for the entire fourteenth century, under the impetus of a triumphant humanism, Sicily enjoyed a cultural flowering in the fifteenth century that resembled the splendid achievements of the age of Frederick II. But a changed historical situation prevented the establishment of a single great center of learning in Sicily. More favorable conditions for such a development existed in various centers in the peninsula and in not-so-distant Naples during the reign of the enlightened statesman, Alfonso the Magnanimous. Although the new learning spread to the main cities on the island, Sicilian humanism was not distinguished for its originality, but was rather a vigorous extension of Italian models. The University of Catania did not support the new philosophical and scientific directions and continued to concentrate on the training of physicians and jurists. Culture remained a monopoly of the nobility and rich bourgeoisie and throughout the sixteenth century maintained a conservative and practical orientation. This was especially apparent in the disciplines where the "Sicilian" aspects were strongest, in historical writing and in the law, intent on exalting the autonomy and traditions of the reign by defending baronial privileges. Anyone who looks at the printing output of the period will note the prevalence of law books, grammars, and devotional books, to the detriment of the classics and the major works of Italian literature.

The spirit with which the educated classes perceived the great religious revolution of the day is echoed in a letter written by the Benedictine abbot, Francesco Maurolico, to the delegates assembled at the Council of Trent. The document, men-

[14]Ibid., document n. 14, 137–38.

tioned earlier, offers a prime example of an intellectual's ability to adapt to the world of the Counter-Reformation. Written a year after the massacre of the Waldensians at San Sisto and Guardia, it does not express a single word of pity for the slaughter of thousands of helpless peasants. On the contrary, the humanist churchman felt only disparagement for them, comparing them to "dogs" chasing a carriage, imitating the teachings and the incredible audaciousness of "the sophist, man-eating" Germans.[15] And then, with customary nationalistic arrogance, he heaped abuses on Melanchthon, Zwingli, and Erasmus, the latter described as presumptuous, ignorant, and a supporter of the Lutherans. Strangely, the writer mentioned neither Luther nor Calvin personally, perhaps so as not to evoke the devil. The letter's anti-Erasmian phobia betrays the renown achieved by the Dutch humanist even in Sicily among the monastic orders, certainly the Benedictines, brother-members of Teofilo Folengo and Benedetto Fontanini, and among intellectuals of the stamp of Boniscontro and Spadafora.

The narrow vision in Maurolico's letter was symptomatic of the confining cultural climate. On 28 January 1543 the inquisitor, Arnaldo Albertini, prohibited laymen and ecclesiastics alike, under the threat of excommunication, from debating and publishing conclusions "whether in theology, philosophy or the liberal arts," a measure intended to oppose "the temerity" of the supporters of heretical theses. Any attempt at discussion in the universities, convents, and academies was being repressed at the outset.

The preponderant presence of theologians, jurists, schoolteachers, priests, and booksellers in the autos da fé of 13 February and 23 December 1547, and 19 May 1549 confirms what the inquisitor feared. On close examination of the list, there are several foreigners: three artisans from Nuremberg, a French engraver, and a Rumanian bookseller. They were condemned alongside the Lombard Calvinist schoolteacher Baldassarre Cazzola, who had broken out of prison; the teacher of grammar, Virgilio Tivoli, and the notary from Syracuse, Giovanni Satalia. Then we read the names of the doctors and masters of theology: the Augustinian, Geremia da Tripedi, a "great Lutheran" and prison breaker; the Franciscan Conventuals, Giovan Battista Vinci and Antonio Bevilacqua; the Augustinian preacher Giacomo Anfulio; the priests Domenico Santoro, Vincenzo Lombardo, Pietro Granata, Giovan Pietro Giardina, Antonino Buscarero, Vincenzo Salvagio, and Cristoforo Gerardo.[16]

Although judges were quick to call all Protestants "Lutherans," the wide appeal of the new ideas among churchmen, schoolteachers, professional men, and artisans should be recognized. Nor should we discount the considerable number of "neophytes" who had relapsed to their old faith. Their punishment was a cause for scandal and the subject of heated discussions among Christians. Many of these Jewish *conversos* had been the fellow workers of "Lutherans," and they often found themselves reunited in prison or as galley slaves. Although the measures adopted by the inquisitor Albertini were aimed at suppressing at birth suspect and dangerous discus-

---

[15]Ibid., 27.
[16]Cf. Garufi I, 282–84.

sions, they left the door open for the clandestine introduction of printed materials. It was impossible to control the arrival of prohibited books concealed among the bales of merchandise in an island with important ports at Messina, Palermo, and Catania, where hundreds of ships arrived from every quarter.

In 1549 the goldsmith Bartolomeo Carpan shipped a large bench concealing books by Luther, Melanchthon, and "such heresiarchs" from Venice to Messina and addressed to the shop of Lauro Orso. At his Venetian trial in 1569, Carpan revealed that he had received the books from Baldassarre Altieri, who as we know, had corresponded with Luther and Melanchthon for years. In their hometown of Treviso, Carpan and his brothers were known as "Lutherans" and proselytizers, and Bartolomeo in particular was considered by his accusers a "great Lutheran." He voiced his views everywhere and in the countryside would actually climb trees to be heard better when "he preached and disseminated his heretical and damned opinions."[17] The efforts of the dynamic Altieri lie behind this episode to disseminate materials for religious instruction and proselytization among the many Venetian goldsmiths working in Sicily.

An even more significant attempt at Protestant propaganda occurred some twenty years later at Messina. In the home of the patrician Filippo Campolo a case was confiscated that contained a commentary on the Pauline Epistles, and a booklet with the unequivocal title, *Qui loci sint docendi pro Evangelio plantando,* concealed among jars of jam. Its author was Georg Rörer (1492–1557), Luther's friend and collaborator at Wittenberg. In ten chapters the small work summarized Lutheran teachings in simple terms, making it an ideal instrument for the instruction of the newly converted.[18] Campolo had shipped it from Naples to his mother and sisters, who were at least intermediaries for the numerous preachers of the clandestine conventicles in Messina.

In 1559 the inquisitor of Messina, having ascertained from the many trials held in his jurisdiction, the crucial role of the printed book in the work of evangelization, issued a peremptory decree ordering the prompt consignment of all suspect literature to the Jesuit College in the city. So many books were turned in, that in September of

---

[17]Quoted from R. Fontana, "'Solo, senza fidel governo et molto inquieto de la mente.' Testimonianze archivistiche su alcuni amici di Lotto processati per eresia," in *Lorenzo Lotto*. Atti del Convegno internazionale di studi, Asolo, 1980 (Treviso, 1981), 279–97. Lauro Orso succeeded in fleeing to Naples, while a friend of his, the Paduan merchant Francesco Vielmo, was arrested in Sicily and condemned to the stake. Although, in the anonymous denunciation of 26 November 1568 we read the name Francesco Vielmo, it is uncertain whether this refers to the person who was sentenced to the stake at Palermo on 8 June 1561. In the inquisitors' memorandum, he is recorded as "Francesco Vicino," Paduan merchant. Cf. ASV, Sant'Uffizio, busta 29, fasc. B. Carpan; list of the auto da fé of 8 June 1561 published in Garufi I, 303.

[18]This small work by the corrector of Luther's manuscripts can be read as an appendix to the first Latin translation of the *Betbüchlein*, published at Wittenberg in 1529 with the title *Enchiridion piarum precationum cum Calendario et passionali ut vocant.* It was reprinted in 1543. Cf. *WA* 10:2, 361. The work circulated in a French version entitled *Quatre Instructions fidèles*, printed between 1529–30. Cf. N. Weiss, "La littérature de la Réforme française," *Bulletin de la Société d'Histoire du Protestantisme Français* 36 (1887) & 37 (1888). On Rörer, see *Deutsche Biographie*, 53: 480–85.

that year, the work of examining them that had begun in June was only halfway completed. Later the search was extended to an inspection of all the bookshops in the realm. Finally in 1571, the inquisitor Giovanni Bezerra de la Quadra assigned Baron della Limina the duty of inspecting all arrivals at the port, authorizing him to confiscate all suspect books, and arrest their owners.

A previously unknown episode helps to illustrate how ideas were channeled into the island: the inquisitorial trial held at Toledo in September 1568 against a Sicilian soldier stationed at Agrigento who was the son of a peasant from Messina.[19] The suspect, thirty-five years old at the time, had himself been an agricultural laborer until age sixteen, when he joined up with a Spanish captain who brought him to Milan, and later to Piedmont and France. Before the youth left Lyons to return to Sicily, a Huguenot entrusted him with Jean Crespin's martyrology, published at Geneva in 1556 with the title *Recueil des Martyrs*. The poor Sicilian peasant-soldier told the powerful inquisitor of Toledo that he could read neither Italian nor French. But this excuse did not hold up after the discovery of two books of anti-Protestant polemic in Italian by the Jesuit Antonio Possevino among the humble belongings in his duffle.[20] This may have been no more than a clever subterfuge suggested by his French contact to direct eventual accusations of heresy away from himself. Whatever the precise explanation, the fact remains that a peasant had become, consciously or not, the bearer of a work of Protestant propaganda as incendiary as Crespin's martyrology, which so infuriated the judges when they read Calvin's letters to the martyr Denis Peloquin, burned alive on 5 September 1553 at Villefranche, and to his prison companions.[21] The story of the soldier from Agrigento, entrusted with the duties of *colporteur* at a time when Spanish inquisitors were in a frenzy of activity, is a useful one because there are no lists of prohibited books confiscated on the island as opposed to the abundant records for Venice and Naples.

FROM THE PREACHING OF THE "MINIMS" TO THE LUTHERAN HERESY

The activity during the 1530s of the order of Minims of San Francesco di Paola, which had spread throughout the island in the early years of the century from neighboring Calabria, is an important element in the early history of the Sicilian Reformation, an aspect of the movement not well known due to the lack of sources. On 30 May 1542, Fra Petruccio Campagna was sentenced to death *"pro heregias lutheranas"* and as an "obstinate member of that sect."[22] This humble, unknown member of the

---

[19]Madrid, Archivo Histórico Nacional, Inquisición de Toledo, Leg. 190, n. 18.
[20]Cf. *Trattato del Santiss. Sacrificio della Messa*. Lione: Michele Giove, 1563; *Risposta a Pietro Vireto, a Nicolò Balbani e a due altri heretici i quali hanno scritto contra il Trattato della Messa di M. Antonio Possevino*. Avignone: Pietro Rosso, 1566.
[21]*Le Recueil de plusieurs personnes qui ont constamment enduré la mort pour le nom du Seigneur...*[Geneva], 1556, contains Calvin's letter to Denis Peloquin, condemned to death at Villefranche on 5 September 1553, and those of his prison mates Louys de Marsac, his cousin, and Estienne Gravot. At the moment of their final ordeal they chanted the canticle of Simeon. See E.& E. Haag, *La France Protestante* (Paris, 1847–58), 8: 183–84.

order was followed to the stake some years later by Francesco Pagliarino, the provincial of the vast province of Messina, which included Catania and Syracuse, who had been born at Savoca, near Messina. In the general chapter of 1542 held at Bologna on 22 July he participated in the election of the general in his capacity as provincial for Sicily. At this point, Pagliarino disappears from the records of his order. We do not know where he first became acquainted with Protestant ideas, but it may have been in Bologna where in the decade between 1530 and 1540 persons influenced by Erasmus and Bucer were active. According to the list of Sicilian victims of the Inquisition, the *Serie dei rilasciati*, at the time that Pagliarino was sentenced to the stake on 5 July 1551, he was a convinced and ardent Lutheran. He in fact "denied that confession was a sacrament...asserted that every Christian was in the grace of God, that faith alone sufficed to justify the Christian without works, and rejected free will."[23] Pagliarino's work of proselytization was so successful that ten years after his death, Jesuits still remembered him as the chief heretic of the region.[24] It is interesting to note the arrival at Geneva in 1558 of another former Minim, Angelo Mangano of Bordonaro, a village near Messina. From 1559 to 1560 we find him enrolled at the University of Basel with the name of Antonius Angelus Messanensis.

The many Protestants discovered and sentenced at Messina over two decades bear witness to the efforts to win conversions made by Pagliarino, Mangano, and Minico Santoro of Mandanici. Messina was particularly troublesome to the inquisitors who frequently stationed themselves there with their entire family of functionaries. Two solemn "spectacles of the faith" were celebrated there in 1555 and 1572. Messina, *Clavis Siciliae*, was the major manufacturing center on the island and it was so successful in extracting privileges from Spain as to assume the characteristics of a virtual aristocratic republic within the viceroyalty, arousing the jealousy of the other cities which led to its eventual ruin after the repression of the 1674 rebellion. But in the sixteenth century Messina reached the apogee of its political and economic power. By the end of the fifteenth century the banks of the river Valdemone had become covered with mulberry trees and Messina shortly became one of the leading European centers of silk production. The trade fair of mid-August was wholly given over to this product. In the first half of the sixteenth century three hundred thousand pounds of finished silk were sold, a figure that doubled in the second half. Raw silk was exported to Genoa, Florence, Lucca, Bologna, Venice, and abroad to England, Holland, and France. Work in silver was second in importance to the silk industry. Keeping pace with the burgeoning economic prosperity was a rapid increase in the population, which tripled in the course of the century to one hundred thousand in 1606. As the great maritime city grew, sumptuous palaces were built and beautiful suburbs sprang up. In many respects, Messina was Sicily's most important urban center, dominated by the nobility and the wealthy mercantile class, while below them

[22]Garufi I, 282 and *Serie dei rilasciati*, n. 391.

[23]*Serie dei rilasciati*, n. 153; Garufi I, 292.

[24]See S. Caponetto, "Le città siciliane dinanzi alla Riforma: Messina," in *Città italiane del '500 tra Riforma e Controriforma*. Atti del Convegno Internazionale di Studi, Lucca, 13–15 ottobre 1983 (Lucca: Pacini, 1988), 103–10.

the poverty of the laborers and peasants, who together with adventurers and job seek-ers constituted the majority of the population, grew more acute. This situation cre-ated difficulties for the spies and informers of the Inquisition because, under the guise of commercial activity, missionaries, distributors of books, merchants, and sol-diers hailing from parts where the Reformation had succeeded, found ways to infil-trate. Significantly the first Italian Protestant martyr was Petruccio Campagna of Messina. In the second half of the century the Protestant movement spread to other urban centers on the island: from the coastal cities of Palermo, Syracuse, Catania, and of course, Messina, the new ideas filtered into the interior and reached the smaller towns.

On 7 May 1557 a new viceroy, Don Giovanni della Cerda, duke of Medinaceli, assumed authority in Sicily, in whom the inquisitors, now freed of his troublesome predecessor, Giovanni Vega, found a staunch ally. Under della Cerda's regime, the Holy Office attained the height of its powers even to the point of being served by royal officials and the Great Court. It prevailed in every jurisdictional conflict, and contrary to the statutes, obtained the privilege of bearing arms for its functionaries. This was an abuse fraught with consequences, since they always claimed to be exempt from the law when they committed their frequent homicides. In 1568 inquisitorial officials in Sicily totaled eight hundred. By 1573 Philip II, well aware of the usefulness of this security force drawn from many ranks of society, but especially from the nobility, had almost doubled their number.

The enormous prestige enjoyed by the Inquisition is demonstrated by the repression of the revolt led by the notary Cataldo Tarsino. On 23 September 1560 the nobility in the Senate, over the opposition of the guild consuls, decreed a reduc-tion in the weight of the loaves of bread to compensate for the grain shortage. The populace of Palermo rose up in fury, and after wounding some of the nobility, com-pelled them to barricade themselves in the castle by the port that housed the prison of the Inquisition. One of the noblemen persuaded the rebel chief Tarsino to embark secretly for his birthplace Paola. Meanwhile, some of the other ringleaders were apprehended and killed. The next day, the sight of their bodies dangling from poles, erected on the main square, quashed any further thought of protest. The inquisitor Ludovico Paramo subsequently claimed that his tribunal had saved the kingdom from the grave threat of revolt.

Under the inquisitor Bezerra de la Quadra (1563–72), born in Estremadura, abbot of the religious house of Magione in Palermo, the pursuit of heresy was con-ducted with unparalleled tenacity and cruelty. Persons penanced totaled more than a hundred, and many others were condemned to capital punishment, as de la Quadra informed the Great Council of Spain in 1566. To strengthen the authorities' control over the religious life every parish was obliged to record the names of its people who had confessed themselves and partaken of communion, who in turn, received a cer-tificate attesting to the fact. This turned out to be a highly effective device, as can be seen by the numbers of suspects turned up between 1566 and 1573.

As the people's interest in religious questions grew, inquisitorial severity increased commensurately, while the dominion of the nobility and rich bourgeoisie also hardened. The spread of sympathy for Reformation ideas, especially among artisans, small merchants, and laborers, reflected their spiritual and economic discontent. It was these groups especially that felt the burdensome tax structure, a consequence of the price revolution, the dramatic increase in the cost of living, and in the countryside, the numberless petty exactions by which dishonest officials swindled the peasants. The discontent found an easier outlet for persons who were in touch with their fellow workers abroad, and many of those prosecuted acknowledged that they had learned about the new religious ideas through contacts made in such places as Genoa, Lucca, Venice, and Lyons. The small bourgeoisie, whose associations never attained the autonomy of their counterparts on the mainland, felt discontent over the unjust fiscal exactions and the obstacles to their fuller participation in public life. Thus this class of small merchants linked itself to the populace whose situation, miserable enough in normal times, became truly tragic as famine and plague beset the island throughout the century. Under these oppressive conditions many persons found in a renewed faith an outlet for their resentment against the prevailing spiritual and political oppression. Both social and religious themes cropped up in their angry discussions, which associated the Church of Rome with Spain, indissolubly united in the repression of every attempt to reform the existing political and ecclesiastical order.

In the second half of the sixteenth century, under the impulse of a vigorous Calvinist missionary effort, the new ideas penetrated precisely among the lower classes, ideas calling for a religious renewal, of a divine justice juxtaposed with human injustice, and of a greater hope in the rediscovery of the Gospel message. This spread of Protestant currents among the populace, which showed itself to be more tenacious and steadfast than other levels of society, was fully explored in the studies on the French Reformation by Henri Hauser and Lucien Febvre,[25] and by Adolfo Omodeo after World War II in a course of university lectures dedicated to John Calvin and the Reformation in Geneva. Treating the popular appeal of Protestant ideas in France, he offered an explanation, which applies as well to the Sicilian and Italian segments of the movement:

> The full vigor of the Protestant Reformation manifested itself…among humble believers, among artisans and the populace for whom the new teachings opened up not only the interpretation of Scripture, but also the autonomous direction of their own consciences. The psychology of these common people is very simple, in certain respects, medieval. It was the custom in the Middle Ages that every person should have his or her own saint in whom to confide and who would offer protection in both spiritual and temporal affairs. The cult of the Virgin, Helper, Patron, Advocate *par excellence* had enjoyed great success. Now the Reformation presented itself in the minds of the people under this aspect: that the true Savior, he who

---

[25]See H. Hauser, *Études sur la Réforme française* (Paris: Picard et Fils, 1909); L. Febvre, "Une question mal posée: Les origines de la Réforme française et le problème des causes de la Réforme," *Revue historique* 161 (1929): 1–73.

alone could bestow salvation through his grace was Jesus Christ, that only in him could one find the confidence to cloak oneself in the only merit which had any value in the eyes of God. The Reformation, thus, presented itself as the expression of a new devotion, unique and unparalleled, which emphasized the same exclusive tendency which the medieval devotions had for their patron saint.[26]

A number of episodes illustrate the people's break from the traditional cult and devotions, and two are especially striking. The Jesuit father Girolamo Nadal, writing from Messina to Ignatius Loyola in 1549, described as an amazing event the substantial participation of the people in a procession honoring the relics of saintly and virgin martyrs.[27] Two years later, on 7 August 1551, the authorities of Messina granted a safe conduct to outlaws who wanted to participate in the Feast of the Assumption on 15 August and benefit from the indulgences that accompanied the occasion. Contemporaneously, under the threat of a fine, "all Turkish Moors and others who work as stevedores" were to come forward and be recorded "so that they could be used to carry the litter and the other objects needed for that festivity."[28] In other words, the authorities had been unable to find among the poor, in spite of their enthusiasm for the Feast Day of the Madonna, a sufficient number to carry her statue in procession. Their refusal is undoubtedly attributable, at least in part, to the insistent preaching on evangelical themes of Fra Francesco Pagliarino, who had been killed at the stake just a month before.

The spread of the Reformation and an accompanying sentiment of skepticism and disbelief towards the rites and precepts of the Roman church among the populace led to even a degradation of the "new Gospel" into materialistic and frequently vulgar forms, as Federico Chabod has so aptly illustrated. Just as the cult of saints in primitive populations often degenerated into idolatrous manifestations, similarly the rejection of the cult of saints and of the Virgin resulted in acts of profanation against images, and irreverent and blasphemous expressions. We can take as an example the case of the Calabrian Cola Pelicano of Sant'Agata, of Clemente Carnoval of Saragozza, of the surgeon of Palermo Vincenzo di Marino, all condemned to many years of galley service for their sacrilegious acts against images of the Virgin and saints.

SYRACUSE AND ENVIRONS

From the mid-1550s on, intense Protestant proselytization took place at Syracuse, Noto, Ferla, Spaccaforno (modern Ispica), and Buscemi. During the same period, while efforts to introduce the Reformation seemed to be at a standstill at Palermo, activity at Messina remained under the surface, and at Catania there were only occa-

---

[26]A. Omodeo, *Giovanni Calvino e la Riforma in Ginevra* (Bari: Laterza, 1947), 45–46.
[27]S. Caponetto, "Le città," 108.
[28]Ibid., 107–8.

sional appearances by dissidents in the convents near Mt. Aetna; in the Syracuse area, instead, clandestine conventicles formed with centers at Syracuse and Noto.

A large number of reconciled heretics appeared in the auto da fé celebrated at Palermo on 18 October 1556: Girolamo Russo of Ferla; Antonino Antonello of Spaccaforno; and eight citizens of Noto, Corrado and Girolamo Luparello, Carlo di Modica, Antonio Caffisi, Nicola di Mineo, Antonio Gambacurta, Pietro Giovanni Tommaso, and Michele Spaccafurno. The schoolteacher, Girolamo Litramo, who had fled prison, and the priest Sebastiano Carbeni, who may have died there, were also from Noto. The priest Giovan Giacomo Petrone of Syracuse, who was reconciled to the church in 1553 and then relapsed, was executed, followed two years later in the auto da fé of 1 May 1558 by Girolamo Russo. Among the "great Lutheran heretics" punished on that occasion, including "some teachers and dogmatizers who had caused great harm," there were the Syracusans Girolamo de Amodeo, the tailor Antonio Junta (or Giunta), Pietro Trapani, and the effigy of the Spanish monk Luis de Castro, "who had been going around teaching the Lutheran sect" and managed to escape.[29] Priests and schoolteachers of the area were joined by platemakers and silversmiths, foreigners, and locals alike, with links to their fellow workers and in constant contact with merchants and sailors. Four of these artisans were reconciled in 1560: Antonio di Antona, Nicola Cassarino, Giovanni Maria Bonello, and Francesco Cascione. They are names on a list of twenty persons who received absolution, but the schematic memorandum sent to the Supreme Council of the Spanish Inquisition on 18 February offers no details about the charges against them, nor for the impenitent prisoners consigned to the secular arm for execution. Many of them are described as "Lutherans" in the *Serie dei rilasciati*, a list that includes Giacomo Bonello and Francesco Gioan Porcaro, both burned alive, who were certainly Calvinists.[30]

It is likely in fact, that all those dubbed "Lutherans" in the Syracuse area were actually members of a Calvinist community. This is suggested by the tenacity with which the silversmiths proselytized for their views, and after abjurations and reconciliations, returned to their faith. Antonio di Antona was sentenced to death in 1564, "first to be hung and then burned until his body be reduced to ashes." Francesco Cascione succeeded in fleeing. In spite of the repression, heretical currents persisted in the Syracuse and Noto area until 1571. Three of the most daring persons met their fate in 1566: on 3 January Michele Giovanni Carobeni, who had been reconciled in 1558 and then "had relapsed into the same errors as an obstinate heretic"; on 26 December, Pietro Giovanni Tommaso, who had been reconciled in 1556, "shoemaker, pertinacious and impenitent Lutheran."[31] Condemned with him was Matteo de Amodeo, first sentenced in 1558, recaptured and reconciled in 1560 together with Girolamo de Amodeo for refusing to fulfill his penances, and finally relapsed,

---

[29]Garufi I, 300.

[30]Ibid., 302. We know the story of Giacomo Bonello. For Francesco Gioan Porcaro, the *Serie dei rilasciati*, n. 140, gives this account: "Francesco Gio. Porcaro, heretic, who denied that Christ was really in the host and rejected indulgences, the pope, praised the things of Luther and other errors...."

[31]S. Caponetto, *Studi sulla Riforma*, 188–90.

still obstinate, six years later. In the same year the notary of Syracuse, Barbato Ungaro, was sentenced in Rome to life in prison.

Even more conclusive evidence that the clandestine community in Syracuse was indeed Calvinist is furnished by the confession made by Antonio Russo of Ferla, known as "the physician." He got off with having to wear the penitential garment for three years because he confessed as soon as he was arrested. The notary of the Inquisition, in listing his beliefs, which included the principal Reformation doctrines, also noted the Calvinist teaching on the Eucharist: the bread is the symbol of the passion of Christ who is present in it only spiritually. The litany of erroneous beliefs also records the customary anticlerical polemic against the papal commerce in jubilees, bulls, and feast days. Some years later, Russo's wife, Margherita, was also charged with heresy. On 21 November 1574 she was burned in effigy at Palermo in the Piazza Ucciardone, because she had died a "Lutheran" in prison during her trial. Only two from the group succeeded in fleeing the island and reaching Geneva: Cesare Lancarbeni of Noto (on 26 June 1559) and Luigi Russo of Ferla.

THE PROTESTANTS OF PALERMO

At Syracuse, Catania, and Messina the Protestant movement was largely indigenous with contributions from outsiders, Calabrians, Venetians, and Genoese. On the contrary, in the capital Palermo and its surrounding areas, a report on the "spectacle of the faith" that occurred on 26 June 1569 revealed a significant number of Frenchmen, Germans, and Flemings living there where they served as soldiers, artisans and merchants. They had formed an association that met in various places for religious purposes and had begun "to infect the kingdom."[32] These outsiders had achieved some successes in Sicilian families, especially among the women who were receptive to the new evangelical message. Meetings occurred in homes or in taverns, such as an inn run by the German Cristoval Pion who served meat even on Fridays and during Lent. At the propitious moment, Bibles and other prohibited books were carefully extracted from their hiding places and discussions then began on the Protestant teachings. The host listened with interest.

Religious services took place in private homes of a certain Brigida da Cascina of Pisa, who later fled to Rome where she was reconciled to the church, and of the Parisian Jacques Ques who must have presided often since he is described as "the person who principally spoke." The doctrines professed by the latter group can be deduced from an account left by Giovanni de Gand, one of the more prominent members of Ques's conventicle, who in addition to his resolute character possessed great physical strength, having twice undergone torture without succumbing. He and his companions denied the existence of purgatory, the intercession of the saints, the primacy of the pope, and the mass for which they substituted personal prayer to God, and to whom alone they offered their adoration. They believed donations collected from

---

[32]"a infettar en el Reyno, mayormente los que eran casados, a sus mugeres." See Garufi I, 309–22. The quote is at 316.

tithes should be given to the poor, rather than to priests and monks. A special characteristic of the group was the total absence of Sicilians, which perhaps was due to diffidence on the part of the organizers towards the islanders who might have been thought less capable of maintaining secrecy and among whom the spies of the Holy Office could more easily infiltrate. These outsiders were joined by a Genoese, a *Mastro* Niccolò, whose profession was carving the stocks of arquebuses. This septuagenarian greeted with enthusiasm the exhilarating news, brought by a German just returned from his homeland, that the prince de Condé was on the verge of conquering France and even Sicily. The old artisan was heard to exclaim that "he will be most welcome, and that for the body of God I and others will furnish him with arquebuses and will join his side."[33] The conventicle, consisting of lay people only, included also a schoolteacher, native of Trent, Giacomo Riis, who knew Latin, Greek, and Hebrew, and was sentenced to wear the penitential garment for three years and perform community service in a hospital. Under torture he had confessed the names of many accomplices. His submission spared him more severe punishment, while several of his brethren were sentenced to languish for years in the galleys of Spain.

Several of the Frenchmen, in addition to Jacques Ques who presided over the meditations on Scripture and prayer, were tenacious Calvinists: Natal Rosano, a servant in the home of the marquis d'Avola, the brother of one of the highest officials in the realm; the merchant Pietro di Arnaldo; and the hosier Carlo Borgognone. The first, who had come from the Huguenot stronghold at La Rochelle, was accused of holding "all the ideas of Calvin," and supporting them with the authority of the Gospels and of the Epistles of Paul. After many entreaties he agreed to abjure his false notions and was sentenced to seven years of galley service. The merchant Pietro di Arnaldo of Angers refused to confess his errors and belatedly asked for mercy in the face of death, but in vain. The Burgundian fared better. Since the wife of the viceroy, the marchioness of Pescara, had asked that one of the less guilty men among the condemned be spared, the execution of the sentence was suspended and he was led back to prison where he revealed the name of a person of "importance." As for the Germans, in addition to the innkeeper Cristoval Pion, two of the viceroy's guards were also punished: Thomas Quifort and a certain Hanzain.

The foregoing account, made possible by the detailed report of the auto da fé, confirms the absence of native Sicilians among the accused. Two precursors, both Frenchmen, had paved the way proselytizing for Calvinism among their fellow nationals in Sicily: the doctor of laws Mariano Olinvoltis, who for many years had been in the service of the viceroy, Giovanni Vega, and Pietro Robert della Goletta of Tunis. Both stood steadfastly for their faith: the jurist abjured only on the scaffold and was spared (1561). Robert, as "an obstinate Huguenot," was executed on 13 January 1566.[34] Still another Frenchman, Giorgio di Avarzo of Toulouse, "a follower of the Lutheran sect" residing in Monreale, fell afoul of the Inquisition in 1573.[35] The

---

[33]"Que fuese el bienvenido que para el cuerpo de Dios, el y otra persona le servirian de escopetas y serian de su parcialidad," ibid., 313.

[34]*Serie dei rilasciati*, n. 396.

[35]Ibid., xiii.

priest Jacopo Cortes, a native of Tropea, a chaplain in the church of San Giovanni in Palermo who had abjured in 1558 and then relapsed, was executed on 1 June 1572.

Echoes at Catania

In the same year that the existence of a Luthero-Calvinist conventicle was exposed in the capital, even Catania, seat of a university, had its own solemn "spectacle of the faith." Unfortunately there are no known official documents connected with the event. A contemporary chronicle reports the arrival of the inquisitor general, Don Giovanni Bezerra, to question the prisoners incarcerated in the Ursino castle. On 13 March 1569, an imposing grandstand was erected facing the bell tower of the cathedral, on which the inquisitor, the episcopal vicar, and a father of the Society of Jesus, the trinity of ecclesiastical authority, took their places. Sixty-seven heretics, of whom fifteen were spared from having to take their places on the platform out of "just considerations," perhaps because they were members of the nobility, heard their sentences to public whipping and to the galleys read out. The administering of the punishments was scheduled for the next day, "but to accommodate the sworn gentlemen (*giurati*) of the city, and many other gentlemen as well," the inquisitor pardoned them all.[36] In this period there does not seem to have been any other case where an inquisitor made such an unexpected gesture. To comprehend fully the reason for such leniency, we would have to explore in greater depth the relationship, which was not always cordial, between the patricians of Catania, defenders of their ancient privileges, and the ecclesiastical authorities. If the names of the defendants were known, it might be possible to say what the limits of inquisitorial clemency were.

Some months later, certain citizens of Vizzini appeared in the auto da fé held at Palermo on 26 June 1569, among whom were relatives and friends of Cannizu, a graduate of the University of Catania and once a member of the Valdesian circle in Naples. Cannizu had been a fiscal advocate in 1541, and subsequent to his trial in 1547 mentioned earlier, a judge of the Great Court. Sometime before 1569, after he had returned to Chiaramonte, not far from Vizzini, he was suspected anew in connection with Protestant infiltrations at Vizzini. Among those who had been absolved with him on the first occasion, were the gentleman Gutiere Laguna, the tailor Pietro Piccolo, and Giuseppe Carnaval. Two years later, two priests were reconciled, Antonio di Pietro and Vincenzo Selvaggio. Three other ecclesiastics who had fled, Don Giuseppe Laquinta, Pietro Giangrosso, and Antonio Astuto, were burned in effigy on 5 July 1551. Authorities were intent on dispersing this embryonic conventicle composed of clergy and laymen drawn from every walk of society. Warned in time, Cannizu managed to avoid being arrested. Since he was an expert in the law and not without powerful patrons, he succeeded in thwarting the law again. But his son Cesare and Francesco Laguna were not so fortunate, both of whom were exiled for two years as abettors of heresy. Battista Gurrisi and Mariano Caruso received long galley sentences. But as late as 1573, there were persons at Vizzini who had not for-

[36]See S. Caponetto, *Studi sulla Riforma*, 61–63.

gotten a simple and fascinating doctrine. Giovanna di Amari was compelled to abjure for having been heard to say that there was neither purgatory nor paradise, because "Christ had sacrificed for all"; the bank clerk, Giulio Azzarello of Paternò, was accused of having said that "the consecrated host does not in reality contain the body of Christ."[37]

CALVINISM AT MESSINA

If the Protestant movement only made sporadic appearances in Catania and neighboring localities, it was more continuous at Messina. During the decade 1563–73, evangelicals who by now had spread to all the surrounding towns, Mandanici, Santa Lucia, Gala, Lipaglara, San Pietro di Monforte, Randazzo, and Taormina, made a strenuous effort to organize and win new converts. The known number of the arrested totaled about seventy, of whom many paid for their hopes of Christian renewal with their lives or with heavy sentences. But there surely were more, because we do not have the report of the auto da fé held in the city by Monsignor Giovanni Retana on 28 November 1568, or any official mention of the many citizens of the city who found refuge in Geneva. However, three distinct, linked groups can be identified: the first located in the city, another at Mandanici, and the third in the Benedictine monastery at San Placido di Colenerò.

The conventicle at Mandanici (situated in the hills forty kilometers from Messina) was the most significant of the three because of its exceptional tenacity during the early struggles and subsequent persecution. This small urban center, which in 1548 totaled 270 family units, produced four martyrs: the priests Domenico (Minico) Santoro and Giacomo Pellizzeri; perhaps Giovan Battista's brother, the schoolteacher Giovan Battista Pellizzeri; and a certain Riccardo Fruxa. The evangelical community had a definite proletarian physiognomy and was composed of peasants, charcoal-burners, masons, bakers, tailors, and barbers who had been won over to the Reformation by G. B. Pellizzeri and Domenico Santoro, who dragged their families into the new faith and subsequent persecution. Both men carried on a vast work of proselytization, only weak echoes of which have filtered through the sparse official records. All those sentenced at Mandanici, who included a small contingent of peasants, and many of those adjudicated at Messina in 1563 and 1568 should be considered their disciples. Two priests, G. B. Castrogiovanni and Giovanni Spataro, should be added to the group.

In 1547 Filippo and Nicola Pellizzeri, assisted by peasants from Santa Lucia and Gala, had rescued G. B. Pellizzeri from the hands of officials. But after resuming a now more concealed ministry, he was apprehended once again, and this time condemned to the stake as "a Lutheran heresiarch." His work was continued by Battista, a peasant; Filippo, a barber; and two priests, Stefano and Giacomo. The latter, who was reconciled to the church in 1551, was also condemned to the stake together with

---

[37] *Serie dei rilasciati*, xiiif.

Messina in the seventeenth century.

his fellow townsman Riccardo Fruxa in the auto da fé celebrated at Palermo on 12 November 1564.

The previous year, the same fate had befallen four others: Minico Santoro, accused of being a "dogmatist" of the Lutheran heresy, who had been the teacher of Stefano and Filippo Pellizzeri; the cloth cutter Antonio Cacoparo; the weaver Nello di Franco; and the coal merchant Giovan Battista Lamberti; all of Messina. Santoro was a country priest from an impoverished family, and although probably meagerly educated, was eloquent and persuasive, as Merlino Nasiti and Filippo Campolo inform us. Other factors might have influenced his success in the small hillside community of Mandanici, numbering about a thousand inhabitants. Could it have been a sympathetic ear and protection from influential members of the community?

In the "spectacle of the faith" at which Santoro was killed, the effigy of the already deceased Giovan Matteo di Micheli, a councilor of Mandanici, was given to the flames, and another councillor, Luciano Mamuni, was reconciled.[38] Five years later, Francesco di Micheli, also of Mandanici, was about to be turned over to the secular arm as a pertinacious heretic when he suddenly asked for mercy. He reappeared the next year and was sentenced to ten years of galley service, but the inquisitor noted, if the judges had known then what Micheli's confessors later revealed, the sentence of death would have been carried out, because he had brought them to the point of despair before finally abjuring his opinions. There had been no way to make him repeat that he believed in the Roman church, and in fact he rejected the interpretations of the Biblical passages quoted to him. Finally, he had interjected, "Which is the Church of Rome, the one that wants to burn me?"[39]

The evangelical community of Messina was composed mostly of artisans, merchants, and laborers, which a few professional men and patricians did not disdain joining. We can call it a community without hesitation, if we think of the solid preparation evidenced by a group of women who quoted confidently from Scripture and held their own against the inquisitor. Among them were Norella Grasso, already mentioned, wife of the weaver Antonio; Caterinella Di Mazio; Giovannella Crapiti, wife of a painter Antonio, a woman "well instructed in the Lutheran sect"; and Caterinella Rizzo, the wife of the salesman Giovanni Antonio, who had become a fervent Calvinist, indoctrinated by her husband and father-in-law. Finally, we should mention Minichella Faraone, the wife of Tommaso who had died in prison after having confessed his errors. Minichella got off with seven years of the penitential garment but was watched over closely because she was even better informed than her husband had been in Lutheran teachings, since she was the sister of the famous proselytizer Fra Francesco Pagliarino, executed in 1551. Twenty years later his followers were still battling to achieve freedom of conscience. Three silversmiths continued in the tradition of their Syracusan colleagues: Fabio lo Aurifice, the Venetian Agostino Grassetto and Pietro Angelo Musco of Reggio, Calabria. Grassetto, after having

---

[38]Garufi I, 305.
[39]Ibid., 319–20.

abjured in 1569, relapsed into the beliefs he had acquired in the workplace in Venice. He fled in 1574.

The long confession left by Giuseppe Stagno, a priest of good family, is the chief source for the clandestine life of Messina's evangelical community and its place in the Calvinist movement. After a first trial in 1558, Stagno was arrested again on 10 January 1568 following accusations made against him by a Benedictine. Under torture, he revealed that for more than twenty years he had belonged to a confraternity where he learned all the points of reformed doctrine, chiefly that one is saved and justified "by being in Christ," and consequently, that there is no purgatory, "because purgatory is the blood of Our Lord, through whom we were saved and justified through faith alone." Later he had gathered with many people in Messina and its surrounding territory where they read "Lutheran books," and a letter from the "minister in Geneva" that exhorted them to be staunch in the "spiritual religion."[40]

Just as in Palermo and Syracuse, at Messina too the cult was celebrated in the Protestant manner in some of the conventicles. Almost certainly, the "minister in Geneva" had to be Calvin, whose preface to the French translation of the Bible executed by his cousin Olivétan, was printed separately in epistolary form. In 1551 it appeared in an Italian version at Lyons with the title, *Come Christo è il fine de la legge*, which was then reprinted at Geneva in 1555 by Gian Luigi Pascale. Presumably he brought copies of it with him during his fatal mission to Calabria.

The discovery, at some point before 1569, that the "Lutheran" heresy had made inroads in the monastery of San Placido di Colenerò, which had been visited some thirty years earlier by Benedetto da Mantova, author of the *Beneficio di Cristo*, offers intriguing possibilities. Even if we cannot establish definite links between this later heterodox infiltration in the religious house and the disciple of Valdés, nevertheless it is another indication of how deeply rooted the Nicodemite phenomenon was in the Benedictine order. Don Nicolò di Alì, who became prior of the monastery at Gangi, was the most prominent of the monks who sought reconciliation with the church. During his trial in 1569 while being questioned under torture, he confessed that he had been instructed some sixteen to twenty years earlier by a fellow member of his order from Trent, to believe "that we are saved and justified through the blood of Christ," that saints cannot intercede for us, and that the pope lacked the authority to issue bulls and proclaim Jubilees. The same opinions were abjured by his fellow Benedictines, Angelo di Alì, dean of San Placido, Don Stefano Pesce, and Ambrogio da Messina, who also disclosed the name of another brother in the order who used to read the Epistles of Paul "in a Lutheran manner."[41]

These Benedictines used to meet with numerous laypeople whom they had instructed during confession, following a method widespread among Nicodemites. Almost all were arrested and tried, and during torture the pupils accused their teachers. The laymen were associated with the monastery for reasons of work and trade, as in the case of the scribe Ferrante Musarra, the shopkeepers Giovanni Antonio Rizzo,

---

[40]See S. Caponetto, *Studi sulla Riforma*, 186–88.
[41]Garufi I, 316–17.

the Frenchman Alessandro Bindon, the coal merchant G. B. Lamberti, and the silk traders Giuseppe Villari and Francesco Salvaricia. Two members of the group died in prison, the barber Francesco Schillaci and A. Bindon, and both appeared in effigy at the auto da fé of 26 June 1569.

Two of the Benedictines of San Placido, Eliseo Manzé and Giambattista Gotto, saved themselves through flight. The latter appeared before the magistrates of Geneva on 12 December 1558, together with his fellow citizens Giovan Pietro Giardina, a former priest who had been reconciled in 1547, Nardo di Mazzeo, and Angelo Mangano, formerly in the order of San Francesco di Paola, whom we mentioned earlier. The most daring were trapped by the network of spies, but others succeeded in remaining concealed until death when they avoided asking for a final confession, as happened in the case of the physician Leone Laganà of Santa Lucia, who "died a Lutheran," and about whom it was learned that he had converted many nuns in the convent of Montevergine.

By the end of the century, defeat of the evangelical cause led many to contemplate seeking a new home in exile. A certain Biagio Corsi, a man of humble origin, had been heard to exclaim that in France and Geneva "there was a good life because people lived in common and he wished to go there to become a Lutheran."[42] A simple liking for this or that Reformation tenet, or pleasure in anticlerical invective, had been replaced by longing for a different life in the fantasies of this man, probably one of the many who did not have steady work in the great port city of Messina. About 1570, the Italian exiles' community in Geneva was completing its second decade. The "life in common" to which Corsi alluded reflected the city's actual democratic organization in which the well-born, merchants, and members of the lower classes lived in common under obedience to the Word of God and the Consistory, to which all could be elected without distinction. It was an economically self-sufficient community with a charitable fund that would endure until 1870. Corsi abjured and his judges showed mercy because they assumed that his wretched condition had made him say desperate things. But inquisitorial persecution and the longing for a better life continued to nurture the notion of emigration. Many decided to face dangers, discomfort, the unknown, the sufferings attending a long journey from a sun-filled island to the damp and cloud-filled skies of the north, all for the love of hearing the pure Word of God preached. Bernardino Ochino, pastor of the Locarnese exile community in Zurich at the time, wrote on 3 February 1556 to the minister of Aarau to recommend a group of refugees from Messina, men, women, and children who had arrived by way of Chiavenna in the dead of winter, prostrate from cold and exhaustion. They were heading for Geneva but hoped they could pause in their journey at Aarau and Bern. Ochino's letter closed with a plea: "Recognize with us, dearest brother, and in them accept the exile Christ, poor, naked, a famished outsider, and you will hear on the last day with all the pious, 'Come, oh blessed of my Father....'"[43] We do not know the names of these hard-pressed travelers, or whether they reached their destination.

[42] S. Caponetto, *Studi sulla Riforma*, 186ff.

Calvinism had become such a powerful force in Messina that thirty of its family groups were induced to emigrate to Geneva. Together with other Sicilians, they comprised the popular element in the Italian refugee colony. It is quite surprising to note that with an occasional exception, the exiles do not turn up in the lists of those tried by the Inquisition. These stalwarts were the tissue of an invisible reformed community who remain hidden even to modern historians.

Spanish Sardinia

Unlike Sicily, there was never a movement of religious protest in Sardinia. The tribunal of the Holy Office there eked out a desultory existence for years, without adequate support, beset by chronic inefficiency; the Supreme Spanish Inquisition had determined that the Catholic faith was not in danger in this culturally backward area. The ecclesiastical hierarchy was in the hands of Spanish bishops named by the sovereign and coming from the local nobility.

Nevertheless, even in the few cases of heterodoxy that have come to light, the Calvinism of the Mediterranean left a trace. The three pairs of Sardinian evangelicals identified by Giorgio Spini, the brothers Nicola and Giovanni Gallo, Sigismondo and Antonio Arquer, and Francesco and Gervaso Vidini finished their days in Geneva, with the exception of Sigismondo Arquer, whose rich life closed tragically at the stake in Toledo in 1571.[44]

In the auto da fé celebrated at Sassari on 2 January 1590, three Piedmontese artisans were reconciled to the church: Ambrogio Veraldo, a native of Altare in the marquisate of Saluzzo; Guglielmo Bormiolo, a glassblower from the same town; and Francesco Bertolucho (or Bertoluccio) of Pinerolo in Piedmont. The first of the three, a convinced Calvinist, had learned his Protestant doctrines at Lyons from a Sicilian glazer, identified only as Ottaviano. The other two were banished from the island.

Nicola Gallo, a physician who had studied in France, was implicated in Geneva in the trial against the antitrinitarian from Cosenza, Valentino Gentile. Even if Gallo manifested some sympathy for Gentile's radical views, he nevertheless quickly subscribed to the confession of faith approved by the Italian exiles' church in Geneva in 1558 in order to nip in the bud the spread of views alien to Calvinist orthodoxy.

Sigismondo Arquer (1530–71), born at Cagliari to the jurist Giovanni Antonio, belonged to a family of urban citizenry that was constantly vying against a nobility closely linked to the church. Sigismondo took a degree *in utroque jure*, in both canon and civil law, at Pisa in 1547 and in theology at Siena, the following year.[45] He promptly set out on a journey meant to take him to the court at Brussels, but lingered for five months in the Grisons, where he met many Italian exiles *religio-*

---

[43]K. Benrath, *Bernardino Ochino von Siena*, 2d ed. (Braunschweig: Schwetschke, 1892), 305–6. See Matt. 25:34.

[44]See G. Spini, "Di Nicola Gallo."

[45]See M. M. Cocco, *Sigismondo Arquer: Dagli studi giovanili all'autodafé* (Cagliari: Edizioni Castello, 1986).

Title page of the *Copilacion delas Instructiones* for the Spanish Inquisition written by the famous monk Tommaso of Torquemada (1420–98), first inquisitor general of Spain (from S. G. Pozhniskii, *Istoria Inkvizitsii* [Moscow, 1914]).

nis causa, including Vergerio, Giulio della Rovere, and Camillo Renato. Reaching Zurich, he was warmly received by Pellikan who recommended him to Boniface Amerbach for assistance from the fund established by Erasmus. Arriving in Basel, he was a guest in the home of C. S. Curione, and was invited by Sebastian Münster to collaborate in his *Cosmographia*. At the age of nineteen, Arquer wrote a history of his island, *Sardiniae brevis historia et descriptio*, but he did not linger long in Basel where he experienced the exiles' difficult existence, nor did he espouse reformed views. In the strenuous defense he would later have to make of his Catholic orthodoxy, this was undoubtedly a decisive point. Philip II, who admired him for his legal knowledge and his scholarship, appointed him fiscal advocate for Sardinia. Arquer now found himself battling with the Aymerich clan, ancient enemies of his own family. He was incarcerated but managed to escape and be restored to the king's good graces.

Arquer was dragged into the inquisitorial trial against the nobleman of Valencia, Gaspar Centelles, sentenced to death for heresy in 1564, after the correspondence between the two men came to light. Arquer himself was then put on trial at Toledo, and after proceedings that dragged on for almost eight years, was executed on 4 June 1571. Humanist, geographer, jurist, poet, widely admired by contemporaries for his lively intellect, his life epitomized that free and anguished search for truth through the Scriptures that he shared with many European intellectuals of his day. From Arquer's doctrinal letters to Gaspar Centelles, we perceive his profound Biblicism, his adherence to the Erasmian *philosophia Christi* and his familiarity with the writings of Valdés and the German reformers.[46] Nevertheless, it remains difficult to come to grips with the actual religious beliefs of a person who, even in the face of death, insisted that he was a loyal Catholic. Although Arquer was acquainted with the thought of the reformers and shared their Christocentrism and belief in the doctrine of justification by faith, he had probably not contemplated separating himself completely from the Church of Rome, also the case with the Valdesians Flaminio, Carnesecchi, Galeota, and Giulia Gonzaga. Proud humanist and learned jurist, Arquer insisted that he was innocent because he was convinced that the essence of Christianity consisted in love of God and of one's neighbor and not in the doctrines of what he esteemed to be a degenerate church. To the end, he failed to comprehend the incompatibility of this Erasmian notion with Tridentine Catholicism.

Another Italian disciple of Valdés, Carlos de Seso (1515–59), although not a Sardinian (he was a nobleman from Verona), met his fate, like Arquer, at the hands of the Spanish Inquisition at Valladolid.[47] The son of Count Ludovico de Seso and Caterina Confalonieri da Sandrigo, de Seso moved to Spain where he married Isabella of Castile, a damsel of royal lineage, and was appointed "*corregidor de Toro*" in 1554. In 1557 he was living at Villamediana (Logroño). It is likely that as a very young man de Seso became acquainted with the ideas of the Reformation in Vicenza in the school run by Fulvio Pellegrino Morato, where he was enrolled. Alongside

---

[46]Ibid., 67–136.
[47]See J. I. Tellechea Idígoras, *Tiempos recios: Inquisición y heterodoxia* (Salamanca: Sigueme, 1977), 53–110.

Cicero, Morato read to his pupils from Calvin's *Institutes of the Christian Religion.* From Spain, de Seso returned to Italy twice and was at Trent during the Council session of 1546, where he met Cardinal Pole and Alvise Priuli, both champions of the doctrine of justification by faith. After his second visit, from 1550 to 1551, he returned to Spain laden with printed works and manuscript writings by Luther, Calvin, Valdés, and many texts in vernacular Italian, almost certainly including the *Beneficio di Cristo.* At home in Logroño he proselytized for the new teachings and joined a conventicle of "true Christians," where he taught the recent converts that only those who believed in justification through Jesus Christ would be saved.

De Seso was arrested in June 1558 at the foot of the Pyrenees while attempting to flee in the company of the monk, Domingo de Rojas. At his trial de Seso mounted an able defense. His "sin, "he said, was that "of exalting the benefit of Christ," whose blood was the sole purgatory for our sins. Any other human work was useless and diminished the unique and exclusive merit of Christ's blood. He declared himself to be a disciple of Valdés and a follower of the spirituality enshrined in the *Beneficio di Cristo.* But his judges confronted him with sixty witnesses who accused him of having taught Lutheran doctrines, from the *sola fides* to the rejection of the mass and the primacy of the pope. Realizing that his fate was sealed, on the eve of his consignment to the stake, undaunted, de Seso presented his judges with a confession of faith in which he thanked God for affording him the opportunity to give witness to his unshakable faith in Jesus Christ and membership in the church of the elect:

> I say and conclude that I place my hopes in Jesus Christ alone, and confide only in him, whom I adore. I embrace him and consider him my sole treasure. And, placing my unworthy hand in his most holy side, thanks to the benefits of his blood, I now go to rejoice in the promises he made to his elect.[48]

The great auto da fé was celebrated at Valladolid in the presence of Philip II and his entire court. The story was told that when de Seso and his other companions in misfortune passed before the king, he reproached the sovereign for permitting him to be killed. To this temerity, Philip II was supposed to have replied, "I would personally carry the wood to burn my own son, if he were as depraved as you." After recounting this "picturesque" episode, de Seso's biographer goes on to conclude: "Going beyond all the tragic confessional disputes, there is magnanimity and beauty in the end of this noble Veronese, whose brief passage through Spain concluded so tragically on an inquisitorial pyre."[49]

---

[48]"Digo e concluyo que en sólo Jesucristo espero, en sólo él confío en él e al adoro, con él me abrazo, a él tengo por único tesoro mio; e puesta mi indigna mano en su sacratismo costado, voy, por el valor de su sangre, a gozar las promesas por él hechas a sus escogidos," ibid., 107.
[49]Ibid., 110.

BIBLIOGRAPHICAL NOTE

The studies of Carlo Alberto Garufi remain fundamental for the history of the Inquisition and Reformation in Sicily. They have been collected and reprinted in volume form as *Fatti e personaggi dell'Inquisizione in Sicilia* (Palermo: Sellerio, 1978).

I have also found useful the essay by N. Giordano, "L'esecuzione in effigie (relaxo in statua): Contributo alla storia della procedura inquisitoriale," *ASS* 18 (1968): 217–66.

On the religious conditions on the island, see M. Scaduto, "La vita religiosa in Sicilia secondo un memoriale inedito del 1563," *RSCI* 28 (1974): 561–81.

For Sicilian history in general, see M. I. Finley and D. Mack Smith, *A History of Sicily*, 3 vols. (London: Chatto & Windus, 1968), and H. Koenigsberger, *The Government of Sicily under Philip II of Spain* (London & New York: Staples Press, 1951).

20

"ECCLESIA PEREGRINORUM"

Olimpia Morato

Arturo Pascal, in his studies on the emigration to Geneva from Lucca, Messina, and Piedmont, called attention to the narrowness of research on the Italian Reformation when limited to names and episodes contained in the few inquisitorial trials that have come down to us—few in respect to the mass of documents accumulated by the Roman Holy Office and its provincial tribunals from 1542 to the end of the seventeenth century. The fact is confirmed merely by noting the almost total absence in inquisitorial inventories of names of persons who found refuge beyond the Alps. Valdo Vinay coined the felicitous phrase "*ecclesia peregrinorum*" to designate the dispersal throughout Europe of Italians who fled their homeland, *causa religionis*.[1]

Small groups of dissidents rebelling against the rigid orthodoxy they encountered in the Italian exiles' churches in the Grisons, Geneva, Zurich, and London generated disturbances and provoked conflicts with their pastors and consistories that led to expulsions and condemnations. But the core of the emigrés remained intact. Even though inexperienced in their new faith, they remained staunchly committed. After the great persecution in Italy during the triennium from 1567 to 1570, which produced hundreds of condemnations from Piedmont to Sicily, many persons who intellectually and sentimentally had been outside of the church for years, came to realize that their Nicodemite practices could not go on indefinitely. They had two choices: the risky and adventurous prospect of flight, or a return to the traditional religion, realizing that a struggle against the Church of Rome in their homeland would be of no avail.

Already in October 1551, Olimpia Morato (1526–55), hearing the news of the martyrdom of the "poor Fanin," wrote to Curione from Schweinfurt that she would rather travel to the ends of the earth than return to Italy where the Antichrist "has so much power that it grows pitiless," not even heeding the requests of princes.[2] In this

---

[1]V. Vinay, *La Riforma protestante*, 2d ed. (Brescia: Paideia, 1982), 399 ff.

severe political judgment by Morato, the daughter of the Vicenza university professor Fulvio Pellegrino Morato and of Lucrezia Gozzi, there are echoes of her painful decision to separate from her family. The elder Morato, who died in 1548, was a distinguished scholar and proselytizer for Calvinism, whose teaching influenced Alessandro and Giulio Trissino, Carlos de Seso, and Niccolò, Marco, and Odoardo Thiene.[3]

Olimpia had been widely admired for her learning at the Ferrarese court of Renée and Ercole II where in her studies she was the companion of their daughter Anna d'Este. After a period of mundane living, immersed in *"illa idolatria Italiae,"* Olimpia espoused the faith of her father, which she would evoke even at the moment of her own death. Olimpia's belief in Scripture and in *"solus Christus"* grew stronger when she married the German Lutheran physician, Andreas Grünthler, who received his degree from Ferrara in 1549. Forced to flee from the court of Renée with so many others because of increasing pressure from the Inquisition, Olimpia, her husband, and her younger brother made their way to Schweinfurt. In 1554 the city found itself trapped in the war between Charles V and the Protestant princes, and the Grünthlers barely managed to save themselves from the fire and pillaging that destroyed almost all of Olimpia's writings, and reach the safety of Heidelberg. But there, at only twenty-nine years of age, ravaged by tuberculosis, she died, one of the most highly cultured persons of her time, a woman of great faith and profound sensibility. A few months before, she had written to Vergerio beseeching him to translate into Italian Luther's *Great Catechism*, a port of refuge for those passionately searching for evangelical truth. Her epigram *Olympiae Votum* dates from the same period:

> Dissolvi cupio, tanta est fiducia menti
> esseque cum Christo, quo mea vita viget.[4]

The Italian Exiles' Church in London

We do not know the full extent of the Italian diaspora since a large part of it has remained without documentation. To reconstruct the story of the Italian refugees abroad, the lives of individual personages for whom there is only fleeting information must be closely examined. Their constancy in the new faith enabled them to overcome many difficulties in adapting to a new environment and surviving among the perils accompanying the religious controversies between Catholics and Protestants.

The travels of two of these wanderers sent to England as pastors for the Italian exiles' church, which had been founded between 1550 to 1551, the subject of a brilliant study by Luigi Firpo, seem to exemplify the far-flung reach of that Mediterranean Calvinism examined in the previous chapter.[5] The first to serve in that position

---

[2] O. Morata, *Opere*, vol. 1 (*Epistolae*) (1540–55), a cura di L. Caretti (Ferrara: Deputazione ferrarese di Storia Patria, 1954), 77.

[3] See M. Cignoni, "Il pensiero di Olimpia Morato nell'ambito della Riforma protestante," *Atti dell'Accademia delle Scienze di Ferrara* 60–61 (1982–83) (1983–84): 191–204.

[4] Morata, *Opere* 2:29.

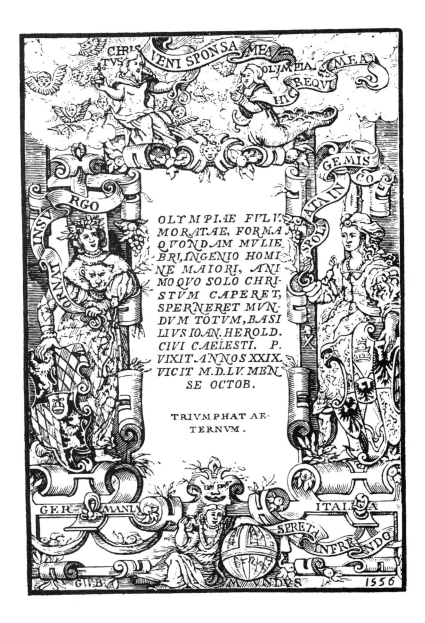

Title page of the *Opera omnia* of Olimpia Morato, published at Basel by Pietro Perna in 1570 (1st ed. 1558). The long epitaph on the Heidelberg monument appears at p. 265 of the work (Yale University, Beinecke Library).

was Michelangelo Florio, a turbulent person, lacking in charity and tact, who would be deposed quickly for moral failings. The "*Ecclesia Londino-Italica*" resurrected itself from this crisis in 1565 thanks to another pastor, Girolamo Ferlito, who had come from Palermo. After leaving Sicily, he had gone to Geneva where he studied theology and married the Venetian Laura Canale. From Castasegna, in Val Bregaglia, where he was serving as minister in 1564, he was sent to London to restore order to the small exiles' church, which was more preoccupied with questions of everyday life than with spiritual matters. Its few Italian members had been joined by Frenchmen and Flemings who found the ecclesiastical discipline less stringent than in their own institutions, and by a few Englishmen, who attended the sermons so they might perfect their Italian, a highly fashionable language at that time.

At his death about 1569, Ferlito was replaced by the Waldensian Gian Battista Aureli (1540–97) from San Sisto in Calabria, one of the few survivors of the massacres in 1561, who was pastor at Saintonge at the time of his call. Following in his predecessor's footsteps, he confronted resolutely the difficulties besetting the cosmopolitan Italian church in London. The year 1572 marked the arrival of many more Frenchmen and six Italians fleeing the St. Bartholomew's Day Massacre. Among them were Francesco Pucci, Michele Clerici, and Filippo Calandrini, all of whom joined the exiles' church. In 1587 the minister Aureli published an *Esamine dei vari giudizi dei politici*, which examined the views of the party of "*politiques*" in France that was willing to compromise if this would end the bitter conflict between Catholics and Protestants. Aureli dedicated his little work to Horatio Pallavicino, a merchant, man of affairs, banker, diplomat, secret agent, and large landowner, the most powerful and affluent Italian exile in England, who had preferred membership in the Anglican church to the smaller dysfunctional community of his compatriots.[6] But with the return of many from its flock to the continent, the precarious existence of the Italian church came to an end in 1598.

The Italian diaspora, drawn from all spheres of society, contributed greatly to the northern diffusion of Renaissance thought. The men of letters, philosophers, jurists, physicians, and engineers left a mark sufficient to permit modern scholars to reconstruct, at least in part, their often troubled and peripatetic careers. More difficult to understand, because the documentation is scarce, are the lives and sacrifices of the many nameless peasants, laborers, and artisans from the Anabaptist colonies in Moravia and Transylvania, whose contributions to the silk industry of Geneva were highly appreciated and often considered indispensable. Even these humble folk, with their wives and children, contributed to European civilization in that fanatical and violent century.

[5]See L. Firpo, "La chiesa italiana di Londra nel Cinquecento e i suoi rapporti con Ginevra," in *Ginevra e l'Italia* (Florence: Sansoni, 1959), 307–412, reprinted in Firpo's *Scritti sulla Riforma in Italia* (Naples: Prismi, 1996), 117–94.

[6]Idem, 405. [On this notable figure, see the full-length study by L. Stone, *An Elizabethan: Sir Horatio Palavicino* (Oxford: Clarendon, 1956). Trans. note.]

LELIO SOZZINI AND THE TOLERATION CONTROVERSY

Even today there are personages from the greater *"ecclesia peregrinorum"* who arouse the historian's strong interest because of their intelligence and noble spirit. Undoubtedly, Lelio Sozzini (1525–62) was the most original and intense theological thinker in the Italian diaspora.[7] Although his point of departure may have been the critical, philological method of Lorenzo Valla, and he assimilated much of the Erasmian approach to New Testament exegesis, his rationalism never departed from the basic principle of the Reformation, namely the bedrock of Scripture. Sozzini's travels through Germany, Switzerland, and Poland, tirelessly searching for the truth of Revelation, led him to discuss all the fundamental principles of the Christian tradition with Melanchthon, Calvin, Bullinger, and Vermigli. Even though these great theologians may have been annoyed and preoccupied by his bold and unfettered inquiries, dangerous for newly established churches, they acknowledged Sozzini's sincerity and solid cultural background. It fell to his nephew, Fausto Sozzini (1539–1604), to systematize his thought and contribute to the development of the Polish Minor Church, rejecting the traditional interpretation of the doctrine of the Trinity, however, without denying the divine value in the message of Jesus, a man directly inspired by God. Socinianism propagated religious rationalism and toleration among all the Christian confessions, in the name of the ethical principles contained in the Sermon on the Mount.

Akin to the Sozzini were two other apostles of religious toleration: Giacomo Aconcio (1492?–1566?) of Trent and the Sienese Mino Celsi (1514–75/76). Aconcio was endowed with versatile intelligence.[8] He studied law and served as secretary to Cardinal Cristoforo Madruzzo at Milan in 1556. But it was in England that he revealed his talents as a military engineer, inventor, and reclaimer of swamplands for which he received important commissions from the Crown. His fame as a religious thinker rests on a work that was reprinted and translated into French, English, and German until the mid–seventeenth century. His *Satanae Stratagemata* offered a radical solution to the sectarian divisions within the Protestant camp provoked by the proliferation of hostile competing denominations. Aconcio came to the conviction that the only path to concord among them was through a return to the simple Gospel message and a reduction in the number of doctrines to a few fundamentals upon which all groups could agree.

In 1569, at age fifty-five, the Sienese Mino Celsi left behind his family and a promising political career and took the road to exile,[9] driven to this perhaps by the arrest of Paleario, with whom he was in contact. From the Grisons, Celsi moved to Basel where he met its progressive Erasmian circles and formed special friendships with Pietro Perna, Boniface and Basil Amerbach, and Giovanni Bernardino Bonifacio, the marquis of Oria, who generously supported him in his moments of greatest need. The *In haereticis coërcendis quatenus progredi liceat...*(1577) brought Celsi post-

[7]See L. Sozzini, *Opere*, a cura di A. Rotondò (Florence: Olschki, 1986).
[8]See the biographical sketch by D. Cantimori, in *DBI* 1:154–59.
[9]See the biographical sketch by P. Bietenholz, in *DBI* 23:478–82.

humous renown and an honorable place in the annals of the long struggle for religious toleration. In the footsteps of Sebastian Castellio, he attacked vigorously the thesis of Calvin and Beza, shared by the Roman church, that it was permissible to punish the heretic. The publisher of the work, Pietro Perna (1520–c. 1582), was one of the leading members of the Basel exile colony.[10] He had arrived from Lucca in 1542 and established a printing house that became influential in the northern diffusion of a host of Italian writers, from such Renaissance giants as Petrarch, Paolo Giovio, and Machiavelli, to Aconcio, Castelvetro, and Ochino.

Three exiles of different geographical and social provenance who shared a Protestant faith unconfined by confessional boundaries, created a network of mutual support among their compatriots in Chiavenna, Basel, and Zurich. They were the Milanese merchant Antonio Besozzi,[11] a friend of Lelio Sozzini, the Roman Francesco Betti,[12] former secretary to Ferdinando Francesco II d'Avalos, marquis of Pescara, and the nobleman from Puglia, Giovanni Bernardino Bonifacio.[13]

Besozzi (d. 1567) helped to organize the emigration to Zurich of one hundred evangelical families from Locarno, where he had settled and married Clara Orelli who belonged to one of the leading families of the city. In Zurich, Besozzi became the group's representative to the government and to the chief minister of the city, Bullinger, vouching for the orthodoxy of the new arrivals. In 1557, with other Italians, among whom was Guarnerio Castiglione, Besozzi organized a large commercial venture for the purchase of cloth at Venice and Milan. It was he who notified Fausto Sozzini in Lyons of the death of his uncle Lelio at Zurich in May 1562. But it was not this friendship that brought on a trial for doctrinal lapses against Besozzi in Zurich, but rather the accusation that he had approved Ochino's ideas in the *Dialogi XXX* (one of the dialogues was thought to advocate polygamy) and had hosted Lelio's brother, Camillo. Besozzi left Zurich for Basel, where he resumed his commercial activity, while continuing to proselytize among his fellow exiles. It appears that in 1564 he helped to draw up a contract for the translation into Italian of Luther's *Commentary on the Epistle to the Galatians*, through the Urach (Tübingen) printing press.

Francesco Betti is primarily remembered for the letter that he wrote from Zurich on 16 October 1557 to the marquis of Pescara, relating the reasons for his flight and his satisfaction in the religious freedom he had found in Switzerland. The document initiated a polemical exchange that would endure for two decades with the Catholic controversialist Girolamo Muzio. Although Betti enjoyed frequent contacts with "heretics," religious radicals in Cantimori's use of the term, Betti remained a loyal member of the reformed community. Unusual for a man of letters and courtier, he expressed regret that he had known nothing about Waldensians before his exile: "Was

---

[10] See L. Perini, "Note e documenti su Pietro Perna, libraio-tipografo a Basilea," *NRS* 50 (1966): 145–200.

[11] See the biographical sketch by J. Tedeschi, in *DBI* 9: 674–75.

[12] See the appropriate entry in *DBI* 9:717–18.

[13] D. Cantimori, *Eretici*, p. 294. On Bonifacio d'Oria, see the sketch by D. Caccamo, in *DBI* 12: 197–201 and the biography by M. Welti, *Dall'umanesimo alla Riforma: Giovanni Bernardino Bonifacio, marchese d'Oria, 1517–57* (Brindisi: De Leo, 1986).

there anyone who knew, before Luther began to preach against the Roman church that in some valleys and mountains of Piedmont there were people called Waldensians, who abominated papist teachings? And yet there were...."[14] Betti may have learned about them after he left Italy, from Scipione Lentolo, a pastor in the Valtellina, who had also ministered to the Waldensians in their valleys.

Among the exiles who were important channels in the diffusion northward of Italian culture, the most singular figure, thanks to his wanderlust, his enormous library that traveled with him, his nonconformity (he was always accompanied by two Berber female slaves), was Marquis Bonifacio d'Oria (1517–97). As a young nobleman he had inherited the title to his feudal domains in Puglia at the death of his father in 1536. After a period of controversy and litigation over the administration of his lands, he withdrew to the area around Otranto where he lived for about a decade. Here Bonifacio dedicated himself to his studies, to book collecting, and corresponding with such literary figures as Paolo Manuzio, Lelio Carani, and Ludovico Dolce. In Naples he was a frequent visitor in the home of Giovanni Maria Bernardo, a gathering place for men of letters and patricians who had been influenced by Valdés, and was present when Lorenzo Romano read from the *Loci* of Melanchthon. When his wife's death freed him from family responsibilities, Bonifacio set out on his travels in 1557. In Basel he found a tolerant climate that was to his liking and where he had the opportunity to express his approval for Sebastian Castellio's toleration plea, the *De haereticis an sint persequendi*, published in 1554. He next went to Zurich and Worms, where he met Melanchthon and further enriched his library.

During a visit to Venice, Bonifacio established contact with the evangelical groups in the city and was denounced to the Inquisition but managed to avoid arrest. In 1561 he was at Kasimirierz, near Cracow. After Poland, he continued his European wanderings, visiting Lyons, Paris, and London as if he was determined never to cease his peregrinations until he found his utopia (*"Nunquam peregrinari desistamus, donec inveniamus Eutopiam"*). From 1565 to 1575 he resided at Lörrach, outside Basel. Subsequently, we shall find him passing through Nuremberg, Vienna, Denmark, Sweden, England again, and even at one point reaching Constantinople. In 1584 he was once more in Poland, as the guest of the antitrinitarian physician, Nicolò Buccella, and then in England, where he lost his eyesight following a sickness. After returning to the continent, he almost drowned when his boat capsized on the Vistula, but miraculously managed to save most of his library.

With his rich experience of life in the Protestant world gained through his travels and personal contacts with persons of different religious persuasions, Bonifacio, without hesitation, threw in his lot with the Lutherans. "These things have led me to decide (through the grace of Our Lord Jesus Christ) to declare myself in favor of the most holy Augsburg Confession, in which I hope he will permit me to die,"[15] he wrote to Basil Amerbach from Brno on 25 April 1564. Filled with an irenic spirit, generous towards all in an epoch of cruel wars and bitter conflicts waged in Christ's

---

[14]D. Cantimori, *Eretici*, 294.
[15]*DBI* 12:200.

name, Bonifacio searched in vain for his utopia. In 1591 he founded the City Library of Danzig through his gift of close to eleven hundred works, including seventy-three Italian authors, accompanied by the stipulation that they should never fall into Jesuit hands. He published the writings of Antonio de Ferraris, better known as Galateo, and left in manuscript a collection of his own hymns, epigrams, and paradoxes, which was published posthumously by A. Welsius two years after Bonifacio's death at Danzig in 1597.

This brief overview of a handful of representatives of the Italian evangelical diaspora omits numerous companions searching with them for a better life in a promised land. But we have to mention at least three others, belonging to the second generation of exiles, who achieved positions of prominence abroad: Alberigo and Scipione Gentili, and Giacomo Castelvetro.

In 1579, the physician Matteo Gentili (1517–1602) was forced to abandon his home in the town of San Ginesio (Marche) and together with his sons Alberigo and Scipione find temporary refuge at Lubiana. He had been accused of participating in a Lutheran conventicle, which included his own brother, Pancrazio, also a physician. We know nothing more about this group, some of whose members are thought to have been tried in Rome and sentenced at the auto da fé held on 9 May 1568. Matteo's Protestant faith prevented him from remaining in Lubiana, and he moved on to Germany with his sons, where at Tübingen he was offered an excellent position. But he chose to continue on to London and settle there permanently where he was highly esteemed, even in court circles, and where he lived to age eighty-five.[16]

Matteo's son Alberigo (1551–1608) had graduated in civil law at the University of Perugia before emigrating. In London he rapidly achieved an enviable reputation as a leading jurist and champion of the Italian legal tradition, and in 1587 accepted the chair of civil law at Oxford. With the publication of his best-known work, *De iure belli* (1589), he gained European fame as a pioneer of international law. In this writing, in the words of Eugenio Garin, "the Ciceronian theme *natura docet* is made the basis of a universal law in which all people are bound by an intimate identity which overcomes any national barrier and any antithesis of faith, celebrated in a perennial human communion. Consequently, war is not natural,"[17] not even against infidels and Turks. Man has forgotten that he was created in God's image (even theologians forget this) and must abide under the unwritten universal law lodged in his very humanity, namely the search for the good and the true. The *De iure belli*, which is still studied today, closes with a prayer to God to make princes desist from war and grant to a sinful humanity the gift of peace through the intercession of the Savior, Jesus Christ.

Alberigo's brother Scipione (1563–1616), who had remained in Germany when the family went on to England, studied law at Tübingen, Wittenberg, and Heidelberg. As disciple of the celebrated jurist Hugo Donellus, he carried on his teaching at Altdorf, refusing invitations from Leyden and Bologna.

---

[16]See E. Comba, "Alberigo Gentili: Cenno sopra la sua vita e le sue opere," *Rivista Cristiana* 4 (1876), 5 (1877); G. Fabiani, "Alberico Gentili e l'eresia in Ascoli," *RSCI* 8 (1954): 397–412.

[17]E. Garin, *Storia della filosofia italiana* (Torino: Einaudi, 1978), 2:737–38.

The Modenese Giacomo Castelvetro (1546–1616), together with his ten-year-old brother Lelio, was reunited in Geneva in 1564 with his uncle Ludovico, the great literary critic and commentator of Aristotle. After Ludovico's death in Chiavenna, Giacomo, like so many others, was attracted to Elizabethan England, where Italian culture was in great vogue. He stayed twelve years teaching the language and championing the publication and diffusion of Italian literature, collaborating on the editions of Giovanni Battista Guarino's *Pastor Fido* and Tasso's *Aminta*. In 1593 we find him at Edinburgh serving as Italian tutor to James VI of Scotland and to his wife, Anne of Denmark, and two years later in Sweden as preceptor to Prince Charles. Castelvetro then returned to Italy where he lived tranquilly for many years in cosmopolitan Venice working for the publisher Giovan Battista Ciotti. This peaceful interlude ended in 1609 when Castelvetro was denounced as a heretic by a prisoner of the Holy Office and subsequently arrested on 4 September 1611. But his detention was short lived. He was a free man again six days later thanks to the forceful intervention of the English ambassador. Castelvetro closed out his life in England, where he was a guest in Kent of Adam Newton, secretary to the prince of Wales. There, between the summer and autumn of 1614, he wrote his only original work, "*Brieve racconto di tutte la radici, di tutte l'erbe, e di tutti i frutti, che crudi o cotti in Italia si mangiano,*" a brief account of all the roots, vegetables, and fruits, that raw or cooked, are eaten in Italy. In the words of a recent biographer of Castelvetro, the piece is "a nostalgic commemoration of a rustic but refined gastronomy, written in a style rich with spontaneity and expressions of tenderness and longing for the two dearest possessions now lost: Italy and youth."[18]

Lelio Castelvetro (1553–1609),[19] who was educated in exile by his uncle, Ludovico, would not be allowed to cling to such childhood memories and dreams. Returning to Modena after the death of his father to oversee family matters, he was arrested at Mantua in March 1604 and forced to abjure his Protestant beliefs, condemned to *carcere perpetuo*, and released from prison after five years but obliged to remain within Mantua's city limits. Just one month later, however, he was accused of not making the sign of the cross at the ringing of the midday Ave Maria. During the interrogations that followed, in an outburst of truthfulness, Lelio recalled the beliefs of his Protestant upbringing. He proclaimed that Theodore Beza was a great man and a famous doctor and preacher, and that Calvin was "another St. Paul." According to our source, the Modenese chronicler G. B. Spaccini, Castelvetro was incarcerated anew and burned at the stake in Mantua in December 1609 as a relapsed heretic.

[18]See the biographical sketch by L. Firpo, in *DBI* 22:1–4. [For a modern English version of the "*Brieve racconto*," see *Giacomo Castelvetro, the Fruits, Herbs and Vegetables of Italy...*, Translated with an introduction by Gillian Riley. Foreword by Jane Grigson (London: Viking–British Museum, Natural History, 1989). Trans. note.]

[19]See the biographical sketch by A. Biondi, in *DBI* 22:6–7.

The Genevan Refuge

It is now proper to turn our attention to the small Italian colony ensconced in the Genevan *Refuge* made up largely of artisans, workers, a few patricians and intellectuals, and an enterprising minority of wealthy merchants. Here is unequivocal confirmation of the prominence of the lower and middle spheres of society in the Italian Protestant movement. The new configuration of the Italian presence in Geneva proposed by William Monter as a revision of the still fundamental work by Galiffe, takes nothing away from the religious, economic, and social significance of the Italian colony, which exceeded a thousand persons in the decade from 1558 to 1568, out of a total population, including many French families attracted by Calvin's fame, of about twenty thousand inhabitants, approximately half of whom consisted of original Genevans.[20]

Although the Italians were a decided minority, their role in Genevan life was significant, especially in the cultural and economic spheres. Unfortunately, the community paid a heavy tribute to the three great ills that beset the city in the course of the century: the plague (1568–71), famine (1586), and the war with the duke of Savoy (1589). Even so, we remain greatly perplexed by the mere 145 votes cast in the general assembly of the Italian church in 1568 in the election of elders and deacons, a number that plummeted to 33 in 1590. Obviously, of the large Italian colony counted in Geneva during the peak years, many of its members chose not to remain permanently in the city, perhaps for work-related reasons, and also to escape from the overcrowded conditions and the chronic shortage of lodgings and provisions.

In a colorful passage Benedetto Croce described the situation in pre-Reformation Geneva and then contrasted it to the changes that followed:

> A few decades earlier [before the arrival of Galeazzo Caracciolo (1517–1586), marquis of Vico, the most illustrious of the Italian exiles], Geneva, though small, was not too different in its life and customs from the cities of southern Italy. It was Catholic, in fact an ecclesiastical city governed by a bishop who, in better times, used to be seen at the head of a mounted troop of soldiers. He had thirty-two parishes each with its own jurisdiction and priest, eleven chaplains called Maccabees from the name of their chapel, possessing seven curates and seven parishes...with five monasteries, two Franciscan, one Dominican, one Augustinian, and one Cluniac, leading a fat and festive life, with their legion of priestly concubines and hordes of brats.[21]

The fun-loving populace took great pleasure from their taverns, brothels, bathhouses, and theaters. But when Geneva espoused the Protestant cause, it underwent

---

[20]See J.-B.-G. Galiffe, *Le refuge italien de Genève aux XVIme et XVIIme siècles* (Geneva: H. Georg, 1881); E. W. Monter, "The Italians in Geneva, 1550–1600: A New Look," in L. Monnier, ed., *Genève et l'Italie: Études publiées à l'occasion du 50e anniversaire de la Société genevoise d'études italiennes* (Geneva: Droz, 1969), 53–77.

[21]B. Croce, *Un Calvinista italiano*, 20–21. Cf. the biographical sketch by E. W. Monter, in *DBI* 19:363–66.

a profound transformation. Monks were chased out, convents torn down, sacred images destroyed, and saintly relics alleged to be from the skull of St. Peter or the arm of St. Anthony, which had been venerated for centuries, were flung into the Rhone. The number of church buildings was reduced to four, "purged of all idolatry," inns were closed, and prostitutes driven off. The city, now freed from the episcopal yoke and from the duke of Savoy, became an independent republic committed to hard work and the meditation of Scripture.

One can ask what impression Reformation Geneva made on Italian exiles, and how they managed to adapt to the strict Genevan discipline. But instructed by the Bible, under the guidance of thoroughly grounded ministers dedicated to the cause of the Gospel, the vast majority accepted the new way of life. Few had to be punished for serious offenses at midcentury. An interesting aspect of this acclimatization, which would deserve further study if the appropriate documentation could be made available, is how the exiles surmounted their regional differences. A variety of customs, dialects, and discrepancies in social and professional standing did not prove to be obstacles to marriage among these Italians, and between Italians and Savoiards, or with French settlers from Provence and the Dauphinée.

In these unions, the common faith for which they had made enormous sacrifices, overcame questions of economic interest and social background, although, of course, marriages were concluded between wealthy mercantile families. Italian women provided a cohesive element. Renea Burlamacchi, the affluent widow of Cesare Balbani, caused a sensation when she accepted the marriage offer from the septuagenarian Théodore Agrippa d'Aubigné, celebrated Huguenot chief, historian, and poet. Although she was twenty years his junior, she felt honored to be loved by a man who had been condemned to death for his valiant battles at the side of Henry IV. At d'Aubigné's passing, after seven years of conjugal life, she spoke moving words of affection and devotion about her departed husband.[22]

Reflecting on the longstanding differences that still separate north and south in Italy, even a century after unification, suggests the healing, educative power of a common faith, encouraged in Geneva by the exercise of the vote in the ecclesiastical assembly where elders and deacons were elected, a system that did not promote divisions of a regional or social nature. The most suitable persons had to be selected to govern the community and oversee poor relief and assistance to widows and the infirm. This communal life, in spite of all its attendant tensions in the face of the inflexible discipline of the Genevan Consistory, was undoubtedly a school in democracy. The Italians gave evidence of spiritual maturity, especially in the sphere of social welfare. Their church, largely composed of modest workers and a minority of more affluent members, managed to look after its own, resolve its problems, and even contribute generously at times of crisis to the appeals of the city government.

---

[22] A. Pascal, "Da Lucca a Ginevra," pt. 1, chap. 3, 49: "Il faut que je vous dise avec une main tremblante et le coeur plein d'engoisse et d'amertume, que Dieu a retiré à soi notre bon seigneur et votre bon et affectioné père et à moi aussi père et mari si cher et bien aimé, que je m'estime bien heureuse de l'avoir servi et malheureuse de ne le servir plus. Hélas! tout d'un coup il m'a été ravi: et il me semble impossible de croire que ce coup soit arrivé..." (letter to her son-in-law, M. de la Villette, dated 14 July 1630).

The Italians did not play a significant political role in the party rivalries of the Republic, as did the French refugees for example, who were closely allied to John Calvin. A few among the former, products of a humanistic education, gave greater attention to doctrinal matters, assailing and annoying Calvin and his ministerial colleagues with their captious queries. The antitrinitarians among the Italians, led by the celebrated physician from Saluzzo, Giorgio Biandrata, brought disarray into the community, and as a consequence, were required on 18 May 1558 to ratify a confession of faith drawn up by the Italian pastor Lattanzio Ragnoni and Calvin himself. After the latter explained the finer points in the document in a session lasting many hours, the Italian congregation accepted it, with seven exceptions. Among these holdouts were Giovan Paolo Alciati and Silvestro Teglio, who had already left the city. They were officially banished from the Republic "for having risen up against the holy reforms."[23] Not even the tragic execution of Servetus could persuade the Italian Genevan community to break with Calvin—sorrow, murmurings, and muted approval for those who had dared to oppose the killing, but nothing more.

One of the most substantial components of the Italian colony was the Piedmontese, thanks both to geographical proximity and to the special bond with Lausanne and Geneva forged by the Waldensians after they threw in their lot with the Reformation at Chanforan in 1532. Many Piedmontese evangelicals found refuge in the Waldensian valleys or in the marquisate of Saluzzo, but the majority emigrated to Geneva, a socially modest contingent, with only few patricians sprinkled among them. But it produced a number of students, some of whom went on to become pastors and were sent out as missionaries to the Waldensian valleys, Saluzzo, the Dauphinée, Calabria, and perhaps even Sicily, according to Arturo Pascal, who probably had the mission of Giacomo Bonello in mind. Francesco Salluardo served as the pastor of the reformed church at Nevers (1561), Lyons (1564–68), and subsequently, Lausanne, Geneva, and Frankfurt.

The Piedmontese dedicated themselves especially to pharmacy, medicine, and printing. But the apothecary's art was their forte, and they accounted for half of the city's practitioners. It was a traditional activity of their region, since "simples," medicinal herbs, were gathered in abundance in the mountains of Piedmont and were then sold at Moncalieri, Pinerolo, Chieri, and other market towns. More than the other Italian regional groups, the Piedmontese, following the French example, were active in politics and served in the Republic's governing councils. A few of them had especially distinguished careers. Ami Varro (1526–93), from Moncalieri, served with Michel Roset as the Republic's official ambassador, and "for over a half century his name filled the annals of Geneva's political and civic history."[24]

The Lucchese contingent in Geneva stood out both quantitatively and qualitatively. It was composed primarily of patrician and wealthy mercantile families, which had traditionally maintained commercial relations with Lyons, Paris, Antwerp, Stras-

[23]Idem, "La colonia piemontese a Ginevra nel secolo XVI," in *Ginevra e l'Italia*, 91.

[24]Ibid., 105–6.

bourg, and London. Before proceeding to Geneva, many of them first settled in that great clearinghouse which was Lyons, or in Antwerp. In both cities they found other Italians who had already broken with the Church of Rome. There is certainly no need, after Arturo Pascal's careful and sympathetic study, to dwell at length on the story of the Lucchese emigration to Geneva. Best known are their contributions in the cultural and theological spheres, thanks to such outstanding personages as Niccolò Balbani (1522–87)[25] and Giovanni Diodati (1576–1649), the translator of the Bible into Italian, which has remained for more than three hundred years the preferred version of Italian Protestants, greatly admired for its literary qualities and faithfulness to the original texts.

Some attention to the considerable economic and social contributions made by the Lucchese men of affairs in their new home is in order. If the Lucchese did not introduce the silk industry to Geneva, they certainly vied with the French emigrés to increase its production and introduce technological innovations. By the end of the century, they enjoyed an almost total monopoly over it.[26] The ties that the Lucchese in Geneva maintained with those family members still residing in Europe's great commercial centers gave them a tremendous advantage. By the second half of the sixteenth century such names as Balbani, Pompeo Diodati, Francesco Turrettini, Michele and Fabrizio Burlamacchi, and Vincenzo Minutoli spread far and wide the fame of Geneva's silk industry.

Francesco Turrettini, who reached Geneva in 1574 after fleeing from Lucca where he had directed his family's business, was one of the most extraordinary of these entrepreneurs. Shortly after his arrival, with limited means at his disposal, he founded a first company in partnership with Carlo and Pompeo Diodati. From 1579 to 1585 he was in Antwerp serving as factor for several Genevan commercial firms. When Antwerp fell to Alessandro Farnese, duke of Parma, Turrettini moved on to Zurich where he established a silk spinning business with the brothers David and Heinrich Werdmüller. The firm, which imported raw silk from Valencia, Genoa, and Amsterdam, and then exported it to France, Germany, and the Low Countries, was a resounding success. In 1592 Turrettini returned to Geneva where his business grew so quickly that his *Grande Boutique* incorporated nine other companies run by Lucchese merchants. The firm continued to prosper until the death of this intrepid man of affairs in 1628.

Though Orazio Micheli, Cesare Balbani, Pompeo Diodati, and the Frenchmen Trembley, Flournois, and Tronchin were no less successful as manufacturers and capitalists, Turrettini's great fame was partly due to his beneficence to the state and charity towards the poor. His son Giovanni recalled in his *Memorie* that the father, deeply moved by a sermon of Theodore Beza concerning the urgency of assisting the many needy in their midst, promptly presented the pastor of the Italian church, Niccolò Balbani, a purse containing fifty *scudi* for the relief of the Italian poor. The good min-

---

[25]See the biographical sketch by C. Ginzburg, in *DBI* 5:336–42.
[26]See L. Mottu-Weber, *Économie et refuge à Genève au siècle de la Réforme: La draperie et la soierie (1540–1630)* (Geneva: Droz; Paris: Champion, 1987).

ister burst into tears and promised him divine blessing. The son dated to that bene-
diction the beginning of his father's successful business ventures, "after having
wandered for a dozen years in the desert of the world." It may be, wrote the son, that
the divine promise delayed its arrival, but Scripture "sings out loud and clear" that
God tests the faithful so as to strengthen their patience, but will never abandon
them. In the *Memorie*, the Burlamacchi, Turrettini, and Balbani recalled tribulations,
adversities, persecutions, but also satisfaction at having accumulated great wealth
from their hard work and sacrifices. Out of gratitude, their generation felt the obligation to provide generously for the less fortunate and for the charitable institutions of
the Republic. This sentiment became distorted in the seventeenth century by the
radicalism of the Puritans for whom the accumulation of wealth was a sign of their
predestination, a concept attributed erroneously to Calvin and still repeated today.[27]

Among the great merchants of the *Refuge*, mention should be made of the Pellizzari brothers of Vicenza and Chiavenna, who constituted a great family constellation
extending throughout Europe—in addition to Geneva—Lyons, Basel, Venice,
Amsterdam, and Lombardy. Taking advantage of their vast commercial network,
they provided couriers to Italy for the evangelicals in the Grisons, Zurich, and
Geneva. After several years of such activity, the incriminating correspondence
between Alessandro Trissino and Giovan Battista Trento was uncovered. In 1562 letters connected with the business dealings of the Pellizzari were discovered in Como.
One of them revealed the existence of an intense traffic in Bibles and prohibited
books between Geneva and Italy.

Studies are still lacking on the other Italian refugee colonies in Geneva, such as
the Ligurian totaling about a hundred members, and the Cremonese, which would
permit further probes into the religious history of these areas, in addition to illuminating still more the life of the exiles in their refuge. We must limit ourselves to the
emigrés from Messina, about eighty strong with their women and children.[28] From
Palermo, Messina, Mazara, and Noto, humble silk workers, boatmen, booksellers,
and former monks chose to face the dangers and discomforts of a long journey to
seek a haven beyond the Alps where they could live out their faith without the threat
of persecution from Spanish inquisitors. Among the few prominent members of this
contingent, we should mention Ludovico Manna, whom we already met in Tuscany
and who became a catechist in Geneva; Francesco Tudesco, a musician, in 1551
among the first to arrive; and the nobleman Giulio Cesare Pascali (1527–1601?).

Pascali may have been a fellow student in Messina of Bartolomeo Spadafora, but
we know with certainty that he was a member of the Valdesian circle in Naples. Pascali
decided on flight after the execution of Fra Pagliarino, during the hunt for Pellizzeri
and while Spadafora was in exile. In the course of his journey, he received the
heartrending news of the death of three of his children. When he arrived in Geneva,
he was in his thirties, broadly educated in the humanities, but well versed also in

---

[27]Ibid., 339. Cf. V. Burlamacchi, *Libro di ricordi*, 44–49.
[28]See A. Pascal, "La colonia messinese di Ginevra e il suo poeta Giulio Cesare Paschali," *BSSV*, nn.
62–66 (1934–36).

archeology, mathematics, and the natural sciences. He formed a firm friendship with Francesco Micheli, who had served as Gonfalonier of Lucca on several occasions, took as wife in second marriage Cecilia, the daughter of the nobleman Jacopo Campagnola from Verona. Although Pascali seemed securely ensconced in his adopted city, he was suspected of antitrinitarian sympathies because he stood up for the Calabrian Valentino Gentile. Even more serious was an accusation lodged against him in 1566 that he had intrigued with his brother who was in the retinue of the Duke of Nemours, a man hostile towards Geneva and the Reformation. The suspicion led to Pascali's expulsion from the city, but subsequently he was permitted to return and enter its service. During the hostilities with the duke of Savoy (1588–89), he pretended to be a supporter of the duke so that he could uncover his battle plans. In 1591 Geneva's government bestowed honorary citizenship on him and tried to alleviate his poverty. His son Giacomo had died *"en allant vers le Duc pour le service de la Seigneurie."*

If Pascali's life seems characterized by "a succession of lights and shadows, of virtues and passions, of truths and errors, of heroism and cowardice,"[29] his writings give a different impression. Principally, we know him as the translator of Calvin's *Institutes*, dedicated to Galeazzo Caracciolo, evidence of his admiration for the great reformer and his thought. In 1592 the printing house of Jacob Stoer published Pascali's verse translation of the *Psalms of David* and a small volume of his religious poetry, *Rime spirituali*. The first of these two works, dedicated to Queen Elizabeth of England, was the fruit of long meditation on the original text, in which the poet identified with the life of the ancient psalmist, at once filled with anxieties and sorrow, and solace in the grace and pardon of God. Pascali claimed to have been inspired to undertake his labors by the desire "that the Lord Our God be commonly sung and celebrated in Italy even by common people, there where everyone knows how to sing lewd verses which offend and obscure his Majesty, and corrupt souls to their eternal damnation."[30] Pascali's distant homeland inspired him with a consuming nostalgia:

Oh worthy David! oh my bounteous and blessed Italy
If you would uphold that, now turn from
A worldly to a celestial spirit!

So that I may wake you. Listen to my discourse,
Apart from living for God, all else is as nothing;
And only He should be celebrated evermore.[31]

Pascali's *Rime spirituali*, dedicated to Orazio Micheli, the son of the Lucchese patrician Francesco, are more enlightening than poetic. The verses are of an autobiographical character, "born from interior, true and living sentiments…now mournful,

---

[29]Ibid., 75.
[30]*De' sacri salmi di Davide, dall'ebreo tradotti, poetica e religiosissima parafrasi del Signor G.C. Paschali.* Geneva: Iacopo Stoer, 1592. See the preface.

[31]Ibid., sonnet introducing the Psalms.

now joyful." A student of the subject, Mario Richter, views Giulio Cesare Pascali as the Italian Theodore Beza, the spokesman of its colony, the poet of a new vision of life and of the world, in the context of Calvin's and Beza's aesthetics.[32] Pascali found himself compelled to abandon the lyrical models of his youth and adapt to new themes and to a new spontaneous and simple style, turning poetry into an instrument of edification. He sought something different from the older poetic tradition, following Beza rather than Ronsard and the Pléiade.

Liliane Mottu-Weber has shed light on the notable contributions made by the Genevan *Refuge*, in which the Italians played a significant role. To be sure, the exiles were people of flesh and blood, with limits and frailties, but many of them also distinguished themselves for their honesty, moral qualities, and generosity towards the less fortunate and the often needy institutions and government of the Republic, drawing deep inspiration from a heartfelt Christian faith.[33] The memoirs and last testaments of the Lucchese testify to a vibrant sense of gratitude towards God and of abandonment to his mercy.[34]

THE MARTYRDOM OF GIACOMO BRUTO

One of the last martyrs of the Italian Reformation, Giacomo Bruto (1551–91) of Villanova d'Asti,[35] had contacts with Geneva and the "*ecclesia peregrinorum*" during his travels through Europe. Restless, yearning for deeper learning and spiritual independence, one could repeat about him what Benedetto Croce said of Giordano Bruno who returned to Italy fascinated with the idea of martyrdom, after rejecting the discipline of Calvin's Geneva.

Bruto had been in Geneva as a boy when he had accompanied his Latin master, Sebastiano Visca, a Calvinist who had gone there to purchase religious books. It may have been at his family's insistence that Bruto had taken the Augustinian habit between sixteen and eighteen years of age. But after studying rhetoric and logic at Paris, he tired of theology, "full of a thousand errors," and withdrew to meditate in a convent on the Adriatic. He then resumed his travels through Europe, as he tells us in a memoir he drew up for inquisitors. He was in Geneva briefly, but could not accept the rigid conditions for enrolling in the Academy. In southern Italy, Sicily, Spain, and Portugal, he sought out evangelicals. He settled finally in Palermo, where he opened a Latin school, and in spite of the prosecutions raging and the ensuing condemnations in 1568 and 1569, made contact with the few surviving Protestants. Bruto was discovered and tried, and on 24 August 1589 signed an abjuration of the

---

[32]M. Richter, "Attività e problemi di un poeta italiano nella Ginevra di Calvino e di Beza," *RSLR* 1 (1965): 234–35.

[33]L. Mottu-Weber, *Économie et refuge*, 439.

[34]Cf. A. Pascal, "Da Lucca a Ginevra," *RSI* 52 (1935): 285 ff.

[35]Cf. C. A. Garufi, "Segundo proceso de Jacobo Bruto...," *Bulletin de la Société d'Histoire Vaudoise*, n. 36 (1916): 68–96; the biographical sketch by A. J. Schutte, in *DBI* 14: 728–30; and S. Caponetto, in *Studi sulla Riforma*, 194–95.

erroneous doctrines he had professed. He was sentenced to serve ten years on the royal galleys, to be followed by life in prison.

After languishing for a year in the galley of Cesare La Torre, he addressed a petition to the Inquisition which succinctly but lucidly explained his faith. He stated that he had tried to repress his Calvinist beliefs more than once, but they continued to fester in his inner being and now he was resolved to profess them openly. He voiced his dismay at the corruption in Sicilian churches and society, sentiments that had been voiced by defendants in many trials before his own, but which cropped up now with renewed vehemence directed against the ecclesiastical hierarchy and the parasitism of the monastic orders, which with their idleness, carnal vices, greed, robberies, seizure of the very "bread out of the mouths of abandoned orphans, waifs and widows" offended the divine Majesty, and provoked it to castigate the world. Bruto lashed out against masses for the dead, a flagrant merchandising conducted by the papacy to the detriment of the poor. Finally, concerning the sacrament of the Eucharist, he affirmed that the host was "the pure bread presented to ignorant people in memory of the bitter Passion of Jesus Christ." On 10 July 1590, Bruto was condemned to death, but the sentence was carried out only a year later, on 28 October 1591. The interval was consumed by theologians and confessors attempting relentlessly to persuade him to recant his errors. But as the compiler of the *Serie dei rilasciati* wrote,[36] Bruto was determined to pay with his life "for Luther," and went bravely to his fate. He may have drawn strength from the case, which he had recounted at his first trial, of the Lutheran preacher who had been condemned to death in Rome and refused to abjure even on the scaffold, a martyrdom that Bruto could have witnessed personally and which would have remained indelibly fixed in his mind.

Bibliographical Note

Much useful information and an exhaustive documentation can be found in J. Tedeschi, "The Cultural Contributions of Italian Protestant Reformers in the Late Renaissance," in *Libri, idee e sentimenti religiosi nel Cinquecento italiano,* ed. A. Prosperi and A. Biondi (Ferrara & Modena: Edizioni Panini, 1987), 81–108. [A revised, corrected, and expanded Italian version appeared in *Italica* 64 (1987): 19–61. Trans. note.]

---

[36] *Serie dei rilasciati,* n. 321.

21

HOPING AGAINST HOPE

The Exiles' Delusion

By the end of the century, the Counter-Reformation had crushed every attempt made by the Protestant movement to establish itself in Italy as it had elsewhere in Europe. All the great northern reformers had known from the very beginning how difficult it would be to achieve their goals without the cooperation of princes or city governments. The ultimate failure of the Italian Reformation, even after it had managed to penetrate everywhere in the peninsula, is proof of this.

The case of the Republic of Venice, which turned a deaf ear to all the appeals made by Italian reformers, from Galateo to Vergerio, from Ochino to Flacius, is exemplary. Realistically, Venice realized that it would be extremely perilous to modify its policy of watchful and cautious neutrality after the defeat of the Schmalkaldic League at Mühlberg in 1547. Church and state were united in Italy in their aversion to heresy, of which they feared the political and social consequences. Flight on the part of the leaders of Italian Protestantism, the martyrdom of some of its greatest preachers and missionaries, the extermination of the Calabrian Waldensians, the forced Catholicization of their brethren in Puglia, the confinement of the Piedmontese Waldensians to their valleys, the ferocious repression of the movement in Sicily, and the systematic destruction of dissent everywhere in Italy, generated a deep-seated sentiment of defeatism among the people and sundered the threads of an incipient network.

Numerous examples demonstrate this ebbing of the tide, but one, cited by P. F. Grendler for Venice where Protestant ideas had penetrated all social classes, seems particularly symptomatic. In 1566 a convicted heretic, wearing the penitential garment and candle in hand, was exhibited in Saint Mark's Square for an entire morning. A tumultuous crowd had gathered to witness the spectacle and was shouting that he should be burned or stoned to death.[1] A quarter of a century earlier a similar crowd had listened enthusiastically to the sermons of Galateo, Ochino, and Giulio della Rovere.

---

[1]See P. F. Grendler, *The Roman Inquisition and the Venetian Press*, 138.

The Reformation did not succeed in sinking lasting roots in Italy. The best educated and most thoroughly indoctrinated among those who sought refuge abroad, after experiencing their new lives in Geneva, Basel, Zurich, Strasbourg, the Grisons, and elsewhere, were fully cognizant of the movement's failure at home. They urged the faithful to emigrate and follow their example. Already in 1553, the anonymous translator of the *De vitandis superstitionibus*, insisted that Italians, compelled at home to practice idolatrous rites, should choose the road into exile:

> We know well that there are churches in Italy and that congregations gather together; we know that the administration of the Word and the sacraments have those few who make a profession of being Christian; we know, I repeat, how everything is meager, cold and of small value, and who does not know it, let him just reflect on the fruits and effects that he sees, and it will all be immediately clear.[2]

Giulio della Rovere is even more explicit in his *Esortazione al martirio*:

> Christians in Italy are like dispersed and dead members, without guide and without head, since the Italian churches are neither organized nor regulated according to the Word of God.... The Gospel is banished and to suffer persecution seems highly strange to us, because we do not feel a living Christ in our hearts.... If our Italians would only congregate, unite and warm themselves in a single body regulated in accordance with the Word of God, faith would take fire....[3]

Even more pitiless was the analysis made by Alessandro Trissino in his *Ragionamento di ritirarsi a vivere nella Chiesa visibile di Gesù Cristo, lasciando il papesimo* (An argument for withdrawing to live in the visible Church of Jesus Christ and abandoning papism) which he sent to the brethren in Italy from Chiavenna on 20 July 1570, just a few days after Paleario had been sentenced to death. For the Vicentine exile the time for organizing evangelical communities in Italy had passed. It was now the moment to flee the spiritual Babylon if one did not want to become "betrayers of the benefit of Christ and idolaters." The time for compromise and Nicodemism was over. This was the voice of a person who had been defeated and overtaken by events, of a survivor, as Achille Olivieri wrote, who felt that the facts were on his side.[4]

Epilogue

The few documents at our disposal, often misleading and lacunose, show that the death sentences emitted by the Roman Inquisition steadily decrease in the seventeenth century, with the last execution occurring in 1761. The majority of the vic-

---

[2] Quoted from D. Cantimori, *Prospettive di storia ereticale del Cinquecento* (Bari: Laterza, 1960), 47.
[3] Quoted from E. Comba, *I nostri protestanti*, 174.
[4] A. Olivieri, "Alessandro Trissino," 75; Idem, "Il Ragionamento di Alessandro Trissino (1570) fra 'Epistola,' ragionamento, discorso politico e religioso," in *Non uno itinere: Studi storici* (Venice, 1993), 73–95.

tims consisted now of foreigners: French, including two women from Montpellier; Spaniards; Portuguese; and English. The registers of the Confraternity of San Giovanni Decollato record the charge of heresy only in a few cases, but some of the victims, with the assistance of complementary sources, are identifiable as Protestants.[5] They were the last to fall after the conclusion of hostilities on the Italian front.

The most glaring example of this omission concerns Teofilo Panarelli of Monopoli, who takes us back to the small world of Venetian heresy, and especially, to the Calvinist movement of which he was a leader.[6] He had been converted through Bartolomeo Fonzio, studied medicine at Padua from 1555 to 1559 where he received his degree. In 1560 he moved to Venice where he joined some "Lutheran" conventicles and established one himself. The membership, which consisted of lawyers, merchants, patricians, and booksellers, had various meeting places, the shop of the printer Arrivabene, a pharmacy, the residence of a nobleman, Marcantonio Canal, or the *Fondaco dei tedeschi*, the enclave of the German merchants, where he purchased books by Bucer, Luther, and Hus. In these gatherings, Panarelli read from the New Testament, Ochino's sermons, and Calvin's catechism, many copies of which had been brought to him by a Venetian merchant from Lyons. One of the questions most actively discussed by the group concerned the merits of flight to Geneva to avoid falling into the "idolatry" of the Roman rites. Panarelli was arrested in 1567, and after a first trial in Venice was extradited to Rome where he was executed on 22 February 1572 after abjuring his errors.

The long testament, which he left with the Confraternity of San Giovanni Decollato, discloses the wealth of this physician and man of affairs, who owned homes, land, and mills at Monopoli, Venice, and Padua. On the eve of his execution, he was tormented by the anxiety to save what he could for his wife, the Venetian Caterina Guarneria, for whom he arranged the return of her dowry of five hundred ducats with interest set at six *lire* and four *soldi* per ducat. Was Panarelli's hope to thus mitigate the ruin of his family by recovering a part of the property confiscated by the Inquisition his motivation in abjuring the evangelical faith he had professed and championed for so many years, or was it the realization that his deviation from the teachings of the Roman church had been folly? In any case, his judges believed that they had to eliminate a dangerous adversary.

If we know little about the Bolognese "heretic" Pompeo Loiani executed at Rome on 12 June 1579, there is much information on Alessandro Jechil of Bassano, an Anabaptist missionary who succeeded in penetrating the convent of the Poor Clares at Udine and converting a number of nuns. He clung "obstinately and pertinaciously to the false opinions…dictated to him by his crazy mind," and faced death at the stake fearlessly on 19 November 1574.[7] A terrible punishment was the lot of

---

[5]In addition to the documents published in D. Orano, *Liberi pensatori*, see the complementary materials in L. Firpo, "Esecuzioni capitali in Roma (1567–1671)," in *Eresia e Riforma nell'Italia del Cinquecento*. Miscellanea I. (Florence: Sansoni; Chicago: The Newberry Library, 1974), 321–42.

[6]D. Orano, *Liberi pensatori*, n. xlvi, 45–49; P. F. Grendler, *The Roman Inquisition and the Venetian Press*, 103–4.

the Englishman Richard Atkinson ("Arctinson"), who could not be persuaded to abjure in spite of the tireless efforts made by four Jesuits, his compatriots. He was conducted to Saint Peter's Square on 2 August 1581, where his right hand was cut off before he was burned alive.[8] At the beginning of the new century, death at the stake in Rome, on the *Campo dei Fiori*, was the punishment for the philosopher Giordano Bruno, followed to his fate by the Jews Nunzio Servadio; Salomone, a Sicilian (13 March 1580); and Jacopo di Elia from San Lorenzo (22 January 1616), who declared "I am a Jew and want to die a Jew."[9]

The number of sentences emitted against foreigners and apostate monks who are not specifically identified as heretics confirms the extinction of the Italian Protestant movement by the century's end. Nevertheless, the Church of Rome did not feel totally at peace because it was experiencing difficulties applying the decrees of the Council of Trent and there remained the thorn of two Protestant enclaves, in the Waldensian valleys and in the Valtellina.

THE "HOLY MASSACRE" IN THE VALTELLINA

To eliminate once and for all the "Lutheran plague" ensconced in the Waldensian valleys, virtually at the gates of Turin, and infiltrating into Lombardy and the Valtellina through the efforts of Italian exiles, became a primary objective for both political and religious authorities in the duchy of Savoy and the State of Milan during the entire sixteenth century. Cardinal Charles Borromeo, whose Milanese diocese extended into the Valtellina as far north as Sondrio and Morbegno, was one of the protagonists in the work of "purification" and reclamation in Lombardy.

The two thrusts of the anti-Protestant offensive were obstructed by a series of disputes and political considerations in the context of the ongoing duel between France and Spain and the inevitable clash with Geneva, with which the Waldensians were intimately linked, and with the Gray Leagues (Grisons), predominantly Protestant, to which the Valtellina had belonged since 1512. Here the situation was even more complicated than in the Waldensian valleys, protected as they were in part by the agreement drawn up at Cavour in 1561. In the Valtellina, the growing number of evangelical communities, while still in a minority, had upset the traditional and somnolent order of the Catholic parishes by carrying a new religious and cultural message to a largely illiterate population of mountaineers.

The hate of the Catholic faction, spurred on by Franciscan and Dominican monks, towards the government of the Grisons, became ever more bitter, aggravated by social and political factors. The proclamation of freedom of religion for both Catholics and Protestants ended by injuring the Catholic majority, compelled to contribute to communal expenses for the salaries of evangelical "preachers." The irenic plea made by Scipione Calandrini, the pastor at Sondrio, for peaceful coexist-

---

[7]D. Orano, *Liberi pensatori*, nn. lxii , lii, 54, 63. For A. Jechil, see G. Paolin, "Dell'ultimo tentativo compiuto in Friuli di formare una comunità anabattista: Note e documenti," *NRS* 62 (1978), 4–28.

[8]D. Orano, *Liberi pensatori*, n. lxv, 67.

[9]Ibid., nn. lxxvii, lxxix, lxiv, lxxxii, 65, 88, 90, 91, 95.

St. Peter's Square and the Apostolic Palaces at Rome towards mid–sixteenth century. The construction of the base of the new cupola planned by Michelangelo has begun, but the square retains its medieval flavor. Engraving by Philippe Galle based on the drawing by Hendrick van Cleef.

"The light shining in the darkness," the Waldensian shield from the "Carta delle tre Valli" (Map of the three Valleys) by Valerio Grosso (1640).

ence between the two confessions was not acceptable to the Catholic party, which twice tried to have him assassinated. Although they did not succeed on these occasions, in 1568, spurred on by Pius V, who had been an inquisitor in Morbegno and kept himself informed about the progress of heresy in the Valtellina, the Dominicans organized the kidnapping of the pastor Francesco Cellario on his way home from the ecclesiastical synod at Chür. He was transported to Rome where he was executed on 25 May 1569, after persistently refusing to be reconciled to the church.[10] There was a tremendous repercussion in the Grisons and in the Protestant cantons to this blatant violation of religious liberty. Reprisals took place at the expense of the monastic orders and threats were made that revenge would be exacted.

The gulf between the two populations was by now unbridgeable and made worse by attempts on the part of both France and Spain to forge an alliance with the Grisons so as to obtain passage for their troops through the Alpine passes. During the night of 18 July the Catholics of Tirano launched a surprise attack against Protestants. The "Holy Massacre" of the Valtellina, as the event was called by Cesare Cantù,[11] in just a few days resulted in the elimination of almost all the evangelicals

---

[10]Ibid., n. xxxiii, 33; A. Pastore, *Nella Valtellina del tardo Cinquecento*, 145, 147.

[11]C. Cantù, *Storia della città di Como*, vol. 2, lib. 8 (Florence, 1856); idem, *Il Sacro Macello di Valtellina: Episodio della Riforma religiosa in Italia* (Florence: Mariani, 1853).

living in Tirano, Teglio, and Sondrio, with pastors and "preachers" the first to perish. In their fanaticism, the Catholics spared neither women nor children. At Teglio the killings, totaling seventy-two dead, took place inside the Protestant place of worship. All told, between three and six hundred evangelicals fell in the "small" St. Bartholomew massacre. On 24 August, Andrea Parravicini was condemned to the stake because he refused to abjure his errors, and at Sondrio entire families, distinguished for their nobility, wealth, and education, were annihilated.

According to a leading authority, E. Besta, the Catholics fought aggressively in order to establish their full rights to religious freedom and political independence from the three Protestant leagues. Spain served merely as "support for the Roman faith against the predominant heresy in the Grisons."[12] In the Valtellina, once the first stage of refuge for the Italian exiles leaving their homeland, the great experiment to establish a Protestant church in a land predominantly Italian in language and culture had concluded. That gateway into Italy, through which so many proselytizers and so much of the literature of the Reformation had passed, was now barred forever.

Survival of the Waldensians

At the opposite end of the Alpine range, in the Waldensian valleys, there remained that small residue of evangelicals protected by the accord reached at Cavour in 1561. In spite of the difficulties ensuing from a juridically inferior status in relation to the other subjects of the duchy of Savoy and the limited geographical area to which they were confined, with all the consequences that followed affecting their capacity to obtain gainful employment or educate their children, the Waldensians, after surviving the terrible crisis of the plague of 1630 (in which their dead totaled about six thousand, including seven pastors), continued to become stronger spiritually and elevate themselves economically. The sect's continuing contacts with the cantons of French-speaking Switzerland and with Geneva in particular, where the community's future ministers were sent to study, allowed them to expand even beyond the limits of their "ghetto." They purchased and built houses and a place of worship at San Giovanni di Luserna, which was easier to reach than the one at Ciabàs.[13] The alarm sent up by Catholic missionaries, the already tense relations with the local population, which could not stand that the "*barbetti*," who were better educated and more enterprising should encroach into Catholic territory, inspired the young ruler, Charles Emanuel II, encouraged by the regent, his mother Christine of France, an intransigent Catholic and daughter of Henry IV, to enforce a strict adherence on the part of Waldensians to the accord of Cavour. The police action subsequently

---

[12]See the posthumous critical reconstruction by E. Besta, *Le valli dell'Adda e della Mera nel corso dei secoli, I: Il dominio grigione* (Milan: Giuffré, 1964), 114 ff., and 176–77 for the opinion cited. For the Protestant viewpoint, cf. E. Camenisch, *Geschichte der Reformation und Gegenreformation in den italienischen Südtälern Graubündens*, 2d ed. (Chur: Bischofberger, 1950).

[13]For this section, I base myself on A. Armand-Hugon, *Storia dei Valdesi*, vol. 2.

entrusted to the bigoted and brutal marquis of Pianezza, governor over Piedmont, turned into an anti-Waldensian crusade.

The Easter campaign, the notorious *"Pasque piemontesi"* of 1655, would have ended in the total annihilation of the Waldensian people if reports of the massacres and of the wanton cruelty committed even against women and children had not horrified Protestant countries. Oliver Cromwell responded to the desperate appeal made by the Waldensian pastors who had fled abroad, and seized the initiative to mobilize Puritan England in the defense of the Waldensian community, *mater Reformationis*.

On 20 May 1655, the princess Christine wrote exultantly to her resident in Rome: "We have crushed the head of the hydra and of the rebellion…the monster of heresy which, with its deadly exhalations, daily contaminated these parts with its deadly poison."[14] But it was only a mirage! The diplomatic efforts of the Lord Protector of England, assisted by his secretary, the ardent Puritan John Milton, impelled Geneva and the Swiss Protestant cantons, the states general of the United Provinces and Cardinal Jules Mazarin to intervene on behalf of the Waldensians, by now reduced to desperation by their losses, by the destruction of their homes, their churches, of all they possessed, by the agonies of prison, and forced conversion. Finally, the duke of Savoy was compelled to grant "Patents of Grace" on 18 August 1655.

The truce lasted only thirty years for the unfortunate survivors among the Waldensians. The Revocation of the Edict of Nantes by Louis XIV in 1685 brought an end to public celebration of the cult for that segment of the community under French control in the Val Chisone and part of the Val Perosa. Under pressure from his powerful neighbor, the young Vittorio Amedeo II reluctantly, because the Waldensian peasants were good and loyal subjects, issued the edict on 31 January 1686 that revoked the concessions that had been made to them well over a century before at Cavour. If the act of revocation calling for the cessation of the cult, the demolition of the churches, the banishment of the pastors and teachers, Catholic baptism of the newborn had been carried out to the letter, it would have meant the end of the Waldensians.

The court of Savoy and the duke himself turned a deaf ear to pleas for mitigation of the edict and finally drove the simple Waldensian mountaineers to desperation, who could not comprehend exactly what their crime had been. Under the guidance of Henri Arnaud, pastor and military leader, hoping against hope, they mounted a desperate resistance against the combined French and Piedmontese troops, which totaled about ten thousand men. The result was a massacre without precedent, involving more than 1,700 persons of both sexes, either killed in battle or murdered after capture; 148 children who were taken from their parents or relatives; 3,000 adults either were forcefully converted or fled. Countless survivors were cast into the ducal dungeons.

The anti-Waldensian crusade finally seemed to have won out over these rebellious and stubborn sectarians. Some survivors languished and died in prison; the

---

[14]Ibid., 87.

"converted" could not find peace in the confines of Vercelli where they had been deported, and fled towards Geneva and Switzerland. It seemed that the roots of the Waldensian "Lutheran" sect had been eradicated. But suddenly, at the end of July 1686 the town of Crissolo was besieged and taken. From that moment on, a vexing guerrilla warfare waged by a few desperate survivors who had come out of their hiding places threw the ducal garrisons into disarray. Officers in the field came to a secret agreement with these "Invincibles": the latter would be allowed to emigrate with their families and those who had been incarcerated were to be freed. In this way, in September 1686 a group of two hundred men, women, and children set out from the Val Pellice on the road to Geneva. Once again, the intervention of Swiss Protestants succeeded in obtaining permission for expatriation, with the exception of a hundred or so prisoners considered to be incorrigible. The edict of 3 January 1687 permitted exile even for the most obdurate rebels.

It can be calculated that the number of persons who reached Geneva and settled either in the city or neighboring cantons totaled a little less than thirty-four hundred. But the edict contained a vexing provision that would come back to haunt its promulgators: it barred pastors and their families from going into exile, as well as all children under twelve years of age, who had to remain behind to be brought up in the Catholic faith. These were enormities that the Swiss negotiators had not succeeded in eliminating. They merely served to make more acute the nostalgia of the exiles and their unquenchable desire to return to the land of their fathers.

Consequently, the Waldensian leaders, encouraged by old Giosuè Janavel, the hero of the "*Pasque piemontesi,*" laid plans for the return, determined on the reconquest of their valleys. Henri Arnaud adroitly exploited the anti-French alliance being formed by William of Orange as he ascended the throne of England and obtained his support. After several early efforts came to nothing, with minute preparation and William's financial contribution for the undertaking, on the night of 26 August 1689, almost a thousand men gathered at Prangins, not far from Nyon, on the north bank of Lake Leman. Inspired by the prayers of Arnaud, the difficult and rash enterprise began, crossing Savoy through the valleys of the Arve, Isère, and Arc, to finally reach Val di Susa, two hundred kilometers of mountains with some passes more than twenty-five hundred meters. It is impossible to describe the extraordinary and moving events of the march, in which a third of the participants did not survive, the bloody skirmishes and the bitter suffering. Before winter set in, the remnant, which had opened up a passage up to the mountain of the Balsiglia in Val Germanasca, took up defensive positions, resolved to perish fighting rather than surrender. At the point that the combined French and Piedmontese forces were about to overwhelm the tiny band of famished and exhausted men, whose ammunition was expended, suddenly in May 1690 the duke offered a cease-fire. The Waldensians had been saved thanks to a congeries of international events.[15] Duke Vittorio Amedeo II had joined England and the Low Countries in the League of Augsburg against France. The duke granted permission to the Waldensians to return to their valleys, undoubtedly hoping to use

---

[15]G. Spini, "Il quadro internazionale," in *Il glorioso rimpatrio* (Turin: Claudiana, 1988), 9–35.

them in the hostilities with France. From prisons in Turin, from Geneva and other Swiss cantons, from distant Brandenburg, after an interval of five years, the remnants of the "Israel of the Alps," who undoubtedly saw the powerful hand of God in this miraculous turn of events, headed homeward. "What had been for decades," as Giorgio Tourn wrote, "a frontier on which were fought great and tragic battles in the seventeenth century, became a small, Alpine ghetto, and like every ghetto it was suffocated by laws, neglect, silence."[16]

But the situation was destined to change. During the course of the eighteenth century, the bonds with the transalpine Protestant churches, always generous with their assistance, grew closer. Thanks to these links with Switzerland and especially with Geneva, where the sons of the leading families went to study theology, law, and medicine, Waldensians passed through a period of notable cultural and economic development, and significant demographic growth. An educated bourgeoisie, which had lived a part of its life abroad, and a class of small-landed proprietors came into being. When the French Revolution reached the Waldensian valleys it found fertile ground long prepared by age-old struggles for the freedom of conscience, and a population lacking the rights enjoyed by other subjects of the house of Savoy. The arrival of the Napoleonic forces, who were received enthusiastically, quickly led to the emancipation of the Waldensians and Jews. Even after the restoration, the former continued to come to the attention of the government leaders because of its contacts with European culture, its thorough indoctrination in the ideas of the Enlightenment, and its commercial contacts with Protestant countries.

The liberal current in the government, headed by Roberto D'Azeglio; Camillo Benso di Cavour, related to a Protestant family in Geneva; and Vincenzo Gioberti succeeded in persuading the sovereign Charles Albert, who had not totally forgotten the progressive education he had received in Geneva in the home of the pastor Jean-Pierre Vaucher, to grant juridical equality to Waldensians and Jews. After the proclamation of the constitution, in a separate decree on 17 February 1848, the king conceded to Waldensians full civic and political rights, eliminating previous restrictions concerning fields of study and professional activities. Full freedom of worship was not yet wholly achieved, but the way had been opened. An enormous assignment now confronted the only Italian evangelical community of the reformed persuasion, previously restricted to "the fringes of Italy," as Edmondo De Amicis would write: to educate their fellow citizens about their faith and spread among the small Italian states, which were beginning to dream of being free, the Sacred Scriptures with their message of human freedom in the profound meaning of the Gospel of John: "The truth will make you free" (8:32).

---

[16]G. Tourn, "L'Esercito dei santi," in *Il glorioso rimpatrio*, 86.

APPENDIX TO THE TEXT

CHAPTER 16. Recent important archival discoveries add significantly to the discussion of Tuscan heterodoxy in the chapter. I refer especially to Gustavo Bertoli's "Luterani e anabattisti processati a Firenze nel 1552," *Archivio Storico Italiano* 154 (1996): 59–122. The study is based on documents of the Florentine Inquisition preserved in the Archivio di Stato, Florence (*Auditore delle Riformagioni*, 4, n. 72). They are part of a memorandum written by Massimiliano Milanesi, who consigned to Duke Cosimo the papers of his father, *Ser* Bernardo, a ducal secretary who died on 16 September 1559. Among the many magistracies he served, Bernardo Milanesi was one of the lay members of the inquisitorial tribunal serving as notary in the capacity of Cosimo's representative. The inventory of the documents records a number of trials and mentions many other important documents, but the fascicle itself only contains a list of names of forty defendants, divided in two parts. A number of persons belonging to the governing class appear among the accused alongside artisans, most of whom are foreigners. In an appendix to his study, the author clarifies the position of Bartolomeo Panciatichi, prosecuted beginning in August 1550, after the revelations made by Lorenzo Davidico, the accuser of the Augustinian Giuliano da Colle and of other Florentines, mentioned in a list shown by the "reformed priest" to Lelio Torelli. The duke intervened firmly with the Inquisition in Rome on Panciatichi's behalf and, in fact, the latter was not forced to appear in the 6 February auto da fé and was released after paying a large fine. The duke also came to the support of Bernardo Ricasoli, a rich merchant who trafficked all over Europe from Palermo to Antwerp, and succeeded in voiding his six-month prison sentence received as a confessed but repentant offender.

Another name on the list of the prosecuted from the ranks of the governing circle is Marcantonio Serrerighi, the *bargello* or chief constable of Pisa, who was condemned to a year's incarceration, but restored to the ranks of the notaries in 1553. Many of the indicted persons are among those betrayed to the Inquisition by the turncoat Anabaptist Pietro Manelfi; others could have been tried after 1552. Two important figures whose names had not appeared previously are Lelio Carani, a literary friend of Domenichi's, who, among other works, translated the *Proverbs* of Erasmus (*DBI* 19: 636–37), and Giovanbattista Giovanni, of an ancient Florentine family, who was a consul in the Wool Guild in 1550.

The great novelty emerging from the recently discovered list concerns the arrest of the Anabaptists, Bartolomeo Ducci of Borgo Buggiano, and Lorenzo Nicolucci of Modigliana, singled out by Manelfi as an "Anabaptist bishop," together with their wives, Giovanna and Elisabetta. The third woman was Antonia, married to Francesco dei Gabellieri, a stocking maker. There is no mention of Panciatichi's wife, Lucrezia Pucci. The duke took harsh action against Ducci and Nicolucci and actually allowed the latter to be extradited to Rome, contrary to the norms that had been established for prisoners of the Florentine Inquisition.

CHAPTER 20. Among the prominent exiles *"religionis causa,"* it would have been proper to mention Giulio Pace (1550–1635) of Vicenza, who joined the Italian church at Geneva in 1573 together with Alessandro Trissino and Niccolò Thiene, became a *bourgeois* in 1576, and married the Lucchese Elisabetta Venturini in 1578. He was invited to teach in the city's academy replacing François Hotman. Pace subsequently taught at Heidelberg, Speyer, Sedan, Nîmes, Montpellier, Padua, and Valencia. "Intelligent jurist and learned and subtle interpreter of Aristotle," as he was described by a recent authority,[1] Pace edited the great philosopher's *Organon* and the *Corpus iuris* (Geneva, 1580). Thanks in part to the academic battles in which he found himself involved, Pace returned to Catholicism, but looked back nostalgically on his decade at Heidelberg. His family, with the exception of his son, Jacopo, chose not to follow him back to the Church of Rome.

[1] C. Vasoli, "Giulio Pace e la diffusione di alcuni temi aristotelici," in *Aristotelismo veneto e scienza moderna*, Atti del 25° anno accademico del Centro per la storia della tradizione aristotelica nel Veneto, 2 vols. (Padua, 1983), 1009–34.

BIBLIOGRAPHICAL APPENDIX

Since the appearance of the first Italian edition of this book in 1992, a great many important works have appeared on the subject of the Italian Reformation. Significant journal articles have been added to the notes in the body of the work. The discussion here is limited to recent full-length books with the exception of note 9 below.

1. Achille Olivieri, *Riforma ed eresia a Vicenza nel Cinquecento* (Rome: Herder, 1992).

   The account searches for ancient roots in history and begins with the penetration of the Cathar heresy in the lands owned by the Trissino family and the birth of the humanistic concept of toleration with Lorenzo Valla, through the establishment of the first Protestant conventicles. The volume is enriched by an important documentary appendix concerned with the trials of Alessandro Trissino and Odoardo Thiene.

2. Massimo Firpo, *Riforma protestante ed eresia nell'Italia del Cinquecento* (Bari: Laterza, 1993).

   An interesting work, with rich bibliography, which attempts to clarify the complex manifestations of Italian religious dissent. The author argues that they cannot be explained simply in terms of a reception and adaptation of northern Protestant doctrines. He views the *Beneficio di Cristo* as the emblematic text of an Italian current aspiring to the reform of the church.

3. Juan de Valdés, *Alfabeto cristiano, Domande e Risposte, Della Predestinazione, Catechismo*, a cura di Massimo Firpo (Turin: Einaudi, 1994).

   In the introduction, the author deals with the theme of the "synthesis of Erasmianism, Lutheranism and *alumbradismo* at the center of the Valdesian experience, profoundly influenced by its Spanish roots" (p. lxvi).

4. Vincenzo Burlamacchi, *Libro di ricordi degnissimi delle nostre famiglie*, a cura di Simonetta Adorni-Braccesi (Rome: Istituto storico italiano per l'età moderna e contemporanea, 1993).

   A truly valuable edition of a fundamental source for the Italian presence in Geneva, with important information on the great Lucchese emigré families (the Balbani, Burlamacchi, Calandrini, Diodati, Turrettini).

5. Simonetta Adorni-Braccesi, *"Una città infetta": La repubblica di Lucca nella crisi religiosa del Cinquecento* (Florence: Olschki, 1994).

   A vast synthesis encompassing previous studies, including the many by the author herself, dedicated to the singular Italian case of an entire city involved in the religious crisis of the century. The episode concludes with the exodus of eighty members from the great patrician and mercantile houses, led by the Arnolfini and Balbani.

6. Susanna Peyronel, ed., "Frontiere geografiche e religiose in Italia: Fattori di conflitto e comunicazione nel XVI e XVII secolo," *BSSV* a. 112, n. 177 (1995).

    This special issue contains the *Atti del XXXIII Convegno di studi sulla Riforma e i movimenti religiosi in Italia (Torre Pellice, 29–31 agosto 1993)*. The contributions are all pertinent to the history of the Italian Reformation.

7. Pierroberto Scaramella, *"Con la croce al core": Inquisizione ed eresia in Terra di Lavoro (1551–1564)* (Naples: La Città del Sole, 1995).

    The discovery of inquisitorial trials, preserved in the Archivio Storico diocesano in Naples and the Archivio arcivescovile in Capua (published in the appendix) permits the author to reconstruct the spread of Lutheran and Calvinist doctrines at Caserta, Capua, and Santa Maria Capuavetere. The chief proselytizer was the ex-Augustinian Lorenzo Romano, formerly a "children's teacher" in the school attached to the hospital of Santa Maria di Loreto at Naples. A Calvinist conventicle was formed in Capua whose leaders fled to Geneva in 1552, including Simone Fiorillo, who would become the catechist of the Italian exiles' church in 1556 and later pastor at Chiavenna. In 1552 death sentences were emitted against the tailor Jacobetto Gentile, who stood up unflinchingly to his judges, and the monk Vincenzo Jannelli. Twenty-seven condemnations followed, of which, for the men, all but five were to galley service. The author claims that the *"ecclesia Cremonensis"* was the only other Italian example, besides the Capuan, of a fully organized evangelical conventicle, forgetting the existence of Messina's strong Calvinist group from which thirty entire families emigrated to Geneva. Scaramella's important contribution confirms the vast Italian extension of Mediterranean Calvinism.

8. Marcantonio Flaminio, *Apologia del Beneficio di Cristo e altri scritti inediti*, a cura di Dario Marcatto (Florence: Olschki, 1996).

    The volume makes a decisive contribution to our understanding of Valdesianism and the thought of Marcantonio Flaminio. In addition to the previously unknown *Apologia*, the edition also publishes for the first time letters of Flaminio that permit us to attribute to him three of the five *Trattatelli*, which had been previously ascribed to Juan de Valdés by Eduard Böhmer in 1870, and reprinted as such by the Claudiana press at Florence in 1873. The introduction provides a complete reconstruction of the genesis and printing of the *Beneficio di Cristo* and wholly confirms its Valdesian character.

9. Carlo De Frede, "Autodafé ed esecuzioni di eretici a Roma nella seconda metà del Cinquecento," *Atti dell'Accademia Pontaniana*, n.s. 38 (1989): 271–311; idem, "Ancora sugli autodafé in Italia durante il Cinquecento," *Atti dell'Accademia Pontaniana*, n.s. 45 (1996).

These essays are rich with information, some of it previously unknown, on almost all Italian sixteenth-century autos da fé, with a detailed description of the ceremony and a reprinting of the relevant illustrations from Philipp van Limborch's *Historia Inquisitionis*. They provide the first biographical sketch of the nobleman Pompeo delli Monti (for whom there is no entry in the *DBI*). The date of his execution is corrected to 27 June 1566.

10. Adriano Prosperi, *Tribunali della coscienza: Inquisitori, confessori, missionari* (Turin: Einaudi, 1996).

The work reconstructs, with a careful analysis of the known documentation, the complex and variegated history of the Counter-Reformation, its victory and pervasive influence on Italian society. With the reconstitution of the Roman Inquisition in 1542 all the states of the peninsula ended up by recognizing in the "sovereign seated on Peter's throne…the right of judicial control over specific subjects" (p. 103), namely the right to investigate opinions, ideas, readings, and religious beliefs. The volume clarifies unequivocally the reasons for the failure of the Italian Protestant movement.

APPENDIX

LORENZO LOTTO PHILO-REFORMER?

by Carlo Papini

SCHOLARSHIP IS VIRTUALLY UNANIMOUS[1] in recognizing the hand of the great Venetian painter Lorenzo Lotto (1480–1556) in the images on the title page of Antonio Brucioli's *Bible* (1st ed.: Venice: Luc'Antonio Giunti, 1532), especially in the depiction of Moses receiving the tablet of the Law. The three upper panels picture the creation of Eve, the fall of Adam and Eve and their expulsion from Eden. Below, at the left, there are three Old Testament episodes: Moses facing Pharaoh, the passage over the Red Sea, and Moses again receiving the tablet of the Law. The panels on the right depict the birth and resurrection of Jesus; below, the apostle Paul preaching to the Athenians. The entire cycle, intimately connected, culminates in this final scene (rather uncommon in Italian iconography), which is intended to emphasize the need to convey the Word of God to the people in the spoken language. This harmonizes perfectly with what Brucioli himself stated in the preface and dedication to the king of France with which the Bible opens, where he argues that the various categories of people who heard the living words of the Messiah at the time of Jesus now had the same right to read those same words in their own vernacular language (see above at p. 28).

In the face of the unwavering hostility on the part of the Roman Curia against any vernacular version of the Sacred Scriptures that did not literally follow the Latin Vulgate, but claimed to be based on the original Hebrew and Greek texts,[2] Lotto's representations assume a disguised but controversial connotation. Moreover, in the opinion of a recent authority, "The close narrative '*continuum*' framing the title and summary of the title page, quite rare in Italy, originated in northern books, suggesting a link, even by this channel, of the "heretic" Brucioli with the Protestant world."[3]

---

[1]The only contrary opinion belongs to Pietro Zampetti, *Lorenzo Lotto nelle Marche: Il suo tempo, il suo influsso* (Florence: Centro DI, 1981), 440–41.

[2]The first instance of Roman censorship against Erasmus's New Testament dates to 1526. Brucioli's Bible was included in Paul IV's *Index* in 1559.

[3]F. Barberi, *Il frontespizio nel libro italiano del Quattrocento e del Cinquecento* (Milan, 1969), 132.

Lotto was a personal friend of the Venetian publishers Giunti, especially with the son of Luc'Antonio, Giovanni Maria. Since the painter had prepared the drawing of their printer's device , it is thus highly possible that they had commissioned him to do the drawings for Brucioli's Bible. The latter had come to Venice, after his expulsion from Florence, with a reputation for heterodoxy (according to Benedetto Varchi, author of the *Storia Fiorentina*, "he was considered a Lutheran"). Therefore, the fact that Lotto had agreed to collaborate in a vernacular version of the Bible, a suspect one no less, suggests, minimally, that he agreed with the reformer's program of making the Scriptures available to the people.

Brucioli's version, and especially his preface, were criticized heavily by the Dominicans. Giunti, who cared greatly about his own good name, since he considered himself the official publisher of the order, quickly regretted having brought out a Bible that smacked of heresy, and he turned to the Florentine convent of San Marco seeking a commission for a new translation of undoubted orthodoxy.[4] The version chosen by the Dominican Sante Marmochino was basically Brucioli's but without the controversial preface, and with modifications that rendered it more faithful to the Vulgate. This new Bible was published by the Giunti in 1538. The rivalry between the two editions was aggravated by the fact that the Venetian publisher used Lotto's title page from the first edition of the Brucioli Bible (1532). He obviously considered himself its legitimate owner, since he employed it in still other books, as was the custom of the day.[5]

Thus, when Brucioli decided to reprint his Bible, he was compelled to find a new publisher, and he found one in the printing establishment of Francesco Bindoni and Maffeo Pasini. Since they were unable to recover the original plates of the title page (and of the text), they had to have it copied by a trusted engraver. The second edition of the Brucioli Bible appeared in 1538, the title page of which is reproduced in this volume (see plate 32 in Italian ed.). If we compare it to the first edition, or to Marmochino's Bible, we note that the new engravings resemble but are not identical to theirs, being inferior to them. We do not know for a fact if Lotto was personally involved in the affair, but it is probable that he authorized the copying of his drawings on the part of the new publishers, even though in this period the artist was principally occupied in the Marche.

That Lotto was sympathetic to the Protestant Reformation, especially during the years from 1540 to 1546, first hypothesized by Bernard Berenson, is asserted by Giovanni Romano and especially by Maria Calì,[6] while the notion is rejected by Francesca Cortesi Bosco and Pietro Zampetti.[7] Their negative viewpoint is based

---

[4]See G. Spini, *Tra Rinascimento e Riforma: Antonio Brucioli* (Florence: "La Nuova Italia," 1940), 70–73.

[5]As an example, for the book by Giovanni Maria Velmazio, *Veteris et Novi Testamenti opus singulare* (Venice, 1538), which was put on the *Index* in 1603.

[6]G. Romano, "La Bibbia di Lotto," *Paragone-Arte* (1976), nn. 317–19: 82–91; M. Calì, "La religione di Lorenzo Lotto," in *Lorenzo Lotto: Atti del convegno internazionale di studi di Asolo, 1980* (Treviso, 1981); idem, "Ancora sulla 'religione' di Lorenzo Lotto," *Ricerche di storia dell'arte*, n. 19 (1983): 37–60.

[7]F. Cortesi Bosco, *Gli affreschi dell'Oratorio Suardi: Lorenzo Lotto nella crisi della Riforma* (Bergamo: Bolis, 1980); L. Lotto, *Libro di spese diverse (1538–1556)*, a cura di P. Zampetti (Venice & Rome, 1969).

principally on Lotto's love for the monastic ideal (conceived as a safe haven from life's troubles), and his generally friendly relations with the religious orders for whom he labored. In fact, in his second testament written in 1546 he asked the Dominicans of San Zanipolo in Venice to assure him "a burial following the customs and habits of the order and clothed in a monk's cassock." Furthermore, the only time that Lotto explicitly dealt with the theme of heterodoxy, in the great fresco in the *Oratorio Suardi* at Trescore (Bergamo) in 1524, the "heretics" are presented negatively, trying to climb into Christ's vineyard to join the grape harvest, but ending up plummeting ruinously to earth in front of an open Bible. However, one can object that: (1) The work dates from Lotto's Bergamo period (1513–25), certainly preceding his encounter with the evangelical movement in Venice; (2) the "heretics" painted at Trescore are those against whom the church fathers, Ambrose and Jerome, battled, and they are specifically named: "Helvidius, Vigilantius, Iuvinianus, Arianus, Sabelianus," etc., in other words the leaders of those movements in the ancient church, which even the Protestant reformers considered heretical.

One thing is certain, namely that Lotto was a convinced Christian, influenced by the "*Devotio Moderna,*" and by Erasmian "evangelism." His favorite reading was the *Imitation of Christ*, then attributed to Jean Gerson, with the title *De contemptu mundi*. Lotto's love for and profound familiarity with the vernacular Bible (he did not know Latin) are well attested.[8] During the time that he was working on the drawings for the wooden marquetry in the choir of Santa Maria Maggiore in Bergamo (1524–32), his letters inform us that he frequently clashed with the Confraternity over the manner, deemed unorthodox by that body, in which he interpreted episodes from the Old Testament.

During the years 1540 to 1542 Lotto was in Venice, a guest in the home of his nephew Mario d'Armano, a prominent lawyer who held the title of "Grand Guardian" of the Confraternity or School of San Marco (just next to San Zanipolo). On 17 October 1540 Lotto copied portraits of Luther and his wife Caterina (perhaps those by Lucas Cranach the Elder, now in the Uffizi) at the request of his nephew, who intended to give them as presents to an admirer of the German reformer, a certain Tristano.[9] Some years later, d'Armano would be denounced to the Holy Office by his daughter and tried, accused of having eaten meat on Fridays. It was during this period that Lotto established friendships with participants in the local Protestant movement, especially with the goldsmith Bartolomeo Carpan (with whom he would

---

[8]In 1542 he spent four *soldi* to acquire a book by Joan. Gerson, *De contemptu mundi*, and three *lire*, four *soldi*, for "the Exposition on the Psalms by Pittorio," namely, *I Salmi di David in forma d'omelie* by Ludovico Pittorio. In 1540, to a niece who has become a novice, Lotto gave "Lives of the Holy fathers," "A Psalmist with Vernacular Commentary Bound in Paperboard," and "Gerson on Contempt for the World." In 1542, after arriving in Treviso, he made a present of "a Psalter" to his host's young house servant, while to the young children of Giovanni del Savon, whose godfather he became, he gave "un donato per Toni et un salterio per Jacomo," in other words the Latin grammar by Donatus and the Book of Psalms (*Libro di spese*, 212, 222, 227, 228).

[9]Lotto recorded in his account book a credit of six ducats, thirty-seven *lire* and a few *soldi* for "two portraits of Martin Luther and his wife which *Misser* Mario gave to Tristan, framed in gold." Various

reside for a month and a half in 1546 during an illness), who was described by his accusers as "a great Lutheran," who clandestinely shipped books by Luther and Melanchthon as far south as Messina. Carpan would be tried alongside his Venetian companions in 1569.[10]

In 1542 Lotto painted for San Zanipolo the *Elemosina di Sant'Antonino*, a painting that vividly represented the necessity of facing up to the plight of the poor so that begging could be eliminated. This was a problem that he felt deeply, since we know that he often gave out of his pocket "to pluck the poor" off the streets, as he recorded in his account book, the *Libro di spese*. The issue, as is well known, had been resolved some time before by the northern reformers, who substituted relief administered by the civic authorities for charity funneled through the parishes.

In October of that year, Lotto left Venice for Treviso where he lodged for three years in the home of Giovanni dal Savon. This is how the artist described the matter in his *Libro*: "I entered the house of *Misser* Joan. dal Savon, my comrade, to remain there forever, to live and die there in his house, in the love and terms of Christian joy, as good friends and companions...." According to Maria Calì, these expressions indicated a fraternal relationship of a religious sort. In his testament Lotto appointed his "comrade" as his universal heir. In 1544 the artist recorded a small expenditure in his account book (10 *soldi*) for the purchase of "5 booklets of the *Instituta Christiana* as presents for the children of Joan. del Savon." Thus, after having already given them a Latin grammar and the Psalter, Lotto now offered them a brief text of "Christian Instruction" (this seems to be what is intended by the title, which is probably abbreviated). But what was the catechism?

The choice is fairly limited, because at the time, shortly before the opening of the Council of Trent, vernacular Italian catechisms were rare and almost exclusively produced by reformers (or by Valdesians).[11] From them originated the *Sommario della santa Scrittura* (1534), Brucioli's *Pia espositione* (1542) (which would later be identified as a compend of three chapters from Calvin's *Institutes*), and the famous *Beneficio di Christo*. But these were rather substantial introductions to the Christian faith, not especially appropriate for children, nor could they have cost a mere two *soldi*. Out of the abundant foreign catechetical production (German or French), inaugurated by Zwingli in 1523, nothing had as yet been translated: an Italian version of Calvin's *Catechism* would not appear in Geneva until 1545. For these reasons,

---

inquisitorial trials provide evidence that the possession of Luther's portrait was a fairly common tradition in the households of Protestant sympathizers in the Veneto (see above p. 161).

[10]See above, p. 351: R. Fontana, "Solo senza fidel governo et molto inquieto de la mente." This sentence, Lotto's own, comes from his second testament (1546) where he described his grave mental anguish when, in the fall of 1542 following the "great worries" he had suffered in the house of his nephew, he decided to move to more peaceful Treviso.

[11]Of the skimpy Catholic output of that time, it is worth mentioning only the *Enchiridio christiano* by the Dominican Vincenzo Giaccheri (1538) and the *Espositioni volgare* by Luigi Lippomano (1541). However, it appears that they had a small impact and very limited circulation. See S. Cavazza, "'Luthero fidelissimo inimico.'" in *Lutero e l'Italia*, a cura di L. Perrone (Casale Monferrato: Marietti, 1983), 74ff.

it seems highly probable to me that the artist was referring to one of the first printed editions of Juan de Valdés's small catechism for the young (only sixteen pages long) which, according to Vergerio, was entitled *In qual maniera si doverebbono instituire i figliuoli de' Christiani,*[12] certainly known in Geneva by 1545, and thus probably printed anonymously the previous year, or at least not long after the death of Valdés (1541), perhaps in Venice itself.

Moreover, in his *Libro di spese*, Lotto described, on three occasions, a certain Zacharia di Bologna as a "new Christian," a conventional way of designating adherents of the Reformation. In his first testament the artist also mentions "the company united in Jesus Christ" and the "brethren in Christ," expressions typically used by the Venetian conventicles of Reformation sympathizers. From this and other evidence, Calì concludes that during this period Lotto was in some way associated with one of these philo-Protestant communities. In opposition, Francesco Colalucci asks us to note that

> Lotto did not need to align himself with one camp or the other, since such a clear-cut antithesis did not exist yet. He seemed to have felt a certain attraction for some aspects of the Reformation; but more than subscribing to the doctrinal or devotional innovations, Lotto shared its fundamental yearning for moral renewal, focused above all on the censure of corruption in the ecclesiastical hierarchy.[13]

In December 1545, the painter decided to leave Treviso "because I did not earn enough from art to support myself." It may also be that his relationship with the dal Savon family had deteriorated, since the next year he wrote a new will naming as executors the governors of San Zanipolo. He returned to rented lodgings in Venice, but in less than three years, he changed his abode four times. He finally decided to move to the Marche in search of new work, and on 30 August 1552 settled in Loreto, in a house put at his disposal by the governor of the *Santuario della Santa Casa*. Here his health quickly took a turn for the worse. On 8 September 1554 he became an oblate at the sanctuary and bequeathed all his property to it. Lotto was appointed "painter of the Santa Casa," but died after only two years. His life presents a striking example of how, at mid–sixteenth century, a convinced and sincere Christian could

---

[12]This small catechism, destined to have great success in various languages, was of clearly Protestant stamp and would soon be condemned and included in the *Index* of Paul III (1549). See P. P. Vergerio, *Il catalogo de' libri...condannati...da M. Giovan della Casa...*[Poschiavo, 1549], fols. 3v–5r. We only know of one surviving sixteenth-century manuscript of this text (Siena, Biblioteca Comunale, MS G VIII 28, fols. 62v–70r), entitled "In che maniera doveriano essere instrutti insino dalla pueritia li figlioli delli christiani nelle cose della religione christiana" (In what manner Christian children should be instructed from childhood in the things of the Christian religion). The title of a printed edition (the only one we know about) has a slightly different title (see, p. 89). In the text, Vald's himself calls it "a brief Christian instruction for children."

[13]F. Colalucci, "Lotto," *Art-dossier*, n. 91 (June 1994), 45. However, where it is considered established that Lotto recognized himself in the brief Valdesian catechism, one cannot state only that he shared the longing for moral renewal. It should be recognized that he accepted also the basic fundamental orientation of the Reformation.

still reconcile a yearning for ecclesiastical reform, with all that implied, with loyalty to its religious tradition and personal acceptance of the monastic ideal.

A COMMENT ON THE ILLUSTRATIONS
HORS-TEXTE

1. The title page of *Uno libretto volgare*, anonymous translation of three writings by Luther (whose name is omitted), printed at Venice in 1525. It is the first known Italian translation of a work by the Saxon reformer (BNF, Biblioteca Guicciardiniana).

2. Second edition of the preceding one (1526), here attributed to Erasmus. The beautiful engraving representing the risen Christ between Saints Andrew and Longinus (the Roman soldier who, according to the Gospel of John, stabbed Jesus in the ribs), was inspired by Andrea Mantegna (Royal Library, The Hague).

3. Title page of the Italian New Testament, translated from the Greek by Antonio Brucioli (1487–1566), published at Venice with the permission of the Venetian Senate by Lucantonio Giunti in 1530. It is dedicated to Cardinal Ercole Gonzaga, and represents the first Italian translation made from the Greek text published by Erasmus in 1516 (BNF, Biblioteca Guicciardiniana).

4. Title page of the second expanded edition of Celio Secondo Curione's *Pasquino in estasi*, published in Italian in 1546 with the false imprint: Rome (BNF).

5. "The creation of Eve and of Jesus Christ, the Savior of humanity," is a preparatory drawing by Jacopo Carucci (Pontormo) for the great cycle of frescoes (no longer extant) from the principal chapel of the church of San Lorenzo in Florence, on which he labored for eleven years, from 1547 until his death. Pontormo, inspired by Valdesian spirituality, combined in a single composition, against every iconographic tradition, the first episode in the history of man and woman and the salvation won by the Redeemer, with the intention of "emphasizing in a symbolic synthesis the close parallelism existing between God's creative act and the new creation brought about by the regenerating sacrifice of Christ." On the basis of the *Beneficio di Cristo* and the last writing from the pen of Valdés, the brief catechism entitled *Qual Maniera...*,

> The entire plan of the cycle appears to affirm precisely this: the Justification which in the Old Testament seemed a hypothesis impossible to realize, since man could not ransom himself from sin solely through the fulfillment of injunctions laid down by the Law, had become actually possible thanks to the soteriological act performed by the Son of God.... By eliminating from the entirety of the composition both the figures of saints, as well as that of the Virgin, Jacopo had also wanted to exclude any allusion to mediating forces, thereby affirming that the problem of forgiveness and that of one's relationship to God, so much discussed

during those years, even at San Lorenzo, had to be resolved exclusively in the direct and immediate encounter between those who were saved and Him who had wanted to save them (Raffaella Corti, "Pontormo a San Lorenzo: Un episodio figurativo dello 'spiritualismo italiano,'" 22–23) (Florence, Galleria degli Uffizi, Gabinetto disegni e stampe).

6.   Emilia Pia (d. 1528), the wife of Count Antonio di Montefeltro, intimate friend of the duchess of Urbino, Elisabetta Gonzaga, who refused to make a confession and receive communion at the time of her death. Medal executed by Adriano Fiorentino (Florence, Museo del Bargello).

7.   Ludovico Domenichi of Piacenza (d. 1564), the man of letters who translated Calvin's book against the Nicodemites, *Nicomediana*. Medal by Domenico Poggini (Florence, Museo del Bargello).

8.   Pier Vettori (1499–1585), the great Florentine writer and philologist, at seventy-nine years of age. Medal by Gasparo Romanelli, 1579 (Florence, Museo del Bargello).

9.   Pier Francesco Riccio of Prato (1501–64), preceptor, and later secretary and majordomo to duke Cosimo I de' Medici. Portrait attributed to Francesco Rossi, known as Cecco di Salviati or "il Salviatino, Florentine (1510–63) (Prato, Palazzo Comunale).

10.   Benedetto Varchi (1503–65), notary, man of letters, historian. Anonymous portrait (Florence, Galleria degli Uffizi).

11.   Pietro Carnesecchi (1508–67), apostolic protonotary during the reign of Clement VII, a member of Duke Cosimo's court, condemned to death as a heretic and executed at Rome in 1567. Portrait by Domenico Ubaldini, known as "il Puligo," c. 1526 (Florence, Galleria degli Uffizi).

12.   Pierre Viret (1511–71) of Orbe (in the Swiss canton of Vaud), reformer and pastor at Lausanne. Contemporary engraving.

13.   Guillaume Farel (1489–1565) of Gap, reformer of Geneva and Neuchâtel. Contemporary engraving.

14.   Marguerite de Valois (1524–74), duchess of Berry and then of Savoy, the daughter of Francis I and the wife of Emanuel Philibert, protectress of Piedmontese Waldensians. Drawing by François Clouet (Museum of Chantilly).

15.   Duke Charles III of Savoy, "the Good" (1486–1533), receiving a book in homage from a Dominican. Luther wrote to him in 1523 inviting him to follow the example of the princes of Saxony. Contemporary miniature.

16.   Martin Luther (on the left) debating the papal diplomat, Cardinal Giovanni Salviati of Florence (1490–1553). Detail from a painting by Francesco Rossi, known as Cecco di Salviati, or "il Salviatino." The painting documents how Luther was imagined in Italy in the sixteenth century. Note the courtier's improbable costume (Rome, Palazzo Farnese).

17.   Interior of Renée de France's chapel in the Este castle at Ferrara (actual state). The walls have been overlaid with polychromatic marbles, in the form of a cross,

perhaps at the order of the duchess who wished to avoid images of any sort, in accordance with Calvinist teachings.

18. Pedro Berruguete, *"Autodafé"* (detail) (c. 1500). A Dominican is conducting two convicted heretics to the stake, while two others are already being consumed by flames. Note the yellow penitential garment and the conical "devil's mitre" with Satan's image (Madrid, Museum of the Prado).

19. Title page of the *Capo Finto*, an Italian translation, probably published at Venice in 1544, of a political oration by Johann Sleidan (BNF, Biblioteca Guicciardiniana).

20. Title page of the *Del fuggir le superstitioni*, the Italian translation of anti-Nicodemite writings by Calvin, various treatises (from the Latin), and four sermons (from the French), probably published at Geneva in 1553 (BNF, Biblioteca Guicciardiniana).

21. Title page of Calvin's *Catechism*, in the Italian translation by Giulio Domenico Gallo of Caramagna (Cuneo), the second edition published in 1551 at Geneva by Adam and Jean Rivery (BNF, Biblioteca Guicciardiniana).

22. Title page of the Italian edition of Calvin's *Institutes*, translated by Giulio Cesare Pascali of Messina, published at Geneva in 1557 (BNF, Biblioteca Guicciardiniana).

23. Renée de France (1510–75), duchess of Ferrara, daughter of Louis XII, the wife of Ercole II (1508–59), duke of Ferrara and Modena, in a portrait by Corneille de Lyons (Museum of Versailles).

24. Reginald Pole (1500–58), English cardinal, humanist, and Catholic reformer (anonymous, London, National Portrait Gallery).

25. Cardinal Girolamo Seripando (1493–1563), general of the Augustinians and defender of the doctrine of justification by faith at the Council of Trent, archbishop of Salerno (contemporary portrait).

26. Cardinal Ercole Gonzaga (1505–63), bishop of Mantua, governor of Tivoli and subsequently of Monferrato. After the death of his brother Federico II (1540), he was regent of the duchy of Mantua for eighteen years on behalf of his nephews Francesco III and Guglielmo. He presided over the final sessions of the Council of Trent. Seventeenth-century print (Milan, Bertarelli collection).

27. Presumed portrait of the refined Florentine man of letters, Giovanni Della Casa (1503–56), archbishop of Benevento, later nuncio to Venice and secretary of state under Paul IV. Drawing by Iacopo Carucci, known as Pontormo (Florence, Galleria degli Uffizi).

28. Gian Matteo Giberti of Palermo (1492–1543), bishop of Verona and Catholic reformer. Painting of the Lombard school, sixteenth century (Museum of Castelvecchio, Verona).

29. The German Jesuit Peter Canisius (1521–97) (Peter de Hondt) of Nimwegen. Contemporary engraving by C. Griter.

30. The Jesuit Alfonso Salmerón (1515–85) of Toledo. Portrait from the edition of his *Commentaries* (Cologne, 1602).

31. Cardinal Charles Borromeo (1538–84) of Arona, archbishop of Milan. Medal by Gasparo Mola, 1610 (Florence, Museo del Bargello).
32. Title page of the second edition of the Italian Bible translated by Antonio Brucioli (1487–1566), published in Venice by Francesco Bindoni and Maffeo Pasini in 1538. (The first edition had appeared in Venice in 1532 from the presses of Luc'Antonio Giunti). Dedicated to Francis I. This is the first appearance of the so-called "apocryphal" books (which the reformers excluded from the canon) grouped separately in an appendix, an arrangement followed by Giovanni Diodati with his Bible (1607). Brucioli even includes book 3 of the Maccabees and book 2 of Esdras. The beautiful engravings on the title page by the Venetian artist Lorenzo Lotto reproduce scenes from the Old and New Testaments. See the appendix to the present work, p. 404, and *Il fondo Guicciardini nella Biblioteca Nazionale Centrale di Firenze, II: Bibbie, Catalogo*, a cura di A. Landi (Florence, 1991) (BNF, Biblioteca Guicciardiniana).
33. Giulia Gonzaga (1513–66), countess of Fondi, widow of Vespasiano Colonna. This famous portrait, perhaps by Agnolo Bronzino, is the best-known copy of the original by Sebastiano del Piombo, lost in France (Florence, Galleria degli Uffizi).
34. The prince-bishop of Trent, Cardinal Cristoforo Madruzzo (1512–78), in a portrait by Titian (1541) (Trent, Museo Diocesano).
35. Cardinal Gian Pietro Carafa (1476–1559) of the dukes of Montorio, Pope Paul IV from 1555 to 1559. Sculpted by Piero Ligorio for the church of Santa Maria sopra Minerva, Rome.
36. Don Pedro de Toledo (1484–1553), grandee of Spain, viceroy of Naples from 1532 to 1553. Sculpture by Giovanni da Nola in the church of San Giacomo degli Spagnoli, Naples.
37. The church of San Giovanni in Bragora, Venice (1505), a few yards from the *Riva degli Schiavoni* (actual state). A neighboring edifice housed the prisons before the completion of the new structure, completed in 1614, adjoining the ducal palace (photo Riccardo Bensi).
38. Church and convent of San Frediano in Lucca (actual state). During the brief priorate of Peter Martyr Vermigli (June 1541–September 1542), with the assistance of Paolo Lazise, Celso Martinengo, and Emmanuele Tremellio, the religious house became a small Protestant "university."
39. Cosimo I de' Medici (1519–74), duke of Florence from 1537 and grand duke from 1569 until his death. Bust in bronze by Benvenuto Cellini (1548) (Florence, Museo del Bargello).
40. Guglielmo Gonzaga (1538–87), duke of Mantua from 1550, but for the first eight years under the regency of his uncle, Cardinal Ercole Gonzaga. In 1574 Guglielmo became duke of Monferrato. Anonymous, contemporary portrait (Vienna, Kunsthistorisches Museum).
41. Alessandro Farnese (1520–89), the son of Pier Luigi the Younger, duke of Parma and Piacenza and nephew of Pope Paul III (after whom he was named), cardinal

from 1534, great patron of the arts and letters (anonymous medal, Florence, Museo del Bargello).

42. Marcello Cervini of Montepulciano (1501–55), cardinal, reigned as pope for a brief twenty days with the name of Marcellus II. Portrait by Francesco Rossi known as Salviatino (Rome, Galleria Borghese).

43. Cardinal Giovanni Angelo Medici of Milan (1499–1565), occupied the papal chair from 1559 to 1565 with the name of Pius IV. An able diplomat, he succeeded in bringing the Council of Trent to a successful conclusion (Vatican commemorative medal).

44. Emperor Maximilian II of Habsburg (1527–76), the son of Ferdinand I, was tolerant towards the Protestants. Portrait by Antonio Mor, detail (Madrid, Museum of the Prado).

45. Théodore Agrippa d'Aubigné (1552–1630), soldier in the Huguenot ranks, historian and poet. In 1620 he took refuge in Geneva where he married Renée Burlamacchi of Lucca, the widow of Cesare Balbani. Painting by Bartholomé Sarburgh (Geneva, Bibliothèque Publique et Universitaire).

46. Clément Marot (1496–1544) of Cahors, Huguenot poet and translator of the Psalms. Portrait attributed to G. B. Moroni (Paris, Société d'Histoire du Protestantisme).

47. Giovanni Diodati (1576–1649), born in Geneva of Lucchese parents, professor and Calvinist theologian, translator of the Bible into Italian from the original languages (1607). English engraving of 1651 from a Biblical anthology annotated by Diodati, here as he appeared at age seventy (BNF, Biblioteca Guicciardiniana).

48. Rome, Castel Sant'Angelo: an arcosolium of the Roman funerary cell for the family of the emperor Hadrian, in the depths of the castle, which was converted in the early fifteenth century into a fearsome, windowless prison called "Sanmarocco" or "Sanmalò." Archbishop Bartolomeo de Flores or Floriano, incarcerated here at the time of Alexander VI, survived only eight months. During the pontificate of Paul IV, Cardinal Giovanni Morone, accused of heresy, was confined in the castle.

49. Letter from P. P. Vergerio to H. Bullinger, 22 December 1563, in which he expresses sorrow for the expulsion of B. Ochino from Zurich. It concludes with the sentence: "Sed quid? fiat iustitia et pereat mundus" (Zurich, Staatsarchiv).

50. "Calvin brought down." Sixteenth-century French print celebrating the triumph of the Counter-Reformation (E. Doumergue, *Iconographie calvinienne* [Lausanne, 1917]).

51. Detail from the "Knight of St. Bartholomew" by Giorgio Vasari (1511–74), painted shortly before his death for the Vatican's *Sala Regia*.

52. "Victory and triumphal chariot of Catholic doctrine over the Lutheran heresy" (1599), engraving by the Franciscan Giacomo Lauro of Bagnacavallo, printed at Rome by the authority of Clement VIII. The chariot of the "Church Militant," supported by the seven sacraments and driven by the four Evangelists, passes under a triumphal arch preceded by Saints Peter and Paul, popes and bishops,

and followed by the Scholastic doctors. Below ground, mingled with devils, the defeated heretics endure great suffering (Herzog August Bibliothek, Wolfenbüttel).

53. The medal coined at the behest of Gregory XIII (Ugo Boncompagni) in 1572 to commemorate the St. Bartholomew's Day Massacre. Above, the caption "*Ugonottorum strages*"; an angel, holding up a cross, and with a raised sword, battles a group of fleeing Huguenots. Medal executed by Giovan Federico Bonzagni of Parma (1508–88) (Florence, Museo del Bargello).

54. Gregory XIII seated on the papal throne blesses a group of Jesuit missionaries (1582). The epithet reads: "Go and labor in the vineyard of the Lord." The medal was coined at the inauguration of the new seat of the Jesuits' *Collegio Romano* (Florence, Museo del Bargello).

55. "The Spanish Inquisition," contemporary Dutch engraving depicting the great Valladolid auto da fé of 21 May 1559. *Center*: The gallery with the seated authorities facing the stands seating the heretics, garbed in their penitential garments and devil's mitres, waiting for the reading of their sentences. *Below*: The solemn procession with the likeness of those condemned in effigy, and *right*: The great collective executions (Bibliothèque Nationale, Paris).

INDEX

M

O